491.59.

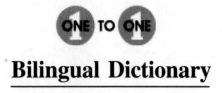

Bilingual Dictionary

English-Pashto
Pashto-English
Dictionary

Compiled by
Amir Khan

ibs BOOKS (UK)

© Publishers

First Edition: 2011
Second Edition: 2012

ISBN : 978-1-905863-93-8

Published by
ibs BOOKS (UK)
55, Warren Street, London W1T 5NW (UK)
e-mail: indbooks@aol.com; starbooksuk@aol.com
www.starbooksuk.com

Printed in India at
Star Print-O-Bind, New Delhi-110020

About this Dictionary

Developments in science and technology today have narrowed down distances between countries, and have made the world a small place. A person living thousands of miles away can learn and understand the culture and lifestyle of another country with ease and without travelling to that country. Languages play an important role as facilitators of communication in this respect.

To promote such an understanding, **ibs BOOKS (UK)** has planned to bring out a series of bilingual dictionaries in which important English words have been translated into other languages, with Roman transliteration in case of languages that have different scripts. This is a humble attempt to bring people of the world closer through the medium of language, thus making communication easy and convenient.

These dictionaries have been compiled and edited by teachers and scholars of relative languages.

Bilingual Dictionaries in this Series

English-Arabic/Arabic-English	Rania-al-Qass
English-Bengali/Bengali-English	Amit Majumdar
English-Cantonese/Cantonese-English	Nisa Yang
English-Dari/Dari-English	Amir Khan
English-Farsi/Farsi-English	Maryam Zamankhani
English-Gujarati/Gujarati-English	Sujata Basaria
English-Hindi/Hindi-English	Sudhakar Chaturvedi
English-Hungarian/Hungarian-English	Lucy Mallows
English-Lithuanian/Lithuanian-English	Regina Kazakeviciute
English-Nepali/Nepali-English	Anil Mandal
English-Panjabi/Panjabi-English	Teja Singh Chatwal
English-Pashto/Pashto-English	Amir Khan
English-Polish/Polish-English	Magdalena Herok
English-Romanian/Romanian-English	Georgeta Laura Dutulescu
English-Somali/Somali-English	Ali Mohamud Omer
English-Tamil/Tamil-English	Sandhya Mahadevan
English-Turkish/Turkish-English	Nagme Yazgin
English-Urdu/Urdu-English	S.A Rahman

More languages in print

ibs BOOKS (UK)
London W1T 5NW (UK)

ENGLISH-PASHTO

A

a *a.* يو yaw
aback *adv.* برته beyrta
abaction *n* په pa sat
abactor *n* تلونکی په pa sat tloonkay
abandon *v.t.* پروول preykhowal
abase *v.t.* يول teetawal
abasement *n* سپکوالی spakwalay
abash *v.t.* شرمول sharmawal
abate *v.t.* لول lagawal
abatement *n.* لونه lagawana
abbey *n.* خانقا khanqa
abbreviate *v.t.* لنول landawal
abbreviation *n* لنيز landeez
abdicate *v.t,* پرودل preykhodal
abdication *n* کيدل وه gokha keydal
abdomen *n* خه kheyta
abdominal *a.* ه ييز geyda yeez
abduct *v.t.* تتول takhtawal
abduction *n* تتونه takhtawana
abed *adv.* کی بستر په pa bistar ki
aberrance *n.* بلارتوب bey laritob
abet *v.t.* لمسول lamsawal
abetment *n.* لمسون lamsoon
abeyance *n.* ال tal
abhor *v.t.* کرکه کول kraka kawal
abhorrence *n.* کرکه kraka
abide *v.i* اوسدل oseydal
abiding *a* پايدار paydar

ability *n* قابليت qabileeyat
abject *a.* خوار khwar
ablaze *adv.* لاند zaland
ablactate *v. t* کوچنی له شدوبلول koochnay la sheydo beylawal
ablactation *n* له شدوبلدا la sheydo beyleyda
able *a و* war
ablush *adv* شرمنده sharminda
ablution *n* اودس awdas
abnegate *v. t* انکارکول inkar kawal
abnegation *n* انکار inkar
abnormal *a* ناسم na sam
aboard *adv* که په pa kakhtay ki
abode *n* مسکن maskan
abolish *v.t* له منه ول la manza wral
abolition *v* له منه ونه la manza wrana
abominable *a* کرکجن krakjan
aboral *adj* له خولی خه ليری la kholi sakha leyri
aborigines *n. pl* پخوانی او سيدونکی pakhwanay useydoonkay
abort *v.i* زيانول zyanawal
abortion *n* بوخته زدنه bey wakhta zeygeydana
abortive *adv* بثمره be samara
abound *v.i.* زياتدل zyateydal
about *adv* تقريباً taqreeban
about *prep* شاوخوا shaw khwa
above *adv* په لوره pa lwara
above *prep.* پورته porta
abreast *adv* سنگ پر سنگ sang par sang
abridge *v.t* لنول landawal
abridgement *n* لنيز landeez
abroad *adv* بهر bahar
abrogate *v. t.* لغوکول lugho kawal

abrupt *a* ناپه nasapa

abruption *n* ناپي nasapee

abscess *n* دانه dana

abscond *v.i* تتدل takhteydal

absence *n* غرحاضري ghayr haziree

absent *a* غرحاضر ghayr hazir

absolute *a* پوره poora

absolutely *adv* بيخي beykhee

absolve *v.t* بخل bakhal

absorb *v.t* جذبول jazbawal

abstain *v.i.* ه کول dada kawal

abstract *a* مختصر mukhtasar

abstract *n* خلاصه khulasa

abstract *adj* مجرد mujarrad

abstraction *n.* بلدنه beyleydana

absurd *a* بمعنی bey mana

absurdity *n* پوچتوب poochtob

abundance *n* پريماني preymanee

abundant *a* زيات zyat

abuse *v.t.* کنل khkanzal

abuse *n* کنا khkanza

abusive *a* ناوه nawara

abut *v* تکيه کول takya kawal

abyss *n* ژورند zhawar dand

academic *a* تحصيلي tahseelee

academy *n* اکاديمي akademee

accede *v.t.* اتفاق ته رسدل etifaq ta raseydal

accelerate *v.t* ندی کول garanday kawal

acceleration *n* نديتوب garandeetob

accent *n* خج khaj

accentuate *v.t* اچول زور zor achawal

accept *&* منل manal

acceptable *a* دمنلو da manalo war

acceptance *n* قبلول qablawal

access *n* لاس رسدنه las raseydana

accession *n* افتخارته رسدنه iftikhar ta raseydana

accessory *n* زيات zyat

accident *n* په peykha

accidental *a* تصادفي tasadufee

acclaim *v.t* چکچکهي کول chakckahi kawal

acclaim *n* چکچک chakchaki

acclamation *n* دشاباسي نار da shabasee narey

acclimatise *v.t* موسم سره مان عادتول mosam sara zan adatawal

accommodate *v.t* ايول zayawal

accommodation *n.* استوزه astoganzay

accompaniment *n* ملتا maltya

accompany *v.t.* مل کيدل mal keydal

accomplice *n* ملری malgaray

accomplish *v.t.*کول بشپ bashpar kawal

accomplished *a* بشپ bashpar

accomplishment *n.* بشپتيا bashpartya

accord *v.t.* موافق کيدل muwafiq keydal

accord *n.* جوجای jor jaray

accordingly *adv.* لهدامله la dey amala

account *n.* حساب heesab

account *v.t.* انيرل angeyral

accountable *a* مسؤل masool

accountancy *n.* حسابداري hisabdaree

accountant *n.* محاسب muhasib

accredit *v.t.* اعتمادكول aytimad kawal

accredited *adj* داعتمادنامخاوند da aytimad namey khawand

accumulate *v.t.* غونول ghondawal

accumulation *n* غونيدنه ghondeydana

accuracy *n.* درستوال drustwalay

accurate *a.* درست drust

accursed *a.* لعنتي lanatee

accusation *n* تورلونه tor lagawana

accuse *v.t.* تورلول tor lagawal

accused *n.* تورن toran

accustom *v.t.* رودول rogdawal

accustomed *a.* رودى rogday

ace *n* ك takay

acerb *adj* ترش torsh

acerbate *v.t* پارول parawal

acescent *adj* تريو treew

acetify *v.* سركهكدل sarka keydal

ache *n.* درد dard

ache *v.i.* خويدل khoogeydal

achieve *v.t.* لاستهراوستل las ta rawastal

achievement *n.* برياليتوب baryaleetob

achromatic *adj* بيرنه beyranga

acid *a* تيزابي tayzabee

acid *n* تيزاب tayzab

acidity *n.* تيزابيت tayzabeeyat

acknowledge *v.* تصديق tasdeeq

acknowledgement *n.* اعتراف aytiraf

acne *n* وانكه zwanaka

acorn *n.* دخرويداز da kharwee daney

acoustic *a* اوازپوهنه awaz pohana

acquaint *v.t.* اشناكول ashna kawal

acquaintance *n.* پژنلوي peyzhandgalwee

acquest *n* لاستهراوستل las ta rawastal

acquiesce *v.i.* غاهايودل ghara eekhodal

acquiescence *n.* غاهايودنه ghara eekhodana

acquire *v.t.* تحصيلول tahseelawal

acquirement *n.* تحصيل tahseel

acquisition *n.* لاستهراوستنه las ta rawastana

acquit *v.t.* ازادول azadawal

acquittal *n.* خلاصون khlasoon

acre *n.* جريب jeereb

acreage *n.* جريبانه jeerebana

acrimony *n* تريخوالي treekhwalay

acrobat *n.* الباز dalbaz

across *adv.* پور pori

across *prep.* پهلنو pa lando

act *n.* عملكول amal kawal

act *v.i.* اغيزهاچول agheyza achawal

acting *n.* عمل amal

action *n.* كنه krana

activate *v.t.* فعالول faalawal

active *a.* فعال faal

activity *n.* فعاليت faaleeyat

actor *n.* فنكار fankar

actress *n.* كاره فن fankara

actual *a.* رتين rakhteenay

actually *adv.* پەرېتیاسره pa reekhtya sara

acumen *n.* ترەوال teyrawalay

acute *a.* تیز teyz

adage *n.* متل matal

adamant *a.* کلک klak

adamant *n.* نەماتدونکی na mateydoonkay

adapt *v.t.* سمول samawal

adaptation *n.* توافق tawafuq

adays *adv* ورځ wrazanay

add *v.t.* زیاتول zyatawal

addict *v.t.* رودول rogdawal

addict *n.* عادت adat

addiction *n.* رودوال rogdwalay

addition *n.* زیاتونه zyatwalay

additional *a.* اضافي izafee

addle *adj* وروست wrost

address *v.t.* خطاب کول khitab kawal

addressee *n.* مخاطب mukhatib

adduce *v.t.* راول rawral

adept *n.* ماهر mahir

adept *a.* تکه takra

adequacy *n.* برابروال barabarwalay

adequate *a.* مناسب munasib

adhere *v.i.* لول lagawal

adherence *n.* طرفداری tarafdaree

adhesion *n.* لاسنیوی las neeway

adhesive *n.* سریخ sareykh

adhesive *a.* سریناک sreykhnak

adhibit *v.t.* قبلول qablawal

adieu *n.* خدایدیمل شه khuday di mal sha

adieu *interj.* خدایپەامانی khuday pa amanee

adjacent *a.* متصل mutasil

adjective *n.* صفت sifat

adjoin *v.t.* متصل کول mutasil kawal

adjourn *v.t.* بلوخت تهنول bal wakht ta zandawal

adjournment *n.* لنمهالی ز land mahalay zand

adjudge *v.t.* قضاوت کول qazawat kawal

adjunct *n.* سنګی سره مرسته sangi sara mrasta

adjuration *n* پرانیستنه pranistana

adjust *v.t.* سمول samawal

adjustment *n.* تعدیل tadeel

administer *v.t.* اداره کول idara kawal

administration *n.* اداره idara

administrative *a.* اداري idaree

administrator *n.* مدیر mudeer

admirable *a.* دخوونو da khwakhay war

admiral *n.* امیرالبحر ameerul bahar

admiration *n.* تحسین tehseen

admire *v.t.* قدرکول qadar kawal

admissible *a.* روا rawa

admission *n.* داخله dakhila

admit *v.t.* اقرارول iqrarawal

admittance *n.* ننوتنه nanawatana

admonish *v.t.* اخطارورکول akhtar warkawal

admonition *n.* تنبه tambeeya

adnascent *adj.*

ado *n.* شورماشور shormashor

adobe *n.* خته khakhta

adolescence *n.* بلوغ balogh

adolescent *a.* بالغ baligh

adopt *v.t.* خپلول khpalawal

adoption *n* خپلونه khpalawana

adorable *a.* مينه‌ناک meenanak

adoration *n.* پرستش parastish

adore *v.t.* قدرکول qadar kawal

adorn *v.t.* سينگارول seengarawal

adscititious *adj* اضافي izafee

adscript *adj.* لمنليک lamanleek

adulation *n* چاپلوسي chaplosee

adult *a* بالغ baligh

adult *n.* بالغ کَس baligh kas

adulterate *v.t.* زناکول zana kawal

adulteration *n.* زنا zana

adultery *n.* زناکاري zana karee

advance *v.t.* مخکېدل makhki keydal

advance *n.* ترقي‌يافته taraqee yafta

advancement *n.* ترقي taraqee

advantage *n.* فايده fayda

advantage *v.t.* گاته‌اخيستل gata akheystal

advantageous *a.* فايده‌مند fayda mand

advent *n.* د مخه د کرسمس ورز da makha da krismas wraz

adventure *n* مهم muhim

adventurous *a.* مهماتي muhimatee

adverb *n.* فعل ته‌اوند؛قد fayl ta arwand; qayd

adverbial *a.* د قدپه‌اوند da qayd pa arwand

adversary *n.* حريف hareef

adverse *a* بدبخت badbakht

adversity *n.* بدمرغي badmarghay

advert *v.* متوجه‌کول mutawajo kawal

advertise *v.t.* اعلانول aylanawal

advertisement *n* اعلان aylan

advice *n* نصيحت naseehat

advisable *a.* مقتضي muqtazee

advisability *n* مصلحت maslihat

advise *v.t.* نصيحت‌کول naseehat kawal

advocacy *n.* قضاوت qazawat

advocate *n* مدافع‌وکيل mudafay wakeel

advocate *v.t.* طرفداري‌کول tarafdaree kawal

aerial *a.* هوايي hawayee

aerial *n.* هوا da hawa

aeriform *adj.* د هوا په‌شان da hawa pa shan

aerify *v.t.* په‌هوااول pa hawa arawal

aerodrome *n* پروازگاه parwazgah

aeronautics *n.pl.* هوابازي hawabazee

aeroplane *n.* الوتکه alwataka

aesthetic *a.* کلاپالونکی khkula

aesthetics *n.pl.* کلاپژندنه khkula peyzhandana

aestival *adj* اونی ornay

afar *adv.* لهورا la wara

affable *a.* خوش‌خلقه khosh khalqa

affair *n.* امر amar

affect *v.t.* اغيزندل agheyz khandal

affectation *n* تصنع tasano

affection *n.* مينه‌توب mayantob

affectionate *a.* مينه‌ناک meenanak

affidavit *n* اعتبار‌ليک aytibar leek

affiliation *n.* تون taroon

affinity *n* قرابت qarabat

affirm *v.t.* ادعاکول ida kawal

affirmation *n* خاطرجمعي khatir jamee

affirmative *a.* مثبت musbat

affix *v.t.* لول lagawal

afflict *v.t.* لتاول latarawal

affliction *n.* بدمرغی bad marghay

affluence *n.* وردنه wareydana

affluent *a.* جاري jaree

afford *v.t.* زغمل zghamal

afforest *v.t.* ځنګل جوړول zangal jorawal

affray *n* جنجال janjal

affront *v.t.* سپکاوی spakaway

affront *n* سپکول spakawal

afield *adv.* په بیدیاک pa beydya ki

aflame *adv.* په شغلو pa shoghlo

afloat *adv.* لاهو lahoo

afoot *adv.* پیاده pyada

afore *prep.* واندینی warandeenay

afraid *a.* ویریدل weyreydal

afresh *adv.* له سره la sara

after *prep.* پسې pasey

after *adv* وروسته wrosta

after *conj.* ورپسې warpasey

afterwards *adv.* پسې pasey

again *adv.* بیا bya

against *prep.* مخالف mukhalif

agamist *n* یوول بوی،پرته له جفت یرزدل yaw dawl bootay; parta la juftgeeray zeygeydalay

agape *adv.,* وته په غا gota pa ghakh

agaze *adv* اندمن andeykhman

age *n.* عمر oomar

aged *a.* زو zor

agency *n.* اژانس azhans

agenda *n.* دغوندبحث مواد da ghondi da behes mawad

agent *n* اجنت ajant

aggravate *v.t.* په غصه کول pa ghosa kawal

aggravation *n.* غصه کونه ghosa kawona

aggregate *v.t.* مجموعه جوول majmooa jorawal

aggression *n* ترى teyray

aggressive *a.* تیری کوونکی teyray kawoonkay

aggressor *n.* یرغلر yarghal gar

aggrieve *v.t.* غمجنول ghamjanawal

aghast *a.* حیران hayran

agile *a.* تکه takra

agility *n.* تکه توب takratob

agitate *v.t.* خوول khotawal

agitation *n* لمسونه lamsawona

agist *v.t.* دمزدپه بدل کرول da mazd pa badal ki sarawal

aglow *adv.* په شغلوروان pa shoghlo rokhan

agnus *n*

ago *adv.* مخک makhki

agog *adj.* بقرار bey qarar

agonist *n* په اضطراب اخته pa iztirab akhta

agonize *v.t.* په عذابول pa azabawal

agony *n.* درد dard

agronomy *n.* کرنپوهنه karanpohana

agoraphobia *n.* ومشتی توب gotmeyshtaytob

agrarian *a.* زراعتي zaratee

agree *v.i.* موافقت کول muwafiqat kawal

agreeable *a.* موافق muwafiq

agreement *n.* تون taroon

agricultural *a* كرنيز karaneez

agriculture *n* كرنه karana

agriculturist *n.* ماهر دكرنه da karani mahir

ague *n* لزنده تبه larzanda taba

ahead *adv.* مخكى makhki

aheap *adv*

aid *n* مرسته mrasta

aid *v.t* مرسته كول mrasta kawal

aigrette *n* جوغه jogha

ail *v.t.* ناروغدل narogheydal

ailment *ŋ.* ناروغي naroghee

aim *n.* موخه mokha

aim *v.i.* مرام moram

air *n* هوا hawa

aircraft *n.* الوتكه alwataka

airy *a.* هوايي hawayee

ajar *adv.* نيم كه neem kakha

akin *a.* شباهت لرل shabahat laral

alacrious *adj* چابك chabak

alacrity *n.* چمتووالى chamtoowalay

alarm *n* دخطرزنگ da khatar zang

alarm *v.t* له خطرخه خبرول la khatar sakha khabrawal

alas *interj.* اى هى ay hay

albeit *conj.* كه هم ka sa ham

album *n.* البوم albom

albumen *n* د هگى سپين da hagay speen

alchemy *n.* كيمياري keemyagaree

alcohol *n* شراب sharab

ale *n* انليسي آبجو eengleesee abjoo

alert *a.* ويخ weekh

alertness *n.* ويخوالى weekhwalay

algebra *n.* الجبر aljabar

alias *n.* فرضي يادروغي نوم farzee ya daroghee noom

alias *adv.* په بل نامه pa bal nama

alibi *n.* د جرم پيدوپه مهال بهانه كول da juram peykheydo pa mahal bahana kawal

alien *a.* پردى praday

alienate *v.t.* دان مخالف جوول da zan mukhalif jorawal

alight *v.i.* روخانول rokhanawal

align *v.t.* په يوه كره كدرول pa yawa karkha ki darawal

alignment *n.* يوه كره يا ليكه كدرونه yawa karkha ya lika ki darawana

alike *a.* يوول،ورته yaw dawal; warta

alike *adv* يوشان yaw shan

aliment *n.* خواه،غذا khwara; ghaza

alimony *n.* خر khars

aliquot *n.* عاد كوونكى عدد ad kawoonkay adad

alive *a* ژوندى،سرشار zhwanday; sarshar

all *a.* بشپول؛ tol; bashpar

all *n* ول tol

all *adv* له يوه سره،هرول la yawa sara; har dawal

all *pron* هروك،هرڅا har sok; har cha

allay *v.t.* آرامول aramawal

allegation *n.* الزام،ادعا ilzam; adaa

allege *v.t.* الزام لول،ادعا كول ilzam lagawal; adaa kawal

allegiance *n.* تابعيت tabieeyat

allegorical *a.* مجازي؛کنايوي majazee; kanayawee

allegory *n.* کنايه؛حکايت kanaya; hikayat

allergy *n.* حساسيتلرنه hasaseeyat larana

alleviate *v.t.* آرامول؛کمول aramawal; kamawal

alleviation *n.* آرام؛کموالی aram; kam walay

alley *n.* کوڅه؛لاره koosa; lara

alliance *n.* پيوستون peywastoon

alligator *n* نهنگ nahang

alliterate *v.* يوورته‌غلرونکي‌توري‌سره دپرله‌پس‌کلمو‌پيلدل yaw warta ghag laroonkee toree sara da parla pasi kalmo peyleydal

alliteration *n.* ورته‌غلرونکي‌توري‌سره دپرله‌پس‌کلمو‌پيلدنه warta ghag laroonkee toree sara da parla pasey kalmo peyleydana

allocate *v.t.* ځانی‌کول zangaray kawal

allocation *n.* ځانه؛با‌کنه zangarana; takana

allot *v.t.* ځانی‌کول zangaray kawal

allotment *n.* وش،تخصيص weysh; takhsees

allow *v.t.* اجازه‌ورکول ijaza warkawal

allowance *n.* مزد؛ډيره mazd; zeyra

alloy *n.* چارج؛الياژ charj

allude *v.i.* نغوته‌کول nghota kawal

allure *v.t.* په‌طمع‌کول pa tama kawal

allurement *n* تطميع؛برامتا tatmee; bramta

allusion *n* نغوته؛اشاره nghota; ishara

allusive *a.* کنايوي؛رمزي kinayawee; ramzee

ally *v.t.* نلول nkhalawal

ally *n.* هم‌تونی؛ژمن ham taroonay; zhman

almanac *n.* کليزه kaleeza

almighty *a.* قادرمطلق qadari mutlaq

almond *n.* بادام badam

almost *adv.* تقريبا taqreeban

alms *n.* خرات kheyrat

aloft *adv.* پورته؛برسره porta; bar seyra

alone *a.* يواز yawazey

along *adv.* ملری؛مل؛ورسره malgaray; mal; warsara

along *prep.* د...په‌او‌دو‌ک؛د...په‌امتداد ک da ... pa oogdo ki; da ... pa imtidad ki

aloof *adv.* لر؛په‌‌ګوه‌ک leyri; pa gokha ki

aloud *adv.* په‌لوغ pa lwar ghag

alp *n.* لوغر lwar ghag

alpha *n* دیوناني‌ابلومی‌توری da yoonanee abeysey loomray toray

alphabet *n.* ابيسي abeysey

alphabetical *a.* دابيه‌اوند da abeysey pa arwand

alpinist *n* غرختونکی ghar khatoonkay

already *adv.* مخکله‌دی؛قبلا makhki la dey; qablan

also *adv.* همداشان؛همداول hamda shan; hamda dawl

altar *n.* قربانای qorban zay

alter *v.t.* بدلول badlawal

alteration *n* بدلون badloon

altercation *n.* شخړه،مباحثه shkhara; mobahisa

alternate *a.* يوپه‌منځ‌ک؛متناوب yaw pa manz ki; motanawab

alternate *v.t.* يوپه‌بل‌پسراتلل yaw pa bal pasey ratlal

alternative *n.* متناوب؛تردوه‌برخوپور motanawab; tar dwa barkho pori zangaray انى

alternative *a.* پرله‌پسواندز parla pasey wrandeyz

although *conj.* كه‌هم ka sa ham

altimeter *n* لووالي‌معلومونكى lwar walay maloomowoonkay

altitude *n.* لووالى lwar walay

alto *n* ترولولوغ tar tolo lwar ghag

altogether *adv.* په‌بشپول pa bashpar dawl

aluminium *n.* دالومينيوم‌فلز da alomeeneeyom filiz

always *adv* تل،همشه tal; hameysha

alveary *n* دشاتولوى da shato lokhay

am (لومړى‌کس؛لکه:زه‌يم) يم yam (loomray kas; laka: za yam)

amalgam *n* دسيمابويوالياژچدغلونو da seemabo yaw alyazh chi da ghakhoonu dakawalo lapara pakareygee کولولپاره‌په‌کاري

amalgamate *v.t.* دسيمابوپه‌دغه‌الياژ da seemabo pa dagha alyazh ghakhoona dakawal غلونه‌کول

amalgamation *n* ونه‌،يواى‌كونه gadawana; yaw zay kawana

amass *v.t.* راغونول raghondawal

amateur *n.* مينه‌وال،شوقين meenawal; shoqeen

amatory *adj* لامينک la meeni dak

amaze *v.t.* حرانول heyranawal

amazement *n.* حرانتيا heyrantya

ambassador *n.* سفير،سياسي‌رى safeer; seeyasee zaray

ambiguity *n.* ابهام،بونتوب ibham; goongtob

ambiguous *a.* مبهم،شکمن mubhim; shakman

ambition *n.* هيله،آرزو heela; arzoo

ambitious *a.* دلوهمت‌خاوند da lwar himat khawand

ambulance *n.* امبولانس ambolans

ambulant *adj* رنده،متحرک garzanda; mutaharik

ambulate *v.t* تګ‌کول tag kawal

ambush *n.* کمين‌ورته‌نيول kameen warta neewal

ameliorate *v.t.* سمول samawal

amelioration *n.* سمونه،جوت samawana; jorakht

amen *interj.* آمين،خداى‌دوکي ameen; khuday di wakree

amenable *a* مسؤلانه masoolana

amend *v.t.* رغول،سمول raghawal; samawal

amendment *n.* سمون،اصلاح samoon; islah

amends *n.pl.* تلافي،جبران talafee; jibran

amiability *n.* لوريني،مهرباني loreenee; mehrabanee

amiable *a.* لوراند،مهربان lorand; mehraban

amicable *adj.* دوستانه dostana

amid *prep.* په منځ pa manz ki

amiss *adv.* ناوه،ناسم nawara; nasam

amity *n.* ملګرتيا،آشنايي malgartya; ashnayee

ammunition *n.* مهمات،اسلحه muhamat; aslaha

amnesia *n* نسيان،هرونه nasyan; heyrawana

amnesty *n.* عمومي بخنه amoomee bakhana

among *prep.* په ... کي؛په ... منځ کې pa ... ki; pa ... manz ki

amongst *prep.* په ... منځ کي؛له ... لخه pa ... manz ki; la ... dali sakha

amoral *a.* غيراخلاقي ghayr akhlaqee

amount *n* کچ؛مقدار kach; miqdar

amount *v.i* صعودکول،مقدارلرل؛ زياتېدل saood kawal; miqdar laral; zyateydal

amount *v.* په مقداريا پيمائش کي برابرېدل pa miqdar ya peymayish ki barabareydal

amorous *a.* عاشقانه ashiqana

amour *n* مينه،عشق meena; ishq

ampere *n* دبرناجريان ياشدت نب کوونکي پيمانه da breykhna jaryan ya shidat nap kawoonki peymana

amphibious *adj* دوه اخيز dwa arkheeza

amphitheatre *n* دننداتون بضوي سالون da nandartoon beyzwee salon

ample *a.* پرمانه،مفصل preymana; mufsal

amplification *n* پراختيا،پياوتيا parakhtya; pyawartya

amplifier *n* پياوي کوونکي، واکمنوونکي pyawaray kawoonkay; zwakmanawoonkey

amplify *v.t.* پراخول parakhawal

amulet *n.* کو،دمډرها kodi; dam durha

amuse *v.t.* مشغولول mashghulawal

amusement *n* مشغولتيا،تفريح mashghultya; tafreeh

an *art* يو (لکه يو کس؛يو کتاب) yaw (laka yaw kas; yaw keetab)

anabaptism *n* دتعميددغسل نه ورکونه da tameed da ghusal na warkawana

anachronism *n* له زوعصرسره اه لرونکي la zor asar sara ara laroonkay

anadem *n* غاک gharakay

anaemia *n* وينه لي weena lagay

anaesthesia *n* هوي ب bey hokhee

anaesthetic *n.* بهوه bey hokha

anal *adj.* دکوندمقعدپه اوند da koni da maqad pa arwand

analogous *a.* دپرتلنو war da partalani

analogy *n.* قياس،پرتلنه qayas; partalana

analyse *v.t.* تجزيه کول tajzeeya kawal

analysis *n.* تجزيه،شننه tajzeeya; shanana

analyst *n* تجزيه نار،روونکي tajzeeya nigar; zeyrowoonkay

analytical *a* شننوونکي،تجزياتي shanawoonkay; tajzeeyatee anamnesis *n* يادآوري yadawaree

anarchism *n.* وي‌پالنه gadwadee palana

anarchist *n* بلوار balwagar

anarchy *n* وي،بغاوت gadwadee; baghawat

anatomy *n.* كالبدپژندنه kalbad peyzhandana

ancestor *n.* پلارنيكونه plar neekoona

ancestral *a.* نيكانه،دپلارنيكه‌په‌اوند neekana; da plar neeka pa arwand

ancestry *n.* پلرنۍ،كورنۍ plaranay; koranay

anchor *n.* دكتلنر da kakhtay langar

anchorage *n* دكتلنرای da kakhtay langarzay

ancient *a.* لرغونی larghonay

ancon *n* نل sangal

and *conj.* او aw

anecdote *n.* لنه‌كيسه landa keesa

anemometer *n* بادمچ bad meych

anew *adv.* له‌سره،دوباره la sara; dobara

anfractuous *adj* خمدار khamdar

angel *n* فرته farikhta

anger *n.* غصه ghusa

angina *n* دزه‌دشريانونودرد da zra da sharyanoonu dard

angle *n.* زاويه zaweeya

angle *n* كونج،گوه konj; gokha

angry *a.* غصه،په‌قهر ghusa; pa qahar

anguish *n.* غمجنی ghamjanee

angular *a.* زاويه‌لرونكی zaweeya laroonkay

anigh *adv.* نژد nazhdey

animal *n.* ناور zanawar

animate *v.t.* ژوندوركول؛ژوندوربخل zhwand warkawal; zhwand warbakhal

animate *a.* ژوندی zhwanday

animation *n* احيا؛پارونه ahya; parawana

animosity *n* دمنی dukhmanee

animus *n* اراده،نيت irada; nyat

aniseed *n* تخم‌بادیان tukhmi badyan

ankle *n.* بجلكه،بنری bajlaka; khangaray

anklet *n* زولانی zolanay

annalist *n.* تاريخليكونكی tareekh leekoonkay

annals *n.pl.* پل،تاريخچه peykh lar; tareekhcha

annex *v.t.* ضميمه‌كول،نلول zameema kawal; nakhlawal

annexation *n* انضمام؛ضميمه‌كونه inzimam; zameema kawana

annihilate *v.t.* له‌منه‌ول la manza waral

annihilation *n* ويجاونه weejarawana

anniversary *n.* كليزه،هركال kaleeza; har kal

announce *v.t.* اعلانول aylanawal

announcement *n.* خبرتيا؛اعلان khabartya; aylan

annoy *v.t.* ورول zorawal

annoyance *n.* ورونه zorawana

annual *a.* كلنی kalanay

annuitant *n* معاش‌اخستونكی moash akheystoonkay

18

annuity *n.* کلنی‌معاش kalanay moash

annul *v.t.* لغوه‌کول lughwa kawal

anoint *v.t.* په‌تلوغوول pa teylu ghwarawal

anomalous *a* له‌دوده‌بهر la dooda bahar

anomaly *n* بترتیبه bey tarteeba

anon *adv.* ورژر deyr zhar

anonymity *n.* بنومتیا bey noomtya

anonymity *n.* نوم‌ورکي noom warakay

anonymous *a.* بنومه؛نارنده beynooma; na sarganda

another *a* یو‌بل yaw bal

answer *n* واب zawab

answer *v.t* واب‌ورکول zawab warkawal

answerable *a.* په‌واب‌مسؤل؛وابده pa zawab masool; zawabday

ant *n* می meygay

antacid *adj.* ضدحموضت ziddi hamoozat

antagonism *n* مخالفت؛دمني mukhalifat; dukhmanee

antagonist *n.* مخالف؛دمن mukhalif; dukhman

antagonize *v.t.* مخالفت‌کول mukhalifat kawal

antarctic *a.* په‌سولي‌قطب‌پوراوند pa sweylee qotab pori arwand

antecede *v.t.* دل‌تروراند tri warandi keydal

antecedent *n.* مخکنی؛واند makhkanay; warandi

antecedent *a.* پخوانی؛مخکنی pakhwanay; makhkanay

antedate *n* له‌ریتني‌تاریخ‌خه‌مخکي la reekhtanee tareekh تاریخ‌ویل sakha makhki tareekh wayal

antelope *n.* غره gharsa

antenatal *adj.* له‌زیدون‌واند la zeygeydoon warandi

antennae *n.* آنن antan

antenuptial *adj.* له‌وادوواند la wada warandi

anthem *n* ملي‌سرود milee sarood

anthology *n.* ادبي‌غورچا adabee ghorchanr

anthropoid *adj.* دانسان‌وله‌بیزو da insan dawla beezo

anti *pref.* مخالف؛پرضد mukhalif; par zid

anti-aircraft *a.* هواضدوسله hawa zid wasla

antic *n* بانوله bey andwala

anticardium *n*

anticipate *v.t.* واندوینه‌کول warandwayana kawal

anticipation *n.* واندوینه warandwayana

antidote *n.* زهرضد zeher zid

antipathy *n.* مخالفانه‌احساس mukhalifana ihsas

antiphony *n.* تهلیل‌وینه tahleel wayana

antipodes *n.* مقابل‌کي muqabil takee

antiquarian *a.* لرغونی larghonay

antiquarian *n* لرغون‌پژندونکی larghon peyzhandoonkay

antiquary *n.* لرغون‌پژندونکی larghon peyzhandoonkay

antiquated *a.* منسوخ‌شوی mansookh shaway

antique *a.* لرغونی larghonay

antiquity *n.* لرغونزمانه larghoni zamana

antiseptic *n.* عفونت ضد afoonat zid

antiseptic *a.* انتان ضددرمل antanzid durmal

antithesis *n.* تضاد tazad

antitheist *n* تضادخوی tazad khwakhay

antonym *n.* ضداونقیض zid aw naqeez

anus *n.* مقعد maqad

anvil *n.* سندان sandan

anxiety *a* اضطراب aztirab

anxious *a.* مضطرب muztarib

any *a.* هي,هر hees; har

any *adv.* هي hees

anyhow *adv.* پهرحال pa har hal

apace *adv.* په چکسره pa chatkay sara

apart *adv.* برسره bar seyra

apartment *n.* اپارتمان apartman

apathy *n.* بحسي bey hisee

ape *n* شادو shado

ape *v.t.* تقلیدکول taqleed kawal

aperture *n.* سوری sooray

apex *n.* وکه,دزاویرأس sooka; da zaweeyi ras

aphorism *n* لنډونا landa weyna

apiary *n.* دشاتودمچیوای da shato da machyo zay

apiculture *n.* دشاتودمچیوروزنه da shato da machyo rozana

apish *a.* ناپوه napoh

apologize *v.i.* بخنه غوتل bakhkhana ghokhtal

apologue *n* اخلاقي کیسه ikhlaqee keesa

apology *n.* بخنه bakhkhana

apostle *n.* استازی,رسول astazay; rasool

apotheosis *n.* له حدسخهزیاته ستاینه la had sakha zyata stayana

apparatus *n.* اسباب,لوازم asbab; lawazim

apparel *n.* اسباب,کالی asbab; kalee

apparent *a.* رند sargand

appeal *n.* التماس,زاري iltimas; zaree

appeal *v.t.* التماس کول,مراجعه کول iltimas kawal; murajia kawal

appear *v.i.* رنډل sargandeydal

appearance *n* ظهور,به zahoor; banra

appease *v.t.* تسکینول,خاموشول taskeenawal; khamoshawal

appellant *n.* مبارزهغوتونکی mobariza ghokhtoonkay

append *v.t.* تاولرل,زیاتول taraw laral; zyatawal

appendage *n.* پایو paysoor

appendicitis *n.* داپانیکس یسوب da apandeeks parsob

appendix *n.* پایو paysoor

appendix *n.* ضمیمه zameema

appetence *n.* هیله,اشتیاق heela; ishteeyaq

appetent *adj.* هیله من,آرزومن heela man; arzoo man

appetite *n.* غذایي اشتها ghazayee ishtiha

appetite *n.* ذاتي لوالتیا zatee leywaltya

appetizer *n* لهخوودمخهاشتها راوستونکیاک la khwaro da makha ishtiha rawastoonkay skhak

applaud *v.t.* آفرین ویل afreen wayal

applause *n.* تحسین;ستاینه tehseen; stayana

apple *n.* مه manra

appliance *n.* آله;وسایل ala; wasayal

applicable *a.* مناسب;داجراو munasib; da ijra war

applicant *n.* غوتونکی;غوتن لیک ورکوونکی ghokhtoonkay; ghokhtan leek warkawoonkay

application *n.* غوتنلیک ghokhtanleek

apply *v.t.* عملي کول;عریضه کول amalee kawal; areeza kawal

appoint *v.t.* ٹاکل;مارل takal; gomaral

appointment *n.* ٹاکنه;دملاقات ژمنه takana; da mulaqat zhmana

apportion *v.t.* وشل weyshal

apposite *adj* مناسب munasib

apposite *a.* پرای par zay

appositely *adv* پهمناسبول pa munasib dawl

approbate *v.t* تصویبول tasweebawal

appraise *v.t.* تخمینول;ارزول takhmeenawal; arzawal

appreciable *a.* دقدردانو da qadardanay war

appreciate *v.t.* قدرداني کول qadardanee kawal

appreciation *n.* قدرداني qadardanee

apprehend *v.t.* پوهدل;دَرَکول poheydal; darakawal

apprehension *n.* پوهاوی;درک pohaway; darak

apprehensive *a.* پوهنیز;اندمن pohaneez; andeykhman

apprentice *n.* شاردي shagardee

apprise *v.t.* خبرول khabrawal

approach *v.t.* نژدکدل nazhdey keydal

approach *n.* نژدوالی;لاسرسدا nazhdeywalay; las raseyda

approbation *n.* تصویب tasweeb

appropriate *v.t.* مناسبول;بانی کول munasibawal; zangaray kawal

appropriate *a.* مناسب munasib

appropriation *n.* مناسبت;وتیا munasibat; wartya

approval *n.* تجویز;تصویب tajweez; tasweeb

approve *v.t.* تصویبول;موافقت کول tasweebawal; muwafiqat kawal

approximate *a.* نژد nazhdey

apricot *n.* زردآلو zard aloo

appurtenance *n* جز;وسایل juz; wasayil

apron *n.* پشبند peysh band

apt *a.* لوال;مناسب leywal; munasib

aptitude *n.* ذهنيتوجه zehnee tawajo

aquarium *n.* دیبکسهچدریائيمخلوق da پکنندارلپارهساتلیشي kheekhey baksa chi daryayee makhlooq paki nandarey lapara satalay shee

aqueduct *n* داوبوبهنز da obo bahanz

arable adj کرنیزهمکه karaneeza zmaka

arbiter n. قاضي qazee

arbitrary a. قضائي،ثالثانه qazayee; salisana

arbitrate v.t. قضاوت کول؛منتوب کول qazawat kawal; manzgartob

arbitration n. منتوب manzgartob

arbitrator n. منی manzgaray

arc n. قوس qos

arcade n کمانيلاره kamanee lara

arch n. کمان kaman

arch v.t. دکمانپهبهاول da kaman pa banra arawal

arch a رئيس؛اصلي rayees; aslee

archaic a. لرغونی؛زو larghonay; zor

archangel n مقربهفرته moqarraba farikhta

archbishop n. لویاسقف loy asqaf

archer n ليندووالا؛خت کاری leenday wala; khakht karay

architect n. معمار maymar

architecture n. معماري maymaree

archives n.pl. دلاسوندونواوپانروضبط da laswandoono aw panro zabat

Arctic n پهشمالیقطبپوراوند pa shumalee qotab pori arwand

ardent a. شوقين؛لوال shawqeen; leywal

ardour n. ولوله؛لوالتيا walwala; leywaltya

arduous a. لهکاوهک la karawa dak

area n مساحت masahat

arena n دلوبور da lobo dagar

argue v.t. بحثکول behes kawal

argument n. مباحثه؛دليل mubahisa; daleel

arid adj. وچ wach

aright adv مستقيم mostaqeem

aright adv. مستقيماً mostaqeeman

arise v.i. پورتهکدل porta keydal

aristocracy n. اشرافواکي ashraf wakee

aristocrat n. داشرافواکپلوی da ashraf wakay palaway

arithmetic n. شمرپوهنه shmeyr pohana

arithmetical a. شمرپوهنيز shmeyr pohaneez

ark n کختی kakhtay

arm n. مه mat

arm v.t. وسلهوالکول wasla wal kawal

armada n. بحريواک behree zwak

armament n. وسله wasla

armature n. زغره؛وسله zghara; wasla

armistice n. زبندي daz bandee

armlet a مهبند mat band

armour n. زغره zghara

armoury n. وسلهتون wasla toon

army n. پو؛لکر poz; lakhkar

around prep. ردچاپره gard chapeyra

around adv پهشاوخواک pa shaw khwa ki

arouse v.t. ويول weekhawal

arraign v. محکمتهحاضرول mahkamey ta hazirawal

arrange v.t. اول odal

arrangement n. اوون odoon

arrant *n.* بدنامه badnama

array *v.t.* اول odal

array *n.* ترتیب tarteeb

arrears *n.pl.* ندلېپوررونه zandeydalee poroona

arrest *v.t.* نيول neewal

arrest *n.* نيونه،توقيف neewana; tawqeef

arrival *n.* رارسدنه raraseydana

arrive *v.i.* رارسدل raraseydal

arrogance *n.* زانليدنه zan leedana

arrogant *a.* كبرجن kabarjan

arrow *n* غشى ghashay

arsenal *n.* وسلهتون waslatoon

arson *n* پهقصديولاوربلوونه pa qasdee dawl orbalawona

art *n.* فن fan

artery *n.* سوررग soor rag

artful *a.* چلباز chalbaz

article *n* مقاله maqala

articulate *a.* ژبور zhabawar

artifice *n.* أستادي ustadee

artificial *a.* مصنوعي masnooee

artillery *n.* توپخانه topkhana

artisan *n.* صنعتگر sanatgar

artist *n.* هنرمند honarmand

artistic *a.* هنري honaree

artless *a.* بهنره bey honara

as *adv.* هغه كچ، كله چ،برنه چ hagha kach; kala chi; saranga chi

as *conj.* رنه چ saranga chi

as *pron.* لكه،غوند laka; ghondi

ascend *v.t.* پورتهتلل porta tlal

ascent *n.* عروج arooj

ascertain *v.t.* معلومول maloomawal

ascetic *n.* رياضت كوونكى reeyazat kawoonkay

ascetic *a.* زاهد zahid

ascribe *v.t.* منسوبول mansoobawal

ash *n.* ایر eerey

ashamed *a.* شرمدلى sharmeydalay

ashore *adv.* پهساحلباند pa sahil bandi

aside *adv.* پهيوهلوري ك pa yawa lori ki

aside *n.* جدلانه judagana

asinine *adj.* خروله khar dawla

ask *v.t.* پوښتل pokhtal

asleep *adv.* ويده weeda

aspect *n.* ره seyra

asperse *v.* بدنامول badnamawal

aspirant *n.* هيلهمن heelaman

aspiration *n.* اخستنه ساه sa akheystana

aspire *v.t.* زهكدل zra keydal

ass *n.* خر khar

assail *v.* بريدكول breed kawal

assassin *n.* قاتل qatil

assassinate *v.t.* قتلول qatlawal

assassination *n* قتل،وژنه qatal; wazhana

assault *n.* بريد breed

assault *v.t.* بريدكول breed kawal

assemble *v.t.* چمتوكول chamtóo kawal

assembly *n.* جره jarga

assent *v.i.* جوجاي كول jor jaree kawal

assent *n.* جوجاي jor jaree

assert *v.t.* پرکنده اظهاركول preykanda izhar kawal

assess *v.t.* تشخيصول tashkheesawal

assessment *n.* مالياتي وضعيت؛اكل malyatee wazeeyat; atkal

asset *n.* پانه panga

assign *v.t.* سپارل sparal

assignee *n.* ګومارل شوی gomaral shaway

assimilate *v.* يو شان كول؛جذب كول yaw shan kawal; jazab kawal

assimilation *n* دخوړ وجذب او تركيب da khwaro jazab aw tarkeeb

assist *v.t.* مرسته كول mrasta kawal

assistance *n.* مرسته mrasta

assistant *n.* مرستيال mrastyal

associate *v.t.* ارتباط لرل irtibat laral

associate *a.* شريك؛مرستندوی shareek; mrastandoy

associate *n.* ونډوال؛شريك wanda wal; shareek

association *n.* پوستون peywastoon

assoil *v.t.* رخصتول rukhsatawal

assort *v.t.* لبندي كول dalbandee kawal

assuage *v.t.* كمول kamawal

assume *v.t.* ومان كول gooman kawal

assumption *n.* ومان؛هو gooman; hod

assurance *n.* داد dad

assure *v.t.* اور كول dad warkawal

asterisk *n.* ستوری(دانه)(*) storgay (da nakha *)

asthma *n.*ساه لنی salanday

astonish *v.t.* حران ول heyranawal

astonishment *n.* حرانتيا heyrantya

astound *v.t* نوسول gangosawal

astray *adv.,* منحرف munharif

astrologer *n.* ستورپوهاند stor pohand

astrology *n.* ستورپوهنه stor pohana

astronaut *n.* ستوريونی stor yoonay

astronomer *n.* ستورپژاند stor peyzhand

astronomy *n.* ستوروين پوه stor ween poh

asunder *adv.* پرته parta

asylum *n* پناهای panahzay

at *prep.* ك؛د...په لور ki; da ... pa lori

atheism *n* ملحدتوب mulhidtob

atheist *n* له خدايه منكر la khudaya monkar

athirst *adj.* تی tagay

athlete *n.* ورزش كار warzish kar

athletic *a.* چست chust

athletics *n.* د ورزش كارعلم da warzish karay ilam

athwart *prep.* له دخوا هغه خواته la dey khwa hagha khwa ta

atlas *n.* د هوادونو دنخچو كتاب da heywadoono da nakhcho keetab

atmosphere *n.* فضا faza

atoll *n.* داپوانو لر da tapoogano lar

atom *n.* ام؛ترولو كوچنی بر كی atam; tar tolo koochnay basarkay

atomic *a.* اومی atomee

atone *v.i.* كفاره ور كول kafara warkawal

atonement *n.* كفاره kafara

atrocious *a.* بی رحمه bey rehma

atrocity *n* بی رحمی bey rehmee

attach *v.t.* نلول nakhlawal

attache *n.* سفيرسره‌اوندچارواکی
safeer sara arwand charwakay

attachment *n.* تاو taraw

attack *n.* برید؛یرغل breed; yarghal

attack *v.t.* یرغلراول yarghal rawral

attain *v.t.* برلاسی کدل barlasay
keydal

attainment *n.* بریالیتوب
baryaleetob

attempt *v.t.* هه‌کول hasa kawal

attempt *n.* هه hasa

attend *v.t.* حاضردل؛پام کول
hazireydal; pam kawal

attendance *n.* حاضري؛ار haziree;
sar

attendant *n.* خدمتار khidmatgar

attention *n.* توجه tawajo

attentive *a.* متوجه mutawajo

attest *v.t.* واهي‌ورکول؛تصدیقول
gawahee warkawal;
tasqeekawal

attire *n.* لباس libas

attire *v.t.* سیناراول seengarawal

attitude *n.* دچلندول da chaland
dawl

attorney *n.* وکیل wakeel

attract *v.t.* زه‌راکل zra rakkhal

attraction *n.* زه‌راکنه zra rakkhana

attractive *a.* زه‌راکوونکی؛جلبوونکی
zra rakkhowoonkay;
jalabowoonkay

attribute *v.t.* تخصیص‌ورکول؛په‌اوند
نل takhsees warkawal; pa
arwand ganral

attribute *n.* انی‌صفت zangaray
sifat

auction *n* لیلام leelam

auction *v.t.* لیلامول leelamawal

audible *a* داوریدو وړ da awreydo war

audience *n.* اوریدوونکي
awreydoonkee

audit *n.* پلنه palatana

audit *v.t.* پلل‌اوسارل palatal aw saral

auditor *n.* دحسابدارارونکی da
hisabdaray saroonkay

auditorium *n.* دکانفرانس‌تالار da
kanfarans talar

auger *n.* برمه barma

aught *n.* هرشی؛په‌هیول har shay; pa
hees dawl

augment *v.t.* زیاتول zyatawal

augmentation *n.* زیادت zyadakht

August *n.* دانرزي‌کال‌اتمه‌میاشت da
angreyzee kal atama myasht

august *n* عظیم؛ستر azeem; star

aunt *n.* ترور tror

aurilave *n.* غوپاکوونکی ghwag
pakowoonkay

aurora *n* سپده‌دا غ speyda dagh

auspicate *v.t.* پرانستنه‌کول
pranistana kawal

auspice *n.* فال fal

auspicious *a.* مبارک mubarak

austere *a.* سخت؛تریخ sakht; treekh

authentic *a.* صحیح sahee

author *n.* لیکوال leekwal

authoritative *a.* واکمن wakman

authority *n.* واک؛پرله wak;
preykhla

authorize *v.t.* واک‌ورکول wak
warkawal

autobiography *n.* خپل‌لاسی‌ژوند
لیک khpal lasay zhwand leek

autocracy *n* خپلواکه‌حکومت khpalwaką hookoomat

autocrat *n* بشپرواکمن bashpar wakman

autocratic *a* زورواکه zorwaka

autograph *n.* دلیکوال‌خپله‌لیکلی لاسلیک da leekwal khpala leekalay lasleek

automatic *a* خپل کاری khpal karay

automobile *n.* موټر motar

autonomous *a* خپلواک‌حکومت khpalwak hukoomat

autumn *n.* مني؛خزان manay; khazan

auxiliary *a.* مرستندویه mrastandoya

auxiliary *n.* مرستندوی mrastandoy

avail *v.t.* تری‌ه‌اخستل tri gata akheystal

available *a* موجود mawjood

avarice *n.* حرص hiras

avenge *v.t.* کسات‌اخستل kasat akheystal

avenue *n.* لوی‌وا loy wat

average *n.* حد مني manzanay had

average *a.* متوسط mutawasit

average *v.t.* اوسط‌اکل awsat takal

averse *a.* بزار beyzar

aversion *n.* بزاري beyzaree

avert *v.t.* دفع کول،برته‌رول dafa kawal; beyrta garzawal

aviary *n.* دالوتونکواله da alwatoonko zala

aviation *n.* هوایون hawayoon

aviator *n.* هوایوني hawayoonee

avid *adj.* هیله‌من heelaman

avidity *adv.* حرص hiras

avidly *adv* په‌هیله‌منه‌توه pa heela mana toga

avoid *v.t.* ه‌کول dada kawal

avoidance *n.* ه،اجتناب dada; ijtinab

avow *v.t.* منته‌کول manakhta kawal

await *v.t.* انتظار‌استل intizar eystal

awake *v.t.* ویدل،ویول weekheydal; weekhawal

awake *a* ویه weekh

award *v.t.* فتواورکول fitwa warkawal

award *n.* فتوا،بنه fitwa; bakhana

aware *a.* باخبر ba khabar

away *adv.* لر؛یولورته leyri; yaw lori ta

awe *n.* ار dar

awful *a.* اروونکی darowoonakay

awhile *adv.* یوه‌موده yaw sa mooda

awkward *a.* بخونده bey khwanda

axe *n.* تبر tabar

axis *n.* چورلیه choorleez

axle *n.* رخ sarkh

B

babble *n.* اپلتوینه apalti wayana

babble *v.i.* اپلتویل apalti wayal

babe *n.* کوچنی koochnay

babel *n* نامفهوم‌شوراوزو namafhooma shor aw zwag

baboon *n.* بیزو beezo

baby *n.* کوچنی koochnay

bachelor *n.* بی bey khazi

back *n.* شا؛ملا sha; mla

26

back *adv.* ترشا tar sha

backbite *v.t.* غیبت کول ghaybat kawal

backbone *n.* ملاتیر da mla teer

background *n.* لرلید lar leed

backhand *n.* دلاس پهوزار da las pa sat goozar

backslide *v.i.* په کوناتو خوایدل pa konato khwayeydal

backward *a.* په pa sat

backward *adv.* مخ پهوره makh pa zwara

bacon *n.* دخوگ دغولاندی da khoog da ghwakhi landay

bacteria *n.* یولنباتی اوحوانی مکروبونه yaw lar nabatee aw heywanee meykroboona

bad *a.* ناوه nawara

badge *n.* علامه؛نه alama; nakha

badger *n.* گرزندپلوروونکی garzand plorowoonkay

badly *adv.* په ناوه دول pa nawara dawl

badminton *n.* دنس لوبه چپه یوسالون کی یوترسره کي da tayna loba chi pa yaw salon ki ta sara keygee

baffle *v.t* گرانه جودل؛بیایلپرودل grana joreydal; bey payle preykhodal

bag *n.* کوه kasora

bag *v. i.* کوه کاچول kasora ki achawal

baggage *n.* دسفرتوه da safar tokha

bagpipe *n.* دموسیقیوول بادي آله da moseeqay yaw dawl badee ala

bail *n.* ضمانت zamanat

bail *v. t.* پهضمانت خلاصول pa zamanat khlasawal

bailable *a.* قابل ضمانت qabili zamanat

bailiff *n.* دجرماندموادوسرکاري ناظر da jormaney da mawado sarkaree nazir

bait *n* ناوریاکبان نیولولپاره پهدام کدخوو مواد zanawar ya kaban neewalo lapara pa dam ki da khwaro mawad

bait *v.t.* کارته دام کدخوومواد ایودل khkar ta dam ki da khwaro mawad eekhodal

bake *v.t.* په سکروو پخول pa skarwato pakhawal

baker *n.* په سکروو پخوونکی؛نانوای pa skarwato pakhowoonkay; nanway

bakery *n* دوپخوناوخووجوولونانوایی da doday pakhawani aw khwago jorawalo nanwayee

balance *n.* تله؛حساب tala; heesab

balance *v.t.* برابرول barabarawal

balcony *n.* دبالاخانبالکن da balakhani balkun

bald *a.* پک؛ینجی pak; ganjay

bale *n.* بلا bala

bale *v.t.* انی کول andi kawal

baleful *a.* ضررناک zararnak

ball *n.* غونسکه ghondaska

ballad *n.* یوول قصیده yaw dawl qaseeda

ballet *sn.* لهدیز ههنري ورزشي نا dala yeeza honaree warzishee nasa

balloon *n.* بوغ boghay

ballot *n* درایپله da rayi panra

ballot *v.i.* پەپلەرای‌ورکول pa panra ray warkawal

balm *n.* ملهم malham

balsam *n.* اوبه‌ملهم oba malham

bamboo *n.* باس banras

ban *n.* بندز bandeyz

ban *n* دبندزپرکه da bandeyz preykra

banal *a.* بی‌خونده bey khwanda

banana *n.* کله kayla

band *n.* پټی؛ک patay; karay

bandage ~*n.* دپ‌تنی da tap tarani patay

bandage *v.t* تپ‌زای‌په‌پتل tap zay pa patay taral

bandit *n.* داه‌مار dara mar

bang *v.t.* دربوول drabowal

bang *n.* دربوونه drabowana

bangle *n.* بنی bangree

banish *v.t.* له‌وطنه‌شل la watana sharal

banishment *n.* له‌وطنه‌شنه la watana sharana

banjo *n.* دموسیقی‌یارچدایروی‌دهلری da moseeqay yaw geetar chi dayrawee geyda laree

bank *n.* بانک،ک bank; kas

bank *v.t.* بانک‌کی‌پسای‌دل bank ki peysey eekhodal

banker *n.* بانکوال bankwal

bankrupt *n.* بی‌ارزښتوب،دوالیه bey arzakhtob; deywaleeya

bankruptcy *n.* دوالیه‌کدژ deywaleeya keydang

banner *n.* بریغ beyragh

banquet *n.* تشریفاتي‌ملمستیا tashreefatee meylmastaya

banquet *v.t.* دتشریفاتي‌ملمستیا da tashreefatee meylmastya bandobast kawal

bantam *n.* کوچني‌کورنی‌چر koochnay koranay charg

banter *v.t.* پري‌توکي‌کول pri toki kawal

banter *n.* توکمار tokmar

bantling *n.* مسخره maskhara

baptism *n.* په‌عیسائیت‌کدتعمیدغسل pa eesaeeyat ki da tameed ghosal

baptize +*v.t.* دتعمیدغسل‌ورکول da tameed ghosal warkawal

bar *n.* پته،کاره pata; katara

bar *v.t* اتل؛ممنوع‌رول taral; mamnoo garzawal

barb *n.* دغشي‌شاتنه da ghashee shatanay sanda

barbarian *a.* وحشیانه wehsheeyana

barbarian *n.* وحشي‌انسان wehshee insan

barbarism *n.* وحشیتوب wehsheetob

barbarity *n* وحشیانه‌عمل wehsheeyana amal

barbarous *a.* وحشي wehshee

barber *n.* ام؛نایي dam; nayee

bard *n.* شاعر shair

bare *a.* لوس،بربند los; barband

bare *v.t.* بربنول barbandawal

barely *adv.* ایله eela

bargain *n.* راکه‌ورکه rakra warkra

bargain *v.t.* راکه‌ورکه‌کول rakra warkra kawal

barge *n.* دمال‌ډولوکت da mal leygdawalo kakhtay

bark *n.* دسپی کونجندنه da spee kuranjeydana

bark *v.t.* غپل؛کونجدل ghapal; kuranjeydal

barley *n.* وربشی warbashi

barn *n.* دغلزرمتون da ghaley zeyrmatoon

barnacles *n* یوول کب چد کتیخ پورنلي yaw dawl kab chi da kakhtay beykh pori nakhalee

barometer *n* هواميچ hawa meych

barouche *n.* یبیزه راربه لورال یوو qaq dol salor araba beza bagai

barrack *n.* دفواستونای da foz astoganzay

barrage *n.* داوبوبند da obo band

barrel *n.* بوئشکه؛تیوب boshka; tyoob

barren *n* شا shar

barricade *n.* دخنونوپه مرسته بندز da khandoono pa mrasta bandeyz

barrier *n.* بندیزلول bandeyz lagawal

barrister n. وکیل wakeel

barter1 *v.t.* دمال دادلون بدلون تجارت کول da mal da adloon badloon tijarat kawal

barter2 *n.* دونجون تجارت da wanjoon tijarat

base *n.* بنس bansat

base *a.* سپک؛ناکس spak; nakas

base *v.t.* بنسایوخدل bansat eekhodal

baseless *a.* بی بنیاده bey boonyada

basement *n.* لاندینی پور landeenay por

bashful *a.* شرمندوکی sharmandookay

basic *a.* بنسیز bansateez

basil *n.* کشمالی kashmalay

basin *n.* تشت tasht

basis *n.* زمینه zameena

bask *v.i.* پتاوی ته کناستل peytawee ta kkheynastal

basket *n.* وکر tokray

bass *n.* دیوکب نوم da yaw kab noom

bastard *n.* ارمونی armoonay

bastard *a* کم اصله kam asla

bat *n* خپرک khaparak

bat *n* دغوندسکوهلونه da ghondaski wahalo danda

bat *v. i* په ده دغوندسکوهلولوبه کول pa danda da ghondaski wahalo loba kawal

batch *n* دلگی dalgay

bath *n* لمبا lamba

bathe *v. t* لمبیدل lambeydal

baton *n* دصاحب منصبانولته da sahib mansabano lakhta

batsman *n.* په ده غوندسکه وهونکی لوبغای pa danda ghondaska wahoonkay lobgharay

battalion *n* کندک kandak

battery *n* بر batray

battle *n* جنگ jang

battle *v. i.* جنگدل jangeydal

bawd *n.* بوا barwa

bawl *n.i.* په چغوفریادکول pa cheygho faryad kawal

bawn *n.*

bay *n* کوچنی خلیج koochnay khaleej

bayonet *n* نزه neyza

be *v.t.* کدل(دشتون رابطه فعل) keydal (da shtoon rabita fayl)

be *pref.* دانرزژبیومختای‌توری da angreyzay zhabi yaw makhtaray toray

beach *n* ددریاب‌سنه da daryab sanda

beacon *n* سمندري‌راغ samandaree sragh

bead *n* دتسبیح‌دانه da tasbeeh dana

beadle *n.* دکلیسانا‌ظم da kaleesa nazim

beak *n* موکه makhooka

beaker *n* کوری katoray

beam *n* تیر teer

beam *v. i* واناچول؛تیراچول warang achawal; teer achawal

bean *n.* لوبیا lobya

bear *n* یږ yag

bear *v.t* زول؛زیدل؛لال galal; zeygeydal; zeygawal

beard *n* یره geera

bearing *n* بردباري bordbaree

beast *n* حیوان heywan

beastly *a* حیوان‌وله heywan dawla

beat *v. t.* وهل wahal

beat *n* ضرب؛وهنه zarb; wahana

beautiful *a* کلی khkulay

beautify *v. t* کلی‌کول khkulay kawal

beauty *n* کلا khkula

beaver *n* بحري‌سپی bahree spay

because *conj.* که zaka

beck *n.* په‌اشاره‌سره‌هر‌کارته‌چمتوکدل pa ishara sara har kar ta chamtoo keydal

beckon *v.t.* اشاره‌ورکول ishara warkawal

become *v. i* کدل keydal

bed *n* پالنگ palang

bedevil *v. t* زورول zorawal

bedding *n.* دویده‌کدوکالی da weeda keydo kalee

bed-time *n.* دخوب‌وخت da khob wakht

bee *n.* مچ machay

beech *n.* دتروپاواودرکونجه‌زي‌لرونگ‌یوه‌ونه da teyro panro aw drey konja zaree laroonki yawa wana

beef *n* دغوایي‌غوه da ghwayee ghwakha

beehive *n.* بین gabeen

beer *n* بیر؛یونالکولی‌اک beer; yaw nalkawalay skhak

beet *n* چغندر chughandar

beetle *n* خزدکه khazdaka

befall *v. t* پدل peykheydal

before *prep* له ... خه‌واند la ... sakha warandi

before *adv.* ‌واند da warandi

before *conj* مخکله‌دچ makhki la dey chi

beforehand *adv.* له‌واند؛د‌مخه warandi; da makha

befriend *v. t.* ورسره‌ملرتیاکول warsara malgartya kawal

beg *v. t.* گدایي‌کول gadayee kawal

beget *v. t* تولیدول tawleedawal

beggar *n* گدا؛درورزر gada; darweyzgar

begin *n* پیل‌کول payl kawal

beginning *n.* پیل؛سر payl; sar

beguile *v. t* غولول gholawal

behalf *n* خاطر؛لوری khatir; loray

behave *v. i.* چلندکول chaland kawal

behaviour *n* چلند،اخلاق chaland; akhlaq

behead *v. t.* سرغوول sar ghosawal

behind *adv* پهشا pa sha

behind *prep* الله___خهشاته ... sakha sha ta

behold *v. t* مشاهده کول moshahida kawal

being *n* شتون؛وجود shtoon; wajood

belabour *v. t* پهسويوهل pa sotee wahal

belated *adj.* ځندلی zandeydalay

belch *v. t* سابندول sabandaval

belief *n* عقیده aqeeda

believe *v. t* عقیدهلرل aqeeda laral

bell *n* زنگ zang

belle *n* کلنجل khkuli najlay

bellicose *a* جاوو jagrawoo

belligerency *n* جهماري jagramaree

belligerent *a* جهییز،جاوو jagrayeez; jagrawoo

belligerent *n* جه کونکی jagra kawoonkay

bellow *v. i* رمباوهل rambari wahal

bellows *n.* دپخ؛سی da pakh banay; sagay

belly *n* هgeyda

belong *v. i* اهلرل ara laral

belongings *n.* کالياوسامان kalee aw saman

beloved *a* محبوب mahboob

beloved *n* معشوق mashooq

below *adv* تر___لاند tar ... landi

below *prep* لاند landi

belt *n* کمربند kamar band

belvedere *n* المرخوال lmar khwalay

bemuse *v. t* مستول mastawal

bench *n* اودموکه oogda sawkay

bend *n* کووالی kogwalay

bend *v. t* کهدل،کول kageydal; kagawal

beneath *adv* تر___لاند tri ... landi

beneath *prep* لاند،یه landi; teet

benefaction *n.* ه kheygara

benefice *n* صوفیانهاوزاهدانهژوند sofiana au zahidana jwand

beneficial *a* ور gatawar

benefit *n* فایده،گاته gata; fayda

benefit *v. t.* گاتهرسول gata rasawal

benevolence *n* سخاوت sakhawat

benevolent *a* سخي sakhee

benevolent *v. t* سخاوتکول sakhawat kawal

benign *adj* مهربان mehraban

benignly *adv* پهمهربانسره mehrabanay sara

bent *n* کووالی kogwalay

bequeath *v. t.* میراثکپرودل meeras ki preykhodal

bereave *v. t.* محرومول mahroomawal

bereavement *n* محرومیت mahroomeeyat

berth *n* داورباياوکتخوبخانه da orgadee aw kakhtay khob khana

beside *prep.* له پرته parta la

besides *prep* برسره bar seyra

besides *adv* پر___برسره par ... bar seyra

besiege *v. t* محاصرهکول muhasira kawal

bestow *v. t* بسپنه‌ورکول baspana warkawal

bestrew *v. t* پوبل;شنل pokhal; shanal

bet *v.i* شرط‌تل shart taral

bet *n* شرط shart

betray *v.t.* خيانت‌كول khayanat kawal

betrayal *n* خيانت;غداري khayanat; ghadaree

betroth *v. t* په‌نامه‌كول pa nama kawal

betrothal *n.* نامزدي namzadgee

better *a* غوره ghwara

better *adv.* په‌غوره‌دول pa ghwara dawl

better *v. t* غوره‌كدل;غوره‌كول ghwara keydal; ghwara kawal

betterment *n* بهتري behtaree

between *prep* په‌منځ pa manz ki

beverage *n* اك skhak

bewail *v. t* ماتم‌كول matam kawal

beware *v.i.* متوجه‌اوسدل mutawajo oseydal

bewilder *v. t* ننس‌كول gangas kawal

bewitch *v.t* جادوكول jadoo kawal

beyond *prep.* هغه‌خوالري hagha khwa leyri

beyond *adv.* اله ... پورته la ... porta

bi *pref* دانرزژبيومختای‌توری da angreyzay zhabi yaw makhtaray toray

biangular *adj.* دوه‌زاويلرونكي dwa zaweeyi laroonkay

bias *n* تعصب tasob

bias *v. t* تعصب‌كول tasob kawal

bible *n* انجيل injeel

bibliography *+n* كتاب‌پژندنه kitab peyzhandana

bibliographer *n* كتاب‌پژاند kitab peyzhand

bicentenary *adj* دوه‌سوه‌كلن dwa sawa kalan

bicker *v.t* شخره‌كول shkhara kawal

bicycle *n.* بايسكل baysakal

bid *v.t* په‌مزايده‌كواندزورکول pa muzayda ki warandeyz warkawal

bid *n* په‌مزايده‌كواندز pa muzayda ki warandeyz

bidder *n* په‌مزايده‌كواندزكوونكی pa muzayda ki warandey kawoonkay

bide *v. t* كامياب‌لپاره‌سخت‌انتظاركول kamyabay lapara sakht intizar kawal

biennial *adj* دوه‌كلن‌وار dwa kalan war

bier *n* دتابوت‌دايودوای da taboot da eekheydo zay

big *a* لوی loy

bigamy *n* دوه‌خزي‌لرنه dwa khazi larana

bight *n* كوراكو kog rakog

bigot *n* متعصب‌كس motasib kas

bigotry *n* تعصب tasob

bile *n* صفرا safra

bilingual *a* دوه‌ژبيز dwa zhabeez

bill *n* قانوني‌لايحه;بل qanoonee layha; bil

billion *n* بيليون;دپسويوشمره beelyoon; da peyso yaw shmeyra

billow *n* لويه‌سپه loya sapa

billow *v.i* پوهل sapey wahal

bilk *v. t.* غولول gholawal

bimonthly adj. دوه میاشتنۍ dwa myashtanay

binary adj لدوه هندسو جو la dwa hindso jor

bind v.t تل taral

binding a پایدار paydar

binocular n. دوه ستریز دوربین dwa stargeez doorbeen

biographer n ژوندلیک لیکونکی zhwand leek leekoonkay

biography n ژوندلیک zhwand leek

biologist n ژوند پوهاند zhwand pohand

biology n ژوند پوهنه zhwand pohana

bioscope n د فلم و دلو پروجکور da filam khodalo projektor

biped n دوه پلرونکی جاندار dwa pkhey laroonkay jandar

birch n. یو دول ونه yaw dawl wana

bird n الوتونکی alwatoonkay

birth n. زیږدنه zeygeydana

biscuit n بسکو biskot

bisect v.t نیمول neemawal

bisexual adj. دوه ره،دوه جنسه dwa raga; dwa jinsa

bishop n اسقف په عیسائیت کی pa eesaeeyat ki asqaf

bison n یو دول غرنی او وحشی بکام لرونکی غوایی yaw dawl gharanay aw wehshee bakam laroonkay ghwayay

bit n یوه توه،لګه برخه yawa tota; laga barkha

bitch n سپی spay

bite v.t. چیچل cheechal

bite n چک؛چیچ chak; cheech

bitter a تریخ treekh

bi-weekly adj دوه اونیزه dwa ooneeza

bizarre adj عجیب ajeeb

blab v.t. & i بی پتی کول bey patee kawal

black a تور tor

blacken v.t. تورول torawal

blackmail n په ارونو دپسو وصولتیا pa darawano da peyso wasooltya

blackmail v.t د بدنامی په دار له چاخه پیسی اخستل da badnamay pa dar la cha sakha peysey akheystal

blacksmith n پ pakh

bladder n مثانه masana

blade n. تغ teygh

blain n التهابی پسوب iltihabee parsob

blame v.t ملامت ملامتول malamat ganral

blame n ملامتیا،الزام malamatya; ilzam

blanch v.t. & i پوستول postawal

bland adj. آرامه arama

blank a ساده،پاک sada; pak

blank n تش ای،نالیکلپاه tash zay; naleekali panra

blanket n ش sharay

blare v.t جار وهل jar wahal

blast n چاودنه chawdana

blast v.i چوول؛چاودل chowal; chawdal

blaze n شوغله shoghla

blaze v.i لمبه کدل؛زور اخستل lamba keydal; zor akheystal

bleach v.t. سپینول؛وینل speenawal; weenzal

blear v.t تاریکول tareekawal

bleat *n* بعبع ba ba

bleat *v. i* بعبع کول،امباامباکول ba ba kawal; amba amba kawal

bleed *v. i* وينکدل weeni keydal

blemish *n* داغ dagh

blend *v. t* مخلوطول makhlootawal

blend *n* مخلوط،وله makhloot; gadola

bless *v. t* برکت ورکول barakat warkawal

blether *v. i* ناوهغدل nawara ghageydal

blight *n* بادوهنه bad wahana

blind *a* وند roond

blindfold *v. t* سترتل stargi taral

blindness *n* نهليدا na leeda

blink *v. t. & i* سترک وهل stargak wahal

bliss *n* کامله خوي kamila khwakhee

blister *n* تاکه tanraka

blizzard *n* دواورتوپان da wawri toopan

bloc *n* کونده konda

block *n* بند،خن band; khand

block *v.t* خن کدل،بندول khand keydal; bandawal

blockade *n* بندز bandeyz

blockhead *n* احمق سی ahmaq saray

blood *n* وينه weena

bloodshed *n* وينهتويونه weena toyawana

bloody *a* پهوينولری pa weeno laralay

bloom *n* غو ghotay

bloom *v.i.* غوکول ghotay kawal

blossom *n* غو ghotay

blossom *v.i* غوکول ghotay kawal

blot *n.* داغ dagh

blot *v. t* داغ لگول dagh lagawal

blouse *n* جاکوله کميس jakat dawla kamees

blow *v.i.* بادچلدل bad chaleydal

blow *n* بادچلدنه bad chaleydana

blue *n* نيل neel

blue *a* آبی رنز abee rang

bluff *v. t* تراستل teyr eystal

bluff *n* تراستنه teyr eystana

blunder *n* لويهتروتنه loya teyrwatana

blunder *v.i* ناوهتروتنه کول nawara teyrwatana kawal

blunt *a* پ pas

blur *n* تتدنه tateydana

blurt *v. t* بيامهغدل bey pama ghageydal

blush *n* دمخ سوروالی da makh soorwalay

blush *v.i* لهشرمدومخ سورمدل la sharmeydo makh sooreydal

boar *n* وحشي خو wahshee khoog

board *n* دبتخته da beyray takhta

board *v. t.* پکسپردل beyray ki spareydal

boast *v.i* لافوهل lafi wahal

boast *n* لاف lafi

boat *n* کوچنی کتی koochnay kakhtay

boat *v.i* کتی چلول kakhtay chalawal

bodice *n* سينهبند seena band

bodily *a* بدني badanee

bodily *adv.* جسمل،يوای jisman; yaw zay

body *n* بدن badan

bodyguard *n.* ساتندوی satandoy

bog *n* جبه jaba

bog *v.i* جبه کودیدل jaba ki doobeydal

bogus *a* درواغ darwagh

boil *n* جوش josh

boil *v.i.* اشول eyshawal

boiler *n* جوشوونکی joshawoonkay

bold *a.* زهور zra war

boldness *n* ورتیا زه zra wartya

bolt *n* دکولپزبانچه da kolp zabancha

bolt *v. t* کولپبندول kolp bandawal

bomb *n* بم bam

bomb *v. t* بمباري کول bambaree kawal

bombard *v. t* بمباري کول bambaree kawal

bombardment *n* بمباري bambaree

bomber *n* بماچوونکالوتکه bam achowoonki alwataka

bonafide *adv* بیبهانی bey bahaney

bonafide *a* سماوجدي sam aw jadee

bond *n* بند،لاسوند band; laswand

bondage *n* مرییتوب mrayeetob

bone *n.* هوکی hadookay

bonfire *n* لوياور loy or

bonnet *n* یوولخوالی yaw dawl khwali

bonus *n* انعام eenam

book *n* لیکی leekay

book *v. t.* درجکول darj kawal

book-keeper *n* الیکیساتونکی leekay satoonkay

book-mark *n.* دلیکینان da leekee nakhan

book-seller *n* لیکيپلورونکی leekee plorowoonkay

book-worm *n* دلیکيچینجی da leekee cheenjay

bookish *n.* کتابی keetab

booklet *n* کتابوی keetabgotay

boon *n* نعمت naymat

boor *n* شلسی shadal saray

boost *n* پرمخوزنه par makh warana

boost *v. t* پرمخول par makh waral

boot *n* بو،فایده boot; fayda

booth *n* پره sapara

booty *n* ولجه walja

booze *v. i* مستول mastawal

border *n* پوله poola

border *v.t* پولهلرل poola laral

bore *v. t* سوری کول sooray kawal

bore *n* دیوهپایپداخليسوری da yawa payp dakhilee sooray

born *v.* زییدل zeygeydal

borne *adj.* زدلی zeygeydalay

borrow *v. t* پوراخستل por akheystal

bosom *n* سینه seena

boss *n* رئیس rayees

botany *n* بوپوهنه bootpohana

botch *v. t* ناماهرانهپوندول namahirana peywandawal

both *a* دواه dwara

both *pron* دواه،هم_هم dwara; ham … ham

both *conj* نهیواز na yawazi

bother *v. t* زحمتول zehmatawal

botheration *n* جنجال janjal

bottle *n* بوتل botal

bottom *n* تل،بخ tal; beykh

35

bough *n* انه sanga

boulder *n* لویهﺭﻩلویه loya gol dabara

bouncer *n* بالو batoo

bound *n.* ﻭپ top

boundary *n* پوله poola

bountiful *a* لورینه lawreena

bounty *n* انعام eenam

bouquet *n* لدسته guldasta

bout *n* نوبت؛حالت nobat; halat

bow *v. t* بیدل teeteydal

bow *n* یت؛کو teet; kog

bow *n* کمان kaman

bowel *n.* ددنبرخه da geydi dananay barkha

bower *n* پره sapara

bowl *n* کاسه kasa

bowl *v.i* دغونسکیپهشانﺍﺭغدل da ghondaski pa shan eyrghareydal

box *n* صندوق sandooq

boxing *n* دسوکﻭهذلوبه da sook wahani loba

boy *n* هلک halak

boycott *v. t.* سرهﺍیکﺥتموﻝ sara areeki khatmawal

boycott *n* دﺍیکوبندز da areeko bandeyz

boyhood *n* هلکتوب halaktob

brace *n* تانه taranga

bracelet *n* وﻯ wakhay

brag *v. i* نازیدل nazeydal

brag *n* ناز؛با naz; bati

braille *n* دندولپارمانیلیک da rando lapara zangaray leek

brain *n* دماغ dimagh

brake *n* دﻣوﺭبریک da motar brayk

brake *v. t* بریکلوﻝ brayk lagawal

branch *n* انه sanga

brand *n* تجارتينه tijaratee nakha

brandy *n* یووﻝشراب yaw dawl sharab

brass *n.* برنج؛ژ birinj; zhar

brave *a* توریالی tooryalay

bravery *n* مانه meyrana

brawl *v. i. & n* ناندﺭﻭهل،ناندﺭ nandaray wahal; nandaray

bray *n* دخرهﺭمبا da khra rambari

bray *v. i* هندل hangeydal

breach *n* نقض nuqz

bread *n* ﻭ doday

breadth *n* پراخوﺍلی parakhwalay

break *v. t* ماتدل،ماتوﻝ mateydal; matawal

break *n* ماتوﺍلی؛بﺩ matwalay; zand

breakage *n* ماتدنه mateydana

breakdown *n* نلاپهخرﺍبتیا nasapa kharabtya

breakfast *n* سهارﻥ saharanay

breakneck *n* ترهوونکی tarhowoonkay

breast *n* ﺗﻲtee

breath *n* ساﻩ sa

breathe *v. i.* ساﻩاخستل sa akheystal

breeches *n.* ترﺯنانهپورلﻥپتلوﻥ tar zangana pori land patloon

breed *v.t* ﺭﻭزﻝ rozal

breed *n* تخم؛ﺭﻭﺯنه tokham; rozana

breeze *n* ﻭمه wagma

breviary *n.* غورﭼاشوﻯکتاب ghorchanr shaway keetab

brevity n لنون landoon

brew v. t. اک‌جوول skhak jorawal

brewery n اک‌جوونه skhak jorawana

bribe n بۍ badi

bribe v. t. بۍ وهل/ورکول badi wahal / warkawal

brick n خته khakhta

bride n ناو nawi

bridegroom n. شلمی shazalmay

bridge n پل pol

bridle n پزوان peyzwan

brief a. مختصر mukhtasar

brigade n. غوز ghond

bright a لاند zaland

brighten v. t روانول rokhanawal

brilliant a نامتو namtoo

brim n سه sanda

brine n اوبه ترو trawey oba

bring v. t راول rawral

brinjal n بانجان banjan

brink n. ژ zhay

brisk adj چک chatak

bristle n وژغونه wazhghona

british adj بریتانوي breetanawee

brittle a. کسن krasan

broad a پراخ prakh

broadcast n خپرونه khparawana

broadcast v. t خپرول khparawal

brocade n کمخاب kimkhab

broccoli n. یو دول بولۍ yaw dawl gopee

brochure n کتابگوتۍ kitabgotay

brochure n رساله risala

broker n سمسار samsar

brood n دجاندارو په‌یوای‌ځای‌دلی‌ماشومان da jandaro pa yaw zay zeygeydalee mashooman

brook n. ویاله wyala

broom n جارو jaroo

bronze n. & adj برونز؛برونزي‌رنۍ bronz; bronzee rang

broth n وروا khorwa

brothel n فاحشه‌خانه fahisha khana

brother n ورور wror

brotherhood n ورورولي wrorwalee

brow n وریز wreez

brown a نصواري naswaree

brown n نصواري‌رنۍ naswaree rang

browse n په‌لوستنه‌پلل pa lostana palatal

bruise n میدیدنه meydeydana

bruit n ونوسی gongosay

brush n برش brash

brutal a برحمه bey rehma

brute n وحشي‌ناور wahshee zanawar

bubble n پوکنه pookanra

bucket n ولچه dolcha

buckle n سک sagak

bud n غنچه ghoncha

budget n بودجه،لخت‌انولتیا bodija; lagakht andwaltya

buff n پیکه‌زیر‌رنۍ peeka zyar rang

buffalo n. مه meykha

buffoon n مسخره maskhara

bug n. خزنده khazanda

bugle n شپل shpeylay

build v. t تعمیرول tameerawal

build n جوت jorakht

building n وداز wadanay

bulb *n.* برنايي،راغ breykhnayee sragh

bulk *n* حجم hojam

bulky *a* وزنلرونکی wazan laroonkay

bull n غوايی ghwayay

bulldog *n* يوولسپی yaw dawl spay

bullet *n* مرمه marmay

bulletin *n* خبرپاه khabar panra

bully *n* دپپهلوان da pkhey palawan

bully *v. t.* تهديدول tahdeedawal

bulwark *n* دبندډوال da band deywal

bumper *n.* فنر،بمپر finar; bampar

bunch *n* وی wagay

bundle *n* keyday

bungalow *n* ما manray

bungle *v. t* خرابول kharabawal

bungle *n* خرابونه kharabawana

bunk *n* هرولراکته کدونکی چپرکیا بستره har dawl rakakhta keydoonkay chaparkat ya bistara

bunker *n* تحويلخانه tahweelkhana

buoy *n* لامبوزنتوکی lambozan tokay

buoyancy *n* لامبووهنه lambowahana

burden *n* بار bar

burden *v. t* بارول barawal

burdensome *a* سخت،ناوه sakht; nawara

bureau *n.* دفتر daftar

Bureacuracy *n.* اداري تأسيسات idaree taseesat

bureaucrat *n* اداريمأمور idaree mamoor

burglar *n* غل ghal

burglary *n* غلا ghla

burial *n* خوونه khakhowana

burn *v. t* سوزول swazawal

burn *n* سون soon

burrow *n* ترمکلاندسوه tar zmakay landi soora

burst *v. i.* چاودېدل chawdeydal

burst *n* چاودنه chawdana

bury *v. t.* خول khakhawal

bus *n* اتوبوس atoboos

bush *n* بوی bootay

business *n* راکهورکه،دنده rakra warkra; danda

businessman *n* تاجر tajir

bustle *v. t* پهجنجالاوډل pa janjal oreydal

busy *a* بوخت bokht

but *prep* مرداچ magar da chi

but *conj.* خو،وا kho; wali

butcher *n* قصاب qasab

butcher *v. t* پهظلموژل pa zolam wazhal

butter *n* کوچ kuch

butter *v. t* چاپلوسيکول chaplosee kawal

butterfly *n* پتنگ patang

buttermilk *n* پروی peyrawee

buttock *n* کونای konatay

button *n* ز tanray

button *v. t.* تبندول tanray bandawal

buy *v. t.* خريداريکول khareedaree kawal

buyer *n.* پرودونکی peyrodoonkay

buzz *v. i* بنډل bangeydal

buzz *n.* بنار bangar

by *prep* د...په وسيله da ... pa waseela

by *adv* لاخه la arakha

bye-bye *interj.* خداى دى مل شه khuday di mal sha

bylaw, bye-law *n* ضمنى قانون،سيمه ييز قانون zimnee qanoon; seemayeez qanoon

bypass *n* فرعي لار faree lar

by-product *n* فرعي محصول faree mahsool

byre *n* غوجله ghojala

byword *n* متل matal

C

cab *n.* د كرايمور da karayi motar

cabaret *n.* موسيقي واله ملمستون moseeqee wala meylmastoon

cabbage *n.* وپي gopee

cabin *n.* كوچنى خونه koochnay khoona

cabinet *n.* د وزيرانو دلگى خونه da wazeerano da dalgay khoona

cable *n.* سيمي پى seemee paray

cable *v. t.* په سيمي پي تل pa seemee paree taral

cache *n* ساتنای satanzay

cachet *n* تپه tapa

cackle *v. i* ككوهل kakari wahal

cactus *n.* زاقوم zaqoom

cad *n* سپک او بي تربيسى spak aw bey tarbeeyey saray

cadge *v. i* گدايي كول gadayee kawal

cafe *n.* قهوه خانه qahwa khana

cage *n.* زندان zandan

cake *n.* كك kayk

calamity *n.* آفت afat

calcium *n* د فلز كلسيم da kilseeyum filiz

calculate *v. t.* شمرل shmeyral

calculator *n* شمرونكى ماشين shmeyroonkay masheen

calculation *n.* شمر shmeyr

calendar *n.* كالهنداره kalhindara

calf *n.* خوسكى khuskay

call *v. t.* رابلل rabalal

call *n.* بلنه balana

caller *n* رابلوونكى rabalowoonkay

calligraphy *n* ليكنه بانره leekanay banra

calling *n.* بلنه؛چغه balana; cheygha

callow *adj* بتجربه bey tajrubey

callous *a.* سخت زړى sakht zaray

calm *n.* آرامت aramakht

calm *n.* خاموشي khamoshee

calm *v. t.* خاموشول khamoshawal

calmative *adj* آراموونكى aramowoonkay

calorie *n.* د تودوخد معلومو ندرجه da tawdokhey da maloomawani daraja

calumniate *v. t.* تورلول tor lagawal

camel *n.* او ookh

camera *n.* د عكاس كامره da akasay kamra

camp *n.* پنغالى pandghalay

camp *v. i.* خمدرول kheymey darawal

campaign *n.* مبارزه mubariza

camphor *n.* كافور kafoor

can *n.* حلبی لوی halbee lokhay

can *v. t.* په حلبي لوي كاچول pa halbee lokhee ki achawal

can *v.* تواندل twaneydal

canal *n.* وياله wyala

canard *n* دروغجن خبر daroghjan khabar

cancel *v. t.* باطلول؛حذفول batilawal; hazafawal

cancellation *n* حذف،فسخ hazaf; faskh

cancer *n.* ناسور؛چنگ nasoor; changakh

candid *a.* لاند zaland

candidate *n.* نوماند noomand

candle *n.* شمع shama

candour *n.* سپین ويي speen goyee

candy *n.* پتاسه patasa

candy *v. t.* شيريني رانيول sheereenee raneewal

cane *n.* لكه،مسافر خانه lakara; musafir khana

cane *v. t.* په لكه وهل pa lakara wahal

canister *n.* دمزري كوچنو كر da meyzaree koochnay tokray

cannon *n.* يو سترو پك yaw star topak

canon *n* مذهبي قانون mazhabee qanoon

canopy *n.* پر sapray

canteen *n.* يو ول خوناى yaw dawl khwaranzay

canter *n* تفريحي چكر tafreehee chakar

canton *n* برخه barkha

cantonment *n.* دنظامي لتمهای da nizamee dalgay tamzay

canvas *n.* تات tat

canvass *v. t.* رايغوتل rayi ghokhtal

cap *n.* خول khwalay

cap *v. t.* په سر خولا يودل pa sar khwali eekhodal

capability *n.* وتيا wartya

capable *a.* ور war

capacious *a.* پراخ prakh

capacity *n.* پراختيا prakhtya

cape *n.* سر sar

capital *n.* پلازمنه،پانه plazmeyna; panga

capital *a.* تورى لوى loy toray

capitalist *n.* پانوال pangawal

capitulate *v. t* تسليمدل tasleemeydal

caprice *n.* وسواس waswas

capricious *a.* وسواسي waswasee

Capricorn *n* دجدي مياشت da jadee myasht

capsize *v. i.* سرچپه كول sar chapa kawal

capsular *adj* د كپسول په شكل da kipsool pa shakal

captain *n.* جتورن،مشر jagtooran; mashar

captaincy *n.* مشري masharee

caption *n.* پركه نيوذ د da neewani preykra

captivate *v. t.* مسحورول mashoorawal

captive *n.* بندي bandee

captive *a.* مسحور mashoor

captivity *n.* زندانيتوب zandaneetob

capture v. t. نيول؛تسخيرول neewal; taskheerawal

capture n. نيونه neewana

car n. موټر motar

carat n. قيراط qeerat

caravan n. قافله qafila

carbon n. د کاربن فلزیاس da karban filiz ya geys

card n. کارت؛پاڼه kart; panra

cardamom n. هل heyl

cardboard n. له سخت کاغذه جوړه شوی نری ګته la sakht kaghaza jora shawi naray gata

cardiacal adjs پهزړهپوراوند pa zra pori arwand

cardinal a. بنسيز bansateez

cardinal n. پهعيسائيت کيو مذهبي مشر pa eesaeeyat ki yaw mazhabee mashar

care n. پام pam

care v. i. پام کول pam kawal

career n. دژوندکنلاره da zhwand kranlar

careful a ږير zeyr

careless a. بېفکره bey fikra

caress v. t. نازول nazawal

caricature n. له هوکو او مسخرو کانور la toko aw maskharo dak anzor

carious adj بوسیده boseeda

carnage n. ټولوژنه tol wazhana

carnival n. جشن jashn

carol n. سرود؛نغمه sarood; naghma

carpenter n. ترکاڼ tarkanr

carpentry n. ترکاڼي tarkanree

carpet n. غال ghalay

carriage n. لادونه leygdawana

carrier n. لادوونکی leygdawoonkay

carrot n. ازره gazara

carry v. t. وړل؛بارول waral; bar waral

cart n. کراچ krachay

carton n پ peytay

cartoon n. کاریکاټور kareekatoor

cartridge n. کارتوس؛مرم kartoos; marmay

carve v. t. تول؛تراشل togal; trashal

cascade n. وبی zarobay

case n. بکس baks

cash n. نغدپسے naghdi peysey

cash v. t. پسنغدول peysey naghdawal

cashier n. خزانهدار khazana dar

casing n. پو pokhakh

cask n دمايعاتو لپاره پايپ da mayato lapara payp

casket n کوچنبکس koochnay baks

cast v. t. اچول؛طرحهکول achawal; tarha kawal

cast n. اچونه؛وضعيت achawana; wozeeyat

caste n نژاد nazhad

castigate v. t. نیوکهکول neewaka kawal

casting n ریختهري؛قالب کاچونه reykhta garee; qalib ki achawana

cast-iron n چدن chadan

castle n. کلا kala

castor oil n. تل ول یو yaw dawl teyl

casual a. تصادفي tasadofee

casualty n. پهمینه peykha; mreena

cat n. پیشو peesho

catalogue n. اليك lar leek

cataract n. دستری‌ل da stargi gol

catch v. t. نیول neewa

catch n. نیونه neewana

categorical a. پرکنده preykanda

category n. طبقه،له dala; tabqa

cater v. i خواه‌چمتو‌کول khwara chamtoo kawal

caterpillar n دورمو‌چینجی da wreykhmo cheenjay

cathedral n. کلیسا عمومی‌amoomee kaleesa

catholic a. کاتولیک عیسائ katoleek eesayee

cattle n. دغوامویله da ghwameykho gala

cauliflower n. گل‌وپی gol gopee

causal adj. سببی sababee

causality n دعلت‌او‌معلول‌ترمنایکه da ilat aw malool tar manz areeka

cause n. سبب sabab

cause v.t لامل‌رڅدل lamal garzeydal

causeway n وچه‌پخه‌لاره wacha pakha lara

caustic a. سوزوونکی sozawoonkay

caution n. خبرداری khabardaray

caution v. t. خبرداری‌ورکول khabardaray warkawal

cautious a. بدار baydar

cavalry n. سپاره‌عسکر spara askar

cave n. سمه smas

cavern n. لوی‌سمه loy askar

cavil v. t عبونه‌پلل ayboona palatal

cavity n. کنده kanda

caw n. کاغ‌کاغ kragh kragh

caw v. i. کاغ‌کاغ‌کول kagh kagh kawal

cease v. i. لاس‌اخستل las akheystal

ceaseless ~a. پرله‌پسی parla pasi

cedar n. سرو sarwa

ceiling n. چت chat

celebrate v. t. & i. لمانل lmanzal

celebration n. لماننه lmanzana

celebrity n نوموی noomawaray

celestial adj آسمانی asmanee

celibacy n. یوازیتوب yawazitob

celibacy n. تنهایی tanhayee

cell n. سلول؛کوچنی‌زندان؛حجره siool; koochnay zandan; hajra

cellar n زیرخانه zeyr khana

cellular adj سلولی siloolee

cement n. سمنټ simant

cement v. t. په‌سمنټوجوول pa simanto jorawal

cemetery n. میستون mreestoon

cense v. t عطرواوخوشبویوسره‌عبادات‌کول atro aw khushbooyo sara ibadat kawal

censer n عطردان atardan

censor n. دمطبوعاتواوچلندونوارونکی da matbooato aw chalandoono saroonkay

censor v. t. دمطبوعاتواوچلندونونارنه‌کول da matbooato aw chalandoono sarana kawal

censorious adj عب‌پلونکی ayb palatoonkay

censorship n. دسانسورجرجه da sansor jargagay

censure n. سخته‌نیوکه sakhta neewaka

42

censure *v. t.* سخته نيو كه كول sakhta neewaka kawal

census *n.* سرشمرنه sar shmeyrana

cent *n* سلمه salama

centenarian *n* سلمه كليزه salama kaleeza

centenary *n.* د سلم كليز جشن da salami kaleezi jashan

centennial *adj.* سل كليزه sal kaleeza

center *n* مركز markaz

centigrade *a.* د تو دو خيو پيمائش da tawdokhay yaw paymayish

centipede *n.* زنزه zanza

central *a.* مركزي markazee

centre *n* مركز markaz

centrifugal *adj.* د له مركز خه راكونك markaz sakha rakhkoonkay

century *n.* پېر سليزه peyray; saleeza

ceramics *n* د كودوي لوي da kawdoree lokhee

cereal *n.* غَله ghala

cereal *a* غَلَه ييز ghalayeez

cerebral *adj* د كوچني دماغ په اوند da koochnee dimagh pa arwand

ceremonial *a.* تشريفاتي tashreefatee

ceremonious *a.* د تشريفاتو پابند da tashreefato paband

ceremony *n.* جشن jashan

certain *a* يقيني yaqeenee

certainly *adv.* يقينا yaqeenan

certainty *n.* پوخ باور pokh bawar

certificate *n.* شهادت نامه shahadat nama

certify *v. t.* تصديق قول tasdeeqawal

cerumen *n* د غوزوه da ghwag zawa

cesspool *n.* د پخلني دلوو وينلو اى da pakhlanzee da lokho weenzalo zay

chain *n* زنير zanzeer

chair *n.* كرسه kursay

chairman *n* رئيس rayees

challenge *n.* مبارزه mubariza

challenge *v. t.* مبارزتهبل mubarizey ta tlal

chamber *n.* خونه khoona

chamberlain *n* ناظر؛ پره دار nazir; peyra dar

champion *n.* اتل atal

champion *v. t.* اتلولى كول atlawali kawal

chance *n.* موقع؛فرصت moqa; fursat

chancellor *n.* لوى منشي؛لومى وزير loy munshee; loomray wazeer

chancery *n* دلوى منشي يالومي وزير دنده يامقام da loy munshee ya loomree wazeer danda ya maqam

change *v. t.* بدلول badlawal

change *n.* بدلون badloon

channel *n* بهن؛وسيله bahanz; waseela

chant *n* سندره sandara

chaos *n.* وي gadwadee

chaotic *adv.* په وسره pa gadwaday sara

chapel *n.* د عبادت كوچنى اى da ibadat koochnay zay

chapter *n.* باب؛درس؛پركى bab; dars; saparkay

character *n.* سيرت seerat

charge *v. t.* دنده سپارل؛تهمت لول danda sparal; tohmat lagawal

charge n. سپارنه،تهمت sparana; tohmat

chariot n جنګي کراچۍ jangee krachay

charitable a. خراتي kheyratee

charity n. خرات kheyrat

charm1 n. سحر،کلا seher; khkula

charm2 v. t. پەسحرمجذوبول pa seher majzoobawal

chart n. دنقشجوولوکاغذ da naqshey jorawalo kaghaz

charter n اجازەلیک،قرارداد eejaza leek; qarardad

chase1 v. t. شارل saral

chase2 n. شارنه،تعقیب sarana; taqeeb

chaste a. پاک pak

chastity n. پاکبازي pakbazee

chat1 n. اترخبر khabari atari

chat2 v. i. خبراترکول khabari atari kawal

chatter v. t. کټپټکول krati prati kawal

chauffeur n. موروان motarwan

cheap a ارزان arzan

cheapen v. t. ارزانول arzanawal

cheat v. t. غولول gholawal

cheat n. دوکه doka

check v. t. معاینهکول moayna kawal

check n معاینه moayna

checkmate n دشطرنجپەلوبەکۍکشتاو مات da shatranj pa loba ki kasht aw mat

cheek n انۍ anangay

cheep v. i چوندل choonreydal

cheer n. دخوچغه da khwakhay cheygha

cheer v. t. پەخوچغەوهل pa khwakhay cheygha wahal

cheerful a. خندان khandan

cheerless a خواشینی khwasheenee

cheese n. پنر paneer

chemical a. کیمیایي keymyayee

chemical n. موادکیمیایي keymyayee mawad

chemise n ترجامولانداچوونکۍکمیس tar jamo landi achowoonkay kamees

chemist n. کمیاپوه keymya poh

chemistry n. کمیاپوهنه keymya pohana

cheque n. چک cheyk

cherish v. t. نازول nazawal

chess n. شطرنج shatranj

chest n ر tatar

chestnut n. بلوط balot

chew v. t ژوول zhowal

chevalier n زەورسرتری zrawar sarteyray

chicken n. چروی chargooray

chide v. t. ملامتول malamatawal

chief a. مهم muhim

chieftain n. سردار sardar

child n ماشوم mashoom

childhood n. ماشومتوب mashoomtob

childish a. ماشومانه mashoomana

chill n. سوخه sarokha

chilli n. مرچ mrich

chilly a یخ yakh

chimney n. پرناه parnara

chimpanzee n. هغەلویبدنەبیزوچپه ونوکژوندکوي hagha loybadana beezo chi pa wano ki zhwand kawee

chin n. زنه zana

china *n.* چینيلوي cheenee lokhee

chirp *v.i.* چرچر کول charchari kawal

chirp *n* چرچر charchari

chisel *n* سکنه sakana

chisel *v. t.* پهسکنهسره پرېکول pa sakani sara prey kawal

chit *n.* وانکه zwanaka

chivalrous *a.* زهور zrawar

chivalry *n.* زهورتوب zrawartob

chlorine *n* یوول کميايي ماده yaw dawl keymyayee mada

chloroform *n* دبهو کميايي ماده da bey hokhay keymyayee mada

choice *n.* غوراوی ghoraway

choir *n* په کليساکسرودي pa kaleesa ki saroodee dalgay

choke *v. t.* زندکول zanday kawal

cholera *n.* دهضوبا da hayzey waba

chocolate *n* چاکلا chaklayt

choose *v. t.* غورهکول ghwara kawal

chop *v. t* وهکول tota kawal

chord *n.* دسرونوجوت da suroonw jorakht

chorus *n.* دسندرغاول da sandar gharo dalgay

Christ *n.* حضرتعیسیعلیهالسلام hazrat eesa alayhissalam

Christendom *n.* مسیحينری maseehee naray

Christian *n* عیسائي eesayee

Christian *a.* عیسوي eesawee

Christianity *n.* عیسائیت eesaeeyat

Christmas *n* کرسمس(دعیسائیانو اختر) krismis (da eesayano akhtar)

chronic *a.* اودمهاله oogad mahala

chronicle *n.* دتاریخاونلهمخدپوليک da tareekh aw neytey la makhi da peykho lar leek

chronology *n.* پلیکنه peykh leekana

chronograph *n* دوختسنجوناآله da wakht sanjawani ala

chuckle *v. i* لمانسرهخندل la zan sara khandal

chum *n* خوملری khog malgaray

church *n.* کليسا kaleesa

churchyard *n.* دکليسااودهغبهرني دوالونومنکچاپرهمکه da kaleesa aw da haghi baharanee deywaloono manz ki chapeyra zmaka

churl *n* سپکشخص spak shakhs

churn *v. t. & i.* شاربل؛کوچجوول sharbal; kuch jorawal

churn *n.* منداو mandaroo

cigar *n.* سر sigrat

cigarette *n.* کوچنیسیار koochnay seegar

cinema *n.* سینما seenama

cinnabar *n* دسیمابوکان da seemabo kan

cinnamon *n* دارچینی darcheenee

cipher, cipher *n.* رمزيتوری ramzee toray

circle *n.* دایره dayra

circuit *n.* دوره؛چاپریال dawra; chapeyryal

circumspect *adj.* محتاط muhtat

circular *a* دایروي dayrawee

circular *n.* مجله mujala

circulate *v. i.* چاپرېدل chapeyr garzeydal

circulation *n* جريان jaryan

circumference *n.* محيط دداير da dayrey muheet

circumstance *n* حال؛صورت؛برنوالى hal; soorat; sarangwalay

circus *n.* سركس sarkas

cist *n* جعبه jaba

citadel *n.* بالاحصار balahisar

cite *v. t* تذكره كول tazkira kawal

citizen *n* اصلي استون aslee astogan

citizenship *n* تابعيت؛مدني حقونه او دند tabieeyat; madanee haqoona aw dandi

city *n* ښار khar

civic *a* مدني madanee

civics *n* مدني علوم madanee oloom

civil *a* مدني؛اولسي madanee; oolasee

civilian *n* ملكي وى malkee wagaray

civilization *n.* ولنيز پرمختہ tolaneez parmakhtag

civilize *v. t* متمدنول garzawal

clack *n. & v. i* ناندر؛ناندروهل nandarey; nandarey wahal

claim *n* ادعا adaa

claim *v. t* ادعا كول adaa kawal

claimant *n* مدعي modaee

clamber *v. i* پهلاسو او پورته تلل pa laso aw pkho porta tlal

clamour *n* وزواگ zwag

clamour *v. i.* وزوول zwag jorawal

clamp *n* لَغتہ laghata

clandestine *adj.* مخفي makhfee

clap *v. i.* لاسونه پكول lasoona parkawal

clap *n* دلاسونو پكار da lasoono parkar

clarify *v. t* وضاحت كول wazahat kawal

clarification *n* وضاحت wazahat

clarity *n* لاندتوب zalandtob

clash *n.* ګر takar

clash *v. t.* ګروهل takar wahal

clasp *n* تسمه؛چنک tasma; chingak

class *n* درجه؛ولى daraja; tolgay

classic *a* غوره او اعلى ghwara aw ala

classic *n* لرغوني علوم larghonee oloom

classical *a* لرغوني larghonee

classification *n* لبندي dalbandee

classify *v. t* لبندي كول dalbandee kawal

clause *n* عبارت ibarat

claw *n* منول mangoley

clay *n* دكلالاخه da kulalay khata

clean *a* پاک pak

clean *v. t* پاكول pakawal

cleanliness *n* صفائي safayee

cleanse *v. t* وينل weenzal

clear *a* لانده zalanda

clear *v. t* روښانول؛پاكول rokhanawal; pakawal

clearance *n* پاكوالى؛چاونه pakwalay; chanrawana

clearly *adv* پهرندول pa sargand dawl

cleft *n* درز darz

clergy *n* روحانيون rohaneeyoon

clerical *a* پہ اوند پهروحانيونو پور pa aond pa rohaneeyoono pori arwand

clerk *n* دفتري منشي daftaree monshee

clever *a.* هوښيار hookhyar

clew *n.* رخی sarkhay

click *n.* کپ krap

client *n..* پرودونکی peyrodoonkay

cliff *n.* ز garang

climate *n.* موسم mosam

climax *n.* اوج oj

climb1 *n.* ورختنه warkhatana

climb *v.i* ورختل warkhatal

cling *v. i.* پوستيدل peywasteydal

clinic *n.* کتنای طبی tibee katanzay

clink *n.* شرنا shranga

cloak *n.* يوول‌چوغه yaw dawl chogha

clock *n.* garay

clod *n.* لوه loota

cloister *n.* خانقا khanqa

close *n.* ای تلی taralay zay

close *a.* بند band

close *v.t* تل taral

closet *n.* المار almaray

closure *n.* محصورای mahsoor zay

clot *n.* دوينپرشووه da weeni pran shawi tota

clot *v. t* پرلدل praneydal

cloth *n.* توکر tokar

clothe *v. t* جاماغوستل jami aghostal

clothes *n.* جام jami

clothing *n* کالی kalee

cloud *n.* ورې wareez

cloudy *a* ورين wareezan

clove *n* لوڼ lawang

clown *n* مسخره maskhara

club *n* انجمن anjuman

clue *n* اثر؛اشاره asar; ishara

clumsy *a* بهنره bey honara

cluster *n* geyday

cluster *v. i.* کول geyday kawal

clutch *n* دموټرکلچ da motar klach

clutter *v. t* شيان‌تيت‌اوپرک‌ايوول shayan teet aw park eekhowal

coach *n* اتوبوس؛أستاد atoboos; ustad

coachman *n* موروان motarwan

coal *n* دبروسکاره da dabaro skara

coalition *n* يوکدنه yaw keydana

coarse *a* شل shalag

coast *n* ساحل sahil

coat *n* کو kot

coating *n* پو pokhakh

coax *v. t* غوهمالی‌کول ghora malee kawal

cobalt *n* دکوبالکميايی‌عنصر da kobalt keymyayee onsar

cobbler *n* موچی mochee

cobra *n* کبرامار kubra mar

cobweb *n* دغاله da ghanrey zala

cocaine *n* دمخدرومواديوقسم da mukhadira mawado yaw qisam

cock *n* چر charg

cocker *v. t* ويدل wyareydal

cockle *n* واه wakha

cockroach *n* سورندی soor garanday

coconut *n* کوپره kopra

code *n* کو؛رمزي‌شمره kod; ramzee shmeyra

co-education *n.* مخلوط‌تعليم makhloot taleem

coefficient *n.* مشترک‌عامل mushtarik amil

co-exist *v. i* ژوندسره کول gad zhwand sara kawal

co-existence *n* ژوندون gad zhwandoon

coffee *n* قهوه qahwa

coffin *n* تابوت taboot

cog *n* دندانه dandana

cogent *adj.* دواکاوزورتن da zwak aw zor sakhtan

cognate *adj* همآره ham ara

cognizance *n* خبرتیا khabartya

cohabit *v. t* پهژوندکول pa gada zhwand kawal

coherent *a* منطقي mantaqee

cohesive *adj* سرښکه sreykhnaka

coif *n* رخچینه rakhchina

coin *n* سکه sika

coinage *n* سکهجوړول sika jorawal

coincide *v. i* توافقسرهپدل tawafuq sara peykheydal

coke *v. t* تکلیسکول taklees kawal

cold *a* سو sor

cold *n* ساه sara

collaborate *v. i* پهکارکول pa gada kar kawal

collaboration *n* ه gadey hasi

collapse *v. i* لهمنهتلل la manza tlal

collar *n* غاه ghara

colleague *n* همکار hamkar

collect *v. t* راغونول raghondawal

collection *n* راغونونه raghondawana

collective *a* ولنیز tolaneez

collector *n* راغونوونکی raghondawoonkay

college *n* پوهنی pohanzay

collide *v. i.* کرکول takar kawal

collision *n* کر takar

collusion *n* دناوردپارهجوجایکول da nawara gato da para jorjaray kawal

colon *n* دلویوکولمولاندینېبرخه da loyo koolmo landeenay barkha

colonial *a* کلاکي khkeylakee

colony *n* کلاکيسیمه khkeylakee seema

colour *n* رن rang

colour *v. t* رنول rangawal

column *n* لیکه leeka

coma *n.* هوي ب bey hokha

comb *n* مز gmanz

combat1 *n* جه jagra

combat *v. t.* جندل jangeydal

combatant1 *n* جهمار jagra mar

combatant *a.* جهماری jagra maree

combination *n* والی gadwalay

combine *v. t* سرهول sara gadawal

come *v. i.* راتلل ratlal

comedian *n.* دخندوونکونندارموهنرمند da khandawoonko nandaro honar mand

comedy *n.* خندوونکننداره khandawoonki nandara

comet *n* لکایولستوری lakay wal storay

comfit *n.* یوولخواه yaw dawl khwaga

comfort1 *n.* آرام aram

comfort *v. t* آرامورکول aram warkawal

comfortable *a* آرامورکونکی aram warkawoonkay

48

comic *a* خندورونکی khandawoonkay

comic *n* کارتون kartoon

comical *a* خندورونکی khandawoonkay

command *n* فرمان؛مشري farman; masharee

command *v. t* فرمان ورکول،مشري کول farman warkawal; masharee kawal

commandant *n* قومندان qomandan

commander *n* سرلکر sar lakhkar

commemorate *v. t* دیادونغونه جوړول da yadawani ghonda jorawal

commemoration *n.* یادغونه yad ghonda

commence *v. t* پیلدل payleydal

commencement *n* پیل payl

commend *v. t* ستایل stayal

commendable *a.* ستایلی stayalay

commendation *n* ستاینه stayana

comment *v. i* رایورکول ray warkawal

comment *n* رای،انتقاد ray; intiqad

commentary *n* تفسیر tafseer

commentator *n* مفسر mufassir

commerce *n* تجارت tijarat

commercial *a* تجارتي tijaratee

commiserate *v. t* زهسوی کول zra saway kawal

commission *n.* مأموریت mamooreeyat

commissioner *n.* مأمور mamoor

commissure *n.* دای پوند د da peywand zay

commit *v. t.* مرتکب کدل murtakib keydal

committee *n* پلاوی plaway

commodity *n.* سوداریزمال sodagareez mal

common *a.* عام am

commoner *n.* عاديوی adee wagaray

commonplace *a.* عادي adee

commonwealth *n.* ولنیزهخره tolaneeza khayr kheygara

commotion *n* غورځ ghorzang

commove *v. t* پرشانهکول preyshana kawal

communal *a* لهییز dalaeez

commune *v. t* دزهخواله کول da zra khwala kawal

communicate *v. t* خبراترکول khabari atari kawal

communication *n.* رابطه rabita

communiqué *n.* دولتي اعلان dawlatee aylan

communism *n* کمونیزم kamooneezam

community *n.* ولنه tolana

commute *v. t* داستوږناودکارایترمنځ سفرکول da astogni aw da kar zay tr manz safar kawal

compact *a.* خلاصهشوی khulasa shaway

compact *n.* ژمنه،معاهده zhmana; moahida

companion *n.* ملری malgary

company *n.* شرکت shirkat

comparative *a* پرتلهییز partalaeez

compare *v. t* سرهسنجول sara sanjawal

comparison *n* سنجوونه sanjawona

compartment *n.* اپارتمان apartman

compass *n* محيط،پركار moheet; parkar

compassion *n* زهسواندي zra swanday

compel *v. t* مجبورول majboorawal

compensate *v.t* جبرانول jibranawal

compensation *n* جبران jibran

compete *v. i* سيالي كول syalee kawal

competence *n* سيالي syalee

competent *a.* دوتياخاوند da wartya khawand

competition *n.* مسابقه musabiqa

competitive *a* مسابقانه musabiqana

compile *v. t* تدوينول tadweenawal

complacent *adj.* راضي razee

complain *v. i* يله كول geela kawal

complaint *n* يله geela

complaisance *n.* مهرباني mehrabanee

complaisant *adj.* مهربان mehraban

complement *n* تشريفات tashreefat

complementary *a* بشپوونكى bashparawoonkay

complete *a* بشپ bashpar

complete *v. t* بشپرول bashparawal

completion *n* پاىتهرسونه pay ta rasawal

complex *a* پچل peychalay

complex *n* فكريتمايل fikree tamayal

complexion *n* درز da seyri rang

compliance *n.* فرمانبرداري farmanbardaree

compliant *adj.* فرمانبردار farmanbardar

complicate *v. t* پچلكول peychalay kawal

complication *n.* پچلتيا peychaltya

compliment *n.* احترام ehtiram

compliment *v. t* احترام اودرناوى كول ehtiram aw dranaway kawal

comply *v.i* غاهايودل ghara eekhodal

component *adj.* اهمجز aham juz

compose *v.t* په كمپيورتصنيفول pa campyootar tasneefawal

composition *n* تركيب tarkeeb

compositor *n* تصنيفوونكى tasneefawoonkay

compost *n* تركيب tarkeeb

composure *n.* آرامت aramakht

compound *n* مركبجسم murakab jisam

compound *a* مركب murakab

compound *n* از angar

compound *v.i* تركيول tarkeebawal

comprehend *v.t* پوهدل poheydal

comprehension *n* پوهه poha

comprehensive *a* پُرفهم purfehem

compress *v. t.* تختهكول takhta kawal

compromise *n* روغهجوه rogha jora

compromise *v.t* روغهجوه كول rogha jora kawal

compulsion *n* زور zor

compulsory *a* لازمي lazmee

compunction *n.* افسوس afsos

computation *n.* له ghanra

compute *v.t* هكول ghanra kawal

comrade *n.* ملرى malgaray

conation *n.* هه hasa

concave *adj.* مقعر maqar

conceal *v. t.* پول patawal

concede *v.t.* تسليمول tasleemawal

conceit *n* غرورلرل gharoor laral

conceive *v. t.* تصوركول tasawor kawal

concentrate *v.t* توجهساتل tawajo satal

concentration *n.* توجه tawajo

concept *n* عقيده aqeeda

conception *n* ادراک idrak

concern *v. t* تشويشلرل tashweesh laral

concern *n* تشويش tashweesh

concert *n.* دموسيقناسته da moseeqay nasta

concert2 *v. t* مرتبكول muratab kawal

concession *n* بخنه bakhkhana

conch *n.* حلزونيصدف hilzonee sadaf

conciliate *v.t.* پخلاكول pukhla kawal

concise *a* مختصر mukhtasar

conclude *v. t* پايلتهرسدل payli ta raseydal

conclusion *n.* نتيجه nateeja

conclusive *a* فصلهكن faysala kun

concoct *v. t* اختراعكول ikhtira kawal

concoction *n.* اختراع ikhtira

concord *n.* توافق tawafuq

concrete *n* دكانكريوماده da kankreeto mada

concrete *a* كلك klak

concrete *v. t* دكانكريوجوول da kankreeto jorawal

concubinage *n.* نامشروعژوند na mashroo gad zhwand

concubine *n* بشرعدوادهژوندترول bey shari da wada zhwand teyrawal

condemn *v.t.* ملامتول malamatawal

condemnation *n* ملامتيا malamatya

condense *v. t* منقبضكول munqabiz kawal

condition *n* حالت،شرط halat; shart

conditional *a* شرطيه sharteeya

condole *v.i* همدرديكول. hamdardee kawal

condolence *n* خواخوي khwakhoogee

condonation *n.* ترناهورترلدنه tar goona warteyridana

conduct *n* خوى khooy

conduct *v. t* چلندكول chaland kawal

conductor *n* چلوونكى chalowoonkay

cone *n.* مخروط makhroot

confectioner *n* خواهجووونكى khwaga jorowoonkay

confectionery *n* دخواوپلورنى da khwago ploranzay

confer *v.i* اعطاكول ata kawal

conference *n* غونه ghonda

confess *v. t.* اقراركول iqrar kawal

confession *n* اقرار iqrar

confidant *n* رازدار razdar

confide *v. i* رازسپارل raz sparal

confidence *n* اطمينان itminan

confident *a.* مطمئن mutmain

confidential *a.* محرمانه mahramana

confine *v. t* محدودول mahdoodawal

confinement *n.* دپولواکنه da poolo takana

confirm *v. t* تائيدول tayeedawal

confirmation *n* تصدیق tasdeeq

confiscate *v. t* مصادره کول musadira kawal

confiscation *n* مصادره musadira

conflict *n.* اختلاف ikhtilaf

conflict *v. i* اختلاف پیداکدل ikhtilaf peyda keydal

confluence *n* جریان gad jaryan

conformity *n.* ورتهوالی warta walay

conformity *n.* رعایت riayat

confraternity *n.* دوروروولوْلنه da wrorwalay tolana

confrontation *n.* مقابله muqabila

confuse *v. t* نسول gangasawal

confusion *n* وارخطايي war khatayee

confute *v.t.* ردول radawal

conge *n.* اجازهلیک eejaza leek

congenial *a* همخویه ham khooya

congratulate *v.t* مبارکيويل mubarakee wayal

congratulation *n* مبارکي mubarakee

congress *n* مجلس majlis

conjecture *n* اکل atkal

conjecture *v. t* ومانکول gooman kawal

conjugal *a* دوادهپهاه da wada pa ara

conjugate *v.t. & i.* صرفکول sarf kawal

conjunct *adj.* متصل mutasil

conjure *v.t.* پهکووحاضرول pa kodo hazirawal

conjure *v.i.* کوکول kodi kawal

connect *v. t.* وصلکول wasl kawal

connection *n* تاو taraw

connivance *n.* پهاجازه pata eejaza

conquer *v. t* غلبهکول ghalaba kawal

conquest *n* غلبه ghalaba

conscience *n* شعور shaoor

conscious *a* باشعوره ba shaoora

consecrate *v.t.* تقدیسول taqdeesawal

consecutive *adj.* متواتر mutawatir

consecutively *adv* پرلهپسې parla pasey

consensus *n.* عمومیخوه amoomee khwakha

consent *n.* کدنه راضي razee keydana

consent *v. i* راضيکدل razee keydal

consent3 *v.t.* راضيکول razee kawal

consequence *n* پایله payla

consequent *a* منتج mantaj

conservative *a* محافظهکار muhafiza kar

conservative *n* محافظهکاري خووونکی muhafiza karee khokhawoonkay

conserve *v. t* ژوندیساتل zhwanday satal

consider *v. t* پهپامکنیول pa pam ki neewal

aconsiderable *a* دپام نه و da pam na war

considerate *a.* احترام ساتوونکی ehtiram satowoonkay

consideration *n* پام pam

considering *prep.* په پام و کچ pa pam war kach

consign *v.t.* امانت سپارل amanat sparal

consign *v. t.* تائیدول tayeedawal

consignment *n.* امانت پلورنه amanat plorana

consist *v. i* شاملدل shamileydal

consistence,-cy *n.* دوام dawam

consistent *a* محکم muhkam

consolation *n* ائنه dadeena

console *v. t* ا ورکول dad warkawal

consolidate *v. t.* ینول teengawal

consolidation *n* ینوالی teengwalay

consonance *n.* هم آهنی ham agangee

consort *n.* همسفر hamsafar

conspectus *n.* زمینه zameena

conspicuous *a.* مالوم maloom

conspiracy *n.* دسیسه daseesa

conspirator *n.* خاین khayin

conspire *v. i.* خیانت کول khyanat kawal

constable *n* د پولس ساندوی da poolas sarandoy

constant *a* مستقل mustaqil

constellation *n.* د ستورو مجمع da storo majma\

constipation *n.* قبض qabz

constituency *n* انتخاباتي حوزه intikhabatee hoza

constitute *v. t* انتخابول intikhabawal

constitution *n* اساسي قانون asasee qanoon

constrict *v.t.* تنول tangawal

construct *v. t.* جورول jorawal

construction *n* ودانی جورول wadanee jorawal

consult *v. t* مشوره کول mashwara kawal

consultation *n* مشوره mashwara

consume *v. t* مصرف کدل masraf keydal

consumption *n* مصرف masraf

consumption *n* لت lagakht

contact *n.* رابطه rabita

contact *v. t* رابطه کول rabita kawal

contain *v.t.* نیول ای zay neewal

contaminate *v.t.* خرابول kharabawal

contemplate *v. t* دایمي پام کول daymee pam kawal

contemplation *n* تفکر tafakur

contemporary *a* هم مهاله ham mahala

contempt *n* حقارت haqarat

contend *v. i* سیالي کول syalee kawal

content *a.* راضی razee

content *v. t* راضي کول razee kawal

content *n* ظرفیت zarfeeyat

content *n.* مفاد mafad

contention *n* مباحثه mubahisa

contentment *n* رضایت reeyazat

contest *v. t* مقابله کول muqabila kawal

contest *n.* مسابقه musabiqa

context *n* زمینه zameena

continent *n* براعظم baryazam

continental *a* براعظم پوراوند baryazam pori arwand

contingency *n.* احتمال ehtimal

continual *adj.* مداوم madawam

continuation *n.* بهیر baheer

continue *v. i.* لرل دوام dawam laral

continuity *n* تسلسل tasalsul

continuous *a* جاري jaree

contour *n* خاکه khaka

contraception *n.* له بلاربت سخه مخنیوی la blarbakht sakha makhneeway

contract *n* عقد aqd

contract *v. t* قرارداد کول qarardad kawal

contrapose *v.t.* مخالف مفهوم ور کول mukhlif mafhoom warkawal

contractor *n* تون کوونکی taroon kawoonkay

contradict *v. t* ماتول matawal

contradiction *n* تکذیب takzeeb

contrary *a* مخالف mukhalif

contrast *v. t* رندتوپیرلرل sargand topeer larl

contrast *n* رندتوپیر sargand topeer

contribute *v. t* ونه ور کول wanda warkawal

contribution *n* ونه wanda

control *n* مخنیوی makhneeway

control *v. t* مخنیوی کول makhneeway kawal

controller *n.* ناظر nazir

controversy *n* مباحثه mubahisa

contuse *v.t.* و کل tokal

conundrum *n.* معما moama

convene *v. t* غوندل ghondeydal

convener *n* د جرگی da jargey gharay

convenience *n.* راحت rahat

convenient *a* باآرام ba aram

convent *n* صومعه somia

convention *n.* کانفرانس kanfarans

conversant *a* د خبرو سی da khabaro saray

conversant *adj.* باخبر ba khabar

conversation *n* مکالمه mukalima

converse *v.t.* خبراتر کول khabari atari kawal

conversion *n* سرچپه کونه sar chapa kawana

convert *v. t* سرچپه کول sar chapa kawal

convert *n* اونه arawana

convey *v. t.* ورر سول warrasawal

conveyance *n* دای سهولت da gaɖee sahoolat

convict *v.t.* ملامتول malamatawal

convict *n* مجرم mujrim

conviction *n* مجرمیت mujrimeeyat

convince *v. t* قانع کول qanay kawal

convivial *adj.* خندان khandan

convocation *n.* راغونونه raghondawana

convoke *v.t.* په دعوت رابلل pa dawat rabalal

convolve *v.t.* تاوول tawowal

coo *n* غومبر ghombar

coo *v. i* غومبر کول ghombar kawal

cook *v. t* پخول pakhawal

cook *n* پخلی pakhlay

cooker *n* ر پخلي pakhleegar

cool *a* سو sor

cool *v. i.* سول sarawal

cooler *n* سوونکی sarowoonkay

coolie *n* پني pandee

co-operate *v. i* همکاري کول hamkaree kawal

co-operation *n* همکاري hamkaree

co-operative *a* مرستندویه mrastandoya

co-ordinate *a.* هم رتبه ham rotba

co-ordinate *v. t* موزونول mawzoonawal

co-ordination *n* همکاري hamkaree

co-partner *n* ونهوال wanda wal

cope *v, i* ورسره مخامخ هدل warsara makhamakheydal

coper *n.* معامله ر moamilagar

copper *n* مس mis

coppice *n.* وڼ ganri wani

copulate *v. i.* پوستدل peywasteydal

copy *n* نقل naqal

copy *v. t* نقل جوول naqal jorawal

coral *n* مرجان marjan

cord *n* رسه rasay

cordial *a* قلبي qalbee

corbel *n.* دودانديرراوتلبرخه da wananay da teer rawatali barkha

core *n.* تخمدان tukhamdan

coriander *n.* دنيا danrya

cork *n.* دبلوطدکورندیوونپوستکی da balot da koranay d yawi wani postakay

corn *n* جواری joowaray

corner *n* و gut

coronation *n* تاج وادنه taj eekhodana

coronet *n.* تاج کوچنی koochnay taj

corporal *a* بدني badanee

corporate *adj.* یوشوی yaw shaway

corporation *n* اتحادیه شرکت etihadeeya shirkat

corps *n* پلاوی plaway

corpse *n* می maray

correct *a* درست drost

correct *v. t* درستول drostawal

correction *n* سمونه samawona

correlate *v.t.* ارتباطورکول irtibat warkawal

correlation *n.* ارتباط irtibat

correspond *v. i* مکاتبه کول makatiba kawal

correspondence *n.* مکاتبه makatiba

correspondent *n.* خبریال khabaryal

corridor *n.* دهلیز dehleez

corroborate *v.t.* غتلی کول ghakhtalay kawal

corrosive *adj.* استحصالي isteyhsalee

corrupt *v. t.* فاسدول fasidawal

corrupt *a.* فاسد fasid

corruption *n.* بد badi

cosmetic *a.* سینروونکی seengarowoonkay

cosmetic *n.* سینار seengar

cosmic *adj.* د کائناتو پهاوند da kaynato pa arwand

cost *v.t.* بیه لرل baya laral

cost *n.* لت lagakht

costal *adj.* ساحلي sahilee

cote *n.* دمرغانوله da marghano zala

costly *a.* قیمتي qeematee

costume n. لباس libas

cosy a. گرماونرم،هوسا garm aw naram; hosa

cot n. اله،پره zala; sapara

cottage n. کوټ kotangay

cotton n. پنبه poonba

couch n. تخت،استراحتای takht; istirahat zay

cough n. وخی tokhay

cough v. i. وخدل tokheydal

council n. شورا shoora

councillor n. دشوراغی da shoora gharay

counsel n. سلاکاري،سلاکار salakaree; salakar

counsel v. t. سلاکاريکول salakaree kawal

counsellor n. سلاکار salakar

count n. شمره shmeyra

count v. t. شمره کول shmeyra kawal

countenance n. رو،قیافه seyra; qeeyafa

counter n. په دفترو کداستقبال او دمز pa daftaro ki da istiqbal oogad meyz

counter v. t. مخالفت کول،وابورکول mukhalifat kawal; zawab warkawal

counteract v.t. باطلول batilawal

countercharge n. وابی تهمت zawabee tuhmat

counterfeit a. مصنوعي masnooee

counterfeiter n. جعل ساز jal saz

countermand v.t. لغوه کول lughwa kawal

counterpart n. نژدملری nazhdey malgaray

countersign v.t. امضاکول imza kawal

countess n. دنواب مرمن da nawab meyrman

countless a. بشمره bey shmeyra

country n. هواد heywad

county n. علاقه ilaqa

coup n. سرچپه پر حکومت باند sar chapa par hookoomat bandi

couple n جوه jora

couple v. t جوه کول jora kawal

couplet n. بت چیوه قافیه ولري beyt chi yawa qafeeya walaree

coupon n. دکاغذیوه رسید da kaghaz yawa raseed

courage n. زوړ توب zra wartob

courageous a. زوړ zra war

courier n. قاصد qasid

course n. دزده کو دوره da zdakro dawra

court n. عدالت،محکمه adalat; mahkama

court v. t. غوه مالي کول ghwaramalee kawal

courteous a. مهربان mehraban

courtesan n. درباري فاحشه darbaree fahisha

courtesy n. احترام ehtiram

courtier n. درباري darbaree

courtship n. واده نه مخکدهلک او نجل تر منمینه ناکخبر wada na makhki da halak aw najlay tar manz meena naki khabari

courtyard n. غولی gholay

cousin *n.* دتره،ماما،یاترورزوی‌یالور da tra, mama, ya tror zoy ya loor

covenant *n.* ژمنه،تون zhmna; taroon

cover *v.t.* پوښل pokhal

cover *n.* پو،جلد pokh; jild

coverlet *n.* بستن brastan

covet *v.t.* آرزوکول arzoo kawal

cow *n.* غوا ghwa

cow *v. t.* ارول،برول darawal; beyrawal

coward *n.* بزه bey zra

cowardice *n.* ارنتوب darantoob

cower *v.i.* ارخه‌زه‌چاودل dar sakha zra chawdal

cozy ساده،آسانه sada; asana

crab *n* چنا changakh

crack *n* درز darz

crack *v. i* درزموندل،ماتدل darz moondal; mateydal

cracker *n* ماتدونکی mateydoonkay

crackle *v.t.* ټکدل trakeydal

cradle *n* زانو zango

craft *n* هنر honar

craftsman *n* هنرمند honar mand

crafty *a* ماهر،چلباز mahir; chalbaz

cram *v. t* زبانی‌یادول zubanee yadawal

crambo *n.* شاعرکی‌هغه‌کلیمه‌چ‌قافیه‌ید بلاهغله‌قافیسره‌جوه‌وی shairay ki hagha kaleema chi qafeeya yi da bali haghi qafeeyi sara jora wee

crane *n* کلن،زاله kalang; zanra

crankle *v.t.* زاویه‌دارکول zaweeyadar kawal

crash *v. i* وهوه‌کدل tota tota keydal

crash *n* ناپهکر nasapa takar

crass *adj.* احمق‌اولوده ahmaq aw lawda

crate *n.* دخوراکی‌موادوصندوق da khorakee mawado sandooq

crave *v.t.* غوتل ghokhtal

craw *n.* ججوره jajoora

crawl *v. t* خاپوکول khapori kawal

crawl *n* خاپو khapori

craze *n* شوق shawq

crazy *a* لونی leywanay

creak *v. i* کنجدل kranjeydal

creak *n* کنجی kranjay

cream *n* پروی peyraway

crease *n* دجاموونجکدووالادرز da jamo gonji keydo wala darz

create *v. t* تولیدول tawleedawal

creation *n* پیدایت peydayakht

creative *adj.* پنوونکی panzowoonkay

creator *n* خالق khaliq

creature *n* مخلوق makhlooq

credible *a* باوري bawaree

credit *n* ارزت،باور arzakht; bawar

creditable *a* معتبر motabar

creditor *n* پوراخستونکی por akhistoonkay

credulity *adj.* زرباوره zar bawara

creed *n.* باورلیک bawar leek

creed *n* اعتقاد aytiqad

creek *n.* کوچنی‌خلیج koochnay khaleej

creep *v.i* پرسینه‌ویدل par seena khwayeydal

creeper *n* خزنده khazanda

cremate *v. t* سوول‌اواير‌كول
sozawal aw eerey kawal

cremation *n* اير‌كوونه eerey
kawona

crest *n* تاج;جوغه taj; jogha

crew *n.* د‌كټ‌كارمندان da kakhtay
karmandan

crib *n.* آخور akhor

cricket *n* كرى karray

crime *n* جنايت janayat

crimp *n* دوتانو‌تاو‌او‌كلوټه da
weykhtano taw aw klokhta

crimple *v.t.* ونور‌كول gònzi
warkawal

criminal *n* جنايت‌كار janayat kar

criminal *a* جنايي janayee

crimson *n* سور‌دنه sooreydana

cringe *v. i.* ان‌راغون‌دول zan
raghondawal

cripple *n* شل‌شو shal shoot

crisis *n* بحران buhran

crisp *a* تاور‌اتاو taw rataw

criterion *n* كچ;مقياس kach;
miqyas

critic *n* دانتقادهنر da intiqad hunar

critical *a* حساس hasas

criticism *n* انتقاد intiqad

criticize *v. t* نيوكه‌كول neewaka
kawal

croak *n.* قر‌قر‌كول qar qar kawal

crockery *n.* خاورن‌لوى khawran
lokhay

crocodile *n* نهڼ nahang

crook *a* بد‌شكله bad shakla

crop *n* غله;فصل ghala; fasal

cross *v. t* پور‌وتل;غوول pori watal;
ghosawal

cross *n* دضرب‌نه;شخه da zarab
nakha; shkhara

cross *a* دوه‌ره;مخالف dwa raga;
mukhalif

crossing *n.* تر‌دنه;دوتلولار;مخالفت
teyreydana; da watalo lar;
mukhalifat

crotchet *n.* چارتاپي‌نو chartapee not

crouch *v. i.* درناوى‌ور‌كول
dranaway warkawal

crow *n* كاغه;كارغه kragha; kargha

crow *v. i* چغوهل cheyghi wahal

crowd *n* ھوه ganra gonra

crown *n* تاج taj

crown *v. t* تاج‌پوشى‌كول taj poshee
kawal

crucial *adj.* ر‌سخت deyr sakht

crude *a* خام kham

cruel *a* ظالم zalim

cruelty *n* ظلم zulm

cruise *v.i.* په‌كټ‌كتفريح‌ته‌تلل pa
kakhtay ki tafree ta tlal

cruiser *n* لويه‌مسافري‌كټ loya
musafiree kakhtay

crumb *n* دوپار‌چه da doday parcha

crumble *v. t* مدول maydawal

crump *adj.* كو kog

crusade *n* صليبي‌جهاد saleebee
jihad

crush *v. t* ماتور‌كول matey
warkawal

crust *n.* خزه‌سطحه khayza satha

crutch *n* دمعذورو‌لكړ da mazooro
lakray

cry *n* چغه cheygha

cry *v. i* چغوهل cheyghi wahal

cryptography *n.* علم ليکنيدرمزيda ramzee leekani ilam

crystal *n* بلور balor

cub *n* دوحشيناوربچی da wahshee zanawar bachay

cube *n* مکعب makab

cubical *a* مکعبي makabee

cubiform *adj.* مکعبوله makab dawla

cuckold *n.* فاحشه fahisha

cuckoo *n* دکوکومرغ da kookoo marghay

cucumber *n* بادرن badrang

cudgel *n* سوی sotay

cue *n* لاروونکیخبره lar khowoonki khabara

cuff *n* لستونرخوله lastonr khula

cuff *v.t* لستونرخولهوراچول lastonr khula warchawal

cuisine *n.* دپخليلارود da pakhlee lar khod

culminate *v.i.* اوجتهرسدل oj ta raseydal

culprit *n* تورن؛غل toran; ghal

cult *n* عبادت ibadat

cultivate *v.t* کرل karal

cultural *a* فرهني farhangee

culture *n* کلتور kaltoor

culvert *n.* کوتره kawtara

cunning *a* چالاک chalak

cunning *n* چالاکي chalakee

cup *n.* پياله pyala

cupboard *n* المار almaray

cupidity *n* شهوت shahwat

curable *a* رغدونکی ragheydoonkay

curative *a* داونديهرغدو da ragheydo pa arwand

curb *n* توقيف tawqeef

curb *v.t* محدودول mahdoodawal

curd *n* مست mastey

cure *n* درملنه darmalana

cure *v.t.* درملنهيکول darmalana yi kawal

curfew *n* ربندي garz bandee

curiosity *n* ظرافت؛دکنجکاوحس zarafat; da kanjkaway his

curious *a* کنجکاو؛دقيق kanjkaw; daqeeq

curl *n.* ک karay

currant *n.* ممبز دازب bey daney mameez

currency *n* دهوادرسميسکه da heywad rasmee sika

current *n* سل؛جريان sayl; jaryan

current *a* موجوده mawjooda

curriculum *n* درسينصاب darsee nisab

curse *n* لعنت lanat

curse *v.t* لعنتورکول lanat warkawal

cursory *a* پهسرسريول pa sarsaree dawl

curt *a* لنډ land

curtain *n* پرده parda

curve *n* کووالی kog walay

curve *v.t* کووالیورکول kog walay warkawal

cushion *n* بالښت balakht

cushion *v.t* پوورکول pokh warkawal

custodian *n* ساتونکی satoonkay

custody v ساتنه کاخیستل satana ki akheystal

custom n. دود dood

customary a رواجي riwajee

customer n پرودونکی peyrodoonkay

cut v. t پرکول prey kawal

cut n چاک؛درز chak; darz

cycle n بایسکل؛چکر baysakal; chakar

cyclic a چکري؛دوروي chakaree

cyclist n بایسکل سوار baysakal sawar

cyclone n. بادوباراني توپان badobaranee toopan

cylinder n تیوب tyoob

cynic n بدو مانه انسان badgoomana insan

D

dabble v. i. لمدول lamdawal

dacoit n. داها چوونکی dara achowoonkay

dacoity n. داه dara

dad, daddy n ابا aba

daffodil n. دزینرسل da zyar nargas gul

daft adj. ملایم mulayam

dagger n. خنجر khanjar

daily a روزانه rozana

daily adv. هرور hara waraz

daily n. ورپله warazpanra

dainty a. لطیف lateef

dainty n. دلطیف ذوق تن da lateef zoq sakhtan

dairy n دشدو اوندشیان da sheydo arwand shayan

dais n. دناستانی مز da nasti zangaray meyz

daisy n داودي ل dawoodee gul

dale n کوچنی دره koochnay dara

dam n داوبوبند da obo band

damage n. نقصان nuqsan

damage v. t. تاوانورکول tawan warkawal

dame n. مرمن meyrman

damn v. t. لعنت ویل lanat wayal

damnation n. غندنه ghandana

damp a نم nam

damp n لمدوالی lamdwalay

damp v. t. لمدول lamdawal

damsel n. پغله peyghla

dance n ابا gada; nasa

dance v. t. ډل gadeydal

dandelion n. یوول یاچزیلان لري yaw dawl gaya chi zyar gulan laree

dandle v.t. لهماشوم سره لوبکول la mashoom sara lobi kawal

dandruff n دسرپخه da sar pakha

dandy n لالی gulalay

danger n. خطر khatar

dangerous a خطرناک khatarnak

dangle v. t وندول zorandawal

dank adj. نمناک namnak

dap v.i.

dare v. i. همت کول himat kawal

daring n. جزأت؛همت jorat; himat

daring a باهمته bahimata

dark *a* تت؛نارند tat; nasargand

dark *n* تیاره tyara

darkle *v.i.* تیاره کېدل tyara ki pateydal

darling *n* محبوب mehboob

darling *a* زه ته نژدې zra ta nazhdey

dart *n.* برغز barghaz

dash *v. i.* په شدت وهل pa shidat wahal

dash *n* برېد breed

date *n* خرما؛نه khorma; neyta

date *v. t* حساب اول،تاریخ معلوم اول hisabawal; tareekh maloomawal

daub *n.* تپنه tapana

daub *v. t.* خرن اول kheyranawal

daughter *n* لور loor

daunt *v. t* ناهیلی کول naheelay kawal

dauntless *a* بی باکه bey baka

dawdle *v.i.* بهوده وخت تېراول bayhooda wakht teyrawal

dawn *n* لمر راختنه lmar rakhatana

dawn *v. i.* دلمرراختل da lmar rakhatana

day *n* ورځ waraz

daze *n* حرانتیا heyrantya

daze *v. t* حران اول heyranawal

dazzle *n* برېدنه breykheydana

dazzle *v. t.* ستر برېدل stargi breykheydal

dead *a* مه mar

deadlock *n* بنست bandakht

deadly *a* ناوه؛وژونکی nawara; wazhoonkay

deaf *a* کوڼ konr

deal *n* معامله moamila

deal *v. i* معامله کول moamila kawal

dealer *n* معامله کوونکی moamila kawoonkay

dealing *n.* سوداریزه راکه ورکه sawdagareeza rakra warkra

dean *n.* د پوهنی رئیس da pohanzee rayees

dear *a* محترم mohtaram

dearth *n* کمت kamakht

death *n* مینه mreena

debar *v. t.* منع کول mana kawal

debase *v. t.* سپک اول spakawal

debate *n.* بحث behes

debate *v. t.* بحث کول behes kawal

debauch *v. t.* خراب اول kharabawal

debauch *n* خرابونه kharabawana

debauchee *n* فاسق fasiq

debauchery *n* فسق fasq

debility *n* کمزورتیا kamzortya

debit *n* پور por

debit *v. t* پور کول por kawal

debris *n* د بی استعمال او خراب اویز و نوری da bey istimala aw kharabo seezoono deyray

debt *n* پور por

debtor *n* پور وری por waray

decade *n* لسیزه laseeza

decadent *a* فسادی fasadee

decamp *v. i* که کول kada kawal

decay زوال zawal

decay *v. i* خراب اېدل kharabeydal

decease *n* مینه mreena

decease *v. i.* مه کېدل mar keydal

deceit *n* دوکه doka

deceive *v. t* دوکه کول doka kawal

december *n* دانزي كال دولسمه da angreyzee kal مياشت dolasama myasht

decency *n* نزاكت nazakat

decent *a* مؤدب moadab

deception *n* چل chal

decide *v. t* پريكه كول preykra kawal

decimal *a* اعشاري aysharee

decimate *v.t.* دلسو كسانو له منځه ديوه هغه وژل da laso kasano la manz sakha da yawa hagha wazhal

decision *n* پريكه preykra

decisive *a* فصله كن faysala kon

deck *n* د كښتۍ عرشه da kakhtay arsha

deck *v. t* عرشه جوړول arsha jorawal

declaration *n* اعلاميه aylameeya

declare *v. t.* اعلانول aylanawal

decline *n* زوال zawal

decline *v.t.* زوال موندل zawal moondal

decompose *v. t.* تجزيه كول tajzeeya kawal

decomposition *n.* تجزيه tajzeeya

decontrol *v.t.* نيو نخه ايستل neewani sakha eystal

decorate *v. t* سينارول seengarawal

decoration *n* سينار seengar

decorum *n* پر اي چلند par zay chaland

decrease *v. t* كمول kamawal

decrease *n* كمت kamakht

decree *n* فرمان farman

decree *v. i* فرمان صادرول farman sadirawal

decrement *n.* نقصان nuqsan

dedicate *v. t.* الكول dalay kawal

dedication *n* وقف waqaf

deduct *v.t.* كمول kamawl

deed *n* چلند؛عمل chaland; amal

deem *v.i.* فرض كول farz kawal

deep *a.* ژور zhawar

deer *n* غره gharsa

defamation *n* تهمت tuhmat

defame *v. t.* تهمت لول tuhmat lagawal

default *n.* قصور؛دوالیه qasoor; deywaleeya

defeat *n* مات mati

defeat *v. t.* ماتورکول mati warkawal

defect *n* نقص nuqs

defence *n* دفاع difa

defend *v. t* دفاع كول difa kawal

defendant *n* دفاع كوونكی difa kawoonkay

defensive *adv.* په دفاعي توه pa difaee toga

deference *n* تواضع tawazo

defiance *n* سركشي sar kashee

deficit *n* نیمتیا neemgartya

deficient *adj.* نقضي nuqzee

defile *n.* خرنتیا kheyrantya

define *v. t* تعريفول tareefawal

definite *a* معين moeen

definition *n* تعريف tareef

deflation *n.* بادوستنه bad weystana

deflect *v.t. & i.* اوډل؛اول awreydal; arawal

deft *adj.* غتلی ghakhtalay

degrade *v. t* عزت كمول eezat kamawal

degree *n* سند؛درجه sanad; daraja

deist *n.* دخدای‌په‌وجودباور da khuday pa wajood bawar

deity *n.* خدای khuday

deject *v. t* مايوسول mayoosawal

dejection *n* مايوسي mayoosee

delay *v.t. & i.* زندول،بندل zandawal; zandeydal

deligate1 *n* له dala

delegate *v. t* په‌له‌تلل pa dala tlal

delegation *n* غونه ghonda

delete *v. t* حذفول hazafawal

deliberate *v. i* قصدي‌کول qasdee kawal

deliberate *a* ارادي iradee

deliberation *n* سنجوونه،چرت sanjawana; churt

delicate *a* لطيف lateef

delicious *a* خوندور khwandawar

delight *n* خوشالي khoshalee

delight *v. t.* خوشالول khoshalawal

deliver *v. t* رسول rasawal

delivery *n* رسونه rasawana

delude *n.t.* دوکه،دوکه‌ورکول doka; doka warkawal

delusion *n.* فريب fareyb

demand *n* غوتنه ghokhtana

demand *v. t* غوتنه‌کول ghokhtana kawal

demarcation *n.* دپولوايودنه da poolo eekhodana

dement *v.t* لوني‌کول leywanay kawal

demerit *n* ناوتيا nawartya

democracy *n* ولسواکي woolaswakee

democratic *a* جمهوري jamhooree

demolish *v. t.* نول rangawal

demon *n.* دو dew

demonetize *v.t.* بارزته‌کول bey arzakhta kawal

demonstrate *v. t* توضيح‌ورکول tawzee warkawal

demonstration *n.* توضيح tawzee

demoralize *v. t.* بداخلاقه‌کول bad akhlaqa kawal

demur *n* اعتراض،شک aytiraz; shak

demur *v.t.* اعتراض‌کول aytiraz kawal

den *n* غار ghar

denial *n* مننه نه na manana

denote *v. i* نه‌ايودل nakha eekhodal

denounce *v. t* تورنول toranawal

dense *a* لوده، lawda; ganr

density *n* ه ganra

dentist *n* دغاونواکر da ghakhoono daktar

denude *v.t.* لول loosawal

denunciation *n.* اخطار،تهديد akhtar; tahdeed

deny *v. t.* انکارکول inkar kawal

depart *v. i.* جلاکدل jala keydal

department *n* اداري‌انه idaree sanga

departure *n* جلاکدنه jala keydana

depauperate *v.t.* ضعيف‌کول zaeef kawal

depend *v. i.* انحصارلرل inhisar laral

dependant *n* انحصارلرونکی inhisar laroonkay

dependence *n* تابعيت،انحصار tabayeeyat; inhisar

dependent *a* تابع tabay

depict *v. t.* رسمول rasmawal

deplorable *a* خواشينوونكى khwasheenawoonkay

deploy *v.t.* پەليکەکشاملول pa leeka ki shamilawal

deponent *n.* شاهديليکونکى shahidee leekoonkay

deport *v.t.* لەوطنەشل la watana sharal

depose *v.t* وەکول gokha kawal

deposit *n.* بانکيحساب bankee hisab

deposit *v.t* بانککحسابايودل bank ki hisab eekhodal

depot *n* تحويلخانه tahweelkhana

depreciate *v.t.i.* بقدرهکدل/کول bey qadra keydal / kawal

depredate *v.t.* لوټل lootal

depress *v.t* فشارلاندراوستل fishar landi rawastal

depression *n* فشار fishar

deprive *v.t* محرومول mehroomawal

depth *n* ژورتيا zhawartya

deputation *n* استازيتوب astazeetob

depute *v.t* استازيتوبورکول astazeetob warkawal

deputy *n* نمائنده numayinda

derail *v.t.* بلارکول bey lari kawal

derive *v.t.* اخذکول akhaz kawal

descend *v.i.* کتهکدل kkhata keydal

descendant *n* اولاد awlad

descent *n.* کتهکدنه،نسل kkhata keydana; nasal

describe *v.t* بيانول bayanawal

description *n* بيان؛توضيح bayan; tawzee

descriptive *a* بيانيه bayaneeya

desert *v.t.* بوفاييکول bey wafayee kawal

desert *n* بديا،بوفايي beydya; bey wafayee

deserve *v.t.* حقدارومدل haqdar garzeydal

design *v.t.* طرحکول tarah kawal

design *n.* طرح؛خاکه tarah; khaka

desirable *a* پهزهپور pa zra pori

desire *n* غوتنه ghokhtana

desire *v.t* آرزولرل arzoo laral

desirous *a* هيلهمن heela man

desk *n* دليکنمز da leekani meyz

despair *n* ناهيلي na heelee

despair *v.i* ناهيلیکدل na heelay keydal

desperate *a* ناميده na oomeeda

despicable *a* خوار khwar

despise *v.t* کرکهکول kraka kawal

despot *n* واکمن؛حاکم wakman; hakim

destination *n* منزل manzil

destiny *n* تقدير taqdeer

destroy *v.t* ويجارول weejarawal

destruction *n* ويجاي weejaree

detach *v.t* انتهکول zanta kawal

detachment *n* بلتون beyltoon

detail *n* تفصيل tafseel

detail *v.t* تفصيلورکول tafseel warkawal

detain *v.t* ايسارول؛بنول eesarawal; zandawal

detect *v.t* معلومول maloomawal

detective *a* تفتيشي tafteeshee

detective *n.* کارپوه karpoh

determination *n.* قصد qasad

determine *v. t* تصميمول tasmeemawal

dethrone *v. t* بېرخه‌كول bey barkhi kawal

develop *v. t.* ترقي‌وركول taraqee warkawal

development *n.* پرمختګ par makhtag

deviate *v. i* منحرف كېدل munharif keydal

deviation *n* سرغونه sar gharawana

device *n* آله،وسيله ala; waseela

devil *n* شطان sheytan

devise *v. t* اختراع‌كول ikhtira kawal

devoid *a* تش،خالي tash; khalee

devote *v. t* وقف‌كول waqaf kawal

devotee *n* وقف‌كوونكى waqaf kawoonkay

devotion *n* اخلاص ikhlas

devour *v. t* جذبول jazbawal

dew *n.* پرخه parkha

diabetes *n* دشكرناروغى da shakari naroghee

diagnose *v. t* معلومول maloomawal

diagnosis *n* تشخيص tashkhees

diagram *n* خاكه khaka

dial *n.* ساعت؛دزنګ‌آواز saat; da zang awaz

dialect *n* دژب‌لهجه da zhabi lahja

dialogue *n* مركه maraka

diameter *n* دقطر داير د da dayri qutar

diamond *n* الماس almas

diarrhoea *n* اسهال ishal

diary *n* ديادتونوكتابوى da yadakhtoono kitabgotay

dice *n.* چكه‌پاو

dictate *v. t* حكم‌چلول hokam chalawal

dictation *n* حكم،حاكميت hokam; hakimeeyat

dictator *n* حاكم hakim

diction *n* دوييوغوره‌كونه da wayyo ghwara kawana

dictionary *n* قاموس qamoos

dictum *n* قضايي‌وينا qazayee wayna

didactic *a* تعليمى taleemee

die *v. i* مړدل mreydal

die *n* مهر،بايه muhar; tapa

diet *n* غذا ghaza

differ *v. i* توپيرلرل tawpeer laral

difference *n* توپير tawpeer

different *a* مختلف mukhtalif

difficult *a* مشكل mushkil

difficulty *n* ستونزه stoonza

dig *n* كيندنه keendana

dig *v.t.* كنستل kanastal

digest *v. t.* هضمول hazmawal

digest *n.* مجله هضم؛ hazam; mujalla

digestion *n* هاضمه hazima

digit *n* عدد adad

dignify *v.t* احترام‌وركول ehtiram warkawal

dignity *n* عزت eezat

dilemma *n* ونه‌ستونزه goonga stoonza

diligence *n* هڅه‌اوهاند hasa aw hand

diligent *a* زيار كښ zeeyar kakh

dilute *v. t* اوبلن‌كول oblan kawal

dilute *a* اوبلن oblan

dim *a* تت tat

dim v. t تتول tatawal

dimension n انداز‌ه؛حجم andaza; hujam

diminish v. t کوچنی کول koochnay kawal

din n غوغا ghawgha

dine v. t. وخول doday khwaral

dinner n ماښامنی makhamanay doday

dip n. غوه؛غوپه ghota; ghopa

dip v. t غوپه کول ghopa kawal

diploma n تعليمي سند taleemee sanad

diplomacy n سفارت کاري safarat karee

diplomat n سفارت کار safarat kar

diplomatic a سفارتي safaratee

dire a رضروري deyr zarooree

direct a نغږه نغه neygh pa neygha

direct v. t امر کول amar kawal

direction n امر؛لارودنه amar; lar khodana

director n. مدير mudeer

directory n لارود کتابوی larkhod keetabgotay

dirt n چرک chark

dirty a چل chatal

disability n ناتواني natwanee

disable v. t ناتوانه کول natwana kawal

disabled a ناتوان natwan

disadvantage n تاوان؛ضرر tawan; zarar

disagree v. i اختلاف لرل ikhtilaf laral

disagreeable a. ناخو nakhwakh

disagreement n. ناخوي nakhwakhee

disappear v. i ورکېدل wrakeydal

disappearance n ورکتوب wraktob

disappoint v. t. مأيوسول mayoosawal

disapproval n ناخوي nakhwakhee

disapprove v. t ردول radawal

disarm v. t بوسلاکول bey wasley kawal

disarmament n. بوسلاکونه bey wasley kawona

disaster n بدمرغي bad marghee

disastrous a تباه کن taba kun

disc n. يکلی؛ڈسک teekalay; disc

discard v. t پرودل preykhodal

discharge v. t رخصتول rukhsatawal

discharge n. رخصت rukhsat

disciple n مريد؛شاگرد mureed; shagard

discipline n نظم؛قاعده nazm; qayda

disclose v. t ښکاره کول khkara kawal

discomfort n ناآرامي naaramee

disconnect v. t ایکغوول areeki ghosawal

discontent n ناآرامه naarama

discontinue v. t ادامه درول idama darawal

discord n اختلاف ikhtilaf

discount n تخفیف takhfeef

discourage v. t. بجرأته کول bey jurata kawal

discourse n موضوع؛ونا mawzoo; wayna

discourteous a بادبه bey adaba

discover v. t افشا کول afsha kawal

discovery n. موندنه moondana

discretion n واک

discriminate v. t. توپيرول tawpeerawal

discrimination n توپيرموندنه tawpeer moondana

discuss v. t. مركه كول maraka kawal

disdain n توهين tawheen

disdain v. t. توهين كول tawheen kawal

disease n رنز ranz

disguise n چماوچل cham aw chal

disguise v. t بهبدلول banra badlawal

dish n لوى lokhay

dishearten v. t زهماتول zra matawal

dishonest a خاين khayin

dishonesty n. خيانت khyanat

dishonour v. t بعزتي كول bey eezatee kawal

dishonour n بعزتي bey eezatee

dislike v. t كركه كول kraka kawal

dislike n كركه،ناخوي kraka; na khwakhee

disloyal a نمک حرام namak haram

dismiss v. t. لهدندرخصتول la dandi rukhsatawal

dismissal n برطرفي bartarfee

disobey v. t سرغونه كول sargharawana kawal

disorder n بنظمي bey nazmee

disparity n ناورتهوالى nawarta walay

dispensary n درملتون darmaltoon

disperse v. t تجزيه كول tajzeeya kawal

displace v. t بهركول bahar kawal

display v. t ننداره ظاهرول nandarey ta zahirawal

display n نمايش numayish

displease v. t خپه كول khapa kawal

displeasure n خپان khapgan

disposal n لركوونه leyri kawona

dispose v. t لركول،غورزول leyri kawal; ghorzawal

disprove v. t باطلول batilawal

dispute n شخره shkhara

dispute v. t شخره كول shkhara kawal

disqualification n ناوتوب nawartob

disqualify v. t. نابريالى بلل nabaryalay balal

disquiet n نارامه na arama

disregard n باعتنائي bey aytinayee

disregard v. t باعتنائي كول bey aytinayee kawal

disrepute n سپک تيا spak tia

disrespect n بى ادبى be adabi

disrupt v. t منقطع كول munqata kawal

dissatisfaction n باطمينائي bey itminanee

dissatisfy v. t. نارضايت كول na razayat kawal

dissect v. t وموه كول tota tota kawal

dissection n غوسونه ghosawana

dissimilar a ناورته nawarta

dissolve v. t حل كول hal kawal

dissuade v. t منع كول mana kawal

distance n وان watan

distant *a* لر leyri
distil *v. t* عرق‌استل arq eystal
distillery *n* تقطیر taqteer
distinct *a* ممتاز mumtaz
distinction *n* امتیاز eemtiyaz
distinguish *v. i* رتبه‌ورکول rutba warkawal
distort *v. t* بدشکله‌کول bad shakla kawal
distress *n* اضطراب iztirab
distress *v. t* مضطرب‌کول muztarib kawal
distribute *v. t* ونه‌ونه‌کول wanda wanda kawal
distribution *n* ویش weysh
district *n* ولسوالي woolaswalee
distrust *n* ناباوري nabawaree
distrust *v. t.* ناباوره‌کول nabawara kawal
disturb *v. t* پرشانه‌کول parayshana kawal
ditch *n* کنده kanda
dive *v. i* غوپه‌وهل ghopa wahal
dive *n* غوپه ghopa
diverse *a* رنارنگ rangarang
divert *v. t* منصرف‌کول munsarif kawal
divide *v. t* جلاکول jala kawal
divine *a* روحاني roohanee
divinity *n* الهي؛خدای ilahee; khuday
division *n* ویش weysh
divorce *n* طلاق talaq
divorce *v. t* طلاق‌قول talaqawal
divulge *v. t* افشاکول afsha kawal
do *v. t* کول kawal

docile *a* فرمانبردار farmanbardar
dock *n.* لنرای langar zay
doctor *n* طبیب؛اکر tabeed; daktar
doctorate *n* داکردرجه da daktaray daraja
doctrine *n* شعائر shaayar
document *n* دستاوز dastawayz
dodge *n* دوکه doka
dodge *v. t* ترابستل teyr eystal
dog *n* سپی spay
dog *v. t* تعقیبول taqeebawal
dogma *n* عقیده دیني deenee aqeeda
dogmatic *a* پردیني‌عقیداوند par deenee aqeedi arwand
doll *n* لانکه lanzaka
dollar *n* دامریکارسمي‌سکه da amreeka rasmee sika
domain *n* قلمرو qalamraw
dome *n* ومبت goombat
domestic *a* کورنی؛اصلي koranay; aslee
domestic *n* کورني‌یز koranay seez
domicile *n* استونه astogna
dominant *a* غالب ghalib
dominate *v. t* غلبه‌لرل ghalaba laral
domination *n* برلاسی barlasay
dominion *n* واکمني wakmanee
donate *v. t* هدیه‌ورکول hadeeya warkawal
donation *n.* بسپنه baspana
donkey *n* خر khar
donor *n* اهدا‌کوونکی ahdaa kawoonkay
doom *n* قیامت qyamat
doom *v. t.* سپارل ته مر marg ta sparal

door *n* ور war

dose *n* ددرملويوخوراک da darmalo yaw khorak

dot *n* ګی takay

dot *v. t* ګيلول takay lagawal

double *a* غبر ghbarg

double *v. t.* غبرول ghbargawal

double *n* دوہاخيز dwa arkheez

doubt *v. i* شکلرل shak laral

doubt *n* شک shak

dough *n* لمدهکياوہ lamda karee ora

dove *n* کوترہ kawtara

down *adv* کته kkhata

down *prep* مخپهزور makh pa zwar

down *v. t* کتهکول،راپرول kkhata kawal; raparzawal

downfall *n* راالوبدنه ralwaydana

downpour *n* زياتورت zyat warakht

downright *adv* کاملا kamilan

downright *a* صادق sadiq

downward *a* کتنی kakhtay

downward *adv* مخپيهکته makh pa kkhata

downwards *adv* الندخواته landi khwa ta

dowry *n* جهز jahayz

doze *n.* چرتوهنه churut wahana

doze *v. i* سپکخوبکول spak khob kawal

dozen *n* درجن darjan

draft *v. t* طرحهکول tarha kawal

draft *n* مسودہ musawida

draftsman *a* مسودهچمتوکوونکی musawida chamtoo kawoonkay

drag *n* راکشونه rakashawana

drag *v. t* راکشول rakashawal

dragon *n* ابامار khamar

drain *n* لت lakhtay

drain *v. t* وچول wachawal

drainage *n* وچونه wachawana

dram *n* دوزنيومقياس da wazan yaw miqyas

drama *n* رامه،ننداره drama; nandara

dramatic *a* نابی nasapee

dramatist *n* ننداره‌جووونکی nandara jorawoonkay

draper *n* وکرپلوروونکی tokar ploroonkay

drastic *a* غتلی ghakhtalay

draught *n* وچتيا wachtya

draw *v. t* انزورول anzorawal

draw *n* پچهاچوونه pacha achowana

drawback *n* بتوب bey gatitob

drawer *n* دراز daraz

drawing *n* انزور anzor

drawing-room *n* دهرکلیخونه da harkalee kota

dread *n* ورہ weyra

dread *v. t* ورول weyrawal

dread *a* ترهوونکی tarhowoonkay

dream *n* خوب khob

dream *v. i.* خوبليدل khob leedal

drench *v. t* اوبهکول oba kawal

dress *n* جامه jami

dress *v. t* جامهاغوستل jami aghostal

dressing *n* کالی؛مرهم kalee; marham

drill *n* برمه barma

drill *v. t.* برمه سره سوری کول barma sara sooray kawal

drink *n* اسک skhak

drink *v. t* سکل skhal

drip *n* څاڅیدنه saseydana

drip *v. i* څاڅیدل saseydal

drive *v. t* چلول ای gaday chalawal

drive *n* موروانی motor wanee

driver *n* موروان motor wan

drizzle *n* ورینی naray warakht

drizzle *v. i* نری ورت ورښدل naray warakht wareydal

drop *n* څاکی saskay

drop *v. i* څاڅیدل؛ له لاسه غورځیدل saseydal; la lasa ghorzeydal

drought *n* وچتیا wachtya

drown *v.i* اوبو کلاهو کیدل obo ki lahoo keydal

drug *n* درمل darmal

druggist *n* درمل پلورونکی darmal ploroonkay

drum *n* ول dol

drum *v.i.* ول وهل dol wahal

drunkard *n* نشه سی nasha saray

dry *a* وچ wach

dry *v. i.* وچدل wacheydal

dual *a* غبر؛دوه کسی ghbarg; dwa kasee

duck *n.* هیل heelay

duck *v.i.* اوبو کغوپه کدل obo ki ghopa keydal

due *a* مناسب munasib

due *n* داداینو da adayani war

due *adv* بالکل bilkul

duel *n* جه تن په تن tan pa tan jagara

duel *v. i* تن په تن جندل tan pa tan jangeydal

duke *n* انلستان کترشاهزاده لاندلقب inglastan kī tar shahzada landi laqab

dull *a* غبی ghabee

dull *v. t.* غبی کول ghabee kawal

duly *adv* پای په خپل pa khpal zay

dumb *a* ونی goongay

dunce *n* پاو غبی سی pas aw ghabee saray

dung *n* خوشایه khooshaya

duplicate *a* نقلي جوه؛ jora; naqlee

duplicate *n* دویمه نسخه dwayma nuskha

duplicate *v. t* نقل جوول naqal jorawal

duplicity *n* دوه مخي dwa makhee

durable *a* پایدار paydar

duration *n* موده mooda

during *prep* ددوران کي dey dawran ki

dusk *n* درنااوتیارترمنوخت da ranra aw tyarey tar manz wakht

dust *n* دو doori

dust *v.t.* دوپاکول doori pakawal

duster *n* دوپاکوونکی doori pakawoonkay

dutiful *a* مطیع mutee

duty *n* وجیبه؛دنده wajeeba; danda

dwarf *n* لویشتکی lweyshtakay

dwell *v. i* ژوندکول zhwand kawal

dwelling *n* مشتای meysht zay

dwindle *v. t* کمول kamawal

dye *v. t* رنول rangawal

dye *n* رنورکونه rang warkowana

dynamic *a* داینامک dainamik

dynamics n. دجسمونودحركت‌مبحث da jismoonu da harkat mubhis

dynamite n منفجره‌مواد munfajira mawad

dynamo n هغه‌ماشین‌چپه‌حرکت‌کولو ترینه‌برناپداکي hagha masheen chi pa harakat kawalo trina breykhna payda keygee

dynasty n دپاچایانوکورنۍ da pachayano koranay

dysentery n خونۍ‌پچش khoonee peychash

E

each a هریو har yaw

each pron. هرکس har kas

eager a لوال leywal

eagle n عقاب oqab

ear n غو ghwag

early adv په‌چکۍ pa chatakay

early a زر؛بینی zar; beeranay

earn v. t په‌لاس‌راول pa las rawral

earnest a مهم muhim

earth n مکه zmaka

earthen a خاورین khawreen

earthly a دنیاوي doonyawee

earthquake n زلزله zalzala

ease n آساني asanee

ease v. t آسانول asanawal

east n ختیځ khateez

east adv دختیځ‌په‌لور da khateez pa lor

east a ختیځوال khateezwal

easter n دمسیحانواختر da maseehano akhtar

eastern a ختیځوال khateezwal

easy a آسان asan

eat v. t خول khwaral

eatable n. دخوويزونه da khwaro seezoona

eatable a دخوړو da khwaro war

ebb n کمدنه kameydana

ebb v. i کمول kamawal

ebony n دآبنوس‌بوی da abnoos bootay

echo n دآوازانعکاس da awaz inikas

echo v. t غته‌انعکاس‌ورکول ghag ta inikas warkawal

eclipse n دسپوږمۍ‌تندرنیونه da spogmay tandar neewana

economic a اقتصادي iqtisadee

economical a کم‌ارزته kam arzakhta

economics n. اقتصادپوهنه iqtisad pohana

economy n اقتصاد iqtisad

edge n پیکه peeska

edible a و خولو د da khwaralo war

edifice n ما manray

edit v. t چاپ‌ته‌چمتوکول chap ta chamtoo kawal

edition n چاپ chap

editor n دمجلې‌خپرونکی da mujaley khparowoonkay

editorial a مديري mudeeree

editorial n دمجلس‌مقاله da mujaley sar maqala

educate v. t تربیه‌ورکول tarbeeya warkawal

education *n* وونه،تربيه khowana; tarbeeya

efface *v. t* پاکول pakawal

effect *n* اغز agheyz

effect *v. t* اغزکول،اجراءکول agheyz kawal; ijra kawal

effective *a* اغزمن agheyz man

effeminate *a* ينه khazeena

efficacy *n* اغزناکتوب agheyznaktob

efficiency *n* فعاليت،پورتوب faaleeyat; gatawartob

efficient *a* فعال،پور faal; gatawar

effigy *n* تمثال timsal

effort *n* هه hasa

egg *n* ه hagay

ego *n* خپلذات khpal zat

egotism *n* ځانغوتنه zan ghokhtana

eight *n* اته ata

eighteen *a* اتلس atalas

eighty *n* اتيا atya

either *a.,* لهدومخيو la dwa sakha yaw

either *adv.* هريو har yaw

eject *v. t.* بهرتهغورول bahar ta ghorzawal

elaborate *v. t* پهمهارتبشپول pa maharat bashparawal

elaborate *a* ماهرانه mahirana

elapse *v. t* لهوختهاوتل la wakhta awookhtal

elastic *a* ژاولن zhawlan

elbow *n* نل sangal

elder *a* مشر mashar

elder *n* سپينيری speen geeray

elderly *a* مشری masharee

elect *v. t* اکل takal

election *n* ولاکنه tol takana

electorate *n* انتخابيپلاوی intikhabee plaway

electric *a* برنايي breykhnayee

electricity *n* برنا breykhna

electrify *v. t* برناورکول breykhna warkawal

elegance *n* ظرافت zarafat

elegant *adj* باذوقه ba zawqa

elegy *n* مرثيه marseeya

element *n* عنصر unsar

elementary *a* ابتدائي ibtidayee

elephant *n* فيل feel

elevate *v. t* لوول lwarawal

elevation *n* لووونه lwarawana

eleven *n* يوولس yawolas

elf *n* پری peyray

eligible *a* حقدار haqdar

eliminate *v. t* لهمنځول la manza wral

elimination *n* وستنه weystana

elope *v. i* لهشهسرهيوایتختدل la shahay sara yaw zay takhteydal

eloquence *n* فصاحتاوبلاغت fasahat aw balaghat

eloquent *a* فصيح fasee

else *a* بل bal

else *adv* پرتهلهدی prata la dey

elucidate *v. t* روانهکول rokhana kawal

elude *v. t* باطلول batilawal

elusion *n* سترپوونه stargi patawana

elusive *a* غولونکی ghawalaunkay

emancipation *n.* نجات nijat

embalm *v. t* خوشبویه‌کول khoshbooya kawal

embankment *n* پشته poshta

embark *v. t* په‌کټ‌کول pa kakhtay ki wral

embarrass *v. t* شرمول sharmawal

embassy *n* سفارت safarat

embitter *v. t* تریخول treekhawal

emblem *n* علامه،نان alama; nakhan

embodiment *n* تجسم tajasum

embody *v. t.* جسم‌ورکول jisam warkawal

embolden *v. t.* زهورتیاورکول zra wartya warkawal

embrace *v. t.* غاهورکول ghara warkawal

embrace *n* غه،غاه gheyga; ghara

embroidery *n* ‌لدوزي guldozee

embryo *n* جنین janeen

emerald *n* زمرد zamrod

emerge *v. i* راختل،راکاردل rakhatal; rakhkareydal

emergency *n* بینی‌حالت beeranay halat

eminance *n* پوی لو lwar poray

eminent *a* نامتو،عالجنابه namtoo; alee janaba

emissary *n* جاسوس jasoos

emit *v. t* خارجول kharijawal

emolument *n* د اجور پس da ajoorey peysey

emotion *n* جذبه jazba

emotional *a* جذباتي jazbatee

emperor *n* ولواک tolwak

emphasis *n* ‌ینار teengar

emphasize *v. t* ‌ینارکول teengar kawal

emphatic *a* زوردار zordar

empire *n* سلطنت saltanat

employ *v. t* کارته‌هول kar ta hasawal

employee *n* کارمند karmand

employer *n* استخدام‌ووونکی istikhdamowoonkay

employment *n* دنده شغل؛ shoghal; danda

empower *v. t* واک‌ورکول wak warkawal

empress *n* ملکه malika

empty *a* تش tash

empty *v* تشول tashawal

emulate *v. t* تقلیدکول taqleed kawal

enable *v. t* وروول war garzawal

enact *v. t* وضع‌کول؛رول‌لوبول waza kawal; rol lobawal

enamel *n* میناکاري meenakaree

enamour *v. t* په‌مینه‌مجذوبول pa meena majzoobawal

encase *v. t* په‌پو‌کاچول pa pokh ki achawal

enchant *v. t* زه‌ترول zra tri wral

encircle *v. t.* راورول rageyrawal

enclose *v. t* بندول bandawal

enclosure *n.* حصار hisar

encompass *v. t* احاطه‌کول ihata kawal

encounter *n.* شخه shkhara

encounter *v. t* شخه‌کول shkhara kawal

encourage *v. t* اوهورکول ooga warkawal

encroach *v. i* ناومه‌پورته‌کول nawara gata porta kawal

73

encumber v. t. په کاواخته کول pa karaw akhta kawal

encyclopaedia n. پوهنغونه pohanghond

end v. t پای‌ته‌رسول pay ta rasawal

end n. پای pay

endanger v. t. له‌خطرسره‌مخامخول la khatar sara makahmakhawal

endear v.t مینه‌ورکول meena warkawal

endearment n. نازوونه nazowana

endeavour n زیار zeeyar

endeavour v.i زیارباسل zeeyar basal

endorse v. t. تصویبول tasweebawal

endow v. t وقف کول waqaf kawal

endurable a بردبار burdbar

endurance n. بردباري brudbaree

endure v.t. زغمل zhghamal

enemy n دښمن dukhman

energetic a قوي qawee

energy n. توان twan

enfeeble v. t. ناتوانه‌کول natwana kawal

enforce v. t. اجراکول ijra kawal

enfranchise v.t. دتابعیت‌حق‌ورکول da tabieeyat haq warqawal

engage v. t استخدامول istikhdamawal

engagement n. تماس tamas

engine n ماشین masheen

engineer n مهندس muhandis

English n انزري angreyzee

engrave v. t حکاکي کول hakakee kawal

engross v.t لوی‌لوی‌لیکل loy loy leekal

engulf v.t راچاپرول rachapeyrawal

enigma n ونبیان goong bayan

enjoy v. t خونداخستل khwand akheystal

enjoyment n لذت lazat

enlarge v. t پراختیاورکول parakhtya warkawal

enlighten v. t. روان‌فکره‌کول rokhan fikra kawal

enlist v. t نوم‌لیکنه‌کول noom leekana kawal

enliven v. t. ژوندوربل zhwand warbakhal

enmity n دښمني dukhmanee

ennoble v. t. رتبه‌ورکول rutba warkawal

enormous a رلوی deyr loy

enough a کافي kafee

enough adv دکفایت‌تر‌کچ da kifayat tar kachi

enrage v.t په‌غصه‌کول pa ghosa kawal

enrapture v. t په‌وجدراوستل pa wajad rawastal

enrich v. t شتمن‌کول shtaman kawal

enrol v. t نوم‌لیکنه‌کول noom leekana kawal

enshrine v. t په‌زیارت‌کایودل pa zyarat ki eekhodal

enslave v.t. غلام‌جورل ghulam jorawal

ensue v.i په‌پایله‌کواقع‌کدل pa payla ki waqay keydal

ensure v. t اینه‌ورکول dadeena warkawal

entangle v.t پراخته‌کول pri akhta kawal

enter v. t داخلدل،ننوتل nanawatal; dakhileydal

enterprise n لويه‌سوداري loya sawdagaree

entertain v. t خاطرداري كول khatirdaree kawal

entertainment n. خاطرداري؛هركلی khatirdaree; har kalay

enthrone v. t پاچاكول pacha kawal

enthusiasm n جوش‌او‌خروش josh aw kharosh

enthusiastic a له‌جوشه‌ک la josha dak

entice v. t. پارول parawal

entire a پوره poora

entirely adv په‌كامله‌توه pa kamila toga

entitle v. t. په‌نوم كول pa noom kawal

entity n هستي hastee

entomology n. د‌حشراتو‌علم da hashrato ilam

entrance n ننوتنه nanawatana

entrap v. t. په‌لومه‌كرول pa looma ki geyrawal

entreat v. t. زاري‌كول zaree kawal

entreaty n. معامله moamila

entrust v. t امانت‌ورسپارل amanat warsparal

entry n ننوتنه nanawatana

enumerate v. t. حسابول heesabawal

envelop v. t په‌لفافه‌كاچول pa lifafa ki achwal

envelope n لفافه lifafa

enviable a د‌كينه‌كو da keena kakhay war

envious a كينه‌ک keena kakh

environment n. چاپريال chapeyryal

envy v سيالكول syalee kawal

envy v. t كينه‌ساتل keena satal

epic n رزمي‌شاعرياشاعري razmee shair ya shairee

epidemic n وبايي wabayee

epigram n خوكلام khog kalam

epilepsy n مري meyrgee

epilogue n د‌شعرورو‌ستبرخه da shayr warostay barkha

episode n ‌توک tok

epitaph n د‌قبربريک da qabar dabarleek

epoch n دوره،دنوي‌موسم‌پيل dawra; da nawee mosam payl

equal a برابر barabar

equal v. t برابرول barabarawal

equal n هم‌پو ham por

equality n برابري barabaree

equalize v. t. مساوي‌كول masawee kawal

equate v. t مساوي‌ل masawee ganral

equation n تساوي tasawee

equator n داستواكره da istiwa karkha

equilateral a متساوی‌الاضلاع mutasavi ul azla

equip v. t آماده‌كول amada kawal

equipment n وسايل wasayil

equitable a يو‌شان yaw shan

equivalent a مساوي masawee

equivocal a دوه‌اخيز dwa arkheez

era n دوران dawran

eradicate *v. t* لهمنهول la manza wral

erase *v. t* محوه كول mahwa kawal

erect *v. t* نصبول nasbawal

erect *a* لك؛نغ lak; neygh

erection *n* درىدا dareyda

erode *v. t* خوساكول؛سولول khoosa kawal; soolawal

erosion *n* سولدنه sooleydana

erotic *a* عشقيه؛جنسي ishqeeya; jinsee

err *v. i* غلطي كول ghalatee kawal

errand *n* پغام paygham

erroneous *a* لارور كى lar wrakay

error *n* غلطي ghalatee

erupt *v. i* لرزىدل larzeydal

eruption *n* لرزىدنه larzeydana

escape *n* تخته teykhta

escape *v.i* تتدل takhteydal

escort *n* بدره؛دسفر ملرى badraga; da safar malgaray

escort *v. t* پهبدرهملرتياكول pa badraga malgartya kawal

especial *a* خصوصي khusoosee

essay *n.* مقاله؛نمونه maqala; namoona

essay *v. t.* مقالهليكل maqala leekal

essayist *n* مقالهليكونكى maqala leekoonkay

essence *n* روح؛اصل rooh; asal

essential *a* ضروري zarooree

establish *v. t.* تأسيسول taseesawal

establishment *n* تأسيس tasees

estate *n* جايداد jaydad

esteem *n* درناوى dranaway

esteem *v. t* درناوىوركول dranaway warkawal

estimate *n.* اندازه andaza

estimate *v. t* اكلول atkalawal

estimation *n* قدر qadar

etcetera *n* اونور؛وغره aw nor; waghayra

eternal *adj* ابدي abadee

eternity *n* ابديت abadeeyat

ether *n* ايتر؛شينآسمان eetar; sheen asman

ethical *a* اخلاقي akhlaqee

ethics *n.* اخلاقپوهنه akhlaq pohana

etiquette *n* دمعاشرتدآدابوعلم da moashirat da adabo ilam

etymology *n* رهپزندنه reykha peyzhandana

eunuch *n* نرى nar khazay

evacuate *v. t* تشول tashawal

evacuation *n* تشونه tashawana

evade *v. t* ستريريوِل stargi pri patawal

evaluate *v. t* ارزول arzawal

evaporate *v. i* پهبخارالوتل pa bukhar alwatal

evasion *n* ه كونه dada kawona

even *a* جفت؛جوه juft; jora

even *v. t* هواروِل hawarawal

even *adv* كاملا؛همدارنه kamilan; hamda ranga

evening *n* ماښام makham

event *n* په؛واقعه peykha; waqia

eventually *adv.* پهپاى ک pa pay ki

ever *adv* تل؛هيكله tal; heeskala

evergreen *a* بادوامه ba dawama

evergreen *n* تلشين tal sheen

everlasting *a.* تل‌پاتی tal pati

every *a* هریو har yaw

evict *v. t* لهقانوني‌لارای‌خه‌وستل la qanoonee lari zay sakha weystal

eviction *n* ایستنه eystana

evidence *n* ثبوت saboot

evident *a.* ر‌نده sarganda

evil *n* بدروح‌؛شطان bad rooh; shaytan

evil *a* ناوه‌؛خراب na wara; kharab

evoke *v. t* حافظته‌راوستل hafizey ta rawastal

evolution *n* بدلون‌؛ارتقا badloon; irtiqa

evolve *v.t* ظاهریدل zahireydal

ewe *n* مه meyga

exact *a* کره kara

exaggerate *v. t.* مبالغه‌کول mubaligha kawal

exaggeration *n.* مبالغه mubaligha

exalt *v. t* دنول dangawal

examination *n.* معاینه‌؛امتحان moayina; imtihan

examine *v. t* امتحان‌اخستل imtihan akheystal

examinee *n* امتحان‌ور‌کوونکی imtihan warkowoonkay

examiner *n* امتحان‌اخستوونکی imtihan akheystoonkay

example *n* ساری saray

excavate *v. t.* کیندول keendawal

excavation *n.* کیندنه keendana

exceed *v.t* زیاتی‌کول zyatee kawal

excel *v.i* تروا‌ندکدل tri wrandi keydal

excellence *n.* برتری bartaree

excellency *n* جناب janab

excellent *a.* اعلی ala

except *v. t* مستثنی‌کول mustasna kawal

except *prep* مر‌؛پر‌ته‌له magar; prata la

exception *n* استثناء istisna

excess *n* افراط afrat

excess *a* زیات zyat

exchange *n* مبادله‌؛صرافي mubadila; safaree

exchange *v. t* مبادله‌کول mubadila kawal

excise *n* غر‌مستقیم‌مالیات geyr mustaqeem maleeyat

excite *v. t* تحریک‌کول tehreekawal

exclaim *v.i* چغه‌وهل cheygha wahal

exclamation *n* چغه cheygha

exclude *v. t* مستثنی‌ر‌ول mustasna garzawal

exclusive *a* یوازی‌؛تنها yawazi; tanha

excommunicate *v. t.* ایکور‌سره شوکول areeki warsara shookawal

excursion *n.* پو‌هنیز‌سر pohaneez sayr

excuse *v.t* معافول maafawal

excuse *n* معافیت‌؛بخنه maafeeyat; bakhana

execute *v. t* تعمیلول tameelawal

execution *n* تعمیل tameel

executioner *n.* جلاد‌؛تعمیلوونکی jalad; tameelawoonkay

exempt *v. t.* مستثنی‌کول mustasna kawal

exempt *adj* معاف،خوندي maaf; khwandee

exercise *n.* ورزش warzish

exercise *v. t* ورزش کول warzish kawal

exhaust *v. t.* ستومانه کول stomana kawal

exhibit *n.* نندارہ nandara

exhibit *v. t* نندارتهواندکول nandari ta wrandi kawal

exhibition *n.* نندارتون nandartoon

exile *n.* جلاوطني jalawatnee

exile *v. t* جلاوطن کول jalawatan kawal

exist *v.i* وجودلرل wajood laral

existence *n* وجود،شتون wajood

exit *n.* دوتنلارہ،اخراج da watani lar; ikhraj

expand *v.t.* پراختیاورکول parakhtya warkawal

expansion *n.* پراختیا parakhtya

ex-parte *a* یواخیز yaw arkheez

ex-parte *adv* دیولورپمه da yaw lori pa gata

expect *v. t* هیله کول heela kawal

expectation *n.* هیله،طمع heela; tama

expedient *a* مصلحتیور maslihatee gatawar

expedite *v. t.* کول ندی garanday kawal

expedition *n* نندیتوب garandeetob

expel *v. t.* اخراجول ikhrajawal

expend *v. t* مصرفول masrafawal

expenditure *n* خر khars

expense *n.* مصرف،لت masraf; lagakht

expensive *a* ران gran

experience *n* تجربه tajroba

experience *v. t.* تجربه کول tajroba kawal

experiment *n* آزموینه azmoyana

expert *a* تجربه کار tajroba kar

expert *n* کارپوه kar poh

expire *v.i.* وخت یپورهکدل wakht yi poora keydal

expiry *n* خاتمه khatima

explain *v. t.* توضیح کول tawzee kawal

explanation *n* توضح،دلیل tawzee; daleel

explicit *a.* سادہ،واضح sada; wazeh

explode *v. t.* چاودول chawdal

exploit *n* کار ستر star kar

exploit *v. t* لوی کار کول loy kar kawal

exploration *n* اکتشاف iktishaf

explore *v.t* اکتشافيسفر کول iktishafee safar kawal

explosion *n.* چاودنه chawdana

explosive *n.* بم،دچاودنمواد bam; da chawdani mawad

explosive *a* انفجاري infijaree

export *n* صادرات sadirat

export *v. t.* بل هوادتهلودول bal haywad ta leygdawal

expose *v. t* رابرسرهکول rabarseyra kawal

express *v. t.* بیانول bayanawal

express *a* چک chatak

express *n* بیان bayan

expression *n.* اظهار izhar

expressive *a.* اخباري،رسا akhbaree; rasa

expulsion *n.* استنه eystana

extend *v. t* اودول oogdawal

extent *n.* حد had

external *a* بهرنی baharanay

extinct *a* نایاب nayab

extinguish *v.t* اوروژل or wazhal

extol *v. t.* زیاته ستاینه کول zyata stayana kawal

extra *a* اضافي izafee

extra *adv* له حده زیات la hada zyat

extract *n* خلاصه،اقتباس khulasa; iqtibas

extract *v. t* اقتباس کول iktibas kawal

extraordinary *a.* مخصوص makhsoos

extravagance *n* اسراف israf

extravagant *a* اسراف کوونکی israf kawoonkay

extreme *a* بحده bey hada

extreme *n* پای،آخر pay; akhar

extremist *n* افراطي شخص afratee shakhs

exult *v. i* ویامدل weeyareydal

eye *n* ستره starga

eyeball *n* د سترګی ګتی da stargi gatay

eyelash *n* د سترګو بڼه da stargo banra

eyewash *n* د سترو وینلو درمل da stargo weenzalo doormal

F

fable *n.* افسانه afsana

fabric *n* وکړ؛کالبد tokar; kalbad

fabricate *v.t* ورته او مشابه کول warta aw mushabay kawal

fabrication *n* جوړونه؛ساخت jorawana; sakht

fabulous *a* افسانوي afsanawee

facade *n* دودانمخ da wadanay makh

face *n* مخ makh

face *v.t* مخامخ کدل makhamakh keydal

facet *n* د معاشرت د آداب و کتاب da moashirat da adabo keetab

facial *a* د مخ سینار کول da makh seengar kawal

facile *a* آسانه asana

facilitate *v.t* آسانول asanawal

facility *n* سهولت sahoolat

fac-simile *n* فاکس ماشین faks masheen

fact *n* حقیقت haqeeqat

faction *n* ګوند gond

factious *a* له یېز dala yeez

factor *n* عامل amil

factory *n* کارخانه karkhana

faculty *n* پوهنیزمانه pohaneeza sanga

fad *n* ذوقي کار zawqee kar

fade *v.i* ماوی کدل mraway keydal

faggot *n* د لریوی da lagyo geyday

fail *v.i* پاتراتلل pati ratlal

failure *n* ناکامي nakamee

faint *a* کمزوری،بزه kamzoray; bey zra

faint *v.i* کمزوری کدل kamzoray keydal

fair *a* لالی؛صفا golalay; safa

fair *n.* ملا mayla

fairly *adv.* په مناسب دول pa munasib dawl

fairy *n* اپر khapeyray

faith *n* ایمان eeman

faithful *a* باایمان،وفادار ba eeman; wafadar

falcon *n* باز baz

fall *v.i.* راغورزېدل raghorzeydal

fall *n* غورزدنه،انحطاط ghorzeydana

fallacy *n* عب ayb

fallow *n* ییوشومکه yeywi shawi zmaka

false *a* غلط ghalat

falter *v.i* تمبدل tambeydal

fame *n* آوازه،شهرت awaza; shohrat

familiar *a* بلد balad

family *n* کورنۍ koranay

famine *n* وچکالي wachkalee

famous *a* نومیالی noomyalay

fan *n* ببوزی babozay

fanatic *a* متعصب،متشدد mutaasib; mutashadad

fanatic *n* متعصب شخص mutaaṣib shakhs

fancy *n* وهم،خیال wehem; khyal

fancy *v.t* ان ته راکل،متاثره کول zan ta rakkhal; mutasira kawal

fantastic *a* شاندار،وسواسي shandar; waswasee

far *adv.* له ـ لر la ... leyri

far *a* لر leyri

far *n* لروالی leyri walay

farce *n* خندوونکنداره khandowoonki nandara

fare *n* کرایه karaya

farewell *n* مخصه makha kha

farewell *interj.* په مخه دی خا pa makha di kha

farm *n* د کرمکه da kar zmaka

farmer *n* کروندر karwandagar

fascinate *v.t زه ول* zra wral

fascination *n.* ونه زه zra wrana

fashion *n* ول،سینار dol; seengar

fashionable *a* سینارپال seengarpal

fast *a* ندی،تز garanday; teyz

fast *adv* په چکسره pa chatakay sara

fast *n* روژه rozha

fast *v.i* روژه نیول rozha neewal

fasten *v.t* تل taral

fat *a* چاغ chagh

fat *n* ورب سی sorb saray

fatal *a* مري margee

fate *n* برخلیک barkhleek

father *n* پلار plar

fathom *v.t* حل کول hal kaval

fathom *n* وازه (قلا چ) waaza (qalach)

fatigue *n* ستوالی stariwalay

fatigue *v.t* ستی کول staray kawal

fault *n* غلطي ghalatee

faulty *a* عیبجن aybjan

fauna *n* دیوسیمدناوروابووقسمونه da yaw seemi da zanawaro aw booto qismoona

favour1 *n* ه kheygara

favour *v.t* ه کول kheygara kawal

favourable *a* واره من wara man

favourite *a* تر ولو خو tar tolo khwakh

favourite *n* په زه پوری pa zra pory

fear *n* وېره weyra

fear *v.i* وېرېدل weyreydal

fearful *a.* ورونكی weyrowoonkay

feasible *a* كيدونكی kedonkay

feast *n* ملمستيا؛جشن meylmastya; jashan

feast *v.i* پهملمستيارابلل pa meylmastya rabalal

feat *n* لويه كارنامه loya karnama

feather *n* وزر؛بكه wazar; banraka

feature *n* ره،شكل seyra; shakal

February *n* دانرزي كال دويمه مياشت da angreyzee kal dwayama myasht

federal *a* ايتلافي aytilafee

federation *n* ايالت ayalat

fee *n* مزد،فيس mazd; fees

feeble *a* كمزورى kamzoray

feed *v.t* خواهوركول khwara warkawal

feed *n* خواه khwara

feel *v.t* لمسول؛درك كول lamsawal; darak kawal

feeling *n* لمس،احساس lams; ehsas

feign *v.t* رياكول reeya kawal

felicitate *v.t* شاباسىوركول shabasay warkawal

felicity *n* شاباسى؛نكمرغي shabasay; neykmarghee

fell *v.t* پرزول parzawal

fellow *n* مل mal

female *a* ينه khazeena

female *n* خه khaza

feminine *a* مؤنث moannas

fence *n* كاره katara

fence *v.t* كارهپررارول katar pri ragarzawal

fend *v.t* دفاع كول difa kawal

ferment *n* تومنه tomna

ferment *v.t* تخمر كول tokhmar kawal

fermentation *n* تخمر،هجان tokhmar; hayjan

ferocious *a* غضبناك ghazabnak

ferry *n* دمسافرو كه da musafiro kakhtay

ferry *v.t* تراتكول tag ratag kawal

fertile *a* رازه khayraza

fertility *n* رازي khayrazee

fertilize *v.t* رازه كول khayraza kawal

fertilizer *n* سره sara

fervent *a* پُرجوش purjosh

fervour *n* ليوالتيا levaltia

festival *n* مله mayla

festive *a* دجشنو da jashan war

festivity *n* دخاص موقعپهاهجشن da khas moqey pa ara jashan

festoon *n* هغهامل چد كپهري hagha ameyl chi da karay pa seyr zareygee

fetch *v.t* راول rawral

fetter *n* زولنه zolana

fetter *v.t* زولانوراچول zolanay warachawal

feud *n.* دنمي dookhmanee

feudal *a* لواكي dalwakee

fever *n* تبه taba

few *a* يوو yaw so

fiasco *n* ناكامي nakamee

fibre *n* تار tar

fickle *a* ناپايدار napaydar

fiction *n* افسانه afsana

fictitious *a* مصنوعي masnooee

fiddle *n* وايلون waylon

81

fiddle *v.i* وايلون غول؛اپلتويل waylon
ghagawal; apalti wayal
fidelity *n* ريتينولي reekhteenwalee
fie *interj* اوشرمه! washarmeyga !
field *n* ر،ممكه dagar; zmaka
fiend *n* دو deyo
fierce *a* غضبناك ghazabnak
fiery *a* سوزنده؛خوني sozanda;
khoonee
fifteen *n* پنلس peenzalas
fifty *n.* پنوس panzos
fig *n* اينر eenzar
fight *n* شخه shkhara
fight *v.t* شخه كول shkhara kawal
figment *n* وهم؛خيال wehem; khyal
figurative *a*
figure *n* نقش؛به naqsh; banra
figure *v.t* بهلرل،ليدل كدل banra
laral; keedal keydal
file *n* دوتن،دوسيه dotanay; doseeya
file *v.t* ثبتول،په ترتيب سره ايودل
sabtawal; pa tarteeb sara
eekhodal
file *n* سوهان sohan
file *v.t* سوهانول sohanawal
file *v.i.* په ليكه تلل pa leeka tlal
fill *v.t* كول dakawal
film *n* دسينمافيلم da sinayma filam
film *v.t* فيلم چمتو كول filam
chamtoo kawal
filter *n* چا chanr
filter *v.t* چاول chanrawal
filth *n* خيرى kheeray
filthy *a* خرن kheyran
final *a* پركنده،آخري preykanda;
akheyree

finance *n* ماليات maleeyat
financial *a* مالياتي maleeyatee
financier *n* پانوال pangawal
find *v.t* موندل moondal
fine *n* جريمه jareema
fine *v.t* جريمه كول jareema kawal
fine *a* شاندار shandar
finger *n* وته gota
finger *v.t* وته ورول gota warwral
finish *v.t* پاى ته رسول pay ta rasawal
finish *n* انتها پاى؛ pay; intiha
finite *a* محدود mahdood
fir *n* نتر nakhtar
fire *n* اور or
fire *v.t* اورلول or lagawal
firm *a* كلك klak
firm *n.* سوداريزه مؤسسه
sawdagareeza moassisa
first *a* لومى loomray
first *n* ور لوم loomray wraz
first *adv* تر هره دمخه tar har sa da
makha
fiscal *a* مالي malee
fish *n* كب kab
fish *v.i* كب نيول kab neewal
fisherman *n* كب نيوونكى kab
neewoonkay
fissure *n* درز darz
fist *n* موى؛سوك mootay; sook
fistula *n* نل؛نيچه nal; necha
fit *v.t* متناسب كول mutanasib kawal
fit *a* مناسب munasib
fit *n* برابر barabar
fitful *a* ناكراره nakarara
fitter *n* نصبوونكى nasbawoonkay
five *n* پنه peenza

fix *v.t* نصبول nasbawal

fix *n* ررراتلنه geyr ratlana

flabby *a* شول‌پول shool pool

flag *n* برغ beyragh

flagrant *a* بدنام badnam

flame *n* لمبه lamba

flame *v.i* لمبه‌ورته‌کول lamba warta kawal

flannel *n* دفلاین‌وکر da flaleen tokar

flare *v.i* ناپه‌لمبیدل nasapa lambey lageydal

flare *n* تزه‌او‌ستروونکی‌را teyza aw stargi wroonki ranra

flash *n* زلیدنه zaleydana

flash *v.t* پک‌وهل park wahal

flask *n* یوبوتل‌چپه‌لابراتوارککاري yaw botal chi pa labratwar ki kareygee

flat *a* پلن plan

flat *n* اپارتمان apartman

flatter *v.t* چاپلوسی‌کول chaplosee

flattery *n* چاپلوسی chaplosee

flavour *n* خوند‌او‌بوی khwand aw booy

flaw *n* چاود؛عیب chawd; ayb

flea *n.* وره wraga

flee *v.i* تتدل takhteydal

fleece *n* و waray

fleece *v.t* وشوکول waray shookawal

fleet *n* جنگي‌بیري jangee beyray

flesh *n* غوه ghwakha

flexible *a* کمیدونکی kamedonkay

flicker *n* دشمالي‌امریکایومارغه‌چپه‌سر سورکی‌لري da shomalee amreeka yaw margha chi pa sar soor takay laree

flicker *v.t* لزیدل larzeydal

flight *n* الوتنه alwatana

flimsy *a* بدوامه bey dawama

fling *v.t* ارتاوول artawol

flippancy *n* ستاخي gustakhee

flirt *n* نخر،مکز nakhrey; makeyz

flirt *v.i* دعشق‌نازنخرکول da ishq naz nakhrey kawal

float *v.i* داوبوپه‌سرلامبووهل da obo pa sar lambo wahal

flock *n* رمه‌بله rama; gala

flock *v.i* غوندیدل ghondeydal

flog *v.t* په‌تزسره‌حرکت‌کول pa teyzay sara harakat kawal

flood *n* خوب،سل kharob; seyl

flood *v.t* داوبوسل‌راتلل da obo seyl ratlal

floor *n* دمکمخ؛پو da zmaki makh; por

floor *v.t* په‌مکه‌وهل pa zmaka wahal

flora *n* دیوسیمدنباتاتوقسمونه da yaw seemi da nabatato qismoona

florist *n* ل‌پلورونکی gul ploroonkay

flour *n* اوه ora

flourish *v.i* وده‌کول wada kawal

flow *n* بهدنگ baheydang

flow *v.i* بهدل baheydal

flower *n* ل gol

fluent *a* روان rawan

fluid *a* سیال،مایع syal; maya

fluid *n* بهاند bahand

flush *v.i* ناساپي‌پکدل‌یابهدل nasapee parkeydal ya baheydal flush *n* نلاپي‌پک‌یابهیر nasapee park ya baheer

flute *n* شپیلۍ shpeylay

flute *v.i* شپیلوهل shpeylay wahal

flutter *n* لرزیدنه larzeydana

flutter *v.t* لرزیدل larzeydal

fly *n* مچ mach

fly *v.i* الوتل alwatal

foam *n* کف، زگ zag; kaf

foam *v.t* زگ کول zag kawal

focal *a* مرکزی markazi

focus *n* توجه tawajo

focus *v.t* توجه کول tawajo kawal

fodder *n* پروه؛بوس parora; boos

foe *n* حریف؛دمن hareef; dukhman

fog *n* بخار؛لوی bokhar; loogay

foil *v.t* جلوه ورکول jalwa warkawal

fold *n* راماتوونه؛راکونه ramatowana; rakagawana

fold *v.t* راتاوول؛راماتول ratawowal; ramatawal

foliage *n* دونو پا da wano panri

follow *v.t* متابعت کول mutabiat kawal

follower *n* مرید mureed

folly *n* ناپوهي napohee

foment *v.t* پەتودواوبووینل pa tawdo obo weenzal

fond *a* شوقین shawqeen

fondle *v.t* نازول nazawal

food *n* خواه khwara

fool *n* ناپوه napoh

foolish *a* احمق ahmaq

foolscap *n* لوبه‌پله loba panra

foot *n* په poomba

for *prep* لپاره lapara

for *conj.* پمای pa zay

forbid *v.t* منع کول mana kawal

force *n* توان؛زور twan; zor

force *v.t* زورکارول zor karawal

forceful *a* قوی qavi

forcible *a* اجباری ajbari

forearm *n* لجه leycha

forearm *v.t* مخکله‌مخکچمتوکول makhki la makhki chamtoo kawal

forecast *n* واندوینه warandwayana

forecast *v.t* واندوینه کول warandwayana kawal

forefather *n* پلارنیکه plarneeka

forefinger *n* دشهادتوته da shahadat gota

forehead *n* تندی tanday

foreign *a* خارجي kharijee

foreigner *n* خارجي هوادوال kharijee heywadwal

foreknowledge *n.* غب‌پوهنه ghayb pohana

foreleg *n* دحواناتومخکۍ da haywanato makhki pkhey

forelock *n* اوربل orbal

foreman *n* جمعدار jamadar

foremost *a* ترولوغوره tar tolo ghwara

forenoon *n* له‌غرمهمخک la gharmey makhki

forerunner *n* لارخود larkhod

foresee *v.t* واندوینه کول warandwayana kawal

foresight *n* واندوینه warandwayana

forest *n* ځل zangal

forestall *v.t* دمخه‌اخستل da makha akheystal

forester n نل وان zangal wan

forestry n نل پوهه zangal poha

foretell v.t واندوينه کول warandwayana kawal

forethought n دراتلونکی غم خونه da ratlonke gham khwarana

forever adv دتل لپاره da tal lapara

forewarn v.t خبر داری ور کول khabardaray warkawal

foreword n سريزه sareeza

forfeit v.t جريمه ور کول jareema warkawal

forfeit n تاوان؛جريمه tawan; jareema

forfeiture n ضبطونه zabtawana

forge n دآهنر کوره da ahangaray kora

forge v.t په سندان باندکول pa sandan bandi takawal

forgery n جعل کاری jal kari

forget v.t هرول heyrawal

forgetful a بی توجه be tawaja

forgive v.t بخل bakhal

forgo v.t تيريدل teredal

forlorn a ناوهسی nawara saray

form n رخت؛ترکيب reykht; tarkeeb

form v.t. ترکيبول؛برهور کول tarkeebawal; seyra warkawal

formal a رسمي rasmee

format n ظاهري بڼه zahiree banra

formation n جوړښت jorakht

former a پخوانی

formerly adv پخوا،دمخه pakhwa; da makha

formidable a اروونکی darowoonkay

formula n قاعده،فارمول qayda; farmool

formulate v.t داصولو په شکل رندول da usoolo pa shakal sargandawal

forsake v.t. ترک کول tark kawal

forswear v.t. توبه کول toba kawal

fort n. کلا kala

forte n. هنر honar

forth adv. له کورخ هلر la kor sakha leyri

forthcoming a. راتلونکی ratloonkay

forthwith adv. ناپه nasapa

fortify v.t. سنرونه جوول sangaroona jorawal

fortitude n. جسمي توان jismee twan

fort-night n. دواوونز dwey oonay

fortress n. سنر،مورچل sangar; morchal

fortunate a. نکمرغه neykmargha

fortune n. قسمت qismat

forty n. سلوت salweykht

forum n. هجره hujra

forward a. پرمخ تللی par makh tlalay

forward adv دمخ خوا ته da makh khwa ta

forward v.t پرمخ تلل؛رسول par makh tlal; rasawal

fossil n. فوسيل fosil

foster v.t. شدور کول sheydey warkawal

foul a. ناولؤ؛خرن nawalay; kheyran

found v.t. بنسايودل bansat eekhodal

foundation *n.* بنياد boonyad

founder *n.* بنسايودونکی bansat eekhodoonkay

foundry *n.* هغمایچهویلیشویفلزپه قالبوکیاچوی hagha zai che weele shavi falz pa qalabo ke achavi

fountain *n.* فواره fawara

four *n.* لمور salor

fourteen *n.* وارلس swarlas

fowl *n.* چره charga

fowler *n.* وحشیمارغانوکاری wahshee marghano khkari

fox *n.* يده gedara

fraction *n.* کسر،ماتدنه kasar; mateydana

fracture *n.* ماتوالی matwalay

fracture *v.t* ماتول matawal

fragile *a.* نازک nazuk

fragment *n.* وه،برخه tota; barkha

fragrance *n.* بوی booy

fragrant *a.* خوشبويه khooshbooya

frail *a.* نازک nazak

frame *v.t.* قالبول qalibawal

frame *n* قالب،چوکا qalib; chawkat

franchise *n.* قانونیحق qanoni haq

frank *a.* ويه سپين speen goya

frantic *a.* هذيانی hazyanee

fraternal *a.* دوستانه dostana

fraternity *n.* اخوت akhoowat

fratricide *n.* ورورۇژنه wror wazhana

fraud *n.* دوکه doka

fraudulent *a.* دوکباز dokey baz

fraught *a.* دک،شتمن dak; shtaman

fray *n* زت zarakht

free *a.* آزاد azad

free *v.t* آزادول azadawal

freedom *n.* آزادي azadee

freeze *v.i.* کنلکدل kangal keydal

freight *n.* دبارونکرايه da barwrani karaya

french *a.* فرانسوي faransawee

French *n* فراسویویاژبه faransawee wagaray ya zhaba

frenzy *n.* شداتوب sheydatob

frequency *n.* فريکوينسی frekvency

frequent *n.* مکرر mukarrar

fresh *a.* تازه taza

fret *n.* زريدوزي zaree dozee

fret *v.t.* زريدوزيکول zaree dozee kawal

friction *n.* مونه mokhana

Friday *n.* جمعه jooma

fridge *n.* يخچال yakhchal

friend *n.* ملری malgaray

fright *n.* ناپيار nasapee dar

frighten *v.t.* ارول ناپي nasapee darawal

frigid *a.* رسو deyr sor

frill *n.* دزلفانوچتر da zulfano chatar

fringe *n.* حاشيه،چرمه hasheeya; charma

fringe *v.t* حاشيهورکول hasheeya warkawal

frivolous *a.* بهوده bayhooda

frock *n.* فراک frak

frog *n.* چنه changakha

frolic *n.* خوشالی khoshalee

frolic *v.i.* خوشايکول khoshalee kawal

from *prep.* له...خه la ... sakha

front *n.* مخه makha

front *a* دمخ،مخامخ da makhi; makhamakh

front *v.t* ورته‌مخ‌کول warta makh kawal

frontier *n.* برید،پوله breed; poola

frost *n.* پرخه parkha

frown *n.* تون‌دخویی،مخالفت tond khooyee; mukhalifat

frown *v.i* مخالفت‌کاره‌کول mukhalifat khkara kawal

frugal *a.* ساده sada

fruit *n.* موه meywa

fruitful *a.* ور gatavar

frustrate *v.t.* کول مأیوسه mayoosa kawal

frustration *n.* مأیوسي mayoosee

fry *v.t.* وریتول wreetawal

fry *n* سره‌کغوه sra kari ghwakha

fuel *n.* دسوخت‌تل da sokht teyl

fugitive *a.* ژرتریدونکی zhar teyreydoonkay

fugitive *n.* تتدونکی takhteydoonkay

fulfil *v.t.* ترسره‌کول tar sara kawal

fulfilment *n.* ترسره‌کوونه tar sara kawona

full *a.* کامل kamil

full *adv.* خورار khora deyr

fullness *n.* تکمیل takmeel

fully *adv.* په‌بشپول pa bashpar dawl

fumble *v.i.* اشتباه‌کول ishtiba kawal

fun *n.* وکی toki

function *n.* کار kar

function *v.i* کارکول kar kawal

functionary *n.* مأمور،عامل mamoor; amil

fund *n.* سرمایه sarmaya

fundamental *a.* بنيادي boonyadee

funeral *n.* دجنازمراسم da janazey marasim

fungus *n.* فنجی funji

funny *n.* خندوونکی khandowoonkay

fur *n.* دناوروپوست‌ویختان da zanawaro post weykhtan

furious *a.* غضبناک ghazabnak

furl *v.t.* غونول،تاوول ghondawal; tawowal

furlong *n.* داودوالی‌یوه‌میچه da ogad wali yawa mecha

furnace *n.* تنور tanoor

furnish *v.t.* آرایش arayish

furniture *n.* دکوراسباب da kor asbab

furrow *n.* یيوشوه‌مکه yeywi shawi zmaka

further *adv.* برسره‌پردی bar seyra par dey

further *a* ترولوږ tar tolo deyr

further *v.t* پرمخ‌ول par makh wral

fury *n.* غصه ghosa

fuse *v.t.* ترکیبول،ویلکول tarkeebawal; weeli kawal

fuse *n* فیوز fyooz

fusion *n.* ویلکیدنه weeli keydana

fuss *n.* شورماشور shor mashor

fuss *v.i* شورماشورجورول shor mashor jorawal

futile *a.* بی‌فایده bey faydey

futility *n.* بی‌فایدیتوب bey faydeytob

future *a.* راتلونکی ratloonkay

future *n* مستقبل mustaqbil

G

gabble *v.i.* بک بک کول bak bak
kawal

gadfly *n.* خرمچ khar mach

gag *v.t.* پوزبندتل pozband taral

gag *n.* پوزبند pozband

gaiety *n.* بادي boonyadee

gain *v.t.* تر لاسه کول tar lasa kawal

gain *n* استفاده istifada

gainsay *v.t.* انکار inkar

gait *n.* ز tak

galaxy *n.* کهکشان kahkashan

gale *n.* سیل selai

gallant *a.* شجاع shoja

gallant *n* مؤدب،ساتندوی moadab;
satandoy

gallantry *n.* بهادري bahadaree

gallery *n.* لوژ lozh

gallon *n.* د پمایش لمن da gaylan
paymayish

gallop *n.* چک غل chatak zghal

gallop *v.t.* چک غلول chatak
zghalawal

gallows *n.* په دارونه. pa dar
zarawona

galore *adv.* په پریماني pa preymanay

galvanize *v.t.* فلز ته اوبه ورکول filiz
ta oba warkawal

gamble *v.i.* قمار کول qomar kawal

gamble *n* قماربازي qomar bazee

gambler *n.* قمارباز qomar baz

game *n.* لوبه؛مسابقه loba; musabiqa

game *v.i* مسابقه کول musabiqa
kawal

gander *n.* قاز(نر) qaz (nar)

gang *n.* له dala

gangster *n.* بدماش badmash

gap *n* رخنه rakhna

gape *v.i.* رخنه پداکول rakhna payda
kawal

garage *n.* د موټررغونياودروناى da
motar raghawani ya darawani
zay

garb *n.* کالي kalee

garb *v.t* کالى په اغوستل kali pa
aghostal

garbage *n.* کثافت kasafat

garden *n.* باغ bagh

gardener *n.* باغوان baghwan

gargle *v.i.* غغه کول ghar ghara
kawal

garland *n.* امل ameyl

garland *v.t.* اميل ameyl

garlic *n.* اوه ooga

garter *n.* د جورابوبند da jorabo
band

gas *n.* ګاز gaz

gasp *n.* تزه ساه اخستنه teyza sa
akheystana

gasp *v.i* تزه ساه اخستل teyza sa
akheystal

gastric *a.* دمعدى da maide

gate *n.* لویه دروازه loya darwaza

gather *v.t.* راولول ratolawal

gaudy *a.* نمايشي numayishee

gauge *n.* اندازه؛درجه andaza; daraja

gauntlet *n.* او ددستکش oogàd
dastkash

gay *a.* خوشاله khoshala

gaze *v.t* —
کيدل یر zer kedal

gaze *n* یریرکتنه zer zer katana

gazette n. مجله mujala

gear n. رار،ابزار gararay; abzar

geld v.t. خصی کول khasee kawal

gem n غمی ghamay

gender n. تذکیراوتأنیث tazkeer aw tanees

general a. عمومي amoomee

generally adv. پهولیزول pa toleez dawl

generate v.t. تولیدول tawleedawal

generation n. نسل nasal

generator n. تولیدوونکی tawleedawoonkay

generosity n. سخاوت sakhawat

generous a. سخي sakhee

genius n. قابل qabil

gentle a. باشرفه ba sharfa

gentleman n. محترم mohtaram

gentry n. تعلیم یافته خلك او دترېیتنان talim yafta khalak au da tarbiye sakhtanan

genuine a. اصلي aslee

geographer n. ـمکپوه zmakpoh

geographical a. دمکپوهنپهاوند da zmakpohani pa arwand

geography n. مکپوهنه zmakpohana

geological a. دمکپژندنپهاوند da zmakpeyzhandani pa arwand

geologist n. مکپژاند zmakpeyzhand

geology n. مکپژندنه zmakpeyzhandana

geometrical a. هندسی hindsi

geometry n. جیومیری geometry

germ n. جرائیم jaraseem

germicide n. جرائیموژونکی jaraseem wazhoonkay

germinate v.i. ودهکول wada kawal

germination n. وده wada

gesture n. اشاره ishara

get v.t. لاستهراول las ta rawral

ghastly a. ویروونکی werawonki

ghost n. اروا arwa

giant n. دو deyw

gibbon n. کیبون gebon

gibe v.i. ملنوهل malandi wahal

gibe n ملذ malandi

giddy a. سربداله sar badala

gift n. ال dalay

gifted a. مستعد mustaid

gigantic a. بدذ لوی loy badanay

giggle v.i. بواکهخنددل bey waka khandeydal

gild v.t. دسروزرواوبهورکول da sro zaro oba warkawal

gilt a. دسروزرواوبهورکشوی da sro zaro oba warkray shaway

ginger n. سوذ sond

giraffe n. زرافه zarafa

gird v.t. پترنهچاپرهکول patay trina chapeyra kawal

girder n. شاهتیر shateer

girdle n. ملاوستنه mla wastanay

girdle v.t کمربندتل kamarband taral

girl n. نجل najlay

girlish a. نجلغوند najlay ghonde

gist n. دکلامنجو da kalam nachor

give v.t. ورکول warkawal

glacier n. یخچال yakhchal

glad a. خوشال khoshal

gladden *v.t.* خوشاله کول khoshala kawal

glamour *n.* طلسم;زهراکنه talasum; zra rakkhana

glance *n.* غلندنظر zghaland nazar

glance *v.i.* غلندنظرکول zghaland nazar kawal

gland *n.* مرغی margharay

glare *n.* لا zala

glare *v.i* لمدل zaleydal

glass *n.* دپیاله;یه da kheekhey pyala; kheekha

glaze *v.t.* لول zalaval

glazier *n.* یهغووونکی kheekha ghosowoonkay

glee *n.* سرور suroor

glide *v.t.* ویدل khwayeydal

glider *n.* بماشینه کوچنالوتکه چدهوایه وسیله الوزي bey masheena koochnay alwataka chi da hawa pa waseela aloozee

glimpse *n.* غلندنظر zghaland nazar

glitter *v.i.* پقدل parqeydal

glitter *n* پقدنه parqeydana

global *a.* نیوال nareewal

globe *n.* ردی garday

gloom *n.* سیوری ganr syoray

gloomy *a.* تیاره tyara

glorification *n.* تجلیل tajleel

glorify *v.t.* تجلیلول tajleelawal

glorious *a.* پرتمین purtameen

glory *n.* عظمت azmat

gloss *n.* توضیح tawzee

glossary *n.* دلغاتونوملیک da lughato noomleek

glossy *a.* لاند zaland

glove *n.* لاسماغو las magho

glow *v.i.* برکیدل breykheydal

glow *n* بر breykh

glucose *n.* لوکوز gulucose

glue *n.* سر sareykh

glut *v.t.* مول marawal

glut *n* زیات خوراک;مت khorak; marakht

glutton *n.* پرخوراک مین par khorak mayan

gluttony *n.* زیات خوراک خونه zyat khorak khwarana

glycerine *n.* لیسرین glicrine

go *v.i.* تلل tlal

goad *n.* مچک machak

goad *v.t* سکونل skoondal

goal *n.* مقصد maqsad

goat *n.* وزه wza

gobble *n.* کریه کول krega kawal

goblet *n.* جام jam

god *n.* خدای khuday

goddess *n.* الهه ilaha

godhead *n.* خدایی khuday

godly *a.* دیندار dendar

godown *n.* زرمتون zeyrmatoon

godsend *n.* خدای ورکیشی khuday warkaray shay

goggles *n.* دستروژغورندویه عنک da stargo zhghorandoya aynaki

gold *n.* سرهزر sra zar

golden *a.* طلایي tilayee

goldsmith *n.* زرگر zargar

golf *n.* دگلف لوبه da gulf loba

gong *n.* جآوازهزنه jag awaza zang

good *a.* ﺵ kha

good *n* نکي neykee

good-bye *interj.* دخدای‌پامان da khuday paman

goodness *n.* هوالی kha walay

goodwill *n.* هنیت kha nyat

goose *n.* بته bata

gooseberry *n.* ازغن‌توت azghan toot

gorgeous *a.* برمناک baramnak

gorilla *n.* وریلابیزو goreela beezo

gospel *n.* انجیل injeel

gossip *n.* بی‌اساسه‌خبری be asasa khabary

gourd *n.* دنسوارو‌کدو da naswaro kadoo

gout *n.* نقرس naqras

govern *v.t.* حکمرانی‌کول hukamranee kawal

governance *n.* حکمرانی hukamranee

governess *n.* وونکۍ khowoonkay

government *n.* حکومت hukoomat

governor *n.* والی walee

gown *n.* دواودجامه da khazo oogdey jamey

grab *v.t.* په‌لاس‌کتول pa las ki takhtawal

grace *n.* عفوه تایید، tayeed; afwa

grace *v.t.* کلاوربل khkula warbakhal

gracious *a.* مهربانه mehrabana

gradation *n.* درجه‌بندي darja bandee

grade *n.* مرتبه martaba

grade *v.t* درجه‌بندي‌کول darja bandee kawal

gradual *a.* ‌گام‌په‌گام gam pa gam

graduate *v.i.* لیسانسه‌سرته‌رسول leesansa sar ta rasawal

graduate *n* زدکوتۍ،لیسانسه zdakrotay; leesansa

graft *n.* پوند peywand

graft *v.t* پوندلول peywand lagawal

grain *n.* غَله ghala

grammar *n.* ژبدود zhabdood

grammarian *n.* ژبود zhabkhod

gramophone *n.* دراموفون‌دموسیقۍآله da gramofon da mawseeqay ala

granary *n.* دغَلودام da ghaley godam

grand *a.* ستر star

grandeur *n.* لویي loyee

grant *v.t.* وربل warbakhal

grant *n* اهداء ihda

grape *n.* انور angoor

graph *n.* هندسي‌نمایش hindsee mumayish

graphic *a.* دهندسواونخچوپه‌اوند da hindso aw nakhcho pa arwand

grapple *n.* لاس‌اوروان‌کدنه las aw greywan keydana

grapple *v.i.* لاس‌اوروان‌کدل las aw greywan keydal

grasp *v.t.* پوهول pohawal

grasp *n* پوهاوی pohaway

grass *n* واه wakha

grate *n.* رنده randa

grate *v.t* رنده‌کول randa kawal

grateful *a.* منندوی manandoy

gratification *n.* مسرت musarat

gratis *adv.* ویا warya

gratitude *n.* حق‌پژندنه haq peyzhandana

gratuity *n.* اجر ajar

grave *n.* قبر qabar

grave *a.* سخت،خطرناک sakht; khatarnak

gravitate *v.i.* دجاذبدقوپه‌وسیله دحرکت کول da jazibey da qawey pa waseela harakat kawal

gravitation *n.* کشش kashish

gravity *n.* وزن wazan

graze *v.i.* رول sarawal

graze *n* روونه sarawana

grease *n* ریس grees

grease *v.t* ریس‌ورکول grees warkawal

greasy *a.* ریس‌ورکی‌شوی grees warkray shaway

great *a* عظیم azeem

greed *n.* حرص hiras

greedy *a.* حرصی hirasee

greek *n.* یونانی‌ویاژبه yoonanee wagaray ya zhaba

Greek *a* یونانی yoonanee

green *a.* زرغون،تازه zarghon; taza

green *n* شین‌رنگ sheen rang

greenery *n.* شینکی sheenkay

greet *v.t.* سلام‌کول salam kawal

grenade *n.* لاسی‌بم lasee bam

grey *a.* خړ khard

greyhound *n.* تازی‌سپی tazee spay

grief *n.* غم gham

grievance *n.* ‌له،شکایت geela; shikayat

grieve *v.t.* غمجنول ghamjanawal

grievous *a.* غمجن ghamjan

grind *v.i.* مده‌کدل mayda keydal

grinder *n.* دژرندماشین da zhrandi masheen

grip *v.t.* په‌لاس‌کنیول pa las ki neewal

grip *n* په‌لاس‌کنیونه pa las ki neewana

groan *v.i.* زروی‌کول zgeyrwee kawal

groan *n* زروی zheyrwee

grocer *n.* سبزي‌پلورونکی sabzee ploroonkay

grocery *n.* سبزي‌پلورنای sabzee ploranzay

groom *n.* شلمی shazalmay

groom *v.t* کلاوربل khkula warbakhal

groove *n.* ناوه،کانال nawa; kanal

grope *v.t.* لاس‌پول las tapawal

gross *n.* اصلي‌برخه،دباریوپمائش aslee barkha; da bar yaw paymayish

gross *a* ناخالص،برجسته nakhalis; barjasta

grotesque *a.* عجیب‌اوغریب ajeeb aw ghareeb

ground *n.* ړ dagar

group *n.* له dala

group *v.t.* په‌لوویشل pa dalo weyshal

grow *v.t.* وده‌کول wada kawal

grower *n.* ودهورکوونکی،پالونکی wada warkawoonkay; paloonkay

growl *v.i.* غړمبدل ghrambeydal

growl *n* غمبار ghrambar

growth *n.* وده،کړه wada; karhanra

grudge *v.t.* بخيلي کول bakheelee kawal

grudge *n* بخل bukhal

grumble *v.i.* وندل doongeydal

grunt *n.* غورغور ghor ghor

grunt *v.i.* غورغورکول ghor ghor kawal

guarantee *n.* ضمانت zamanat

guarantee *v.t* ضمانت ورکول zamanat warkawal

guard *v.i.* ژغورل zhghoral

guard *n* ژغورونکی،ساتونکی zhghoroonkay; satoonkay

guardian *n.* ولي walee

guava *n.* امرود amrood

guerilla *n.* نارسمي جنيالی narasmee jangyalay

guess *n.* اکل atkal

guess *v.i* اکل کول atkal kawal

guest *n.* ملمه meylma

guidance *n.* لاروونه lar khowana

guide *v.t.* لاروونه کول lar khowana kawal

guide *n.* ود لار lar khod

guild *n.* صنف،ولی sanf; tolay

guile *n.* مکر،حيله makar; heela

guilt *n.* جرم juram

guilty *a.* مجرم mujrim

guise *n.* ظاهر،شکل zahir; shakal

guitar *n.* دارد موسيقی آله da geetar da mawseeqay ala

gulf *n.* خليج khaleej

gull *n.* ساده saada

gull *v.t* غولول ghwalaval

gulp *n.* لويه نمه loya namray

gum *n.* اور،سر ooray; sareykh

gun *n.* ويک topak

gust *n.* سيل seelay

gutter *n.* لتی lakhtay

guttural *a.* ستونيز stoonez

gymnasium *n.* لوبغالی lobghalay

gymnast *n.* دجمناسک دلوبو ماهر da jamnastic da lobo mahir

gymnastic *a.* اوند، په جمناسک د پ چست da jamnastic pa arwand; chust

gymnastics *n.* دجمناسک لوب da jamnastic lobi

habit *n.* عادت adat

habitable *a.* داستوگنو da astogni war

habitat *n.* دناورو او مارغانو داوسدوای da zanawaro aw marghano da oseydo zay

habitation *n.* استوگنای astoganzay

habituate *v. t.* رودی کول rogday kawal

hack *v.t.* پ جوول؛غوول tap jorawal; ghosawal

hag *n.* غوروی ghoravy

haggard *a.* نر dangar

haggle *v.i.* اصرارکول israr kawal

hail *n.* ل galay

hail *v.i* لورېدل galay wareydal

hail *v.t* سلام اچول salam achawal

hair *n* وته weykhta

hale *a.* لالی gulalay

half *n.* نيمايي neemayee

half *a* نیم neem
hall *n.* دالان،تالار dalan; talar
hallmark *n.* دطلااوسپینوزروباندجو نان da tila aw speeno zaro bandi jor nakhan
hallow *v.t.* تقدیسول taqdeesawal
halt *v. t.* درمدل dareydal
halt *n* درمدنه dareydana
halve *v.t.* نیمایي کول neemayee kawal
hamlet *n.* کوچنی کلی koochnay kalay
hammer *n.* ستک satak
hand *n* لاس laas
hand *v.t* مرسته کول mrasta kawal
handbill *n.* لاس په لاس خپرونکخبرتیا laas pa las khparowoonki khabartya
handbook *n.* لاسی کتاب laasi kitab
handcuff *n.* اتک atkaray
handcuff *v.t* اتکاچول atkaray achawal
handful *n.* لشان lag shan
handicap *v.t.* کمزوری کول kamzoray
handicap *n* معذور mazoor
handicraft *n.* لاسي صنعت laasee sanat
handiwork *n.* لاسی کار laasee kaar
handkerchief *n.* دستمال dastmal
handle *n.* لاستی lastay
handle *v.t* په لاس سمول pa las samawal
handsome *a.* للالی gulalay
handy *a.* آسانه asana
hang *v.t.* وندول zwarandawal
hanker *v.i.* هوس کول hawas kawal

haphazard *a.* ناپایی nasapi
happen *v.t.* پدل peykheydal
happening *n.* پدنه peykheydana
happiness *n.* خوي khwakhee
happy *a.* خو khwakh
harass *v.t.* اذیتول azeeyatawal
harassment *n.* اذیت azeeyat
harbour *n.* لنرای langarzay
harbour *v.t* پناهور کول pana warkawal
hard *a.* سخت sakht
harden *v.t.* سختول sakhtawal
hardihood *n.* بباکي bey bakee
hardly *adv.* په سختسره pa sakhtay sara
hardship *n.* ربه rabra
hardy *adj.* جسور jasoor
hare *n.* سویه soya
harm *n.* تاوان tawan
harm *v.t* تاوان رسول tawan rasawal
harmonious *a.* همغای hamghardi
harmonium *n.* دهارمونیومدموسیقهآله da harmoneeyom da mawseeqay ala
harmony *n.* جوجای jor jaray
harness *n.* پزوان peyzwan
harness *v.t* رامول ramawal
harp *n.* چ chang
harsh *a.* شدید shadeed
harvest *n.* دفصلونولو da fasloono law
haverster *n.* دلوماشین،لوری da law masheen; law garay
haste *n.* بیه beera
hasten *v.i.* بیه کول beera kawal
hasty *a.* بیهناک beeranak

hat n. خول khwalay

hatchet n. تشه،کور teysha; kawdar

hate n. کرکه kraka

hate v.t. کرکه کول kraka kawal

haughty a. کبرجن kabarjan

haunt v.t. تراتگ کول tag ratag kawal

haunt n تراتگ tag ratag

have v.t. درلودل darlodal

haven n. پناهای panazay

havoc n. چپاول chapawal

hawk n شاهين shaheen

hawker n رندپلورونکی garzand ploroonkay

hay n. پروه prora

hazard n. خطر khatar

hazard v.t خطرسره مخامخول khata sara makhamakhawal

haze n. غبار ghobar

hazy a. ردجن gardjan

he pron. هغه hagha

head n. سر sar

head v.t رهبري کول rahbaree kawal

headache n. دسرخوږدنه da sar khoogeydana

heading n. سرليک sarleek

headlong adv. بهناك bera naak

headstrong a. خپل سری khpal saray

heal v.i. رغول raghawal

health n. روغتيا roghtya

healthy a. سلامت salamat

heap n. زيات مقدار zyat

heap v.t زيات مقدار ور کول zyat miqdar warkawal

hear v.t. اورول awrawal

hearsay n. آواز ه،بنوسی awaza; gangosay

heart n. ز زره zra

hearth n. منقل،نغری munqal; nagharay

heartily adv. په زه ورتوب pa zarawartob

heat n. تودوخه tawdokha

heat v.t تودول tawdawal

heave v.i. هسکول hasakaval

heaven n. جنت janat

heavenly a. آسماني asmanee

hedge n. خڼ،کاره khand; katara

hedge v.t خنياکاره راتاوول khand ya katara ratawowal

heed v.t. توجه کول tawajo kawal

heed n توجه tawajo

heel n. پونده poonda

hefty a. دروند droond

height n. لوواليی lwarwalay

heighten v.t. لوول lwarawal

heinous a. ناوه nawara

heir n. وارث waris

hell a. دوزخ dozakh

helm n. دکتسرنه da kakhtay stayring

helmet n. فلزي خول filizee khwalay

help v.t. مرسته کول mrasta kawal

help n مرسته mrasta

helpful a. کومکي komakee

helpless a. بیاره،بمدداره bey yara; bey madadgara

helpmate n. دژوندملری da zhwand malgaray

hemisphere n. ژ jai

hemp n. بنگ bang

hen *n.* چرګه charga
hence *adv.* لددلامله la dey lamala
henceforth *adv.* پس لددی pas la dey
henceforward *adv.* پس لددی pas la dey
henchman *n.* باوريلاروی bawaree laraway
henpeck *a.* پرميهبرچوهل pa merda barach wahal
her *pron.* دهغ،هغته da haghey; haghey ta
her *a* دهغ da haghey
herald *n.* جارچي،الجي jarchee; aylchee
herald *v.t* زریورکول zeyray warkawal
herb *n.* طبيبوی tibee botay
herculean *a.* ران gran
herd *n.* رمه rama
herdsman *n.* شپون shpoon
here *adv.* دخوا،دلته deykhwa; dalta
hereabouts *adv.* پهدشاوخواک pa dey shawkhwa ki
hereafter *adv.* تردوروسته tar dey wrosta
hereditary *n.* موروثي mawroosee
heredity *n.* ميراث meeras
heritage *n.* ميراث meeras
hermit *n.* وشهنشينزاهد gosha nasheen zahid
hermitage *n.* دانزوامای da anzwa zay
hernia *n.* چوره،فتق choora; fataq
hero *n.* اتل،قهرمان atal; qaharman
heroic *a.* قهرماني qaharmanee
heroine *n.* تله،قهرمانه tala; qaharmana

heroism *n.* اتلوي،قهرماني atlawee; qaharmanee
herring *n.* یوولکب yaw dol kab
hesitant *a.* دشمالي امریکايوولکب da shomalee amreeka yaw dawl kab
hesitate *v.i.* زهنازه کدل zra na zra keydal
hesitation *n.* زهنازهتوب zra na zratob
hew *v.t.* قطع کول،غوول qata kawal; ghosawal
heyday *n.* دنکمرغاوج da naykmarghay oj
hibernation *n.* دژميموسمپهخوب تروونه da zhamee mosam pa khob teyrowana
hiccup *n.* سله salgay
hide *n.* پونه patawana
hide *v.t* پول patawal
hideous *a.* ربدشکله deyr bad shakla
hierarchy *n.* مذهبيحکومت mazhabee hukoomat
high *a.* عالي،لو alee; lwar
highly *adv.* پهلوی کچ pa loy kach
Highness *n.* عزتمأب eezat mab
highway *n.* لويهلار loya lar
hilarious *a.* رخندوونکی deyr khandowoonkay
hilarity *n.* خوشالي khoshalee
hill *n.* غوز ghonday
hillock *n.* کوچنغوز koochnay ghonday
him *pron.* هغهته hagha ta
hinder *v.t.* نارامه کول narama kawal

hindrance *n.* خنډ،مزاحمت khand; muzahimat

hint *n.* اشاره ishara

hint *v.i* اشاره کول ishara kawal

hip *n* کونای konatay

hire *n.* کرایه،اجاره karaya; eejara

hire *v.t* کرایه کول karaya kawal

hireling *n.* مزدور mazdoor

his *pron.* دهغه da hagha

hiss *n* سوډنه sonreydana

hiss *v.i* سوډل sonreydal

historian *n.* تاریخ لیکونکی tareekh leekoonkay

historic *a.* تاریخي tareekhee

historical *a.* تاریخي tareekhee

history *n.* تاریخ،پلار tareekh; peykhlar

hit *v.t.* ګرکول takar kawal

hit *n* ګر،تصادف takar; tasadof

hitch *n.* کان،جکه takan; jatka

hither *adv.* دغای ته dagha zay ta

hitherto *adv.* تراوسه tar osa

hive *n.* دمچیو کور da muchyo kor

hoarse *a.* زیه zeg

hoax *n.* وکه toka

hoax *v.t* وکه کول toka kawal

hobby *n.* مشغولا mashghola

hockey *n.* دهاکی لوبه da hakay loba

hoist *v.t.* پورته کول porta kawal

hold *n.* پورته کونه porta kawona

hold *v.t* په واک کی لرل pa wak ki laral

hole *n* سوری sooray

hole *v.t* سوری کول sooray kawal

holiday *n.* دآرام ورز da aram wraz

hollow *a.* خالي،پوده khalee; pooda

hollow *n.* سوری sooray

hollow *v.t* تشول،خالي کول tashawal; khalee kawal

holocaust *n.* عام وژنه am wazhna

holy *a.* مقدس muqadas

homage *n.* احترام ehtiram

home *n.* کور kor

homicide *n.* وژنه wazhana

homogeneous *a.* همجنسه hamjinsa

honest *a.* امین ameen

honesty *n.* دیانت deeyanat

honey *n.* شهد shehed

honeycomb *n.* دشاتوبین da shato gabeen

honeymoon *n.* دوادهلومنیاشت da wada loomranay myasht

honorarium *i.* حق الوکاله haqul wakala

honorary *a.* اعزازي ayzazee

honour *n.* احترام ehtiram

honour *v.t* درناوی ورته کول dranaway warta kawal

honourable *a.* محترم mohtaram

hood *n.* پوني،اوباش paroonay; obash

hoodwink *v.t.* دوکه کول doka kawal

hoof *n.* سوه،کومه swa; korma

hook *n.* چنګ changak

hooligan *n.* لوچک او کوهبی وان loochak aw koosa dabay zwan

hoot *n.* دتحقیر چغه da tehqeer cheygha

hoot *v.i* دتحقیرچغه وهل da tehqeer cheygha wahal

hop *v.i* وپونه وهل topoona wahal

hop *n* بیر،افین؛غوری‌پری beer; afeen; ghorzay parzay

hope *v.t.* ورته‌هیله‌لرل warta heela laral

hope *n* امید omeed

hopeful *a.* هیله‌من heelaman

hopeless *a.* ناامیده na omeeda

horde *n.* قبیله qabeela

horizon *n.* افقي‌کره ofqee karkha

horn *n.* کر khkar

hornet *n.* یوول‌ستره‌غومبسه yaw dawl stara ghombasa

horrible *a.* هیبتناک haybatnak

horrify *v.t.* ترهول tarhawal

horror *n.* ترهه tarha

horse *n.* آس as

horticulture *n.* پوهنیزه‌باغواني pohaneeza baghwanee

hose *n.* داوبوشیندنانی‌پلاستیکي‌نل da obo sheendani zangaray plasteekee nal

hosiery *n.* دجورابواوبنینونوجوورنه‌یا پلورنی da jorabo aw banaynoono jorawona ya ploranzay

hospitable *a.* ملمه‌پال meylma pal

hospital *n.* روغتون roghtoon

hospitality *n.* ملمستیا meylmastya

host *n.* کوربه korba

hostage *n.* یرغمل yarghmal

hostel *n.* دپوهنتون‌یاووني‌لیله da pohantoon ya khowonzee laylya

hostile *a.* مخالف mukhalif

hostility *n.* مخالفت mukhalifat

hot *a.* گرم‌اوتود garam aw tod

hotchpotch *n.* گوآش gadwad ash

hotel *n.* ملمستون meylmastoon

hound *n.* ‌کاري‌سپی khkaree spay

hour *n.* یوساعت yaw saat

house *n* کور؛سرای kor; sray

house *v.t* مشت‌کول meysht kawal

how *adv.* په‌هول؛‌څنه pa sa dawl; sanga

however *adv.* خوبیاهم kho bya ham

however *conj* که‌هم ka sa ham

howl *v.t.* کوکول،چغوهل kooki kawal; cheyghi wahal

howl *n* کوک kooki

hub *n.* دفعالیت‌مرکز da faaleeyat markaz

hubbub *n.* غرو،هیاهو ghreew; hya hoo

huge *a.* پیاوی،لوی pyawaray; loy

hum *v. i* بندل bangeydal

hum *n* بندنه bangeydana

human *a.* انساني insanee

humane *a.* مهربان mehraban

humanitarian *a* بشرپال bashar pal

humanity *n.* بشریت bashareeyat

humanize *v.t.* انسانول؛سی‌کول insanawal; saray kawal

humble *a.* خاکسار khaksar

humdrum *a.* بخونده bey khwanda

humid *a.* نمجن،لوند namjan; loond

humidity *n.* رطوبت ratoobat

humiliate *v.t.* توهینول tawheenawal

humiliation *n.* توهین tawheen

humility *n.* خاکساري khaksaree

humorist *n.* وکمار tokmar

humorous *a.* توکی toki

humour *n.* خوش طبعي khush tabee

hunch *n.* بوكام،راوتلتيا bokam; rawataltya

hundred *n.* سل sal

hunger *n* لوه loga

hungry *a.* وى wagay

hunt *v.t.* كار كول khkar kawal

hunt *n* كار khkar

hunter *n.* كاري khkaree

huntsman *n.* كاريسى khkaree saray

hurdle1 *n.* خند،كاره تاوونه khand; katara tawowan

hurdle2 *v.t* خندروال،كاره ترتاوول khand darawal; katara tri tawowal

hurl *v.t.* شل،ايستل sharal; eystal

hurrah *interj.* شاباش،دخوشاليو آواز shabash; da khoshalay yaw awaz

hurricane *n.* تونداوتزباد tond aw teyz awaz

hurry *v.t.* توندي كول tondee kawal

hurry *n* توندي tondee

hurt *v.t.* ژوبلول zhoblawal

hurt *n* شوبل shobal

husband *n* مه meyra

husbandry *n.* كرهه،باغباني karhanra; baghbanee

hush *n* چوپتيا choptya

hush *v.i* خاموشول khamoshawal

husk *n.* پوستكى postakay

husky *a.* وچ،آواز wach; dad awaz

hut *n.* كوله koodala

hyaena, hyena *n.* كو،دسپيپهريوناور kog; da spee pa seyr yaw zanawar

hybrid *a.* پوندي،دوهرى peywandee; dwa ragay

hybrid *n* پوندي بوي يافصل peywandee bootay ya fasal

hydrogen *n.* دهايروجنباز da haydrojan gaz

hygiene *n.* روغتياپوهنه roghtya pohana

hygienic *a.* پا پهروغتياپوراوند roghtya pori arwand

hymn *n.* مذهبي ترانه mazhabee tarana

hyperbole *n.* مبالغهونا mubaligha wayna

hypnotism *n.* پهمصنوعيولدويده pa masnooee dawl da weeda kawalo amal aw ilam

hypnotize *v.t.* پهمصنوعيولويدهكول pa masnooee dawl weeda kawal

hypocrisy *n.* پهريا كارانبريالي كونه pa reeyakaray zan baryalay kawona

hypocrite *n.* رياكارسى reeyakar saray

hypocritical *a.* رياكارانهاودوهمخي reeyakarana aw dwa makhee

hypothesis *n.* مفروضه،يوخيال mafrooza; yaw khyal

hypothetical *a.* خيالي،مفروضي khyalee; mafroozee

hysteria *n.* دتشنجرز da tashannuj ranz

hysterical *a.* تشنجوهلىشخص tashannuj wahalay shakhs

I

I *pron.* زه za
ice *n.* واوره wawra
iceberg *n.* د واوری وو کی غر da wawri warookay ghar
icicle *n.* ونده کنل شوی واوره zwaranda kangal shawi wawra
icy *a.* واورین wawreen
idea *n.* خيال؛فکر khyal; fikar
ideal *a.* خيالي؛تصوري khyalee; tasawwuree
ideal *n* مکمل او بشرانسان mukamal aw bashbar insan
idealism *n.* خيال پالنه khyal palana
idealist *n.* خيالي انسان khyalee insan
idealistic *a.* انريال؛تصوري angeyryal; tasawwuree
idealize *v.t.* خيالي به ورکول khyalee banra warkawal
identical *a.* مشابه mushabay
indentification *n.* پژندلوي؛شناخت peyzhandgalwee; shanakht
identify *v.t.* شناخت کول shanakht kawal
identity *n.* شناخت shanakht
idiom *n.* لهجه؛نه lehja; garana
idiomatic *a.* لهجوي lehjawee
idiot *n.* لو ده lawda
idiotic *a.* بعقله bey aqla
idle *a.* بکاره bey kara
idleness *n.* بکاري bey karee
idler *n.* بکاره bey kara
idol *n.* بت boot

idolater *n.* بت پرست boot parast
if *conj.* کاش؛ای که ka; ay kash
ignoble *a.* کم اصل kam asal
ignorance *n.* ناپوهي napohee
ignorant *a.* ناپوه napoh
ignore *v.t.* سترپرپول stargey pri patawal
ill *a.* رنزور ranzoor
ill *adv.* ناسم؛ناجو nasam; najor
ill *n* بده چاره bada chara
illegal *a.* غرقانوني gheyr qanoonee
illegibility *n.* نه لوستل کدل na lostal keydal
illegible *a.* نه لوستل کدونکی na lostal keydoonkay
illegitimate *a.* ناروا؛ارموني narawa; armoonay
illicit *a.* ارموني؛غرقانوني armoonay; gheyr qanoonee
illiteracy *n.* ناپوهي؛کم تعليمي napohee; kam taleemee
illiterate *a.* بتعليمه bey taleema
illness *n.* بيماري beemaree
illogical *a.* نامعقول namaqool
illuminate *v.t.* لانده کول zalanda kawal
illumination *n.* روانتيا rokhantya
illusion *n.* فرب؛وهم farayb; wehem
illustrate *v.t.* شرحه کول sharha kawal
illustration *n.* شرحه؛توضيح sharha; tawzee
image *n.* تصوير؛شکل tasweer; shakal
imagery *n.* تصور؛خيال tasawwur; khyal

imaginary *a.* خيالي khyalee

imagination *n.* تصور،ګومان tasawwur; gooman

imaginative *a.* تصوري tasawwuree

imagine *v.t.* ګومان اواكل كول gooman aw atkal kawal

imitate *v.t.* پروي كول،نقل كول peyrawee kawal; naqal kawal

imitation *n.* پروي،تقليد peyrawee; taqleed

imitator *n.* تقليد كوونكى taqleed kawoonkay

immaterial *a.* غير مادي gheyr madee

immature *a.* ناپخته napukhta

immaturity *n.* ناپختي napukhtagee

immeasurable *a.* لامحدود lamehdood

immediate *a* فوري fawree

immemorial *a.* ديرپخوانى deyr pakhwanay

immense *a.* خورا ډير khora deyr

immensity *n.* ډيرت deyrakht

immerse *v.t.* جذبول،غرقول jazbawal; gharqawal

immersion *n.* غوپه كوونه ghopa kawona

immigrant *n.* كوال kadwal

immigrate *v.i.* كوچيدل koocheydal

immigration *n.* كوالتوب kadwaltob

imminent *a.* خطرناك،نژدې khatarnak; nazhdey

immodest *a.* بحيا bey haya

immodesty *n.* بحيايي bey hayayee

immoral *a.* بداخلاق bad akhlaq

immorality *n.* بداخلاقي bad akhlaqee

immortal *a.* تل ژوندى tal zhwanday

immortality *n.* تلپاتتوب talpatitob

immortalize *v.t.* تلپاتى كول talpati kawal

immovable *a.* بحركت bey harakat

immune *a.* محفوظ mehfooz

immunity *n.* حفاظت،مصئونتيا heefazat; masuntya

immunize *v.t.* درنپرضدواكسين وركول da ranz pr zid wakseen warkawal

impact *n.* اثر،فشار asar; fishar

impart *v.t.* ونه وركول،په برخه كول wanda warkawal; gata pa barkha kawal

impartial *a.* بطرفه bey tarafa

impartiality *n.* بطرفي bey tarafee

impassable *a.* ناشوني nashoonay

impasse *n.* بلاريای be lari zai

impatience *n.* بصبري bey sabree

impatient *a.* بصبره bey sabra

impeach *v.t.* تورنول toranawal

impeachment *n.* تورونه،تعقيب torawona; taqeeb

impede *v.t.* مانع كدل manay keydal

impediment *n.* خنډ كدنه khand keydana

impenetrable *a.* راسخ او كلك klak aw rasikh

imperative *a.* امري،لازمي amaree; lazimee

imperfect *a.* ناقص naqis

imperfection *n.* نيمګرتيا neemgartya

imperial *a.* پاچاهي pachahee

imperialism *n.* امپراطوري ampratooree

imperil *v.t.* په‌خطركاچول pa khatar ke achaval

imperishable *a.* تلپاتـ talpati

impersonal *a.* غرشخصي gheyr shakhsee

impersonate *v.t.* شخصيت‌نه‌وركول shakhseeyat na warkawal

impersonation *n.* اندبل‌شخصيت‌په رمل zan da bal shakhseeyat pa seyra ganral

impertinence *n.* بادبي bey adabee

impertinent *a.* بادبه bey adaba

impetuosity *n.* سختي‌اوشدت sakhtee aw shiddat

impetuous *a.* سخت‌اوشديد sakht aw shadeed

implement *n.* كارونه karawona

implement *v.t.* كارول؛عمل‌كراوستل karawal; amal ki rawastal

implicate *v.t.* په‌جنايت‌كلاس‌لرل pa jinayat ki las laral

implication *n.* په‌جنايت‌كگتيا pa jinayat kakartya

implicit *a.* كامل؛مكمل kamil; mukamal

implore *v.t.* زاركول zaray kawal

imply *v.t.* ضمن‌مفهوم zaman mafhoom

impolite *a.* بادبه bey adaba

import *v.t.* واردول waridawal

import *n.* واردات waridat

importance *n.* اهميت ahmeeyat

important *a.* اهم aham

impose *v.t.* مسلطول musallatawal

imposing *a.* مسلط musallat

imposition *n.* لازمي‌كوونه lazimee kawona

impossibility *n.* ناشونتيا nashoontya

impossible *a.* ناشونى nashoonay

impostor *n.* چلباز chalbaz

imposture *n.* چلبازي chalbazee

impotence *n.* جنسي‌كمزورتيا jinsee kamzortya

impotent *a.* په‌جنسي‌توه‌كمزورى pa jinsee toga kamzoray

impoverish *v.t.* ناتوان‌كول natwan kawal

impracticability *n.* ناعملي‌توب na amaleetob

impracticable *a.* ناعملي na amalee

impress *v.t.* متاثرول mutasirawal

impression *n.* اثر،خيال asar; khyal

impressive *a.* مؤثر moassar

imprint *v.t.* په‌فشارسره‌جوول pa fishar sara jorawal

imprint *n.* چاپ‌شوى‌شى chap shaway shay

imprison *v.t.* زنداني‌كول zandanee kawal

improper *a.* نامناسب na munasib

impropriety *n.* ناوتوب nawartob

improve *v.t.* سمول؛سمسورول samawal; samsorawal

improvement *n.* سمسورتيا samsortya

imprudence *n.* بپامي bey pamee

imprudent *a.* بپامه bey pama

impulse *n.* انزه angeyza

impulsive *a.* انزوي angeyzwee

impunity *n.* له‌سزاخه‌بنه la saza sakha bakhana

impure *a.* ناولى nawalay

impurity *n.* ناپاكي napakee

impute *v.t.* ملامتول malamatawal

in *prep.* په كى pa ki

inability *n.* ناتواني natwanee

inaccurate *a.* ناسم nasam

inaction *n.* بكارى bey karee

inactive *a.* بكاره bey kara

inadmissible *a.* ناروا narawa

inanimate *a.* بروحه،جامد bey rooha; jamid

inapplicable *a.* نا جو na jor

inattentive *a.* بپامه bey pama

inaudible *a.* ناواورلدونكى na awreydoonkay

inaugural *a.* په پرانستىپوراوند pa pranistani pori arwand

inauguration *n.* پرانستنه pranistana

inauspicious *a.* بدمرغه badmargha

inborn *a.* فطري fitree

incalculable *a.* بشماره bey shmara

incapable *a.* ناتوان natwan

incapacity *n.* كمزورتيا kamzortia

incarnate *a.* مجسم mujassam

incarnate *v.t.* مجسمكول mujassam kawal

incarnation *n.* وجودوركوونه wajood warkowana

incense *v.t.* فتنهاچول fitna achawal

incense *n.* فتنه fitna

incentive *n.* محرك mohrik

inception *n.* آغاز aghaz

inch *n.* دواتنيوپمائش da watan yaw paymayish

incident *n.* حادثه hadisa

incidental *a.* حادثاتي hadisatee

incite *v.t.* لمسول lamsawal

inclination *n.* آمادي،ميلان amadagee; meelan

incline *v.i.* هول،كوپول hasawal; kropawal

include *v.t.* شاملول shamilawal

inclusion *n.* شمولتيا shamooltya

inclusive *a.* شامل shamil

incoherent *a.* ناوارند na arwand

income *n.* ده،حاصل gata; hasil

incomparable *a.* بجو bey jorey

incompetent *a.* نالائق nalayiq

incomplete *a.* ناتكميل natakmeel

inconsiderate *a.* بااحتياطه bey ehteeyata

inconvenient *a.* نارامه narama

incorporate *v.t.* يوكول yaw kawal

incorporate *a.* يوشوى yaw shaway

incorporation *n.* پوستون،يوكدا peywastoon; yaw keyda

incorrect *a.* غلط ghalat

incorrigible *a.* نه نهرغدونكى na ragheydoonkay

incorruptible *a.* نه نهخرابدونكى na kharabeydoonkay

increase *v.t.* زياتول zyatawal

increase *n* زيادت zyadakht

incredible *a.* دنهمنني da na manani war

increment *n.* رت deyrakht

incriminate *v.t.* تورنول toranawal

incubate *v.i.* چروياستل chargooree eystal

inculcate *v.t.* تلقينكول talqeen kawal

incur *v.t.* خواشيني كول khwasheenee kawal

incurable *a.* لاعلاج la ilaj

indebted *a.* قرضدار qarzdar

indecency *n.* بنزاكتي bey nazakatee

indecent *a.* بنزاكته bey nazakata

indecision *n.* بى عزمى be azami

indeed *adv.* پەريتينى ول pa reekhteenee dawl

indefensible *a.* نه ژغورونكى na zhghoroonkay

indefinite *a.* غرمحدود gheyr mehdood

indemnity *n.* تاوان،جبران tawan; jibran

independence *n.* خپلواكي khpalwakee

independent *a.* خپلواكه khpalwaka

indescribable *a.* نه شرحه كدونكى na sharha keydoonkay

index *n.* لارودليك lar khod lar leek

Indian *a.* هندي،هندوستاني hindee; hindoostanee

indicate *v.t.* رندول،دلالت كول sargandawal; dalalat kawal

indication *n.* دلالت،اشاره dalalat; ishara

indicative *a.* اشاره كوونكى ishara kawoonkay

indicator *n.* اشاره كوونكى ishara kawoonkay

indict *v.t.* دادعاليك له مختورنول da ida leek la makhi toranawal

indictment *n.* په ادعاليك سره مخ تورنونه pa ida leek sara makh torawona

indifference *n.* بتفاوتي bey tafawatee

indifferent *a.* بتفاوت bey tafawat

indigenous *a.* سوچه اصلي؛ aslee; soocha

indigestible *a.* نه هضمدونكى na hazmeydoonkay

indigestion *n.* نه هضمدنه na hazmeydana

indignant *a.* قهردلى qahreydalay

indignation *n.* قهر qahar

indigo *n.* تز آسماني رنـ teyz asmanee rang

indirect *a.* نامستقيم na mustaqeem

indiscipline *n.* بنظمي bey nazmee

indiscriminate *a.* لوده،بعقل lawda; bey aqla

indispensable *a.* ضروري zarooree

indisposed *a.* ناساز nasaz

indisputable *a.* مسلم musallam

indistinct *a.* نامشخص na mushakhkhas

individual *a.* انى،يوازان zanee; yawazi zan

individualism *n.* يوازتوب yawazitob

individuality *n.* انى،فردي zan zanee; fardee

indolent *a.* كاهل kahil

indoor *a.* دننى،داخلي danananay; dakhilee

indoors *adv.* په كوردنه pa kor danana

induce *v.t.* مجبورول majboorawal

inducement *n.* سبب sabab

induct *v.t.* داخلول؛درك كول dakhilawal; darak kawal

induction *n.* داخلدا dakhileyda

indulge *v.t.* خپلواكهپرودل khpalwaka preykhodal

indulgence *n.* اجازهوركونه eejaza warkawona

indulgent *a.* خپلواكهپرودلىشوى khpalwaka preykhodalay shaway

industrial *a.* صنعتي sanatee

industrious *a.* زيارك zeeyar kakh

industry *n.* صنعت sanat

ineffective *a.* غرمؤثر ghayr moassar

inertia *n.* عطالت italat

inevitable *a.* ناچار nachar

inexact *a.* نادرست nadrust

inexorable *a.* برحم bey rehem

inexpensive *a.* كمخره kam kharsa

inexperience *n.* ناتجربهكار na tajroba kar

inexplicable *a.* ستونزمن stoonzman

infallible *a.* نهغولدونكى na gholeydoonkay

infamous *a.* بدنام badnam

infamy *n.* بدنامي badnamee

infancy *n.* كوچنيتوب koochneetob

infant *n.* كوچنى koochnay

infanticide *n.* دكوچنووژنه da koochno wazhana

infantile *a.* دكوچنوپهاوند da koochno pa arwand

infantry *n.* پوپياده pyada pawz

infatuate *v.t.* حماقتكول himaqat kawal

infatuation *n.* حماقت himaqat

infect *v.t.* ككول kakarawal

infection *n.* ككنيا kakartya

infectious *a.* ككر kakar

inference *n.* استنباط istimbat

inferior *a.* كمتر kamtar

inferiority *n.* كمتري kamtaree

infernal *a.* دوزخي dozakhee

infinite *a.* لامحدود la mehdood

infinity *n.* لامحدوديت la mehdoodeeyat

infirm *a.* ضعيف zaeef

infirmity *n.* ضعف zof

inflame *v.t.* پارول parawal

inflammable *a.* اوراخيستونكى or akheystoonkay

inflammation *n.* التهاب،بسودنه iltihab; sozeydana

inflammatory *a.* التهابى iltihabee

inflation *n.* اقتصاديپسوب iqtisadee parsob

inflexible *a.* نهبدلدونكى،نهكدونكى na badleydoonkay; na kageydoonkay

inflict *v.t.* سزاوركول saza warkawal

influence *n.* اغز agheyz

influence *v.t.* اغزلرل agheyz laral

influential *a.* اغزناك agheyznak

influenza *n.* زكام zukam

influx *n.* بهير،جريان baheer; jaryan

inform *v.t.* خبرول khabrawal

informal *a.* غررسمي ghayr rasmee

information *n.* معلومات maloomat

informative *a.* باخبر ba khabar

informer *n.* خبروونكى khabrawoonkay

infringe *v.t.* لاساچول laas achawal

infuriate *v.t.* قهرول qahrawal

infuse v.t. دمول damaval

ingrained a. پوخ pokh

ingratitude n. ناشكري na shukree

ingredient n. ترکيبي‌جز tarkeebee joz

inhabit v.t. استونه‌کول astogna kawal

inhabitable a. داستوڼو da astogni war

inhabitant n. استوڼ astogan

inhale v.i. بويول booyawal

inherent a. ميراثي meerasee

inherit v.t. په‌ميراث‌راول pa meeras rawral

inheritance n. ميراث meeras

inhibit v.t. مخنيوی‌کول makhneeway kawal

inhibition n. مخنيوی makhneeway

inhospitable a. نامهربان na mehraban

inhuman a. غرانساني ghayr insanee

inimical a. زيانمن zeeyanman

inimitable a. بساريتوب beysareetob

initial a. بنيادي،ابتدايي boonyadee; ibtidayee

initial n. آغاز؛شروع aghaz; shoro

initial v.t شروع‌کول shoro kawal

initiate v.t. لومړی‌ام‌پورته‌کول loomray gam porta kawal

initiative n. آغاز aghaz

inject v.t. ستنه‌وهل stana wahal

injection n. اماله؛تزريق imala; tazreeq

injudicious a. بانصافه bey insafa

injunction n. دنيونحکم da neewani hokam

injure v.t. پی‌کول tapee kawal

injurious a. وروونکی zorowoonkay

injury n. زخم zakham

injustice n. بانصافي bey insafee

ink n. سياهي seeyahee

inkling n. راپور rapor

inland a. دمکبريدونو کدننه da zmaki breedoono ki danana

inland adv. دهوادخواته da haywad khwa ta

in-laws n. دکوروداﻧﺮونه‌اوخوند da korwadani ronra aw khwayndi

inmate n. استوڼ astogan

inmost a. په‌منځ‌کی pa manz ke

inn n. مسافرخانه moosafar khana

innate a. طبيعي tibbee

inner a. داخلي dakhilee

innermost a. منډبرخه manzanay barkha

innocence n. بناهتوب bey goonahtob

innocent a. بناه bey goona

innovate v.t. بدلون‌راوستل badloon rawastal

innovation n. بدلون؛نوی‌شی badloon; naway shay

innovator n. بدلون‌راوستونکی badloon rawastoonkay

innumerable a. بشمره bey shmeyra

inoculate v.t. خال‌وهل khal wahal

inoculation n. خال‌وهنه khal wahana

inoperative *a.* غرفعال ghayr faal

inopportune *a.* بوخته،بموقع bey wakhta; bey moqa

input *n.* ونه،بولتونه wanda; tol lagakhtoona

inquest *n.* رونه garweygna

inquire *v.t.* پوتل pokhtal

inquiry *n.* تحقیق tehqeeq

inquisition *n.* پوتنه pokhtana

inquisitive *a.* تحقیقي،تفتیشي tehqeeqee; tafteeshee

insane *a.* نده ganda

insanity *n.* خچنتوب khachantob

insatiable *a.* نه راضه کدونکی na razee keydoonkay

inscribe *v.t.* نقش کول naqsh kawal

inscription *n.* کتیبه kateeba

insect *n.* حشره hashra

insecticide *n.* حشره وژونکی hashra wazhoonkay

insecure *a.* غرمحفوظ ghayr mehfooz

insecurity *n.* باطمیناني bey itmaynanee

insensibility *n.* بحسي bey hisee

insensible *a.* بحس bey his

inseparable *a.* نه بلدونکی na beyleydoonkay

insert *v.t.* ننوستل،زایول nanaweystal; zayawal

insertion *n.* ننوستنه nanaweystana

inside *n.* کولمه واحشاء koolmey aw ahsha

inside *prep.* دننه danana

inside *a* دننی؛داخلي danananay; dakhilee

inside *adv.* په داخل پوراوند pa dakhil pori arwand

insight *n.* بصیرت baseerat

insignificance *n.* بماناتوب bey manatob

insignificant *a.* بمانا bey mana

insincere *a.* ریاکار،بمخلص reeyakar; bey mukhlis

insincerity *n.* دوه مخي،ریا dwa makhay; reeya

insinuate *v.t.* چاپلوسي کول chaplosee kawal

insinuation *n.* چاپلوسي chaplosee

insipid *a.* بخونده bey khwanda

insipidity *n.* بخوندي bey khwandee

insist *v.t.* اصرار کول israr kawal

insistence *n.* اصرار israr

insistent *a.* اصرار کوونکی israr kawoonkay

insolence *n.* اهانت ihanat

insolent *a.* ستاخ gostakh

insoluble *n.* نه ویلا کدونکی na waylay keydoonkay

insolvency *n.* نه ویلا کدنه na wayla keydana

insolvent *a.* نابسیا،پاتراغلی na basya; pati raghalay

inspect *v.t.* پلنه کول palatana kawal

inspection *n.* پلنه palatana

inspector *n.* پلونکی palatoonkay

inspiration *n.* اثر asar

inspire *v.t.* متاثرول mutasirawal

instability *n.* نایکاوتوب nateekawtob

install *v.t.* په کار اچول pa kar achawal

installation *n.* په کاراچوونه pa kar achawona

instalment *n.* قسط qist

instance *n.* نمونه،بله namoona; beylga

instant *n.* جاري jaree

instant *a.* این areen

instantly *adv.* ژرترژره zhar tar zhara

instigate *v.t.* لمسول lamsawal

instigation *n.* لمسون lamsoon

instil *v.t.* تدریجيتلقینکول tadreejee talqeen kawal

instinct *n.* حوانيشعور haywanee shaoor

instinctive *a.* حوانيشعورلرونکی haywanee shaoor laroonkay

institute *n.* مؤسسه moassisa

institution *n.* مرکز،سازمان markaz; sazman

instruct *v.t.* وونهکول khowana kawal

instruction *n.* درس،هدایت dars; hidayat

instructor *n.* درسورکوونکی dars warkowoonkay

instrument *n.* آله،وسیله ala; waseela

instrumental *a.* آلاتي alatee

instrumentalist *n.* دموسیقدآلاتو ماهر da mawseeqay da alato mahir

insubordinate *a.* نافرمان nafarman

insubordination *n.* نافرماني nafarmanee

insufficient *a.* ناکافي nakafee

insular *a.* لنفکری land fikray

insularity *n.* لنفکري land fikree

insulate *v.t.* جلاکول jala kawal

insulation *n.* بلتون beyltoon

insulator *n.* جلاکوونکی jala kawoonkay

insult *n.* سپکاوی spakaway

insult *v.t.* بدردويل badi radi wayal

insurance *n.* بیمه beema

insure *v.t.* بیمهکول beema kawal

insurgent *a.* باغیانه baghyana

insurgent *n.* باغ baghee

insurrection *n.* بلواري balwagaree

intact *a.* سالم salim

intangible *a.* نامحسوس na mehsoos

integral *a.* ضروري zarooree

integrity *n.* ایمانداري eemandaree

intellect *n.* فهم fehem

intellectual *a.* فکري fikree

intellectual *n.* مفکر mufakkir

intelligence *n.* استخبارات istikhbarat

intelligent *a.* هوښیار hookhyar

intelligentsia *n.* قابلخلک qabil khalk

intelligible *a.* واضح wazeh

intend *v.t.* ارادهکول irada kawal

intense *a.* شدید shadeed

intensify *v.t.* شدتزیاتول shiddat zyatawal

intensity *n.* تزي،شدت teyzee; shiddat

intensive *a.* شدید shadeed

intent *n.* هو hod

intent *a.* منظور manzoor

intention *n.* قصد qasad

intentional *a.* قصدي qasdee

intercept *v.t.* رابطه‌شنول rabita shandawal

interception *n.* مخنيوى makhneeway

interchange *n.* مبادل mubadil

interchange *v.* مبادله‌كول mubadila kawal

intercourse *n.* مقاربت؛معامله muqaribat; moamila

interdependence *n.* يوپه‌بل‌باندتكيه yaw pa bal bandi takia

interdependent *a.* يوپه‌بل‌باندتكيه yaw pa bal bandi takia

interest *n.* جاليبيت jalibeeyat

interested *a.* جالب jalib

interesting *a.* په‌زه‌پور pa zra pori

interfere *v.i.* دخالت‌كول dakhalat kawal

interference *n.* دخالت dakhalat

interim *n.* عارضي‌مدت arzee mudat

interior *a.* داخلي dakhilee

interior *n.* دننه danana

interjection *n.* حرف‌ندا؛دخالت harfi nida; dakhalat

interlock *v.t.* په‌قلف‌بندول pa qulf bandawal

interlude *n.* كوونكى‌وان dakowoonkay watan

intermediary *n.* مصالحت‌كوونكى musalihat kawoonkay

intermediate *a.* منى manzgaray

interminable *a.* پايدار paydar

intermingle *v.t.* ول gadaval

intern *v.t.* توقيف‌كول tawqeef kawal

internal *a.* داخلي dakhilee

international *a.* نړيوال nareewal

interplay *n.* دوه‌اخيزاغز dwa arkheez agheyz

interpret *v.t.* ژبانه‌كول zhbarana kawal

interpreter *n.* ژبان zhbaran

interrogate *v.t.* تفتيش‌كول tafteesh kawal

interrogation *n.* رونه garweygna

interrogative *a.* پوتونكى pokhtoonkay

interrogative *n* دپوتنه da pokhtani nakha

interrupt *v.t.* قطع‌كول qata kawal

interruption *n.* پرېكون preykoon

intersect *v.t.* قطع‌كول qata kawal

intersection *n.* تقاطع taqato

interval *n.* موده؛دمه mooda; dama

intervene *v.i.* مداخله‌كول mudakhila kawal

intervention *n.* مداخله mudakhila

interview *n.* مركه maraka

interview *v.t.* مركه‌كول maraka kaval

intestinal *a.* دكولموپه‌اوند da koolmo pa arwand

intestine *n.* كولمې koolmey

intimacy *n.* نژداشناتوب nazhdey ashnatob

intimate *a.* اشنا؛نژد ashna; nazhdey

intimate *v.t.* مطلب‌رسول matlab rasawal

intimation *n.* اشاره؛خبرتيا ishara; khabartya

intimidate *v.t.* ترهول tarhawal

intimidation *n.* ترهه tarha

into *prep.* دننه،په‍_‍ک danana; pa
... ki

intolerable *a.* نه‌زغمو‌ونکی na
zghamowoonkay

intolerance *n.* نه‌زغمنه na
zghamana

intolerant *a.* نه‌زغمو‌ونکی na
zghamowoonkay

intoxicant *n.* نشه‌یاک nashayee
skhak

intoxicate *v.t.* نشه‌کول nasha
kawal

intoxication *n.* نشه‌کو‌ونه nasha
kawona

intransitive *a.* *verb* لازمي‌فعل
lazimee fayl

intrepid *a.* بور bey weyri

intrepidity *n.* نه‌ارنه na darana

intricate *a.* پچلی peychalay

intrigue *v.t.* پچلی‌کول peychalay
kawal

intrigue *n* پچلتیا peychaltya

intrinsic *a.* حقیقی haqiki

introduce *v.t.* معرفي‌کول marifee
kawal

introduction *n.* پژندلوي
peyzhandgalwee

introductory *a.* سریزه،ابتدایي
sareeza; ibtidayee

introspect *v.i.* ځان‌ل zan seyral

introspection *n.* ځان‌نه zan seyrana

intrude *v.t.* تری‌کول teyray kawal

intrusion *n.* تری teyray

intuition *n.* فراست firasat

intuitive *a.* بصیرت‌لرونکی baseerat
laroonkay

invade *v.t.* برید‌کول breed kawal

invalid *a.* بی‌بنیاده bey boonyada

invalid *a.* غرقانوني ghayr qanoonee

invalid *n* بیمار beemar

invalidate *v.t.* باطلول batilawal

invaluable *a.* بارزته bey arzakhta

invasion *n.* حمله hamla

invective *n.* بده‌ژبه bada zhaba

invent *v.t.* اختراع‌کول ikhtira kawal

invention *n.* نوت nawakht

inventive *a.* اختراعي ikhtiraee

inventor *n.* نوتر nawakhtgar

invert *v.t.* تحریفول tehreefawal

invest *v.t.* پانسمانول pansmanawal

investigate *v.t.* تحقیق‌کول tehqeeq
kawal

investigation *n.* تحقیق tehqeeq

investment *n.* پانه‌اچوونه panga
achowana

invigilate *v.t.* ‍ارل saral

invigilation *n.* ‍ارنه sarana

invigilator *n.* ‍ارن saran

invincible *a.* نه‌لیدونکی na
leedoonkay

inviolable *a.* منزه،محفوظ munazza;
mehfooz

invisible *a.* نالیدلی naleedalay

invitation *v.* بلنه balana

invite *v.t.* بلنه‌ورکول balana
warkawal

invocation *n.* دم،دعا dam; doa

invoice *n.* بجک beyjak

invoke *v.t.* مرسته‌غوشتل mrasta
ghoshtal

involve *v.t.* ونه‌ورکول wanda
warkawal

inward *a.* دننه danana

inwards *adv.* دننه‌خواته danana khwa ta

irate *a.* قارشوى qarshavi

ire *n.* غضب ghazab

Irish *a.* ايرليني eerlayndee

Irish *n.* ايرليني‌وى‌ياژبه eerlayndee wagaray ya zhaba

irksome *a.* ستومانه‌كوونكى stomana kawoonkay

iron *n.* اوسپنه ospana

iron *v.t.* اوتوكول oto kawal

ironical *a.* پغور peghor

irony *n.* پغور peghor

irradiate *v.i.* وانه‌اچول waranga achawal

irrational *a.* نامعقوله namaqoola

irreconcilable *a.* ته‌پخلاكيدونكى ta pakhula kedonkay

irrefutable *a.* نه‌ردېدونكى na radeydoonkay

irregular *a.* بقاعد bey qaydey

irregularity *n.* بقاعلى bey qaydagee

irrelevant *a.* نامناسب namunasib

irrespective *a.* باعتنا bey aytina

irresponsible *a.* بپروا bey parwa

irrigate *v.t.* اوبول obawal

irrigation *n.* اوبورنه obawana

irritable *a.* عصباني asbanee

irritant *a.* فسخ‌كوونكى fasakh kawoonkay

irritant *n.* پاروونكى parowoonkay

irritate *v.t.* په‌قارول pa qaraval

irritation *n.* پارونه parawana

irruption *n.* هجوم hajoom

island *n.* ټاپو tapoo

isle *n.* ټاپوزمه tapoo wazma

isolate *v.t.* وه gokha

isolation *n.* يوازېتوب yawazitob

issue *v.i.* صادرول sadirawal

issue *n.* معامله maamila

it *pron.* دا،هغه da; hagha

Italian *a.* ايالوي eetalwee

Italian *n.* ايالوي‌وى‌ياژبه eetalwee wagaray ya zhaba

italic *a.* په‌لرغونوايالويانوپوراوند pa larghono eetalweeyano pori arwand

italics *n.* رنده‌كاه‌توري reykhanda kaga toree

itch *n.* خار kharakh

itch *v.i.* خارلرل kharakh laral

item *n.* شى shay

ivory *n.* دفيل‌غا da feel ghakh

ivy *n* يوول‌بوى‌چه‌تل‌شين‌وى yaw dol botay che tal sheen we

J

jab *v.t.* ننه‌ايستنه nana estana

jabber *v.t.* ناشمېرخبركول na shmeyri khabari kawal

jack *n.* دموترجك da motar jak

jack *v.t.* په‌جك‌سره‌پورته‌كول pa jak sara

jackal *n.* شغال shaghal

jacket *n.* جاك jakat

jade *n.* يوقيمتى‌كانى yaw qeematee kanray

jail *n.* بنديخانه bandeekhana

jailer *n.* دبنديخانهمسؤل da bandeekhaney masool

jam *n.* مربا muraba

jam *v.t.* چيتول،بندول cheetawal; bandawal

jar *n.* يووڵديبوتل yaw dawl da kheekhey botal

jargon *n.* ډانرهنريژبه zangari honaree zhaba

jasmine, jessamine *n.* دياسمينګل da yasmeen gul

jaundice *n.* دزيږيرنز da zyaree ranz

jaundice *v.t.* پهزيږياختهكوڵ pa zyaree akhta kawal

javelin *n.* نزهلاسيسپكه spaka lasee nayza

jaw *n.* ژامه zhama

jay *n.* لهكاغذكورنيومارغه la kraghi da koranay yaw margha

jealous *a.* نيتبدى nyat baday

jealousy *n.* نيتبدي nyat badee

jean *n.* يووڵپتلون yaw dawl patloon

jeer *v.i.* پغورورکوڵ peyghor warkawal

jelly *n.* يووڵخواهخواه yaw dawl khwaga khwara

jeopardize *v.t.* خطرسرهمخامخوڵ khatar sara makhamakhawal

jeopardy *n.* خطر khatar

jerk *n.* جكه jaka

jerkin *n.* چرميواسک charmee waskat

jerky *a.* كدلى takeydalay

jersey *n.* اوبدلشوىينهجاک obdal shaway khazeena jakat

jest *n.* پغور peyghor

jest *v.i.* پغورورکوڵ peyghor warkawal

jet *n.* تورهكهربا tora kahruba

Jew *n.* يهودي yahoodee

jewel *n.* قيمتيكانى qeematee kanray

jewel *v.t.* پهغميوكلىكوڵ pa ghamyo khkulay kawal

jeweller *n.* زرګر zargar

jewellery *n.* جواهراتپلورنى jawahirat ploranzay

jingle *n.* شرنهار shranghar

jingle *v.i.* شرندل shrangeydal

job *n.* دنده danda

jobber *n.* قاچاقچي qachaqchee

jobbery *n.* دقاچاقدنده da qachaq danda

jocular *a.* خندونکى khandoonkay

jog *v.t.* ورول khorawal

join *v.t.* پوندول peywandawal

joiner *n.* ترکا tarkanr

joint *n.* مفصل mafsal

jointly *adv.* پههسره pa gada sara

joke *n.* وکه toka

joke *v.i.* وککوڵ toki kawal

joker *n.* مسخره maskhara

jollity *n.* عش aysh

jolly *a.* مست mast

jolt *n.* ناپهمکان nasapa takan

jolt *v.t.* چدل racheydal

jostle *n.* ويدا khwayeyda

jostle *v.t.* خوتورکوڵ khozakht warkawal

jot *n.* برکى basarkay

jot *v.t.* مختصرليکل mukhtasar leekal

journal *n.* جريده jareeda

journalism *n.* پليکنه peykh leekana

journalist *n.* پليکونکی peykh leekoonkay

journey *n.* سفر safar

journey *v.i.* سفرکول safar kawal

jovial *a.* عش اوعشرت کول aysh aw ishrat kawal

joviality *n.* عش اوعشرت aysh aw ishrat

joy *n.* لذت lazat

joyful, joyous *n.* خوندور khwandawar

jubilant *a.* خوشاله khoshala

jubilation *n.* خوي khwakhee

jubilee *n.* يوخاص کليزه yaw khas kaleeza

judge *n.* قضايي حکم qazayee hukam

judge *v.i.* قضايي فصله کول qazayee faysala kawal

judgement *n.* قضاوت qazawat

judicature *n.* دقاضيانوپلاوی da qazyano plaway

judicial *a.* قضايي qazayee

judiciary *n.* قضايي واک qazayee zwak

judicious *a.* قضاپوراوند qaza pori arwand

jug *n.* لاستي لويه پياله lastee loya pyala

juggle *v.t.* شعبده بازي کول shobda bazee kawal

juggler *n.* شعبده باز shobda baz

juice *n* دميوه اوبه da meywey oba

juicy *a.* دمواوبه لرونکی da meywey oba laroonkay

jumble *v.t.* وکول gadwad kawal

jump *n.* وپ top

jump *v.i.* وپ وهل top wahal

junction *n.* دپوستون ای da peywastoon zay

juncture *n.* اتصال itisal

jungle *n.* ځل zangal

junior *a.* ناتجربه کار na tajruba kar

junior *n.* کشر kashar

junk *n.* دره darga

jupiter *n.* مشتري mushtree

jurisdiction *n.* قانوني واک qanoonee wak

jurisprudence *n.* قانون پوهنه qanoon pohana

jurist *n.* قانونپوه qanoonpoh

juror *n.* دمنصفه پلاوي غی da munsifa plawee gharay

jury *n.* قضايي ل qazayee dalgay

juryman *n.* دمنصفه پلاوي غی da munsifa plawee gharay

just *a.* نياور nyawgar

just *adv.* سمدلاسه samdalasa

justice *n.* نياو nyaw

justifiable *a.* دسپينونو da speenawani war

justification *n.* سپينونه speenawana

justify *v.t.* سپينول speenawal

justly *adv.* په عادلانه توه pa adilana toga

jute *n.* سن sand

juvenile *a.* دځوانو da zwanay war

K

keen *a.* حاد had

keenness *n.* فراست firasat

keep *v.t.* ساتل satal

keeper *n.* ساتونکی satoonkay

keepsake *n.* یادار yadgar

kennel *n.* دسپي‌خونه da spee khoona

kerchief *n.* دسمال dasmal

kernel *n.* هسته hasta

kerosene *n.* دخاوروتل da khawro teyl

ketchup *n.* دپیازماراومسالوروب da pyaz tamatar aw masalo roob

kettle *n.* جوشه چای chay josha

key *n.* کلي kalee

key *v.t* په‌کلي‌سره‌خلاصول pa kalee sara khlasawal

kick *n.* لغته laghata

kick *v.t.* لغته‌وهل laghata wahal

kid *n.* ماشوم mashoom

kidnap *v.t.* تتول takhtawal

kidney *n.* پوتوری pokhtawargay

kill *v.t.* وژل wazhal

kill *n.* وژنه wazhana

kiln *n.* بټ batai

kin *n.* خپلوان khpalwan

kind *n.* قسم qisam

kind *a* مهربان mehraban

kindergarten *n.* وکتون waraktoon

kindle *v.t.* اوربلول or balawal

kindly *adv.* په‌مهربانۍسره pa mehrabanay sara

king *n.* پاچا pacha

kingdom *n.* پاچاهي pachahee

kinship *n.* خپلولي khpalwalee

kiss *n.* مچو macho

kiss *v.t.* مچوکول macho kawal

kit *n.* تغاره taghara

kitchen *n.* پخلنای pakhlanzay

kite *n.* کاغذباد kaghaz bad

kith *n.* اونیان gawandyan

kitten *n.* دپیشوبچی da peesho bachay

knave *n.* بدماش badmash

knavery *n.* بدماشي badmashee

knee *n.* ونه gonda

kneel *v.i.* ونه‌کیدل gonda kedal

knife *n.* چاقو chaqoo

knight *n.* قهرمان qahraman

knight *v.t.* قهرماني‌کول qahramanee kawal

knit *v.t.* اوبدل obdal

knock *v.t.* کول takawal

knot *n.* غوه ghota

knot *v.t.* کول غوه ghota kawal

know *v.t.* پوهدل poheydal

knowledge *n.* پوهه poha

L

label *n.* تاپه tapa

label *v.t.* تاپه‌لول tapa lagawal

laboratory *n.* آزموینتون azmoyantoon

laborious *a.* خواري‌کی khwaree ke

labour *n.* کاو؛مزدوري karaw; mazdooree

labour v.i. مزدوري کول mazdooree kawal

labourer n. مزدور mazdoor

labyrinth n. کلج kagleych

lac, lakh n لاک lak

lace n. د بو بند da boot band

lace v.t. د بو بند تل da boot band taral

lacerate v.t. شکیدل shkeydal

lack n. کمت kamakht

lack v.t. کمول kamawal

lackey n. نو کر nawkar

lacklustre a. د روانتیانشتوالی da rokhantya nashtwalay

laconic a. په خبرو اتروکله pa khabaro ataro ki land

lactate v.i. شدورکول sheydey warkawal

lactose n. د شدوقند da sheydo qand

lad n. وان هلک zwan halak

ladder n. پو poray

lade v.t. چارجورکول charge warkawal

ladle n. مه samsa

lady n. مرمن meyrman

lag v.i. شاته پاتکدل shata pati keydal

laggard n. شاته پاتشخص shata pati shakhs

lagoon n. ز dand

lair n. د وحشیناوراله da wahshee zanawar zala

lake n. جیل jeel

lama n. دتبت او منولیاهوادونوبودایی ملا da tibat aw mangoleeya haywanoono boodayee mula

lamb n. وری wray

lambaste v.t. په مترو که وهل pa matrooka wahal

lame a. وزن وهلی goozan wahalay

lame v.t. وزن وهل goozan wahal

lament v.i. ویر کول weer kawal

lament n. ویر weer

lamentable a. غمجن ghamjan

lamentation n. ماتم matam

lambkin n. تندیوری tandi wari

laminate v.t. په مختلفو طبقوباندجلا pa mukhtalifo tabqo bandi jala kawal کول

lamp n. راغ sragh

lampoon n. ملذ malande

lampoon v.t. ملذکول malande kawal

lance n. نزه neyza

lance v.t. په نزه وهل pa neyza wahal

lancer n. نزه وهونکی neyza wahoonkay

lancet n. نتر neykhtar

land n. زمکه zmaka

land v.i. په زمکه کناستل pa zmaka kkheynastal

landing n. وچه ته وتنه wachi ta watana

landscape n. لرلید larleed

lane n. کوه koosa

language n. ژبه zhaba

languish v.i. ماوی کدل mraway keydal

lank a. اوگد او دنگر oogad aw dangar

lantern n. دیوه deewa

lap n. غ gheyg

lapse v.i. د وخت تر وتل da wakht teyr watal

lapse n انحراف inhiraf

115

lard *n.* دخووازده da khoog wazda

large *a.* پراخ parakh

largesse *n.* ال‌ dalay

lark *n.* دسندربولومارغانویوهله da sandar bolo marghano yawa dala

lascivious *a.* شهواني shahwanee

lash *a.* شلاخه shlakha

lash *n* باله banra

lass *n.* وانهنجل zwana najlay

last1 *a.* وروستی wrostay

last *adv.* پهپایلهک pa payla ki

last *v.i.* اداملرل idama laral

last *n* وروستنی wrostanay

lastly *adv.* ترولوآخر tar tolo akheyr

lasting *a.* دوامدار dawamdar

latch *n.* قفلچلهدواوخواوخهپرانستل شي qufal chi la dwaro khwaw sakha pranistal shee

late *a.* ندلی zandeydalay

late *adv.* ترندوروسته tar zand wrosta

lately *adv.* پهوروستیووختونوک pa wrostyo wakhtoono ki

latent *a.* مکنون maknoon

lath *n.* دلرينرپ da largee naray patay

lathe *n.* دخراطمشین da kharatay masheen

lathe *n.* دغلودانوزرمه da ghalo dano zeyrma

lather *n.* دصابون da saboon zag

latitude *n.* عرضالبلد arzul balad

latrine *n.* بیتالخلا baytul khala

latter *a.* آخري akheyree

lattice *n.* شبکه shabaka

laud *v.t.* دستایندسندرهویل da stayani sandara wayal

laud *n* دستاینسندره da stayani sandara

laudable *a.* دستاینو da stayani war

laugh *n.* خندا khanda

laugh *v.i* خندل khandal

laughable *a.* خندونکی khandoonkay

laughter *n.* دخندیدوغ da khandeydo ghag

launch *v.t.* توغول toghawal

launch *n.* توغونه toghawana

launder *v.t.* وینل weenzal

laundress *n.* کاليوینونکه kalee weenzoonki khaza

laundry *n.* دوبيخانه dobee khana

laurel *n.* یوهتلشنهونه yawa tal shna wana

laureate *a.* دلارلدونپهپلوپسوللشوی da laril da wani pa panro psolal shaway

laureate *n* ملکالشعرا malakush shoara

lava *n.* داورشیندیغرهویليمواد da or sheendee ghra weelee mawad

lavatory *n.* دمخلاسوینلوخونه da makh las weenzalo khoona

lavish *a.* اسرافي israfee

lavish *v.t.* اسرافکول israf kawal

law *n* قانون qanoon

lawful *a.* روا rawa

lawless *a.* بقانونه bey qanoona

lawn *n.* چمن chaman

lawyer *n.* قانونپوه qanoonpoh

lax *a.* شل shal

laxative *n.* قبضنرموونکی qabz narmowoonkay

laxative *a* قبضیتضد qabzeeyat zid

laxity *n.* نرمي narmee
lay *v.t.* سملاستل samlastal
layer *n.* لايه laya
layman *n.* بمهارته كس bey maharata kas
laze *v.i.* مبلي كول tambalee kawal
laziness *n.* ستوماني stomanee
lazy *n.* مبل tambal
lea *n.* چمنزار chamanzar
leach *v.t.* مينل meenzal
lead *n.* لاروونه lar khowana
lead *v.t.* رهبري كول rehbaree kawal
lead *n.* سيم هادي hadee seem
leaden *a.* سربي sarpee
leader *n.* لارود larkhod
leadership *n.* لاروونه larkhowana
leaf *n.* پاه panra
leaflet *n.* پاه كوچه koochnay panra
league *n.* اتحاديه itehadeeya
leak *n.* رخنه rakhna
leak *v.i.* لد saseydal
leakage *n.* رخنه rakhna
lean *n.* تكيه كوونه takeeya kawona
lean *v.i.* تكيه كول takeeya kawal
leap *v.i.* وپ top
leap *n* وپوهل top wahal
learn *v.i.* زده كول zda kawal
learned *a.* عالم alim
learner *n.* زده كوونكى zda kawoonkay
learning *n.* كه زده zdakra
lease *n.* اجاره eejara
lease *v.t.* اجاره كول eejara kawal
least *a.* كوچنى koochnay
leather *n.* رمن sarman
leave *n.* رخصت rukhsat

leave *v.t.* پرودل preykhodal
lecture *n.* درس dars
lecture *v* درس وركول dars warkawal
lecturer *n.* مدرس mudarris
ledger *n.* دحسابونوثبت كتاب da heesaboono sabt keetab
lee *n.* لهبادخهخونديهاى la bad sakha khwandee zay
leech *n.* جراثيم jaraseem
leek *n.* پهپيازپوراوندبوولسبزي pa pyaz pori arwand yaw dawl sabzee
left *a.* كير keenr
left *n.* دهرشي كيهخوا da har shee keenra khwa
leftist *n* پهسياست كآزادخوىشخص pa seeyasat ki azad khwakhay shakhs
leg *n.* په pkha
legacy *n.* ميراث meeras
legal *a.* قانوني qanoonee
legality *n.* قانونيت qanooneeyat
legalize *v.t.* قانوني كول qanoonee kawal
legend *n.* افسانه afsana
legendary *a.* افسانوي afsanawee
leghorn *n.* يوولمارغه yaw dawl margha
legible *a.* خوانا khwana
legion *n.* دپوىلكريوهطبقه da pawzee lakhkar yawa tabqa
legionary *n.* طبقه يو دلكر پوى د تشكيل da pawzee lakhkar da yaw tabqey tashkeel
legislate *v.i.* قانونوضعكول qanoon waza kawal

legislation *n.* قانون وضع کوونه qanoon waza kawona

legislative *a.* قانوني qanoonee

legislator *n.* قانون‌ساز qanoonsaz

legislature *n.* مقننه‌پلاوی muqannana plaway

legitimacy *n.* قانونیتوب qanooneetob

legitimate *a.* روا rawa

leisure *n.* آرامت aramakht

leisure *a* فارغ farigh

leisurely *a.* آرامه arama

leisurely *adv.* په‌آرامسره pa aram sara

lemon *n.* لیمو leemoo

lemonade *n.* دلیموشربت da leemoo sharbat

lend *v.t.* پوروركول por warkawal

length *n.* اودوالی oogadwalay

lengthen *v.t.* اودول oogdawal

lengthy *a.* اود oogad

lenience, leniency *n.* نرمت narmakht

lenient *a.* نرم naram

lens *n.* عدسه adsa

lentil *n.* دمسوردال da masoor dal

Leo *n.* دزمري‌برج da zmaree burj

leopard *n.* پاز prang

leper *n.* جذامي jazamee

leprosy *n.* جذام jazam

leprous *a.* جذامي jazamee

less *a.* ل lag

less *n* یوكم‌مقدار yaw kam miqdar

less *adv.* په‌كم‌مقدار pa kam miqdar

less *prep.* ترلگ‌مقدار tar lag miqdar

lessee *n.* اجاره‌كوونكی ijara kaonke

lessen *v.t* كمول kamawal

lesser *a.* كم kam

lesson *n.* لوست lost

lest *conj.* داسنه‌چ dasi na chi

let *v.t.* اجازه‌وركول eejaza warkawal

lethal *a.* وژونكی wazhoonkay

lethargic *a.* ستومانه stomana

lethargy *n.* ستوماني stomanee

letter *n* لیک leek

level *n.* سطح sata

level *a* اوار awar

level *v.t.* اوارول awarawal

lever *n.* ام aram

lever *v.t.* پورته‌كول porta kawal

leverage *n.* دام‌كار da aram kar

levity *n.* سپكوالی spakwalay

levy *v.t.* مالیات‌لول maleeyat lagawal

levy *n.* مالیات maleeyat

lewd *a.* شهوت‌پرست shahwat parast

lexicography *n.* سیندكنه seend kakhana

lexicon *n.* قاموس qamoos

liability *n.* مسؤلیت masooleeyat

liable *a.* مسؤل masool

liaison *n.* رابطه rabita

liar *n.* دروغجن daroghjan

libel *n.* تهمت tuhmat

libel *v.t.* تهمت‌لول tuhmat lagawal

liberal *a.* روآندی roonr anday

liberalism *n.* روان‌فكري rokhan fikray

liberality *n.* آزادپالنه azad palana

liberate *v.t.* آزادول azadawal

liberation *n.* آزادي azadee

liberator *n.* آزاديبخوونکی azadee bakhkhoonkay

libertine *n.* عياش ayash

liberty *n.* اختيار ikhtyar

librarian *n.* دکتابتونچارواکی da keetabtoon charwakay

library *n.* کتابتون keetabtoon

licence *n.* دکاراجازهليک da kar eejaza leek

license *v.t.* اجازهليکورکول eejaza leek warkawal

licensee *n.* اجازهليکاخستونکی eejaza leek akheystoonkay

licentious *a.* شهوتي shahwatee

lick *v.t.* پهژبمل pa zhaba satal

lick *n* نه satana

lid *n.* سرپو sar pokh

lie *v.i.* دروغويل darogh wayal

lie *v.i* غدل ghazeydal

lie *n* دروغ darogh

lien *n.* دنيوونحق da neewani haq

lieu *n.* عوض؛ای zay; iwaz

lieutenant *n.* دويمبريدمن dwayam breedman

life *n* ژوند zhwand

lifeless *a.* بيژونده bey zhwanda

lifelong *a.* ولعمري tol umree

lift *n.* پورتهکوونه porta kawona

lift *v.t.* پورتهکول porta kawal

light *n.* را ranra

light *a* برندوی breykhandoy

light *v.t.* رول ranrawal

lighten *v.i.* بلدل baleydal

lighter *n.* اورک ortak

lightening *n.* پکدنه parkeydana

lignite *n.* يوولدبروسکاره yaw dawl da dabaro skara

like *a.* ورته warta

like *n.* ورتهوالی warta walay

like *v.t.* خوول khwakhawal

like *prep* پهورتهول pa warta dawl

likelihood *n.* شونتيا shoontya

likely *a.* کدونی keydoonay

liken *v.t.* ورتهکول warta kawal

likeness *n.* ورتهتوب wartatob

likewise *adv.* همداشان hamda shan

liking *n.* مل meyl

lilac *n.* پيکهبنفشرنز peeka banafsh rang

lily *n.* دسپينسوسنگل da speen sosan gul

limb *n.* دبدنغی da badan gharay

limber *v.t.* ورزشتهزانچمتوکول warzash ta zan chamtoo kawal

lime *n.* آهک ahak

lime *v.t* آهککول ahak kawal

lime *n.* ماله malta

limelight *n.* دپامولامل da pam war lamal

limit *n.* حد had

limit *v.t.* محدودول mahdoodawal

limitation *n.* محدوديت mahdoodeeyat

limited *a.* محدود mahdood

limitless *a.* لامحدود la mehdood

line *n.* کره karkha

line *v.t.* پهليکهدرول pa leeka darawal

line *v.t.* ليکهپرکل leeka pri kakhal

lineage *n.* پت pakht

linen n. کتانيوکر katanee tokar

linger v.i. وختـنول wakht zandawal

lingo n. ژبه ناز zangari zhaba

lingua franca n. دعام کارونژبه da am karawani zhaba

lingual a. ژبنى zhabanay

linguist n. ژبپوه zhabpoh

linguistic a. ژبپوهنيز zhabpohaneez

linguistics n. ژبپوهنه zhabpohan

lining n خط کشي khat kashee

link n. ک karay

link v.t یو کول yaw kawal

linseed n. دکتان تخم da katan tukham

lintel n. ددروازدسرتير da darwazey da sar teer

lion n زمرى zmaray

lioness n. زمر zmaray

lip n. شونه shoonda

liquefy v.t. مايع کول maya kawal

liquid a. سيال شى syal shay

liquid n مايع maya

liquidate v.t. مايع کول maya kawal

liquidation n. دحسابونو تصفيه da heesaboono tasfeeya

liquor n. مشروب mashroob

lisp v.t. دژبپهوکه خبر کول da zhabi pa sooka khabari kawal

lisp n دژبپهوکه خبر کونه da zhabi pa sooka khabari kawona

list n. نوملیک noomleek

list v.t. نومونه لیکل noomoona leekal

listen v.i. اوريدل awreydal

listener n. اوريدونکى awreydoonkay

listless a. بـميله be mela

literacy n. ليک لوست leek lost

literal a. لفظي lafzee

literary a. ادبي adabee

literate a. لوستى lostay

literature n. دادبياتوعلم da adabeeyato ilam

litigant n. مرافعه کوونکى murafia kawoonkay

litigate v.t. مرافعه کول murafia kawal

litigation n. مرافعه murafia

litre n. دمايعشي دپيمائش يوهيمانه da maya shee da paymayish yawa paymana

litter n. دناروغانو دولو دپاره يوول ک da naroghano da wralo dapara yaw dol kat

litter v.t. په فاضله شيانو ديوا ىلال pa fuzla shayano da yaw zai laral

litterateur n. اديب adeeb

little a. ل lag

little adv. له lag sa

little n. لمقدار lag miqdar

littoral a. تانه taranga

liturgical a. عبادتي ibadatee

live v.i. ژوند کول zhwand kawal

live a. ژوندى zhwanday

livelihood n. معاش muash

lively a. چک او چابک chatak aw chabak

liver n. ينه yana

livery n. جامه از zangari jamey

living a. ژوندى zhwanday

living n ژوندون zhwandoon

lizard n. سمساره samsara

load *n.* بار bar

load *v.t.* بارول barawal

loadstar *n.* قطبی‌ستوری qutbee storay

loadstone *n.* آهن‌ربا ahan ruba

loaf *n.* ټیکله teekala

loaf *v.i.* وخت‌ضائع‌کول wakht zaya kawal

loafer *n.* کوهبی‌سی koosa dabay saray

loan *n.* پور por

loan *v.t.* پورکول por kawal

loath *a.* غصه‌ناک ghusanak

loathe *v.t.* غصه‌کدل ghusa keydal

loathsome *a.* زه‌تورووونکی zra torowoonkay

lobby *n.* دالان dalan

lobe *n.* پرده parda

lobster *n.* سمندري‌چنا samandaree changakh

local *a.* سیمه‌ییز seemayeez

locale *n.* سیمه seema

locality *n.* محل mahal

localize *v.t.* سیمه‌ییزکول seemayeez kawal

locate *v.t.* ځای‌کل zay takal

location *n.* موقعیت moqeeyat

lock *n.* کولپ kolp

lock *v.t* کولپول kolpawal

lock *n* کو kawsay

locker *n.* کولپ‌لرونکالماراء kolp laroonki almaray

locket *n.* امل ameyl

locomotive *n.* محرک mahrak

locus *n.* هندسی‌ای hindsee zay

locust *n.* ملخ moolakh

locution *n.* وينا wayna

lodge *n.* کوچنی‌استونای koochnay astoganzay

lodge *v.t.* لنمهاله‌استونه‌کول land mahala astogna kawal

lodging *n.* مشتای meysht zay

loft *n.* ترچت‌لاندای tar chat landi zay

lofty *a.* مغرورانه maghroorana

log *n.* کونده konda

logarithim *n.* لواريتم logareetam

loggerhead *n.* احمق‌سی ahmaq saray

logic *n.* منطق mantaq

logical *a.* منطقي mantaqee

logician *n.* منطق‌پوه mantaq poh

loin *n.* صلب salb

loiter *v.i.* وزاروخت‌ترول wazgar wakht teyrawal

loll *v.i.* غدل ghazeydal

lollipop *n.* خوه‌پتاسه khwaga patasa

lone *a.* تنها tanha

loneliness *n.* تنهايي tanhayee

lonely *a.* يواز yawazi

lonesome *a.* بياره bey yara

long *a.* اود oogda

long *adv* په‌اودوالي pa oogadwalee

long *v.i* هيله‌لرل heela laral

longevity *n.* اودژوند oogad zhwand

longing *n.* هوس hawas

longitude *n.* طول‌البلد toolul balad

look *v.i* کتل katal

look *a* کتنه katana

loom *n* داودماشين da obdani masheen

loom *v.i.* معلومدل maloomeydal

loop *n.* وَل wal

loop-hole *n.* روندان rokhandan

loose *a.* سست sast

loose *v.t.* سستول sastawal

loosen *v.t.* پرانستل pranistal

loot *n.* چپاول chapawal

loot *v.i.* چپاوکول chapaw kawal

lop *v.t.* دسراڼغوول da sar sangi ghosawal

lop *n.* دسمندرنرمپ da samandar narmi sapey

lord *n.* ارباب arbab

lordship *n.* اربابتوب arbabtob

lore *n.* وونهاوروزنه khowana aw rozana

lorry *n.* لاړ laray

lose *v.t.* لهلاسهورکول la lasa wrakawal

loss *n.* زیان zyan

lot *n.* ونه wanda

lot *n* پچه pacha

lotion *n.* پاکوونه pakowana

lottery *n.* پچهاچونه pacha ahowana

loud *a.* لواوازی lwar awazay

lounge *v.i.* زمبدل zambeydal

lounge *n.* دراحتخونه da rahat khoona

louse *n.* سپه spaga

lovable *a.* محبوب mehboob

love *n* مینه meena

love *v.t.* مینهکول meena kawal

lovely *a.* ران gran

lover *n.* مین mayan

loving *a.* مینهناک meenanak

low *a.* کته kkhata

low *v.i.* خرابدل kharabeydal

low *n.* ماوی mraway

lower *v.t.* کتهکول kkhata kawal

lowliness *n.* کتهوالی kkhata walay

lowly *a.* دتواضعلهمخ da tawazo la makhi

loyal *a.* باوفا bawafa

loyalist *n.* وفادار wafadar

loyalty *n.* وفاداري wafadaree

lubricant *n.* غووونکیمواد ghwarowoonkay mawad

lubricate *v.t.* غوول ghwarawal

lubrication *n.* غوونه ghwarowana

lucent *a.* شفاف shafaf

lucerne *n.*

lucidity *n.* روتیا roonrtya

luck *n.* بخت bakht

luckily *adv.* خوشبختسره khoshbakhtee

luckless *a.* بدقسمته bad qismata

lucky *a.* نکمرغه neykmargha

lucrative *a.* ور gatavar

lucre *n.* مال mal

luggage *n.* سامان saman

lukewarm *a.* تمن tarman

lull *v.t.* خاموشول khamoshawal

lull *n.* آرامت aramakht

lullaby *n.* للو للو lalo lalo

luminary *n.* روښانهجسم rokhana jisam

luminous *a.* روښانه rokhana

lump *n.* لویهلوه loya tota

lump *v.t.* لویدل loyidal

lunacy *n.* لونتوب leywantob

lunar *a.* سپوږمیز spogmeez

lunatic *n.* لونیکس leywanay kas

lunatic *a.* لونی leywanay

lunch *n.* دغرمو da gharmey doday

lunch *v.i.* دغرموخول da gharmey doday khwaral

lung *n* سی sagay

lunge *n.* ناپتوغونه nasapee toghawona

lunge *v.i* بریدکول breed kawal

lurch *n.* چل chal

lurch *v.i.* رخدل sarkheydal

lure *n.* غولونه gholowona

lure *v.t.* دوکهکول doka kawal

lurk *v.i.* چاتهپدل cha ta pateydal

luscious *a.* شیرین sheereen

lush *a.* شاداب shadab

lust *n.* شهوت shahwat

lustful *a.* شهوانی shahwanee

lustre *n.* رووالی rond walay

lustrous *a.* لاند zaland

lusty *a.* شهوتپاروونکی shahwat parowoonkay

lute *n.* دختوددرزونودنیوانلپارهزانخه da khakhto da darzoono da neewani lapara zangari khata

luxuriance *n.* عظمت azmat

luxuriant *a.* عظیم azeem

luxurious *a.* تجمل tajamulee

luxury *n.* تجمل tajamul

lynch *v.t.* بیدمحاکمیلهحکمهدچاوژل be da muhakimy la hukma da cha wajal

lyre *n.* دبربطدرباببخوازآله da barbat da rabab pakhwanay ala

lyric *a.* غنایی ghanayee

lyric *n.* غوونه ghagowona

lyrical *a.* احساساتیاوغنایی ehsasatee aw ghinayee

lyricist *n.* غزللیکونکی ghazal leekoonkay

M

magical *a.* جادویی jadooyee

magician *n.* رکو kodgar

magisterial *a.* آمرانه amirana

magistracy *n.* دناحیدمحکمریاست da naheeyey da mahkamey reeyasat

magistrate *n.* قاضي qazee

magnanimity *n.* لویی loyee

magnanimous *a.* عظیم azeem

magnate *n.* نجیبزاده najeeb zada

magnet *n.* مقناطیس miqnatees

magnetic *a.* مقناطیسي miqnatees

magnetism *n.* مقناطیسیت miqnateeseeyat

magnificent *a.* عظیم azeem

magnify *v.t.* عظمتوربل azmat warbakhal

magnitude *n.* پراختیا parakhtya

magpie *n.* یوولکورنتورهاوسپینهکوتره yaw dawl koranay toora aw speena kawtara

mahogany *n.* سوربخنقهوهییرن soorbakhan qahwayee rang

mahout *n.* فیلوان feelwan

maid *n.* ناوادهشوه na wada shawi khaza

maiden *n.* پغله peyghla

maiden *a* رمروغ rogh ramat

mail *n.* پُست pust
mail *v.t.* پُستلل pust leygal
mail *n* زغره zghara
main *a* اصلي او ضروري aslee aw zarooree
main *n* توان twan
mainly *adv.* په اصل که pa asal ki
mainstay *n.* اصلي تابعیت aslee tabieeyat
maintain *v.t.* ادامه ورکول idama warkawal
maintenance *n.* ساتنه satana
maize *n.* جوار joowar
majestic *a.* شاهانه shahana
majesty *n.* اعلیحضرت aleehazrat
major *a.* ضروري zarooree
major *n* جن jagran
majority *n.* ډېرکی deyrkay
make *v.t.* جوړول jorawal
make *n* جوړ jor
maker *n.* جوړوونکی jorowoonkay
mal adjustment *n.* ناسمي nasamee
mal administration *n.* ناتنظیمي natanzeemee
malady *n.* خرابتیا kharabtya
malaria *n.* تبه نوبتي nobatee taba
maladroit *a.* خام او ناوه kham aw nawara
malafide *a.* ناوه نیت na wara nyat
malafide *adv* په ناوه توګه pa nawara toga
malaise *n.* ناقراري na qararee
malcontent *a.* ناراضه na raza
malcontent *n* ناراض na raz
male *a.* نارینه nareena
male *n* سړی saray

malediction *n.* بدوینه bad wayana
malefactor *n.* بدکار bad kar
maleficent *a.* تباه کار tabah kar
malice *n.* کرکه kraka
malicious *a.* کرکجن krakjan
malign *v.t.* بدغوتل bad ghokhtal
malign *a* پلید paleed
malignancy *n.* پلیدي paleedgee
malignant *a.* خبیث khabees
malignity *n.* خباثت khabasat
malleable *a.* سوک خوړونکی sotak khwaroonkay
malmsey *n.* قبرسي خواه شراب qabrasee khwaga sharab
malnutrition *n.* کم خوراکي kam khorakee
malpractice *n.* ناوه کار کوونه na wara kar kawona
malt *n.* مالت لرونکی اک جوړول malt laroonkay skhak jorawal
mal-treatment *n.* بدچلند bad chaland
mamma *n.* تی tay
mammal *n.* تي لرونکی tay laroonkay
mammon *n.* شتمني shtamanee
mammoth *n.* له تاریخ سخه د مخه دوري لوی فیل la tareekh sakha da makha dawri loy feel
mammoth *a* ډېر لوی deyr loy
man *n.* انسان insan
man *v.t.* د انسان په وسیله په کاروول da insan pa waseela pa karowal
manage *v.t.* انتظام کول intizam kawal
manageable *a.* د چلونقابل da chalowani qabil

management *n.* مديريت mudeereeyat

manager *n.* مدير mudeer

managerial *a.* مديري mudeeree

mandate *n.* امريه amreeya

mandatory *a.* امر amree

mane *n.* دسيوتان da saree weykhtan

manes *n.* دماروواني da maro arwagani

manful *a.* دمازخاوند da meyrani khawand

manganese *n.* يوعنصر yaw unsar

manger *n.* آخور akhor

mangle *v.t.* اوتوكول oto kawal

mango *n* ام am

manhandle *v.t.* پهزورسرهاداره کول pa zor sara idara kawal

manhole *n.* دنکاسياوبوسوری da nikasee obo sooray

manhood *n.* نارينتوب nareentob

mania *n* لونتوب leywantob

maniac *n.* لونی leywanay

manicure *n.* لاسونهاونوکانسيناروال lasoona aw nookan seengarawal

manifest *a.* رند sargand

manifest *v.t.* حاضرول hazirawal

manifestation *n.* نمايش numayish

manifesto *n.* اعلاميه aylameeya

manifold *a.* و چنده so chanda

manipulate *v.t.* پهلاسسرهسمول pa las sara samawal

manipulation *n.* مهارت maharat

mankind *n.* انسانينژاد insanee nizhad

manlike *a.* انسانی insanee

manliness *n* نارينتوب nareentob

manly *a.* پهنارينتوبسره pa nareentob sara

manna *n.* منواوسلوا man aw salwa

mannequin *n.* دنندارفنکارهنجل da nandarey fankara najlay

manner *n.* طريقه tareeqa

mannerism *n.* ادب adab

mannerly *a.* پهادبسره pa adab sara

manoeuvre *n.* پهتدبيرسرهکاراخستنه pa tadbeer sara kar akheystana

manoeuvre *v.i.* پهتدبيرسرهکار اخستل pa tadbeer sara kar akheystal

manor *n.* لوىجاير loy jageer

manorial *a.* جايردارانه jageerdarana

mansion *n.* قصر qasar

mantel *n.* ادر sadar

mantle *n* چوغه chogha

mantle *v.t* چوغهاغوستل chogha aghostal

manual *a.* لاسی lasee

manual *n* لاسکنه las kakhana

manufacture *v.t.* توليدول tawleedawal

manufacture *n* توليدوونه tawleedawana

manufacturer *n* توليدوونکی tawleedawoonkay

manumission *n.* آزادي azadee

manumit *v.t.* غلامآزادول gholam azadawal

manure *n.* پارو paro

manure *v.t.* کوورکول kod warkawal

manuscript *n.* خطي khatee

many *a.* متعدد mutaadad

map *n* نخچه nakhcha

map *v.t.* نخچه‌جوول ṇakhcha jorawal

mar *v.t.* مانع‌کول manay kawal

marathon *n.* یوغاستي‌سیالي yaw zghastee syalee

maraud *v.i.* لوبل lootal

marauder *n.* لو� lootmar

marble *n.* دمرمرکاڼی da marmar kanray

march *n* لاریون laryoon

march *n.* منظم‌حرکت munazzam harakat

march *v.i* په‌موزون‌قدم‌تلل pa mawzoon qadam tlal

mare *n.* دخرینه da khra khazeena

margarine *n.* نباتي‌کوچ nabatee koch

margin *n.* حاشیه hasheeya

marginal *a.* حاشیوي hasheeyawee

marigold *n.* همشه‌بهارل hamaysha bahar gul

marine *a.* سمندري samandaree

mariner *n.* ماو manroo

marionette *n.* یوول‌هیله yaw dawl heelay

marital *a.* ازدواجي azdawajee

maritime *a.* سمندري samandaree

mark *n.* نان nakhan

mark *v.t* نان‌لول nakhan lagawal

marker *n.* نه‌ایودونکی nakha eekhoodoonkay

market *n* بازار bazar

market *v.t* سوداري‌کول sawdagaree kawal

marketable *a.* دسودارو da sawdagaray war

marksman *n.* نه‌ویشتونکی nakha weeshtoonkay

marl *n.* طناب‌اوپی‌غل tanab aw paray gharal

marmalade *n.* دنارنج‌مربا da naranj murabba

maroon *n.* تورپوستي‌غلام tor postay ghulam

maroon *a* سوربخن‌خرمایي‌رڼ soorbakhan khurmayee rang

maroon *v.t* بایه‌زدل bey zaya garzeydal

marriage *n.* واده wada

marriageable *a.* دوادهو da wada war

marry *v.t.* واده‌کول wada kawal

Mars *n* دمریخ‌سیاره da mareekh seeyara

marsh *n.* لجنزار lajanzar

marshal *n* سرلکر sar lakhkar

marshal *v.t* تنظیمول tanzeemawal

marshy *a.* لجنزاره lajanzara

marsupial *n.* کوهلرونکی kasora laroonkay

mart *n.* سودا sawda

marten *n.* موش‌خرما mosh khurma

martial *a.* جني jangee

martinet *n.* سختیر sakhtgeer

martyr *n.* شهید shaheed

martyrdom *n.* شهادت shahadat

marvel *n.* حرانوونکی heyranawoonkay

marvel *v.i* حراندل heyraneydal

marvellous *a.* حيرانوونکی hayranawoonkay

mascot *n.* ښه‌شون kha shagoon

masculine *a.* نرينه nareena

mash *n.* اوبلن‌خوراک oblan khorak

mash *v.t* مدول maydawal

mask *n.* نقاب naqab

mask *v.t.* نقاب‌اچول naqab achowal

mason *n.* خر khatgar

masonry *n.* خري khatgaree

masquerade *n.* يووول‌وين‌کالي yaw dawl wareen kalee

mass *n.* ولی tolay

mass *v.i* ونه‌اخستل wanda akheystal

massacre *n.* ول‌وژنه tol wazhana

massacre *v.t.* قتلول qatlawal

massage *n.* مونه mokhana

massage *v.t.* مول mokhal

masseur *n.* موووونکی mokhowoonkay

massive *a.* لوی‌او‌عظيم loy aw azeem

massy *a.* لوی‌بدنی loy badanay

mast *n.* دبخاده da beyray khada

master *n.* استاد ustad

master *v.t.* استادي‌کول ustadee kawal

masterly *a.* استادانه ustadana

masterpiece *n.* شاهکار shahkar

mastery *n.* مهارت maharat

masticate *v.t.* نرمول narmawal

masturbate *v.i.* مویوهل mootay wahal

mat *n.* پوز poozay

matador *n.* غوبی‌سره‌لوبه‌کوونکی ghwayee sara loba kawoonkay

match *n.* اورليت orlageet

match *v.i.* اورليت‌بلوول orlageet balowal

match *n* مسابقه musabiqa

matchless *a.* بی‌ساری bey saray

mate *n.* ملری malgaray

mate *v.t.* وول gadwadawal

mate *n* جوه jora

mate *v.t.* جوه‌کول jora kawal

material *a.* مادي madee

material *n* ماده mada

materialism *n.* ماده‌پرستي mada parastee

materialize *v.t.* مجسم‌کول mujassam kawal

maternal *a.* مورنی moranay

maternity *n.* زنتون zeygantoon

mathematical *a.* درياضي‌په‌اوند da reeyazii pa arwand

mathematician *n.* reeyazee poh

mathematics *n* رياضي reeyazee

matinee *n.* مازدير‌ملمستيا mazdeegaray meylmastya

matriarch *n.* دتبرمشره da tabar mashra

matricidal *a.* مورو‌ژونکی mor wazhoonkay

matricide *n.* موروژنه mor wazhana

matriculate *v.t.* وونی‌ترسره‌کول khowanzay tar sara kawal

matriculation *n.* دخووني‌پورزده‌ک da khowanzee pori zdakri

matrimonial *a.* ازدواجي azdawajee

matrimony *n.* واده wada

matrix *n* تخمدان tukhamdan

matron *n.* دکوره ka kor khaza

matter *n.* ماده mada

matter *v.i.* اهميتلرل ahmeeyat laral

mattock *n.* دوهسرىكلد dwa saray kalang

mattress *n.* توشکه toshaka

mature *a.* پوخشوى pokh shaway

mature *v.i* پخدل pakheydal

maturity *n.* بلوغ balogh

maudlin *a* ينمائىنوم khazeena zangaray noom

maul *n.* لرينسک largeen satak

maul *v.t* پهسکوهل pa satak wahal

maulstick *n.* دلاستکيه da las takya

maunder *v.t.* کول دايي gadayee kawal

mausoleum *n.* مقبره maqbara

mawkish *a.* ستومانهکوونکى stomana kawoonkay

maxilla *n.* پورتنزامه portanay zama

maxim *n.* نصيحت naseehat

maximize *v.t.* اخرىحدپورىرسول akhiree had pori rasawal

maximum *a.* اخرىحد akhiree had

maximum *n* زياتنهزيات zyat na zyat

May *n.* دانرزيکالدريمهمياشت da angreyzee kal dreyma myasht

may *v* تواندل twaneydal

mayor *n.* دارناظم da khar nazim

maze *n.* تاوراتاوزينه taw rataw zeena

me *pron.* ماله ma la

mead *n.* دمالتاوخمرىهاک da malt aw khumree skhak

meadow *n.* لوىچمنزار loy chamanzar

meal *n.* خوراک khorak

mealy *a.* اوهوله ora dawla

mean *a.* معمولى mamoli

mean *n.* مننىکى manzani takay

mean *v.t* مانااخستل mana akheystal

meander *v.i.* چکروهل chakar wahal

meaning *n.* مانا mana

meaningful *a.* پُرمانا pur mana

meaningless *a.* بمانا bey maney

meanness *n.* کمينهتوب kameenatob

means *n* وسايل wasayil

meanwhile *adv.* پهدهدوران pa dey dawran

measles *n* شرى sharay

measurable *a.* دسنجونو da sanjawani war

measure *n.* پمائش paymayish

measure *v.t* پمائشکول paymayish kawal

measureless *a.* بيماز bey paymani

measurement *n.* پمائش paymayish

meat *n.* غوه ghwakha

mechanic *n.* ماشينپوه masheen poh

mechanic *a* ميخانيکى meykhanikee

mechanical *a.* ميخانيکى meykhanikee

mechanics *n.* دماشينوعلم da masheeno ilam

mechanism *n.* طريقهکار tareeqa kar

medal *n.* مال midal

medallist *n.* دمالخاوند da midal khawand

meddle *v.i.* مداخلهکونکی mudakhila kawoonkay

medieval *a.* دمننیوپیوتاریخپوراوند da manzanyo peyryo tareekh pori arwand

medieval *a.* دمننیوپیوتاریخپوراوند da manzanyo peyryo tareekh pori arwand

median *a.* وسطی wastee

mediate *v.i.* جوهکول jora kawal

mediation *n.* جوه jora

mediator *n.* منی manzgaray

medical *a.* طبي tibee

medicament *n.* درملنه darmalana

medicinal *a.* ددرملپهاوند da darmal pa arwand

medicine *n.* درمل darmal

medico *n.* طبیب tabeeb

mediocre *a.* معتدل motadil

mediocrity *n.* اعتدال aytidal

meditate *v.t.* ذکرکول zikar kawal

mediation *n.* ذکر zikar

meditative *a.* تفکري tafakurree

medium *n* ذریعه zareeya

medium *a* دمنندرجه da manzanay darajey

meek *a.* حلیم haleem

meet *n.* ملاقات mulaqat

meet *v.t.* ملاوول milawawal

meeting *n.* لیدنهکتنه leedana katana

megalith *n.* یادگاريبره yadgaree dabara

megaphone *n.* غرساند ghag rasand

melancholia *n.* وسواس waswas

melancholic *a.* وسواسي waswasee

melancholy *n.* وسواس waswas

melancholy *adj* وسواسي waswasee

melee *n.* تنپهتنجگه tan pa tan jagara

meliorate *v.t.* ترقۀکول taraqee kawal

mellow *a.* نرم naram

melodious *a.* پرآهنـ pur ahang

melodrama *n.* بریالمینه baryalay meena

melodramatic *a.* عاشقانه ashiqana

melody *n.* خوهسندره khwaga sandara

melon *n.* هندوانه hindwana

melt *v.i.* ویلاکدل weeli keydal

member *n.* غی gharay

membership *n.* غیتوب ghareetob

membrane *n.* غشا ghasha

memento *n.* دمودعا da maro dua

memoir *n.* یادت yadakht

memorable *a.* یاداري yadgaree

memorandum *n* یادت yadakht

memorial *n.* یادار yadgar

memorial *a* یاداريبرلیک yadgaree dabar leek

memory *n.* حافظه hafiza

menace *n* تهدید tahdeed

menace *v.t* تهدیدول tanhdeedawal

mend *v.t.* رغول raghawal

menial *a.* پست past

menial *n* نوکر nawkar

meningitis *n.* دمغزوالتهاب da maghzo iltihab

menopause *n.* دحضبندیدا da hayz bandeyda

menses *n.* حض hayz

menstrual *a.* دحض پەاوند da hayz pa arwand

menstruation *n.* دحض جريان da hayz jaryan

mental *a.* ذهني zehnee

mentality *n.* فكري توان fikree twan

mention *n.* يادوونه yadowana

mention *v.t.* ذكر كول zikar kawal

mentor *n.* قابل سلاكار qabil salakar

menu *n.* دخواونيوليک da khwaro naywleek

mercantile *a.* تجارتي tijaratee

mercenary *a.* دبهرو ادمزدور da bahar haywad mazdoor

merchandise *n.* سوداري سامان sawdagaree saman

merchant *n.* سودار sawdagar

merciful *a.* لوراند lorand

merciless *adj.* برحمه bey rehma

mercurial *a.* سيمابي seemabee

mercury *n.* سيماب seemab

mercy *n.* زه سوی؛رحم zra saway; rehem

mere *a.* ايله؛بس هم دومره eela; bas ham domra

merge *v.t.* شاملول shamilawal

merger *n.* شاملوونکی shamilawoonkay

meridian *a.* دنصف النهار کره؛غرمه da nisfun nihar karkha; gharma

merit *n.* لياقت leeyaqat

merit *v.t* لياقت لرل leeyaqat laral

mermaid *n.* سمندري حوره samandaree hoora

merman *n.* سمندري نارينه مخلوق samandaree nareena makhlooq

merriment *n.* خوشالي khoshalee

merry *a* خوشاله khoshala

mesh *n.* جال؛لومه jal; looma

mesh *v.t* پەلومه سره نيول pa loomi sara neewal

mesmerism *n.* مصنوعي خوبونه masnooee khobawana

mesmerize *v.t.* پەمقناطيسي خوب ويدول pa miqnateesee khob weedawal

mess *n.* ناولشی nawalay shay

mess *v.i* ککول kakarawal

message *n.* پغام paygham

messenger *n.* پغام وونکی paygham wroonkay

messiah *n.* مسيح عليه السلام masee alayhis salam

Messrs *n.* اغلي khaghalay

metabolism *n.* حياتي اوتون hayatee awakhtoon

metal *n.* فلز filiz

metallic *a.* فلزي filizee

metallurgy *n.* دفلزاتو داستنا او ويل کونه پوهه da filizato da eystani aw weeli kawoni poha

metamorphosis *n.* دشکل او بدلوونه da shakal aw banri badlawona

metaphor *n.* استعاره istiara

metaphysical *a.* ماورايي طبيعت پور اوند mawarayee tabeeyat pori arwand

metaphysics *n.* دماورايي طبيعت علم da mawarayee tabeeyat ilam

mete *v.t* اندازه کول andaza kawal

meteor *n.* لکوال ستوری lakay wal storay

meteoric *a.* دستورو پەاوند da storo pa arwand

meteorologist *n.* هواپژاند hawa peyzhand

meteorology *n.* هواپژندنه hawa peyzhandana

meter *n.* مقياس miqyas

method *n.* طريقه tareeqa

methodical *a.* طريقهلرونکی tareeqa laroonkay

metre *n.* دوايوپمائش da wat yaw paymayish

metric *a.* دشعردبحراووزنعلم da shayr da bahar aw wazan ilam

metrical *a.* دوزناوکچپهاوند da wazan aw kach pa arwand

metropolis *n.* پلازمنه plazmayna

metropolitan *a.* لوىخارپوراوند loy khar pori arwand

metropolitan *n.* اصليخوبى aslee tatobay

mettle *n.* فطرت fitrat

mettlesome *a.* سرکخ sar kakh

mew *v.i.* دپيشوغکول da peesho ghag kawal

mew *n.* دپيشوغ da peesho ghag

mezzanine *n.* دلومنياودويمپورترمنزنيم پو da loomranee aw dwayam por tar manz neem por

mica *n.* کانيیه kanee kheekha

microfilm *n.* دعکسونولپارهيوکوچنى فيلم da aksoono lapara yaw koochnay filam

micrology *n.* دکوچنيوشيانوعلم da koochnyo shayano ilam

micrometer *n.* دکوچنيوشيانودانداز آله da koochnyo shayano da andazey ala

microphone *n.* دغلوولوآله da ghag lwarawalo ala

microscope *n.* دکوچنيوشيانودوربين da koochnyo shayano doorbeen

microscopic *a.* دوربينى doorbeenee

microwave *n.* کوچنىمقناطيسىپه koochnay miqnateesee sapa

mid *a.* منز manz

midday *n.* نيمايىور neemayee wraz

middle *a.* منز manz

middle *n* مرکز markaz

middleman *n.* دلال dalal

middling *a.* وسط wast

midget *n.* لوېشتکىسى lweyshtakay saray

midland *n.* دهوادننبرخه da haywad dananay barkha

midnight *n.* نيمهشپه neema shpa

mid-off *n.* دمرکزىلاسته da markaz khee las ta

mid-on *n.* دمرکزکيلاسته da markaz keenr las ta

midriff *n.* بلوونى beylowanay

midst *n.* مرکزيبرخه markazee barkha

midwife *n.* دايى dayee

might *n.* توان twan

mighty *adj.* زورور zorawar

migraine *n.* سرخوى sar khoogay

migrant *n.* کوال kadwal

migrate *v.i.* که کول kada kawal

migration *n.* کوالي kadwalee

milch *a.* شدورکوونکى sheydey warkowoonkay

mild *a.* نرم naram

mildew *n.* چاس chanrasay

mile *n.* داودوالي يوپمائش da oogadwalee yaw paymayish

mileage *n.* دميل لەمخسنجوونه da meel la makhi sanjawana

milestone *n.* دژوندمهمهدوره da zhwand muhima dawra

milieu *n.* محيط muhcct

militant *a.* جهمار jagra mar

militant *n* جهماری jagra maree

military *a.* پو pawz

military *n* پوي pawzee

militate *v.i.* جندل jangeydal

militia *n.* نظامي واک nizamee zwak

milk *n.* شد sheydey

milk *v.t.* شدورکول sheydey warkawal

milky *a.* لەشدوک la sheydo dak

mill *n.* ژرنده zhranda

mill *v.t.* ژرندەکول zhranda kawal

millennium *n.* زرکاله zar kala

miller *n.* ژرندی zhrandagaray

millet *n.* دن،باجره gdan; bajra

milliner *n.* ينەخوﻻجووونکی khazeena khwali jorawoonkay

millinery *n.* ينەخوﻻپلورونه khazeena khwali plorawana

million *n.* لسلکه las laka

millionaire *n.* مالدار،شتمن maldara; shtaman

millipede *n.* نه zanza

mime *n.* خندوونکننداره khandowoonkay

mime *v.i* وککول toki kawal

mimesis *n.* پکوونه peykhi kawona

mimic *a.* تقليدي taqleedee

mimic *n* وکمار tokmar

mimic *v.t* پکول peykhi kawal

mimicry *n* وکماري tokmaree

minaret *n.* مناره munara

mince *v.t.* مدهمدهکول meyda meyda kawal

mind *n.* ذهن،خيال zehen; khyal

mind *v.t.* پامکول،فکرکول pam kawal; fikar kawal

mindful *a.* فکرمند fikarmand

mindless *a.* بيپروا bey parwa

mine *pron.* زما zama

mine *n* کان،معدن kan; madan

miner *n.* کان کيندوونکی kan keendoonkay

mineral *n.* کاني بر kanee dabar

mineral *a* کاني،معدني kanee; madanee

mineralogist *n.* کانپژندونکی kan peyzhandoonkay

mineralogy *n.* کانپژندنه kan peyzhandana

mingle *v.t.* ترکيبول tarkeebawal

miniature *n.* کوچني برليک koochnay dabarleek

miniature *a.* ميناتوري meena toree

minim *n.* ترولو کوچنی tar tolo koochnay

minimal *a.* ترولو لو tar tolo lag

minimize *v.t.* ترولو کم کچ تەرسول tar tolo kam kach ta rasawal

minimum *n.* ترولو کممقدار tar tolo kam miqdar

minimum *a* کمنه کمحد kam na kam had

minion *n.* غوهمال ghwara mal

minister *n.* وزير wazeer

minister *v.i.* سمبالول sambalawal

ministrant *a.* خادم khadim

ministry *n.* وزارت wazarat

mink *n.* يوولغموشخرما yaw dawl ghat mosh khurma

minor *a.* کم،لا kam; lag

minor *n* کوچنی koochnay

minority *n.* لکی lagkay

minster *n.* دراهبانونمزدک da rahibanu namazdak

mint *n.* ضرابخانه zarabkhana

mint *n* پودينه podeena

mint *v.t.* سکهجوول sika jorawal

minus *prep.* ترصفرکم tar sifar kam

minus *a* منفي manfee

minus *n* نشتون،دمنفيعلامه nashtoon; da manfee alama

minuscule *a.* کوچنی،ووکی koochnay; warookay

minute *a.* ډيرکوچنی deyr koochnay

minute *n.* شيبه sheyba

minutely *adv.* پهدقيقهتوه pa daqeeqa toga

minx *n.* ستاخسیيابهخاز gustakh saray ya khaza

miracle *n.* معجزه mojiza

miraculous *a.* معجزاتي mojizatee

mirage *n.* سراب sarab

mire *n.* چيکر cheekar

mire *v.t.* پهچيکوننوستل pa cheekaro nanawistal

mirror *n* ييخه kheekha

mirror *v.t.* منعکسول munakisawal

mirth *n.* عيش aysh

mirthful *a.* پرعيش puraysh

misadventure *n.* ناوهپه nawara peykha

misalliance *n.* ناوهيووالی nawara yawwalay

misanthrope *n.* لهانسانانواوبشريپولد خهبزارانسان la insanano aw basharee tolani sakha beyzara insan

misapplication *n.* ناوهاستعمال nawara istimal

misapprehend *v.t.* ناسمدرککول nasam darak kawal

misapprehension *n* تروتنه teyr watana

misappropriate *v.t.* بخول badi khwaral

misappropriation *n.* بد،رشوت badi; rishwat

misbehave *v.i.* ناسمچلندکول nasam chaland kawal

misbehaviour *n.* ناوهچلند nawara chaland

misbelief *n.* ناوهباور nawara bawar

miscalculate *v.t.* ناسمشمرل nasam shmeyral

miscalculation *n.* ناسمهشمره nasama shmeyra

miscall *v.t.* پهغلطهغکول pa ghalata ghag kawal

miscarriage *n.* ناوهچلند nawara chaland

miscarry *v.i.* دماشومدزوناميدشنول da mashoom da zeygoon omeed shandawal

miscellaneous *a.* متنوع mutanaway

miscellany *n.* درنارنشيانووله da rangarang shayano gadola

mischance *n.* بدبختي bad bakhtee

mischief *n* ضرر zarar

mischievous *a.* شریر shareer

misconceive *v.t.* ناسم پوهېدل nasam poheydal

misconception *n.* غلط ومان ghalat goomat

misconduct *n.* بداخلاقي کول bad akhlaqee kawal

misconstrue *v.t.* تعبيرول ناسم nasam tabeerawal

miscreant *n.* بوجدانه bey wajdana

misdeed *n.* بدچلند bad chaland

misdemeanour *n.* ناہ goona

misdirect *v.t.* غلطه لاروونه کول ghalata larkhowana kawal

misdirection *n.* ناسمه لاروونه nasama larkhowana

miser *n.* کنجوس kanjoos

miserable *a.* بخته بد bad bakhta

miserly *a.* خسيس، کنجوس khasees; kanjoos

misery *n.* بدبختي badbakhtee

misfire *v.i.* سم کار نه کول sam kar na kawal

misfit *n.* ناسم شی nasam shay

misfortune *n.* بدمرغي bad marghee

misgive *v.t.* غلط خبرور کول ghalat khabar warkawal

misgiving *n.* بدوماني bad goomanee

misguide *v.t.* بلاري کول bey lari kawal

mishap *n.* بدهپه bada peykha

misjudge *v.t.* غلط قضاوت کول ghalat qazawat kawal

mislead *v.t.* مراه کول gomra kawal

mismanagement *n.* ناوه چلوونه nawara chalowana

mismatch *v.t.* سره نه جوړدل sara na joreydal

misnomer *n.* غلط نوم ghalat noom

misplace *v.t.* په ناسمه ای کی کارول pa nasam zay ki karawal

misprint *n.* غلط چاپ ghalat chap

misprint *v.t.* غلط چاپول ghalat chapawal

misrepresent *v.t.* ناسم ودل nasam khodal

misrule *n.* بنظمي bey nazmee

miss *n.* پغله peyghla

miss *v.t.* له لاسه ورکول la lasa warkawal

missile *n.* توغوندی toghanday

mission *n.* استوونه، داستازو پنغالی astawana; da astazo pandghalay

missionary *n.* تبليغاتي پلاوی tableeghatee plaway

missis, missus *n..* ترخپل اغزلاند tar khpal سيموته دپاچارنداستازی agheyz landi seemo ta da pacha garzand astazay

missive *n.* پغام لرونکليکنه paygham laroonki leekana

mist *n.* ګرد gard

mistake *n.* تروتنه teyr watana

mistake *v.t.* تروتل teyr watal

mister *n.* اغلی khaghalay

mistletoe *n.* يوول بوی yaw dawl bootay

mistreat *v.t.* بدسلوک کول bad salook kawal

mistress *n.* مرمن meyrman

mistrust *n.* بباوري bey bawaree

mistrust *v.t.* پربادرنه کول pri bawar na kawal

misty *a.* لمړدهک la garda dak

misunderstand *v.t.* ناسم پوهدل nasam poheydal

misunderstanding *n.* غلط تعبیر ghalat tabeer

misuse *n.* ناسم کارونه nasam karowana

misuse *v.t.* ناسم کارول nasam karawal

mite *n.* ر کوچنی چینجی deyr koochnay cheenjay

mite *n* ذره zara

mithridate *n.* زهرضد zahar zad

mitigate *v.t.* تخفیفول takhfeefawal

mitigation *n.* کمت kamakht

mitre *n.*

mitten *n.* یوول دستکش yaw dawl dastkash

mix *v.i* وول gadwadawal

mixture *n.* مرکب؛وله murakab; gadola

moan *v.i.* زیروي کول zgeyrwee kawal

moan *n.* زیروی؛فریاد zgeyrway; faryad

moat *n.* کنده kanda

moat *v.t.* کنده کیندل kanda keendal

mob *n.* وه ه ganra goonra

mob *v.t.* ههوه کول ganra goonra kawal

mobile *a.* رند؛متحرک garzand; mutaharik

mobility *n.* رلدنه garzeydana

mobilize *v.t.* په جریان راوستل pa jaryan rawastal

mock *v.i.* ملنپر کول malandi pri kawal

mock *adj* ملن؛پغور malandi; peyghor

mockery *n.* پخهکول peykhey kawal

modality *n.* کفیت kayfeeyat

mode *n.* طرز؛دود tarz; dood

mode *n.* ول؛بان سمبالونه dol; zan sambalawana

model *v.t.* تنظیم کول tanzeem kawal

moderate *a.* معتدل motadil

moderate *v.t.* معتدل کول motadil kawal

moderation *n.* اعتدال aytidal

modern *a.* تازه؛نوی taza; naway

modernity *n.* تجدد؛تازہ توب tajaddud; tazatob

modernize *v.t.* نوبهورکول nawi banra warkawal

modest *a.* حیاناک hayanak

modesty *n* حیا haya

modicum *n.* ذره zara

modification *n.* اصلاح isla

modify *v.t.* اصلاح کول isla kawal

modulate *v.t.* تعدیلول tadeelawal

moil *v.i.* ستومانه کدل stomana keydal

moist *a.* نمجن namjan

moisten *v.t.* نم پیداکول nam payda kawal

moisture *n.* نم nam

molar *a* مډونکی meydawoonkay

molasses *n* شات؛شیره shat; sheera

mole *n.* خال khal

molecular *a.* ذروي zarawee

molecule *n.* ذره zara

molest *v.t.* ظلم کول zulam kawal

molestation *n.* ظلمزیاتی zulam zyatay

molten *a.* ویلیشوی weeli shaway

moment *n.* شبه sheyba

momentary *a.* ژرترډونکی zhar teyreydoonkay

momentous *a.* دآنيحرکتپهقوپور اوند da anee harakat pa qawey pori arwand

momentum *n.* دآنيحرکتقوه da anee harakat qawa

monarch *n.* ولواک tolwak

monarchy *n.* ولواکي tolwakee

monastery *n.* خانقا khanqa

monasticism *n* رهبانيت rehbaneeyat

Monday *n.* دوشنبه doshamba

monetary *a.* پولي polee

money *n.* پسے peysey

monger *n.* دلال dalal

mongoose *n.* موشخرما mosh khurma

mongrel *a* دوهرهحوان dwa raga haywan

monitor *n.* وونکی khowoonkay

monitory *a.* دارنهکوونکی sarana kawoonkay

monk *n.* راهب rahib

monkey *n.* بیزو beezo

monochromatic *a.* ابوالیککیچنوالی abwalay karkeychanwalay

monocle *n.* یوستریزهعینک yaw stargeeza aynak

monocular *a.* یوستریز yaw stargeez

monody *n.* مرثیه marseeya

monogamy *n.* دیولرنه da yawey khazi larana

monogram *n.* طغرا taghara

monograph *n.* هنريلاسليک honaree lasleek

monogynous *a.* یومهلرونکی yawa khaza laroonkay

monolatry *n.* دیوخدایعبادت da yaw khuday ibadat

monolith *n.* یوهوه yawa tota

monologue *n.* یوکسیزونا yaw kaseez wayna

monopolist *n.* دامتیازخاوند da eemteeyaz khawand

monopolize *v.t.* انحصاريامتیاز اخستل inhisaree eemteeyaz akheystal

monopoly *n.* اجارهداري eejara daree

monosyllable *n.* یوهجا yaw hija

monosyllabic *a.* یوهجايي کلمه yaw hijayee kalma

monotheism *n.* توحید tawheed

monotheist *n.* مؤمن momin

monotonous *a.* یوآوازی yaw awazay

monotony *n* یوآوازلرنه yaw awaz larana

monsoon *n.* نوبتيبادوباران nobatee bad wa baran

monster *n.* بلا bala

monstrous *a.* بلايي balayee

month *n.* میاشت myasht

monthly *a.* میاشتنی myashtanay

monthly *adv* هرهمیاشت hara myasht

monthly *n* میاشتنمجله myashtanay mujala

monument *n.* تاریخي یادگار tareekhee yadgar

monumental *a.* یادگاري yadgaree

mouse *v.i* یوول امریکایي غرﻨ yaw dawl amreekayee gharsanay

mood *n.* مزاج mizaj

moody *a.* پرشانه parayshana

moon *n.* سپوږمی spogmay

moor *n.* ‍ dag

moor *v.t* پزوانول peyzwanawal

moot *n.* مناظره munazira

mop *n.* صفاکوونکی وکر safa kawoonkay tokar

mop *v.t.* صفاکول safa kawal

mope *v.i.* پرشانه کدل parayshana keydal

moral *a.* اخلاقي akhlaqee

moral *n.* پند pand

morale *n.* اخلاقیات akhlaqeeyat

moralist *n.* اخلاق وونکی akhlaq khowoonkay

morality *n.* اخلاقي چلند akhlaqee chaland

moralize *v.t.* اخلاقي فکرورکول akhlaqee fikar warkawal

morbid *a.* خوسا khosa

morbidity *n* ناروغوالی na roghwalay

more *a.* نور nor

more *adv* په زیادتر مقدار سره pa zyadtar miqdar sara

moreover *adv.* برسره پر دی barseyra par dey

morganatic *a.* له ناسیال سره واده کوونکی la nasyal sara wada kawoonkay

morgue *n.* میستون mreestoon

moribund *a.* مري حال margee hal

morning *n.* ﻬ gaheez

moron *n.* ساده sada

morose *a.* بدخویه bad khooya

morrow *n.* بله ورځ bala wraz

morsel *n.* ﻣ maray

mortal *a.* فاني fanee

mortal *n* فاني بشر fanee bashar

mortality *n.* مینه mreena

mortar *v.t.* لنړ،هاون langaree; hawan

mortgage *n.* رهن rehen

mortgage *v.t.* رهن کول rehen kawal

mortagagee *n.* مرتهن murtahin

mortify *v.t.* تباه کول taba kawal

mortuary *n.* مرده خانه murda khana

mosaic *n.* د موزائیک انور da mozayeek anzor

mosque *n.* جومات joomat

mosquito *n.* میاشی myashay

moss *n.* سنډل gul sang

most *a.* زیات تر zyat tar

most *adv.* زیاتره zyattara

most *n* تر ولولوی مقدار tar tolo loy miqdar

mote *n.* خاشه khasha

motel *n.* د سرک دغامل مستون da sarak da ghari meylmastoon

moth *n.* حشره hashra

mother *n* مور mor

mother *v.t.* پالل؛روزل palal; rozal

motherhood *n.* موروالی morwalay

motherlike *a.* د موربه شان da mor pa shan

motherly *a.* مورنۍ moranay

motif *n.* اصلي به aslee banra
motion *n.* حرکت harakat
motion *v.i.* حرکت کول harakat kawal
motionless *a.* بحرکته bey harakata
motivate *v* پاروول parawal
motivation *n.* پاروونه parowana
motive *n.* محرک muhrak
motley *a.* رنارنگ rangarang
motor *n.* خوزنده وسیله khozanda waseela
motor *v.i.* حرکت ورکول harakat warkawal
motorist *n.* موټرچلوونکی motar chalowoonkay
mottle *n.* خال خال khal khal
motto *n.* شعار shaar
mould *n.* قالب qalib
mould *v.t.* قالبول qalibawal
mould *n* ترکیب tarkeeb
mould *n* نمونه namoona
moult *v.i.* پوستکی اچول postakay achawal
mound *n.* خاکریز khakrayz
mount *n.* غوڼ ghonday
mount *v.t.* پرختل pri khatal
mount *n* صعود saood
mountain *n.* غر ghar
mountaineer *n.* غرختونکی ghar khatoonkay
mountainous *a.* غرهییز gharayeez
mourn *v.i.* ماتم کول matam kawal
mourner *n.* ماتم کوونکی matam kawoonkay
mournful *n.* ماتمي matamee
mourning *n.* ماتم matam

mouse *n.* موګ mogak
moustache *n.* برت breyt
mouth *n.* خوله khola
mouth *v.t.* پس پس کول pas pas kawal
mouthful *n.* لقمه luqma
movable *a.* خوت منونکی khozakht manoonkay
movables *n.* د کورمالونه اولوازم da kor maloona aw lawazim
move *n.* حرکت؛کان harakat; takan
move *v.t.* ای بدلول zay badlawal
movement *n.* حرکت harakat
mover *n.* خوزوونکی khozawoonkay
movies *n.* سینما sinama
mow *v.t.* کوه کول koota kawal
much *a* زیات zyat
much *adv* زیاتره zyattara
mucilage *n.* لعاب loab
muck *n.* توره خاوره tora khawra
mucus *n.* دغوخیری da ghwag kheeray
mud *n.* خه khata
muddle *n.* وي gadwadee
muddle *v.t.* ککول kakarawal
muffle *v.t.* پچل peychal
muffler *n.* دغادسمال da ghari dasmal
mug *n.* غه پیاله ghata pyala
muggy *a.* خپه کوونکی khapa kawoonkay
mulberry *n.* توت toot
mule *n.* کچر kachar
mulish *a.* دوه رده dwa raga
mull *n.* ململ malmal
mull *v.t.* غور کول ghor kawal

mullah *n.* دمسلمانانو ديني‌عالم da moosalmanano deenee alim

mullion *n.* دچوکاعمودي‌برخه da chawkat amoodee barkha

multifarious *a.* رنارنگ rangarang

multiform *n.* وشکلی so shaklay

multilateral *a.* واخیز so arkheez

multiparous *a.* په‌يوای‌ربچیان‌زونکی pa yaw zay deyr bachyan zeygoonkay

multiple *a.* وونی so goonay

multiple *n* مرکب murakab

multiplicand *n.* مضروب mazroob

multiplication *n.* ضرب zarab

multiplicity *n.* زيات‌شمر zyat shmeyr

multiply *v.t.* ضرب‌کول zarab kawal

multitude *n.* يوزيات‌مقدار yaw zyat miqdar

mum *a.* خاموش khamosh

mum *n* مور mor

mumble *v.i.* ژولاخبری‌کول zhowali khabari kawal

mummer *n.* ماسک‌اغوستی‌لوبغای mask aghostay lobgharay

mummy *n.* مومیایی‌شوی‌می momyayee shaway maray

mummy *n* مور mor

mumps *n.* دغومبری‌رنز da sat dad ghmbaray ranz

munch *v.t.* دغوایي‌په‌شان‌شخوندوهل da ghwayee pa shan shkhwand wahal

mundane *a.* دنیوي doonyawee

municipal *a.* ‌ناري kharee

municipality *n.* ناروالي kharwalee

munificent *a.* بونکی bakhoonkay

muniment *n.* سند sanad

munitions *n.* وسلي wasley

mural *a.* ديوالي deywalee

mural *n.* ديوال deywal

murder *n.* وژنه wazhana

murder *v.t.* وژل wazhal

murderer *n.* وژونکی wazhoonkay

murderous *a.* قاتلانه qatilana

murmur *n.* بزهار bazhar

murmur *v.t.* وکول zwag kawal

muscle *n.* دبدن‌په da badan pata

muscovite *n.* دماسکوخاراوسدونکی da masko khar oseydoonkee

muscular *a.* عضلاتي uzlatee

muse *v.i.* فکرکول fikar kawal

muse *n* فکر،غور fikar; ghor

museum *n.* دلرغونوشيانونندارای da larghono shayano nandarzay

mush *n.* په‌اوبوياشدوکاشدلي‌دجوارو اوه pa obo ya sheydo ki eysheydalee da joowaro ora

mushroom *n.* مرخی markheyray

music *n.* موسيقي mawseeqee

musical *a.* دموسيقۍپه‌اوند da mawseeqay pa arwand

musician *n.* موسيقي‌جوورونکی mawseeqee jorawoonkay

musk *n.* مشک mushk

musket *n.* داودميل‌وپک da oogad meel topak

musketeer *n.* وپکوال topak wal

muslin *n.* سان san

must *v.* بايد bayad

must *n.* دانوروشيره da angooro sheera

must *n* لزوم lazoom

mustache *n.* برتونه breytoona

mustang *n.* يووحشي آس yaw wahshee as

mustard *n.* خردل khardal

muster *v.t.* راغوښتل raghokhtal

muster n راغونوونه raghondawana

musty *a.* پوپنک وهلی popanak wahalay

mutation *n.* اوتون awakhtoon

mutative *a.*

mute *a.* خاموش khamosh

mute *n.* بغه توری bey ghaga toray

mutilate *v.t.* فلجول faljawal

mutilation *n.* فالج falij

mutinous *a.* باغيانه baghyana

mutiny *n.* بغاوت baghawat

mutiny *v. i* بغاوت کول baghawat kawal

mutter *v.i.* ژوولخبر zhowali khabari

mutton *n.* دپسه غوه da psa ghwakha

mutual *a.* شريک shareek

muzzle *n.* پوزبند pozband

muzzle *v.t* پوزبندوراچول pozband warachawal

my *a.* زما zama

myalgia *n.* دعضلاوماهيچدرد da uzley aw maheechey dard

myopia *n.* نژدليدنه nazhdey leedana

myopic *a.* نژدليدی nazhdey leeday

myosis *n.*

myriad *n.* لس زره las zara

myriad *a* لس زريز las zareez

myrrh *n.* يوه سرنا که خوشبويه ماده yawa sreykhnaka khoshbooya mada

myrtle *n.* نکريز nakreezi

myself *pron.* ماخپله ma khpala

mysterious *a.* پراسرار purasrar

mystery *n.* راز raz

mystic *a.* صوفيانه soofyana

mystic *n* صوفي soofee

mysticism *n.* تصوف tasawwuf

mystify *v.t.* حرانول hayranawal

myth *n.* خيالي کيسه khyalee keesa

mythical *a.* افسانوي afsanawee

mythological *a.* افسانوي afsanawee

mythology *n.* افسانه پژندنه afsana peyzhandana

N

nab *v.t.* نيول neewal

nabob *n.* نواب nawab

nadir *n.* ره کته برخه deyra kkhata barkha

nag *n.* وردلی شخص zoreydalay shakhs

nag *v.t.* مسلسل دردلرل musalsal dard laral

nail *n.* نوک nook

nail *v.t.* په نوکانونلول pa nookano nakhlawal

naive *a.* ساده sada

naivete *n.* سادهتوب sadatob

naivety *n.* ناتجربه کاري natajruba karee

naked *a.* بربند barband

name *n.* نوم noom

name *v.t.* نوم‌ورکول noom warkawal

namely *adv.* دسارپه‌توه da sari pa toga

namesake *n.* هم‌نومه ham nooma

nap *v.i.* ستره‌پول starga patawal

nap *n.* ستره‌پوونه starga patawana

nap *n* وین‌استر wareen astar

nape *n.* ورم wurmeyg

napkin *n.* دسمال dasmal

narcissism *n.* ځان‌ستاینه zan stayana

narcissus *n* دنرسل da nargas gul

narcosis *n.* نشه‌یي‌مواد nashayee mawad

narcotic *n.* نشه‌یي‌مواد nashayee mawad

narrate *v.t.* کیسه‌کول keesa kawal

narration *n.* کیسه،بیان keesa; bayan

narrative *n.* داستان dastan

narrative *a.* داستاني dastanee

narrator *n.* بیانوونکی bayanawoonkay

narrow *a.* تنگ tang

narrow *v.t.* تنول tangawal

nasal *a.* په‌پوزه‌پوراوند pa poza pori arwand

nasal *n* دپوزدننه da pozi danana

nascent *a.* پندلی panzeydalay

nasty *a.* ککه kakar

natal *a.* پدایشي paydayshee

nation *n.* قام qam

national *a.* قامي qamee

nationalism *n.* قام پالنه qam palana

nationalist *n.* قام‌پال qam pal

nationality *n.* ملیت mileeyat

nationalization *n.* ملي‌کدنه milee keydana

nationalize *v.t.* ملي‌کول milee kawal

native *a.* اصلي aslee

native *n* وطني watanee

nativity *n.* زدنه zeygeydana

natural *a.* فطري fitree

naturalist *n.* پنون‌پال panzoon pal

naturalize *v.t.* طبیعي‌کول tabiee kawal

naturally *adv.* په‌طبیعي‌ول pa tabiee dawl

nature *n.* قدرت qudrat

naughty *a.* شریر shareer

nausea *n.* زړه‌اهسکدنه zra rahaskeydana

nautical *a.* سمندري samandaree

naval *a.* سمندري samandaree

nave *n.* دکلیسامرکز da kaleesa markaz

navigable *a.* دکتچلوونو da kakhtay chalowani war

navigate *v.i.* کتچلول kakhtay chalawal

navigation *n.* سمندریون samandaryoon

navigator *n.* مانو manroo

navy *n.* سمندري‌واک samandaree zwak

nay *adv.* دانکارتوری‌نه da inkar toray na

neap *a.* دسمندریه‌یه da samandar teeta sapa

near *a.* نژد nazhdey

near *prep.* ورته deyr warta

near *adv.* تقریباً taqreeban

near *v.i.* نژدکدل nazhdey keydal

nearly *adv.* تقریباً taqreeban

neat *a.* پاک pak

nebula *n.* د دشپه اسمان کتہ ردد da shpey pa asman ki tat gard

necessary *n.* ضروری شی zarooree shay

necessary *a* ضروري zarooree

necessitate *v.t.* اکول ar kawal

necessity *n.* محتاجي muhtajee

neck *n.* غاہ، ghara; sat

necklace *n.* امل ameyl

necromancer *n.* د مو په مرسته غب وینه da maro pa mrasta ghayb wayana

necropolis *n.* هدیره hadeera

nectar *n.* خوندورشراب khwandawar sharab

need *n.* اتیا artya

need *v.t.* اتیالرل artya laral

needful *a.* مجبور majboor

needle *n.* ستن stan

needless *a.* غرضروري ghayr zarooree

needs *adv.* لهناچارخه la nacharay sakha

needy *a.* محتاج muhtaj

nefarious *a.* بدکاره badkara

negation *n.* نفي nafee

negative *a.* منفي manfee

negative *n.* عدد منفي manfee adad

negative *v.t.* ردول radawal

neglect *v.t.* غفلت کول ghaflat kawal

neglect *n* غفلت ghaflat

negligence *n.* بېپروايي bey parwayee

negligent *a.* بېپروا bey parwa

negligible *a.* ناچیز na cheez

negotiable *a.* د خبرواترو و da khabaro ataro war

negotiate *v.t.* مذاکره کول muzakira kawal

nagotiation *n.* مذاکره muzakira

negotiator *n.* جوجای کوونکی jor jaray kawoonkay

negress *n.* تورپوسته tor posti khaza

negro *n.* تورپوستی سی tor postay saray

neigh *v.i.* د اس شیشنل da as sheeshneydal

neigh *n.* د اس شیشنه da as sheeshney

neighbour *n.* ګاونډي gawandee

neighbourhood *n.* ګاونډ gawand

neighbourly *a.* د ګاونډپه اوند da gawand pa arwand

neither *conj.* نهخو na khu

neolithic *a.* دانسانانو دژونددنوبرینه دوره da insanano da zhwand da nawi dabareeney dawra

neon *n.* یوعنصر yaw unsar

nephew *n.* وراره wrara

nepotism *n.* خپل پالنه khpal palana

Neptune *n.* دنپتون سیاره da niptoon seeyara

Nerve *n.* عصب asb

nerveless *a.* بې عصبه bey asba

nervous *a.* عصبي asbee

nescience *n.* جهالت jahalat

nest *n.* ځاله zala

nest *v.t.* ځاله جوول zala jorawal

nether *a.* لاندینی landeenay

nestle *v.i.* الهجوول zala jorawal

nestling *n.* دمرغبچی da marghay bachay

net *n.* جال jal

net *v.t.* جالغوول jal ghorawal

net *a* خالص khalis

net *v.t.* سوچمهلاستهراول soocha gata las ta rawral

nettle *n.* له laramay

nettle *v.t.* اذاراول azarawal

network *n.* جال jal

neurologist *n.* عصبپژاند asb peyzhandana

neurology *n.* عصبپژندنه asb peyzhandana

neurosis *n.* ارواییزهناروغي arwayeeza naroghee

neuter *a.* بغرضه bey gharaza

neuter *n* بجنسهنوم bey jinsa noom

neutral *a.* بطرفه bey tarafa

neutralize *v.t.* بطرفهكول bey tarafa kawal

neutron *n.* داومیوهمننذره da atom yawa manzanay zara

never *adv.* هیكله،هیوخت heeskala; hees wakht

nevertheless *conj.* كمههم ka sa ham

new *a.* نوی naway

news *n.* خبرونه khabrawona

next *a.* راتلونكی ratloonkay

next *adv.* وروستهله wrosta la

nib *n.* ترموكه teyra sooka

nibble *v.t.* پهغاوشكول pa ghakho shkawal

nibble *n* وموه wara tota

nice *a.* ورین wreen

nicety *n.* ورینتوب wreentob

niche *n.* تاخچه takhcha

nick *n.* دچاودونه da chawdo nakha

nickel *n.* دنكلعنصر da nikal unsar

nickname *n.* كورنینوم koranay noom

nickname *v.t.* كورنینومایودل koranay noom eekhodal

nicotine *n.* یوزهرجنهماده yaw zaharjana mada

niece *n.* وروه wreyra

niggard *n.* بخیل bakheel

niggardly *a.* پهبدنیتهسره pa badnyatay sara

nigger *n.* تورپوستكی tor postakay

nigh *adv.* تقریبا taqreeban

nigh *prep.* نژد nazhdey

night *n.* شپه shpa

nightingale *n.* بلبل bulbul

nightly *adv.* دشپ da shpey

nightmare *n.* اروونكیخوب darowoonkay khob

nightie *n.* دخوبكالی da khob kalee

nihilism *n.* دماداوندشتوننهمننه da madey aw naray da shtoon na manana

nil *n.* نشت nasht

nimble *a.* چك chatak

nimbus *n.* نورانيشپول nooranee shpol

nine *n.* نهه naha

nineteen *n.* نولس noolas

nineteenth *a.* نولسم noolasam

ninetieth *a.* نویم nawyam

ninth *a.* نهم naham

ninety *n.* نوي nawee

nip *v.t* نتل nakhteyzal

nipple *n.* دتي وکه da tee sooka

nitrogen *n.* دنايتروجن ګاز da naytrojan gaz

no *a.* منفي manfee

no *adv.* نه na

no *n* هي،نفي hees; nafee

nobility *n.* نجابت najabat

noble *a.* شريف shareef

noble *n.* شريف سى shareef saray

nobleman *n.* شريف سى shareef saray

nobody *pron.* هيوک heesok

nocturnal *a.* دشپ da shpey

nod *v.i.* سرخوول sar khozawal

node *n.* سرخوونه sar khozawana

noise *n.* و zwag

noisy *a.* غالمغالي ghalmaghalee

nomad *n.* کوچی kochay

nomadic *a.* کوچيانه kochyana

nomenclature *n.* نوم لر noom lar

nominal *a.* نوميز noomeez

nominate *v.t.* نوماندکول noomand kawal

nomination *n.* نومونه noomawana

nominee *n* نومند noomand

non-alignment *n.* نه پيوستون na peywastoon

nonchalance *n.* بپروايي bey parwayee

nonchalant *a.* بپروا bey parwa

none *pron.* هييو hees yaw

none *adv.* هيکله heeskala

nonetheless *adv.* لهدسره سره la dey sara sara

nonpareil *a.* غرمساوي ghayr masawee

nonpareil *n.* يوولمه yaw dawl manra

nonplus *v.t.* پرشانه کول pareyshana kawal

nonsense *n.* چي chatee

nonsensical *a.* بايه bey zaya

nook *n.* دمستطيلي شکل کونج da mustateelee shakal konj

noon *n.* غرمه gharma

noose *n.* لومه looma

noose *v.t.* په لومه کرول pa looma ki geyrawal

nor *conj* خو نه na khu

norm *n.* جوت او ترکيب jorakht aw tarkeeb

norm *n.* اخلاقي معيار akhlaqee mayar

normal *a.* عادي adee

normalcy *n.* عادي حالت adee halat

normalize *v.t.* قانون لاندراوستل qanoon landi rawastal

north *n.* شمال shomal

north *a* شمالي shomalee

north *adv.* مخ په شمال makh pa shomal

northerly *a.* په شمال ک pa shomal ki

northerly *adv.* دشمال په لور da shomal pa lor

northern *a.* شمالي shomalee

nose *n.* پوزه poza

nose *v.t* پوزه مولل poza mokhal

nosegay *n.* ګل سانه gul sanga

nosy *a.* بدبويه bad booya

nostalgia *n.* دپرديتوب احساس da pradeetob ehsas

nostril *n.* دپوزسورى da pozi sooray

nostrum *n.* دهردرددوااومعالجدرمل da har dard dwa aw moalij darmal

not *adv.* دنه‌منفي‌كلمه da na manfee kalma

notability *n.* اهميت ahmeeyat

notable *a.* ديادوونو da yadawani war

notary *n.* ليكوونكى leekoonkay

notation *n.* ياشت yadakht

notch *n.* چوله chola

note *n.* چوله‌كول chola kawal

note *v.t.* يادتول yadakhtawal

noteworthy *a.* دتوجهو da tawajo war

nothing *n.* بارزتهشى bey arzakhta shay

nothing *adv.* هيكله heeskala

notice *a.* خبرتيا khabartya

notice *v.t.* خبرول khabrawal

notification *n.* خبروونه khabrawana

notify *v.t.* اعلانول aylanawal

notion *n.* فكر،آند fikar; and

notional *a.* فكري fikree

notoriety *n.* بدنامتوب badnamtob

notorious *a.* بدنام badnam

notwithstanding *prep.* چ ار agar chay

notwithstanding *adv.* لهدسرهسره la dey sara sara

notwithstanding *conj.* كمههم ka sa ham

nought *n.* نشت،صفر nasht; sifar

noun *n.* اسم،نوم isam; noom

nourish *v.t.* خواهوركول khwara warkawal

nourishment *n.* روزنه rozana

novel *a.* نوى naway

novel *n.* رُمان،عشقيه‌كيسه ruman; ishqeeya keesa

novelette *n.* لنه‌كيسه landa keesa

novelist *n.* كيسه‌ليكوونكى keesa leekoonkay

novelty *n.* نوت nawakht

november *n.* دانرزي‌كال‌يوولسمه میاشت da angreyzee kal yawolasama myasht

novice *n.* نوى‌كار naway kar

now *adv.* اوس os

now *conj.* داچ da chi

nowhere *adv.* هيچرته hees cheyrta

noxious *a.* تاوان‌اوونكى tawan arowoonkay

nozzle *n.* نلى nalay

nuance *n.* جزيى juzee

nubile *a.* دوادهو da wada war

nuclear *a.* هستوي hastawee

nucleus *n.* مركزي‌هسته markazee hasta

nude *a.* لغ laghar

nude` *n.* لغه‌مجسمه laghara mujasima

nudity *n.* لغتوب laghartob

nudge *v.t.* پهنل‌وهل pa sangal wahal

nugget *n.* قطعه qita

nuisance *n.* ور،خوابدوونه zor; khwa badowana

null *a.* باطل batil

nullification *n.* باطلوونه batilawona

nullify *v.t.* باطلول batilawal

numb *a.* بحسه bey hisa

number *n.* شمیر shmeyr

number *v.t.* شمرل shmeyral

numberless *a.* بشمره bey shmeyra

numeral *a.* عددي adadee

numerator *n.* شمرونکی shmeyroonkay

numerical *a.* عددي adadee

numerous *a.* بشمره bey shmeyra

nun *n.* راهبه rahiba khaza

nunnery *n.* ینه‌صومعه khazeena somia

nuptial *a.* په‌نکاح‌پوراوند pa nika pori arwand

nuptials *n.* دوادهرسم da wada rasam

nurse *n.* رنورپال ranzoor pal

nurse *v.t* خدمت‌کول khidmat kawal

nursery *n.* روزنتون rozantoon

nurture *n.* پالنه palana

nurture *v.t.* پالل palal

nut *n* چارمغز char maghaz

nutrition *n.* غذا ghaza

nutritious *a.* غذايي ghazayee

nutritive *a.* دغذاپه‌اوند da ghaza pa arwand

nuzzle *v.* په‌خاوره‌باندپوزه‌مول pa khawra bandi poza mokhal

nylon *n.* نايلون naylon

nymph *n.* سمندري‌پر samandaree khapeyray

O

oak *n.* ونه seyray wuna

oar *n.* دکتراشپل da kakhtay rashpeyl

oarsman *n.* راشپل‌وهونکی rashpeyl wahoonkay

oasis *n.* رغیله raghyanra

oat *n.* سارايي‌اوربشه sarayee orbasha

oath *n.* لوه lora

obduracy *n.* سرتمبي sartambagee

obdurate *a.* برزی dabar zaray

obedience *n.* اطاعت itaat

obedient *a.* تابع tabay

obeisance *n.* احترام ehtiram

obesity *n.* چاغت chaghakht

obey *v.t.* غاه‌ايودل ghara eekhodal

obituary *a.* دمیناعلان da mreeni aylan

object *n.* شی shay

object *v.t.* اعتراض‌کول aytiraz kawal

objection *n.* نیوکه neewaka

objectionable *a.* داعتراض‌و da aytiraz war

objective *n.* هدف hadaf

objective *a.* واقعي waqiee

oblation *n.* نذر nazar

obligation *n.* احسان؛ژمنه ehsan; zhmana

obligatory *a.* واجب wajib

oblige *v.t.* ناچارکول nachar kawal

oblique *a.* ریبند reyband

obliterate *v.t.* محوه‌کول mahwa kawal

obliteration *n.* پاکوونه pakowana

oblivion *n.* هروونه heyrawana

oblivious *a.* بخبره bey khabara

oblong *a.* اوډ oogda

oblong *n.* مستطيل mustateel

obnoxious *a.* کرغن kargheyran

obscene *a.* فاحش fahish

obscenity *n.* فحشتوب fahashtob

obscure *a.* مبهم mubhim

obscure *v.t.* تتول tatawal

obscurity *n.* ابهام ibham

observance *n.* رسمپالنه rasam palana

observant *a.* اوار awsar

observation *n.* پاملرنه pam larana

observatory *n.* ارمای sar zay

observe *v.t.* معاينه کول muayna kawal

obsess *v.t.* نارامه کول narama kawal

obsession *n.* سودا sawda

obsolete *a.* له کاره لوېدلی la kara lweydalay

obstacle *n.* مانع manay

obstinacy *n.* سرغاوی sar gharaway

obstinate *a.* سرتمبه sar tamba

obstruct *v.t.* مانع کدل manay keydal

obstruction *n.* بندست bandakht

obstructive *a.* مخنيوی کوونکی makhneeway kawoonkay

obtain *v.t.* لاس ته راول las ta rawral

obtainable *a.* شونی shoonay

obtuse *a.* کرخت karakht

obvious *a.* واضح wazay

occasion *n.* موقع moqa

occasion *v.t* موقع راپدل moqa rapeykheydal

occasional *a.* اتفاقي itifaqee

occasionally *adv.* اتفاقا itifaqan

occident *n.* لوديز lweydeez

occidental *a.* لوديزه naray lweydeeza naray

occult *a.* مخفي makhfee

occupancy *n.* خپلونه khpalawana

occupant *n.* نيوونکی neewoonkay

occupation *n.* دنده danda

occupier *n.* نيوونکی neewoonkay

occupy *v.t.* کول لا lagya kawal

occur *v.i.* پدل peykheydal

occurrence *n.* په peykha

ocean *n.* لوی سمندر loy samandar

oceanic *a.* سمندري samandaree

octagon *n.* اته مخيز ata makheez

octangular *a.* اته وير ata guteez

octave *n.* اته سطري شعر ata satree shayr

October *n.* دانزي کال لسمه مياشت da angreyzee kal lasama myasht

octogenarian *a.* اتيا کلن atya kalan

octogenarian *a* اتيا کلن انسان atya kalan insan

octroi *n.* بخشش bakhshish

ocular *a.* بصري basree

oculist *n.* دستروا کر da stargo dakdar

odd *a.* طاق taq

oddity *n.* عجيب او غريب شی ajeeb aw ghareeb shay

odds *n.* ناانولتوب na andwaltob

ode *n.* قصيده qaseeda

odious *a.* خوابدوونکی khwa badoonkay

odium *n.* عداوت adawat

odorous *a.* خوشبويه khoshbooya

odour *n.* خوشبو khoshbooya

offence *n.* جرم juram

offend *v.t.* ګناه کول goona kawal

offender *n.* ګناهګار goona gar

offensive *a.* کرغن kargheyran

offensive *n* يرغلګر yarghalgar

offer *v.t.* واندزکول warandeyz kawal

offer *n* پشنهاد payshnihad

offering *n.* هديه hadeeya

office *n.* کاراى،دفتر karzay; daftar

officer *n.* ددفترچارواکى da daftar charwakay

official *a.* دفترى daftaree

official *n* ادارى چارواکى idaree charwakay

officially *adv.* په رسمي توه pa rasmee toga

officiate *v.i.* رسمي مقام نيول rasmee maqam neewal

officious *a.* ادارى،مسؤولي idaree; masoolee

offing *n.* ساحلي اوبه sahilee oba

offset *v.t.* ورسره برابرى کول warsara barabaray kawal

offset *n* برابرى،نيالى barabaree; nyalgee

offshoot *n.* بچى bachgay

offspring *n.* بچى bachgay

oft *adv.* ډله deyr zala

often *adv.* ډله deyr zala

ogle *v.t.* په نخرو کتل pa nakhro katal

ogle *n* ناز نخره naz nakhra

oil *n.* تل teyl

oil *v.t* په تيلوغوول pa teylo ghwarawal

oily *a.* غو ghwar

ointment *n.* ملهم malham

old *a.* عمرخولى oomar khwaralay

oligarchy *n.* د شتمنو واکمني da shtamano wakmanee

olive *n.* زتون zaytoon

olympiad *n.* دالمپيک دنيو الوسيالو لوبغاى da ulampeek da nareewalo syalo lobgharay

omega *n.* ديونانى ابآخري توري da yoonanee abeysey akhiree toray

omelette *n.* خاينه khageena

omen *n.* پال pal

ominous *a.* بدمرغه bad margha

omission *n.* حذفونه hazafawana

omit *v.t.* حذفول hazafawal

omnipotence *n.* بشپرواکمني bashpar wakmanee

omnipotent *a.* بشپرواکمن bashpar wakman

omnipresence *n.* هرځاى موجودي har zay mawjoodgee

omnipresent *a.* هرځايته حاضر har zay ta hazir

omniscience *n.* لاپايه پوهنه lapaya pohana

omniscient *a.* په هرسه پوه pa har sa poh

on *prep.* پر،باند par; bandi

on *adv.* سربره sar beyra

once *adv.* پخوا pakhwa

one *a.* يو yaw

one *pron.* وک،يوکس sok; yaw kas

oneness *n.* يوتوب yawtob

onerous *a.* سخت sakht

onion *n.* پياز pyaz

on-looker *n.* کتونکى katoonkay

only *a.* يوازى yawazi

only *adv.* پهيواز pa yawazi

only *conj.* صرف siraf

onrush *n.* غيزهنومومونه ghageeza noomawana

onset *n.* حمله hamla

onslaught *n.* سختهحمله sakhta hamla

onus *n.* ژمنه zhmana

onward *a.* مخخواته makh khwa ta

onwards *adv.* دمخپلوهته da makh palwa ta

ooze *n.* نرمهخه narma khata

ooze *v.i.* نندل naneydal

opacity *n.* تتوالى tatwalay

opal *n.* يورنارنگليرنونهلرونكمادهچ غميترجوي yaw rangarang khkulee rangoona laroonki mada chi ghamee tri joreygee

opaque *a.* تت tat

open *a.* پرانستى pranistay

open *v.t.* پرانستل pranistal

opening *n.* پرانستنه؛سورى pranistana; sooray

openly *adv.* پهكارهول pa khkara dawl

opera *n.* موزيكالهرامه mozeekala drama

operate *v.t.* پهكاراچول pa kar achowana

operation *n.* عمليات amaleeyat

operative *a.* عملي amalee

operator *n.* ادارهكوونكى idara kawoonkay

opine *v.t.* رسميبيانوركول rasmee bayan warkawal

opinion *n.* رايه raya

opium *n.* افيون afyoon

opponent *n.* مخالف mukhalif

opportune *a.* پرزاى par zay

opportunism *n.* مصلحت maslihat

opportunity *n.* موقع moqa

oppose *v.t.* مخالفتكول mukhalifat kawal

opposite *a.* مخالف mukhalif

opposition *n.* مقاومت muqawmat

oppress *v.t.* ظلمكول zulam kawal

oppression *n.* ظلم zulam

oppressive *a.* ظالمانه zalimana

oppressor *n.* ظالم zalim

opt *v.i.* اكل takal

optic *a.* پهليدپوراوند pa leed pori arwand

optician *n.* عينكجووونكى aynak jorawoonkay

optimism *n.* اميدپُر pur omeed

optimist *n.* باورى bawaree

optimistic *a.* اميدلرونكى omeed laroonkay

optimum *n.* اينكچ areen kach

optimum *a* مناسب munasib

option *n.* غوراوى ghoraway

optional *a.* اختياري ikhtyaree

opulence *n.* بايتوب badaytob

opulent *a.* شتمن shtaman

oracle *n.* الهام ilham

oracular *a.* الهامي ilhamee

oral *a.* ژبنى zhabanay

orally *adv.* پهژبنيول pa zhabanee dawl

orange *n.* نارنج naranj

orange *a* نارنجي naranjee

oration *n.* وينا wayna

orator *n.* وناول waynawal

oratorical *a.* ادیبانه adeebana

oratory *n.* دونافن da wayna fan

orb *n.* کُره kura

orbit *n.* تلوری،مَدار tag loray; madar

orchard *n.* دموه باغ da meywa bagh

orchestra *n.* دموسیقله da mawseeqay dala

orchestral *a.* دهیزه موسیقي dala yeeza mawseeqee

ordeal *n.* له کاوه که آزموینه la karawa daka azmoyana

order *n.* فرمان farman

order *v.t* فرمان ورکول farman warkawal

orderly *a.* په منظمه توه pa munazzama toga

orderly *n.* تنظیم tanzeem

ordinance *n.* حکم hukam

ordinarily *adv.* په عادت سره pa adat sara

ordinary *a.* معمولي mamoolee

ordnance *n.* توپخانه topkhana

ore *n.* کاني بره kanee dabara

organ *n.* غی،هه gharay; had

organic *a.* عضوي uzwee

organism *n.* ژوندی وجود zhwanday wajood

organization *n.* اداره idara

organize *v.t.* ترتیبول tarteebawal

orient *n.* ختیز khateez

orient *v.t.* ختیزته تلل khateez ta tlal

oriental *a.* ختیزوال khateezwal

oriental *n* آسیا aseeya

orientate *v.t.* لارموندل lar moondal

origin *n.* اصل؛آر asal; ar

original *a.* اصلي aslee

original *n* اصل او سیدونکی asal oseydoonkay

originality *n.* اصالت asalat

originate *v.t.* سرچینه کدل sar cheena keydal

originator *n.* سرچینه sar cheena

ornament *n.* زور zaywar

ornament *v.t.* سینارول seengarawal

ornamental *a.* سینارپوراوند seengar pori arwand

ornamentation *n.* زبائش zaybayish

orphan *n.* یتیم yateem

orphan *v.t* یتیم کول،یتیم کدل yateem kawal; yateem keydal

orphanage *n.* یتیمانو داستوګنای yateemano da astogni zay

orthodox *a.* په دودیز دین باوري pa doodeez deen bawaree

orthodoxy *n.* په دودیز دین باورلرونکی pa doodeez deen bawar laroonkay

oscillate *v.i.* رددل reygdeydal

oscillation *n.* رددنه reygdeydana

ossify *v.t.* هوکیز کول hadokeez kawal

ostracize *v.t.* په عمومي رایو سره شل pa amoomee rayo sara sharal

ostrich *n.* شترمرغ shutar murgh

other *a.* بل؛جدا bal; juda

other *pron.* بل؛نور bal; nor

otherwise *adv.* له دې پرته la dey parta

otherwise *conj.* او که نه aw ka na

otter *n.* دحشراتولاروا da hashrato larwa

150

ottoman *n.* عثماني تركيه usmanee turkeeya

ounce *n.* دوزن يو پيمانه da wazan yaw paymana

our *pron.* زموږ zamoong

oust *v.t.* بهر كول bahar kawal

out *adv.* دباند da bandi

out-balance *v.t.* پر درندل pri draneydal

outbid *v.t.* لونر خواندكول lwar narkh warandi kawal

outbreak *n.* پيلدنه payleydana

outburst *n.* پاون اوبلوا pasoon aw balwa

outcast *n.* شل شوى sharal shaway

outcast *a* بكوره bey kora

outcome *n.* پايله payla

outcry *a.* نارسور narey soorey

outdated *a.* منسوخ mansookh

outdo *v.t.* زيات كاركول zyat kar kawal

outdoor *a.* دباند da bandi

outer *a.* باندينى bandeenay

outfit *n.* اسباب؛لوازم asbab; lawazim

outfit *v.t* وسايل په لاس وركول wasayil pa las warkawal

outgrow *v.t.* زياته پراختياموندل zyata parakhtya moondal

outhouse *n.* انگر angar

outing *n.* تفريحي چكر tafreehee chakar

outlandish *a.* پردى praday

outlaw *n.* شل شوى كس sharal shaway kas

outlaw *v.t* له حقوقو محروم ول la haqooqo mahroomawal

outline *n.* شكل بندي shakal bandee

outline *v.t.* طرح كول tarha kawal

outlive *v.i.* ر عمرلرل deyr oomar laral

outlook *n.* لرليد larleed

outmoded *a.* نادوده nadooda

outnumber *v.t.* له شمره اولدل la shmeyra awreydal

outpatient *n.* دروغتون سرپايي ناروغ da roghtoon sarpayee narogh

outpost *n.* سرحدي وكى sarhadee sawkay

output *n.* حاصل hasil

outrage *n.* غضب ghazab

outrage *v.t.* په غضب كول pa ghazab kawal

outright *adv.* مستقيما mustaqeeman

outright *a* په يوه دم pa yawa dam

outrun *v.t.* په منده واندكدل pa manda warandi keydal

outset *n.* شروع shuro

outshine *v.t.* زيات لدل zyat zaleydal

outside *a.* بهرنى baharanay

outside *n* دبهر da bahar

outside *adv* بهرته bahar ta

outside *prep.* دباند da bandi

outsider *n.* پردى praday

outsize *a.* غرمعمولي ghayr mamoolee

outskirts *n.pl.* داربانددبرخ da khar bandanay barkhi

outspoken *a.* سپينه ونا كوونكى speena wayna kawoonkay

outstanding *a.* هسك؛وتلى hask; watalay

outward *a.* بهرنی baharanay

outward *adv* بهرلورته bahar lor ta

outwards *adv* بهرته bahar ta

outwardly *adv.* بهرلورته bahar lor ta

outweigh *v.t.* ورخهدرندل warsakha draneydal

outwit *v.t.* ترچادمخهکدل tar cha da makha keydal

oval *a.* هوله hagay dawla

oval *n* بيضوي‌جسم bayzwee jisam

ovary *n.* تخمدان tukhamdan

ovation *n.* عمومي‌هر‌کلی amoomee har kalay

oven *n.* تنور tanoor

over *prep.* سربرهپرد sar beyra par dey

over *adv* پهدبرخهکی pa dey barkha ki

over *n* هسک hask

overact *v.t.* زياتکارکول zyat kar kawal

overall *n.* سرجمع sar jama

overall *a* جامع jamay

overboard *adv.* دسيندپهلوری da seend pa lori

overburden *v.t.* زياتبارول zyat barawal

overcast *a.* ترسيوري‌لاند tar syooree landi

overcharge *v.t.* زياتلتراوستل zyat lagakht rawastal

overcharge *n* زياتلت zyat lagakht

overcoat *n.* بالاپوش balaposh

overcome *v.t.* برلاسی‌کدل barlasay keydal

overdo *v.t.* زياتکارکول zyat kar kawal

overdose *n.* زياتدرملخول zyat darmal khwaral

overdose *v.t.* زياتدرملخول zyat darmal khwaral

overdraft *n.* لهاعتبارسخهزياتترلاسه شوی la aytibar sakha zyat tar lasa shaway

overdraw *v.t.* لهشتهپانخهراخستل la shta pangi sakha deyr akheystal

overdue *a.* زندیدلی zandeydaly

overhaul *v.t.* ولوبرخوکبدلونونه راوستل tolo barkho ki badloonoona rawastal

overhaul *n.* لهسرهبياسنجونه la sara bya sanjawana

overhear *v.t.* ترآخرهاورلدل tar akhira awreydal

overjoyed *a* زياتخوشاله zyat khoshala

overlap *v.t.* زياتپچل zyat peychal

overlap *n* زياتسرهنلدلی zyat sara nakhleydalay

overleaf *adv.* پهبلهپله pa bala panra

overload *v.t.* زياتبارول zyat barawal

overload *n* زياتبار zyat bar

overlook *v.t.* متوجهکدل mutawajo keydal

overnight *adv.* دشپهلهمخ da shpey la makhi

overnight *a* دشپ da shpey

overpower *v.t.* فتحکول fata kawal

overrate *v.t.* لوهبيهورکول lwara baya warkawal

overrule *v.t.* پرمسلط کول pri musallat kawal

overrun *v.t* پربريد کول pri breed kawal

oversee *v.t.* ارل saral

overseer *n.* سرپرست sar parast

overshadow *v.t.* تياره کول tyara kawal

oversight *n.* تروتنه نظري nazaree teyrwatana

overt *a.* معلوم maloom

overtake *v.t.* لاند کول landi kawal

overthrow *v.t.* لهپواچول la pkho achawal

overthrow *n* غورونه ghorzawana

overtime *adv.* ترا کلي وخت زيات takalee wakht zyat

overtime *n* اضافي کار izafee kar

overture *n.* پيلامه؛سريزه peelama; sareeza

overwhelm *v.t.* بشپغوپه کول bashpar ghopa kawal

overwork *v.i.* اضافي کار کول izafee kar kawal

overwork *n.* زيات کار zyat kar

owe *v.t* پوروی کدل por waray keydal

owl *n.* وز goong

own *a.* خپل؛ماني khpal; zanee

own *v.t.* لرل laral

owner *n.* لرونکی؛مالک laroonkay; malik

ownership *n.* ملکيت milkeeyat

ox *n.* غويی ghwayay

oxygen *n.* دآکسيجن ازda akseejan gaz

oyster *n.* يوسمندري صدف yaw samandaree sadaf

pace *n* دتلورفتار da tlo raftar

pace *v.i.* په يو خاص اندازه تلل pa yaw khas andaza tlal

pacific *a.* آرام سمندر aram samandar

pacify *v.t.* خاموشول khamoshawal

pack *n.* بنل bandal

pack *v.t.* بنل کول bandal kawal

package *n.* ی geyday

packet *n.* کوچنی بی koochnay dabay

packing *n.* باربندي barbandee

pact *n.* معاهده muahida

pad *n.* توشکچه toshakcha

pad *v.t.* پلی سفر کول pali safar kawal

padding *n.* دناليدجوونچاره da naleegay da jorawani chara

paddle *v.i.* راشپل وهل rashpeyl wahal

paddle *n* پلنه تخته plana takhta

paddy *n.* نه ژرنده شو وريج na zhranda shawi wareeji

page *n.* پله panra

page *v.t.* په لو غ معلومات ور کول pa lwar ghag maloomat warkawal

pageant *n.* و دنه khodana

pageantry *n.* پرتمينه ندا ره purtameena nandara

pagoda *n.* دبودايانوبُتخانه da boodayano butkhana

pail *n.* ولچه dolcha

pain *n.* درد dard

pain *v.t.* دردول dardawal

painful *a.* دردناک dardnak

painstaking *a.* محتاط muhtat

paint *n.* رن rang

paint *v.t.* رنول rangawal

painter *n.* رنوونکی rangawoonkay

painting *n.* نقاشي،انوروري naqashee; anzorgaree

pair *n.* جوه jora

pair *v.t.* جوه کدل jora keydal

pal *n.* يار،شريک yar; shareek

palace *n.* ما manray

palanquin *n.* ول dolay

palatable *a.* مزهناک mazanak

palatal *a.* پهتالوپوراوند pa taloo pori arwand

palate *n.* تالو taloo

palatial *a.* هواادارسترای hawadar star zay

pale *n.* زِي zyar

pale *a* پيکه peeka

pale *v.i.* پيکهکدل peeka keydal

palette *n.* دنقاشدرنونوخهکاراخستنه da naqashay da rangoono sakha kar akheystana

palm *n.* کجوره kajoora

palm *v.t.* لاسورکول las warkawal

palm *n.* دلاسورغوى da las warghaway

palmist *n.* ورغوىکتونکى warghaway katoonkay

palmistry *n.* ورغوىکتنه warghaway katana

palpable *a.* دلمسور da lams war

palpitate *v.i.* درزدل drazeydal

palpitation *n.* دزهدرزا da zra draza

palsy *n.* وز goozanr

paltry *a.* کثافاتاوچل kasafat aw chatalay

pamper *v.t.* پهنازپالل pa naz palal

pamphlet *n.* رساله risala

pamphleteer *n.* رسالهليکونکى risala leekoonkay

panacea *n.* دوامرضهرد da har maraz dawa

pandemonium *n.* دشطانما da shaytan manray

pane *n.* يوملورکونجموه yawa salor konja tota

panegyric *n.* مدحه madha

panel *n.* چوکا،بلورکونجهده chawkat; salor konja dara

panel *v.t.* کتهپرايودل kata pri eekhodal

pang *n.* يکه sreeka

panic *n.* اضطراب iztirab

panorama *n.* هراخيزهمنظره har arkheeza manzara

pant *v.i.* لهاوتزهساهاخستل landa aw teyza sa akheystal

pantaloon *n.* پتلون patloon

pantheism *n.* دخدایدولوپواوواکونو da khuday da tolo peykho aw zwakoono majmoo ganral مجموعهبلل

pantheist *n.* دخدایپهقدرتباوري da khuday pa qudrat bawaree

panther *n.* پاز prang

pantomime *n.* ماسکونهاغوستيلوبغاى maskoona aghostee lobgharee

pantry *n.* دلوخونه da lokho khoona

papacy *n.* دکلیساداپاپ‌مقام da kaleesa da pap maqam

papal *a.* دکلیساداپاپ‌پوراوند da kaleesa da pap pori arwand

paper *n.* کاغذ kaghaz

par *n.* یوشانوالی yawshanwalay

parable *n.* نمونه namoona

parachute *n.* دژغورنی‌چتر da zhghorani chatray

parachutist *n.* چترباز chatarbaz

parade *n.* رسم‌گشت rasam gasht

parade *v.t.* رسم‌گشت‌کول rasam gasht kawal

paradise *n.* جنت janat

paradox *n.* متقابل‌واندز mutaqabil warandeyz

paradoxical *a.* متضاد mutazad

paraffin *n.* یوه‌موم‌وله‌ماده yawa mom dawla mada

paragon *n.* نمونه؛معیار namoona; mayar

paragraph *n.* دلیکنی‌وه‌برخه da leekani yawa barkha

parallel *a.* برابر barabar

parallel *v.t.* برابرول barabarawal

parallelism *n.* یوشانتوب yawshantob

parallelogram *n.* متوازی‌الاضلاع mutawazeeul azla

paralyse *v.t.* وزوهل goozanr wahal

paralysis *n.* وز goozanr

paralytic *a.* وزوهلی goozanr wahalay

paramount *n.* لوپوی‌حاکم lwar poray hakim

paramour *n.* شه shahay

paraphernalia *n. pl* جهز jahayz

paraphrase *n.* آزاده‌لیکنه azada leekana

paraphrase *v.t.* شرحه‌کول،آزادلیکل sharha kawal; azada leekal

parasite *n.* جراثیم jaraseem

parcel *n.* پنډکی pandukay

parcel *v.t.* په‌ووویشل pa toto weyshal

parch *v.t.* وریتول wreetawal

pardon *v.t.* بنه‌کول bakhana kawal

pardon *n.* مغفرت maghfirat

pardonable *a.* دمغفرت‌و da maghfirat war

parent *n.* مورپلار mor plar

parentage *n.* نسب nasab

parental *a.* دمورپلارپه‌اوند da mor plar pa arwand

parenthesis *n.* لیندکی leendakay

parish *n.* ناحیه،علاقه naheeya; ilaqa

parity *n.* مساویتوب masaweetob

park *n.* دعمومی‌تفریح‌ځای da amoomee tafree zay

park *v.t.* په‌یوای‌کی‌درول pa yaw zay ki darawal

parlance *n.* وینا؛بیان wayna; bayan

parley *n.* مکالمه makalima

parley *v.i* مذاکره‌کول muzakira kawal

parliament *n.* ملی‌شورا milee shoora

parliamentarian *n.* دملی‌شوراغړی da milee shoora gharay

parliamentary *a.* شورایی shoorayee

parlour *n.* دسينارخونه da seengar khoona

parody *n.* دنورودسبک‌تقليد da noro da subak taqleed

parody *v.t.* خندوونکهنري‌ننداره‌واند کول khandawoonki hunaree nandara warandi kawal

parole *n.* ضمانت zamanat

parole *v.t.* په‌ضمانت‌پرول pa zamanat preykhwal

parricide *n.* دمورپلاروژنه da mor plar wazhana

parrot *n.* طوطي totee

parry *v.t.* اوسپکول oogey spakawal

parry *n.* دفاعي‌خوت difaee khozakht

parson *n.* سيمه‌ييزپادري seemayeez padree

part *n.* برخه barkha

part *v.t.* برخه‌اخستل barkha akheystal

partake *v.i.* شريکيدل shareekeydal

partial *a.* برخيز؛جزيي barkheez; juzayee

partiality *n.* پلويتوب palaweetob

participate *v.i.* شرکتلرل shirkat laral

participant *n.* شرکت‌کوونکی shirkat kawoonkay

participation *n.* شرکت shirkat

particle *a.* ذره zara

particular *a.* خاص khas

particular *n.* خاص‌سی khas saray

partisan *n.* پلوی palaway

partisan *a.* طرفدار tarafdar

partition *n.* وش weysh

partition *v.t.* وشل weyshal

partner *n.* ونهوال wandawal

partnership *n.* شراکت shirakat

party *n.* وند gond

pass *v.i.* پوروتل pori watal

pass *n* پوروتنه pori watana

passage *n.* دوتولاره da wato lara

passenger *n.* لاروی laraway

passion *n.* جذبه jazba

passionate *a.* جذباتي jazbatee

passive *a.* غرفعال ghayr faal

passport *n.* پژنديپه peyzhandana

past *a.* تر teyr

past *n.* ترمهال teyr mahal

past *prep.* دمخه da makha

paste *n.* خميره khameera

paste *v.t.* سرول sreykhawal

pastel *n.* رنه‌انور ranga anzor

pastime *n.* بوختيا bokhtya

pastoral *a.* روحاني‌لارود roohanee larkhod

pasture *n.* ‌سر‌زی sar zay

pasture *v.t.* رول sarawal

pat *v.t.* نازول nazawal

pat *n* نازوونه nazawana

pat *adv* په‌مناسبه‌توه pa munasiba toga

patch *v.t.* پوندلول peywand lagawal

patch *n* وه؛پينه tota; peena

patent *a.* واضح wazeh

patent *n* دکارحق da kar haq

patent *v.t.* انحصاري‌حق‌ورکول inhisaree haq warkawal

paternal *a.* پلرني plaranay

path *n.* تلوری؛لار tagloray; lar

pathetic *a.* غرور اوستونکی ghreew rawastoonkay

pathos *n.* شفقت shafqat

patience *n.* صبر sabar

patient *a.* صبر کوونکی sabar kawoonkay

patient *n* مریض mareez

patricide *n.* دپلاروژنه da plar wazhana

patrimony *n.* پلرنی میراث plaranay meeras

patriot *n.* هوادوال haywad wal

patriotic *a.* هوادپال haywad pal

partiotism *n.* هوادپالنه haywad palana

patrol *v.i.* شت کول gasht kawal

patrol *n* شت gasht

patron *n.* ساتندوی satandoy

patronage *n.* پالنه palana

patronize *v.t.* ساتل؛پالل satal; palal

pattern *n.* طرحه؛نمونه tarha; namoona

paucity *n.* لتوب lagtob

pauper *n.* تش لاسی tash lasay

pause *n.* وقفه waqfa

pause *v.i.* وقفه کول waqfa kawal

pave *v.t.* پهبروپول pa dabaro pokhal

pavement *n.* سنفرشي sangfarshee

pavilion *n.* لویه کد loya keygday

paw *n.* خپه khapara

paw *v.t.* منولپرخول mangoli prey khakhawal

pay *v.t.* اداکول ada kawal

pay *n* ادینه؛جبران adayana; jibran

payable *a.* داداینو da adayani war

payee *n.* پستر لاسه کوونکی peysey tar lasa kawoonkay

payment *n.* دپسو اداینه da peyso adayana

pea *n.* یوول چ yaw dawl chanrey

peace n. پخلاینه؛سوله pukhlayana; sola

peaceable *a.* دسولو da soli war

peaceful *a.* سولهییز solayeez

peach *n.* شفتالو shaftaloo

peacock *n.* طاوس tawas

peahen *n.* ینهطاوس khazeena tawas

peak *n.* و که؛موکه sooka; makhooka

pear *n.* ناک nak

pearl *n.* ملغلره malghalara

peasant *n.* کلیوال kaleewal

peasantry *n.* کلیوالهخوی kaleewala khooy

pebble *n.* شه shaga

peck *n.* سطل تهورتهلوی satal ta warta lokhay

peck *v.i.* پهموکهوهل pa makhooka wahal

peculiar *a.* خاص khas

peculiarity *n.* خاصیت khaseeyat

pecuniary *a.* نغدي naghdey

pedagogue *n.* وونکی khowoonkay

pedagogy *n.* وونهاوروزنه khowana aw rozana

pedal *n.* رکاب rakab

pedal *v.t.* دبایسکل رکاب پهپووهل da baysakal rakab pa pkho wahal

pedant *n.* کورنیوونکی koranay khowoonkay

pedantry *n.* دخپلپوهبایمودنه da khpali pohi bey zaya khodana

pedestal *n.* پایه،ستون paya; satoon

pedestrian *n.* پلاره pali lara

pedigree *n.* نسبنامه nasabnama

peel *v.t.* پوستکیاچول postakay achawal

peel *n.* پوستکی postakay

peep *v.i.* پهغلاغلاکتل pa ghla ghla katal

peep *n* پهغلاکتنه pa ghla katana

peer *n.* سیال،جوه syal; jora

peerless *a.* بیجو bey jorey

peg *n.* موی،سنجاق magaway; sanjaq

peg *v.t.* پهموي،راوندول pa magwee razwarandawal

pelf *n.* دنیاییمال doonyayee mal

pell-mell *adv.* پهوول pa gadwad dawl

pen *n.* قلم qalam

pen *v.t.* لیکل،پهبندکاچول leekal; pa band ki achawal

penal *a.* جزایی jazayee

penalize *v.t.* جریمهکول jareema kawal

penalty *n.* جریمه jareema

pencil *n.* پنسل،دنقاشبرس pensal; da naqashay burs

pencil *v.t.* پهپنسلجوولیالیکل pa pensal jorawal ya leekal

pending *prep.* معلق moallaq

pending *a* نااجرا na ijra

pendulum *n.* بنول bandol

penetrate *v.t.* پکنفوذکول paki nafooz kawal

penetration *n.* نفوذ،ننوتنه nafooz; nanawatana

penis *n.* دنارینهجنسيآله da nareena jinsee ala

penniless *a.* تشلاسی tash lasay

penny *n.* یوهپسه،دامریکاسکه yawa paysa; da amreeka sika

pension *n.* دتقاعدتنخوا da taqaid tankha

pension *v.t.* دتقاعدتنخوااخستل da taqaid tankha akheystal

pensioner *n.* متقاعد mutaqaid

pensive *a.* پرشان parayshan

pentagon *n.* پنځوی peenza gotay

peon *n.* ددفترقاصد da daftar qasid

people *n.* خلک khalq

people *v.t.* آبادول،مشتکول abadawal; meysht kawal

pepper *n.* مرچ mrich

pepper *v.t.* تریخوال treekhawal

per *prep.* پهوسیله pa waseela

perambulator *n.* دماشومانوټانه da mashoomano tanga

perceive *v.t.* درککول،موندل darak kawal; moondal

perceptible *adj* ددرکو da darak war

per cent *adv.* سلنه،فیصدي salana; feesadee

percentage *n.* دسلولهمخ da salo la makhi

perception *n.* درک،احساس darak; ehsas

perceptive *a.* ادراکي idrakee

perch *n.* دلرييتیر da largee teer

perch *v.i.* پهیوخوندیایکنستل pa yaw khwandee zay kkheynastal

perennial *a.* پايت لرونکی payakht laroonkay

perennial *n.* دوامدارشی dawamdar shay

perfect *a.* زبردست پوره، poora; zabardast

perfect *v.t.* پوره کول؛بشپول poora kawal; bashparawal

perfection *n.* پورهوالی؛کمال poora walay; kamal

perfidy *n.* بی وفايي bey wafayee

perforate *v.t.* سوری کول sooray kawal

perforce *adv.* لهناکامخه la nakamay sakha

perform *v.t.* اجراکول ijra kawal

performance *n.* سرتهرسونه؛اجرا sar ta rasawana; ijra

performer *n.* اجراکوونکی ijra kawoonkay

perfume *n.* عطر atar

perfume *v.t.* دعطروبوی ورکول da atro booy warkawal

perhaps *adv.* کدای شي،شايد keyday shee; shayad

peril *n.* خطر khatar

peril *v.t.* پهخطرکاچول pa khatar ki achawal

perilous *a.* خطرناک khatarnak

period *n.* وخت؛دوران wakht; dawran

periodical *n.* مهاليز mahaleez

periodical *a.* نوبتي nawbatee

periphery *n.* چاپريال chapeyryal

perish *v.i.* تلف کول talf kawal

perishable *a.* لهمنهتلونکی la manza tloonkay

perjure *v.i.* ژمنهماتول zhmana matawal

perjury *n.* ژمنهماتوونه zhmana matawana

permanence *n.* دوام dawam

permanent *a.* دايمي daymee

permissible *a.* داجازو da eejazey war

permission *n.* اجازه eejaza

permit *v.t.* اجازهورکول eejaza warkawal

permit *n.* اجازه eejaza

permutation *n.* اوتوناوونجون awakhtoon aw wanjoon

pernicious *a.* زیاناوونکی zyan arowoonkay

perpendicular *a.* ولا walar

perpendicular *n.* شاقول shaqol

perpetual *a.* دايمي daymee

perpetuate *v.t.* بقاوربل baqa warbakhal

perplex *v.t.* حرانول hayranawal

perplexity *n.* پچلتيا peychaltya

persecute *v.t.* شکنجه کول shkanja kawal

persecution *n.* شکنجه shkanja

perseverance *n.* یکاو teekaw

persevere *v.i.* استقامتلرل istiqamat laral

persist *v.i.* اصرارکول israr kawal

persistence *n.* اصرار israr

persistent *a.* یندونکی teengeydoonkay

person *n.* نفر،شخص nafar; shakhs

personage *n.* مهمشخصیت muhim shakhseeyat

personal *a.* شخصي shakhsee

piles *n.* بواسير bawaseer

pilfer *v.t.* دکمشيغلاکول da kam shee ghla kawal

pilgrim *n.* زيارت;حج zyarat; haj

pilgrimage *n.* زيارت;حج zyarat; haj

pill *n.* دانه dana

pillar *n.* ستنه,پايه stana; paya

pillow *n* بالت balakht

pillow *v.t.* پهبالتسرايودل pa balakht sar eekhodal

pilot *n.* پيلو,جالهوان paylot; jalawan

pilot *v.t.* پيلويکول;رهنماييکول paylotee kawal; rehnumayee kawal

pimple *n.* رمکه,دانه garmaka; dana

pin *n.* کوچنیمخ koochnay meykh

pin *v.t.* مخټومبل meykh toombal

pinch *v.t.* چيچل cheechal

pinch *v.* غلاکول ghla kawal

pine *n.* دصنوبرونه da sanobar wana

pine *v.i.* کول karawal

pineapple *n.* اناناس ananas

pink *n.* رنلابي gulabee rang

pink *a* لابي gulabee

pinkish *a.* لابيرنتهمايل gulabee rang ta mayil

pinnacle *n.* اوج;ترهوکه oj; teyra sooka

pioneer *n.* مخکخ makhkakh

pioneer *v.t.* رهبريکول rehbaree kawal

pious *a.* پرهزار parhayzgar

pipe *n.* نل;سوری nal; soornray

pipe *v.i* نلونوکاوبهرسول naloono ki oba rasawal

piquant *a.* تريخاوخوندور treekh aw khwandawar

piracy *n.* دحقغلا da haq ghla

pirate *n.* غل ghal

pirate *v.t* غلاکول ghla kawal

pistol *n.* تمانچه tamancha

piston *n.* خوندهميله khozanda meela

pit *n.* کنده kanda

pit *v.t.* پهکندهکاچول pa kanda ki achawal

pitch *n.* نصبشوىای nasab shaway zay

pitch *v.t.* نصبکول,توغول nasab kawal; toghawal

pitcher *n.* کوزه kooza

piteous *a.* زاهد zahiḍ

pitfall *n.* دام dam

pitiable *a.* درحمو da rehem war

pitiful *a.* زهسواندی zra swanday

pitiless *a.* برحمه bey rehma

pitman *n.* کيندونکی keendoonkay

pittance *n.* پهميپسخرات pa maree pasi khayrat

pity *n.* خويزه zra khoogee

pity *v.t.* سزلزه zra seyzal

pivot *n.* چورليز choorleez

pivot *v.t.* پهمحورتاودل pa mehwar taweydal

place *n.* ربای dagar; zay

place *v.t.* پمایکول pa zay kawal

placid *a.* امن dadman

plague *a.* وبا;طاعون waba; taoon

plague *v.t.* پهبلااختهکول pa bala akhta kawal

plain *a.* د) dag

plain *n.* هوار hawar

plaintiff *n.* دعواکوونکی dawa kawoonkay

plan *n.* تدبیر tadbeer

plan *v.t.* تدبیرکول tadbeer kawal

plane *n.* الوتکه alwataka

plane *v.t.* الوتل؛رنده کول alwatal; randa kawal

plane *a.* هوارهسطح hawara sata

plane *n* دترکارنده da tarkanray randa

planet *n.* سیاره seeyara

planetary *a.* سیاروي seeyarawee

plank *n.* دلرېهوارهتخته da largee hawara takhta

plank *v.t.* پهدودوویشل pa daro daro weyshal

plant *n.* بوی bootay

plant *v.t.* کرل؛نیالول karal; nyalawal

plantain *n.* کله kayla

plantation *n.* کرونده karwanda

plaster *n.* پلستر؛لو palistar; leyw

plaster *v.t.* پلسترول palistarawal

plate *n.* لوخی lokhay

plate *v.t.* فلزيپوورکول filizee pokh warkawal

plateau *n.* لوهسطح lwara sata

platform *n.* کنلاره؛منبر kranlara; mimbar

platonic *a.* دافلاطوندلارلاروی da aflatoon da lari laraway

platoon *n.* بلوک؛یوهدلههمکاراشخاص blok; yawa dala hamkar ashkhas

play *n.* لوبه loba

play *v.i.* لوبکول lobi kawal

player *n.* لوبغای lobgharay

plea *n.* حقوقيدعوا haqooqee dawa

plead *v.i.* دفاعکول difa kawal

pleader *n.* مدافعوکیل mudafay wakeel

pleasant *a.* پهزهپور pa zra pori

pleasantry *n.* خوطبعي khwakh tabee

please *v.t.* خوندورکول khwand warkawal

pleasure *n.* لذت lazat

plebiscite *n.* دعاموورایه da am wagaro raya

pledge *n.* تعهد؛ژمنه taahud; zhmana

pledge *v.t.* تعهدکول taahud kawal

plenty *n.* زیاتکچ zyat kach

plight *n.* تون؛بیعت taroon; beyt

plod *v.i.* نوهدل nagokheydal

plot *n.* زمینه؛دمکيوهوه zameena; da zmaki yawa tota

plot *v.t.* پلانجوول plan jorawal

plough *n.* یو yeywi

plough *v.i* ځمکهیوکول zmaka yeywi kawal

ploughman *n.* کروندر karwandagar

pluck *v.t.* شکول؛وولول shukawal; tolawal

pluck *n* وولونه tolawana

plug *n.* خولپوی؛پل kholpotay; plag

plug *v.t.* خولپويپکایوودل kholpotay paki eekhodal

plum *n.* آلوچه aloocha

plumber *n.* نلدوان؛سرپکار naldawan; sarp kar

plunder *v.t.* لول lootal

plunder *n* غنيمت،ولجه walja; ghaneemat

plunge *v.t.* غوه کول ghota kawal

plunge *n* غوه،غوپه ghota; ghopa

plural *a.* جمع jama

plurality *n.* پهجمعپوراوند pa jama pori arwand

plus *a.* مثبت musbat

plus *n* دجمعنه،مثبت da jama nakha; musbat

ply *v.t.* اوزارپه کارول،پهاکلالارسفرکول awzar pa karawal; pa takali lar safar kawal

ply *n* دلریيوپه da largee yaw pata

pneumonia *n* دسوالتهاب da sago iltihab

pocket *n.* جب jeyb

pocket *v.t.* جب کایودل jeyb ki eekhodal

pod *n.* پو،تکی pokh; teykay

poem *n.* شعر shayr

poesy *n.* شاعري،دیوان shairee; deewan

poet *n.* شاعر shair

poetaster *n.* شاعروی shair gotay

poetess *n.* شاعره shaira khaza

poetic *a.* شاعرانه shairana

poetics *n.* شاعرانهکلا shairana khkula

poetry *n.* شاعري shairee

poignancy *n.* توندي tondee

poignant *a.* توند tond

point *n.* کی،وکه takay; sooka

point *v.t.* کی،لول،اشارهکول takay lagawal; ishara kawal

poise *v.t.* ثابتقدمساتل sabit qadam satal

poise *n* وضعيت،وقار wuzeeyat; waqar

poison *n.* زهر zahar

poison *v.t.* زهرورکول zahar warkawal

poisonous *a.* زهرجن zaharjan

poke *v.t.* بایهپلنهکول bey zaya palatana kawal

poke *n.* چوخوونه chokhawana

polar *n.* شمالیياسولمیقطب shumalee ya sweylee qutab

pole *n.* قطب،ستن qutab; stan

police *n.* امنيتيواک،پوليس amneeyatee zwak; polees

policeman *n.* امنيتيمامور amneeyatee mamoor

policy *n.* کنلاره kranlara

polish *v.t.* صقليکول sayqalee kawal

polish *n* رنگ،صقل rang; sayqal

polite *a.* نرم naram

politeness *n.* نرمي narmee

politic *a.* مهذب muhazzab

political *a.* سياسي seeyasee

politician *n.* سياستوال seeyasatwal

politics *n.* سياستپوهنه seeyasat pohana

polity *n.* سياستداري seeyasatdaree

poll *n.* رایه raya

poll *v.t.* رایهورکول raya warkawal

pollen *n.* نباتيکوچنيسپرورونه nabatee koochnee sporawan

pollute *v.t.* ناولیکول nawalay kawal

pollution *n.* ناولیتوب nawaleetob

polo *n.* دهاکیوهلوبه da hagay yawa loba

polygamous *a.* شمرلرونکی ganr shmeyr khazi laroonkay

polygamy *n.* شمرلرنه ganr shmeyr khazi larana

polyglot1 *n.* پهوژبوپوه pa so zhabo poh

polyglot2 *a.* پهوژبوپوهدنه pa so zhabo poheydana

polytechnic *a.* راخیزفنونوپوراوند deyr arkheez fanoono pori arwand

polytechnic *n.* راخیزفنياوتخنیکي پوهنتون deyr arkheez fanee aw takhneekee pohantoon

polytheism *n.* پهوخدایانوباور pa ganro khudayano bawar

polytheist *n.* پهوخدایانوباورلرونکی pa ganro khudayano bawar laroonkay

polytheistic *a.* پهوخدایانوپوراوند pa ganro khudayano pori arwand

pomp *n.* دبدبه dabdaba

pomposity *n.* شان؛شوکت shan; shawkat

pompous *a.* شاندار shandar

pond *n.* ډند dand

ponder *v.t.* غورکول ghor kawal

pony *n.* کوچنیاس koochnay as

poor *a.* مسکین miskeen

pop *v.i.* پهزورهتپول pa zora trapawal

pop *n* پهزورهدرزونه pa zora drazawana

pope *n.* دکاتولیکيعیسائیانورهبر da katoleekee eesayano rehbar

poplar *n.* سپدار sapeedar

poplin *n.* دپوپلینوکر da poplayn tokar

populace *n.* عاموی am wagaray

popular *a.* عمومي؛نوموی amoomee; noomawaray

popularity *n.* شهرت shuhrat

popularize *v.t.* مشهورول mashhoorawal

populate *v.t.* مشتکول meysht kawal

population *n.* نفوس nafoos

populous *a.* نفوسه ganr nafoosa

porcelain *n.* چینيلوي cheenee lokhee

porch *n.* دالان dalan

pore *n.* کوچنیسوری koochnay sooray

pork *n.* دخوغوه da khoog ghwakha

porridge *n.* مخلوطشوشوربا makhloot shaway shorba

port *n.* بندر bandar

portable *a.* دلدونو da leygdawani war

portage *n.* لدونه leygdawana

portal *n.* ور؛کمانلرونکیور war; kaman laroonkay war

portend *v.t.* ورخهخبرول warsakha khabrawal

porter *n.* پني pandee

portfolio *n.* داسنادواوکاغذوبکس؛د وزارتدندهاومقام da asnado aw kaghazo bakas; da wazarat danda aw maqam

portico *n.* برنه baranda

portion *n* جز juz

portion *v.t.* پهبرخوویشل pa barkho weyshal

portrait *n.* دمخعكس da makh aks

portraiture *n.* دمخدبرخنقاشي da makh da barkhi naqashee

portray *v.t.* دمخانوراستل da makh anzor eystal

portrayal *n.* مجسم كوونه mujassam kawana

pose *v.i.* پهيومانيوضعيت كانوراستل pa yawa zangaree wuzeeyat ki anzor eystal

pose *n.* اقامه،يومانيوضعيت iqama; yawa zangaray wuzeeyat

position *n.* مقام،حالت maqam; halat

position *v.t.* ايودل eekhodal

positive *a.* مثبت musbat

possess *v.t.* پهواكـكلرل pa wak ki laral

possession *n.* لرنه،نيونه larana; neewana

possibility *n.* كدون keydoon

possible *a.* كدوني keydoonay

post *n.* پست،دپستاداره pust; da pust idara

post *v.t.* ليكـياسامانپهپستلدول leek ya saman pa pust leygdawal

post *n* مسؤليت masooleeyat

post *v.t.* پهمسؤليتاكل pa masooleeyat takal

post *adv.* وروسته،بعدل wrusta; badan

postage *n.* پستيكـ pustee tikat

postal *a.* پستي pustee

post-date *v.t.* دپدتاريخپهزندليكل da peykhi da tareekh pa zand leekal

poster *n.* اعلان aylan

posterity *n.* نسل nasal

posthumous *a.* دپلارمينوروستهزمدلى da plar mreeni wrusta zeygeydalay

postman *n.* پست رسان pust rasan

postmaster *n.* دپسترئيس da pust rayees

post-mortem *a.* ترمينوروسته tar mreeni wrusta

post-mortem *n.* دترمينوروستهمعاينه tar mreeni wrusta moayna

post-office *n.* دپستاداره da pust idara

postpone *v.t.* زندول zandawal

postponement *n.* تاخير takheer

postscript *n.* دكتابپايو da keetab paysoor

posture *n.* حالت،كفيت halat; keyfeeyat

pot *n.* لوى lokhay

pot *v.t.* پهلوىكاچول pa lokhee ki achawal

potash *n.* دپاسفلز da putas filiz

potassium *n.* دپسيمعنصر da putasyum unsar

potato *n.* الو aloo

potency *n.* لياقت،توان leeyaqat; twan

potent *a.* پياورى pyawaray

potential *a.* پياوى،زورلرونكى pyawaray; zorlaroonkay

potential *n.* زور،استعداد zor; istaydad

pontentiality *n.* پياوتيا pyawartya

potter *n.* كلال kulal

pottery *n.* كلالي kulalee

pouch *n.* كوه kasora

poultry *n.* چرګان‌ساتنه chargan satana

pounce *v.i.* په‌یوشي‌ورغورځدل pa yaw shee warghorzeydal

pounce *n* ناپه‌برید nasapa breed

pound *n.* درونډوزار droond goozar

pound *v.t.* پرله‌پسوزارونه‌ورکول parla pasi goozaroona warkawal

pour *v.i.* ورځدل wareydal

poverty *n.* تنسه tangsa

powder *n.* دوه doora

powder *v.t.* دوه‌اچول؛شیندل doora achawal; sheendal

power *n.* طاقت taqat

powerful *a.* طاقتور taqatwar

practicability *n.* عملیتوب amaleetob

practicable *a.* کارېدونکی kareydoonkay

practical *a.* عملي amalee

practice *n.* مشق،تجربه mashq; tajruba

practise *v.t.* مشق‌کول mashq kawal

practitioner *n.* وکالت‌کوونکی؛ماهر wakalat kawoonkay; mahir

pragmatic *a.* دعملي‌فلسفه‌اوند da amalee falsafey pa arwand

pragmatism *n.* عملي‌فلسفه amalee falsafa

praise *n.* تحسین tehseen

praise *v.t.* ارزول arzawal

praiseworthy *q.* د ستاینه و da stayani war

prank *n.* شرارت shararat

prattle *v.i.* زیات‌غدل zyat ghageydal

prattle *n.* بایه‌خبر bey zaya‌khabari

pray *v.i.* لمونځ‌کول lmoonz kawal

prayer *n.* لمونځ lmoonz

preach *v.i.* وعظ‌کول waaz kawal

preacher *n.* واعظ waiz

preamble *n.* دکتاب‌سریزه da keetab sareeza

precaution *n.* احتیاط ehteeyat

precautionary *a.* احتیاطي ehteeyatee

precede *v.* مخک‌کدل makhki keydal

precedence *n.* واندتوب wranditob

precedent *n.* واند wrandi

precept *n.* حکم hukam

precepter *n.* لارود larkhod

precious *a.* قیمتي qeematee

precis *n.* لنون؛غورچا landoon; ghorchanr

precise *n.* جامع jamay

precision *n.* کره‌والی karawalay

precursor *n.* منادي manadee

predecessor *n.* نیکونه‌او‌پلرونه neekoona aw plaroona

predestination *n.* سرنوت sarnawakht

predetermine *v.t.* دمخه‌بر‌خلیک‌اکل da makha barkhleek takal

predicament *n.* نامساعد‌حالت namasaid halat

predicate *n.* مسند masnad

predict *v.t.* اکل‌کول atkal kawal

prediction *n.* اکل atkal

predominance *n.* برتري bartaree

predominant *a.* برتر bartar

predominate *v.i.* برلاسی‌کدل barlasay keydal

pre-eminence *n.* غوراوی ghoraway

pre-eminent *a.* ترولوغوره tar tolo ghwara

preface *n.* سريزه sareeza

preface *v.t.* سريزهليكل sareeza leekal

prefect *n.* قوماندان qomandan

prefer *v.t.* ترجيحوركول tarjee warkawal

preference *n.* غوراوی ghoraway

preferential *a.* امتيازي imteeyazee

prefix *n.* مختای makhtaray

prefix *v.t.* پرمختایزياتول pri makhtaray zyatawal

pregnancy *n.* بلاربت blarbakht

pregnant *a.* اميدواره umeedwara

prehistoric *a.* تاريخخهمخكينی tareekh sakha makhkeenay

prejudice *n.* لهپلنپرتهقضاوتكول la palatani parta qazawat kawal

prelate *n.* خليفه khaleefa

preliminary *a.* ابتدايي ibtidayee

preliminary *n* لومی loomray

prelude *n.* مقدمه muqadima

prelude *v.t.* مقدمهچمتوكول muqadima chamtoo kawal

premarital *a.* لهوادهمخكينی la wada makhkeenay

premature *a.* نابالغ nabaligh

premeditate *v.t.* دمخهسنجول da makha sanjawal

premeditation *n.* دمخهسوچ da makha soch

premier *a.* لومنی loomranay

premier *n* مشر،رهبر mashar; rahbar

premiere *n.* مشره،رهبره mashra; rahbara

premium *n.* دبيمهپيسی da beemey peysey

premonition *n.* خبرداري khabardaree

preoccupation *n.* تصرف،دلوميتوب حق tasarruf; da loomreetob haq

preoccupy *v.t.* تصرفكول tasarruf kawal

preparation *n.* تياری tayaray

preparatory *a.* ابتدايي ibtidayee

prepare *v.t.* تيارول tayarawal

preponderance *n.* زياتوالی zyatwalay

preponderate *v.i.* زياتدل zyateydal

preposition *n.* داضافتتوری da izafat toray

prerequisite *a.* اين،شرطيه areen; sharteeya

prerequisite *n* شرطاين areen shart

prerogative *n.* رسميحق rasmee haq

prescience *n.* دغبوعلم da ghaybo ilam

prescribe *v.t.* نسخهوركول nuskha warkawal

prescription *n.* نسخه nuskha

presence *n.* موجودي mawjoodgee

present *a.* موجود mawjood

present *n.* ال dalay

present *v.t.* رسمواندكول rasman warandi kawal

presentation *n.* پژندنه peyzhandana

presently *adv.* اوسمهال os mahal

preservation *n.* خوندیینه
khwandeeyeena

preservative *n.* خوندي کوونکی
khwandee kawoonkay

preservative *a.* دخرابیدومخنیوونکی
da kharabeydo
makhneewoonkay

preserve *v.t.* خوندیساتل
khwandee satal

preserve *n.* مُرباباذانحصاريسیمه
muraba; zangari inhisaree
seema

preside *v.i.* مشريکول masharee
kawal

president *n.* ولسمشر woolas
mashr

presidential *a.* ریاستي reeyasatee

press *v.t.* زورورکول،تخته کول zor
warkawal; takhta kawal

press *n* زور،مطبوعات zor; matbooat

pressure *n.* فشار fishar

pressurize *v.t.* فشاراچول fishar
achawal

prestige *n.* آبرو abroo

prestigious *a.* دعزتپهاوند da eezat
pa arwand

presume *v.t.* مُسلمل،صحیحوومانکول
musallam ganral; sahee
gooman kawal

presumption *n.* احتمال،صحیحوومان
ehtimal; sahee gooman

presuppose *v.t.* واندخمومانکول
wrandi sakha gooman kawal

presupposition *n.* واندخمومان
wrandi sakha gooman

pretence *n.* وډنه ان zan khodana

prtend *v.t.* تظاهرکول tazahar
kawal

pretension *n.* تظاهر،بهانه tazahar;
bahana

pretentious *a.* ذانودنپوراوند zan
khodani pori arwand

pretext *n* بهانه bahana

prettiness *n.* ښکلا khkula

pretty *a* لالی gulalay

pretty *adv.* پهانداز pa kha andaz

prevail *v.i.* دودیدل doodeydal

prevalance *n.* خپراوی khparaway

prevalent *a.* دودشوی dood shaway

prevent *v.t.* مخنیویکول
makhneeway kawal

prevention *n.* مخنیوی
makhneeway

preventive *a.* مخنیوونکی
makhneewoonkay

previous *a.* پخوانی pakhwanay

prey *n.* ښکار khkar

prey *v.i.* ښکارکول khkar kawal

price *n.* بیه baya

price *v.t.* بیهموندل baya moondal

prick *n.* دسکوڼلویاربدلونه da
skoondalo ya gareydalo
nakha

prick *v.t.* سکوڼل،چوخول skoondal;
chokhawal

pride *n.* کبر kabar

pride *v.t.* کبرکول kabar kawal

priest *n.* پادري padree

priestess *n.* ینهپادري khazeena
padree

priesthood *n.* کاهنتوب،مُلاتوب
kahintob; mulatob

prima facie *adv.* پهیوهنظر pa yawa
nazar

primarily *adv.* په ابتدايي توه pa ibtidayee toga

primary *a.* ابتدايي ibtidayee

prime *a.* لومړنی؛مهم loomranay; muhim

prime *n.* اوج؛غوړه وخت oj; ghwara wakht

primer *n.* د ابکتاب da abisi keetab

primeval *a.* د ابتدايي بشريت دور da ibtidayee bashareeyat dawr

primitive *a.* لرغوني تمدن پور اوند larghonee tamaddun pori arwand

prince *n.* شاهزاده shahzada

princely *a.* د شاهزاده په شان da shahzada pa shan

princess *n.* شاهزادۍ shahzadgay

principal *n.* د ووني رئيس da khowanzee rayees

principal *a* مهم muhim

principle *n.* اصول usool

print *v.t.* چاپول chapawal

print *n* چاپ؛خپرونه chap; khparawana

printer *n.* چاپوونکی chapawoonkay

prior *a.* وانديني wrandeenay

prior *n* لوپوی راهب lwar poray rahib

prioress *n.* لوپور اهبه lwar pori rahiba

priority *n.* ترجيح tarjee

prison *n.* بنديخانه bandeekhana

prisoner *n.* بندي bandee

privacy *n.* خلوت khilwat

private *a.* خصوصي؛خپل ذاتي khasoosee; khpal zatee

privation *n.* بې برخوالی bey barkhiwalay

privilege *n.* امتياز eemteeyaz

prize *n.* انعام eenam

prize *v.t.* انعام ورکول eenam warkawal

probability *n.* احتمال ehtimal

probable *a.* شونی shoonay

probably *adv.* احتمالاً ehtimalan

probation *n.* آزمايت azmayakht

probationer *n.* تر آزمايت لاند کارمندیا زنداني tar azmayakht landi karmand ya zandanee

probe *v.t.* آزمويل azmoyal

probe *n* د جراحميله meela da jarahay

problem *n.* ستونزه stoonza

problematic *a.* ستونزمن stoonzman

procedure *n.* طريقه tareeqa

proceed *v.i.* پر مخ تلل par makh tlal

proceeding *n.* کاري بهير karee baheer

proceeds *n.* عايداتي محصول ayidatee mahsool

process *n.* کاري دوره karee dawra

procession *n.* لهيزخوت dalayeez khozakht

proclaim *v.t.* اعلانول aylanawal

proclamation *n.* بيانيه bayaneeya

proclivity *n.* په ذات باند خبيثتوب pa zat bandi khabeestob

procrastinate *v.i.* الدل taleydal

procrastination *n.* ال tal

proctor *n.* ناظر؛قانوني وکيل nazir; qanoonee wakeel

procure *v.t.* موندل moondal

procurement *n.* موندنه moondana

prodigal *a.* مُسرف musraf

prodigality *n.* بدخرﻪسی bad kharsa saray

produce *v.t.* تولیدول tawleedawal

produce *n.* تولید،حاصل tawleed; hasil

product *n.* حاصل hasil

production *n.* تولیدشوی‌مواد tawleed shaway mawad

productive *a.* تولیدي tawleedee

productivity *n.* سرشاري،تولیدي‌وتیا sar sharee; tawleedee wartya

profane *a.* بعزته،کفریه bey eezata; kufreeya

profane *v.t.* کفر کول kufar kawal

profession *n.* کسب،دنده kasab; danda

professional *a.* کسبي،ماهر kasabee; mahir

professor *n.* پوهاند pohand

proficiency *n.* مهارت maharat

proficient *a.* ماهر mahir

profile *n.* دکردار کتنه،نیمرخ‌انور da kirdar katana; neemrukh anzor

profile *v.t.* په‌مقطعي‌ول‌ودل pa maqtaee dawl khodal

profit *n.* ﻪ gata

profit *v.t.* ﻪکول gata kawal

profitable *a.* ﻨدویه gatandoya

profiteer *n.* ﻨدویي gatandoyay

profiteer *v.i.* زیاته‌ﻪکول zyata gata kawal

profligacy *n.* لوچکي loochkay

profligate *a.* لوچک loochak

profound *a.* ژورفکره،روآنده zhawar fikra; roonr anda

profundity *n.* معرفت،فکري‌ژوروالی marifat;fikree zhawarwalay

profuse *a.* سرشار sarshar

profusion *n.* سخاوت sakhawat

progeny *n.* اولاد،بای‌ناستی awlad; zay nastay

programme *n.* کاري‌پلان karee plan

programme *v.t.* کاري‌پلان‌جوول karee plan jorawal

progress *n.* جریان jaryan

progress *v.i.* جریان‌لرل jaryan laral

progressive *a.* پرمختیایي parmakhtyayee

prohibit *v.t.* بندزلول bandeyz lagawal

prohibition *n.* بندز bandeyz

prohibitive *a.* ممنوعه mamnooa

prohibitory *a.* ممنوعه mamnooa

project *n.* پروژه parozha

project *v.t.* پروژه‌جوول parozha jorawal

projectile *n.* توغول‌کدونکي‌جسم toghawal keydoonkay jisam

projectile *a* توغول‌شوی toghawal shaway

projection *n.* طرحه‌جوونه tarha jorawana

projector *n.* دسینماماشین da seenama masheen

proliferate *v.i.* زیاتدل zyateydal

proliferation *n.* زیاتدا zyateyda

prolific *a.* حاصل‌ورکوونکی hasil warkawoonkay

prologue *n.* سریزه sareeza

prolong *v.t.* اودول oogdawal

prolongation *n.* اودوالى oogadwalay

prominence *n.* نوميالیتوب noomyaleetob

prominent *a.* وتلى او برجسته watalay aw barjasta

promise *n* وعده wada

promise *v.t* وعده کول wada kawal

promising *a.* امیدبونکى umeed bakhoonkay

promissory *a.* د اقرار da iqrar

promote *v.t.* پرمخ بيول par makh beywal

promotion *n.* وده wada

prompt *a.* فوري fawree

prompt *v.t.* په فعالیت راوستل pa faaleeyat rawastal

prompter *n.* پراختیاور کوونکى parakhtya warkawoonkay

prone *a.* مستعد mustaid

pronoun *n.* نومری noomzaray

pronounce *v.t.* تلفظ کول talaffuz kawal

pronunciation *n.* تلفظ talaffuz

proof *n.* دليل daleel

proof *a* له زيان خه خوندي la zyan sakha khwandee

prop *n.* ستنه،ملاتی stana; mlataráy

prop *v.t.* ملاتړ کول mlatar kawal

propaganda *n.* تبليغات tableeghat

propagandist *n.* آواز خپروونکى awazey khparawoonkay

propagate *v.t.* تبليغول tableeghawal

propagation *n.* انتشار،تبليغ intishar; tableegh

propel *v.t.* په حرکت راوستل pa harakat rawastal

proper *a.* مناسب munasib

property *n.* جايداد jaydad

prophecy *n.* نبوت naboowat

prophesy *v.t.* پغمبري کول peyghambaree kawal

prophet *n.* نبي nabee

prophetic *a.* نبوي nabawee

proportion *n.* تناسب tanasub

proportion *v.t.* متناسب کول mutanasib kawal

proportional *a.* متناسب mutanasib

proportionate *a.* متناسب mutanasib

proposal *n.* تجويز tajweez

propose *v.t.* تجويزورکول tajweez warkawal

proposition *n.* سکاله،پشنهاد skala; payshnihad

propound *v.t.* مطرح کول matrah kawal

proprietary *a.* اختصاصي،ملکيتي ikhtisasee; malkeeyatee

proprietor *n.* مالک malik

propriety *n.* خصوصي مالکيت khasoosee malkeeyat

prorogue *v.t.* زندول zandawal

prosaic *a.* بي خونده bey khwanda

prose *n.* نثر nasar

prosecute *v.t.* په قانوني پلوه تعقيبول pa qanoonee palwa taqeebawal

prosecution *n.* تعقيب قانوني qanoonee taqeeb

prosecutor *n.* قانوني وکيل qanoonee wakeel

172

prosody *n.* دعروضوعلم da aroozo
ilam
prospect *n.* لرليد،قيافه larleed;
qyafa
prospective *a.* پهراتلونكيپوراوند pa
ratloonkee pori arwand
prospectus *n.* خبرپاه khabar panra
prosper *v.i.* كاميابدل kamyabeydal
prosperity *n.* خوشحالي khoshhalee
prosperous *a.* موفق،خوشحاله
muwafaq; khoshhala
prostitute *n.* فاحشانسان fahish
insan
prostitute *v.t.* پيسولپارهزناكول peyso
lapara zana kawal
prostitution *n.* بدلمني bad
lamanee
prostrate *a.* پهمكهپروت pa zmaka
prot
prostrate *v.t.* سجدهكول sajeeda
kawal
prostration *n.* سجده،فرمانبرداري
sajeeda; farmanbardaree
protagonist *n.* سردنه sar danga
protect *v.t.* ژغورل zhghoral
protection *n.* ژغورنه zhghorana
protective *a.* ژغورندوى
zhghorandoy
protector *n.* ژغورونكى
zhghoroonkay
protein *n.* پروتين proteen
protest *n.* شكايت shikayat
protest *v.i.* شكايتكول shikayat
kawal
protestation *n.* شكايت،رندهناخوي
shikayat; sarganda
nakhwakhee

prototype *n.* اصلينمونه aslee
namoona
proud *a.* ځانوډى zankhoday
prove *v.t.* ثابتول sabitawal
proverb *n.* متل،زرينهوينا matal;
zareena wayna
proverbial *a.* دمتلپهاوند da matal
pa arwand
provide *v.i.* ورتهبرابرول warta
barabarawal
providence *n.* دخدایقدرت da
khuday qudrat
province *n.* ولايت wilayat
provincial *a.* ولايتي wilayatee
provincialism *n.* پهولايتاوونه pa
wilayat arawana
provision *n.* تياري،مقرراتاكل
tayaree; muqarrarat takal
provisional *a.* لنمهاليبندوبست land
mahalee bandobast
proviso *n.* شرط shart
provocation *n.* لمسوونه
lamsawana
provocative *a.* لمسوونكى
lamsawoonkay
provoke *v.t.* تحريكول tahreekawal
prowess *n.* لياقت leeyaqat
proximate *a.* نژدې nazhdey
proximity *n.* نژدوالى
nazhdeywalay
proxy *n.* نماينده numayinda
prude *n.* محتاطانسان muhtat insan
prudence *n.* احتياط ehteeyat
prudent *a.* محتاط muhtat
prudential *a.* محتاط muhtat
prune *v.t.* سينارول seengarawal

pry *v.i.* په‌دقت‌سره‌پلل pa diqat sara palatal

psalm *n.* زبور zaboor

pseudonym *n.* تخلص takhallus

psyche *n.* فکر،اروا fikar; arwa

psychiatrist *n.* داروااييزونارو‌غيواکر da arwayeezo naroghyo daktar

psychiatry *n.* ارواييزطبابت arwayeez tababat

psychic *a.* روحي roohee

psychological *a.* ارواپوهنيز arwa pohaneez

psychologist *n.* پوه اروا arwa poh

psychology *n.* ارواپوهنه arwa pohana

psychopath *n.* ارواييزنارو‌غ arwayeez narogh

psychosis *n.* لونتوب leywantob

psychotherapy *n.* روحي‌تداوي roohee tadawee

puberty *n.* بلوغت baloghat

public *a.* ملي،عمومي milee; amoomee

public *n.* ولس woolas

publication *n.* نشر،خپراوی nashar; khparaway

publicity *n.* تبليغات tableeghat

publicize *v.t.* عام‌خلک‌پر‌خبرول am khalk pri khabrawal

publish *v.t.* نشرول nashrawal

publisher *n.* خپرندوی khparandoy

pudding *n.* يوول‌غوين‌ساس yaw dawl ghwakheen sas

puddle *n.* دبدرفت‌ساه da badraft sah

puddle *v.t.* خو‌کلو‌دل khato ki lweydal

puerile *a.* ماشومانه mashoomana

puff *n.* پف،دخولادهوااواز paf; da khuley da hawa awaz

puff *v.i.* دپف‌اوازخولنه‌وتل da paf awaz khuley na watal

pull *v.t.* کول

pull *n.* کوونه

pulley *n.* خ رخ sarkh

pullover *n.* يوول‌جاک yaw dawl jakat

Shankar *n.* دمو‌غونه‌برخه da meywey ghwakhana barkha

pulp *v.t.* غوین‌کدل ghwakhan keydal

pulpit *a.* دریٔ،منبر dareez; mimbar

pulpy *a.* غوین ghwakhan

pulsate *v.i.* لزدل larzeydal

pulsation *n.* رددا reygdeyda

pulse *n.* نبض nabaz

pulse *v.i.* درزدل drazeydal

pulse *n* رددا reygdeyda

pump *n.* داوبوراستنه‌ماشين da obo raeystani masheen

pump *v.t.* دپمپ‌په‌وسيله‌راستل da pamp pa waseela raeystal

pumpkin *n.* کدو kadoo

pun *n.* دلفظونو‌لوب da lafzoono lobey

pun *v.i.* دلفظونو‌لوب‌کول da lafzoono lobey kawal

punch *n.* دسوک‌وزار da sook goozar

punch *v.t.* په‌سوک‌وهل pa sook wahal

punctual *a.* پروخت،دوخت‌پابند par wakht; da wakht paband

punctuality *n.* وخت‌پژندنه wakht peyzhandana

punctuate *v.t.* کی او نقطې ايودل takee aw nuqtey eekhodal

punctuation *n.* نقطې ايودنه nuqtey eekhodana

puncture *n.* سوری،شلدلی sooray; shleydalay

puncture *v.t.* سوری کدل،شلدل sooray keydal; shleydal

pungency *n.* تريخوالی treekhwalay

pungent *a.* تريخ treekh

punish *v.t.* سزا ورکول saza warkawal

punishment *n.* سزا saza

punitive *a.* سزايی sazayee

puny *a.* لنډی يا کوچنی landay ya koochnay

pupil *n.* زده کوونکی zda kawoonkay

puppet *n.* لاسپوی،ای lasposay; goodagay

puppy *n.* دسپي‌بچی da spee bachay

purblind *n.* کاملاوند kamilan roond

purchase *n.* پرودنه peyrodana

purchase *v.t.* پرودل peyrodal

pure *a* سوچه soocha

purgation *n.* چاوونه،سپينوونه chanrowana; speenawana

purgative *n.* داماله‌درمل da imaley darmal

purgative *a* مُسهل،پاکوونکی mushal; pakowoonkay

purgatory *n.* ن برزخي barzakhee naray

purge *v.t.* پاکول،اماله‌کول pakawal; imala kawal

purification *n.* وينزنه weenzana

purify *v.t.* پاکول pakawal

purist *n.* سوچه‌والی‌غوتونکی soochawalay ghokhtoonkay

puritan *n.* اخلاقي‌اصيلوالی‌غوتونکی شخص akhlaqee aseelwalay ghokhtoonkay shakhs

purity *n.* سوچه‌والی soochawalay

purple *adj./n.* ن ارغواني،ارغواني‌رنگ arghawanee; arghawanee rang

purport *n.* مفهوم،مانا mafhoom; mana

purport *v.t.* مفهومي‌کول mafhoomee kawal

purpose *n.* موخه،هدف mokha; hadaf

purpose *v.t.* هودلرل hod laral

purposely *adv.* په‌هومن‌ول pa hodman dawl

purr *n.* دپيشوغ‌غر da peesho ghur ghur

purr *v.i.* دپيشوغ‌دل da peesho ghureydal

purse *n.* دپيسو‌کوه da peyso kasora

purse *v.t.* راورل،جب‌وهل rageyrawal; jeyb wahal

pursuance *n.* پس‌کدنه pasi keydana

pursue *v.t.* پس‌کدل pasi keydal

pursuit *n.* پس‌کدنه pasi keydana

purview *n.* بريدونه‌او‌حدود breedoona aw hadood

pus *n.* چرک،زوه chark; zoh

push *v.t.* ټیله‌کول teyla kawal

push *n.* ټیله،کو teyla; kokhakh

put *v.t.* ايودل eekhodal

puzzle *n.* ستوب gangastob

puzzle *v.t.* نس کول gangas kawal

pygmy *n.* لوشتینک،انسان lweyshteenak insan

pyorrhoea *n.* دغاچرک da ghakh chark

pyramid *n.* مصري‌هرم misree haram

pyre *n.* دمي‌سوونلپاره‌دلریوازکوه da maree sozawani lapara da largyo zangari kota

python *n.* لوی‌امار loy khamar

Q

quack *v.i.* دهیلاغدل da heelay ghageydal

quack *n* دهیاغ da heelay ghag

quackery *n.* چلبازي chalbazee

quadrangle *n.* وی لور salor gotay

quadrangular *a.* لوروییز salor goteez

quadrilateral *a. & n.* پملورویپور اوند pa salor gotee pori arwand

quadruped *n.* ساروی،لورپلرونکی sarway; salor pkhey laroonkay

quadruple *a.* لوربرخیز salor barkheez

quadruple *v.t.* لورغبره کول salor ghbarga kawal

quail *n.* مز؛کرک maraz; krak

quaint *a.* پوه؛عاقل poh; aqil

quake *v.i.* لزدل larzeydal

quake *n* لزدنه larzeydana

qualification *n.* صلاحیت،تعلیم salaheeyat; taleem

qualify *v.i.* ورملدل،رتبه‌موندل war garzeydal; rutba moondal

qualitative *a.* رنیز srangeez

quality *n.* رنوالی،معیار srangwalay; mayar

quandary *n.* سرردانی sargardanee

quantitative *a.* ومره‌ییز somrayeez

quantity *n.* ومره‌والی somrawalay

quantum *n.* کچ؛مقدار kach; miqdar

quarrel *n.* شخړه shkhara

quarrel *v.i.* جنجال کول janjal kawal

quarrelsome *a.* جنجالي janjalee

quarry *n.* ككارشوی‌ناوریاانسان khkar shaway zanawar ya insan

quarry *v.i.* کاني‌بررایستل kanree dabari raistal

quarter *n.* لورمه salorama

quarter *v.t.* پملوروبرخووشل pa saloro barkho weyshal

quarterly *a.* لورمیاشتنی salor myashtanay

queen *n.* ملکه malika

queer *a.* عجیب ajeeb

quell *v.t.* آرامول aramawal

quench *v.t.* آرامول،مول aramawal; marawal

query *n.* پوتنروز pokhtani garweygni

query *v.t* ترپوتنلاندنیول tar pokhtani landi neewal

quest *n.* کو kokhakh

quest *v.t.* کوکول kokhakh kawal

question *n.* سوال؛پوښتنه sawal; pokhtana

question *v.t.* پوښتل pokhtal

questionable *a.* د و پوښتنه da pokhtani war

questionnaire *n.* پوښتنليک pokhtanleek

queue *n.* کتار،لیکه katar; leeka

quibble *n.* کنایه kinaya

quibble *v.i.* ابهامویل ibham wayal

quick *a.* چک chatak

quick *n* هاند hasand

quicksand *n.* خوندهاووینده شه khozanda aw khwayanda shaga

quicksilver *n.* سیماب seemab

quiet *a.* ساکن؛غلی ghalay; sakin

quiet *n.* چوپتیا choptya

quiet *v.t.* آرامول aramawal

quilt *n.* بالاپو balapokh

quinine *n.* د کونینبوټی da koneen bootay

quintessence *n.* د وجودپنمعنصر da wajood peenzam unsar

quit *v.t.* لاس ورخه اخستل las warsakha akheystal

quite *adv.* پهرتینیول pa rakhteenee dawl

quiver *n.* لزه larza

quiver *v.i.* لزدل larzeydal

quixotic *a.* خیالپرسته khyal parasta

quiz *n.* لنهآزموینه landa azmoyana

quiz *v.t.* آزموینهکول azmoyana kawal

quorum *n.* نصاب nisab

quota *n.* برخه barkha

quotation *n.* اقتباس؛بیان iqtibas; bayan

quote *v.t.* رانقلول ranaqlawal

quotient *n.* خارجقسمت kharij qismat

R

rabbit *n.* سویه soya

rabies *n.* د لوني سپي ناروغي da leywanee spee naroghee

race *n.* سیالي؛دمنمسابقه syalee; da mandi musabiqa

race *v.i* دمنمسابقهکول da mandi musabiqa kawal

racial *a.* توکمیز؛نژادي tokmeez; nazhadee

racialism *n.* توکمپالنه tokampalana

rack *v.t.* شکنجهکول shkanja kawal

rack *n.* طاقچه taqcha

racket *n.* ښنس teynas

radiance *n.* نورانیت nooraneeyat

radiant *a.* نوراني nooranee

radiate *v.t.* لدل zaleydal

radiation *n.* لا zala

radical *a.* بنسیزسمونپال bansateez samoonpal

radio *n.* رایو radeeyo

radio *v.t.* پهرایوخپرول pa radeeyo khparawal

radish *n.* مول moolay

radium *m.* یورایواکتیفاوتشعشعي عنصر yaw radyoekteef aw tashashee unsar

radius *n.* دقطرنيمايي da qutar neemayee

rag *n.* دزوو كروه da zor tokar tota

rag *v.t.* زوو كرپوندول zor tokar peywandawal

rage *n.* غصه ghusa

rage *v.i.* غصهناك كدل ghusanak keydal

raid *n.* يرغل yarghal

raid *v.t.* يرغل كول yarghal kawal

rail *n.* اورای orgaday

rail *v.t.* داوسپنپلاغول da ospani patlay ghazawal

railing *n.* كاره katara

raillery *n.* مسخر maskharey

railway *n.* داوراي كره da orgadee karkha

rain *v.i.* اورتوريدل orakht wareydal

rain *n* اورت orakht

rainy *a.* باراني baranee

raise *v.t.* پورته كول porta kawal

raisin *n.* مويز maweez

rally *v.t.* لهييزهغونهراولول dalayeeza ghonda ratolawal

rally *n* لهييزهغونه dalayeeza ghonda

ram *n.* مغ؛وری mag; wray

ram *v.t.* پهسختسرهوهل pa sakhtay sara wahal

ramble *v.t.* سروردان كول sargardan kawal

ramble *n* سروداني sargardanee

rampage *v.i.* لونتوب كول leywantob

rampage *n.* غالمغالي ghalmaghalee

rampant *a.* خپورشوی؛پراخ khpor shaway; parakh

rampart *n.* دخاوروواوشوحفاظتي دوال da khawro aw shago hifazatee deywal

rancour *n.* كينه keena

random *a.* بترتيبه bey tarteeba

range *v.t.* ترتيبول tarteebawal

range *n.* لړ؛ترتيب laray; tarteeb

ranger *n.* ترتيبوونكي؛ساتندوی tarteebawoonkay; satandoy

rank *n.* مقام؛پو maqam; poray

rank *v.t.* مقاملرل maqam laral

rank *a* ژرستردونكی zhar stareydoonkay

ransack *v.t.* مالونهلول maloona lootal

ransom *n.* دتاوانپس da tawan peysey

ransom *v.t.* تاواناخستل tawan akheystal

rape *n.* دزورزياتيزنا da zor zyatee zana

rape *v.t.* پهزورزناكول pa zor zana kawal

rapid *a.* تز teyz

rapidity *n.* چكتيا chataktya

rapier *n.* يوولنرسپكهتوره yaw dawl naray spaka toora

rapport *n.* موافقايك mawafiqi areeki

rapt *a.* غلاشوی ghla shaway

rapture *n.* وجد wajad

rare *a.* ناياب nayab

rascal *n.* دوكهماراوبحيا dokamar aw bey haya

rash *a.* بپامه bey pama

rat *n.* موك mogak

rate *v.t.* بيهايودل baya eekhodal

rate *n.* نرخ؛شرح narkh; sharah

rather *adv.* مخكله؛البته makhki la; albata

ratify *v.t.* تصويبول tasweebawal

ratio *n.* نسبت؛شرح nisbat; sharah

ration *n.* دخواوكلونه da khwaro takali wanda

rational *a.* پەدلايلورلا pa dalayalo walar

rationale *n.* آراوبنست ar aw bansat

rationality *n.* اصوليت؛عقلانيت usooleeyat; aqlaneeyat

rationalize *v.t.* منطقيبەوركول mantaqee banra warkawal

rattle *v.i.* پەلوغويل pa lwar ghag wayal

rattle *n* دتقتقغ da traq traq ghag

ravage *n.* لوتالان loot talan

ravage *v.t.* لولل؛تالاكول lootal; tala kawal

rave *v.i.* پەغصەكدل pa ghusa keydal

raven *n.* توركارغه tor kargha

ravine *n.* اودەژورەدره oogda zhawara dara

raw *a.* خام kham

ray *n.* وانه waranga

raze *v.t.* ويجاول weejarawal

razor *n.* پل؛نرڅاه pal; naray chara

reach *v.t.* رسدل raseydal

react *v.i.* غبرونوول ghbargoon khowal

reaction *n.* غبرون ghbargoon

reactionary *a.* پرشاتى؛مخالف par sha tagay; mukhalif

... *v.t.* لوستل lostal

... *n.* لوستونكى lostoonkay

readily *adv.* پەآسانتياسره pa asantya sara

readiness *n.* چمتووالى chamtoowalay

ready *a.* چمتو chamtoo

real *a.* حقيقي haqeeqee

realism *n.* رتياپاله rakhtyapala

realist *n.* رتياپال rakhtyapal

realistic a. حقيقي haqeeqee

reality *n.* حقيقت haqeeqat

realization *n.* ادراک idrak

realize *v.t.* درککول darak kawal

really *adv.* پەرتينيول pa rakhteenee dawl

realm *a.* سلطنت saltanat

ream *n.* د۵۰۰كاغذونوبنل da peenzo sawo kaghazoonu bandal

reap *v.t.* ربل reybal

reaper *n.* لورى؛دلوماشين lawgaree; da law masheen

rear *n.* وروستەبرخه wrostanay barkha

rear *v.t.* روزل؛تربيەوركول rozal; tarbeeya warkawal

reason *n.* سبب؛دليل sabab; daleel

reason *v.i.* دليلواندکول daleel wrandi kawal

reasonable *a.* معقول maqool

reassure *v.t.* بياتسلوركول bya tasal warkawal

rabate *n.* كمت kamakht

rebel *v.i.* سرغاويكول sar gharaway kawal

rebel *n.* سرغاوى sar gharaway

rebellion *n.* بغاوت baghawat

rebellious *a.* باغيانه baghyana

rebirth *n.* بيازون bya zeygoon

rebound *v.i.* برتەراستدل beyrta rastaneydal

rebound *n.* پرشاتب؛برتەرلدنه par shatag; beyrta garzeydana

rebuff *n.* منع؛ردونه mana; radawana

rebuff *v.t.* منع كول mana kawal

rebuke *v.t.* ملامتول malamatawal

rebuke *n.* ملامتيا malamatya

recall *v.t.* برتەراغوتل beyrta raghokhtal

recall *n.* پەيادراوستنه pa yad rawastana

recede *v.i.* پەشاكدل pa sha keydal

receipt *n.* رسيد raseed

receive *v.t.* ترلاسه كول tar lasa kawal

receiver *n.* ترلاسه كوونكى tar lasa kawoonkay

recent *a.* تازه؛نوى taza; naway

recently *adv.* لوخت مخكا lag wakht makhki

reception *n.* هەراغلى؛هر كلى kha raghalay; har kalay

receptive *a.* منونكى؛درك كوونكى manoonkay; darak kawoonkay

recess *n.* وقفه waqfa

recession *n.* پەشاتلنه pa sha tlana

recipe *n.* نسخه؛فورمول nuskha; formool

recipient *n.* اخستونكى akheystoonkay

reciprocal *a.* متقابل؛متناوب mutaqabal; mutanawab

reciprocate *v.t.* متقابل عمل كول mutaqabal amal kawal

recital *n.* راپور؛مفصل بيان rapor; mufassil bayan

recitation *n.* لەيادەلوستل la yada lostal

recite *v.t.* لەيادەويل la yada wayal

reckless *a.* بى پروا bey parwa

reckon *v.t.* شمرل؛اندازەلول shmeyral; andaza lagawal

reclaim *v.t.* بيارستندل bya rastaneydal

reclamation *n* بيارستندنه؛مكسمون bya rastaneydana; zmaksamoon

recluse *n.* يوازانسان yawazi insan

recognition *n.* پژندنه peyzhandana

recognize *v.t.* تصديق كول tasdeeq kawal

recoil *v.i.* پەشاتلل؛منعكس كدل pa sha tlal; munakkis keydal

recoil *adv.* پەشاتگ pa shatag

recollect *v.t.* دوباره راغونول dobara raghondawal

recollection *n.* پەيادراوستنه pa yad rawastana

recommend *v.t.* سپارتنه ورته كول sparakhtana warta kawal

recommendation *n.* سپارتنه؛توصيه sparakhtana; tawseeya

recompense *v.t.* حساب سپينول heesab speenawal

recompense *n.* تاوان؛عوض tawan; awaz

reconcile *v.t.* سره پخلا كول sara pukhla kawal

reconciliation *n.* پخلاينه pukhlayana

record *v.t.* ثبتول؛پەيادراوستل sabtawal; pa yad rawastal

record *n.* ثبت،یادت sabt; yadakht

recorder *n.* ثبتوونکی sabtawoonkay

recount *v.t.* له‌سره‌شمرل la sara shmeyral

recoup *v.t.* جبرانول jibranawal

recourse *n.* مراجعه murajia

recover *v.t.* برته‌ترلاسه‌کول beyrta tar lasa kawal

recovery *n.* تلافي talafee

recreation *n.* تفریح tafree

recruit *n.* نوی‌عسکر naway askar

recruit *v.t.* تازه‌انتخابول taza intikhabawal

rectangle *n.* مستطیل mustateel

rectangular *a.* مستطیل‌شکل‌لرونکی mustateel shakal laroonkay

rectification *n.* اصلاح؛سموونکی isla; samowoonkay

rectify *v.i.* اصلاح‌کول isla kawal

rectum *n.* دکولمای‌اخري‌برخه da koolmey akhiree barkha

recur *v.i.* ستندل staneydal

recurrence *n.* ستندنه staneydana

recurrent *a.* ستندونکی staneydoonkay

red *a.* سور soor

red *n.* رنگ سور soor rang

redden *v.t.* سورکول soor kawal

reddish *a.* سوربخن soorbakhan

redeem *v.t.* لاله‌روخه‌خلاصول la garway sakha khlasawal

redemption *n.* لاله‌روخه‌خلاصون la garway sakha khlasoon

redouble *v.t.* دوه‌چنده‌کول dwa chanda kawal

redress *v.t.* تداوي‌کول tadawee kawal

redress *n.* تداوي،تلافي tadawee; talafee

reduce *v.t.* کمول kamawal

reduction *n.* کمی kamay

redundance *n.* نه‌استعمال‌دا na istimaleyda

redundant *a.* بی کاره bey kara

reel *n.* رخ،دعکاس‌دفیلم‌رخ sarkh; da akasay da feelam sarkh

reel *v.i.* رخدل sarkheydal

refer *v.t.* مراجعه‌کول،برته‌کتنه‌کول murajia kawal; beyrta katana kawal

referee *n.* لوباری lobsaray

reference *n.* ورتلنه wartlana

referendum *n.* ولپوختنه tolpokhtana

refine *v.t.* تزکیه‌کول tazkeeya kawal

refinement *n.* تزکیه tazkeeya

refinery *n.* چلای chanrzay

reflect *v.t.* منعکس‌کول munakis kawal

reflection *n.* انعکاس inikas

reflective *a.* انعکاسي inikasee

reflector *n.* منعکس‌جسم munakis jisam

reflex *n.* انعکاس inikas

reflex *a* منعکس‌شوی munakis shaway

reflexive *a* معکوس،معکوس‌فعل makoos; makoos fayl

reform *v.t.* سمونتیارامنته‌کول samoontya ramanz ta kawal

reform *n.* سمونتیا samoontya

reformation *n.* اصلاح isla

reformatory *n.* اصلاح کوونکی isla kawoonkay

reformatory *a* اصلاح کوونکی isla kawoonkay

reformer *n.* سمونپال samoonpal

refrain *v.i.* اجتناب کول ijtinab kawal

refrain *n* اجتناب ijtinab

refresh *v.t.* تازه کول taza kawal

refreshment *n.* تازه کونه taza kawana

refrigerate *v.t.* ساتل یخ yakh satal

refrigeration *n.* یخ او تازه ساتنه yakh aw taza satana

refrigerator *n.* یخچال yakhchal

refuge *n.* پناه؛ کوالتوب pana; kadwaltob

refugee *n.* پناه غوتونکی pana ghokhtoonkay

refulgence *n.* بریدنه breykheydana

refulgent *a.* پرکند parkand

refund *v.t.* حساب برته ورکول heesab beyrta warkawal

refund *n.* برته اداشوی حساب beyrta ada shaway heesab

refusal *n.* مننه نه na manana

refuse *v.t.* ردول radawal

refuse *n.* رد؛انکار rad; inkar

refutation *n.* نه مننه na manana

refute *v.t.* ردول radawal

regal *a.* پاچاهي pachahee

regard *v.t.* رعایت کول؛احترام کول riayat kawal; ehtiram kawal

regard *n.* رعایت؛احترام riayat; ehtiram

regenerate *v.t.* بیاتولیدول؛بیازدل bya tawleedawal; bya zeygeydal

regeneration *n.* نوی تولید naway tawleed

regicide *n.* پاچاوژونکی pacha wazhoonkay

regime *n.* حکومتي نظام hukoomatee nizam

regiment *n.* غن؛دحکومت واکمني ghwand; da hukoomat wakmanee

regiment *v.t.* اداره کول؛په وغنونو وشل idara kawal; pa so ghwandoono weyshal

region *n.* ناحیه naheeya

regional *a.* سیمه ییز seemayeez

register *n.* دثبت دفتر da sabt daftar

register *v.t.* په دفتر کثیتول pa daftar ki sabtawal

registrar *n.* ثبتونکی sabtawoonkay

registration *n.* نوم لیکنه noom leekana

registry *n.* دلاسوندونو دثبت اداره da laswandoono da sabt idara

regret *v.i.* خپان کول khapgan kawal

regret *n* خپان؛پماني khapgan; pkheymanee

regular *a.* منظم munazzam

regularity *n.* قاعده؛تنظیم qayda; tanzeem

regulate *v.t.* لا له قانون سره برابرول la qanoon sara barabarawal

regulation *n.* تنظیم tanzeem

regulator *n.* برابروونکی barabarawoonkay

rehabilitate v.t. بیاودانول bya wadanawal

rehabilitation n. بیاودانتیا bya wadantya

rehearsal n. تکرار،تمرین takrar; tamreen

rehearse v.t. تمرین کول tamreen kawal

reign v.i. حکومت کول hukoomat kawal

reign n پاچاهي دوره pachahee dawra

reimburse v.t. برتەورکول beyrta warkawal

rein n. وا wagi

rein v.t. مخەیرارول makha yi ragarzawal

reinforce v.t. واکوربل zwak warbakhal

reinforcement n. وربنه واک zwak warbakhana

reinstate v.t. لومني مقامتەستنول loomranee maqam ta stanawal

reinstatement n. بحالي،برتەمارنه bahalee; beyrta gumarana

reiterate v.t. یوکارتکرارول yaw kar takrarawal

reiteration n. دکارتکرار da kar takrar

reject v.t. ردول radawal

rejection n. ردوونه radawana

rejoice v.i. خوشالدل khoshaleydal

rejoin v.t. دوبارەیوکدل dobara yaw keydal

rejoinder n. دفاعي واب difaee zawab

rejuvenate v.t. دوبارەموانول dobara zwanawal

rejuvenation n. نووانی nawi zwanee

relapse v.i. زوحالتتەستندل zor halat ta staneydal

relapse n. برتەستندنه beyrta staneydana

relate v.t. ارتباطلرل irtibat laral

relation n. ارتباط،نسبت irtibat; nisbat

relative a. مربوط marboot

relative n. خپلوان khpalwan

relax v.t. دمەکول dama kawal

relaxation n. دمه،ارام dama; aram

relay n. دمەکوونکی dama kawoonkay

relay v.t. پماکلیوختدمەکول pa takalee wakht dama kawal

release v.t. پرودل preykhodal

release n پرودنه preykhodana

relent v.i. نرمدل narmeydal

relentless a. سختزی sakht zaray

relevance n. مناسبت munasibat

relevant a. مطابق،اوند mutabiq; arwand

reliable a. باوري bawaree

reliance n. توکل tawkal

relic n. لرغوني آثار larghonee asar

relief n. آرام aram

relieve v.t. آراموربل aram warbakhal

religion n. دین deen

religious a. دیني deenee

relinquish v.t. خوشی کول khoshay kawal

relish v.t. خونداخستل khwand akheystal

relish n خوند،ذوق zoq; khwand

reluctance n. ناخوي nakhwakhee

reluctant a. زتورى zratoray

rely v.i. لرل ا dad laral

remain v.i. پاته کدل pata keydal

remainder n. پاتهشوى pata shaway

remains n. پاتهشوي،مي pata shawee; maree

remand v.t. دوبارهزندانتهاستول dobara zandan ta astawal

remand n بيانيوونه bya neewana

remark n. پام،يادوونه pam; yadawana

remark v.t. پامورته کول،نظرورکول pam warta kawal; nazar warkawal

remarkable a. پهزهپور pa zra pori

remedial a. درملنه کوونکى darmalana kawoonkay

remedy n. علاج ilaj

remedy v.t شفاوربل shafa warbakhal

remember v.t. پهيادراوستل pa yad rawastal

remembrance n. حافظه hafiza

remind v.t. ورپهيادول warpayadawal

reminder n. پهيادراوستونکى pa yad rawastoonkay

reminiscence n. خاطره،يادار khatira; yadgar

reminiscent a. تذکري tazkiree

remission n. معافيت maafeeyat

remit v.t. معافول،تخفيفول maafawal; takhfeefawal

remittance n. پساستوونه peysey astawana

remorse n. افسوس afsos

remote a. لرى leyri

removable a. دلر کدنو da leyri keydani war

removal n. لهمنهوونه la manza wrana

remove v.t. لمايهپورته کول la zaya porta kawal

remunerate v.t. تاوانورکول tawan warkawal

remuneration n. تاوانورکوونه tawan warkawana

remunerative a. پهجبرانپوراوند pa jibran pori arwand

renaissance n. ادبياوفرهنينوت adabee aw farhangee nawakht

render v.t. سهولتورکول،تحويلول sahoolat warkawal; tahweelawal

rendezvous n. ملاقاتاوخبراتر mulaqat aw khabari atari

renew v.t. تازه کول taza kawal

renewal n. تازه کوونه taza kawana

renounce v.t. انکارکول inkar kawal

renovate v.t. لهنويسرهرغول nawee sara raghawal

renovation n. سموونه samawana

renown n. شهرت shohrat

renowned a. مشهور mashahoor

rent n. کرايه karaya

rent v.t. کرايه کول karaya kawal

renunciation n. پروونه،لاستراخستنه preykhowana; las tri akheystana

repair v.t. تعميرول tameerawal

repair *n.* رغوونه raghawana

raparable *a.* دتعميرلدوو da
tameereydo war

repartee *n.* حاضروابي hazir
zawabee

repatriate *v.t.* خپل هوادته برته راولدل
khpal haywad ta beyrta
ragarzeydal

repatriate *n.* خپل هوادته برته ستندونكى
khpal haywad ta
staneydoonkay

repatriation *n.* خپل هوادته برته استندنه
khpal haywad ta beyrta
staneydana

repay *v.t.* لهسره اداكول la sara ada
kawal

repayment *n.* لهسره ادايي la sara
adaygee

repeal *v.t.* نهمنل،لغوه كول na manal;
lughwa kawal

repeal *n* نهمننه na manana

repeat *v.t.* خبرهيالوست تكرارول
khabara ya lost takrarawal

repel *v.t.* پهشاتمبول pa sha
tambawal

repellent *a.* مخنيوونكى
makhneewoonkay

repellent *n* شونكى sharoonkay

repent *v.i.* پماندل pkheymaneydal

repentance *n.* پماني pkheymanee

repentant *a.* ار توبه tobagar

repercussion *n.* مخنيوى او وقايه
makhneeway aw waqaya

repetition *n.* تكرار takrar

replace *v.t.* ای نيول zay neewal

replacement *n.* ای نيوونه،تعويض zay
neewana; taweez

replenish *v.t.* لهسرهزرمه كول la sara
zeyrma kawal

replete *a.* ترزرموك tar zeyrmo
dak

replica *n.* نسخه،نقل nuskha; naqal

reply *v.i.* واب ور كول zawab
warkawal

reply *n* واب،دفا ع zawab; difa

report *v.t.* راپرور كول rapor
warkawal

report *n.* راپور؛خبر rapor; khabar

reporter *n.* خبريال khabaryal

repose *n.* استراحت istirahat

repose *v.i.* استراحت كول istirahat
kawal

repository *n.* زرمتون zeyramtoon

represent *v.t.* بيانول bayanawal

representation *n.* معرفي كوونه
marifee kawana

representative *n.* نماينده
numayanda

representative *a.* نماينلي كوونكى
numayindagee kawoonkay

repress *v.t.* پهشاتمبول pa sha
tambawal

repression *n.* جلويري jilogeeree

reprimand *n.* رنه ratana

reprimand *v.t.* رل ratal

reprint *v.t.* بياچاپول bya chapawal

reprint *n.* دوباره چاپ dobara chap

reproach *v.t.* شرمول؛رسواكول
sharmawal; ruswa kawal

reproach *n.* ملامتي malamatee

reproduce *v.t.* بياتوليدول bya
tawleedawal

reproduction *n* بياتوليدوونه bya
tawleedawana

185

reproductive *a.* زوونکی zeygowoonkay

reproof *n.* غندنه ghandana

reptile *n.* رمکه sarmakhkay

republic *n.* جمهوري jamhooree

republican *a.* ولسپاله woolaspala

republican *n.* ولسپال woolaspal

repudiate *v.t.* انکارکول inkar kawal

repudiation *n.* انکار inkar

repugnance *n.* نفرت nafrat

repugnant *a.* مخالف mukhalif

repulse *v.t.* دفع کول dafa kawal

repulse *n.* تمبوونه tambawana

repulsion *n.* تمبوونه tambawana

repulsive *a.* تمبوونکی tambawoonkay

reputation *n.* هنوم،اعتبار kha noom; aytibar

repute *v.t.* هنوملرل kha noom laral

repute *n.* آبرو abroo

request *v.t.* تقاضاکول taqaza kawal

request *n* تقاضا taqaza

requiem *n.* دجنازلمونز da janazey lmoonz

require *v.t.* اتیاورتهلرل artya warta laral

requirement *n.* شرط،اتیا shart; artya

requisite *a.* اینشرط areen shart

requiste *n* احتیاج ehteeyaj

requisition *n.* مصادره masadira

requisition *v.t.* مصادرهکول masadira kawal

requite *v.t.* بدلهورکول badla warkawal

rescue *v.t.* نجاتورکول nijat warkawal

rescue *n* نجات،خلاصون nijat; khlasoon

research *v.i.* شنلاوسپل shanal aw sparal

research *n* شننداوسپنه shanana aw sparana

resemblance *n.* یورنوالی yawrangwalay

resemble *v.t.* یورنوالیلرل yawrangwalay laral

resent *v.t.* ناخویکارهکول na khwakhee khkara kawal

resentment *n.* خوابدي khwabadee

reservation *n.* زانسرهخوندیساتنه zan sara khwandee satana

reserve *v.t.* زانسرهخوندیساتل،زرمه کول zan sara khwandee satal; zeyrga kawal

rservoir *n.* داوبوزرمه da obo zeyrma

reside *v.i.* استونهلرل astogna laral

residence *n.* مشتای meysht zay

resident *a.* استونپوراوند astogni pori arwand

resident *n* اوسدوونکی oseydoonkay

residual *a.* پاتهشوی pata shaway

residue *n.* پاتهشوبرخه pata shaway barkha

resign *v.t.* زانشاتهکول zan sha ta kawal

resignation *n.* استعفا istifa

resist *v.t.* مخهپکول makha dap kawal

resistance *n.* مقاومت maqawmat

resistant *a.* مقاوم،پایند maqawam; payand

resolute *a.* ينعزمه،سرپه‌لاس teeng azama; sar pa las

resolution *n.* عزم‌رندوونه،قرارداد azam sargandawana; qarardad

resolve *v.t.* حل‌کول hal kawal

resonance *n.* دغازه da ghag angaza

resonant *a.* انازه‌کوونکی angaza kawoonkey

resort *v.i.* پناه‌ورول pana warwaral

resort *n* دتفریحای da tafree zay

resound *v.i.* منعکس‌کدل munakkis keydal

resource *n.* وسیله waseela

resourceful *a.* چاره‌ساز chara saz

respect *v.t.* درناوی‌کول dranaway kawal

respect *n.* احترام ehtiram

respectful *a.* محترم muhtaram

respective *a.* خصوصي khasoosee

respiration *n.* کنه‌ساه sa kakhana

respire *v.i.* ساه‌اخستل sa akeystal

resplendent *a.* زلاند zaland

respond *v.i.* واب‌ورکول zawab warkawal

respondent *n.* واب‌ورکوونکی zawab warkawoonkey

response *n.* واب zawab

responsibility *n.* ذمه‌واري zima waree

responsible *a.* ذمه‌وار zima war

rest *v.i.* سملاستل samlastal

rest *n* آرام aram

restaurant *n.* خونای khwaranzay

restive *a.* نارامه narama

restoration *n.* بیارغاوونه bya raghawana

restore *v.t.* اصلاح‌کول isla kawal

restrain *v.t.* مخه‌پ‌کول makha dap kawal

restrict *v.t.* محدودول mahdoodawal

restriction *n.* بندښت bandakht

restrictive *a.* محدودوونکی mahdoodawoonkay

result *v.i.* نتیجه‌ورکول nateeja warkawal

result *n.* نتیجه nateeja

resume *v.t.* بیاپیلول bya paylawal

resume *n.* ادامه idama

resumption *n.* بیاپیلوونه bya paylawana

resurgence *n.* بیاراژوندی‌کدنه bya razhwanday keydana

resurgent *a.* بیاراژوندی‌شوی bya razhwanday shaway

retail *v.t.* په‌پرچون‌ول‌پلورل pa parchoon dawl ploral

retail *n.* پرچون‌پلورنه parchoon plorana

retail *adv.* په‌سو‌سو‌زله pa so so zala

retail *a* پرچون‌پلورونکی parchoon ploroonkay

retailer *n.* دپرچون‌سودار da parchoon sawdagar

retain *v.t.* ان‌سره‌ساتل zan sara satal

retaliate *v.i.* تاوان‌ورکول tawan warkawal

retaliation *n.* تاوان‌ورکوونه tawan warkawana

retard *v.t.* سوکه‌کول sawka kawal

retardation *n.* سوکه،پوونه sawka; pasawana

retention *n.* ساتنه satana

retentive *a.* ساتونکی satoonkay

reticence *n.* خاموشي khamoshee

reticent *a.* خاموش khamosh

retina *n.* دسترشبکیه da stargey shabkeeya

retinue *n.* ملازم؛نوکر mulazim; nawkar

retire *v.i.* وناستی کدل got nastay keydal

retirement *n.* پهوناستی pa got nastay

retort *v.t.* متقابل‌جواب‌ورکول mutaqabil zawab warkawal

retort *n.* متقابل‌جواب mutaqabil zawab

retouch *v.t.* لاس‌پکوهل las paki wahal

retrace *v.t.* ورباندبرته‌تلل warbandi beyrta tlal

retread *v.t.* ځان‌شاته‌کول zan sha ta kawal

retread *n.* ټشا shatag

retreat *v.i.* پرشاتلل par sha tlal

retrench *v.t.* لتونډکمول lagakhtoona kamawal

retrenchment *n.* کمت؛سپما kamakht; sapma

retrieve *v.t.* برته‌اخستل beyrta akheystal

retrospect *n.* ترمهال‌ته‌ستندا teyr mahal ta staneyda

retrospection *n.* ترمهال‌ته‌نظراچوونه teyr mahal ta nazar achawana

retrospective *a.* تروپوپوراوند teyro peykho pori arwand

return *v.i.* ستندل staneydal

return *n.* راردنه؛بدله ragarzeydana; badla

revel *v.i.* عیاشي‌کول ayashee kawal

revel *n.* عیاشي ayashee

revelation *n.* مکاشفه makashifa

reveller *n.* عیاش ayash

revelry *n.* خوی khwakhee

revenge *v.t.* کسات‌اخستل kasat akheystal

revenge *n.* کسات؛غچ kasat; ghach

revengeful *a.* کرکجن krakjan

revenue *n.* مالیه maleeya

revere *v.t.* احترام‌کول ehtiram kawal

reverence *n.* لواوی lwaraway

reverend *a.* داحترامو da ehtiram war

reverent *a.* پاس‌لرونکی pas laronki

reverential *a.* درناوی dranaway

reverie *n.* دورخوب da wrazi khob

reversal *n.* معکوسوونه makoosawana

reverse *a.* ضد؛معکوس zid; makoos

reverse *n* په‌کدنه؛شکست pa sat keydana; shakast

reverse *v.t.* په‌کدل pa sat keydana

reversible *a.* په‌کدونکی pa sat keydoonkay

revert *v.i.* رجوع‌کول rujoo kawal

review *v.t.* بیاکتل bya katal

review *n* بیاکتنه bya katana

revise *v.t.* اصلاح‌کول isla kawal

revision *n.* اصلاح؛نوی‌نظر isla; naway nazar

revival *n.* بیاراژوندی‌کدنه bya razhwanday keydana

revive *v.i.* بیاراژوندی‌کدل bya razhwanday keydal

revocable *a.* دفسخ‌كوونو da faskh kawoni war

revocation *n.* فسخ‌كوونه faskh kawana

revoke *v.t.* فسخ‌كول faskh kawal

revolt *v.i.* پاون‌كول pasoon kawal

revolt *n.* پاون pasoon

revolution *n.* پاون pasoon

revolutionary *a.* انقلابي inqilabee

revolutionary *n* انقلابي‌وى inqilabee wagaray

revolve *v.i.* چورلېدل choorleydal

revolver *n.* رخندوى sarkhandoy

reward *n.* اجر؛جزا ajar; jaza

reward *v.t.* اجرورکول ajar warkawal

rhetoric *n.* دبديع‌علم da badee ilam

rhetorical *a.* فصاحت‌اوبلاغت fasahat aw balaghat

rheumatic *a.* دبندونوپه‌دردداخته‌کس da bandoono pa dard akhta kas

rheumatism *n.* دبندونودددرنز da bandoono da dard ranz

rhinoceros *n.* کرګدن kargadan

rhyme *n.* قافيه qafeeya

rhyme *v.i.* قافيه‌جوول qafeeya jorawal

rhymester *n.* قافيه‌سازي qafeeya sazee

rhythm b. وزني‌هم ham waznee

rhythmic *a.* موزون؛هم‌وزن mawzoon; ham wazan

rib *n.* پوټه pokhtay

ribbon *n.* پټانه patay; taranga

rice *n.* وريژ wareezhi

rich *a.* باى baday

riches *n.* شتمني shtamanee

richness *a.* شتمني shtamanee

rick *n.* دخش‌خش‌غ da khash khash ghag

rickets *n.* دهوكي‌دپوستوالي‌رنز da hadookee da postwalee ranz

rickety *a.* نرمت narmakht

rickshaw *n.* كوچني‌درپايلرونكي‌اى koochnay drey payey laroonkay gaday

rid *v.t.* آزادول azadawal

riddle *n.* غلبل ghalbeyl

riddle *v.i.* غلبلول ghalbeylawal

ride *v.t.* سپرلدل spareydal

ride *n* سپرل sparlay

rider *n.* چلوونكى؛سپور chalowoonkay; spor

ridge *n.* دغونيوياغروونل da ghondyo ya ghroono laray

ridicule *v.t.* ورپورخندل warpori khandal

ridicule *n.* مسخر maskharey

ridiculous *a.* له‌مسخروك la maskharo dak

rifle *v.t.* په‌توندپل pa tonday palatal

rifle *n* وپك topak

rift *n.* غووالى ghoswalay

right *a.* نغ؛سم neygh; sam

right *adv* په‌سمه‌توه pa sama toga

right *n* خى‌لاس؛سم‌كار khay las; sam kar

right *v.t.* سمدل sameydal

righteous *a.* پرهزار parhayzgar

rigid *a.* سخت sakht

rigorous *a.* سخت sakht

rigour *n.* شخوالى shakhwalay

rim *n.* ژ zhay
ring *n.* کړ karay
ring *v.t.* زنوهل zang wahal
ringlet *n.* کيزه‌نه kareeza nakha
ringworm *n.* دپوستکي‌يوه‌چاسي‌ساري ناروغي da postakee yawa chanrasee saree naroghee
rinse *v.t.* په‌اوبووينل pa obo weenzal
riot *n.* بلوا balwa
riot *v.t.* بلواکول balwa kawal
rip *v.t.* غوول ghosawal
ripe *a* پوخ pokh
ripen *v.i.* پخدل pakheydal
ripple *n.* په sapa
ripple *v.t.* په‌پداکول sapa payda kawal
rise *v.* راختل rakhatal
rise *n.* راختنه rakhatana
risk *v.t.* خطرسره‌مخامخول khatar sara makhamakhawal
risk *n.* خطر khatar
risky *a.* خطرناک khatarnak
rite *n.* مذهبي‌تشريفات mazhabee tashreefat
ritual *n.* دعبادت‌مراسم da ibadat marasim
ritual *a.* دعبادت‌مراسموپوراوند da ibadat marasimo pori arwand
rival *n.* رقيب raqeeb
rival *v.t.* رقابت‌کول raqabat kawal
rivalry *n.* رقابت raqabat
river *n.* سيند seend
rivet *n.* رپ reypat
rivet *v.t.* سره‌ نل sara gandal
rivulet *n.* وياله wyala
road *n.* سک sarak
roam *v.i.* شت‌کول gasht kawal
roar *n.* غوردنه ghoreydana
roar *v.i.* غوردل ghoreydal
roast *v.t.* وريتول wreetawal
roast *a* وريت‌شوی wreet shaway
roast *n* وريته‌شوغوه wreeta shawi ghwakha
rob *v.t.* لول lootal
robber *n.* شوکمار shookmar
robbery *n.* شوکه shooka
robe *n.* اوداوازادکميس oogad aw azad kamees
robe *v.t.* اوداوازادکميس‌اغوستل oogad aw azad kamees aghostal
robot *n.* ماشيني‌سی masheenee saray
robust *a.* صحت‌من؛قوي sayhat man; qawee
rock *v.t.* هغه‌خوادخواخودل hagha khwa deykhwa khozeydal
rock *n.* کاڼی kanray
rocket *n.* توغندی toghanday
rod *n.* ميله،لکه meela; lakara
rodent *n.* شخوندوهونکی shkhwand wahoonkay
roe *n.* يواروپايي‌کوچنغره yaw aroopayee koochnay gharsa
rogue *n.* رذيل‌سی razeel saray
roguery *n.* رذالت razalat
roguish *a.* چلباز chalbaz
role n. وظيفه،رول wazeefa; rol
roll *n.* تاوشوی‌يز taw shaway seez
roll *v.i.* چورلدل choorleydal
roll-call *n.* حاضري‌اخستنه haziree akheystana

roller n. ویندوی khwayandoy

romance n. رومان؛دمینکیسه roman; da meeni keesa

romantic a. افسانه‌وله afsana dawla

romp v.i. په‌مینه‌اوشورماشورسره‌لوبدل pa meena aw shor mashor sara lobeydal

romp n. غالمغال‌غلدنه ghalmaghal zghaleydana

rood n. صلیب saleeb

roof n. چت chat

roof v.t. چت‌جوول chat jorawal

rook n. تورکارغه tor kargha

rook v.t. دوکه‌کول doka kawal

room n. خونه khoona

roomy a. ای‌لرونکی؛هوادار zay laroonkay; hawadar

roost n. دمرغانواله da marghano zala

roost v.i. شپه‌ترول؛ای‌ورکول shpa teyrawal; zay warkawal

root n. ریه reykha

root v.i. ریغول reykhi ghazawal

rope n. پی paray

rope v.t. په‌پی‌تل pa paree taral

rosary n. تسبیح tasbee

rose n. گلاب gulab

roseate a. گلورین؛گلوزمه gulwareen; gulwazma

rostrum n. ممبر؛دریه mimbar; dareez

rosy a. گلورین gulwareen

rot n. خرابدا kharabeyda

rot v.i. خرابدل؛ورستدل kharabeydal; wrusteydal

rotary a. چورلدونکی choorleydoonkay

rotate v.i. چورلدل choorleydal

rotation n. چورلدنه choorleydana

rote n. رودتیا rogdtya

rouble n. دروسیسکه da rooseeyi sika

rough a. لوارژور lwar zhawar

round a. ردبول gard; golay

round adv. هرلورته har lori ta

round n. کرای؛دوره karay; dawra

round v.t. ردول؛راغونول gardawal; raghondawal

rouse v.i. په‌هجان‌راپادل pa hayjan rapaseydal

rout v.t. بشپه‌ماتورکول bashpara mati warkawal

rout n. کامله‌ماته kamila mati

route n. تلوری tagloray

routine n. ورنجار wrazanay chari

routine a. رودیز rogdeez

rove v.i. سره‌تاوول sara tawawal

rover n. رند garzand

row n. لیکه leeka

row v.t. دکتراشپل‌وهل da kakhtay rashpeyl wahal

row n. لفظی‌شخره lafzee shkhara

row n. دکتراشپل da kakhtay rashpeyl

rowdy a. فریادی faryadee

royal a. شاهی shahee

royalist n. ولواکپال tolwakpal

royalty n. پاچاهی pachahee

rub v.t. سولول soolawal

rub n. سولوونه soolawana

rubber n. وچکپاک wachkakhpak

rubbish n. ناولی nawalay

rubble n. دکانوبرویوغوند da kanro dabaro yaw ghond

ruby n. یاقوت yaqoot

rude a. بتربیه bey tarbeeyey

rudiment n. سرچینه sar cheena

rudimentary a. بنسیز bansateez

rue v.t. کول افسوس afsos kawal

rueful a. غمجن ghamjan

ruffian n. بشرفه bey sharafa

ruffle v.t. ناهوارول nahawarawal

rug n. غال ghalay

rugged a. ناهوار nahawar

ruin n. ویجای weejaree

ruin v.t. ویجاول weejarawal

rule n. واک؛حکومت wak; hookoomat

rule v.t. حکومت کول hookoomat kawal

ruler n. واکمن wakman

ruling n. حکم hukam

rum n. اداري چارواکی idaree charwakay

rum a. منظم munazzam

rumble v.i. غومبدل ghroombeydal

rumble n. غمبهار ghrambahar

ruminant a. شخوندوهونکی shkhwand wahoonkay

ruminant n. شخوندوهونکی اروی shkhwand wahoonkay sarway

ruminate v.i. شخوندوهل shkhwand wahal

rumination n. شخوندوهنه shkhwand wahana

rummage v.i. لاوسپل seyral aw sparal

rummage n. سپنه او نه seyrana aw sparana

rummy n. دپتویورل لوبه da pato yaw dawl loba

rumour n. اوازه awaza

rumour v.t. اوازخپرول awazey khparawal

run v.i. منډه وهل manda wahal

run n. منډه manda

rung n. دپوردستکي da poray dastakee

runner n. غاستونکی zghastoonkay

rupee n. دهندواوپاکستان سکه da hind aw pakistan sika

rupture n. یروالی seeriwalay

rupture v.t. یرکول seeri kawal

rural a. کلیوال kaleewal

ruse n. چل؛چلباز chal; chalbaz

rush n. نلاپي او وحرکت nasapee aw gadwad harakat

rush v.t. جنجال جوړدل؛تصادم کول janjal joreydal; tasadum kawal

rush n یوول ونه yaw dawl wana

rust n. زن zang

rust v.i زنوهل zang wahal

rustic a. ساده؛خندوني sada; khandoonay

rustic n کلیوال سی kaleewal saray

rusticate v.t. کلیوال ژوندکول kaleewal zhwand kawal

rustication n. کلیوالي به ور کوونه kaleewalee banra warkawana

rusticity n. زنوهنه zang wahana

rusty a. زنوهلی zang wahalay

rut n. پهمکه درخنه pa zmaka da sarkh nakha

ruthless a. برحمه bey rahma

rye *n.* جودر،تورغنم joodar; tor ghanam

S

sabbath *n.* دشنبور da shambey wraz

sabotage *n.* تخریب takhreeb

sabotage *v.t.* تخریبول takhreebawal

sabre *n.* درنەتوره drana toora

sabre *v.t.* پەتورەوهل pa toora wahal

saccharin *n.* یوەقندیماده yawa qandee mada

saccharine *a.* قندلرونکی qand laroonkay

sack *n.* بوجۀ bojay

sack *v.t.* لەدندخەخارجول la dandi sakha kharijawal

sacrament *n.* دینياومذهبیدود deenee aw mazhabee dood

sacred *a.* مقدس muqaddas

sacrifice *n.* قربانی qurbanee

sacrifice *v.t.* قربانول qurbanawal

sacrificial *a.* فداکارانه fidakarana

sacrilege *n.* دمقدسویزونوغلا da muqadaso seezoonu ghla

sacrilegious *a.* دمقدسویزونوغلا کوونکی da muqadaso seezoonu ghla kawoonkey

sacrosanct *a.* مقدس،نابدلدونکی muqaddas; na badleydoonkey

sad *a.* خپه khapa

sadden *v.t.* خپەکول khapa kawal

saddle *n.* زین zeen

saddle *v.t.* زینیاکتەایودل zeen ya kata eekhodal

sadism *n.* دبرحمجنسیمینه da bey rahmay jinsee meena

sadist *n.* پەبرحمسرەجنسیخوند اخستونکی pa bey rahmay sara jinsee khwand akheystoonkey

safe *a.* محفوظ mahfooz

safe *n.* تجر tajaray

safeguard *n.* ساتندوی satandoy

safety *n.* امنیت amneeyat

saffron *n.* زعفران zafran

saffron *a* دزعفرانپەشان da zafran pa shan

sagacious *a.* هوشیار hookhyar

sagacity *n.* فراست firasat

sage *n.* یوولبوی yaw dawl bootay

sage *a.* هوشیار hookhyar

sail *n.* پەکتۀکسفر pa kakhtay ki safar

sail *v.i.* کتۀکتلل kakhtay ki tlal

sailor *n.* کتۀچلوونکی kakhtay chalawoonkey

saint *n.* ولی،بزر walee; buzurg

saintly *a.* دیندار deendar

sake *n.* لپاره،حق lapara; haq

salable *a.* دلیلامو da leelam war

salad *n.* سلاته salata

salary *n.* تنخوا،اجوره tankha; ajoora

sale *n.* پلورنه plorana

salesman *n.* پلورونکی ploroonkey

salient *a.* مهم ر deyr muhim

saline *a.* مالین malgeen

salinity *n.* تریووالی treewwalay

saliva *n.* لا lari

sally *n.* ناپاوچکفعاليت nasapee aw chatak faaleeyat

sally *v.i.* غورزکول ghorzang kawal

saloon *n.* لويهخونه loya khoona

salt *n.* ماله malga

salt *v.t* مالهپرمول malga pri mokhal

salty *a.* مالين malgeen

salutary *a.* مثبتاغزلرونکی musbat agheyz laroonkay

salutation *n.* سلامدعا salam dua

salute *v.t.* سلاماچول salam achawal

salute *n* سلام؛درناوی salam; dranaway

salvage *n.* دکتيادماليادانزغورنه da kakhtay ya da mal ya da zan zhghorana

salvage *v.t.* دکتاومالاوانزغورل da kakhtay aw mal aw zan zhghoral

salvation *n.* خلاصون khlasoon

same *a.* شان يو yaw shan

sample *n.* نمونه namoona

sample *v.t.* بلهآزمويل beylga azmoyal

sanatorium *n.* دنړيرنددرملناى da naree ranz da darmalani zay

sanctification *n.* تقديس taqdees

sanctify *v.t.* تقديسول taqdeesawal

sanction *n.* بندیز bandeyz

sanction *v.t.* بندیزلول bandeyz lagawal

sanctity *n.* پرهزباري parheyzgaree

sanctuary *n.* عبادتاى ibadatzay

sand *n.* شه shaga

sandal *n.* سپکپل spaki saplay

sandalwood *n.* سپينصندل speen sandal

sandwich *n.* دکوچسلاتواوخوراکي موادوخهجوهو da koch salatoaw khorakee mawado sakha jora doday

sandwich *v.t.* ددوهشيانومنکايودل da dwa shayano manz ki eekhodal

sandy *a.* شلنه shaglana

sane *a.* رمروغ rogh ramat

sanguine *a.* وينهييز weenayeez

sanitary *a.* روغتياي roghtyayee

sanity *n.* روغتيا roghtya

sap *n.* نباتيشيره nabatee sheera

sap *v.t.* شيرهتراستل sheera tri eystal

sapling *n.* نيال؛قلمه nyal; qalma

sapphire *n.* شينياقوت sheen yaqoot

sarcasm *n.* پغور peyghor

sarcastic *a.* کنايي kinayee

sardonic *a.* پغوروزمه peyghor wazma

satan *n.* شطان shaytan

satchel *n.* دووني دکتابونوکوه da khowanzee da keetabono kasora

satellite *n.* سپوگمک;پليونی spogmakay; pleewanay

satiable *a.* قانعکدونکی qanay keydoonkay

satiate *v.t.* قانعکول qanay kawal

satiety *n.* قناعت؛مت qanaat; marakht

satire *n.* غندنليک ghandanleek

satirical *a.* طنزيه tanzeeya

satirist *n.* هجوليکونکی hijoleekoonkay

satirize v.t. مسخره کول maskhara kawal

satisfaction n. رضايت rizayat

satisfactory a. قانع؛رضايي qanay; rizayee

satisfy v.t. راضي کول razee kawal

saturate v.t. مشبوع کول mashboo kawal

saturation n. اشباع ashba

Saturday n. دشنبور da shambey wraz

sauce n. ساس sas

saucer n. نالبکی nalbakay

saunter v.t. چکروهل chakar wahal

savage a. وحشي wahshee

savage n. وحشي؛ناوریاانسان wahshee zanawar ya insan

savagery n. وحشت wahshat

save v.t. ژغورل zhghoral

save prep چ دا مر magar da chi

saviour n. ژغورندوی zhghorandoy

savour n. ذايقه zayqa

savour v.t. مزه اخستل maza akheystal

saw n. اره ara

saw v.t. په ارهرېبل pa ara reybal

say v.t. ويل wayal

say n. ونا؛خبره wayna; khabara

scabbard n. دتوریو da toori pokh

scabies n. دخارترنز da kharakht ranz

scaffold n. دغلودسزاچوبندي da ghlo da saza chawbandee

scale n. تله؛پمانه tala; paymana

scale v.t. ناپول؛وزن کول napawal; wazan kawal

scalp n. کوپړ kopray

scamper v.i. پهبيسرهتتدل pa beeri sara takhteydal

scamper n چکهتته chataka teykhta

scan v.t. ګامپهګام gam pa gam seyral

scandal n رسوايي ruswayee

scandalize v.t. رسواکول ruswa kawal

scant a. لږکم lag; kam

scanty a. ناکافي nakafee

scapegoat n. فديه feedeeya

scar n دپهایيادا غ da tap zay ya dagh

scar v.t. داغلول dagh lagawal

scarce a. کمياب kamyab

scarcely adv. پهمشکلسره pa mushkil sara

scarcity n. قلت qilat

scare n. ترهه tarha

scare v.t. ترهول tarhawal

scarf n. دوتانوپولودسمال da weykhtano patawalo dasmal

scatter v.t. وشنل؛بایپمایکول weyshnal; zay pa zay kawal

scavenger n. لاشخورناوریامارغه lashkhor zanawar ya margha

scene n. منظره manzara

scenery n. منظر manzar

scenic a. ښکليمنظرهلرونکی khkuli manzara laroonkay

scent n. عطر atar

scent v.t. معطرکول moattar kawal

sceptic n. دبدوينددفلسفيليوني da badwayani da falsafey pleewanay

sceptical a. شکمن shakman

scepticism n. شکمني shakmanee

schedule *n.* مهالوېش mahalweysh

schedule *v.t.* مهالوېش‌کوخت‌ورکول mahalweysh ki wakht warkawal

scheme *n.* تدبير،طرحه tadbeer; tarha

scheme *v.i.* تدبيرجوړول tadbeer jorawal

schism *n.* باتفاقي bey itifaqee

scholar *n.* اديب،محقق adeeb; muhaqqiq

scholarly *a.* عالمانه alimana

scholarship *n.* زده‌کولپاره‌مالي‌مرسته، تحصيل zdakro lapara malee mrasta; tehseel

scholastic *a.* استادانه ustadana

school *n.* ووني khowanzay

science *n.* دساينس‌علم da sayins ilam

scientific *a.* ساينسي sayinsee

scientist *n.* ساينس‌پوه sayins poh

scintillate *v.i.* سپرغبادول sparghay badawal

scintillation *n.* برېخدنه breykheydana

scissors *n.* قيچي qeechee

scoff *n.* طنز tanz

scoff *v.i.* طنزکول tanz kawal

scold *v.t.* کنل‌کول kanzal kawal

scooter *n.* دﺩوه‌پايومورسايکل da dwa payo motarsaykal

scope *n.* مفاداوه mafad aw gata

scorch *v.t.* په‌سطح‌سوول pa sata swazawal

score *n.* شمره؛کره shmeyra; karkha

score *v.t.* شمېرل shmeyral

scorer *n.* شمرونکی shmeyroonkay

scorn *n.* تحقير tehqeer

scorn *v.t.* لسپک spak ganral

scorpion *n.* لم laram

Scot *n.* اسکلنډيوی skatlandee wagaray

scotch *a.* دمخنيوي‌وسيله da makhneewee waseela

scotch *n.* درز؛چاود darz; chawd

scot-free *a.* له‌مالي‌خه‌معاف la maleeyey sakha maf

scoundrel *n.* لوچك lochak

scourge *n.* مترو که matrooka

scourge *v.t.* ويجاول weejarawal

scout *n* اړوری sargaray

scout *v.i* اړري‌کول sargaree kawal

scowl *v.i.* تروهنه‌نيول trawa tanda neewal

scowl *n.* ه‌ تروه trawa tanda

scramble *v.i.* په‌زحمت‌سره‌پرمخ‌تلل pa zehmat sara par makh tlal

scramble *n* په‌لاسواوپوتلنه pa laso aw pkho tlana

scrap *n.* خوزاوخوشايه khasozey aw khoshaya

scratch *n.* رﻟدنه،نشت gareydana; nasht

scratch *v.t.* رﻟدل،رول gareydal; garawal

scrawl *v.t.* په‌بيه‌ليکل pa beera leekal

scrawl *n* ناوه‌ليکنه nawara leekana

scream *v.i.* چغوهل cheyghey wahal

scream *n* چغه‌سوره cheygha soora

screen *n.* دسينماياتلويزيون‌پرده da seenama ya talweezyon parda screen v.t. پهپردسرهپول pa pardey sara pokhal

screw n. پچ peych

screw v.t. پهپچنلول pa peych nakhlawal

scribble v.t. پهبیهلیکل pa beera leekal

scribble n. بداوناوهلیکنه bad aw nawara leekana

script n. مسوده musawwida

scripture n. اسماني کتاب asmanee keetab

scroll n. طوماريحرکت toomaree harakat

scrutinize v.t. کره کتنه کول kara katana kawal

scrutiny n. کره کتنه kara katana

scuffle n. مزاحمت؛شورماشور muzahimat; shormashor

scuffle v.i. مزاحمت کول muzahimat kawal

sculptor n. مجسمهجووونکی mujassima jorawoonkay

sculptural a. مجسمهوله mujassima dawla

sculpture n. مجسمه mujassima

scythe n. لور lor

scythe v.t. پهلورسرهربل pa lor sara reybal

sea n. سمندر samandar

seal n. سمندريخو samandaree khoog

seal n. مهرباپه muhur; tapa

seal v.t. تل؛بندول taral; bandawal

seam n. دجامودرز da jamo darz

seam v.t. درزونهبندول darzoona bandawal

seamy a.

search n. تفتیش،؛پلنه tafteesh; palatana

search v.t. پلل palatal

season n. موسم mosam

season v.t. ماله پري مول malga pri mokhal

seasonable a. دموسمسرهسم da mosam sara sam

seasonal a. موسمي mosamee

seat n. چوکۍ chawkay

seat v.t. چوکورکول chawkay warkawal

secede v.i. ورخمونه کدل warsakha gokha keydal

secession n. بیلدا byaleyda

secessionist n. بلتونپال beyltoonpal

seclude v.t. جلاکول jala kawal

secluded a. جلاشوی jala shaway

seclusion n. جلاتوب jalatob

second a. دویم dwayam

second n ثانیه saneeya

second v.t. یو دندخهعارضي بلدندتهاول yaw dandi sakha arzee bali dandi ta arawal

secondary a. ثانوي،ددویمدرج sanwee; da dwayami darajey

secrecy n. رازساتنه raz satana

secret a. خفیه khoofeeya

secret n. راز raz

secretariat e n. ددفتري کارمندانو پلاوییاادارۍای da daftaree karmandano plaway ya idaree zay

secretary n. منشي munshee

secrete v.t. رازساتل raz satal

secretion n. رازساتنه raz satana

secretive *a.* خفيه khoofeeya

sect *n.* مسلک maslak

sectarian *a.* مسلکي maslakee

section *n.* برخه barkha

sector *n.* ناحيه naheeya

secure *a.* محفوظ mehfooz

secure *v.t.* حفاظت کول heefazat kawal

security *n.* امنيت amneeyat

sedan *n.* کجاوه kajawa

sedate *a.* نرماوينه naram aw teeng

sedate *v.t.* دتسکين درمل ورکول da taskeen darmal warkawal

sedative *a.* آرامبونکی aram bakhoonkay

sedative *n* مسکن درمل musakkan darmal

sedentary *a.* کورناستی kornastay

sediment *n.* شنشوب shanshob

sedition *n.* بلوا balwa

seditious *a.* بلوارانه balwagarana

seduce *n.* بدکار badkar

seduction *n.* بدکاري badkaree

seductive *a* بدکارانه badkarana

see *v.t.* کتل،ليدل katal; leedal

seed *n.* زی zaray

seed *v.t.* زيشيندل zaree sheendal

seek *v.t.* پناه ورول pana warwral

seem *v.i.* په نظر راتلل pa nazar ratlal

seemly *a.* په مناسب ډول pa munasib dawl

seep *v.i.* راڅڅيدل rasaseydal

seer *n.* ليدونکی leedoonkay

seethe *v.i.* اشلدل eysheydal

segment *n.* برخه barkha

segment *v.t.* په برخو ويشل pa barkho weyshal

segregate *v.t.* نوروخه جلا کول noro sakha jala kawal

segregation *n.* جلاتوب jalatob

seismic *a.* لړزند larzand

seize *v.t.* لاس ته راول las ta rawral

seizure *n.* نيونه neewana

seldom *adv.* ډير کم deyr kam

select *v.t.* غوره کول ghwara kawal

select *a* غوره ghwara

selection *n.* انتخاب intikhab

selective *a.* انتخابي intikhabee

self *n.* ځان،نفس zan; nafas

selfish *a.* ځانغوای zanghwaray

selfless *a.* بې غرضه bey gharaza

sell *v.t.* خرڅول kharsawal

seller *n.* پلورونکی ploroonkay

semblance *n.* قيافه qeeyafa

semen *n.* نطفه،تخم nutfa; tukham

semester *n.* دزده کدوره da zdakri dawra

seminal *a.* نطفوي nutfawee

seminar *n.* د غونه بحث da behes ghonda

senate *n.* دسپين ورجره da speengeero jarga

senator *n.* دسپين ورد جرغی da speengeero da jargey gharay

senatorial *a.* سناتوري sanatoree

senatorial *a* دمشرانو جرپوراوند da masharano jargey pori arwand

send *v.t.* لدول leygdawal

senile *a.* عمرخولی انسان oomar khwaralay insan

senility *n.* زڼت zarakht

senior *a.* مشر؛زو mashar; zor

senior *n.* سی مشر mashar saray

seniority *n.* مشرتوب mashartob

sensation *n.* هجان hayjan

sensational *a.* هجاني hayjanee

sense *n.* حس his

sense *v.t.* محسوسول mehsoosawal

senseless *a.* بې حسه bey hisa

sensibility *n.* حساسیت hasaseeyat

sensible *a.* باخبر؛حساس bakhabar; hasas

sensitive *a.* حساس؛نازك hasas; nazak

sensual *a.* شهواني shahwanee

sensualist *n.* شهوت پرست shahwat parast

sensuality *n.* شهوت پرستي shahwat parastee

sensuous *a.* شهواني shahwanee

sentence *n.* غونله؛سزا ghondla; saza

sentence *v.t.* غونله جوول؛سزاورکول ghondla jorawal; saza warkawal

sentience *n.* ادراك idrak

sentient *a.* ادراكي idrakee

sentiment *n.* احساس ehsas

sentimental *a.* احساسي؛جذباتي ehsasee; jazbatee

sentinel *n.* ارندوی سرتری sarandoy sarteyray

sentry *n.* و کیدار sawkeedar

separable *a.* جلا کدونکی jala keydoonkay

separate *v.t.* جلاکول jala kawal

separate *a.* جلاشوی jala shaway

separation *n.* جلاتوب jalatob

sepsis *n.* وینه ننوتلی چرک weeney ta nanawatalay chark

September *n.* دانرزي کال نهمه میاشت da angreyzee kal nahama myasht

septic *a.* انتاني او عفوني جسم antanee aw afoonee jisam

sepulchre *n.* مقبره maqbara

sepulture *n.* مقبره maqbara

sequel *n.* راتلونكي؛افسانه ratloonki peykhey; afsana

sequence *n.* لړ؛تسلسل laray; tasalsul

sequester *v.t.* جلا کول jala kawal

serene *a.* خاموش khamosh

serenity *n.* آرامت aramakht

serf *n.* مریی mrayay

serge *n.* وین وکر wareen tokar

sergeant *n.* اجرايوي چارواكی ijraywee charwakay

serial *a.* دوره يي؛مسلسل dawrayee; musalsal

serial *n.* سلسله؛سوبرخيزه فيلم يا کيسه silsila; so barkheeza feelam ya keesa

series *n.* لړ laray

serious *a* خطرناك khatarnak

sermon *n.* وعظ waaz

sermonize *v.i.* وعظ کول waaz kawal

serpent *n.* مار mar

serpentine *n.* د مار غونده تاو راتاو da mar ghonda tawrataw

servant *n.* خدمتار khidmatgar

serve *v.t.* خدمت کول khidmat kawal

serve *n.* دنس لوبه کدغونسکوهنه da taynas loba ki da ghondaski wahana

service *n.* خدمت khidmat

service *v.t* چوپورته‌کول chopar warta kawal

serviceable *a.* چوپته‌چمتو chopar ta chamtoo

servile *a.* خدمتارانه khidmatgarana

servility *n.* نوکرصفتي nawkar sifatee

session *n.* مجلس majlis

set *v.t* جوول؛ودانول jorawal; wadanawal

set *a* له‌واندچمتوشوی؛معین la wrandi chamtoo shaway; muayyan

set *n* وله tolga

settle *v.i.* آبادول؛تصفیه‌کول abadawal; tasfeeya kawal

settlement *n.* جوجای؛استونه jorjaray; astogna

settler *n.* نوی‌کوال naway kadwal

seven *n.* اووه owa

seven *a* اوومه owama

seventeen *n., a* اولس owallas

seventeenth *a.* اولسم owallasam

seventh *a.* اووم owam

seventieth *a.* اویایم awyayam

seventy *n., a* اویا awya

sever *v.t.* پرانستل pranistal

several *a* وږووڼ so; so goonay

severance *n.* جلاکونه jala kawal

severe *a.* شدید shadeed

severity *n.* شدت shidat

sew *v.t.* ګنل gandal

sewage *n.* ناولاوچلاوبه nawali aw chatali oba

sewer *n* دناولواوبوبهنونه da nawalo obo bahanzoona

sewerage *n.* دناولواوبودمکلاندبهنونه da nawalo obo da zmaki landi bahanzoona

sex *n.* جنس؛شهوت jins; shahwat

sexual *a.* شهواني shahwanee

sexuality *n.* شهوانیت shahwaneeyat

sexy *n.* شهوت‌پاری shahwat paray

shabby *a.* بشرم bey sharam

shackle *n.* اتک؛زولا atkaray; zolanay

shackle *v.t.* اتکاچول atkaray achawal

shade *n.* سیوری syoray

shade *v.t.* په‌سیوري‌کساتل pa syoree ki satal

shadow *n.* سیوری syoray

shadow *v.t* سیوری‌پراچول syoray pri achawal

shadowy *a.* سیوری‌لرونکی syoray laroonkay

shaft *n.* استوانه astawana

shake *v.i.* لړزیدل larzeydal

shake *n* لړه larza

shaky *a.* لړزیدونکی larzeydoonkay

shallow *a.* سرسري؛کمژور sarsaree; kam zhawar

sham *v.i.* تظاهرکول tazahur kawal

sham *n* دروغ؛پلمه darogh; palma

sham *a* ناریتونی nareekhtoonay

shame *n.* شرم sharam

shame *v.t.* شرمول sharmawal

shameful *a.* شرمناک sharamnak

shameless *a.* بی‌شرمه bey sharma

shampoo *n.* دوتووینلومایعمرکب da weykhto weenzalo maya murakkab

shampoo *v.t.* پهشامپوويتهوینل pa shampoo weykhta weenzal

shanty *a.* جونه jongara

shape *n.* شکل shakal

shape *v.t* شکلورکول shakal warkawal

shapely *a.* دکلبخاوند da khkuli banri khawand

share *n.* ونه،سکت wand; skakht

share *v.t.* لهنوروسرهوشل la noro sara weyshal

share *n* دشرمای‌هوکی da sharamzay hadookay

shark *n.* یولوی‌سمندري‌کب yaw loy samandaree kab

sharp *a.* تره teyra

sharp *adv.* لهکمت‌اوزیادت‌پرته la kamakht aw zyadakht parta

sharpen *v.t.* ترهکول teyra kawal

sharpener *n.* ترهکوونکی teyra kawoonkay

sharper *n.* پنسل‌تراشی pensal tarashay

shatter *v.t.* مدول maydawal

shave *v.t.* تراشل،حجامت‌جوول trashal; hajamat jorawal

shave *n* یرهخرینه geera khrayna

shawl *n.* شال shal

she *pron.* هغه khaza hagha khaza

sheaf *n.* دسته،بنل dasta; bandal

shear *v.t.* بیاتي‌کول،سکولل byatee kawal; skwalal

shears *n. pl.* سترییاتي stari byatee

shed *v.t.* بهول،پاشل bahawal; pashal

shed *n* بهدنه،پره baheydana; sapara

sheep *n.* پسه psa

sheepish *a.* ساده sada

sheer *a.* نازک،ورمین nazak; wreykhmeen

sheet *n.* پلنهپاه plana panra

sheet *v.t.* پول،بادرپرغوول pokhal; sadar pri ghwarawal

shelf *n.* تاخچه takhcha

shell *n.* قشر،پوستکی qashar; postakay

shell *v.t.* قشرترسپینول qashar tri speenawal

shelter *n.* پناهای panazay

shelter *v.t.* پناهورکول pana warkawal

shelve *v.t.* تاخچهجوول takhcha jorawal

shepherd *n.* شپون shpoon

shield *n.* ال dal

shield *v.t.* پهال‌سرهژغورل pa dal sara zhghoral

shift *v.t.* ای‌بدلول zay badlawal

shift *n* دای‌بدلون da zay badloon

shifty *a.* چلباز chalbaz

shilling *n.* دبریتانیدسکشلمهبرخه da breetaneeyey da sikey shalama barkha

shilly-shally *v.i.* زهنازهتوب‌کول zra nazratob kawal

shilly-shally *n.* دوهزی dwa zaray

shin *n.* لینی leengay

shine *v.i.* پکدل parkeydal

shine *n* پک،بلدنه park; zaleydana

shiny *a.* لمرین lmareen

ship *n.* کښتۍ kakhtay

ship *v.t.* په کښتۍ کې لودول pa kakhtay ki leygdawal

shipment *n.* د کښتۍ بار،محموله da kakhtay bar; mahmoola

shire *n.* ایالت ayalat

shirk *v.t.* ناغيي کول nagheeree kawal

shirker *n.* ناغيي کوونکی nagheeree kawoonkay

shirt *n.* کميس kamees

shiver *v.i.* ارتعاش irtiash

shoal *n.* لژور lag zhawar

shoal *n* له dala

shock *n.* صدمه،بوزار sadma; goozar

shock *v.t.* سخت بوزار خول sakht goozar khwaral

shoe *n.* بو boot

shoe *v.t.* بوان په پو کول bootan pa pkho kawal

shoot *v.t.* توغول،ويشتل toghawal; weeshtal

shoot *n* ويشتنه،دبوو راوتلتيا weeshtana; da booto rawataltya

shop *n.* پلورنی ploranzay

shop *v.i.* پلورل ploral

shore *n.* ساحل sahil

short *a.* لنډ land

short *adv.* په لنډه توګه pa landa toga

shortage *n.* کمت kamakht

shortcoming *n.* کم راتلنه kam ratlana

shorten *v.t.* لنډول landawal

shortly *adv.* په لنډه توګه pa landa toga

shorts *n. pl.* جانۍ،ترزنونانولډپتلون jangay; tar zangoonano land patloon

shot *n.* مرم،دنويشتنه marmay; da nakhi weeshtana

shoulder *n.* اوه،ولی ooga; walay

shoulder *v.t.* په او سره زور کول pa oogey sara zor kawal

shout *n.* کريکه،فرياد kreeka; faryad

shout *v.i.* کريکه وهل kreeka wahal

shove *v.t.* په زور سره پر مخ بیول pa zor sara par makh beywal

shove *n.* غلوونه zghalawana

shovel *n.* بلچه beylcha

shovel *v.t.* بلچ سره لر کول beylchey sara leyri kawal

show *v.t.* وول khowal

show *n.* وونه khowana

shower *n.* سخت باران sakht baran

shower *v.t.* باران ورېدل baran wareydal

shrew *n.* حشره خوری موک hashara khoray mogak

shrewd *a.* پر پلمه palmagar

shriek *n.* چغاو کريک cheyghey aw kreeki

shriek *v.i.* چغاو کريکوهل cheyghey aw kreeki wahal

shrill *a.* تېز؛فريادي teyz; faryadee

shrine *n.* زيارتای zyaratzay

shrink *v.i* ونزکېدل gonzi keydal

shrinkage *n.* ونزکوونه gonzi kawana

shroud *n.* کفن؛پو kafan; pokh

shroud *v.t.* کفن وراغوستل kafan waraghostal

shrub *n.* لەسرکاومو جوباک la sarkey aw meywey jor skhak

shrug *v.t.* اوپورتەخوول oogey porta khozawal

shrug *n.* داوپورتەحرکت da oogo porta harakat

shudder *v.i.* لپدل lapreydal

shudder *n.* لپدنه lapreydana

shuffle *v.i.* هخواد خواحرکت کول hakhwa deykhwa harakat kawal

shuffle *n.* ھبدنه؛نوۍدنه zambeydana; ngokheydana

shun *v.t.* ازنترساتل zan tri satal

shunt *v.t.* منحرف کول munharif kawal

shut *v.t.* بندول؛راکتهکول bandawal; rakkhata kawal

shutter *n.* راکتهکدونکیاوسپنیزہور rakkhata keydoonkay aw ospaneeza war

shuttle *n.* ماکو makoo

shuttle *v.t.* دماکوسفرکول da makoo safar kawal

shuttlecock *n.* دبمنوندلوبپرلرونک غوٮسکه da baydminton da lobey parey laroonki ghondaska

shy *n.* شرمندوکی sharmindookay

shy *v.i.* شرمدل sharmeydal

sick *a.* ناروغه narogha

sickle *n.* لور lor

sickly *a.* کمزوریانسان kamzoray insan

sickness *n.* کمزورتیا kamzortya

side *n.* خوا؛اخ khwa; arkh

side *v.i.* یوخواتهتلل yawey khwa ta tlal

siege *n.* محاصره؛کلابند muhasira; kalabandee

siesta *n.* غرمنیخوب gharmanay khob

sieve *n.* غلبل ghalbeyl

sieve *v.t.* غلبلول ghalbeylawal

sift *v.t.* شيندل sheendal

sigh *n.* آہکنه ah kkhana

sigh *v.i.* افسوسکول؛آہکل afsos kawal; ah kkhal

sight *n.* لیدنه leedana

sight *v.t.* لیدل leedal

sightly *a.* لیدلکدونی؛ترپاملاند leedal keydoonay; tar pam landi

sign *n.* علامه؛نه alama; nakha

sign *v.t.* پهنونانوسرهپوهول pa nakho nakhano sara pohawal

signal *n.* علامه؛لارود alama; larkhod

signal *a.* وتلی؛رمزي watalay; ramzee

signal *v.t.* پهاشاروپوهول pa isharo pohawal

signatory *n.* لاسلیکونکی lasleekoonkay

signature *n.* لاسلیک lasleek

significance *n.* قدر؛مفهوم؛اهمیت qadar; mafhoom; ahmeeyat

significant *a.* مهم muhim

signification *n.* مانا؛لویت mana; loyakht

signify *v.t.* ماناورکول mana warkawal

silence *n.* چوپتیا choptya

silence *v.t.* غلیکول ghalay kawal

silencer n. غلی کوونکی ghalay kawoonkay

silent a. بغه bey ghaga

silhouette n. دهرهنیم‌مخ da har sa neem makh

silk n. ورم wreykham

silken a. ورمین wreykhmeen

silky a. ورمین wreykhmeen

silly a. بعقل bey aqal

silt n. خه،لهه khata; laha

silt v.t. په‌خولل pa khato laral

silver n. سپین‌زر speen zar

silver a. نقرهیی naqrayee

silver v.t. په‌سپینوزروپولل pa speeno zaro pokhal

similar a. پهر،یوشان pa seyr; yaw shan

similarity n. ورتهوالی wartawalay

simile n. تشبیه tashbee

similitude n. دبیورنوالی da banri yaw rangwalay

simmer v.i. له‌غصه‌خولل la ghusey khoteydal

simple a. ساده،آسان sada; asan

simpleton n. احمق ahmaq

simplicity n. ساده‌توب sadatob

simplification n. ساده‌کون sada kawang

simplify v.t. ساده‌کول sada kawal

simultaneous a. په‌یوه‌وخت pa yawa wakht

sin n. ناه goona

sin v.i. ناه‌کول goona kawal

since prep. وروسته‌له wrusta la

since conj. چ دا da chi

since adv. له‌هغه‌وخته‌چ la hagha wakhta chi

sincere a. مخلص mukhlis

sincerity n. خلوص khuloos

sinful a. ناهار goonagar

sing v.i. سندره‌ویل sandara wayal

singe v.t. سوزول sozawal

singe n. سوزدنه sozeydana

singer n. سندرغای sandargharay

single a. یواز؛یوکسیز yawazi; yaw kaseez

single n. یو،تنها yaw; tanha

single v.t. یوازتلل؛یوکدل yawazi tlal; yaw keydal

singular a. مفرد؛یو mufrad; yaw

singularity n. یوازتوب yawazeytob

singularly adv. په‌یوازسره pa yawazi sara

sinister a. کیلاسی keenr lasay

sink v.i. غرقدل؛تنزل‌کول gharqeydal; tanazzul kawal

sink n. وبدنه doobeydana

sinner n. نهار goonagar

sinuous a. پهییز؛دموجونوپه‌اوند sapayeez; da mawjoono pa arwand

sip v.t. په‌غپ‌غپ‌ل pa ghrap ghrap skhal

sip n. غپ ghrap

sir n. اغلی؛حضرت khaghalay; hazrat

siren n. هارن haran

sister n. خور khor

sisterhood n. خورولی khorwalee

sisterly a. دخورپه‌شان da khor pa shan

sit v.i. کناستل kkheynastal

site n. مکان؛ترودازلاندمکه makan; tar wadanay landi zmaka

situation *n.* حالت halat

six *n., a* شپ،شپم shpag; shpagam

sixteen *n., a.* شپاس؛شپاسم shparas; shparasam

sixteenth *a.* شپاسم shparasam

sixth *a.* شپم shpagam

sixtieth *a.* شپتم shpeytam

sixty *n., a.* شپته shpeyta

sizable *a.* نسبتاًلوی nisbatan loy

size *n.* اندازه؛کچ andaza; kach

size *v.t.* اندازه کول andaza kawal

sizzle *v.i.* غدل zghageydal

sizzle *n.* غ غ zagh zagh

skate *n.* ناوه او پست سرى nawara aw past saray

skate *v.t.* په یخ خویدل pa yakh khwayeydal

skein *n.* لاستى،کلاوه lastay; kalawa

skeleton *n.* کالبد؛جوت kalbad; jorakht

sketch *n.* ساده نخچه،طرحه sada nakhcha; tarha

sketch *v.t.* ساده نخچه جوړول sada nakhcha jorawal

sketchy *a.* نیمى neemgaray

skid *v.i.* پاىورکول payey warkawal

skid *n* دپاىتیر da payey teer

skilful *a.* کارپوه karpoh

skill *n.* هنر hunar

skin *n.* رمن sarman

skin *v.t* پوکىتراول patokay tri arawal

skip *v.i.* وپونه وهل toopoona wahal

skip *n* کته اوپورته top kkhata aw porta top

skipper *n.* وپوهونکى top wahoonkay

skirmish *n.* جزیي جه juzyee jagara

skirmish *v.t.* سرسرى جندل sarsaree jangeydal

skirt *n.* دپرانستلمنزنانه کو da pranasti lamani zanana kot

skirt *v.t.* لمن وراچول laman warachawal

skit *n.* پغور peyghor

skull *n.* کوپ kopray

sky *n.* اسمان asman

sky *v.t.* رپورته کول deyr porta kawal

slab *n.* برینه تخته dabareena takhta

slack *a.* سستي sastee

slacken *v.t.* سوکه کول؛سستول sawka kawal; sastawal

slacks *n.* چکر باندتلو پتلون chakar bandi da tlo patloon

slake *v.t.* خاموشول khamoshawal

slam *v.t.* په زوراولوارغسره بندول pa zor aw lwar ghag sara bandawal

slam *n* دسخت اوتزغاواز da sakht aw teyz ghag awaz

slander *n.* بدنامي badnamee

slander *v.t.* بدنامول badnamawal

slanderous *a.* تومتي tomatee

slang *n.* عامه ژبه ama zhaba

slant *v.t.* رېبندکول؛کوواوپه دتلل reyband kawal; kog aw pa dada tlal

slant *n* که کرخه kaga karkha

slap *n.* سپ sapeyra

slap *v.t.* سپېره پورته کول sapeyra porta kawal

slash *v.t.* په تکان سره غوسول pa takan sara ghosawal

slash *n* چکـوزار chatak goozar

slate *n.* يوه‌برينه‌پاه yawa dabareena panra

slattern *n.* تمبل‌سى tambal saray

slatternly *a.* په‌مبل‌سره pa tambal sara

slaughter *n.* تول‌وژنه tol wazhna

slaughter *v.t.* په‌تول‌وژنه‌لاس‌پور‌كول pa tol wazhna las pori kawal

slave *n.* مریی mrayay

slave *v.i.* مرییتوب‌ته‌ول mrayeetob ta wral

slavery *n.* مرییتوب mrayeetob

slavish *a.* مریی‌ول‌ه mrayay dawla

slay *v.t.* له‌منه‌ول la manza wral

sleek *a.* نرم؛صیقلی naram; sayqalee

sleep *v.i.* ویده‌كدل weeda keydal

sleep *n.* خوب khob

sleeper *n.* د‌ویده‌كدنى‌واون da weeda keydani wagon

sleepy *a.* خوبولی khobawalay

sleeve *n* لستوی lastonray

sleight *n.* مهارت maharat

slender *n.* نر dangar

slice *n.* قاش qash

slice *v.t.* پركول preykawal

slick *a* ساده؛مطلق sada; mutlaq

slide *v.i.* رغدل raghreydal

slide *n* خوایدنه khwayeydana

slight *a.* كم؛نایز kam; naseez

slight *n.* پست؛لر past; lag

slight *v.t.* سپک‌نظركول spak nazar kawal

slim *a.* نازک nazuk

slim *v.i.* نركدل dangar keydal

slime *n.* چكه؛لعاب chakara; luab

slimy *a.* سرناك sreykhnak

sling *n.* مچنوغزه machnoghza

slip *v.i.* ویدل؛خوشی‌كول khwayeydal; khoshay kawal

slip *n.* رغدنه؛بلارتوب raghreydana; bey laritob

slipper *n.* د‌كور‌داستعمال‌سپكپل da kor da istimal spaki saplay

slippery *a.* خوایند khwayand

slipshod *a.* پروت؛بپروا prot; bey parwa

slit *n.* چاود؛غووالی chawd; ghoswalay

slit *v.t.* سوری‌كول sooray kawal

slogan *n.* ناره؛شعار nara; shuar

slope *n.* ر‌بنده‌همكه reybanda zmaka

slope *v.i.* ر‌بندتوب‌پداكول reybandtob payda kawal

sloth *n.* كاهلی kahilee

slothful *n.* كاهل kahil

slough *n.* له‌خوا‌و‌لهو‌كسای la khato aw laho dak zay

slough *n.* اخلاقی‌فساد akhlaqee fasad

slough *v.t.* مپوستكی‌غورول mar postakay ghorzawal

slovenly *a.* و‌نونه gonzi gonzi

slow *a* ورو؛سست wro; sast

slow *v.i.* په‌ورووورو‌تلل pa wro wro tlal

slowly *adv.* په‌قراره pa qarara

slowness *n.* سستی sastee

sluggard *n.* لت‌سى lat saray

sluggish *a.* ناكار؛لت nakar; lat

sluice *n.* ورخ؛پم warkh; patam

slum *n.* چله‌یاجونه chatala ya jongara

slumber *v.i.* سپک‌خوب‌کول spak khob kawal

slumber *n.* سپک‌خوب spak khob

slump *n.* دپام‌ومقدار da pam war miqdar

slump *v.i.* په‌یوه‌دم‌ندل pa yawa dam nareydal

slur *n.* اشاره؛پوند ishara; peywand

slush *n.* احمقانه‌احساسات ahmaqana ehsasat

slushy *a.*

slut *n.* بدلمنه bad lamana khaza

sly *a.* مکار؛موذي makar; mozee

smack *n.* کلونه‌او‌مچکه khkulawana aw machaka

smack *v.i.* غنه‌مچوتراخستل ghagana macho tri akheystal

smack *n* خوند khwand

smack *n.* سطحي‌مالومات sathee maloomat

smack *v.t.* په‌چپ‌چپ‌سره‌خوال pa chrap chrap sara khwaral

small *a.* کوچنی koochnay

small *n* ووکی‌شی‌یاانسان warookay shay ya insan

smallness *adv.* ووکتیا warooktya

smallpox *n.* دچیچک‌ناروغي da cheechak naroghee

smart *a.* توند؛تز؛چالاک tond; teyz; chalak

smart *v.i* خوږدل khoogeydal

smart *n* لالی‌انسان gulalay insan

smash *v.t.* دوکول dari wari kawal

smash *n* تکر؛مده‌شوووه takar; mayda shawi tota

smear *v.t.* داغي‌کول daghee kawal

smear *n.* داغ؛ککتیا dagh; kakartya

smell *n.* بوی booy

smell *v.t.* بویول؛بوی‌ورکول booyawal; booy warkawal

smelt *v.t.* یوول‌کوچني‌خوراکي‌کب yaw dawl koochnay khorakee kab

smile *n.* خندا khanda

smile *v.i.* موسکاکول moska kawal

smith *n.* مسر misgar

smock *n.* ینه‌زرپراهني khazeena zayr parahanee

smog *n.* غلیظه‌او‌تته‌له ghaleeza aw tata lara

smoke *n.* لوی loogay

smoke *v.i.* لوی‌کدل loogay keydal

smoky *a.* لوی‌وهلی loogay wahalay

smooth *a.* سلیس؛هوار salees; hawar

smooth *v.t.* نرمول narmawal

smother *v.t.* دلوی‌له‌کبله‌ساه‌بندیدل da loogee la kabala sa bandeydal

smoulder *v.i.* سوزیدل‌او‌لوی‌کول sozeydal aw loogay kawal

smug *a.* پرهیزگارسی parheyzgar saray

smuggle *v.t.* قاچاقول qachaqawal

smuggler *n.* قاچاق‌کوونکی qachaq kawoonkay

snack *n.* له‌خواه lag sa khwara

snag *n.* دغابخ da ghakh beykh

snail *n.* ژوره zhawara

snake *n.* مار mar

snake *v.i.* په‌مارپچي‌ول‌حرکت‌کول pa marpeychee dawl harakat kawal

snap *v.t.* له‌تکهارسره‌ماتول la trakahar sara matawal

snap *n* اواز دتک‌تک da trak trak awaz

snap *a* نابي،لدمهالي land mahalay; nasapee

snare *n.* لومه looma

snare *v.t.* په‌لومه‌کرارول pa looma ki rageyrawal

snarl *n.* دام dam

snarl *v.i.* ستونزمنول stoonzmanawal

snatch *v.t.* برمته‌کول barmata kawal

snatch *n.* شوکونه،تتوونه shookawana; takhtawana

sneak *v.i.* په‌غلاغلاتلل pa ghla ghla tlal

sneak *n* پت‌حرکت pat harakat

sneer *v.i* په‌مسخرو‌سره‌غدل pa maskharo sara ghageydal

sneer *n* مسخره،ملنه maskhara; malanda

sneeze *v.i.* پرنجدل pranjeydal

sneeze *n* پرنج pranj

sniff *v.i.* بویول booyawal

sniff *n* په‌پوزه‌کش‌کوونه pa poza kash kawana

snob *n.* غراشرافی‌شخص ghayr ashrafee shakhs

snobbery *n.* عاموی am wagaray

snobbish *v* کبرجن،عادي kabarjan; adee

snore *v.i.* خرهارکول kharhar kawal

snore *n* خرخر khar khar

snort *v.i.* غوریدل ghoreydal

snort *n.* خرهار kharhar

snout *n.* شونک،پوز shoondak; poz

snow *n.* واوره wawra

snow *v.i.* واوره‌وریدل wawra wareydal

snowy *a.* واورین wawreen

snub *v.t.* رټل،ردول ratal; radawal

snub *n.* رټنه؛ردوونه ratana; radawana

snuff *n.* نسوار naswar

snug *n.* کوچنی‌خونه koochnay khoona

so *adv.* لهدکبله؛پر‌داساس la dey kabala; par dey asas

so *conj.* که zaka

soak *v.t.* لمدول lamdawal

soak *n.* غوپه‌کوونه ghopa kawana

soap *n.* صابون saboon

soap *v.t.* صابون‌پرمول saboon pri mokhal

soapy *a.* صابوني saboonee

soar *v.i.* لوه‌الوتنه‌کول lwara alwatana kawal

sob *v.i.* لمدیدل lamdeydal

sob *n* سل salgay

sober *a.* عاقل aqil

sobriety *n.* معقولیت؛هویاري maqooleeyat; hookhyaree

sociability *n.* دژوندوتیا da gad zhwand wartya

sociable *a.* مینه‌ناک meenanak

social *n.* ولنیز tolaneez

socialism *n* پرنپالي parganpalee

socialist *n,a* پرنپال parganpal

society *n.* ولنه tolana

sociology *n.* ولنپوهنه tolanpohana

sock *n.* جوراب jorabey

socket *n.* ژورغالی؛کاسه zhawarghalay; kasa

sod *n.* چمن chaman

sodomite *n.* بچهباز؛کوني bachabaz; koonee

sodomy *n.* بچهبازي؛کونیتوب bachabazee; kooneetob

sofa *n.* نرمهاودهوکۍ narma oogda sawkay

soft *n.* لطیف نرم؛ naram; lateef

soften *v.t.* نرمول،ملایم کدل narmawal; mulayim keydal

soil *n.* خاوره khawra

soil *v.t.* خرندل kheyraneydal

sojourn *v.i.* ای‌ناستی کول zay nastay kawal

sojourn *n.* لنمهالي‌استونه land mahalee astogna

solace *v.t.* تسکینول taskeenawal

solace *n.* تسکین taskeen

solar *a.* لمرین lmareen

solder *n.* کوشر kawsheyr

solder *v.t.* کوشرول kawsheyrawal

soldier *n.* سپایي spayee

soldier *v.i.* سپای‌جوړل spayee joreydal

sole *n.* دپیابوتلی da pkhey ya boot talay

sole *v.t* بوتهتلی‌اچول boot ta talay achawal

sole *a* تنها tanha

solemn *a.* سنین؛جدي sangeen; jiddee

solemnity *n.* وقار،تشریفات waqar; tashreefat

solemnize *v.t.* لهتشریفاتوسرهترسره کول la tashreefato sara tar sara kawal

solicit *v.t.* تقاضاکول؛زارکول taqaza kawal; zaray kawal

solicitation *n.* غوتنه؛زار ghokhtana; zaray

solicitor *n.* حقوقي‌سلاکار haqooqee salakar

solicitious *a.* هیلهمن؛نارامه heelaman; narama

solicitude *n.* پرشاني؛زیات‌دقت parayshanee; zyat diqat

solid *a.* جامد jamid

solid *n* سخت‌شی sakht shay

solidarity *n.* غمرازي؛مسؤلیت ghamrazee; gad masooleeyat

soliloquy *n.* لمان‌سرهغدنه la zan sara ghageydana

solitary *a.* تنها tanha

solitude *n.* خلوت khilwat

solo *n* یو کسیزهسندره yaw kaseeza sandara

solo *a.* یوازینی؛انفرادي yawazeenay; infiradee

solo *adv.* پهانفرادي‌توه pa infiradee toga

soloist *n.*

solubility *n.* دویلاکدنوورتیا da weeli keydano wartya

soluble *a.* دویلاکدنوور da weeli keydano war

solution *n.* حل‌لاره hal lara

solve *v.t.* حل‌لاره‌ورتهموندل hal lara warta moondal

solvency *n.* حلدنه haleydana

solvent *a.* ویلاکدونکی؛حلوونکی weelikeydoonkay; halawoonkay

solvent *n* محلل muhlal

sombre *a.* سیوری‌لرونکی syoray laroonkay

some a. يو شمير؛ينی zeeni; yaw shmeyr

some pron. وک؛کوميو sok; kom yaw

somebody pron. کوم کس kom kas

somebody n. يووک yaw sok

somehow adv. په يو هول pa yaw dawl

someone pron. کوم کس؛يووکkom kas; yaw sok

somersault n. سرکوز sarkondai

something pron. يو شی؛يوسيز yaw seez; yaw shay

something adv. تريواندازtar yawey andazey

sometime adv. کله ناکله kala na kala

sometimes adv. زينی وختونه zeeni wakhtoona

somewhat adv. تريوه حده tar yawa hada

somewhere adv. يو چر؛په کومای کyaw cheyri; pa kom zay ki

somnambulism n. په خوب کرېدنه pa khob ki garzeydana

somnambulist n. ک خوب په رېدونکیpa khob ki garzeydoonkay

somnolence n. خوبولی حالت khobawalay halat

somnolent n. خوبولی khobawalay

son n. زوی zoy

song n. سندره sandara

songster n. سندربول sandarbol

sonic a. اورلدييز awreydyeez

sonnet n. غزل ghazal

sonority n. غنتوب ghagantob

soon adv. ژر و deyr zhar

soot n. لوی loogay

soot v.t. دبخار دنل لوی da bukharay da nal loogay

soothe v.t. آرامول aramawal

sophism n. تراستنه teyr eystana

sophist n. فسطايي fastayee

sophisticate v.t. تراستل teyr eystal

sophisticated a. غولوونکی gholawoonkay

sophistication n. تحريف؛غولوونه tahreef; gholawana

sorcerer n. کوډگر kodgar

sorcery n. کوډري kodgaree

sordid a. خسيس؛بدلاری khasees; badlaray

sore a. دردناک؛پی dardnak; tapee

sore n زخم zakham

sorrow n. خپان khapgan

sorrow v.i. غمجنېدل ghamjaneydal

sorry a. خواشيني khwasheenee

sort n. جنس؛قسم jins; qisam

sort v.t په قسمونو کوشل pa qismoono ki weyshal

soul n. روح rooh

sound a. روغ rogh

sound v.i. غږبرېدل ghag khpareydal

sound n غ ghag

soup n. وروا khorwa

sour a. تريو treew

sour v.t. تروشول؛ناراضه کول troshawal; naraza kawal

source n. سرچينه sar cheena

south n. سول swayl

south n. سولی swaylee

south *adv* دسويل لورته da swayl lor ta

southerly *a.* په سويل كپروت pa swayl ki prot

southern *a.* سولي swaylee

souvenir *n.* يادگار yadgar

sovereign *n.* پاچا pacha

sovereign *a* واكمن zwakman

sovereignty *n.* پاچاهي pachahee

sow *v.t.* تخم شنل tukham shanal

sow *n.* خوينه khazeena khoog

space *n.* د هواچاپريال da hawa chapeyryal

space *v.t.* فضا كردل،پای ورکول faza ki garzeydal; zay warkawal

spacious *a.* زای لرونكی zay laroonkay

spade *n.* بلچه beylcha

spade *v.t.* په بلچی سره اول pa beylchey sara arawal

span *n.* مدت،باكل شوی وخت mudat; takal shaway wakht

span *v.t.* پراختيا ورکول parakhtya warkawal

Spaniard *n.* اسپانوي aspanawee

spaniel *n.* ژوی ببرسپی zwar ghwagay babar spay

Spanish *a.* اسپانوي aspanawee

Spanish *n.* اسپانوي وی يا ژبه aspanawee wagaray ya zhaba

spanner *n.* پیچ كش peych kash

spare *v.t.* وربل warbakhal

spare *a* اضافي izafee

spare *n.* پرهیز parheyz

spark *n.* سكروه skarwata

spark *v.i.* سرک كول srak kawal

spark *n.* برکی basarkay

sparkle *v.i.* سركدل srakeydal

sparkle *n.* سركدنه srakeydana

sparrow *n.* كورنمرغ koranay marghay

sparse *a.* تيت پرک teet park

spasm *n.* د اضطراب حالت da iztirab halat

spasmodic *a.* تشنجي tashannujee

spate *n.* سل seyl

spatial *a.* هوايي hawayee

spawn *n.* د كبه هگی da kab hagay

spawn *v.i.* د كب هاچول da kab hagay achawal

speak *v.i.* غدل ghageydal

speaker *n.* غدونكی ghageydoonkay

spear *n.* نزه neyza

spear *v.t.* په نزه غوول pa neyza ghosawal

spearhead *n.* د نزوكه da neyzey sooka

spearhead *v.t.* بريد كول breed kawal

special *a.* خاص khas

specialist *n.* كاروه karpoh

speciality *n.* مهارت maharat

specialization *n.* اختصاص ikhtisas

specialize *v.i.* متخصص كدل mutakhassas keydal

species *n.* د ساه لرونكو د نو قسمونه da sa laroonko da noogi qismoona

specific *a.* مخصوص makhsoos

specification *n.* تعيين taayyun

specify *v.t.* تعيين كول taayyun kawal

specimen *n.* بله beylga

speck n. ‏پی‎ tapay

spectacle n. ‏منظره،تماشا‎ manzara; tamasha

spectacular a. ‏دلیدومنظره‎ da leed war manzara

spectator n. ‏لیدونکی‎ leedoonkay

spectre n. ‏ارواء،پری‎ arwa; peyray

speculate v.i. ‏اندنهکول‎ andeykhna kawal

speculation n. ‏احتکار‎ ehtikar

speech n. ‏وناکوونه‎ wayna kawana

speed n. ‏رفتار‎ raftar

speed v.i. ‏پهچکسرهغلدل‎ pa chatakay sara zghaleydal

speedily adv. ‏پهچکسره‎ pa chatakay sara

speedy a. ‏چابک‎ chabak

spell n. ‏اپ‎ abeysey

spell v.t. ‏ابکول،املاکول‎ abeysey kawal; imla kawal

spell n ‏دوره،دوران‎ dawra; dawran

spend v.t. ‏مصرفول‎ masrafawal

spendthrift n. ‏زیاتلتکوونکی‎ zyat lagakht kawoonkay

sperm n. ‏نطفه‎ nutfa

sphere n. ‏دایره‎ dayra

spherical a. ‏دایروی‎ dayrawee

spice n. ‏مساله‎ masala

spice v.t. ‏مسالهپردوول‎ masala pri doorawal

spicy a. ‏مسالدار،خوندور‎ masaleydar; khwandawar

spider n. ‏غه‎ ghanra

spike n. ‏دغنمویاجواروی‎ da ghanamo ya joowaro wagay

spike v.t. ‏پهنزهغوول‎ pa neyza ghosawal

spill v.i. ‏تویول،نول‎ toyawal; narawal

spill n ‏توىشوىیز‎ toy shaway seez

spin v.i. ‏رخول،تاوول‎ sarkhawal; tawawal

spin n. ‏تاوخونه‎ taw khwarana

spinach n. ‏سابه‎ saba

spinal a. ‏دملاتیرپوراوند‎ da mla teer pori arwand

spindle n. ‏دوک‎ dok

spine n. ‏دملاتیر‎ da mla teer

spinner n. ‏سنغونکی،تاوورکوونکی‎ sanay gharoonkay; taw warkawoonkay

spinster n. ‏ناوادهکنجل‎ nawada kari najlay

spiral n. ‏ماریچ،بنول‎ mar peych; bandol

spiral a. ‏تاوراتاو‎ taw rataw

spirit n. ‏روا،جذبه‎ arwa; jazba

spirited a. ‏فکری،جذباتي‎ fikree; jazbatee

spiritual a. ‏روحاني‎ roohanee

spiritualism n. ‏داروالانوپهنباور‎ da arwagano pa naray bawar

spiritualist n. ‏روحانيپال‎ roohanee pal

spirituality n. ‏روحانیت‎ roohaneeyat

spit v.i. ‏توکانریکل‎ tookanri tookal

spit n ‏توکا،لا‎ tookanri; lari

spite n. ‏کینه‎ keena

spittle n ‏توکا‎ tookanri

spittoon n. ‏توکا‎ tookanri

splash v.i. ‏افرازول،چپچپکول‎ afrazawal; chrap chrap kawal

splash *n* افراز؛چپ چپ afraz; chrap chrap

spleen *n.* توری؛طحال toray; tahal

splendid *a.* باعظمت ba azmat

splendour *n.* عظمت azmat

splinter *n.* دلري ده da largee dara

splinter *v.t.* وموه كول tota tota kawal

split *v.i.* ماتول؛بلول matawal; beylawal

split *n* درز؛نفاق darz; nifaq

spoil *v.t.* ورستول؛خرابول wrustawal; kharabawal

spoil *n* خرابي kharabee

spoke *n.* درخ پره يا ميله da sarkh para ya meela

spokesman *n.* وياند wayand

sponge *n.* سفنج sfanj

sponge *v.t.* په سفنج پاكول pa sfanj pakawal

sponsor *n.* ژمن پلار يا مور zhman plar ya mor

sponsor *v.t.* مسؤليت وركول masooleeyat warkawal

spontaneity *n.* ناپي توب nasapeetob

spontaneous *a.* په ماني توه،باختياره pa zanee toga; bey ikhtyara

spoon *n.* كاشوغه kashogha

spoon *v.t.* په كاشوغه سره خول kashoga sara khwaral

spoonful *n.* ديو كاشوغه په اندازه da yaw kashoghi pa andaza

sporadic *a.* انفرادي infiradee

sport *n.* لوبه loba

sport *v.i.* لوبه كول loba kawal

sportive *a.* ورزشي warzashee

sportsman *n.* لوبغای lobgharay

spot *n.* كی،بای takay; zay

spot *v.t.* په نه كول،داغي كول pa nakha kawal; daghee kawal

spotless *a.* داغه بے bey dagha

spousal *n.* واده wada

spouse *n.* دژوندملری da zhwand malgaray

spout *n.* نل،ناوه،فواره nal; nawa; fawara

spout *v.i.* دچينه په شكل ورلدل da cheeney pa shakal wareydal

sprain *n.* دردرد da rag dard

sprain *v.t.* په دردراوستل،راوتل pa dard rawastal; rag awakhtal

spray *n.* نندنه،شيندنه naneydana; sheendana

spray *n* دحشراتوزهرجن درمل da hasharato zaharjan darmal

spray *v.t.* شيندل؛دحشراتوزهرجن درمل پاشل sheendal; da hasharato zaharjan darmal pashal

spread *v.i.* ويول؛غوول weerawal; ghwarawal

spread *n.* پراختيا،انتشار parakhtya; intishar

spree *n.* مستي mastee

sprig *n.* دبوي كوچنانه da bootee koochnay sanga

sprightly *a.* تراوتازه tar aw taza

spring *v.i.* سرچينه اخستل،بوپوهل sar cheena akheysta; top wahal

spring *n* چينه،پسرلی cheena; pasarlay

sprinkle *v.t.* نندل،تيتول naneydal; teetawal

sprint *v.i.* چک‌غلدل chatak zghaleydal

sprint *n* چکي‌غاستي‌سيالي chatakee zghastee syalee

sprout *v.i.* وکدل،نوتکول tookeydal; notaki kawal

sprout *n* نوتکه،نيال،بوکه notaka; nyal; sooka

spur *n.* سيخک،ترەراوتلتيا seekhak; teyra rawataltya

spur *v.t.*

spurious *a.* ناريتوني،ارموني nareekhtoonay; armoonay

spurn *v.t.* ردول،په‌لغته‌وهل radawal; pa laghata wahal

spurt *v.i.* ناپه‌سرعت‌زياتول nasapa surat zyatawal

spurt *n* ناپي‌هه nasapee hasa

sputnik *n.* سپوږمکی spogmakay

sputum *n.* خراشکی kharashkay

spy *n.* سارر sargar

spy *v.i.* ساري‌کول sargaree kawal

squad *n.* ل نظامي nizamee dalgay

squadron *n.* دنظامي‌مشرانويوه‌ل da nizamee masharano yawa dalgay

squalid *a.* خيرن kheeran

squalor *n.* مرداري murdaree

squander *v.t.* کول تلف talf kawal

square *n.* وی‌لمور salor gotay

square *a* لمورويز salor goteez

square *v.t.* لمورويزه‌بهورکول؛جوجای کول salor gooteeza banra warkawal; jor jaray kawal

squash *v.t.* خچ‌پچ‌کول khach pach kawal

squash *n* خچ‌پچ‌شوی khach pach shaway

squat *v.i.* دپوپه‌پنجوکناستل da pkho pa panjo kkheynastal

squeak *v.i.* چغسوروهل cheyghi soorey wahal

squeak *n* چغن‌غ؛فرياد chaghan ghag; faryad

squeeze *v.t.* چيتول cheetawal

squint *v.i.* کوستری‌کدل kog stargay keydal

squint *n* کوسترتوب kog stargtob

squire *n.* ملک،خان malak; khan

squirrel *n.* موش‌خرما mosh khurma

stab *v.t.* په‌خنجروهل pa khanjar wahal

stab *n.* دحمله‌هه da hamley hasa

stability *n.* ‌ټکاو teekaw

stabilization *n.* ‌ټنت teengakht

stabilize *v.t.* ‌ټکاووربل teekaw warbakhal

stable *a.* تثبيت‌شوی tasbeet shaway

stable *n* غوجل،پنغالی ghojal; pand ghalay

stable *v.t.* ‌ټناوورکول teengar warkawal

stadium *n.* لوبغالی lobghalay

staff *n.* کارمندان karmandan

staff *v.t.* مرسته‌ورسره‌کول mrasta warsara kawal

stag *n.* نارينه‌سرغوزه nareena sra gowaza

stage *n.* دنندارصحنه da nandarey sahna

stage *v.t.* دريورته‌ايوودل dareez warta eekhodal

stagger *v.i.* ميدل،نتلل zambeydal;
rang rang tlal

stagger *n.* ميدنه zambeydana

stagnant *a.* بحركته،ولا bey
harakata; walar

stagnate *v.i.* راكدكدل،بحركته كدل
rakad keydal; bey harakata
keydal

stagnation *n.* كساد،ركود kasad;
rakood

staid *a.* دروند،ثابت droond; sabit

stain *n.* داغ dagh

stain *v.t.* خيرنول kheyranawal

stainless *a.* زنگ‌نه‌اخستونکی zang na
akheystoonkay

stair *n.* پوړ،مرتبه poray; martaba

stake *n* لرينه‌لکه largeena lakara

stake *v.t.* په‌لري‌يالکپورتل pa largee
ya lakari pori taral

stale *a.* زو،پاته‌شوی zor; pata
shaway

stale *v.t.* زول،له‌موه‌لويدل zarawal; la
moda lweydal

stalemate *n.* په‌شطرنج کمات‌او‌مبهوت
pa shatranj ki mat aw
mabhoot

stalk *n.* داانستن da adaney stan

stalk *v.i.* ارل،په‌نازنخروتلل saral; pa
naz nakhro tlal

stalk *n* دشرابوجام da sharabo jam

stall *n.* کوچنی‌لرينه‌خونه koochnay
largeena khoona

stall *v.t.* له‌حرکته‌غورول la harakata
ghorzawal

stallion *n.* نارينه‌اس nareena as

stalwart *a.* غتلی،هومن ghakhtalay;
hodman

stalwart *n* زور،برم zrawar; garam

stamina *n.* توان،ژوندواک twan;
zhwand zwak

stammer *v.i.* توتله‌کدل totla keydal

stammer *n* توتله‌توب totlatob

stamp *n.* نقش،مهر naqsh; muhar

stamp *v.i.* مهرلول muhar lagawal

stampede *n.* نا‌اپی‌له‌ييز‌حرکت
nasapee dalayeez harakat

stampede *v.i* له‌ييز‌حرکت‌کول
dalayeez harakat kawal

stand *v.i.* دردل dareydal

stand *n.* دردنه،دردوای dareydana;
da dareydo zay

standard *n.* معيار mayar

standard *a* معياري mayaree

standardization *n.* دمعيارلبندي da
mayar dalbandee

standardize *v.t.* معياري‌کول
mayaree kawal

standing *n.* حالت halat

standpoint *n.* ثابت‌تمای sabit
tamzay

standstill *n.* سکون،دردنه sakoon;
dareydana

stanza *n.* شعری‌بند shayree band

staple *n.* پايه،اوسپنيزه‌را paya;
ospaneeza geera

staple *a* اهم،اصلي aham; aslee

star *n.* ستوری storay

star *v.t.* ملدل،شهرت‌پداکول
zaleydal; shuhrat payda
kawal

starch *n.* نشاسته nishasta

starch *v.t.* په‌نشاسته‌کلکول pa
nishasta klakawal

stare *v.i.* يريريريرکتل zeyr zeyr katal

stare *n.* وانه؛رركتنه rad rad katana; waranga

stark *n.* وچكلك؛تنها wach klak; tanha

stark *adv.* پهبشپول pa bashpar dawl

starry *a.* لهستوروك la storo dak

start *v.t.* پيلكول payl kawal

start *n* پيل payl

startle *v.t.* لامايموپوهل la zaya top wahal

starvation *n.* لوه؛قحطي lwaga; qahtee

starve *v.i.* لهلومدل la lwagi mreydal

state *n.* حالت؛رياست؛دولت halat; reeyasat; dawlat

state *v.t* بيانول bayanawal

stately *a.* عالي alee

statement *n.* بيان bayan

statesman *n.* سياستوال seeyasatwal

static *n.* ساكن sakin

statics *n.* دساكنوجسمونونيزمانه da sakino jismoono seyraneeza sanga

station *n.* تماى؛مركز tamzay; markaz

station *v.t.* مستقركول؛تماىكپرول mustaqar kawal; tamzay ki preykhwal

stationary *a.* ساكن sakin

stationer *n.* كتابپلورى keetabploray

stationery *n.* دليكنيزووسايلو پلورونكى da leekaneezo wasayalo plooroonkey

statistical *a.* سرشمرنه sar shmeyrana

statistician *n.* دسرشمرنكارپوه da sar shmeyrani karpoh

statistics *n.* دشمرنعلم da shmeyrani ilam

statue *n.* مجسمه mujassima

stature *n.* قد؛بدنيبه qad; badanee banra

status *n.* حالت؛مرتبه halat; martaba

statute *n.* قانون qanoon

statutory *a.* لهقانونسرهسم la qanoon sara sam

staunch *a.* وفادار؛ثابتقدم wafadar; sabit qadam

stay *v.i.* پاتكدل؛مشتكدل pati keydal; meysht keydal

stay *n* درمدنه؛قيام dareydana; qayam

steadfast *a.* ثابتقدم sabit qadam

steadiness *n.* پياوىعظم pyawaray azam

steady *a.* يونواخت؛امن yaw nawakht; dadman

steady *v.t.* ثابتقدمساتل sabit qadam satal

steal *v.i.* غلاكول ghla kawal

stealthily *adv.* پهپهسره pa pata sara

steam *n* بخار؛له bukhar; lara

steam *v.i.* بخاركول bukhar kawal

steamer *n.* بخاركوونكى bukhar kawoonkay

steed *n.* اس as

steel *n.* پولاد pawlad

steep *a.* ژور zhawar

steep *v.t.* لمدول lamdawal

steeple *n.* برج؛مناره burj; munara

steer *v.t.* چلول chalawal

stellar *a.* پاياوستنتهورته payey aw stani ta warta

stem *n.* رګه،تنه reekha; tana

stem *v.i.* تنهپدا کول tana payda kawal

stench *n.* بدبويي bad booyee

stencil *n.* دتورواوشکلونودمنقوشپله da toro aw shakloono da manqooshay panra

stencil *v.i.* دتورواوشکلونودمنقوشپاپه مرستهنقشجوول da toro aw shakloono da manqooshay panri pa mrasta naqsh jorawal

stenographer *n.* چکلیکونکی chatak leekoonkay

stenography *n.* چکلیکنه chatak leekana

step *n.* پل،بام pal; gam

step *v.i.* پلیرردل،بام اخستل palee garzeydal; gam akheystal

steppe *n.* بونواوپراخهاوزمهجله bey wano aw parakha dag wazma jalga

stereotype *n.* کلیشه،دکلیشهجووانفن kaleesha; da kaleeshey jorawani fan

stereotype *v.t.* کلیشهاوفیلمبرابرول kaleesha aw feelam barabarawal

stereotyped *a.* تقلیدشوی taqleed shaway

sterile *a.* شن،بحاصله shand; bey hasila

sterility *n.* شنتوب shandtob

sterilization *n.* لهکارهغورونه la kara ghorzawana

sterilize *v.t.* بحاصلهکول bey hasila kawal

sterling *a.* دقانونيمعیارخاوند da qanoonee mayar khawand

sterling *n.* دبریتانیرسميسکه da breetaneeyey rasmee sika

stern *a.* سختیر sakhtgeer

stern *n.* سختیرانسان sakhtgeer insan

stethoscope *n.* طبيغو tibee ghwagay

stew *n.* ورواپخوونکی khorwa pakhowoonkay

stew *v.t.* ورووواشول wro wro eyshawal

steward *n.* خادم khadim

stick *n.* لکه،امسا lakara; amsa

stick *v.t.* نلدل،پهلکوهل nakhleydal; pa lakari wahal

sticker *n.* سردونکیکاغذ sreykheydoonkay kaghaz

stickler *n.* اصرارکوونکیشخص israr kawoonkay shakhs

sticky *n.* سرناک sreykhnak

stiff *n.* شخ؛نغ shakh; neygh

stiffen *v.t.* کلکول klakawal

stifle *v.t.* زندکول؛خاموشول zanday kawal; khamoshawal

stigma *n.* دشرمداغ da sharam dagh

still *a.* غلی،ساکت ghalay; sakit

still *adv.* همشه،تردچ hamaysha; tar dey chi

still *v.t.* آرامول aramawal

still *n.* چوپتیا choptya

stillness *n.* خاموشي khamoshee

stilt *n.* یواودپلرونکیمارغه yaw oogdey pkhey laroonkay margha

stimulant *n.* پاروونکی parawoonkay

stimulate *v.t.* پارول parawal

stimulus *n.* دپاريدنوسيله da pareydani waseela

sting *v.t.* چيچل cheechal

sting *n.* چيچ cheech

stingy *a.* لرونکی نـ neykh laroonkay

stink *v.i.* بدبوىلرل bad booy laral

stink *n* بدبويي bad booyee

stipend *n.* تنخوا tankha

stipulate *v.t.* تونلاسليکول taroon lasleekawal

stipulation *n.* دتونماده da taroon mada

stir *v.i.* حرکتورکول harakat warkawal

stirrup *n.* رکاب rakab

stitch *n.* ګنه gandana

stitch *v.t.* پوندول،ګنل peywandawal; gandal

stock *n.* ذخيره zakheera

stock *v.t.* ذخيرهکول zakheera kawal

stock *a.* موجود،زرمهشوى mawjood; zeyrma shaway

stocking *n.* اودينهجوراب oogdey khazeena jorabey

stoic *n.* خاموشاوجنجالخهلرىپروت انسان khamosh aw janjal sakha leyri prot insan

stoke *v.t.* پهاورتلاچول pa or teyl achawal

stoker *n.* دسوزولومواد da sozawalo mawad

stomach *n.* خه kheyta

stomach *v.t.* زغمل zghamal

stone *n.* برہ،کانئ dabara; kanray

stone *v.t.* پهبرووېشتلیاموخل pa dabaro weeshtal ya mokhal

stony *a.* برين dabareen

stool *n.* لوموک lwara sawkay

stoop *v.i.* کدل kageydal

stoop *n* کونه kagawana

stop *v.t.* درول darawal

stop *n* درندنه dareydana

stoppage *n* توقف tawaquf

storage *n.* ودام godam

store *n.* سترپلورنی star ploranzay

store *v.t.* ودامکساتل godam ki satal

storey *n.* طبقه،پو tabqa; por

stork *n.* لاگ lag lag

storm *n.* توپان،سوران toopan; sooran

storm *v.i.* نناپريدکول nasapaee breed kawal

stormy *a.* توپاني،هجاني toopanee; hayjanee

story *n.* کيسه keesa

stout *a.* شجاع shuja

stove *n.* بخار bukharay

stow *v.t.* مخفيکول،پول makhfee kawal; patawal

straggle *v.i.* بايهودهکول،بترتيبهودهکول bey zaya wada kawal; bey tarteeba wada kawal

straggler *n.* کوهبی،وروستوپاتشوى koosa dabay; wrusto pati shaway

straight *a.* نغ neygh

straight *adv.* پهمستقيمول pa mustaqeem dawl

straighten *v.t.* تنظيمول tanzeemawal

straightforward *a.* پهانپيلي pa dang peyalee

straightway *adv.* مستقیما mustaqeeman

strain *v.t.* فشارلاندراوستل fishar landi rawastal

strain *n* فشار؛زور fishar; zor

strait *n.* دمکنرتانه da zmaki naray taranga

straiten *v.t.* پەتنسەکاچول pa tangsa ki achawal

strand *v.i.* یوازپرودل yawazi preykhodal

strand *n* دسیندغاه da seend ghara

strange *a.* ناآشنا naashna

stranger *n.* پردی praday

strangle *v.t.* دچاغاەتختەکول da cha ghara takhta kawal

strangulation *n.* زندکوونه zanday kawana

strap *n.* ریتاه؛تسمه reetara; tasma

strap *v.t.* پەتسمەسرەتل pa tasmey sara taral

strategem *n.* جنیچال jangee chal

strategic *a.* تدبیري tadbeeree

strategist *n.* دجنيتدبیرونوماهر da jangee tadbeeroono mahir

strategy *n.* دجنيتدبیرونوفن da jangee tadbeeroono fan

stratum *n.* طبقه؛قشر tabqa; qashar

straw *n.* پوزی؛مزری pozay; meyzaray

strawberry *n.*

stray *v.i.* درپەدررودل dar pa dar garzeydal

stray *a* سردان؛کوهی sargardan; koosa dabay

stray *n* سرردانی sargardanee

stream *n.* ویاله wyala

stream *v.i.* بهدل؛جاريکدل baheydal; jaree keydal

streamer *n.* دجامودلبووپ da jamo da gul booto patay

streamlet *n.* کوچنویاله koochnay wyala

street *n.* کوه koosa

strength *n.* قوت؛پایت qoowat; payakht

strengthen *v.t.* قويکدل؛قويکول qawee keydal; qawee kawal

strenuous *a.* فعال faal

stress *n.* کو؛فشار kokhakh; fishar

stress *v.t* ترفشارلاندراوستل tar fishar landi rawastal

stretch *v.t.* غول؛پراختیاورکول ghazawal; parakhtya warkawal

stretch *n* غوونه ghazawana

stretcher *n.* درنوردولودلاسيوسیله da ranzoor da wralo lasee waseela

strew *v.t.* تیتول؛شنل teetawal; shanal

strict *a.* سخت sakht

stricture *n.* زورزیاتی zor zyatay

stride *v.i.* لويلويءامونەاخستل loy loy gamoona akheystal

stride *n* پەامونوسرەاندازەنیونه pa gamoono sara andaza neewana

strident *a.* کوکوونکيغ koonr kawoonkay ghag

strife *n.* جنجال؛هەاوهاند janjal; hasa aw hand

strike *v.t.* کاربندزکول؛ویشتل kar bandeyz kawal; weeshtal strike n وهل بول،کاربدنز wahal dabawal; kar bandeyz

striker n. وهونکی wahoonkay

string n. مزی،تار mazay; tar

string v.t. سیمیامزی وراچول،کش کول seem ya mazay warachawal; kash kawal

stringency n. سختيري sakhtgeeree

stringent a. سخت،کنجوس sakht; kanjoos

strip n. پ،نرتسمه patay; naray tasma

strip v.t. بربنول barbandawal

stripe n. اودهمختلف رنونهلرونکپ oogda mukhtalif rangoona laroonki patay

stripe v.t. لیکهلیکهکول leeka leeka kawal

strive v.i. زیارکل zyar kakhal

stroke n. ضربه،بوزار zarba; goozar

stroke v.t. وزارکول،لاس پرراکل goozar kawal; las pri rakakhal

stroke n دزنغ،حمله hamla; da zang ghag

stroll v.i. وروورو چکروهل wro wro chakar wahal

stroll n چکروهنه chakar wahana

strong a. زورور zorawar

stronghold n. پنای،مورچل patanzay; morchal

structural a. جوتیز jorakhtaneez

structure n. جوت jorakht

struggle v.i. زیارکل zyar kakhal

struggle n زیار zyar

strumpet n. فاحشه fahisha

strut v.i. پهنازنخروتلل pa naz nakhro tlal

strut n دناز نخروتگ da naz nakhro tag

stub n. کونده،ریه koonda; reekha

stubble n. ببرهیره babara geera

stubborn a. خپلسری khpal saray

stud n. مخل gul meykhay

stud v.t. پهل مخوسیناورل pa gul meykho seengarawal

student n. زدکيال zdakryal

studio n. کاريخونه karee khoona

studious a. کتابلوستی keetab lostay

study v.i. زدکهکول،لوستل zdakra kawal; lostal

study n. مطالعه،لوست mutalia; lost

stuff n. ماده،بیز mada; seez

stuff 2 v.t. پهزورهکول pa zora dakawal

stuffy a. زندشوی zanday shaway

stumble v.i. تروتل teyr watal

stumble n. پرشاني parayshanee

stump n. دونکونده da wani koonda

stump v.t پهلوغسرهرالودل pa lwar ghag sara ralwaydal

stun v.t. حرانول hayranawal

stunt v.t. حرانوونکیورزشيکرتب کول hayranawoonkay warzashee kartab kawal

stunt n شهکارکرتب shahkar kartab

stupefy v.t. حرانول hayranawal

stupendous a. حرانوونکی،عجیب hayranawoonkay; ajeeb

stupid a لوده lawda

stupidity n. لودهتوب lawdatob

sturdy a. سرمبه sar tamba

sty n. دخواستونای da khoog astoganzay

stye *n.* دخواستونای da khoog astoganzay

style *n.* طرز tarz

subdue *v.t.* مطیع کول mutee kawal

subject *n.* تبعه،وی،ماده،جسم taba; wagaray; mada; jisam

subject *a* مسند،مطیع masnad; mutee

subject *v.t.* په واک کراوستل pa wak ki rawastal

subjection *n.* اطاعت itaat

subjective *a.* موضوعی،فاعلی mawzooee; failee

subjudice *a.* له قضایی پرکاو هو پرته la qazayee preykri aw hod parta

subjugate *v.t.* رام کول ram kawal

subjugation *n.* اطاعت itaat

sublet *v.t.* فرعی مستاجر ته داجار حق ورکول faree mustajar ta da eejarey haq warkawal

sublimate *v.t.* تصفیه کول tasfeeya kawal

sublime *a.* تصفیه کوونکی tasfeeya kawoonkey

sublime *n* چلونه chanrawana

sublimity *n.* رفعت rifat

submarine *n.* سمندر لاندپوړۍ samandar landi pawzee beyray

submarine *a* ترسمندر لاند tar samandar landi

submerge *v.i.* په اوبو کغوپه کدل pa obo ki ghopa keydal

submission *n.* غاه ایودنه ghara eekhodana

submissive *a.* مطیع mutee

submit *v.t.* تسلیم کدل tasleem keydal

subordinate *a.* تابع tabay

subordinate *n* اطاعت کوونکی itaat kawoonkey

subordinate *v.t.* اطاعت کول itaat kawal

subordination *n.* اطاعت itaat

subscribe *v.t.* تصویبول tasweebawal

subscription *n.* دورپاونبیه،نسخه لیکنه da warzpanri gadoonbaya; nuskha leekana

subsequent *a.* ورپسی warpasey

subservience *n.* په درد خونه pa dard khwarana

subservient *a.* مفید mufeed

subside *v.i.* خاموشدل khamosheydal

subsidiary *a.* کومکی komakee

subsidize *v.t.* مالی مرسته کول malee mrasta kawal

subsidy *n.* مالی مرسته malee mrasta

subsist *v.i.* ژوند کول zhwand kawal

subsistence *n.* ژوند zhwand

substance *n.* ماده،ذات mada; zat

substantial *a.* واقعی،موثق waqiee; muwassaq

substantially *adv.* په حقیقت ک pa haqeeqat ki

substantiate *v.t.* مادی به ورکول madee banra warkawal

substantiation *n.* تجسم tajassum

substitute *n.* ایناستی zaynastay

substitute *v.t.* دبل پرای ایودل da bal par zay eekhodal

substitution *n.* تبدیل tabdeel

subterranean *a.* پات او غلی pat aw ghalay

subtle *n.* دقیق،پلمر palmagar; daqeeq

subtlety *n.* زیات دقت zyat diqat

subtract *v.t.* تفریقول tafreeqawal

subtraction *n.* تفریق tafreeq

suburb *n.* داردشاوخواسیمه da khar da shawkhwa seema

suburban *a.* داردشاوخواسیماستون da khar da shawkhwa seemi astogan

subversion *n.* انهدام inhidam

subversive *a.* ندلی nareydalay

subvert *v.t.* نول narawal

succeed *v.i.* بریالی کدل baryalay keydal

success *n.* بریا barya

successful *a* بریالی baryalay

succession *n.* پرلهپستوب parla pasitob

successive *a.* پرلهپس parla pasi

successor *n.* ایناستی zaynastay

succumb *v.i.* لهپولودل la pkho lweydal

such *a.* همداشان،دارنه hamda shan; da ranga

such *pron.* داول خلک؛داول شیان da dawl khalk; da dawl shayan

suck *v.t.* رودل،تی رودل rodal; tay rodal

suck *n.* رودنه rodana

suckle *v.t.* شدورکول sheydey warkawal

sudden *n.* ناپی په nasapee peykha

suddenly *adv.* پهندیول،ناپه pa garandee dawl; nasapa

sue *v.t.* تعقیبول taqeebawal

suffer *v.t.* وربدل،زغمل zoreydal; zghamal

suffice *v.i.* کافی کدل kafee keydal

sufficiency *n.* کفایت،کافی مقدار kifayat; kafee miqdar

sufficient *a.* کافی؛پوره kafee; poora

suffix *n.* روستای rostaray

suffix *v.t.* روستای جوول rostaray jorawal

suffocate *v.t.* ساهیوربندول sa yi warbandawal

suffocation *n.* ساهوربندوونه sa warbandawana

suffrage *n.* پهول اکنوکدرای ورکولو حق pa tol takano ki da ray warkawalo haq

sugar *n.* بوره،قند boora; qand

sugar *v.t.* بورهورکول boora warkawal

suggest *v.t.* خپلهروهمکارهکول khpala groha khkara kawal

suggestion *n.* روههرندوونه groha sargandawana

suggestive *a.* نغوتهکوونکی naghota kawoonkay

suicidal *a.* ازنوژني zan wazhnee

suicide *n.* زنوژنه ان zan wazhna

suit *n.* مرافعه،یوهجوجام murafia; yawa jor jamey

suit *v.t.* راضی کول razee kawal

suitability *n.* موافقت muwafiqat

suitable *a.* موافق muwafiq

suite *n.* اپارتمان او دهغلوازم apartman aw da haghey lawazim

suitor *n.* مدعي mudaee

sullen *a.* توندخویه tond khooya

sulphur *n.* دسلفرباز da salfar gaz

sulphuric *a.* سلفرلرونکی salfar laroonkay

sultry *a.* رماونمجن garam aw namjan

sum *n.* ولپس؛مجموعه toley peysey; majmooa

sum *v.t.* جمع کول jama kawal

summarily *adv.* په لنډه توګه pa landa toga

summarize *v.t.* په لنډه توګه بیانول pa landa toga bayanawal

summary *n.* لنون landoon

summary *a.* لنډ land

summer *n.* درموسم da garmay mosam

summit *n.* دلوي درجغونه da loyi darajey ghonda

summon *v.t.* غایو دلوتوه رابلل ghari eekhodalo ta rabalal

summons *n.* دقانوني رابلنچه da qanoonee rabalani cheetay

sumptuous *a.* عیاش؛مسرفي ayash; masrafee

sun *n.* لمر lmar

sun *v.t.* لمر ته ایودل lmar ta eekhodal

Sunday *n.* یک شنبه؛یونۍ yak shamba; yoonay

sunder *v.t.* بلول beylawal

sundry *a.* رنارنۍ؛بلابل ranga rang; beyla beyl

sunny *a.* لمرین lmareen

sup *v.i.* غوپ غوپ سکل ghorap ghorap skhal

superabundance *n.* ډېررت deyrakht

superabundant *a.* خوراډېر khora deyr

superb *a.* درونداوپتمن droond aw patman

superficial *a.* برسرن؛سطحي barseyran; sathee

superficiality *n.* برسرنتوب barseyrantob

superfine *a.* غوره او ممتاز ghwara aw mumtaz

superfluity *n.* زیادت zyadakht

superfluous *a.* اضافي izafee

superhuman *a.* فوق بشر foq bashar

superintend *v.t.* سرپرستي کول sarparastee kawal

superintendence *n.* مدیریت mudeereeyat

superintendent *n.* سرپرست sarparast

superior *a.* پورتنی؛غوره portanay; ghwara

superiority *n.* پورته والی portawalay

superlative *a.* تر ټولو kha tar tolo kha

superlative *n.* تفضیلي tafzeelee

superman *n.* فوق بشر خصوصیات لرونکی انسان foq bashar khusooseeyat laroonkay insan

supernatural *a.* فوق العاده foqul ada

supersede *v.t.* دبل پای نیول da bal seez zay neewal

supersonic *a.* له غږ پورته la ghag porta

superstition *n.* موهوم پرستي mawhoom parastee

superstitious *a.* موهوم پرست mawhoom parast

supertax *n.* پر اضافي عایداتو مالیه par izafee aydato maleeya

supervise *v.t.* نظارت کول nazarat kawal

supervision *n.* نظارت nazarat

supervisor *n.* ناظر nazir

supper *n.* ماښام makham

supple *a.* غوړخوونکی ghozh khwaroonkay

supplement *n.* تکمیل؛ضمیمه takmeel; zameema

supplement *v.t.* کول تکمیل takmeel kawal

supplementary *a.* اضافي izafee

supplier *n.* رسوونکی؛دتدارکاتومسؤل rasawoonkay; da tadarikato masool

supply *v.t.* رسول rasawal

supply *n* تدارکات؛جنس tadarikat; jins

support *v.t.* ملاتړکول mlatar kawal

support *n.* ملاتړ mlataray

suppose *v.t.* تصورکول tasawwur kawal

supposition *n.* تصور؛فرض؛خیال tasawwur; farz; khyal

suppress *v.t.* پایمالول paymalawal

suppression *n.* پایمالوونه paymalawana

supremacy *n.* لواوی lwaraway

supreme *a.* متعال؛تروـلولو mutaal; tar tolo lwar

surcharge *n.* اضافي ماليه izafee maleeya

surcharge *v.t.* اضافي ماليه لول izafee maleeya lagawal

sure *a.* امن؛یقیني dadman; yaqeenee

surely *adv.* په امن ول pa dadman dawl

surety *n.* اطمینان itmaynan

surf *n.* په sapa

surface *n.* برسرن مخ؛سطح barseyran makh; sata

surface *v.i* باندنی مخ ورکول bandinay makh warkawal

surfeit *n.* بزاره کول؛مول beyzara kawal; marawal

surge *n.* لوهپه lwara sapa

surge *v.i.* پچوول؛پاند کدل sapey jorawal; sapand keydal

surgeon *n.* دجراحاکر da jarahay daktar

surgery *n.* جراحي jarahee

surmise *n.* اکل atkal

surmise *v.t.* اکل کول atkal kawal

surmount *v.t.* پرزیاتدل pri zyateydal

surname *n.* کورنی نوم koranay noom

surpass *v.t.* ورخه مخکاکدل warsakha makhki keydal

surplus *n.* پاته شوني؛اضافي pata shoonay; izafee

surprise *n.* حرانتیا hayrantya

surprise *v.t.* حرانول hayranawal

surrender *v.t.* تسلیمدل tasleemeydal

surrender *n* سپارنه sparana

surround *v.t.* احاطه کول ihata kawal

surroundings *n.* چاپریال chapeyryal

surtax *n.* مالیاتي جریمه maleeyatee jareema

surveillance *n.* نظارت nazarat

survey *n.* اندازه‌ميري،درجه‌بندي andaza geyree; daraja bandee

survey *v.t.* اندازه‌ميري‌كول andaza geyree kawal

survival *n.* بقا baqa

survive *v.i.* ژوندي‌پاته‌كدل zhwanday pati keydal

suspect *v.t.* بدلومانه‌كدل badgoomana keydal

suspect *a.* مشكوك mashkook

suspect *n* شكمن shakman

suspend *v.t.* معلق‌كول،بنول muallaq kawal; zandawal

suspense *n.* معلق muallaq

suspension *n.* تعليق،درونه taleeq; darawana

suspicion *n.* شك shak

suspicious *a.* شكمن shakman

sustain *v.t.* ادامه‌وركول،خوندي‌ساتل idama warkawal; khwandee satal

sustenance *n.* خوندينه،ساتنه khwandeyana; satana

swagger *v.i.* په‌تكبرتلل pa takabbur tlal

swagger *n* مغرور maghroor

swallow *v.t.* دچڼچڼري‌اوازونه‌كول da chanrchanri pa shan awazoona kawal

swallow *n.* چڼه chanrchanra

swallow *n.* دچڼاواز ونه da chanrchanri awazoona

swamp *n.* دناولواوبو نه da nawalo obo dand

swamp *v.t.* وبدل doobeydal

swan *n.* يو مارغه yaw margha

swarm *n.* وهه ganra goonra

swarm *v.i.* موه‌جوول ganra goonra jorawal

swarthy *a.* تورربنى tor rangay

sway *v.i.* هخواده‌خوامبدل hakhwa deykhwa zambeydal

sway *n* موجي‌حركت mojee harakat

swear *v.t.* قسم‌خول qasam khwaral

sweat *n.* خولى khwaley

sweat *v.i.* خولاكدل khwaley keydal

sweater *n.* هغه‌كس‌چه‌خواكوي، رموونكى‌جاك hagha kas chi khwaley kawee; garmowoonkay jakat

sweep *v.i.* رېبول reybazawal

sweep *n.* رب reybaz

sweeper *n.* رېوهونكى reybaz wahoonkay

sweet *a.* خو khog

sweet *n* محبوب mahboob

sweeten *v.t.* خوول khwagawal

sweetmeat *n.* حلويات halweeyat

sweetness *n.* خووالى khogwalay

swell *v.i.* تسپودداكدل taspod payda keydal

swell *n* پسوب parsob

swift *a.* چك chatak

swim *v.i.* لامبووهل lambo wahal

swim *n* لامبووهنه lambo wahana

swimmer *n.* لامبووهونكى lambo wahoonkay

swindle *v.t.* غولول gholawal

swindle *n.* فرب farayb

swindler *n.* غولوونكى gholawoonkay

swine *n.* سركوزى sar koozay

swing *v.i.* تاوخول taw khwaral

swing *n* تاو،دفعاليت‌دوره taw; da faaleeyat dawra

swiss *n.* سویسی‌وی‌باژبه sweesee wagaray ya zhaba

swiss *a* سویسی sweesee

switch *n.* سوچ؛زر swich; tanray

switch *v.t.* بدلول؛دبرښناتکته‌پورته‌کول badlawal; da breykhna tanray kkhata porta kawal

swoon *n.* کمزورتیا kamzortya

swoon *v.i* بهوه‌کدل bey hokha keydal

swoop *v.i.* نیول لاند برید ناپه nasapa breed landi neewal

swoop *n* ناپی‌برید nasapee breed

sword *n.* توره toora

sycamore *n.* یومصری‌اینر yaw misree eenzar

sycophancy *n.* چاپلوسی chaplosee

sycophant *n.* چاپلوسه‌سی chaplosa saray

syllabic *n.* هجایی؛دیوپاستازی hijayee; da yawey sapey astazay

syllable *n.* هجا؛په hija; sapa

syllabus *n.* دزدکددورمضامین da zdakri da dawrey mazameen

sylph *n.* حوره hoora

sylvan *a.* نلمشتی zangal meyshtay

symbol *n.* علامه alama

symbolic *a.* نهلرونکی nakha laroonkay

symbolism *n.* په‌نوعلامومکاره‌کونه pa nakho alamo khkara kawana

symbolize *v.t.* ترکیبول tarkeebawal

symmetrical *a.* متناسب mutanasib

symmetry *n.* تطابق tatabuq

sympathetic *a.* زسواند zraswand

sympathize *v.i.* خواخوي‌ي‌کاره‌کول khwakhoogee khkara kawal

sympathy *n.* هم‌اندتوب ham andtob

symphony *n.* له‌ییزساز dalayeez saz

symposium *n.* دوستانه‌مجلس dostana majlis

symptom *n.* علامه alama

symptomatic *a.* دناروغنه‌اوعرض da naroghay nakha aw arz

synonym *n.* هم‌مانیزویی ham maneez wayay

synonymous *a.* هم‌مانا ham mana

synopsis *n.* اجمال؛لنون ajmal; landoon

syntax *n.* غونله‌پوهه؛دنحوعلم ghondla poha; da nahwi ilam

synthesis *n.* ترکیب؛یوایت tarkeeb; yaw zayakht

synthetic *a.* مصنوعي masnooee

synthetic *n* مصنوعي‌یز masnooee seez

syringe *n.* سرنج sirinj

syringe *v.t.* سرنج‌وهل sirinj wahal

syrup *n.* درملیزمحلول darmaleez mahlool

system *n.* قاعده؛نظام qayda; nizam

systematic *a.* له‌نظام‌سره‌سم la nizam sara sam

systematize *v.t.* کنلاره‌ورته‌جوول kranlara warta jorawal

T

table *n.* مز meyz

table *v.t.* سره نلول sara nakhlawal

tablet *n.* ګولۍ golay

taboo *n.* پرهز،تقديس parheyz; taqdees

taboo *a.* حرام haram

taboo *v.t.* حرام لل haram ganral

tabular *a.* جدولي jadwalee

tabulate *v.t.* په نوم لکايول pa noom lar ki zayawal

tabulation *n.* لتليک جوړونه lakhtleek jorawana

tabulator *n.* لتليک جوړوونکى lakhtleek jorawoonkay

tacit *a.* ضمني،اخيز zimnee; arkheez

taciturn *a.* خاموش khamosh

tackle *n.* مخه نيونه،کاري وسايل makha neewana; karee wasayal

tackle *v.t.* مخه نيول makha neewal

tact *n.* مهارت maharat

tactful *a.* ماهرانه mahirana

tactician *n.* کارپوه شخص karpoh shakhs

tactics *n.* مهارتونه او تدبيرونه maharatoona aw tadbeeroona

tactile *a.* دلمس حس پوراوند da lams his pori arwand

tag *n.* ريتاه،پ reetara; patay

tag *v.t.* پټى لول patay pri lagawal

tail *n.* لکۍ lakay

tailor *n.* ګنډونکى gandoonkay

tailor *v.t.* خياطي کول khayatee kawal

taint *n.* داغ،ککتيا dagh; kakartya

taint *v.t.* ملوث کول mulawwis kawal

take *v.t* اخستل،نيول akheystal; neewal

tale *n.* کيسه keesa

talent *n.* وتيا wartya

talisman *n.* کوي kodi

talk *v.i.* غدل،خبر کول ghageydal; khabari kawal

talk *n* خبر khabari

talkative *a.* ژبغاند zhabgharand

tall *a.* هسک،ج hask; jag

tallow *n.* وازده ويلکونه او غوروونه wazda weeli kawana aw ghwarawana

tally *n.* چوبخط،شمره chobkhat; shmeyra

tally *v.t.* تطبيقول tatbeeqawal

tamarind *n.* هندي املي hindee imlee

tame *a.* کورنى،اهلي koranay; ahlee

tame *v.t.* اهلي کول ahlee kawal

tamper *v.i.* جوجاى کول jor jaray kawal

tan *v.i.* دلمررا کبدنخدل da lmar ranra ki badan khareydal

tan *n., a.* قهويي،قهويي رن qahwayee; qahwayee rang

tangent *n.* مماس mamas

tangible *a.* دلمس ويز،محسوس da lams seez; mahsoos

tangle *n.* اختهاومبتلا،تاوراتاو akhta aw mubtila; tawrataw

tangle *v.t.* په جال کرارول،اخته کول pa jal ki rageyrawal; akhta kawal tank *n.* داوبوزرمتون،بانک da obo zeyramtoon; tank

tanker *n.* دتلولدونکلار da teylo leygdawoonki laray

tanner *n.* دباغ dabagh

tannery *n.* درمنوآش کوونه da sarmano ash kawana

tantalize *v.t.* چاته‌لاس‌وراچول cha ta law warachawal

tantamount *a.* انول،معادل andwal; muadil

tap *n.* شیردان،سوری،نلکه sheerdan; sooray; nalka

tap *v.t.* ول،ورووروهل sasawal; wro wro wahal

tape *n.* پ،تار patay; tar

tape *v.t* په‌پسره‌تل pa patay sara taral

taper *v.i.* نری کول naray kawal

taper *n* کوچنیشمع koochnay shama

tapestry *n.* غالوله‌پرده ghalay dawla parda

tar *n.* قیر،تارکول qeer; tarkol

tar *v.t.* په‌قیرولل،تارکول‌لول pa qeero laral; tarkol lagawal

target *n.* موخه،هدف mokha; hadaf

tariff *n.* محصول mahsool

tarnish *v.t.* کدرکول،داغي‌کول kadar kawal; daghee kawal

task *n.* کار،چاره kar; chara

task *v.t.* په‌کوم‌کارمارل pa kom kar gumaral

taste *n.* ذایقه zayqa

taste *v.t.* ذایقه‌لرل zayqa laral

tasteful *a.* خوندور khwandawar

tasty *a.* خوندور khwandawar

tatter *n.* یرویرشی seeri weeri shay

tatter *v.t* یرویرکول seeri weeri kawal

tattoo *n.* خال khal

tattoo *v.i.* خال‌وهل khal wahal

taunt *v.t.* رل ratal

taunt *n* رنه ratana

tavern *n.* شرابخانه sharabkhana

tax *n.* مالیه maleeya

tax *v.t.* مالیه‌لول maleeya lagawal

taxable *a.* دمالیو da maleeyey war

taxation *n.* مالیه‌ایودنه maleeya eekhodana

taxi *n.* کسي tiksee

taxi *v.i.* کسي‌کتلل tiksee ki tlal

tea *n* چای chay

teach *v.t.* ورزده‌کول warzda kawal

teacher *n.* وونکی khowoonkay

teak *n.* یوول‌ونه yaw dawl wana

team *n.* له dala

tear *v.t.* شلول،شکول shlawal; shkawal

tear *n.* اوکه ookhka

tear *n.* قهر،پ qahar; tap

tearful *a.* ژغونی zharghonay

tease *v.t.* اذارول azarawal

teat *n.* دتیوکه da tee sooka

technical *n.* تخنیکي takhneekee

technicality *n.* نه‌تخنیکي takhneekee garana

technician *n.* تخنیکي‌کارپوه takhneekee karpoh

technique *n.* فن،طریقه fan; tareeqa

technological *a.* تخنیک‌پوراوند takhneek pori arwand

technologist *n.* تخنیکي‌کارپوه takhneekee karpoh

technology *n.* تخنیک پژندنه takhneekee peyzhandana

tedious *a.* ستومانه کوونکی stomana kawoonkay

tedium *n.* ستومانی stomana

teem *v.i.* تشول tashawal

teenager *n.* نویزوان naway zwan

teens *n. pl.* نورلس کلنزوان noorlas kalan zwan

teethe *v.i.* غاوونه کول ghakhoona kawal

teetotal *a.* دنشهیموادودپرولوپهاوند da nashayee mawado da preykhwalo pa arwand

teetotaller *n.* دنشهیموادودپرولوملاتی da nashayee mawado da preykhwalo mlataray

telecast *n.* درایویيیالمویزیونيپرورامخپرونه da radyoyee ya talweezyonee parogram khparawana

telecast *v.t.* رایویيیالمویزیونيپرورامخپرول radyoyee ya talweezyonee parogram khparawal

telecommunications *n.* لفونياودرابطایک taylafoonee aw da rabitey areeki

telegram *n.* لرلیکنی lar leekanay

telegraph *n.* لمراف talgaraf

telegraph *v.t.* پهلمرافخبرول pa talgaraf khabrawal

telegraphic *a.* لمرافی talgarafee

telegraphist *n.* لمرافکارپوه talgaraf karpoh

telegraphy *n.* دلمراففن da talgaraf fan

telepathic *a.* فکريتاولروونکی fikree taraw laroonkay

telepathist *n.* پهفکريتاوباوري pa fikree taraw bawaree

telepathy *n.* دانسانيفکريتاوفن da insanee fikree taraw fan

telephone *n.* لفون taylafoon

telephone *v.t.* پهلفونغدل pa taylafoon ghageydal

telescope *n.* ستوراريلروین storsaray larween

telescopic *a.* ستوراريلروینی storsaray larweenee

televise *v.t.* پهملویزیونخپرول pa talweezyon khparawal

television *n.* لمویزیون talweezyon

tell *v.t.* ویل wayal

teller *n.* ویاند،شمرونکی wayand; shmeyroonkay

temper *n.* مزاج mizaj

temper *v.t.* فلزتهاوبهورکول filiz ta oba warkawal

temperament *n.* خوی khooy

temperamental *a.* مزاجي mizajee

temperance *n.* طبیعت tabyat

temperate *a.* ملایم mulayim

temperature *n.* تودوخي tawdokhee

tempest *n.* توپان toopan

tempestuous *a.* توپاني toopanee

temple *n.* عبادتزای ibadat zay

temple *n* روکی ranrookay

temporal *a.* مهالیز mahaleez

temporary *a.* لنمهالي land mahalee

tempt *v.t.* تحریکول tahreekawal

temptation *n.* لمسون lamsoon

tempter *n.* لمسوونکی lamsawoonkay

ten *n., a* لس،لسمهشمره las; lasama shmeyra

tenable *a.* دساتنو da satani war

tenacious *a.* محکم muhkam

tenacity *n.* ینت teengakht

tenancy *n.* اجارهداري eejaradaree

tenant *n.* اجارهدار eejara

tend *v.i.* میللرل mayl laral

tendency *n.* توجه tawajo

tender *n* دداوطلبمزایده da dawtalbay muzayda

tender *v.t.* دلیلامیاداوطلبپهمزایدهکونه داستل da leelam ya dawtalbay pa muzayda ki wanda akheystal

tender *n* داجناسولدوونکته da ajnaso leygdawani kakhtay

tender *a* نرم،لطیف naram; lateef

tenet *n.* عقیده aqeeda

tennis *n.* دنسلوبه da taynas loba

tense *n.* شدت،دفعلزمانه shiddat; da fayl zamana

tense *a.* شدید shadeed

tension *n.* فشار fishar

tent *n.* خیمه khayma

tentative *a.* تجربوي tajrubawee

tenure *n.* دتصرفوخت da tasarruf wakht

term *n.* موده mooda

term *v.t.* نومپرایودل noom pri eekhodal

terminable *a.* پایتهرسدونی pay ta rasawal

terminal *a.* پهبخکپروت pa beykh ki prot

terminal *n* آخر akhir

terminate *v.t.* ختمول khatmawal

termination *n.* پای،ختمدا pay; khatmeyda

terminological *a.* نومپوهنیز noompohaneez

terminology *n.* نومپوهنه noompohana

terminus *n.* وروستنیتمای wrustanay tamzay

terrace *n.* چوتره،برنه chawtra; baranda

terrible *a.* وحشتناک wahshatnak

terrier *n.* یوولکلیکوچنیکاريسپی yaw dawl khkulay koochnay khkaree spay

terrific *a.* فوقالعاده fawqul ada

terrify *v.t.* ترهول tarhawal

territorial *a.* سیمهییز seemayeez

territory *n.* سیمه seema

terror *n.* ار dar

terrorism *n.* ترهري tarhagaree

terrorist *n.* ترهر tarhagar

terrorize *v.t.* ترهول tarhawal

terse *a.* ک،روزلشوی dak; rozal shaway

test *v.t.* آزمویل azmoyal

test *n* امتحان،آزموینه imtihan; azmoyana

testament *n.* انجیل injeel

testicle *n.* خوه،خصیه khota; khuseeya

testify *v.i.* تصدیقول tasdeeqawal

testimonial *n.* شهادتنامه shahadat nama

testimony *n.* تصدیق tasdeeq

tete-a-tete *n.* دوهپهدوه dwa pa dwa

tether n. پی paray

tether v.t. پزواني کول peyzwanee kawal

text n. عبارت؛متن ibarat; matan

textile a. اوبدلشوی obdal shaway

textile n منسوجات؛توکر mansoojat; tokar

textual n. لفظي lafzee

texture n. اوبدنه؛تنسته obdana; tanasta

thank v.t. مننه ورته ويل manana warta wayal

thanks n. مننه manana

thankful a. منندوی manandoy

thankless a. ناشکره nashukra

that a. بل bal

that dem. pron. هغه hagha

that rel. pron. يو هغه hagha yaw

that adv. داولچ da dawl chi

that conj. چ دا da chi

thatch n. کال؛لوخه kagal; lookha

thatch v.t. اخول akheyrawal

thaw v.i ويلاکيدل weeli keydal

thaw n رمموسم garam mosam

theatre n. تياتر tyatar

theatrical a. تياترپوراوند tyatar pori arwand

theft n. غلا ghla

their a. دهغوي da haghwee

theirs pron. د هغوي da haghwee

theism n. په‌خدای‌باور pa khuday bawar

theist n. په‌خدای‌باورلرونکی pa khuday bawar laroonkay

them pron. ته هغوي haghwee ta

thematic a. موضوعي mawzooee

theme n. موضوع؛مقاله mawzoo

then adv. کله‌چي kala chi

then a بيا bya

thence adv. لههغهلوري‌چ la hagha lori chi

theocracy n. دروحانيونوواکمني da roohaneeyoonu wakmanee

theologian n. ددينی‌علومو‌کارپوه da deenee uloomu karpoh

theological a. په‌الهي‌چاروپوراوند pa ilahee charo pori arwand

theology n. دين‌پوهنه deen pohana

theorem n. مسئله؛قاعده masala; qayda

theoretical a. نظري nazaree

theorist n. په‌نظري‌علم‌پوه pa nazaree ilam poh

theorize v.i. نظري‌کول nazaree seyrani kawal

theory n. نظري‌علم nazaree ilam

therapy n. معالجه mualija

there adv. هلته halta

thereabouts adv. په‌هغه‌شاوخواک pa hagha shawkhwa ki

thereafter adv. ورسته‌له wrusta la

thereby adv. له‌دکبله la dey kabala

therefore adv. له‌دلامله la dey lamala

thermal a. حرارتي hararatee

thermometer n. تودوخمج tawdokhmeych

thermos flask n. دتودوخدرجهپه‌خپل دای‌خونديساتونکی‌لوی da tawdokhay daraja pa khpal zay khwandee satoonkay lokhay

thesis n. پوهنليک pohanleek

thick *a.* راغوند raghond

thick *n.* غليظ ghaleez

thick *adv.* پهغليظول pa ghaleez dawl

thicken *v.i.* ضخيم كول zakheem kawal

thicket *n.* بوي ganr bootee

thief *n.* غل ghal

thigh *n.* ورون؛پنه wroon; panday

thimble *n.* وتمو gotmo

thin *a.* نرى naray

thin *v.t.* نرول dangarawal

thing *n.* شى؛يز shay; seez

think *v.t.* فكركول fikar kawal

thinker *n.* انزيال angeyryal

third *a.* دريم dreyam

third *n.* دريمهبرخه dreyama barkha

thirdly *adv.* دريمداچ dreyam da chi

thirst *n.* تنده tanda

thirst *v.i.* تىكدل tagay keydal

thirsty *a.* تى tagay

thirteen *n.* ديارلس dyarlas

thirteen *a* ديارلس dyarlas

thirteenth *a.* ديارلسم dyarlasam

thirtieth *a.* درشم deyrsham

thirtieth *n* درشمهبرخه deyrshama barkha

thirty *n.* درش deyrsh

thirty *a* درش deyrsh

thistle *n.* اغزى aghzay

thither *adv.* ته هخوا hakhwa ta

thorn *n.* اغزى aghzay

thorny *a.* اغزن aghzan

thorough *a* پوره؛مطلق poora; mutlaq

thoroughfare *n.* لويهلاره loya lara

though *conj.* ارچه agar chay

though *adv.* كههم ka sa ham

thought *n* اند،فكر and; fikar

thoughtful *a.* اندپال andpal

thousand *n.* زر zar

thousand *a* دزروشمر da zaro shmeyr

thrall *n.* مرىى mrayay

thralldom *n.* اسارت؛مرييتوب asarat; mrayeetob

thrash *v.t.* دبلاودرزول dabawal aw drazawal

thread *n.* تار tar

thread *v.t* تارپكاچول tar paki achawal

threadbare *a.* شلشل shalag shalag

threat *n.* خطر khatar

threaten *v.t.* وال gwakhal

three *n.* در drey

three *a* ددروشمر da dreyo shmeyr

thresh *v.t.* كول؛كوترهكول takawal; kotra kawal

thresher *n.* دغلكولوماشين da galey masheen

threshold *n.* درشل darshal

thrice *adv.* درلهزر drey zala

thrift *n.* پاسرهشوشتمنى pasra shawi shtamanee

thrifty *a.* پاسرهكوونكى pasra kawoonkay

thrill *n.* چ؛لز rach; larz

thrill *v.t.* چول rachawal

thrive *v.i.* وودهكول kha wada kawal

throat *n.* ستونى؛مر stoonay

throaty *a.* دلوی‌مرخاوند،غلوملی da loy maray khawand; ghag lweydalay

throb *v.i.* درزیدل drazeydal

throb *n.* درز؛ضرب draz; zarb

throe *n.* ددردیکه da dard sreeka

throne *n.* لد،دپاچاتخت gaday; da pacha takht

throne *v.t.* پاچاکول pacha kawal

throng *n.* زیات‌خلک zyat khalk

throng *v.t.* ګنوه‌جوول ganra goonra jorawal

throttle *n.* ستونی؛غاه stoonay; ghara

throttle *v.t.* ستونی‌ورتخته‌کول stoonay wartakhta kawal

through *prep.* له‌لور،به‌واسطه la lori; pa wasta

through *adv.* سرترسره،له‌پیله‌ترپایه sar tar sara; la payla tar paya

through *a* مستقیم mustaqeem

throughout *adv.* په‌ملنیزول pa tolaneez dawl

throughout *prep.* سرترسره sar tar sara

throw *v.t.* غورول ghorzawal

throw *n.* غوروونه ghorzawana

thrust *v.t.* په‌زورسره‌منل pa zor sara mandal

thrust *n* مننه،دننه‌کوونه mandana; danana kawana

thud *n.* درب‌درب drab drab

thud *v.i.* درب‌درب‌کول drab drab kawal

thug *n.* خونی،انسان‌وژونکی khoonee; insan wazhoonkay

thumb *n.* بموته bata gota

thumb *v.t.* په‌بموته‌سولول pa bata gota soolawal

thump *n.* درب،خرپ drab; khrap

thump *v.t.* درزول drazawal

thunder *n.* تندر tandar

thunder *v.i.* دتندرپه‌شان‌غګ‌کول da tandar pa shan ghag kawal

thunderous *a.* تندرته‌ورته tandar ta warta

Thursday *n.* پنجشنبه،دزیارت‌ور panjshamba; da zyarat wraz

thus *adv.* په‌دی‌دول pa dey dawl

thwart *v.t.* لاره‌یی‌بندول lara yi bandawal

tiara *n.* شاهی‌تاج shahee taj

tick *n.* دسمون‌نه da samoon nakha

tick *v.i.* دسمون‌نه‌لول da samoon nakha lagawal

ticket *n.* ک teekat

tickle *v.t.* تخول takhnrawal

ticklish *a.* ‌خانوزمه khangar wazma

tidal *a.* په‌جذراومدپوراوند pa jazar aw mad pori arwand

tide *n.* دسمندرپه da samandar sapa

tidings *n. pl.* خبرونه khabroona

tidiness *n.* منظموالی munazzamwalay

tidy *a.* منظم munazzam

tidy *v.t.* منظم‌کول munazzam kawal

tie *v.t.* غوه‌کول ghota kawal

tie *n* غوه،بند ghota; band

tier *n.* صف،کتار saf; katar

tiger *n.* پاز prang

tight *a.* کلک klak

tighten *v.t.* کلکول klakawal

tigress *n.* پازینه khazeena prang

tile *n.* کاشی کودوی kashee kawdoray

tile *v.t.* کاشی کودوی لول kashee kawdoray lagawal

till *prep.* ترهغه مهاله tar hagha mahala

till *n. conj.* چ د تر tar dey chi

till *v.t.* زمکه دکت لپاره تیارول zmaka da kakht lapara tayarawal

tilt *v.i.* کدل kageydal

tilt *n.* کوروالی kogwalay

timber *n.* لری largay

time *n.* مهال mahal

time *v.t.* وخت برابرول؛وخت اکل wakht barabarawal

timely *a.* پرخپل وخت par khpal wakht

timid *a.* بزه bey zra

timidity *n.* بزه توب bey zratob

timorous *a.* شرمیندوکی sharmeendookay

tin *n.* قلعی qalee

tin *v.t.* په قلعی سره پول pa qalee sara pokhal

tincture *n.* یوول درمل yaw dawl darmal

tincture *v.t.* رنول rangawal

tinge *n.* جزیی رنز juzyee rang

tinge *v.t.* جزیی رنور کول juzyee rang warkawal

tinker *n.* تار tatar

tinsel *n.* دفلس زلاندپ da filas zalanda patay

tint *n.* رنز پیکه peeka rang

tint *v.t.* پیکه رنور کول peeka rang warkawal

tiny *a.* کوچنی koochnay

tip *n.* سوکه sooka

tip *v.t.* بتو اکدو لاملهراغورزدل bey toley keydo lamala raghorzeydal

tip *n.* انعام eenam

tip *v.t.* انعام ورکول eenam warkawal

tip *n.* مشوره mashwara

tip *v.t.* مشوره ورکول mashwara warkawal

tipsy *a.* مست،نشه mast; nasha

tirade *n.* اودهاو لهقهره کهونا oogda aw la qahra daka wayna

tire *v.t.* ستی کدل،ستی کول staray keydal; staray kawal

tiresome *a.* ستومانه کوونکی stomana kawoonkay

tissue *n.* نسج nasj

titanic *a.* ډیر غټ deyr ghat

tithe *n.* لسمه برخه lasama barkha

title *n.* لقب laqab

titular *a.* افتخاري،رسمي iftikharee; rasmee

toad *n.* مکمشتی حشره خور zmakmeyshtay hashra khor

toast *n.* یوول پسته و yaw dawl pasta doday

toast *v.t.* په هور وریتول pa hor wreetawal

tobacco *n.* تنباکو tambakoo

today *adv.* په دوختونوک pa dey wakhtoono ki

today *n.* ور نن nan wraz

toe *n.* منول mangol

toe *v.t.* منول لول mangol lagawal

toffee *n.* کوچنکلکه شیریني koochnay klaka sheereenee

toga *n.* اوڊادر oogad sadar

together *adv.* پهسره pa gada sara

toil *n.* کار،لهزحمتهککار karaw; la zehmata dak kar

toil *v.i.* دکختهککارکول da karakhta dak kar kawal

toilet *n.* tatay

token *n.* کنانه، nakhana; teekat

tolerable *a.* دتحملو da tahammul war

tolerance *n.* زغم zgham

tolerant *a.* زغمونکی zghamoonkay

tolerate *v.t.* زغمل zghamal

toleration *n.* حوصله،صبر hawsala; sabar

toll *n.* دسکباج da sarak baj

toll *n* دبدپلهکبلهزیاناوتلفات da badi peykhi la kabala zyan aw talfat

toll *v.t.* دزنپهکنولوسرهاعلانول da zang pa krangawalo sara aylanawal

tomato *n.* سوربانجان soor banjan

tomb *n.* قبر qabar

tomboy *n.* بدلمنیهلک badlamanay halak

tomcat *n.* نرپشی nar pashay

tome *n.* دکتابدوتن da keetab dotanay

tomorrow *n.* سبا saba

tomorrow *adv.* ته سبا saba ta

ton *n.* دوزنیوهپمانه da wazan yawa paymana

tone *n.* غ،آهن ghag; ahang

tone *v.t.* دبدنپمضبوطول،رنورکول da badan pati mazbootawal; rang warkawal

tongs *n. pl.* انبور amboor

tongue *n.* ژبه zhaba

tonic *a.* مقوي،غن muqawee; ghagan

tonic *n.* مقويدرمل muqawee darmal

to-night *n.* ننشپه nan shpa

tonight *adv.* نندشپ nan da shpey

tonne *n.*

tonsil *n.* بغو baghot

tonsure *n.* سرخرینه sar khreyana

too *adv.* هم ham

tool *n.* آله ala

tooth *n.* غا ghakh

toothache *n.* دغاخو da ghakh khoog

top *n.* وکه،اوج sooka; oj

top *v.t.* تروولوای موندل tar tolo lwar zay moondal

top *n.* چت،بام chat; bam

topaz *n.* زیاقوت zeyr yaqoot

topic *n.* موضوع،مبحث mawzoo; mubhas

topical *a.* موضوعاتي mawzooatee

topographer *n.* نخچهکخ nakhcha kakh

topographical *a.* نخچهاخیستنوپور اوند nakhcha akheestano pori arwand

topography *n.* نخچهاخیستنه nakhcha akheestana

topple *v.i.* ندل nareydal

topsy turvy *a.* سرچپه sar chapa

topsy turvy *adv* پهسرچپهول pa sar chapa dawl

torch *n.* راغ sragh

torment *n.* کاو karaw

torment *v.t.* کول karawal

tornado *n.* هوايي‌توپان hawayee toopan

torpedo *n.* سمندريوني‌توغوندی samandaryoonay toghonday

torpedo *v.t.* پەسمندريوني‌توغوندي ویشتل pa samandaryoonee toghondee weeshtal

torrent *n.* سلاب saylab

torrential *a.* سلابي saylabee

torrid *a.* توده،برم tawda; deyr garam

tortoise *n.* مكمشتەشمشتة zmakmeyshtay shamshatay

tortuous *a.* كلج‌لرونكی kagleych laroonkay

torture *n.* شكنجه،ربوونه shkanja; rabrawana

torture *v.t.* شكنجه‌كول shkanja kawal

toss *v.t.* شرخط‌كول sheyr khat

toss *n* شرخط sheyr khat

total *a.* ول tol

total *n.* حاصل،جمع hasil; jama

total *v.t.* جمع‌كول jama kawal

totality *n.* بشپتوب bashpartob

touch *v.t.* لمس‌كول lams kawal

touch *n* لمس lams

touchy *a.* حساس،نازک hasas; nazak

tough *a.* توانمند twanmand

toughen *v.t.* كلكول،توانول klakawal; twanawal

tour *n.* يون؛سفر yoon; safar

tour *v.i.* سفركول safar kawal

tourism *n.* رندويي garzandoyee

tourist *n.* سيلاني seelanee

tournament *n.* ورزشي‌سيالي warzishee syalee

towards *prep.* لورته lor ta

towel *n.* مان‌پاک zan pak

towel *v.t.* پمان‌پاک‌وچول pa zan pak wachawal

tower *n.* برج braj

tower *v.i.* هسكول haskawal

town *n.* ارووی khargotay

township *a.* ارووی khargotay

toy *n.* لوبتكه lobtaka

toy *v.i.* لوبدل lobeydal

trace *n.* خاپ،اثر khap; asar

trace *v.t.* تعقيبول taqeebawal

traceable *a.* دموندنو da moondani war

track *n.* مند،دپای mand; da pkhey zay

track *v.t.* تعقيبول taqeebawal

tract *n.* دمكپراختیا da zmaki parakhtya

tract *n* مقاله maqala

traction *n.* كشش kashish

tractor *n.* دیيوماشين da yeywi masheen

trade *n.* تجارت tijarat

trade *v.i* تجارت‌كول tijarat kawal

trader *n.* سودار sawdagar

tradesman *n.* سودار sawdagar

tradition *n.* دود،روایت dood; riwayat

traditional *a.* روایتي riwayatee

traffic *n.* ونهراونه،تراڼ wrana rawrana; tag ratag

traffic *v.i.* تراڼ‌كول tag ratag kawal

tragedian *n.* غم‌لپليكونكی gham larali peykhi leekoonkay

tragedy *n.* ویرلالپه weer larali peykha

tragic *a.* ویرلالی weer laralay

trail *n.* دپخاپونه؛جوهشولاره da pkhey khapoona; jora shawi lara

trail *v.t.* ان‌پس‌كال zan pasi kagal

trailer *n.* بحركتهواون bey harakata wagon

train *n.* اورای orgaday

train *v.t.* تربیهورکول tarbeeya warkawal

trainee *n.* زده‌كوونكی zda kawoonkay

training *n.* زده‌كه؛تربیت zdakra; tarbeeyat

trait *n.* خصوصیت khasooseeyat

traitor *n.* خاین khayin

tram *n.* داردننه‌چلدونكی‌برنایي‌واون da khar danana chaleydoonkay breykhnayee wagon

trample *v.t.* پایمالول paymalawal

trance *n.* جذبه؛بهوي jazba; bey hokhee

tranquil *a.* آسوده asooda

tranquility *n.* سكون sakoon

tranquillize *v.t.* دسكون‌درملورکول da sakoon darmal warkawal

transact *v.t.* دپسوراكوهركه‌كول da peyso rakra warkra kawal

transaction *n.* دپسوراكوهركه da peyso rakra warkra

transcend *v.t.* پرمخكه‌كدل pri makhki keydal

transcendent *a.* برلاسی bar lasay

transcribe *v.t.* په‌لیكلی‌شكل‌كراوستل pa leekalee shakal ki rawastal

transcription *n.* نقل‌جوونه naqal jorawana

transfer *n.* وراستول؛منتقلي warastawal; muntaqilee

transfer *v.t.* منتقل‌كول muntaqil kawal

transferable *a.* انتقال‌كدونكی intiqal keydoonkay

transfiguration *n.* دشكل‌اوربدلون da shakal aw seyrey badloon

transfigure *v.t.* نورانی‌كول nooranee kawal

transform *v.* نوبهورکول nawi banra warkawal

transformation *n.* دببدلون da banri badloon

transgress *v.t.* ترتری‌كول tri teyray kawal

transgression *n.* سرغاوی sar gharaway

transit *n.* تردنه teyreydana

transition *n.* انتقال؛بدلون intiqal; badloon

transitive *n.* ژرتردونكی؛متعدي‌فعل zhar teyreydoonkay; mutadee fayl

transitory *n.* ناپایدار napaydar

translate *v.t.* ژبال zhbaral

translation *n.* ژباه zhbara

transmigration *n.* داروانويوبل‌ته دانوتل da arwagano yaw bal ta nanawatal

transmission *n.* دمخابراتي‌پولادراد da mukhabiratee sapo leygd raleygd

transmit *v.t.* داوسپنیزلارپه‌مرسته استول da ospaneezi lari pa mrasta astawal

transmitter *n.* مخابراتي‌پلدوونکی‌او استوونکی‌ماشین mukhabiratee sapey leygdawoonkay aw astawoonkay masheen

transparent *a.* رو roonr

transplant *v.t.* پوندول peywandawal

transport *v.t.* لدول leygdawal

transport *n.* دلدولوسیله da leygdawalo waseela

transportation *n.* لدرالد leygd raleygd

trap *n.* دام dam

trap *v.t.* دام‌کرول dam ki geyrawal

trash *n.* ناکاره‌شی nakara shay

travel *v.i.* سفرکول safar kawal

travel *n* سفر safar

traveller *n.* مسافر musafar

tray *n.* پتنوس patnoos

treacherous *a.* خاینانه khaynana

treachery *n.* خیانت khyanat

tread *v.t.* پهرایودل pkhey pri eekhodal

tread *n* داماخیستنآواز da gam akheestani awaz

treason *n.* ژمنه‌ماتوونه zhmana matawana

treasure *n.* خزانه khazana

treasure *v.t.* ‌خهارزښت‌ورکول kha arzakht warkawal

treasurer *n.* خزانه‌دار khazanadar

treasury *n.* خزانه‌داري khazana daree

treat *v.t.* چلندکول chaland kawal

treat *n* چلند؛رویه chaland; riwayya

treatise *n.* لیکلژمنه leekali zhmana

treatment *n.* چلند؛ملمستیا chaland; meylmastya

treaty *n.* میثاق meesaq

tree *n.* ونه wana

trek *v.i.* ستومانه‌سفر stomana safar

trek *n.* ستومانه‌کوونکی‌سفرکول stomana kawoonkay safar kawal

tremble *v.i.* رېدل reygdeydal

tremendous *a.* شاندار shandar

tremor *n.* رېدنه reygdeydana

trench *n.* مورچل morchal

trench *v.t.* مورچل‌جورول morchal jorawal

trend *n.* میلان meelan

trespass *v.i.* یوه‌لورته‌میلان‌لرل yawa lor ta meelan laral

trespass *n.* ترۍکول teyray kawal

trial *n.* محاکمه muhakama

triangle *n.* درۍ‌ګوټی drey gotay

triangular *a.* درۍ‌ګوټیز drey goteez

tribal *a.* قبیلوي qabeelawee

tribe *n.* قبیله qabeela

tribulation *n.* سخته‌آزمویینه sakhta azmoyana

tribunal *n.* محکمه mahkama

tributary *n.* دعزت‌پرزوینه da eezat peyrzoyana

tributary *a.* فرعي؛مرستیال faree; mrastyal

trick *n* چل؛دوکه chal; doka

trick *v.t.* چل‌کول chal kawal

trickery *n.* چلبازي chalbazee

trickle *v.i.* لراتلل؛بدل lag lag ratlal; saseydal

trickster *n.* دوکه‌مار dokamar

tricky *a.* چلباز chalbaz

tricolour *a.* دررني drey rangee

tricolour *n* دررنی drey rangay

tricycle *n.* ددريو دورونو خاوند da dreyo dawro khawand

trifle *n.* کم ارزتهیز kam arzakhta seez

trifle *v.i* نایزل na seez ganral

trigger *n.* دوسلامشه da wasley masha

trim *a.* متعادل؛ زهراکونکی mutaadil; zra rakhkoonkay

trim *n* سینار؛سموونه seengar; samawana

trim *v.t.* تراشل؛ترتیبول trashal; tarteebawal

trinity *n.* درونی توب؛تثلیث drey goonaytob; taslees

trio *n.* درکسیزه له drey kaseeza dala

trip *v.t.* ویدل؛بکرخول khwayeydal; takar khwaral

trip *n.* سفر safar

tripartite *a.* دراخیز drey arkheez

triple *a.* درونی drey goonay

triple *v.t.,* درچنده کول drey chanda kawal

triplicate *a.* درچنده drey chanda

triplicate *n* دراخیزهتون drey arkheeza taroon

triplicate *v.t.* درچندهکول drey chanda kawal

triplication *n.* درچندهکوونه drey chanda kawana

tripod *n.* درپایه drey paya

triumph *n.* بریا؛فتح barya; fata

triumph *v.i.* بریاکدل barya keydal

triumphal *a.* بریالی،فاتح baryalay; fatay

triumphant *a.* بریالی،فاتح baryalay; fatay

trivial *a.* بارزته bey arzakhta

troop *n.* دپویانوله da pawzyano dala

troop *v.i* پهلهکحرکتکول pa dala ki harakat kawal

trooper *n.* سرتری sar teyray

trophy *n.* دبریالیتوبیادار da baryaleetob yadgar

tropic *n.* دناستوایسیم da naray ustawayee seema

tropical *a.* استوای ustawayee

trot *v.i.* چکتلل chatak tlal

trot *n* چکت؛داسغوندهتلل chatak tag; da as ghonda tlal

trouble *n.* ربوونه rabrawana

trouble *v.t.* ربول rabrawal

troublesome *a.* ربوونکی rabrawoonkay

troupe *n.* دسندرغاوله da sandar gharo dala

trousers *n. pl* پتلون patloon

trowel *n.* دباغوانبلچه da baghwanay beylcha

truce *n.* لنمهالیاوربند lang mahalee orband

truck *n.* لار laray

true *a.* رتونی rakhtoonay

trump *n.* دلوبویوولپهبهاواهمسی da lobo yaw dawl panra; kha aw aham saray

trump *v.t.* بهتانلول buhtan lagawal

trumpet *n.* تروم؛شپیل trom; shpeylay

trumpet *v.i.* پهلوغاعلانول pa lwar ghag aylanawal

use *v.t.* په کاراچول pa kar achawal
useful *a.* مفید mufeed
usher *n.* لاړود larkhod
usher *v.t.* رهنمايکول rehnumayee kawal
usual *a.* عادي adee
usually *adv.* معمولاً mamoolan
usurer *n.* سودخور sood khor
usurp *v.t.* غصب کول ghasab kawal
usurpation *n.* پهزوراخيستنه pa zor akheestana
usury *n.* سودخونه sood khwarana
utensil *n.* لوىاولري lokhee aw largee
uterus *n.* تخمدان tukhamdan
utilitarian *a.* دکوميزدورتوبلهمخد هغهمطلوبيت da kom seez da gatawartob la makhi da hagha matloobeeyat
utility *n.* مفيديت mufeedeeyat
utilization *n.* کاروونه karawana
utilize *v.t.* کارول karawal
utmost *a.* ترولوړ tar tolo deyr
utmost *n* اعظمي azamee
utopia *n* يوخيالىهواد. yaw khyalee haywad
utopian *a.* خيالي khyalee
utter *v.t.* مکملکول،اداکول mukamal kawal; ada kawal
utter *a* کامل kamil
utterance *n.* خپراوى،ونا khparaway; wayna
utterly *adv.* کاملاً kamilan

V

vacancy *n.* ای تش tash zay
vacant *a.* خالي تش،؛ tash; khalee
vacate *v.t.* کول کاره ب تشول،؛ tashawal; bey kara kawal
vacation *n.* رخصتي وزبارتوب،؛ wuzgartob; rukhsatee
vaccinate *v.t.* ورکول واکسين wakseen warkawal
vaccination *n.* ورکوونه واکسين wakseen warkawana
vaccinator *n.* پهواکسينورکولومامور pa wakseen warkawalo mamoor
vaccine *n.* واکسين wakseen
vacillate *v.i.* زهنازهکدل zra nazra keydal
vacuum *n.* تشيال،خلا tashyal; khala
vagabond *n.* کوچى؛کوال kochay; kadwal
vagabond *a* درپهدر؛کوهبى dar pa dar; koosa dabay
vagary *n.* خيالپرستي khyal parastee
vagina *n.* مهبل،تکى mahbal; teykay
vague *a.* ميبهم؛وز mubhim; goong
vagueness *n.* ونتوب goongtob
vain *a.* بايه bey zaya
vainglorious *a.* ځانکارى؛باو zankhkaray; batoo

vainglory *n.* لاف او بتی lafi aw bati

vainly *adv.* بنتیجه bey nateejey

vale *n.* دره dara

valiant *a.* مېنی meyranay

valid *a.* معتبر motabar

validate *v.t.* اعتبار ورکول؛نافذکول aytibar warkawal; nafiz kawal

validity *n.* اعتبار،تنفیذ aytibar; tanfeez

valley *n.* دره،وادي dara; wadee

valour *n.* مانه meyrana

valuable *a.* قیمتی qeematee

valuation *n.* ارزوونه arzawana

value *n.* بیه baya

value *v.t.* ارزت ورکول؛نرخ اکل arzakht warkawal; narkh takal

valve *n.* ورخ warkh

van *n.* سرغندوی،سرلاری sar ghandaway; sar laray

vanish *v.i.* ورکدل wrakeydal

vanity *n.* فنا fana

vanquish *v.t.* بریالی کدل baryalay keydal

vaporize *v.t.* په بخار اول pa bukhar arawal

vaporous *a.* لوی لرونکی loogay laroonkay

vapour *n.* باس،لوی baras; loogay

variable *a.* بدلدونکی badleydoonkay

variance *n.* اختلاف،توپیر ikhtilaf; tawpeer

variation *n.* تغییر taghayyur

varied *a.* رنارنا ranga rang

variety *n.* قسم؛خل qisam; kheyl

various *a.* رنزرنا ranga rang

varnish *n.* یوول لاور کوونکماده yaw dawl zala warkawoonki mada

varnish *v.t.* لاور کول zala warkawal

vary *v.t.* توپیرلرل tawpeer laral

vaseline *n.* واسلین wasleen

vast *a.* پراخ prakh

vault *n.* ومبته،مغاره gombata; maghara

vault *n.* وپ top

vault *v.i.* وپ وهل top wahal

vegetable *n.* سبزي sabzee

vegetable *a.* نباتی؛سبزپوراروند nabatee; sabzay pori arwand

vegetarian *n.* سبزي خور sabzee khor

vegetarian *a* سبزي خور sabzee khor

vegetation *n.* نباتي ژوند nabatee zhwand

vehemence *n.* شدت،پیاوتیا shiddat; pyawartya

vehement *a.* شدید،توند shadeed; tond

vehicle *n.* ای gaday

vehicular *a.* داوپه اوند da gado pa arwand

veil *n.* پرده،برقع parda; burqa

veil *v.t.* پرده کول parda kawal

vein *n.* ر،ورید rag; wareed

velocity *n.* تزوالی teyzwalay

velvet *n.* بخمل bakhmal

velvety *a.* بخملي bakhmalee

venal *a.* فاسد،پسه خور fasid; paysa khor

venality *n.* بخونه badi khwarana

vendor *n.* لاسپلوری lasploray

venerable *a.* محترم؛معزز muhtaram; moazzaz

venerate *v.t.* احترام،کول ehtiram yi kawal

veneration *n.* احترام ehtiram

vengeance *n.* کینه keena

venial *a.* دبنو da bakhani war

venom *n.* زهر zahar

venomous *a.* زهرجن zaharjan

vent *n.* هواکش؛سومه hawakash

ventilate *v.t.* هواورکول hawa warkawal

ventilation *n.* هوارسوونه hawa rasawana

ventilator *n.* هوارساند hawa rasand

venture *n.* لهخطره کهچاره la khatara daka chara

venture *v.t.* خطرناک کارتهلاساچول khatarnak kar ta las achawal

venturesome *a.* خطرناک khatarnak

venturous *a.* خطرناک khatarnak

venue *n.* دلیدذکتناکلیۍای da leedani katani takalay zay

veracity *n.* رتیاوینه rakhtya wayana

verendah *n.* برنه baranda

verb *n.* فعل؛کوۍ fayl; kroyay

verbal *a.* فعلوزمه؛کوزمه faylwazma; karwazma

verbally *adv.* پهژبنيتوه pa zhabanee toga

verbatim *a.* کۍپمکی takay pa takay

verbatim *adv.* وییپهویی wayay pa wayay

verbose *a.* اود oogad

verbosity *n.* خبرهاودونه khabara oogdawana

verdant *a.* تکشین tak sheen

verdict *n.* دقاضيحکم da qazee hukam

verge *n.* ۵ sanda

verification *n.* تصدیق tasdeeq

verify *v.t.* تصدیقول tasdeeqawal

verisimilitude *n.* دسموالیشونتیا da samwalee shoontya

veritable *a.* رتینی rakhteenay

vermillion *n.* سوررنهحشرات soor ranga hashrat

vermillion *a.* تکسور tak soor

vernacular *n.* سیمهییزهلهجهاووینه seemayeeza lahja aw wayang

vernacular *a.* سیمهییز؛محلي seemayeez; mahalee

vernal *a.* پسرلنی،تازهاوتاند pasarlanay; taza aw tand

versatile *a.* واخیز so arkheez

versatility *n.* رنارنتوب ranga rangtob

verse *n.* نظم nazam

versed *a.* ماهر mahir

versification *n.* نظملیکنه nazam leekana

versify *v.t.* نظملیکل nazam leekal

version *n.* روایت نسخه؛ nuskha; riwayat

versus *prep.* پهوراند pa wrandi

vertical *a.* عمودي؛نغ amoodee; neygh

verve *n.* جوشاوشوق josh aw kharosh

very *a.* ور؛زیات deyr; zyat

vessel *n.* لوۍ lokhay

vest *n.* واسکه waskat

vest *v.t.* سپارل sparal

vestige *n.* آثار،نه asar; nakha

vestment *n.* رسمي يا روحاني كالي rasmee ya roohanee kalee

veteran *n.* عسكري دوره پای ته رسولی پوری askaree dawra pay ta rasawalay pawzee

veteran *a.* تجربه کار tajruba kar

veterinary *a.* د ارويو طبابت پور اوند da sarwayo tababat pori arwand

veto *n.* مخالفه رايه mukhalifa raya

veto *v.t.* مخالفه رايه ورکول mukhalifa raya warkawal

vex *v.t.* پرېشانه کول parayshana kawal

vexation *n* پرېشاني parayshanee

via *prep.* له لارٍ la lari

viable *a.* وده کوونکی؛عملي wada kawoonkay; amalee

vial *n.* کوچنی بوتل koochnay botal

vibrate *v.i.* رډدل reygdeydal

vibration *n.* رډدنه reygdeydana

vicar *n.* نايب،باٍناستی nayib; zaynastay

vicarious *a.* نيابتي nyabatee

vice *n.* اخلاقي فساد،ګناه akhlaqee fasad; goona

viceroy *n.* د سلطنت نايب da saltanat nayib

vice-versa *adv.* برعکس baraks

vicinity *n.* نژدوالی nazhdeywalay

vicious *a.* شرير،خبيث shareer; khabees

vicissitude *n.* بدلون،لوو badloon; lwar zawar

victim *n.* ښکار khkar

victimize *v.t.* ښکار کول khkar kawal

victor *n.* بريالی baryalay

victorious *a.* بريالی baryalay

victory *n.* سوبه،کامٍابي soba; kamyabee

victuals *n. pl* رنارنخواه،ماکولات ranga rang khwara; makoolat

vie *v.i.* سٍالی،رقابت syalee; raqabat

view *n.* منظر،نظر manzar; nazar

view *v.t.* لٍدل leedal

vigil *n.* ښار نلپاره ویٍپاټ کدنه sarani lapara weekh pati keydana

vigilance *n.* وٍتوب،ښار نته ویٍپاټ کدنه weekhtob; sarani ta weekh pati keydana

vigilant *a.* بٍدار baydar

vigorous *a.* غتلی،ځواکمن ghakhtalay; zwakman

vile *a.* ناهار goonagar

vilify *v.t.* تورنول toranawal

villa *n.* کلٍوالی کور kaleewalee kor

village *n.* کلی kalay

villager *n.* کلٍوال kaleewal

villain *n.* فاسدسری fasid saray

vindicate *v.t.* تور ٍا بدګومانی لری کول tor ya badgoomanee leyri kawal

vindication *n.* دفاع،رٍتٍنوالی difa; rakhteenwalee

vine *n.* نرم ساقه،تاک naram saqa; tak

vinegar *n.* سرکه sarka

vintage *n.* د شراب جوړونو موسم da sharab jorawani mawsam

violate *v.t.* تری کول؛توهٍن کول teyray kawal; tawheen kawal

violation *n.* سرغاوی؛تری sar gharaway; teyray

violence *n.* زورزیاتی zor zyatay

violent *a.* غصهناک ghusanak

violet *n.* بنفشرنز banafsh rang

violin *n.* د موسیقۍآلهویلون da mawseeqay ala wayloon

violinist *n.* ویلونغوونکی wayloon ghagoonkay

virgin *n.* پغله؛پاکلمنه peyghla; pak lamana

virgin *n* سوچه soocha

virginity *n.* بکارت؛پغلتوب bakarat; peyghaltob

virile *a.* مردانه؛لهجنسيپلوهفعال mardana; la jinsee palwa faal

virility *n.* نارینهجنسيواک؛نارینتوب nareena jinsee zwak; nareentob

virtual *a* مجازي؛واقعی majazee; waqiee

virtue *n.* کلا؛فضیلت khkula; fazeelat

virtuous *a.* فضیلتلرونکی؛متقی fazeelat laroonkay; muttaqee

virulence *n.* زهرجنتوب؛ویروسيتوب zaharjantob; wayrooseetob

virulent *a.* زهرجن zaharjan

virus *n.* ویروس؛دفسادتومنه wayroos; da fasad tomna

visage *n.* ره؛ظاهريبه seyra; zahiree banra

visibility *n.* دلیدوتیا da leed wartya

visible *a.* دلیدو da leed war

vision *n.* بصیرت baseerat

visionary *a.* تصوري؛خیالي tasawwuree; khyalee

visionary *n.* خیاليانسان khyalee insan

visit *n.* راشهدرشه rasha darsha

visit *v.t.* راشهدرشهکول rasha darsha kawal

visitor *n.* ملمه؛لیدونکیاوکتونکی melma; leedoonkay aw katoonkay

vista *n.* منظره؛لرلید manzara; larleed

visual *a.* بصري basree

visualize *v.t.* مجسمکول mujassam kawal

vital *a.* اصلياومهم aslee aw muhim

vitality *n.* دپایتاوبقاواک da payakht aw baqa zwak

vitalize *v.t.* ژوندیکول zhwanday kawal

vitamin *n.* ویامین weetameen

vitiate *v.t.* خرابول kharabawal

vivacious *a.* خوشاله khoshala

vivacity *n.* تازهتوب؛مستي tazatob; mastee

viva-voce *adv.* پهژبسره pa zhabi sara

viva-voce *a* ژبنی zhabanay

viva-voce *n* شفاهيآزموینه shafahee azmoyana

vivid *a.* فعال؛هاند faal; hasand

vixen *n.* یده geedara

vocabulary *n.* ویيپانه؛قاموس wayee panga; qamoos

vocal *a.* غیز ghageez

vocalist *n.* سندربول؛سندرغای sandarbol; sandar gharay

vocation *n.* رسالت؛خدمتتهلوالتیا risalat; khidmat ta leywaltya

vogue *n.* دودیز؛رواجي doodeez; riwajee

voice *n.* انسانيغ insanee ghag

voice *v.t.* بیانول؛غیزه‌به‌ورکول bayanawal; ghageeza banra warkawal

void *a.* بی‌گټی؛پوچ bey gati; pooch

void *v.t.* باطلول batilawal

void *n.* بقانوني bey qanoonee

volcanic *a.* اورشیندی orsheenday

volcano *n.* اورشیندیغر orsheenday ghar

volition *n.* غوت؛اراده ghokht; irada

volley *n.* باران؛پرله‌پسز baran; parla pasi dazi

volley *v.t* پرله‌پسزکول parla pasi dazi kawal

volt *n.* دبرنایوپیمانه da breykhna yaw paymana

voltage *n.* قوه برنایي breykhnayee qawa

volume *n.* حجم؛مقدار؛بوله؛جلد hujam; miqdar; tolga; jild

voluminous *a.* لوی؛حجیم loy; hajeem

voluntarily *adv.* په‌داوطلبانه‌ول pa daw talbana dawl

voluntary *a.* داوطلبانه؛خپل‌په‌خوه daw talbana; khpal pa khwakha

volunteer *n.* داوطلب؛خپل‌په‌خوی daw talab; khpal pa khwakhi

volunteer *v.t.* داوطلب‌کدل daw talab keydal

voluptuary *n.* شهوتران shahwatran

voluptuous *a.* شهواني shahwanee

vomit *v.t.* کازکول kangi kawal

vomit *n* کاز kangi

voracious *a.* حریص harees

votary *n.* راهب؛راهبه rahib; rahiba

vote *n.* رایه raya

vote *v.i.* رایه‌ورکول raya warkawal

voter *n.* رایه‌ورکوونکی raya warkawoonkay

vouch *v.i.* ضمانت‌ورکول zamanat warkawal

voucher *n.* ضمانت‌لیک zamanat leek

vouchsafe *v.t.* اعطاکول ata kawal

vow *n.* کلک‌هو klak hod

vow *v.t.* په‌ینارسره‌ژمنه‌کول pa teengar sara zhmana kawal

vowel *n.* غنتوری ghagan toray

voyage *n.* هوایي‌یاسمندري‌یون hawayee ya samandaree yoon

voyage *v.i.* هوایي‌یاسمندري‌یون‌کول hawayee ya samandaree yoon kawal

voyager *n.* مسافر musafar

vulgar *a.* پوچ؛بادبه pooch; bey adaba

vulgarity *n.* بادبي؛پوچ‌خولتوب bey adabee; pooch khuleytob

vulnerable *a.* خرابدونکی kharabeydoonkay

vulture *n.* کجیر kajeer

wade *v.i.* خوچیکوکردل khato cheekaro ki garzeydal

waddle *v.i.* دبتیهپهشانتلل da bati pa shan tlal

waft *v.t.* دبادیهپهشانترلدل da bad pa shan teyreydal

waft *n.* نرمباد naram bad

wag *v.i.* مخاوشاتهحرکتکول makh aw sha ta harakat kawal

wag *n.* وکمار tokmar

wage *v.t.* جهکول jagara kawal

wage *n.* اجوره ajoora

wager *n.* شرطتنه shart tarana

wager *v.i.* شرطتل shart taral

wagon *n.* واون،بارلدوونکوسیله wagon; bar leygdawoonki waseela

wail *v.i.* ویرکول weer kawal

wail *n.* ویر weer

wain *n.* ا gaday

waist *n.* ملا mla

waistband *n.* ملاوستن،کمربند mla wastanay; kamar band

waistcoat *n.* بلستووکو bey lastonro kot

wait *v.i.* انتظارایستل intizar eestal

wait *n.* انتظار intizar

waiter *n.* دملمستونیاخونای‌خدمتار da meylmastoon ya khwaranzay khidmatgar

waitress *n.* دملمستونیاخونای‌خدمتاره da meylmastoon ya khwaranzay khidmatgara

waive *v.t.* مستثنیکول،صرف‌نظرکول mustasna kawal; sarf nazar kawal

wake *v.t.* ویول،ویدل weekhawal; weekheydal

wake *n.* ویوالی weekhwalay

wake *n.* منړاثر mand; asar

wakeful *a.* بدار baydar

walk *v.i.* رلدل garzeydal

walk *n.* چکر،پلیة chakar; pali tag

wall *n.* دوال deywal

wall *v.t.* دوال‌جوول deywal jorawal

wallet *n.* دپسوکوه da peyso kasora

wallop *v.t.* تزخودل teyz khwazeydal

wallow *v.i.* پهخوکرغدل pa khato ki raghreydal

walnut *n.* چارمغز char maghaz

walrus *n.* سمندریفیل samandaree feel

wan *a.* رنالوتی،نر rang alwatay; dangar

wand *n.* لته lakhta

wander *v.i.* سروردانرلدل sargardan garzeydal

wane *v.i.* کمزوریکدل kamzoray keydal

wane *n.* انحطاط،کمزورتیا inhitat; kamzortya

want *v.t.* غوتل ghokhtal

want *n.* غوتنه ghokhtana

wanton *a.* جنایتکار،بنظمه janayatkar; bey nazma

war *n.* جن jang

war *v.i.* جندل jangeydal

warble *v.i.* یوخاص‌طرزکسندره‌ویل yaw khas tarz ki sandara wayal

warble *n.* سرود،چوهار sarood; choonrar

warbler *n.* یوولسندربولهمرغ yaw dawl sandar bola marghay

ward *n.* حصار،خونه hisar; khoona

ward v.t. حفاظت کساتل hifazat ki satal

warden n. سرپرست sar parast

warder n. ساتندوی satandoy

wardrobe n. دجاموالمار da jamo almaray

wardship n. سرپرستي sar parastee

ware n. آلات؛ییزونه alat; seezoona

warehouse v.t پهودام کساتل pa godam ki satal

warfare n. جه jagara

warlike a. جهپال jagara pal

warm1 a. تود؛ برم tod; garam

warm v.t. تودول؛ برمول todawal; garmawal

warmth n. تودوخه tawdokha

warn v.t. خبرداری ورکول khabardaree warkawal

warning n. خبرداری khabardaree

warrant n. حواله؛ رسمي حکم hawala; rasmee hukam

warrant v.t. رسمي اجازت لرل، تضمینول rasmee eejazat laral; tazmeenawal

warrantee n. ضمانت zamanat

warrantor n. ضامن zamin

warranty n. ضمانت zamanat

warren n. دسویو دروزلوبای da soyo da rozalo zay

warrior n. جنیالی jangyalay

wart n. زخه zakha

wary a. متوجه mutawajo

wash v.t. وینل weenzal

wash n ویننه weenzana

washable a. دوینلوو war da weenzalo war

washer n. دوبی dobee

wasp n. غومبسه ghombasa

waspish a. غومبستهورته ghombasi ta warta

wassail n. دشرابخورجشن da sharabkhoray jashan

wastage n. تلف کوونه talf kawana

waste a. ضایع؛شا zaya; shar

waste n. ضایع کوونه zaya kawana

waste v.t. تلف کول talf kawal

wasteful a. بایه bey zaya

watch v.t. لیدل؛کتل leedal; katal

watch n. لیدنه؛ساعت leedana; saat

watchful a. بدار؛بارو baydar; saro

watchword n. شعار shaar

water n. اوبه oba

water v.t. اوبهورکول oba warkawal

waterfall n. وبی zarobay

water-melon n. هندواه hindwanra

waterproof a. اوبضد؛نهلونددونکی obzad; na loondeydoonkay

waterproof n بارانيوکر baranee tokar

waterproof v.t. اوبضدرول obzad garzawal

watertight a. اوبهنهاخیستونکی oba na akheestoonkay

watery a. اوبلن oblan

watt n. دبرنانابولویوپیمانه da breykhna napawalo yaw paymana

wave n. چه sapa

wave v.t. چاندکدل؛کانخول sapand keydal; takan khwaral

waver v.i. زهنازهکدل zra nazra keydal

wax n. موم mom

wax v.t. موم ورکول mom warkawal

way n. لاره lara
wayfarer n. لاروی laraway
waylay v.t. چاته‌لاره‌نیول cha ta lara neewal
wayward a. نافرمان nafarman
weak a. کمزوری kamzoray
weaken v.t. & i ناتوانه‌کول،ناتوانه کدل natwana kawal; natwana keydal
weakling n. کمزوری kamzoray
weakness n. کمزوري kamzoree
weal n. پسوب،سوکالي parsob; sokalee
wealth n. مال،شتمني mal; shtamanee
wealthy a. بای baday
wean v.t. ماشوم‌له‌شدوورکولوبیلول mashoom la sheydo warkawalo beylawal
weapon n. وسله wasla
wear v.t. اغوستل aghostal
weary a. ستی،بزاره staray; beyzara
weary v.t. & i ستومانه‌کول،بزاره‌کدل stomana kawal; beyzara keydal
weary a. زتوری‌کوونکی zartoray kawoonkay
weary v.t. کرکه‌کول kraka kawal
weather n موسم mosam
weather v.t. دموسم‌په‌وراندبدلدل، زغمل da mosam pa wrandi badleydal; zghamal
weave v.t. تارونه‌سرهندل taroona sara gandal
weaver n. جولا،اوبدونکی jola; obdoonkay
web n. جال،تنسته jal; tanasta

webby a. جال‌ته‌ورته jal ta warta
wed v.t. واده‌کول wada kawal
wedding n. واده wada
wedge n. دلري‌یااوسپنپله‌یاوه da largee ya ospani panra ya tota
wedge v.t. په‌پانه‌ماتول pa pana matawal
wedlock n. نکاح nika
Wednesday n. چارشنبه charshamba
weed n. یوول‌سارانی‌بوی yaw dawl saranay bootay
weed v.t. ندهشی‌لمایه‌ایستل ganda shay la zaya eestal
week n. اوونۍ oonay
weekly a. اوونیز ooneez
weekly adv. په‌اووه‌ورو‌کی pa owa wrazo ki
weekly n. هره‌اوونۍ hara oonay
weep v.i. ژل zharal
weevil n. یوول‌کوچنونه yaw dawl koochnay goongata
weigh v.t. وزن‌کول wazan kawal
weight n. وزن wazan
weightage n. وزنلرنه wazan larana
weighty a. دروند droond
weir n. داوبوکوچنی‌بند da obo koochnay band
weird a. عجیب ajeeb
welcome a. مهربانی،هرکلی mehrabanee; har kalay
welcome n هرکلی har kalay
welcome v.t استقبال‌کول istiqbal kawal
weld v.t. سره‌پوندول sara peywandawal
weld n یوکوونه yaw kawana

welfare *n.* ه kheygara

well *a.* نک،غوره،که kha; ghwara; nayk

well *adv.* ه kha

well *n.* کوهی koohay

well *v.i.* داوبوسرتهراخوئدل da obo sar ta rakhoteydal

wellington *n.* دنیوزیلنپلازمنه،یوول آزادخولموزه da nyoozeelaynd plazmayna; yaw dawl azad khuley mooza

well-known *a.* مشهور mashahoor

well-read *a.* باخبر،کتابلوستی ba khabar; keetab lostay

well-timed *a.* پرای،پهمناسبوخت par zay; pa munasib wakht

well-to-do *a.* کامیاب kamyab

welt *n.* دبوئلواوجامونلوکییوولتغمه da boot gandalo aw jamo gandalo ki yaw dawl taghma

welter *n.* وساماننیااسباب gadwad saman ya asbab

wen *n.* دانرزيژبد توری w da angreyzay zhabi da w toray

wench *n.* ماشوم؛خدمتار mashoom; khidmatgar

west *n.* لویدیز lweydeez

west *a.* لویدیزوال lweydeez wal

west *adv.* دلودیپهلور da lweydeez pa lor

westerly *a.* لویدیپوراوند lweydeez pori arwand

westerly *adv.* دلودیپهلور da lweydeez pa lor

western *a.* لویدیه lweydeeza

wet *a.* لوند loond

wet *v.t.* لونداول loondawal

wetness *n.* لونداوالی loondwalay

whack *v.t.* پهپهوهل pa sapeyra wahal

whale *n.* یورستربدنیکب yaw deyr star badanay kab

wharfage *n.* پهلنرایکدکتدرولولت pa langar zay ki da kakhtay darawalo lagakht

what *a.* کوم؛کومیز kom; kom seez

what *pron.* شی،به sa shay; sa

what *interj.* ه sa

whatever *pron.* کومه چ،هره چ kom sa chi; har sa chi

wheat *n.* غنم ghanam

wheedle *v.t.* غولول gholawal

wheel *a.* رخ،پایه sarkh; paya

wheel *v.t.* رخول sarkhawal

whelm *v.t.* چپه کول chapa kawal

whelp *n.* دسپیبچی da spee bachay

when *adv.* هوخت،کله sa wakht; kala

when *conj.* کله چ kala chi

whence *adv.* له کومایه la koma zaya

whenever *adv. conj* هروخت،هرکله، کله har wakht; har kala; kala

where *adv.* چر cheyri

where *conj.* چرته،هلته charta; halta

whereabout *adv.* چرته cheyrta

whereas *conj.* کههم ka sa ham

whereat *conj.* کله چ kala chi

wherein *adv.* به sanga

whereupon *conj.* لهمخي la makhi yi

wherever *adv.* هرچرته har cheyrta

whet *v.t.* ترهکول؛پارول teyra kawal; parawal

whether *conj.* آیا،پههرصورت aya; pa har soorat

which *pron.* کوم kom

which *a* کوم يو چ kom yaw chi

whichever *pron* هريو har yaw

whiff *n.* ومه wagma

while *n.* موده،بهوخت mooda; sa wakht

while *conj.* کله چ kala chi

while *v.t.* وخت ترول wakht teyrawal

whim *n.* هوس hawas

whimper *v.i.* غوريدل ghoreydal

whimsical *a.* هوس باز hawasbaz

whine *v.i.* کونجدل koranjeydal

whine *n* کونجدنه koranjeydana

whip *v.t.* په قمچينه وهل pa qamcheena wahal

whip *n.* قمچينه،شلاخه qamcheena; shalakha

whipcord *n.* غل شوی پندمزی gharal shaway pand mazay

whir *n.* چک پرواز chatak parwaz

whirl *n.i.* په دايروي لور باند حرکت کول pa dayrawee lori bandi harakat kawal

whirl *n* دايروي حرکت dayrawee harakat

whirligig *n.* رخنی sarkhanay

whirlpool *n.* اوبرنی obgarzanay

whirlwind *n.* ببو ک barbokay

whisk *v.t.* په چک حرکت لر کول pa chatak harakat leyri kawal

whisk *n* کوچنی ربزبورس koochnay reybaz; bors

whisker *n.* دزمري ياپيشو برت da zmaree ya peesho breyt

whisky *n.* يوول شراب yaw dawl sharab

whisper *v.t.* پس پس کول pas pas kawal

whisper *n* پس پسی،پخبر pas pasay; pati khabari

whistle *v.i.* شپيلک وهل shpeylak wahal

whistle *n* شپيلک shpeylak

white *a.* سپين speen

white *n* سپين رنگ speen rang

whiten *v.t.* سپين رنور کول speen rang warkawal

whitewash *n.* دچوناوبه da chooney oba

whitewash *v.t.* دچونپهاوبورنول da chooney pa obo rangawal

whither *adv.* کوم ځای kom zay

whitish *a.* سپين وزمه speen wazma

whittle *v.t.* تراشل trashal

whiz *v.i.* بزيدل bazeydal

who *pron.* وک،کوم يو sok; kom yaw

whoever *pron.* هروک چ،هر چا چ har sok chi; har cha chi

whole *a.* سالم،روغ رمه salam; rogh ramat

whole *n* ول tol

whole-hearted *a.* صميمانه sameemana

wholesale *n.* غونپلورنه ghond plorana

wholesale *a* غونپلورونکی ghond ploroonkay

wholesale *adv.* په پراخه کچه pa parakha kacha

wholesaler *n.* غونپلوری ghond ploray

wholesome *a.* روغ رمه rogh ramat

wholly *adv.* كاملاً kamilan

whom *pron.* چاته،چالپاره cha ta; cha lapara

whore *n.* فاحشه fahisha

whose *pron.* د چا da cha

why *adv.* ولي،دەلپاره wali; da sa lapara

wick *n.* با،فتيله،اورلوونی batay; fateela; orlagawoonay

wicked *a.* خبيث khabees

wicker *n.* چوکه chooka

wicket *n.* کوچندروازه،دکرکدلوبدر چوک koochnay darwaza; da krikat da lobi drey chooki

wide *a.* ارت،پلن art; plan

wide *adv.* په‌پلنوالي‌سره pa planwalee sara

widen *v.t.* پلنول planawal

widespread *a.* پرانستی pranistay

widow *n.* کونه konda

widow *v.t.* کونول kondawal

widower *n.* کونز kond

width *n.* پلنوالی planwalay

wield *v.t.* په‌مهارت‌سره‌کارول pa maharat sara karawal

wife *n.* ماينه mayna

wig *n.* مصنوعي‌ويتان masnooee weykhtan

wight *n.* ژوندی‌موجود zhwanday mawjood

wigwam *n.* خمه‌وله‌کور khayma dawla kor

wild *a.* سارانی،وحشي saranay; wahshee

wilderness *n.* وحشيتوب،بيابان wahsheetob; bayaban

wile *n.* دوکه doka

will *n.* ارمان arman

will *v.t.* وصيت‌کول waseeyat kawal

willing *a.* راضي razee

willingness *n.* رضا raza

willow *n.* دولونه da wali wana

wily *a.* مار دوکه dokamar

wimble *n.* برمه barma

wimple *n.* سرپونی sar patoonay

win *v.t.* کاميابدل kamyabeydal

win *n* کاميابي kamyabee

wince *v.i.* زانلزول zan larzawal

winch *n.* لاستی،موی lastay; mootay

wind *n.* باد bad

wind *v.t.* کووتلل kogwog tlal

wind *v.t.* بادته‌ایودل bad ta eekhodal

windbag *n.* پاوو gapawoo

winder *n.* پچوونکی peychowoonkay

windlass *v.t.* دکوهي‌رخ da koohee sarkh

windmill *n.* بادي‌ژرنده badee zhranda

window *n.* کک karkay

windy *a.* توپانی toopanee

wine *n.* سره‌شراب sra sharab

wing *n.* وزر wazar

wink *v.i.* سترک‌وهل stargak wahal

wink *n* سترک stargak

winner *n.* ونکی gatoonkay

winnow *v.t.* غله‌بادول gala badawal

winsome *a.* زه‌راکونی zra rakhkoonay

winter *n.* ژمی zhamay

winter *v.i* ژمی‌ترول zhamay teyrawal

wintry *a.* ژمنی zhamanay

zigzag *n.* خط منكسر او مات‌هوايه so
zaya mat aw munkasir khat

zigzag *a.* په زيزاول pa zeegzag dawl

zigzag *v.i.* په زيزاول حركت كول pa
zeegzag dawl harakat kawal

zinc *n.* دجست‌عنصر da jast unsar

zip *n.* زيپ، كشك zeep; kashak

zip *v.t.* په كشك‌تل pa kashak taral

zip *n* فشار fishar

zonal *a.* مذاومنطقپوراوند mayni aw
mantaqey pori arwand

zone *n.* منطقه mantaqa

zoo *n.* ژوب zhobanr

zoological *a.* ژوپوهنپوراوند
zhopohani pori arwand

zoologist *n.* ژوپوه zhopoh

zoology *n.* ژوپوهنه zhopohana

zoom *n.* لويدنه، تزحركت loyeydana;
teyz harakat

zoom *v.i.* لويول، لويدل loyawal;
loyeydal

Pushto to English

A

aba *n* ابا dad, daddy

abadawal; meysht kawal *v.t.*
آبادول،مشت کول people

abadawal; tasfeeya kawal *v.i.*
آبادول،تصفیه کول settle

abadee *adj* ابدي eternal

abadeeyat *n* ابدیت eternity

abee rang *a* آبي رنز blue

abeysey *n.* اب alphabet

abeysey *n.* اب spell

abeysey kawal; imla kawal *v.t.* اب
کول،املاکول spell

abroo *n.* آبرو repute

abroo *n.* آبرو prestige

abwalay karkeychanwalay *a.*
ابوالی ککیچنوالی
monochromatic

achar *n.* اچار pickle

achawal; tarha kawal *v. t.* اچول؛
طرحه کول cast

achawana; wozeeyat *n.* اچونه،
وضعیت cast

ad kawoonkay adad *n.* عادکوونکی
عدد aliquot

ada kawal *v.t.* اداکول pay

adaa *n* ادعا claim

adaa kawal *v. t* ادعاکول claim

adab *n.* ادب mannerism

adabee *a.* ادبي literary

adabee aw farhangee nawakht
n. ادبي او فرهنينوت renaissance

adabee ghorchanr *n.* ادبيغورچا
anthology

adad *n* عدد digit

adadee *a.* عددي numeral

adadee *a.* عددي numerical

adalat; mahkama *n.* عدالت،
محکمه court

adat *n.* عادت addict

adat *n.* عادت habit

adat *n* عادت wont

adawat *n.* عداوت odium

adayana; jibran *n* اداینه،جبران pay

adee *a.* عادي normal

adee *a.* عادي commonplace

adee *a.* عادي usual

adee halat *n.* عاديحالت normalcy

adee wagaray *n.* عاديوی
commoner

adeeb *n.* ادیب litterateur

adeeb; muhaqqiq *n.* ادیب،محقق
scholar

adeebana *a.* ادیبانه oratorical

adsa *n.* عدسه lens

afat *n.* آفت calamity

afoonat zid *n.* عفونتضد antiseptic

afrat *n* افراط excess

afratee shakhs *n* افراطيشخص
extremist

afraz; chrap chrap *n* افراز،چپ
چپ splash

afrazawal; chrap chrap kawal
v.i. افرازول،چپچپ کول splash

afreen wayal *v.t.* آفرینویل applaud

afsana *n.* افسانه fable

afsana *n* افسانه fiction

afsana *n.* افسانه legend

afsana dawla *a.* افسانهوله romantic

afsana peyzhandana *n.* افسانه پژندنه mythology

afsanawee *a* افسانوي fabulous

afsanawee *a.* افسانوي legendary

afsanawee *a.* افسانوي mythical

afsanawee *a.* افسانوي mythological

afsha kawal *v. t* افشا کول discover

afsha kawal *v. t* افشا کول divulge

afsos *n.* افسوس compunction

afsos *n.* افسوس remorse

afsos kawal *v.t.* کول افسوس rue

afsos kawal; ah kkhal *v.i.* افسوس کول،آه کل sigh

afyoon *n.* افیون opium

agar chay *prep.* اګر چ notwithstanding

agar chay *conj.* ارچه though

aghaz *n.* آغاز inception

aghaz *n.* آغاز initiative

aghaz; shoro *n.* آغاز،شروع initial

agheyz *n* اغز effect

agheyz *n.* اغز influence

agheyz kawal; ijra kawal *v. t* اغز کول،اجراءکول effect

agheyz khandal *v.t.* اغیزندل affect

agheyz laral *v.t.* اغزلرل influence

agheyz man *a* اغزمن effective

agheyza achawal *v.i.* اغیزهاچول act

agheyznak *a.* اغزناک influential

agheyznaktob *n* اغزناکتوب efficacy

aghostal *v.t.* اغوستل wear

aghzan *a.* اغزن thorny

aghzay *n.* اغزی thistle

aghzay *n.* اغزی thorn

ah kkhana *n.* آه کنه sigh

ahak *n.* آهک lime

ahak kawal *v.t* آهک کول lime

aham *a.* اهم important

aham juz *adj.* اهمجز component

aham; aslee *a* اهم،اصلي staple

ahan ruba *n.* آهنربا loadstone

ahdaa kawoonkay *n* اهداکوونکی donor

ahlee kawal *v.t.* اهلي کول tame

ahmaq *a* احمق foolish

ahmaq *n.* احمق simpleton

ahmaq aw lawda *adj.* احمقاولوده crass

ahmaq saray *n* احمقسی blockhead

ahmaq saray *n.* سی احمق loggerhead

ahmaqana ehsasat *n.* احمقانه احساسات slush

ahmeeyat *n.* اهمیت importance

ahmeeyat *n.* اهمیت notability

ahmeeyat laral *v.i.* اهمیتلرل matter

ahya; parawana *n* احیا،پارونه animation

ajant *n* اجنت agent

ajar *n.* اجر gratuity

ajar warkawal *v.t.* اجرورکول reward

ajar; jaza *n.* اجر،جزا reward

ajbari *a* اجباری forcible

ajeeb *adj* عجیب bizarre

ajeeb *a.* عجیب queer

ajeeb *a.* عجیب weird

ajeeb aw ghareeb *a.* عجیباوغریب grotesque

ajeeb aw ghareeb shay *n.* عجيب او غريب شی oddity

ajmal; landoon *n.* اجمال؛لنون synopsis

ajoora *n.* اجوره wage

akademee *n* اکاديمي academy

akasee *n.* عکاسي photography

akhaz kawal *v. t.* اخذکول derive

akhbaree; rasa *a.* اخباري؛رسا expressive

akheyrawal *v.t.* اخول thatch

akheyree *a.* آخري latter

akheystal; neewal *v.t* اخستل؛نيول take

akheystoonkay *n.* اخستونکی recipient

akhir *n* آخر terminal

akhiree *a.* آخري ultimate

akhiree had *a.* اخريحد maximum

akhiree had pori rasawal *v.t.* اخريحدپوررسول maximize

akhlaq khowoonkay *n.* اخلاق وونکی moralist

akhlaq pohana *n.* اخلاق پوهنه ethics

akhlaqee *a* اخلاقي ethical

akhlaqee *a.* اخلاقي moral

akhlaqee aseelwalay ghokhtoonkay shakhs *n.* اخلاقي اصيلولی غوتونکی شخص puritan

akhlaqee chaland *n.* اخلاقي چلند morality

akhlaqee fasad *n.* اخلاقي فساد slough

akhlaqee fasad; goona *n.* اخلاقي فساد؛بناه vice

akhlaqee fikar warkawal *v.t.* اخلاقي فکرورکول moralize

akhlaqee mayar *n.* اخلاقي معيار norm

akhlaqeeyat *n.* اخلاقيات morale

akhoowat *n.* اخوت fraternity

akhor *n.* آخور crib

akhor *n.* آخور manger

akhta aw mubtila; tawrataw *n.* اختهاومبتلا؛تاوراتاو tangle

akhtar warkawal *v.t.* اخطارورکول admonish

akhtar; tahdeed *n.* اخطار؛تهديد denunciation

aks *n* عکس photograph

aks akheystal *v.t.* عکساخستل photograph

aks jorawoonkay *n.* عکس جوروونکی photographer

aksee *a.* عکسي photographic

ala *a.* اعلی excellent

ala *n.* آله tool

ala; wasayal *n.* آله؛وسايل appliance

ala; waseela *n* آله؛وسيله device

ala; waseela *n.* آله؛وسيله instrument

alama *n.* علامه symbol

alama *n.* علامه symptom

alama; larkhod *n.* علامه؛لارود signal

alama; nakha *n.* علامه؛نه badge

alama; nakha *n.* علامه؛نه sign

alama; nakhan *n* علامه؛نان emblem

alat; seezoona *n.* آلات؛بيزونه ware

alatee *a.* آلاتي instrumental

albom *n.* البوم album

alee *a.* عالي stately

alee; lwar *a.* عالي،لو high

aleehazrat *n.* اعليحضرت majesty

alim *a.* عالم learned

alimana *a.* عالمانه scholarly

aljabar *n.* الجبر algebra

almaray *n.* المار closet

almaray *n* المار cupboard

almas *n* الماس diamond

aloo *n.* الو potato

aloocha *n.* آلوچه plum

alwataka *n.* الوتکه aircraft

alwataka *n.* الوتکه aeroplane

alwataka *n.* الوتکه plane

alwatal *v.i* الوتل fly

alwatal; randa kawal *v.t.* الوتل، رنده کول plane

alwatana *n* الوتنه flight

alwatoonkay *n* الوتونکی bird

am *n* ام mango

am *a.* عام common

am khalk pri khabrawal *v.t.* عام خلک پرخبرول publicize

am wagaray *n.* عاموی populace

am wagaray *n.* snobbery

am wazhna *n.* عاموژنه holocaust

ama zhaba *n.* عامهژبه slang

amada kawal *v. t* آماده کول equip

amadagee; meelan *n.* آمادی؛میلان inclination

amal *n.* عمل acting

amal kawal *n.* عمل کول act

amalee *a.* عملي practical

amalee *a.* عملي operative

amalee falsafa *n.* عملي فلسفه pragmatism

amalee kawal; areeza kawal *v.t.* عملي کول؛عريضه کول apply

amaleetob *n.* عمليتوب practicability

amaleeyat *n.* عمليات operation

amanat plorana *n.* امانت پلورنه consignment

amanat sparal *v.t.* امانت سپارل consign

amanat warsparal *v. t* امانت ورسپارل entrust

amar *n.* امر affair

amar kawal *v. t* امر کول direct

amar; lar khodana *n* امر،لارو دنه direction

amaree; lazimee *a.* امري؛لازمي imperative

ambolans *n.* امبولانس ambulance

amboor *n. pl.* انبور tongs

ameen *a.* امين honest

ameen *n.* امين trustee

ameen *a.* امين trustful

ameen; khuday di wakree *interj.* آمين،خدای دو کي amen

ameerul bahar *n.* امير البحر admiral

ameyl *n.* امل garland

ameyl *n.* امل locket

ameyl *n.* امل necklace

ameyl *v.t.* اميل garland

amil *n* عامل factor

amirana *a.* آمرانه magisterial

amneeyat *n.* امنيت safety

amneeyat *n.* امنيت security

amneeyatee mamoor *n.* امنيتي مامور policeman

amneeyatee zwak; polees *n.* امنيتي واک؛پوليس police

amoodee; neygh *a.* عمودي؛نغ vertical

amoomee *a.* عمومي general

amoomee bakhana *n.* عمومي بخنه amnesty

amoomee har kalay *n.* عمومي هر کلی ovation

amoomee kaleesa *n.* عمومي کليسا cathedral

amoomee khwakha *n.* عمومي خوه consensus

amoomee; noomawaray *a.* عمومي؛نوموی popular

ampratooree *n.* امپراطوري imperialism

amree *a.* امر mandatory

amreeya *n.* امريه mandate

amrood *n.* امرود guava

ananas *n.* اناناس pineapple

anangay *n* اننی cheek

and; fikar *n* اند؛فکر thought

andaza *n.* اندازه estimate

andaza geyree kawal *v.t.* اندازه يری کول survey

andaza geyree; daraja bandee *n.* اندازه ميري؛درجه بندي survey

andaza kawal *v.t* اندازه کول mete

andaza kawal *v.t.* اندازه کول size

andaza; daraja *n.* اندازه؛درجه gauge

andaza; hujam *n* اندازه؛حجم dimension

andaza; kach *n.* اندازه؛کچ size

andeykhman *adv* اندمن agaze

andeykhna kawal *v.i.* اندنه کول speculate

andi kawal *v.t.* انڈی کول bale

andpal *a.* اندپال thoughtful

andwal; muadil *a.* انول؛معادل tantamount

angar *n* از compound

angar *n.* از outhouse

angaza kawoonkay *a.* انازه کوونکی resonant

angeyral *v.t.* انيرل account

angeyryal *n.* انريال thinker

angeyryal; tasawwuree *a.* انريال؛ تصوري idealistic

angeyza *n.* انزه impulse

angeyzwee *a.* انزوي impulsive

angoor *n.* انور grape

angreyzee *n* انزري English

anjuman *n* انجمن club

antan *n.* آنن antennae

antanee aw afoonee jisam *a.* انتاني او عفوني جسم septic

antanzid durmal *a.* انتان ضد درمل antiseptic

anzor *n* انور drawing

anzor *n.* انور picture

anzor akheystal *v.t.* انور اخستل picture

anzorawal *v.t* انورول draw

anzoreez *a.* انوريز pictorical

apalti wayal *v.i.* اپلتويل babble

apalti wayana *n.* اپلتوينه babble

apartman *n.* اپارتمان apartment

apartman *n.* اپارتمان compartment

apartman *n* اپارتمان flat

apartman aw da haghey lawazim *n.* اپارتمان او دهغلوازم suite

aqal; hikmat *n.* عقل؛حکمت wisdom

aqalman *a.* عقلمن wise

aqd *n* عقد contract

aqeeda *n* عقیده belief

aqeeda *n* عقیده concept

aqeeda *n.* عقیده tenet

aqeeda laral *v. t* عقیدهلرل believe

aqil *a.* عاقل sober

ar aw bansat *n.* آراوبنسـ rationale

ar kawal *v.t.* اکول necessitate

ara *n.* اره saw

ara laral *v. i* اهلرل belong

ara laral *v.i.* اهلرل pertain

aram *n.* ام lever

aram *n.* آرام comfort1

aram *n.* آرام relief

aram *n* آرام rest

aram bakhoonkay *a.* آرامبونکی sedative

aram samandar *a.* آرامسمندر pacific

aram warbakhal *v.t.* آراموربل relieve

aram warkawal *v. t* آراموركول comfort

aram warkawoonkay *a* آرام وركوونکی comfortable

aram; kam walay *n.* آرام؛کموالی alleviation

arama *adj.* آرامه bland

arama *a.* آرامه leisurely

aramakht *n.* آرامت composure

aramakht *n.* آرامت leisure

aramakht *n.* آرامت lull

aramakht *n.* آرامت serenity

aramakht *n.* آرامت calm

aramawal *v.t.* آرامول allay

aramawal *v.t.* آرامول quell

aramawal *v.t.* آرامول quiet

aramawal *v.t.* آرامول soothe

aramawal *v.t.* آرامول still

aramawal; kamawal *v.t.* آرامول؛ کمول alleviate

aramawal; marawal *v.t.* آرامول؛ مول quench

aramowoonkay *adj* آراموونکی calmative

arawana *n* اونه convert

arayish *v.t.* آرایش furnish

arbab *n.* ارباب lord

arbabtob *n.* اربابتوب lordship

areeki ghosawal *v. t* ايکغوول disconnect

areeki warsara shookawal *v. t.* ايکورسرهشوکول excommunicate

areen *a.* این instant

areen *a.* این urgent

areen kach *n.* این کچ optimum

areen shart *n* اینشرط prerequisite

areen shart *a.* اینشرط requisite

areen; sharteeya *a.* این؛شرطیه prerequisite

areentob *n.* اینتوب urgency

argamay *n.* ارمی yawn

argamay eystal *v.i.* ارمیاستل yawn

arghawanee; arghawanee rang *adj./n.* ارغوانی؛ارغوانیرنـ purple arman *n.* ارمان will

armoonay *n.* ارمونی bastard

armoonay; gheyr qanoonee *a.* ارمونی؛غرقانوني illicit

arooj *n.* عروج ascent

arq eystal *v. t* عرقاستل distil

arsha jorawal *v. t* عرشهجوول deck

art; plan *a.* ارت؛پلن wide

artawol *v.t* ارتاوول fling

artya *n.* اتیا need

artya laral *v.t.* اتیالرل need

artya warta laral *v.t.* اتیاورتهلرل require

arwa *n.* اروا ghost

arwa poh *n.* ارواپوه psychologist

arwa pohana *n.* ارواپوهنه psychology

arwa pohaneez *a.* ارواپوهنیز psychological

arwa; jazba *n.* اروا؛جذبه spirit

arwa; peyray *n.* اروا؛پری spectre

arwayeez narogh *n.* اروایيزنارو غ psychopath

arwayeez tababat *n.* اروایيزطبابت psychiatry

arwayeeza naroghee *n.* اروایيزه ناروغي neurosis

arz kawoonkay *n.* عرض کوونکی petitioner

arzakht warkawal; narkh takal *v.t.* ارزتورکول؛نرخاکل value

arzakht; bawar *n* ارزت؛باور credit

arzakhtman *a* ارزتمن worth

arzakhtman *a.* ارزتمن worthy

arzan *a* ارزان cheap

arzanawal *v. t.* ارزانول cheapen

arzawal *v. t* ارزول evaluate

arzawal *v.t.* ارزول praise

arzawana *n.* ارزوونه valuation

arzee mudat *n.* عارضيمدت interim

arzoo *n.* آرزو yearning

arzoo kawal *v.t.* آرزوکول covet

arzoo laral *v.t* آرزولرل desire

arzul balad *n.* عرضالبلد latitude

as *n.* آس horse

as *n.* اس steed

asal oseydoonkay *n* اصل اوسیدونکی original

asal; ar *n.* اصل؛آر origin

asalat *n.* اصالت originality

asan *a* آسان easy

asana *a* آسانه facile

asana *a.* آسانه handy

asanawal *v. t* آسانول ease

asanawal *v.t* آسانول facilitate

asanee *n* آساني ease

asar *n.* اثر inspiration

asar; fishar *n.* اثر؛فشار impact

asar; ishara *n* اثر؛اشاره clue

asar; khyal *n.* اثر؛خيال impression

asar; nakha *n.* vestige

asarat; mrayeetob *n.* اسارت؛ مریيتوب thralldom

asasee qanoon *n* اساسيقانون constitution

asb *n.* عصب Nerve

asb peyzhandana *n.* عصبپژاند neurologist

asb peyzhandana *n.* عصبپژندنه neurology

asbab; kalee *n.* اسباب؛کالي apparel

asbab; lawazim *n.* اسباب،لوازم
apparatus

asbab; lawazim *n.* اسباب،لوازم
outfit

asbanee *a.* عصباني irritable

asbee *a.* عصبي nervous

aseeya *n* آسيا oriental

ashba *n.* اشباع saturation

ashiqana *a.* عاشقانه amorous

ashiqana *a.* عاشقانه melodramatic

ashna kawal *v.t.* اشناکول acquaint

ashna; nazhdey *a.* اشنا،نژده
intimate

ashraf wakee *n.* اشراف واکي
aristocracy

askaree dawra pay ta rasawalay
pawzee *n.* عسکري دوره پای ته
رسولي پوي veteran

aslee *a.* اصلي genuine

aslee *a.* اصلي native

aslee *a.* اصلي original

aslee astogan *n* اصلي استون citizen

aslee aw muhim *a.* اصلي اومهم vital

aslee aw zarooree *a* اصلي او ضروري
main

aslee banra *n.* اصلي به motif

aslee barkha; da bar yaw
paymayish *n.* اصلي برخه،دباريو
پمائش gross

aslee namoona *n.* اصلي نمونه
prototype

aslee tabieeyat *n.* اصلي تابعيت
mainstay

aslee tatobay *n.* اصلي ماوبی
metropolitan

aslee; soocha *a.* اصلي،سوچه
indigenous

asman *n.* اسمان sky

asmanee *adj* آسماني celestial

asmanee *a.* آسماني heavenly

asmanee keetab *n.* اسماني کتاب
scripture

asooda *a.* آسوده tranquil

aspanawee *n.* اسپانوي Spaniard

aspanawee *a.* اسپانوي Spanish

aspanawee wagaray ya zhaba *n.*
اسپانوي وی یاژبه Spanish

astawana *n.* استوانه shaft

astawana; da astazo pandghalay
n. استوونه،داستازوپنغالی mission

astazay; rasool *n.* استازی،رسول
apostle

astazeetob *n* استازیتوب deputation

astazeetob warkawal *v. t*
استازیتوب ورکول depute

astogan *n.* استون inhabitant

astogan *n.* استون inmate

astoganzay *n.* استونای habitation

astoganzay *n.* استونـة
accommodation

astogna *n* استونه domicile

astogna kawal *v.t.* استونه کول
inhabit

astogna laral *v.i.* استونه لرل reside

astogni pori arwand *a.* استونه پور
اوند resident

ata *n* اته eight

ata guteez *a.* اته ويز octangular

ata kawal *v. i* اعطاکول confer

ata kawal *v.t.* اعطاکول vouchsafe

ata makheez *n.* اته مخيز octagon

ata satree shayr *n.* اته سطري شعر
octave

atal *n.* اتل champion

atal; qaharman *n.* اتل؛قهرمان hero

atalas *a* اتلس eighteen

atam; tar tolo koochnay basarkay *n.* اتم؛ترولوکوچنی برکی atom

atar *n.* عطر perfume

atar *n.* عطر scent

atardan *n* عطردان censer

atkal *n* اکل conjecture

atkal *n.* اکل guess

atkal *n.* اکل surmise

atkal *n.* اکل prediction

atkal kawal *v.i* اکل کول guess

atkal kawal *v.t.* اکل کول predict

atkal kawal *v.t.* اکل کول surmise

atkalawal *v. t* اکلول estimate

atkaray *n.* اتک handcuff

atkaray achawal *v.t* اتکاچول handcuff

atkaray achawal *v.t.* اتکاچول shackle

atkaray; zolanay *n.* اتک؛زولان shackle

atlawali kawal *v. t.* اتلولی کول champion

atlawee; qaharmanee *n.* اتلوي؛ قهرماني heroism

atoboos *n* اتوبوس bus

atoboos; ustad *n* اتوبوس؛أستاد coach

atomee *a.* اومي atomic

atro aw khushbooyo sara ibadat kawal *v. t* عطرواوخوشبويوسره عبادت کول cense

atya *n* اتیا eighty

atya kalan *a.* اتیاکلن octogenarian

atya kalan insan *a* اتیاکلن انسان octogenarian

aw *conj.* او and

aw ka na *conj.* اوکهنه otherwise

aw nor; waghayra *n* اونور؛وغره etcetera

awakhtoon *n.* اوتون mutation

awakhtoon aw wanjoon *n.* اوتون اوونجون permutation

awar *a* اوار level

awarawal *v.t.* اوارول level

awaz pohana *a* اوازپوهنه acoustic

awaza *n.* اوازه rumour

awaza; gangosay *n.* آوازه؛بنوسی hearsay

awaza; shohrat *n* آوازه؛شهرت fame

awazey khparawal *v.t.* اوازخپرول rumour

awazey khparawoonkay *n.* آواز خپروونکی propagandist

awdas *n* اودس ablution

awlad *n* اولاد descendant

awlad; zay nastay *n.* اولاد؛بای ناستی progeny

awrawal *v.t.* اورول hear

awreydal *v.i.* اوردل listen

awreydal; arawal *v.t. & i.* اولدل؛اول deflect

awreydoonkay *n.* اوردونکی listener

awreydoonkee *n.* اوردونکي audience

awreydyeez *a.* اورلدییز sonic

awsar *a.* اوار observant

awsat takal *v.t.* اوسطاکل average

awya *n., a* اويا seventy

awyayam *a.* اويايم seventieth

awzar pa karawal; pa takali lar safar kawal *v.t.* اوزارپه‌کارول؛ پماکلالرسفرکول ply

ay hay *interj.* ای‌هی alas

aya; pa har soorat *conj.* آيا،په‌هر صورت whether

ayalat *n* ايالت federation

ayalat *n.* ايالت shire

ayash *n.* عياش libertine

ayash *n.* عياش reveller

ayash; masrafee *a.* عياش،مسرفي sumptuous

ayashee *n.* عياشي revel

ayashee kawal *v.i.* عياشي‌کول revel

ayb *n* عب fallacy

ayb palatoonkay *adj* عب‌پلونکی censorious

aybjan *a* عبجن faulty

ayboona palatal *v. t* عبونه‌پلل cavil

ayidatee mahsool *n.* عايداتي محصول proceeds

aylameeya *n* اعلاميه declaration

aylameeya *n.* اعلاميه manifesto

aylan *n.* اعلان poster

aylan *n* اعلان advertisement

aylanawal *v.t.* اعلانول advertise

aylanawal *v.t.* اعلانول announce

aylanawal *v. t.* اعلانول declare

aylanawal *v.t.* اعلانول notify

aylanawal *v.t.* اعلانول proclaim

aynak jorawoonkay *n.* عينک جوروونکی optician

aysh *n.* عش jollity

aysh *n.* عيش mirth

aysh aw ishrat *n.* عش‌او‌عشرت joviality

aysh aw ishrat kawal *a.* عش‌او عشرت‌کول jovial

aysharee *a* اعشاري decimal

aytibar leek *n* اعتبارليک affidavit

aytibar warkawal; nafiz kawal *v.t.* اعتباروركول،نافذکول validate

aytibar; tanfeez *n.* اعتبار،تنفيذ validity

aytidal *n.* اعتدال mediocrity

aytidal *n.* اعتدال moderation

aytilafee *a* ايتلافي federal

aytimad *n.* اعتماد trust

aytimad kawal *v.t.* اعتمادکول accredit

aytimad kawal *v.t* اعتمادکول trust

aytiqad *n* اعتقاد creed

aytiraf *n.* اعتراف acknowledgement

aytiraz kawal *v. t* اعتراض‌کول demur

aytiraz kawal *v.t.* اعتراض‌کول object

aytiraz; shak *n* اعتراض،شک demur

ayzazee *a.* اعزازي honorary

azad *a.* آزاد free

azad palana *n.* آزادپالنه liberality

azada leekana *n.* آزاده‌ليکنه paraphrase

azadawal *v.t.* ازادول acquit

azadawal *v.t* آزادول free

azadawal *v.t.* آزادول liberate

azadawal *v.t.* آزادول rid

azadee *n.* آزادي liberation

azadee *n.* آزادي manumission

azadee *n.* آزادي freedom

azadee bakhkhoonkay *n.* آزادي
بخوونکی liberator

azam sargandawana; qarardad
n. عزمهرندوونه،قرارداد resolution

azamee *n* اعظمي utmost

azarawal *v.t.* اذارول nettle

azarawal *v.t.* اذارول tease

azdawajee *a.* ازدواجي marital

azdawajee *a.* ازدواجي matrimonial

azeem *a* عظیم great

azeem *a.* عظیم luxuriant

azeem *a.* عظیم magnanimous

azeem *a.* عظیم magnificent

azeem; star *n* عظیم،ستر august

azeeyat *n.* اذیت harassment

azeeyatawal *v.t.* اذیتول harass

azghan toot *n.* ازغنتوت
gooseberry

azhans *n.* اژانس agency

azmat *n.* عظمت glory

azmat *n.* عظمت luxuriance

azmat *n.* عظمت splendour

azmat warbakhal *v.t.* عظمتوربل
magnify

azmayakht *n.* آزمایت probation

azmoyal *v.t.* آزمویل probe

azmoyal *v.t.* آزمویل test

azmoyana *n* آزمینه experiment

azmoyana kawal *v.t.* آزمینهکول
quiz

azmoyantoon *n.* آزموینتون
laboratory

aztirab *a* اضطراب anxiety

ba aram *a* باآرام convenient

ba azmat *a.* باعظمت splendid

ba ba *n* بع بع bleat

ba ba kawal; amba amba kawal
v. i بعبعکول،امباامباکول bleat

ba dawama *a* بادوامه evergreen

ba eeman; wafadar *a* باایمان،وفادار
faithful

ba khabar *a.* باخبر aware

ba khabar *adj.* باخبر conversant

ba khabar *a.* باخبر informative

ba khabar; keetab lostay *a.* با
خبر،کتابلوستی well-read

ba shaoora *a* باشعوره conscious

ba sharfa *a.* باشرفه gentle

ba zawqa *adj* باذوقه elegant

bab; dars; saparkay *n.* باب،درس،
پرکی chapter

babara geera *n.* بیرهیره stubble

babozay *n* بیوزی fan

bachabaz; koonee *n.* بچهباز،کوني
sodomite

bachabazee; kooneetob *n.* بچه
بازي،کونیتوب sodomy

bachgay *n.* بچی offshoot

bachgay *n.* بچی offspring

bad *n.* باد wind

bad akhlaq *a.* بداخلاق immoral

bad akhlaqa kawal v. t. بداخلاقه کول demoralize

bad akhlaqee n. بداخلاقي immorality

bad akhlaqee kawal n. بداخلاقي کول misconduct

bad aw nawara leekana n. بداو ناوهليکنه scribble

bad bakht a. بدبخت wretched

bad bakhta a. بدبخته miserable

bad bakhtee n. بدبختي mischance

bad been a. بدبين pessimistic

bad been kas n. بدبين کس pessimist

bad beenee n. بدبيني pessimism

bad booy laral v.i. بدبوىلرل stink

bad booya a. بدبويه nosy

bad booyee n. بدبويي stench

bad booyee n بدبوي stink

bad chaland n. بدچلند mal-treatment

bad chaland n. بدچلند misdeed

bad chaleydal v.i. بادچللل blow

bad chaleydana n بادچلدنه blow

bad ghokhtal v.t. بدغوتل malign

bad goomanee n. بدلوماني misgiving

bad kar n. بدکار malefactor

bad kharsa saray n. بدخرهسى prodigality

bad khooya a. بدخويه morose

bad lamana khaza n. بدلمنه slut

bad lamanee n. بدلمني prostitution

bad margha a. بدمرغه unfortunate

bad margha a. بدمرغه ominous

bad ma· بدم affliction

bad marghee n بدمرغي disaster

bad marghee n. بدمرغي misfortune

bad meych n بادمچ anemometer

bad qismata a. بدقسمته luckless

bad rang; weejar a. بدرن،ويجا uncouth

bad rooh; shaytan n بدروح،شطان evil

bad salook kawal v.t. بدسلوک کول mistreat

bad shakla a بدشکله crook

bad shakla a. بدشکله ugly

bad shakla kawal v. t بدشکلهکول distort

bad shaklee n. بدشکلي ugliness

bad ta eekhodal v.t. بادتهايودل wind

bad tara kawal; la kharabawal v.t. بدتراکول،لاخرابول worsen

bad tareen shay n. بدترينشى worst

bad wahana n بادوهنه blight

bad wayana n. بدوينه malediction

bad weystana n. بادوستنه deflation

bada chara n بدهچاره ill

bada peykha n. بدهپه mishap

bada zhaba n. بدهژبه invective

badam n. بادام almond

badan n بدن body

badanee a بدني bodily

badanee a بدني corporal

badanee a. بدني physical

baday a. باى rich

baday a. باى wealthy

badaytob n. بايتوب opulence

badr ht بدت ad rse

badbakhtee *n.* بدبختي misery

badee zhranda *n.* بادي‌ژرنده windmill

badee; leyri *a.* بعدي،لر ulterior

badgoomana insan *n* بدومانه‌انسان cynic

badgoomana keydal *v.t.* بدومانه كدل suspect

badi *n* بِ bribe

badi *n.* بِ corruption

badi khwaral *v.t.* بخول misappropriate

badi khwarana *n.* بخونه venality

badi radi wayal *v.t.* بدردويل insult

badi wahal / warkawal *v. t.* بوهل /وركول bribe

badi; rishwat *n.* بِ،رشوت misappropriation

badkar *n.* بدكار seduce

badkara *a.* بدكاره nefarious

badkarana *a* بدكارانه seductive

badkaree *n.* بدكاري seduction

badla warkawal *v.t.* بدله‌وركول requite

badlamanay halak *n.* بدلمنی‌هلك tomboy

badlawal *v. t.* بدلول change

badlawal *v.t.* بدلول alter

badlawal; da breykhna tanray kkhata porta kawal *v.t.* بدلول،دبریناتكته‌پورته‌كول switch

badleydoonkay *a.* بدلدونكی variable

badloon *n.* بدلون change

badloon *n* بدلون alteration

badloon rawastal *v.t.* بدلون‌راوستل innovate

badloon rawastoonkay *n.* بدلون راوستونكی innovator

badloon; irtiqa *n* بدلون،ارتقا evolution

badloon; lwar zawar *n.* بدلون،لوو vicissitude

badloon; naway shay *n.* بدلون، نوی‌شی innovation

badmargha *a.* بدمرغه inauspicious

badmarghay *n.* بدمرغی adversity

badmash *n.* بدماش gangster

badmash *n.* بدماش knave

badmashee *n.* بدماشي knavery

badnam *a.* نام بد infamous

badnam *a* بدنام flagrant

badnam *a.* بدنام notorious

badnama *n.* بدنامه arrant

badnamawal *v.* بدنامول asperse

badnamawal *v.t.* بدنامول slander

badnamee *n.* بدنامي infamy

badnamee *n.* بدنامي slander

badnamtob *n.* بدنامتوب notoriety

badobaranee toopan *n.* بادوباراني توپان cyclone

badraga; da safar malgaray *n* بدرګه،دسفرملری escort

badrang *n* بادرنز cucumber

bagh *n.* باغ garden

baghawat *n.* بغاوت mutiny

baghawat *n.* بغاوت rebellion

baghawat kawal *v.* بغاوت‌كول mutiny

baghee *n.* باغ insurgent

baghot *n.* بغو tonsil

baghwan *n.* باغوان gardener

baghyana *a.* باغیانه insurgent

baghyana *a.* باغيانه mutinous

baghyana *a.* باغيانه rebellious

bahadaree *n.* بهادري gallantry

bahalee; beyrta gumarana *n.* بحالي؛برتهمارنه reinstatement

bahana *n* بهانه pretext

bahand *n* بهاند fluid

bahanz; waseela *n* بهن؛وسيله channel

bahar *adv* بهر abroad

bahar kawal *v. t* بهركول displace

bahar kawal *v.t.* بهركول oust

bahar lor ta *adv* بهرلورته outward

bahar lor ta *adv.* بهرلورته outwardly

bahar ta *adv* بهرته outside

bahar ta *adv* بهرته outwards

bahar ta ghorzawal *v. t.* بهرته غورول eject

baharanay *a* بهرنى external

baharanay *a.* بهرنى outside

baharanay *a.* بهرنى outward

bahawal; pashal *v.t.* بهول؛باشل shed

baheer *n.* بهير continuation

baheer; jaryan *n.* بهير؛جريان influx

baheydal *v.i* بهدل flow

baheydal; jaree keydal *v.i.* بهدل، جاري كدل stream

baheydana; sapara *n* بهدنه؛پره shed

baheydang *n* بهدنگ flow

bahimata *a* باهمته daring

bahree spay *n* بحريسپى beaver

bajlaka; khangaray *n.* بجلكه؛بنرى ankle

bak bak kawal *v.i.* بك بك كول gabble

bakarat; peyghaltob *n.* بكارت، پغلتوب virginity

bakhabar; hasas *a.* باخبر؛حساس sensible

bakhal *v.t* بخل absolve

bakhal *v.t* بخل forgive

bakhana kawal *v.t.* بنه كول pardon

bakheel *n.* بخيل niggard

bakheelee kawal *v.t.* بخيلي كول grudge

bakhkhana *n.* بخنه apology

bakhkhana *n* بخنه concession

bakhkhana ghokhtal *v.i.* بخنه غوتل apologize

bakhmal *n.* بخمل velvet

bakhmalee *a.* بخملي velvety

bakhoonkay *a.* بونكى munificent

bakhshish *n.* بخشش octroi

bakht *n.* بخت luck

baks *n.* بكس case

bal *a* بل else

bal *a.* بل that

bal haywad ta leygdawal *v. t.* بل هوادتهلدول export

bal wakht ta zandawal *v.t.* بل وخت تهنول adjourn

bal; juda *a.* بل،جدا other

bal; nor *pron.* بل؛نور other

bala *n.* بلا bale

bala *n.* بلا monster

bala wraz *n.* بلهور morrow

balad *a* بلد familiar

balahisar *n.* بالاحصار citadel

balakht *n* بالت cushion

balakht *n* بالت pillow
balana *n.* بلنه call
balana *v.* بلنه invitation
balana warkawal *v.t.* بلنه‌ورکول invite
balana; cheygha *n.* بلنه؛چغه calling
balapokh *n.* بالاپو quilt
balaposh *n.* بالاپوش overcoat
balayee *a.* بلایي monstrous
baleydal *v.i.* بلدل lighten
baligh *a.* بالغ adolescent
baligh *a* بالغ adult
baligh kas *n.* بالغ کس adult
balogh *n.* بلوغ adolescence
balogh *n.* بلوغ maturity
baloghat *n.* بلوغت puberty
balor *n* بلور crystal
balot *n.* بلوط chestnut
balwa *n.* بلوا riot
balwa *n.* بلوا turbulence
balwa *n.* بلوا sedition
balwa kawal *v.t.* بلواکول riot
balwagar *n* بلوار anarchist
balwagarana *a.* بلوارانه seditious
balwagaree *n.* بلواري insurrection
balwayee *a.* بلوایي turbulent
bam *n* بم bomb
bam achowoonki alwataka *n* بم اچوونکالوتکه bomber
bam; da chawdani mawad *n.* بم؛ دچاودنمواد explosive
bambaree *n* بمباري bombardment
bambaree kawal *v. t* بمباري کول bomb
bambaree kawal *v. t* بمباري کول bombard

banafsh rang *n.* رنگ بنفش violet
band *a.* بند close
band; khand *n* بند؛خ block
band; laswand *n* بند؛لاسوند bond
bandakht *n* بندست deadlock
bandakht *n.* بندست restriction
bandakht *n.* بندست obstruction
bandal *n.* بنل pack
bandal kawal *v.t.* بنل کول pack
bandar *n.* بندر port
bandawal *v. t* بندول enclose
bandawal; rakkhata kawal *v.t.* بندول؛راکته‌کول shut
bandee *n.* بندي captive
bandee *n.* بندي prisoner
bandeekhana *n.* بندیخانه jail
bandeekhana *n.* بندیخانه prison
bandeenay *a.* باندیني outer
bandeyz *n.* بندز ban
bandeyz *n* بندز blockade
bandeyz *n.* بندز sanction
bandeyz *n.* بندز prohibition
bandeyz lagawal *n.* بندزلول barrier
bandeyz lagawal *v.t.* بندزلول prohibit
bandeyz lagawal *v.t.* بندزلول sanction
bandinay makh warkawal *v.i* باندیني مخ ورکول surface
bandol *n.* بنول pendulum
bang *n.* بنگ hemp
bangar *n.* بنار buzz
bangeydal *v. i* بندل buzz
bangeydal *v. i* بندل hum
bangeydana *n* بندنه hum

bangree *n.* بنگی bangle

banjan *n* بانجان brinjal

bank ki hisab eekhodal *v. t* بانک کحساب‌ایودل deposit

bank ki peysey eekhodal *v.t.* بانک کپسی‌ایودل bank

bank; kas *n.* بانک؛ک bank

bankee hisab *n.* بانکی‌حساب deposit

bankwal *n.* بانکوال banker

banra *n* بله lash

banra badlawal *v. t* به‌بدلول disguise

banra laral; keedal keydal *v.t* به لرل؛لیدل‌کدل figure

banras *n.* باس bamboo

bansat *n.* بنس base

bansat eekhodal *v.t.* بنسای‌ودل base

bansat eekhodal *v.t.* بنسای‌ودل found

bansat eekhodoonkay *n.* بنس ایودونکی founder

bansateez *a.* بنسیز basic

bansateez *a.* بنسیز cardinal

bansateez *a.* بنسیز rudimentary

bansateez samoonpal *a.* بنسیز سمونپال radical

baqa *n.* بقا survival

baqa warbakhal *v.t.* بقاوربل perpetuate

bar *n* بار burden

bar *n.* بار load

bar aks *prep* برعکس unlike

bar koozawal *v.t.* بارکوزول unburden

bar lasay *a.* برلاسی transcendent

bar seyra *adv.* برسره apart

bar seyra *prep* برسره besides

bar seyra par dey *adv.* برسره‌پردی further

bar seyra par dey *adv.* برسره‌پردی withal

barabar *a* برابر equal

barabar *n* برابر fit

barabar *a.* برابر parallel

barabarawal *v.t.* برابرول balance

barabarawal *v. t* برابرول equal

barabarawal *v.t.* برابرول parallel

barabarawoonkay *n.* برابروونکی regulator

barabaree *n* برابری equality

barabaree; nyalgee *n* برابری؛نیالی offset

barabarwalay *n.* برابروال adequacy

barakat warkawal *v. t* برکت ورکول bless

baraks *adv.* برعکس vice-versa

baramnak *a.* برمناک gorgeous

baran wareydal *v.t.* باران‌وردل shower

baran; parla pasi dazi *n.* باران؛ پرله‌پسز volley

baranda *n.* برنه portico

baranda *n.* برنه verendah

baranee *a.* بارانی rainy

baranee tokar *n* بارانی‌وکر waterproof

baras; loogay *n.* باس؛لوی vapour

barawal *v. t* بارول burden

barawal *v.t.* بارول load

barband *a.* برند naked

barbandawal *v.t.* بربنول bare

barbandawal *v.t.* برينول strip

barbandee *n.* باربندي packing

barbokay *n.* بوکه whirlwind

barghaz *n.* برغز dart

barkha *n* برخه canton

barkha *n.* برخه quota

barkha *n.* برخه section

barkha *n.* برخه segment

barkha *n.* برخه part

barkha akheystal *v.t.* برخهاخستل part

barkheez; juzayee *a.* برخيز؛جزيي partial

barkhleek *n* برخليک fate

barlasay *n* برلاسى domination

barlasay keydal *v.t.* برلاسىکدل attain

barlasay keydal *v.t.* برلاسىکدل overcome

barlasay keydal *v.i.* برلاسىکدل predominate

barma *n.* برمه auger

barma *n* برمه drill

barma *n.* برمه wimble

barma sara sooray kawal *v. t.* برمهسرهسورىکول drill

barmata kawal *v.t.* برمتهکول snatch

barseyra par dey *adv.* برسرهپردى moreover

barseyran makh; sata *n.* برسرن مخ؛سطح surface

barseyran; sathee *a.* برسرن؛سطحي superficial

barseyrantob *n.* برسرنتوب superficiality

bartar *a.* برتر predominant

bartaree *n.* برترى excellence

bartaree *n.* برترى predominance

bartarfee *n* برطرفي dismissal

barwa *n.* بوا bawd

barya *n.* بريا success

barya keydal *v.i.* برياکدل triumph

barya; fata *n.* بريا؛فتح triumph

baryalay *a* بريالى successful

baryalay *a.* بريالى victorious

baryalay *n.* بريالى victor

baryalay keydal *v.i.* بريالىکدل succeed

baryalay keydal *v.t.* بريالىکدل vanquish

baryalay meena *n.* بريالمينه melodrama

baryalay; fatay *a.* بريالى؛فاتح triumphal

baryalay; fatay *a.* بريالى؛فاتح triumphant

baryaleetob *n.* بريالىتوب achievement

baryaleetob *n.* بريالىتوب attainment

baryazam *n* براعظم continent

baryazam pori arwand *a* براعظم پوراوند continental

barzakhee naray *n.* برزخينرى purgatory

basarkay *n.* برکى jot

basarkay *n.* برکى spark

baseerat *n.* بصيرت insight

baseerat *n.* بصيرت vision

baseerat laroonkay *a.* بصيرت لرونکى intuitive

bashar dosta *n.* بشردوسته philanthropy

bashar pal *a* بشرپال humanitarian

bashareeyat *n.* بشريت humanity

bashpar *a* بشپ accomplished

bashpar *a* بشپ complete

bashpar ghopa kawal *v.t.* بشپغوپه کول overwhelm

bashpar kawal *v.t.* بشپکول accomplish

bashpar wakman *n* بشپواکمن autocrat

bashpar wakman *a.* بشپواکمن omnipotent

bashpar wakmanee *n.* بشپواکمني omnipotence

bashpara mati warkawal *v.t.* بشپهماتورکول rout

bashparawal *v. t* بشپول complete

bashparawoonkay *a* بشپوونکی complementary

bashpartob *n.* بشپتوب totality

bashpartya *n.* بشپتيا accomplishment

baspana *n.* بسپنه donation

baspana warkawal *v. t* بسپنه ورکول bestow

basree *a.* بصري ocular

basree *a.* بصري visual

bata *n.* بته goose

bata gota *n.* بهوته thumb

batai *n.* بـ kiln

batay; fateela; orlagawoonay *n.* باـ؛فتيله؛اورلوونى wick

batil *a.* باطل null

batilawal *v.t.* باطلول counteract

batilawal *v. t* باطلول disprove

batilawal *v. t* باطلول elude

batilawal *v.t.* باطلول invalidate

batilawal *v.t.* باطلول undo

batilawal *v.t.* باطلول void

batilawal *v.t.* باطلول nullify

batilawal; hazafawal *v. t.* باطلول؛ حذفول cancel

batilawona *n.* باطلوونه nullification

batoo *n* باو bouncer

batray *n* بر battery

bawafa *a.* باوفا loyal

bawar leek *n.* باورليک creed

bawaree *a* باوري credible

bawaree *a.* باوري reliable

bawaree *n.* باوري optimist

bawaree laraway *n.* باوريلاروى henchman

bawaseer *n.* بواسير piles

baya *n.* بيه price

baya *n.* بيه value

baya eekhodal *v.t.* بيهايودل rate

baya laral *v.t.* بيهلرل cost

baya moondal *v.t.* بيهموندل price

bayad *v.* بايد must

bayan *n* بيان express

bayan *n.* بيان statement

bayan; tawzee *n* بيان؛توضيح description

bayanawal *v. t* بيانول describe

bayanawal *v. t.* بيانول express

bayanawal *v.t* بيانول state

bayanawal *v.t.* بيانول represent

bayanawal; ghageeza banra warkawal *v.t.* بيانول،غيزه به وركول voice

bayanawoonkay *n.* بيانوونكى narrator

bayaneeya *a* بيانيه descriptive

bayaneeya *n.* بيانيه proclamation

baydar *a.* بدار cautious

baydar *a.* بدار vigilant

baydar *a.* بدار wakeful

baydar; saro *a.* بدار،سارو watchful

bayhooda *a.* بهوده frivolous

bayhooda wakht teyrawal *v.i.* بهوده وخت تيرول dawdle

baysakal *n.* بايسكل bicycle

baysakal sawar *n* بايسكل سوار cyclist

baysakal; chakar *n* بايسكل،چكر cycle

baytul khala *n.* بيت الخلا latrine

bayzwee jisam *n* بضوي جسم oval

baz *n* باز falcon

bazar *n* بازار market

bazeydal *v.i.* بزيدل whiz

bazhar *n.* بزهار murmur

be adabi *n* بى ادبى disrespect

be asasa khabary *n.* بى اساسه خبرى gossip

be azami *n.* بى عزمى indecision

be da muhakimy la hukma da cha wajal *v.t.* بى دمحاكمى له حكمه دچاوژل lynch

be lari zai *n.* بلارى زاى impasse

be mela *a.* بمیله listless

be samara *adv* بثمره abortive

be tawaja *a* بى توجه forgetful

beelyoon; da peyso yaw shmeyra *n* بيليون،دپسو يوشمره billion

beema *n.* بيمه insurance

beema kawal *v.t.* بيمه كول insure

beemar *n* بيمار invalid

beemaree *n.* بيمارى illness

beer; afeen; ghorzay parzay *n* بير،افين،غورى پرى hop

beer; yaw nalkawalay skhak *n* بير،يونالكولى اک beer

beera *n.* بيه haste

beera kawal *v.i.* بيه كول hasten

beeranak *a.* ناک بيه hasty

beeranay halat *n* بينى حالت emergency

beezo *n.* بيزو monkey

beezo *n.* بيزو baboon

behes *n.* بحث debate

behes kawal *v. t.* بحث كول debate

behes kawal *v.t.* بحث كول argue

behree zwak *n.* بحرى واک armada

behtaree *n* بهترى betterment

benzeen; naft *n.* بنزين،نفت petrol

bera naak *adv.* بهناك headlong

bey adaba *a* بادبه discourteous

bey adaba *a.* بادبه impertinent

bey adaba *a.* بادبه impolite

bey adabee *n.* بادبي impertinence

bey adabee *a* بادبي unmannerly

bey adabee; pooch khuleytob *n.* بادبي،پوچ خولتوب vulgarity

bey andwala *n* بانوله antic

bey aqal *a.* بعقل silly

bey aqal *a.* بعقل zany

bey aqla *a.* بعقله idiotic

bey arzakhta *a.* بارزته invaluable

bey arzakhta *a.* بارزته trivial

bey arzakhta *a.* بارزته worthless

bey arzakhta kawal *v.t.* بارزته کول demonetize

bey arzakhta shay *n.* بارزتهشی nothing

bey arzakhtob; deywaleeya *n.* بـ ارزتوب،ډواليه bankrupt

bey asba *a.* بعصبه nerveless

bey aytibara *a.* باعتباره unreliable

bey aytina *a.* باعتنا irrespective

bey aytinayee *n* باعتنائي disregard

bey aytinayee kawal *v. t* باعتنائي کول disregard

bey bahaney *adv* ببهانې bonafide

bey baka *a* بباکه dauntless

bey bakee *n.* بباکي hardihood

bey barkhi kawal *v. t* ببرخهکول dethrone

bey barkhiwalay *n.* ببرخوالی privation

bey bawaree *n.* بباوري mistrust

bey boonyada *a.* ببنياده baseless

bey boonyada *a.* ببنياده invalid

bey dagha *a.* بداغه spotless

bey daney mameez *n.* بدانهميز currant

bey dawama *a* بدوامه flimsy

bey eezata; kufreeya *a.* بعزته، کفريه profane

bey eezatee *n* بعزتي dishonour

bey eezatee kawal *v. t* بعزتيکول dishonour

bey ehteeyata *a.* باحتياطه inconsiderate

bey faydey *a.* بفايد futile

bey faydeytob *n.* بفايدتوب futility

bey fikra *a.* بفکره careless

bey gati; pooch *a.* بـﭘوچ void

bey gatitob *n* بتوب drawback

bey ghaga *a.* بغه silent

bey ghaga toray *n.* بغهتوری mute

bey gharaza *a.* بغرضه neuter

bey gharaza *a.* بغرضه selfless

bey goona *a.* بناه innocent

bey goonahtob *n.* بناهتوب innocence

bey hada *a* بحده extreme

bey harakat *a.* بحرکت immovable

bey harakata *a.* بحرکته motionless

bey harakata wagon *n.* بحرکته واون trailer

bey harakata; walar *a.* بحرکته،ولا stagnant

bey hasila kawal *v.t.* بحاصلهکول sterilize

bey haya *a.* بحيا immodest

bey hayayee *n.* بحيايي immodesty

bey his *a.* بحس insensible

bey hisa *a.* بحسه numb

bey hisa *a.* بحسه senseless

bey hisee *n.* بحسي apathy

bey hisee *n.* بحسي insensibility

bey hokha *n.* بهوه anaesthetic

bey hokha *n.* بهوي coma

bey hokha keydal *v.i* بهوهکدل swoon

bey hokhee *n* بهوي anaesthesia

bey honara *a.* بهنره artless

bey honara *a* بهنره clumsy

bey insafa *a.* بانصافه injudicious
bey insafa *a* بانصافه unfair
bey insafee *n.* بانصافي injustice
bey itifaqee *n.* باتفاقي schism
bey itmaynanee *n.* باطميناني insecurity
bey itminanee *n* باطميناني dissatisfaction
bey jinsa noom *n* بجنسهنوم neuter
bey jorey *a.* بجو incomparable
bey jorey *a.* بجو peerless
bey jurata kawal *v. t.* بجرأتهکول discourage
bey kara *a.* بکاره idle
bey kara *n.* بکاره idler
bey kara *a.* بکاره inactive
bey kara *a.* بکاره redundant
bey karee *n.* بکاري idleness
bey karee *n.* بکاري inaction
bey khabara *a.* بخبره oblivious
bey khabaray sara *adv.* بخبرسره unwittingly
bey khazi *n.* ب bachelor
bey khwanda *a.* بخونده banal
bey khwanda *a.* بخونده humdrum
bey khwanda *a.* بخونده insipid
bey khwanda *a.* بخونده awkward
bey khwanda *a.* بخونده prosaic
bey khwandee *n.* بخوندي insipidity
bey kora *a* بکوره outcast
bey lari *a.* بلار unprincipled
bey lari kawal *v. t.* بلارکول derail
bey lari kawal *v.t.* بلارکول misguide
bey laritob *n.* بلارتوب aberrance

bey lastonro kot *n.* بلستووکو waistcoat
bey maharata *a.* بمهارته gainly
bey maharata kas *n.* بمهارته کس layman
bey mana *a* بمعنی absurd
bey mana *a.* بمانا insignificant
bey manatob *n.* بماناتوب insignificance
bey maney *a.* بماز meaningless
bey masheena koochnay alwataka chi da hawa pa waseela aloozee *n.* بماشينه کوچدالوتکهچدهواپهوسيلهالوزي glider
bey misla *a.* بمثله unique
bey nateejey *adv.* بنتيج vainly
bey nazakata *a.* بنزاکته indecent
bey nazakatee *n.* بنزاکتي indecency
bey nazma *a.* بنظمه tumultuous
bey nazmee *n* بنظمي disorder
bey nazmee *n.* بنظمي indiscipline
bey nazmee *n.* بنظمي misrule
bey noomtya *n.* بنومتيا anonymity
bey pama *a.* بپامه imprudent
bey pama *a.* بپامه inattentive
bey pama *a.* بپامه rash
bey pama ghageydal *v. t* بپامهغدل blurt
bey pama; na khabar *a.* بپامه،نا خبر unaware
bey pamee *n.* بپامي imprudence
bey parwa *a.* بپروا irresponsible
bey parwa *a.* بپروا mindless
bey parwa *a.* بپروا reckless

bey parwa *a.* بپروا nonchalant

bey parwa *a.* بپروا negligent

bey parwayee *n.* بپرويي negligence

bey parwayee *n.* بپروايي nonchalance

bey patee kawal *v. t. & i* بپتي کول blab

bey paymani *a.* بپيماڼ measureless

bey qadra keydal / kawal *v.t.i.* بـ قدره کدل/کول depreciate

bey qanoona *a.* بقانونه lawless

bey qanoonee *n.* بقانوني void

bey qarar *adj.* بقرار agog

bey qaydagee *n.* بقاعلي irregularity

bey qaydey *a.* بقاعد irregular

bey rahma *a.* برحمه ruthless

bey rehem *a.* برحم inexorable

bey rehma *a.* برحمهatrocious

bey rehma *a* برحمه brutal

bey rehma *adj.* برحمه merciless

bey rehma *a.* برحمه pitiless

bey rehmee *n* برحمي atrocity

bey rooha; jamid *a.* بروحه؛جامد inanimate

bey sabra *a.* بصبره impatient

bey sabree *n.* بصبري impatience

bey saray *a.* بساری matchless

bey seem *a.* بسيم wireless

bey seem mukhabira *n* بسيممخابره wireless

bey sharafa *n.* بشرفه ruffian

bey sharam *a.* بشرم shabby

bey shari da wada zhwand teyrawal *n* بشرعدوادهژوندترول concubine

bey sharma *a.* بشرمه shameless

bey shmara *a.* بشماره incalculable

bey shmeyra *a.* بشمره countless

bey shmeyra *a.* بشمرهinnumerable

bey shmeyra *a.* بشمره numberless

bey shmeyra *a.* بشمره numerous

bey tafawat *a.* بتفاوت indifferent

bey tafawatee *n.* بتفاوتي indifference

bey tajrubey *adj* بتجرب callow

bey taleema *a.* بتعلمه illiterate

bey tarafa *a.* بطرفه impartial

bey tarafa *a.* بطرفه neutral

bey tarafa kawal *v.t.* بطرفهکول neutralize

bey tarafee *n.* بطرفي impartiality

bey tarbeeyey *a.* بتربيه rude

bey tarteeba *n* بترتيبه anomaly

bey tarteeba *a.* بترتيبه random

bey toley keydo lamala raghorzeydal *v.t.* بتواکدولامله راغوردل tip

bey wafayee *n.* بوفايي perfidy

bey wafayee kawal *v. t.* بوفاييکول desert

bey wajdana *n.* بوجدانه miscreant

bey waka khandeydal *v.i.* بواکه خندیدل giggle

bey wakhta zeygeydana *n* بوخته زیدنه abortion

bey wakhta; bey moqa *a.* بوخته؛بې موقع inopportune

bey wano aw parakha dag wazma jalga *n.* بونواوپراخها وزمهجله steppe

bey wasley kawal *v. t* بوسلکول disarm

bey wasley kawona *n.* بوسلکوونه disarmament

bey weyri *a.* بوړ intrepid

bey yara *a.* بیاره lonesome

bey yara; bey madadgara *a.* بي یاره،بمدداره helpless

bey zaya *a.* بایه nonsensical

bey zaya *a.* بایه wasteful

bey zaya *a.* بایه vain

bey zaya garzeydal *v.t* بایهرلدل maroon

bey zaya khabari *n.* بایهخبر prattle

bey zaya palatana kawal *v.t.* بایه پلنهکول poke

bey zaya wada kawal; bey tarteeba wada kawal *v.i.* بایه وده کول،بترتیبهوده کول straggle

bey zaya; bey wakhta *a.* بایه،بوخته undue

bey zhwanda *a.* بژونده lifeless

bey zra *n.* بزه coward

bey zra *a.* بزه timid

bey zratob *n.* بزهتوب timidity

beydya; bey wafayee *n* بدیا،بوفایي desert

beyjak *n.* بجک invoice

beykhee *adv* بیخي absolutely

beylawal *v.t.* بلول sunder

beylcha *n.* بلچه shovel

beylcha *n.* بلچه spade

beylchey sara leyri kawal *v.t.* بلچ سرهلرکول shovel

beyleydana *n.* بلدنه abstraction

beylga *n.* بله specimen

beylga azmoyal *v.t.* بلهآزمویل sample

beylowanay *n.* بلوونی midriff

beyltoon *n* بلتون detachment

beyltoon *n.* بلتون insulation

beyltoonpal *n.* بلتونپال secessionist

beynooma; na sarganda *a.* بنومه، نارنده anonymous

beyragh *n.* برغ banner

beyragh *n* برغ flag

beyranga *adj* بیرنه achromatic

beyray ki spareydal *v. t.* بکسپرلدل board

beyrta *adv.* برته aback

beyrta ada shaway heesab *n.* برته اداشویحساب refund

beyrta akheestal *v.t.* برتهاخیستل withdraw

beyrta akheystal *v.t.* برتهاخستل retrieve

beyrta raghokhtal *v.t.* برتهراغوتل recall

beyrta rastaneydal *v.i.* برته راستندل rebound

beyrta staneydana *n.* برتهستندنه relapse

beyrta tar lasa kawal *v.t.* برتهتر لاسهکول recover

beyrta warkawal *v.t.* برتهورکول reimburse

beysareetob *a.* بساریتوب inimitable

beyt chi yawa qafeeya walaree *n.* بت چیوهقافیهولري couplet

beyzar *a.* بزار averse

beyzara kawal; marawal *n.* بزاره
کول؛مول surfeit

beyzaree *n.* بزاري aversion

bilkul *adv* بالکل due

birinj; zhar *n.* ژ؛برنج brass

biskot *n* بسکو biscuit

blarbakht *n.* بلاربت pregnancy

**blok; yawa dala hamkar
ashkhas** *n.* بلوک؛يوهلههمکار
اشخاص platoon

bodija; lagakht andwaltya *n*
بودجه؛لختانولتيا budget

boghay *n.* بوغ balloon

bojay *n.* بوج sack

bokam; rawataltya *n.* بوکام؛
راوتلتيا hunch

bokhar; loogay *n* بخار؛لوی fog

bokht *a* بوخت busy

bokhtya *n.* بوختيا pastime

boonyad *n.* بنياد foundation

boonyadee *a.* بنيادي fundamental

boonyadee *n.* ادي gaiety

boonyadee; ibtidayee *a.* بنيادي؛
ابتدايي initial

boora warkawal *v.t.* بورهورکول
sugar

boora; qand *n.* بوره،قند sugar

boot *n.* بت idol

boot *n.* بو shoe

boot parast *n.* بتپرست idolater

boot ta talay achawal *v.t* بوتهتلی
اچول sole

boot; fayda *n* بو،فايده boot

bootan pa pkho kawal *v.t.* بوانپه
پوکول shoe

bootay *n* بوی bush

bootay *n.* بوی plant

bootpohana *n* بوپوهنه botany

booy *n.* بوی fragrance

booy *n.* بوی smell

booyawal *v.i.* بويول inhale

booyawal *v.i.* بويول sniff

booyawal; booy warkawal *v.t.*
بويول؛بویورکول smell

bordbaree *n* بردباري bearing

boseeda *adj* بوسيده carious

boshka; tyoob *n.* بوشکه؛تيوب barrel

botal *n* بوتل bottle

braj *n.* برج tower

brash *n* برش brush

brastan *n.* بستن coverlet

brayk lagawal *v. t* بريکلول brake

breed *n.* بريد assault

breed *n* بريد dash

breed kawal *v.* بريدکول assail

breed kawal *v.t.* بريدکول assault

breed kawal *v.t.* بريدکول invade

breed kawal *v.i* بريدکول lunge

breed kawal *v.t.* بريدکول
spearhead

breed; poola *n.* بريد،پوله frontier

breed; yarghal *n.* بريد،يرغل attack

breedoona aw hadood *n.* بريدونهاو
حدود purview

breetanawee *adj* بريتانوي british

breykh *n* بر glow

breykhandoy *a* برندوی light

breykheydal *v.i.* بردل glow

breykheydana *n* بردنه dazzle

breykheydana *n.* بردنه
scintillation

breykheydana *n.* بریدنه refulgence
breykhna *n* برنا electricity
breykhna warkawal *v. t* برنا
ورکول electrify
breykhnayee *a* برنایي electric
breykhnayee qawa *n.* برنایيقوه
voltage
breykhnayee sragh *n.* برنایيراغ
bulb
breyt *n.* برت moustache
breytoona *n.* برتونه mustache
bronz; bronzee rang *n. & adj*
برونز؛برونزيرنگ bronze
brudbaree *n.* بردباري endurance
buhran *n* بحران crisis
buhtan lagawal *v.t.* بهتانلول trump
bukhal *n* بخل grudge
bukhar kawal *v.i.* بخارکول steam
bukhar kawoonkay *n.* بخار
کوونکی steamer
bukhar; lara *n* بخار؛له steam
bukharay *n.* بخار stove
bulbul *n.* بلبل nightingale
burdbar *a* بردبار endurable
burj; munara *n.* برج؛مناره steeple
bya *adv.* بیا again
bya *a* بیا then
bya chapawal *v.t.* بیاچاپول reprint
bya katal *v.t.* بیاکتل review
bya katana *n* بیاکتنه review
bya neewana *n* بیانیوونه remand
bya paylawal *v.t.* بیاپیلول resume
bya paylawana *n.* بیاپیلونه
resumption
bya raghawana *n.* بیارغاوونه
restoration

bya rastaneydal *v.t.* بیاراستندل
reclaim
bya rastaneydana; zmaksamoon
n بیاراستندنه؛مکسمون
reclamation
bya razhwanday keydal *v.i.* بیا
راژوندیکدل revive
bya razhwanday keydana *n.* بیا
راژوندیکدنه resurgence
bya razhwanday keydana *n.* بیا
راژوندیکدنه revival
bya razhwanday shaway *a.* بیا
راژوندیشوی resurgent
bya tasal warkawal *v.t.* بیاتسل
ورکول reassure
bya tawleedawal *v.t.* بیاتولیدول
reproduce
bya tawleedawal; bya zeygeydal
v.t. بیاتولیدول؛بیازدل regenerate
bya tawleedawana *n* بیاتولیدوونه
reproduction
bya wadanawal *v.t.* بیاودانول
rehabilitate
bya wadantya *n.* بیاودانتیا
rehabilitation
bya zeygoon *n.* بیازون rebirth
byaleyda *n.* بیلدا secession
byatee kawal; skwalal *v.t.* بیاتي
کول؛سکولل shear

C

cha ta lara neewal *v.t.* چاتهلارهنیول
waylay

cha ta law warachawal *v.t.* چاته لاسوراچول tantalize

cha ta pateydal *v.i.* چاته پدل lurk

cha ta; cha lapara *pron.* چاته،چا لپاره whom

chabak *adj* چابک alacrious

chabak *a.* چابک speedy

chadan *n* چدن cast-iron

chagh *a* چاغ fat

chaghakht *n* چاغت obesity

chaghan ghag; faryad *n* چغن غ،فرياد squeak

chak; cheech *n* چک،چيچ bite

chak; darz *n* چاک،درز cut

chakar bandi da tlo patloon *n.* چکربانددتلوپتلون slacks

chakar wahal *v.i.* چکروهل meander

chakar wahal *v.t.* چکروهل saunter

chakar wahana *n* چکروهنه stroll

chakar; pali tag *n* چکر،پلی ز walk

chakara; luab *n.* چکه،لعاب slime

chakaree *a* چکري،دوروي cyclic

chakchaki *n* چکچک acclaim

chakckahi kawal *v.t* چکچکه کول acclaim

chaklayt *n* چاکلا chocolate

chal *n* چل deception

chal *n.* چل lurch

chal kawal *v.t.* چل کول trick

chal; chalbaz *n.* چل،چلباز ruse

chal; doka *n* چل،دوکه trick

chalak *a* چالاک cunning

chalakee *n* چالاکي cunning

chaland kawal *v.t* چلند کول conduct

chaland kawai *v. i.* چلند کول behave

chaland kawal *v.t.* چلند کول treat

chaland; akhlaq *n* چلند،اخلاق behaviour

chaland; amal *n* چلند،عمل deed

chaland; meylmastya *n.* چلند، ملمستيا treatment

chaland; riwayya *n* چلند،رويه treat

chalawal *v.t.* چلول steer

chalbaz *a.* چلباز artful

chalbaz *n.* چلباز impostor

chalbaz *a.* چلباز roguish

chalbaz *a.* چلباز shifty

chalbaz *a.* چلباز tricky

chalbazee *n.* چلبازي imposture

chalbazee *n.* چلبازي quackery

chalbazee *n.* چلبازي trickery

chalowoonkay *n* چلوونکی conductor

chalowoonkay; spor *n.* چلوونکی، سپور rider

cham aw chal *n* چماوچل disguise

chaman *n.* چمن lawn

chaman *n.* چمن sod

chamanzar *n.* چمنزار lea

chamtoo *a.* چمتو ready

chamtoo kawal *v.t.* چمتو کول assemble

chamtoowalay *n.* چمتووالی alacrity

chamtoowalay *n.* چمتووالی readiness

chang *n.* چن harp

changak *n.* چنک hook

changakh *n* چنا crab

changakha *n.* چنه frog

chanr *n* چا filter

chanrasay *n.* چاس mildew

chanrawal *v.t* چاول filter

chanrawana *n* چاونه sublime

chanrchanra *n.* چچه swallow

chanrowana; speenawana *n.*
چاوونه؛سپینوونه purgation

chanrzay *n.* چای refinery

chap *n* چاپ edition

chap shaway shay *n.* چاپ شوی شی
imprint

chap ta chamtoo kawal *v. t* چاپ
ته چمتو کول edit

chap; khparawana *n* چاپ؛خپرونه
print

chapa kawal *v.t.* چپه کول whelm

chapaw kawal *v.i.* چپاو کول loot

chapawal *v.t.* چاپول print

chapawal *n.* چپاول havoc

chapawal *n.* چپاول loot

chapawal; dalbandee kawal *v.t.*
چاپول؛لبندي کول type

chapawoonkay *n.* چاپوونکی
printer

chapawoonkay *n.* چاپوونکی typist

chapeyr garzeydal *v. i.* چاپیرګرزیدل
circulate

chapeyryal *n.* چاپیریال
environment

chapeyryal *n.* چاپیریال periphery

chapeyryal *n.* چاپیریال
surroundings

chaplosa saray *n.* چاپلوسه سی
sycophant

chaplosee *n* چاپلوسی flattery

chaplosee *v.t* چاپلوسي کول flatter

chaplosee *n* چاپلوسی adulation

chaplosee *n.* چاپلوسي sycophancy

chaplosee *n.* چاپلوسي insinuation

chaplosee kawal *v. t* چاپلوسي کول
butter

chaplosee kawal *v.t.* چاپلوسي کول
insinuate

chaqoo *n.* چاقو knife

char maghaz *n* چارمغز nut

char maghaz *n.* چارمغز walnut

chara saz *a.* چاره ساز resourceful

charchari *n* چرچر chirp

charchari kawal *v.i.* چرچر کول
chirp

charg *n* چرګ cock

charga *n.* چره fowl

charga *n.* چره hen

chargan satana *n.* چرګان ساتنه
poultry

charge warkawal *v.t.* چارج ورکول
lade

chargooray *n.* چروی chicken

chargooree eystal *v.i.* چروي استل
incubate

charj *n.* الیاژ چارج؛ alloy

chark *n* چرک dirt

chark; zoh *n.* چرک؛زوه pus

charmee waskat *n.* چرمي واسکټ
jerkin

charshamba *n.* چارشنبه
Wednesday

charta; halta *conj.* چرته؛هلته where

chartapee not *n.* چارتاپي نو crotchet

chat *n.* چَت ceiling

chat *n.* چت roof

chat jorawal *v.t.* چت جوول roof

chat; bam *n.* چت،بام top

chatak *adj* چک brisk

chatak *a* چک express

chatak *a.* چک nimble

chatak *a.* چک quick

chatak *a.* چک swift

chatak aw chabak *a.* چک او
چابک lively

chatak goozar *n* چک،وزار slash

chatak leekana *n.* چک لیکنه
stenography

chatak leekoonkay *n.* چک
لیکونکی stenographer

chatak parwaz *n.* چک پرواز whir

chatak tag; da as ghonda tlal *n*
چک ت،داس غونده تلل trot

chatak tlal *v.i.* چک تلل trot

chatak zghal *n.* چک غل gallop

chatak zghalawal *v.t.* چک غلول
gallop

chatak zghaleydal *v.i.* چک غلدل
sprint

chataka teykhta *n* چکه تنه scamper

chatakee zghastee syalee *n* چکی
غاستی سیالي sprint

chataktya *n.* چکتیا rapidity

chatal *a* چل dirty

chatala ya jongara *n.* چله یاجونه
slum

chatarbaz *n.* چترباز parachutist

chatee *n.* چی nonsense

chatray *n.* چتر umbrella

chawd; ayb *n* چاود،عیب flaw

chawd; ghoswalay *n.* چاود،غووالی
slit

chawdal *v. t.* چاودول explode

chawdana *n* چاودنه blast

chawdana *n* چاودنه burst

chawdana *n.* چاودنه explosion

chawdeydal *v. i.* چاوددل burst

chawkat; salor konja dara *n.*
چوکا، بلور کونجه ده panel

chawkay *n.* چوکی seat

chawkay warkawal *v.t.* چوکی
ورکول seat

chawtra; baranda *n.* چوتره،برنه
terrace

chay *n* چای tea

chay josha *n.* چای جوشه kettle

cheech *n.* چیچ sting

cheechal *v. t.* چیچل bite

cheechal *v.t.* چیچل pinch

cheechal *v.t.* چیچل sting

cheekar *n.* چیک mire

cheena; pasarlay *n* چینه،پسرلی
spring

cheenee lokhee *n.* چینی لوی
porcelain

cheenee lokhee *n.* چینی لوي china

cheenjay *n.* چینجی worm

cheetawal *v.t.* چیتول squeeze

cheetawal; bandawal *v.t.* چیتول،
بندول jam

cheygha *n* چغه cry

cheygha *n* چغه exclamation

cheygha soora *n* چغه سوره scream

cheygha wahal *v.i* چغه وهل
exclaim

cheyghey aw kreeki *n.* چغاو کریک
shriek

cheyghey aw kreeki wahal *v.i.* چغ
او کریکوهل shriek

cheyghey wahal *v.i.* چغوهلscream

cheyghi soorey wahal *v.i.* چغسور
وهل squeak

cheyghi wahal *v. i* چغوهل crow

cheyghi wahal *v. i* چغوهل cry

cheyk *n.* چک cheque

cheyri *adv.* چر where

cheyrta *adv.* چرته whereabout

chobkhat; shmeyra *n.* چوبخط،
شمره tally

chogha *n* چوغه mantle

chogha aghostal *v.t* چوغهاغوستل
mantle

chokhawana *n.* چوخوونه poke

chola *n.* چوله notch

chola kawal *n.* چولهکول note

chooka *n.* چوکه wicker

choonrar *n.* چوهار twitter

choonreydal *v. i* چوندل cheep

choonreydal *v.i.* چوندل twitter

choora; fataq *n.* چوره،فتق hernia

choorleez *n.* چورلې axis

choorleez *n.* چورلې pivot

choorleydal *v.i.* چورلدل revolve

choorleydal *v.i.* چورلدل roll

choorleydal *v.i.* چورلدل rotate

choorleydana *n.* چورلدنه rotation

choorleydana; badloon; taw *n*
چورلدنه،بدلون،تاو turn

choorleydoonkay *a.* چورلدونکی
rotary

chopar ta chamtoo *a.* چوپتهچمتو
serviceable

chopar warta kawal *v.t* چوپورته
کول service

choptya *n* چوپتيا hush

choptya *n.* چوپتيا quiet

choptya *n.* چوپتيا still

choptya *n.* چوپتيا silence

chowal; chawdal *v.i* چوول،چاودل
blast

chughandar *n* چغندر beet

churut wahana *n.* چرتوهنه doze

chust *a.* چست athletic

da payakht aw baqa zwak *n.* د
پايتاوبقاواک vitality

da ... pa oogdo ki; da ... pa
imtidad ki *prep.* د،په اودوک‍،د
په امتدادک... along

da ... pa waseela *prep* د__په وسيله
by

da abeysey pa arwand *a.* دابپه اوند
alphabetical

da abisi keetab *n.* دابکتاب primer

da abnoos bootay *n* دآبنوسبوی
ebony

da adabeeyato ilam *n.* دادبياتوعلم
literature

da adaney stan *n.* دااننستن stalk

da adayani war *n* دادينو due

da adayani war *a.* دادادينوpayable

da aflatoon da lari laraway *a.* د
افلاطوندلارلاروی platonic

da ahangaray kora *n* دآهنرکوره
forge

da ajnaso leygdawani kakhtay *n*
داجناسولدوونکت tender

da ajoorey peysey *n* داجورپس
emolument

da akasay kamra *n.* دعکاسکامره
camera

da akseejan gaz *n.* دآکسیجنباز
oxygen

**da aksoono lapara yaw
koochnay filam** *n.* دعکسونو
لپارهیوکوچنیفیلم microfilm

da alomeeneeyom filiz *n.* د
الومینیومفلز aluminium

da alwatoonko zala *n.* دالوتونکوباله
aviary

da am karawani zhaba *n.* دعام
کارونژبه lingua franca

da am wagaro raya *n.* دعامووورایه
plebiscite

da amalee falsafey pa arwand *a.*
دعملیفلسفیپهاوند pragmatic

da amoomee tafree zay *n.* دعمومي
تفریحای park

da amreeka rasmee sika *n* دامریکا
رسمیسکه dollar

**da anee harakat pa qawey pori
arwand** *a.* دآنيحرکتپهقویپور
اوند momentous

da anee harakat qawa *n.* دآني
حرکتقوه momentum

da angooro sheera *n.* دانوروشیره
must

da angreyzay zhabi da w toray
n. توریwدانرزيژبد wen

**da angreyzay zhabi yaw
makhtaray toray** *pref.* دانرز
ژبیومختایتوری be

**da angreyzay zhabi yaw
makhtaray toray** *pref* دانرزژب
یومختایتوری bi

da angreyzee kal atama myasht
n. دانرزيکالاتمهمیاشت August

**da angreyzee kal dolasama
myasht** *n* دانرزيکالدولسمه
میاشت december

**da angreyzee kal dreyma
myasht** *n.* دانرزيکالدریمه
میاشت May

**da angreyzee kal dwayama
myasht** *n* دانرزيکالدویمه
میاشت February

da angreyzee kal lasama myasht
n. دانرزيکاللسمهمیاشت
October

**da angreyzee kal nahama
myasht** *n.* دانرزيکالنهمه
میاشت September

**da angreyzee kal yawolasama
myasht** *n.* دانرزيکالیوولسمه
میاشت november

da anzor akheystanai war *a.* د
انوراخستنو picturesque

da anzwa zay *n.* دانزوامای
hermitage

da apandeeks parsob *n.* داپانیکس
پسوب appendicitis

da aqal ghakh *n.* دعقلغا
wisdom-tooth

da aram kar *n.* دامکار leverage

da aram wraz *n.* دآرامور holiday

da areeko bandeyz *n* دایکوبندز
boycott

da aroozo ilam *n.* دعروضوعلم
prosody

da arwagano pa naray bawar *n.*
داروګانوپهنباور spiritualism

da arwagano yaw bal ta nanawatal *n.* داروګانویوبلته
ننوتل transmigration

da arwayeezo naroghyo daktar
n. داروايیزوناروغیواکر
psychiatrist

da as sheeshney *n.* داسشیشنۍneigh

da as sheeshneydal *v.i.* داسشیشنل
neigh

da ashraf wakay palaway *n.* د
اشرافواکپلوی aristocrat

da asnado aw kaghazo bakas; da wazarat danda aw maqam *n.* داسنادواوکاغذو
بکس،دوزارتدندهاومقام
portfolio

da astogni aw da kar zay tr manz safar kawal *v. t* داستوݢ
اودکاریترمنسفرکول commute

da astogni war *a.* داستوݢو
habitable

da astogni war *a.* داستوݢو
inhabitable

da atom yawa manzanay zara *n.*
داوميوهمنذره neutron

da atro booy warkawal *v.t.* د
عطروبویورکول perfume

da awaz inikas *n* دآوازانعکاس echo

da awreydo war *a* داوريدووو audible

da aytimad namey khawand *adj*
داعتمادنامهخاوند accredited

da aytiraz war *a.* داعتراضو
objectionable

da bad pa shan teyreydal *v.t.* دباد
پهشانترېدل waft

da badan gharay *n.* دبدنغی limb

da badan jorakht *n.* دبدنجوت
physique

da badan pata *n.* دبدنپه muscle

da badan pati mazbootawal; rang warkawal *v.t.* دبدنپ
مضبوطول؛رنورکول tone

da badee ilam *n.* دبدیععلم rhetoric

da badi peykhi la kabala zyan aw talfat *n* دبدپلهزیاناو
تلفات toll

da badnamay pa dar la cha sakha peysey akheystal *v.t* د
بدنامهپهارلهچاخهپساخستل
blackmail

da badraft sah *n.* دبدرفتماه puddle

da badwayani da falsafey pleewanay *n.* دبدويندفلسفه
پلیونی sceptic

da baghwanay beylcha *n.* دباغوان
بلچه trowel

da bahar *n* دبهر outside

da bahar haywad mazdoor *a.* د
بهرهوادمزدور mercenary

da bakhani war *a.* دبنو venial

da bal par zay eekhodal *v.t.* دبل
پراییودل substitute

da bal seez zay neewal *v.t.* دبلیز
اینیول supersede

da balakhani balkun *n.* دبالاخان
بالکن balcony

da balot da koranay d yawi wani postakay *n.* دبلوطدکورن
پوستکیدیوون cork

da band deywal *n* دبندوال
bulwark

da bandeekhaney masool *n.* د بنديخانهمسؤل jailer

da bandeyz preykra *n* دبندىزپركه ban

da bandi *adv.* دباند out

da bandi *a.* دباند outdoor

da bandi *prep* دباند outside

da bandi *prep.* دباند without

da bandoono da dard ranz *n.* د بندونو ددردرنز rheumatism

da bandoono pa dard akhta kas *a.* دبندونوپهدردآختهکس rheumatic

da banri badloon *n.* دببدلون transformation

da banri yaw rangwalay *n.* دبيو رنوالى similitude

da barbat da rabab pakhwanay ala *n.* دبربطدرباببخوازآله lyre

da barwrani karaya *n.* دبارونکرايه freight

da baryaleetob yadgar *n.* د بريالیتوبيادار trophy

da bati pa shan tlal *v.i.* دبتپهشان تلل waddle

da bawar war *a.* دباورو trustworthy

da bawar war saray *n.* دباوروسى trusty

da baydminton da lobey parey laroonki ghondaska *n.* دبمنون دلوبپرلرونکغونسکه shuttlecock

da baysakal rakab pa pkho wahal *v.t.* دبايسکلرکاببپهو وهل pedal

da beemey peysey *n.* دبيمپس premium

da behes ghonda *n.* دبحثغونه seminar

da bey hokhay keymyayee mada *n* دبهوکميايىماده chloroform

da bey istimala aw kharabo seezoono deyray *n* دباستعماله اوخرابويزونورى debris

da bey rahmay jinsee meena *n.* د برحمجنسیمینه sadism

da beyray khada *n.* دبخاده mast

da beyray takhta *n* دبتخته board

da boodayano butkhana *n.* د بودايانوبتخانه pagoda

da boot band *n.* دبوبند lace

da boot band taral *v.t.* دبوبندتل lace

da boot gandalo aw jamo gandalo ki yaw dawl taghma *n.* دبوةلو اوجامونلوکیيو ولتغمه welt

da bootee koochnay sanga *n.* د بوي کوچنانه sprig

da breetaneeyey da sikey shalama barkha *n.* دبريتانید سکشلمهبرخه shilling

da breetaneeyey rasmee sika *n.* د سکه رسمي بريتانيى sterling

da breykhna jaryan ya shidat nap kawoonki peymana *n* د برناجريانياشدتناپ کوونکپمانه ampere

dabreykhnan apawalo yawpaymana *n.* دبرنخاناپهلوليويوپيمانه watt

da breykhna yaw paymana *n.* د برنايوپمانه volt

da bukharay da nal loogay *v.t.* د بخاردنللوى soot

da cha *pron.* د چا whose

da cha ghara takhta kawal *v.t.* د
چاغاهتخته کول strangle
da chaland dawl *n.* دچلندول
attitude
da chalowani qabil *a.* دچلونقابل
manageable
da chanrchanri awazoona *n.* د
چڼچاوازونه swallow
**da chanrchanri pa shan
awazoona kawal** *v.t.* دچڼچپه
شاناوازونه کول swallow
da chawdo nakha *n.* دچاودونه nick
da chawkat amoodee barkha *n.*
دچوکاعمودي برخه mullion
da cheechak naroghee *n.* د
چيچک ناروغي smallpox
da cheen rasmee sika *n.* دچين
رسمي سکه Yen
da cheeney pa shakal wareydal
v.i. دچينه به شکل وردل spout
da chi *conj.* داچ since
da chi *conj.* داچ that
da chi *conj.* داچ now
da chooney oba *n.* دچوناوبه
whitewash
da chooney pa obo rangawal *v.t.*
دچونپه اوبورنول whitewash
da dabaro skara *n* دبروسکاره coal
da daftar charwakay *n.* ددفتر
چارواکی officer
da daftar qasid *n.* ددفترقاصد peon
**da daftaree karmandano
plaway ya idaree zay** *n.* د
دفتري کارمندانوپلاوی یااداریهای
secretariat e
da daktaray daraja *n* داکردرجه
doctorate

da darak war *adj* ددرک و
perceptible
da dard sreeka *n.* ددردیکه throe
da darmal pa arwand *a.* ددرمل په
اوند medicinal
da darmalo yaw khorak *n* ددرملو
یوخوراک dose
da darwazey da sar teer *n.* ددرواز
دسرتیر lintel
da daryab sanda *n* ددریاببنه beach
da dawl chi *adv.* داولچ that
da dawl khalk; da dawl shayan
pron. داولخلک،داولشیان such
da dawtalbay muzayda *n* دداوطلبه
مزایده tender
da dayrey muheet *n.* ددایرمحیط
circumference
da dayri qutar *n* ددایرقطر diameter
da deenee uloomu karpoh *n.* د
دینيعلومو کارپوه theologian
da dey naray *a.* ددز worldly
**da doday pakhawani aw
khwago jorawalo nanwayee**
n دوپخوناوخووجوولونانوايي
bakery
da doday parcha *n* دوپارچه crumb
da dreyo dawro khawand *n.* د
دریودورونوخاوند tricycle
da dreyo shmeyr *a* ددروشمر three
da dwa payo motarsaykal *n.* ددوه
پایوموررسایکل scooter
**da dwa shayano manz ki
eekhodal** *v.t.* ددوهشیانومنزک
ایودل sandwich
da eejazey war *a.* داجازو
permissible

da eemteeyaz khawand n. دامتیاز خاوند monopolist

da eesayano akhtar n. دعیسائیانو اختر Xmas

da eezat pa arwand a. دعزت په اوند prestigious

da eezat peyrzoyana n. دعزت پرزوینه tributary

da ehtiram war a. داحترامو reverend

da faaleeyat markaz n. دفعالیت مرکز hub

da fasfureek aseed malga n. د فسفریک اسیدماله phosphate

da faskh kawoni war a. دفسخ کوونو revocable

da fasloono law n. دفصلونولو harvest

da feel ghakh n. دفیلغا ivory

da filam khodalo projektor n. د فلمودلوپروجکور bioscope

da filas zalanda patay n. دفلس لاندهپ tinsel

da filizato da eystani aw weeli kawoni poha n. دفلزاتو داستناو ویلکوونپوهه metallurgy

da flaleen tokar n. دفلالین وکر flannel

da foz astoganzay n. دفو استونای barrack

da gad zhwand wartya n. دژوند وتیا sociability

da gadee paya n. دایپایه tyre

da gadee sahoolat n. دایسهولت conveyance

da gado pa arwand a. داوپهاوند vehicular

da galey masheen n. دغلکولوماشین thresher

da gam akheestani awaz n. دام اخیستنآواز tread

da garmay mosam n. درمموسم summer

da gawand pa arwand a. داونپه اوند neighbourly

da gaylan paymayish n. دلنپمایش gallon

da geetar da mawseeqay ala n. د باردموسیقهآله guitar

da geydi dananay barkha n. ددنه برخه bowel

da ghag angaza n. دغاانازه resonance

da ghag lwarawalo ala n. دغلوولو آله microphone

da ghagoono da tarkeeb aw harfoono da wayang ilam n. دغونودترکیباوحرفونودوینعلم phonetics

da ghakh beykh n. دغابخ snag

da ghakh chark n. دغاچرک pyorrhoea

da ghakh khoog n. دغاخو toothache

da ghakhoono daktar n. دغاونواکر dentist

da ghaley godam n. دغَلودام granary

da ghaley zeyrmatoon n. دغل زرمتون barn

da ghalo dano zeyrma n. دغلودانو زرمه lathe

da ghanamo ya joowaro wagay n. دغنمویاجوارووی spike

da ghanrey zala n. دغاله cobweb

da ghari dasmal *n.* دغادسمال muffler

da gharmey doday *n.* دغرمو lunch

da gharmey doday khwaral *v.i.* د غرمو خول lunch

da ghashee shatanay sanda *n.* د غشی‌شاتننه barb

da ghaybo ilam *n.* دغبوعلم prescience

da ghaza pa arwand *a.* دغذاپه‌اوند nutritive

da ghlo da saza chawbandee *n.* د غلو دسزاچوبندي scaffold

da ghondaski pa shan eyrghareydal *v.i* دغونسکپه‌شان ارغدل bowl

da ghondaski wahalo danda *n* د غونسکوهلونه bat

da ghondi da behes mawad *n.* دغوندبحث‌مواد agenda

da ghondyo ya ghroono laray *n.* دغونیویاغرونول ridge

da ghwag kheeray *n.* دغوخیری mucus

da ghwag zawa *n* دغوزوه cerumen

da ghwameykho gala *n.* دغواموله cattle

da ghwayee ghwakha *n* دغوایی‌غوه beef

da ghwayee pa shan shkhwand wahal *v.t.* دغوایی‌په‌شان‌شخوند وهل munch

da gramofon da mawseeqay ala *n.* دراموفون‌دموسیقۀآله gramophone

da gul panra *n.* دل پاه petal

da gulf loba *n.* دلف‌لوبه golf

da guloono taj *n.* دلونوتاج wreath

da guloono taj jorawal *v.t.* دلونو تاج‌جوول wreathe

da hadookee da postwalee ranz *n.* دهوکی‌دپوستوالی‌رنز rickets

da hagay speen *n* دهسپین albumen

da hagay yawa loba *n.* دهاکیوه‌لوبه polo

da hagay zeyr *n.* دهزیر yolk

da hagha *pron.* دهغه his

da haghey *a* دهغ her

da haghey; haghey ta *pron.* دهغۀ هغته her

da haghwee *a.* دهغوي their

da haghwee *pron.* دهغوي theirs

da hakay loba *n.* دهاکلوبه hockey

da hamley hasa *n.* دحملهه stab

da haq ghla *n.* دحق‌غلا piracy

da har dard dwa aw moalij darmal *n.* دهردردو او معالج درمل nostrum

da har maraz dawa *n.* دهرمرض دوا panacea

da har sa neem makh *n.* دهره‌نیم مخ silhouette

da har shee keenra khwa *n.* دهر شی کیه‌خوا left

da harkalee kota *n* دهرکلي‌خونه drawing-room

da harmoneeyom da mawseeqay ala *n.* دهارمونیوم‌دموسیقۀآله harmonium

da hasharato zaharjan darmal *n* دحشراتوزهرجن‌درمل spray

da hashrato ilam *n.* دحشراتوعلم entomology

da hashrato larwa *n.* دحشراتولاروا otter

da hawa *n.* دهوا aerial

da hawa chapeyryal *n.* دهوا چاپريال space

da hawa pa shan *adj.* دهواپهشان aeriform

da haydrojan gaz *n.* دهايروجنباز hydrogen

da haywad dananay barkha *n.* د هوادننبرخه midland

da haywad khwa ta *adv.* دهوادخوا ته inland

da haywanato makhki pkhey *n* د حواناتومخکپ foreleg

da hayz bandeyda *n.* دحضبندلا menopause

da hayz jaryan *n.* دحضجريان menstruation

da hayz pa arwand *a.* دحضپهاوند menstrual

da hayzey waba *n.* دهضوبا cholera

da heelay ghag *n* دهيلغ quack

da heelay ghageydal *v.i.* دهياغدل quack

da heesaboono sabt keetab *n.* د حسابونوثبتکتاب ledger

da heesaboono tasfeeya *n.* د حسابونوتصفيه liquidation

da heywad rasmee sika *n* دهواد رسميسکه currency

da heywadoono da nakhcho keetab *n.* دهوادونودنخچوکتاب atlas

da hind aw pakistan sika *n.* دهند اوپاکستانسکه rupee

da hindso aw nakhcho pa arwand *a.* دهندسواونخچوپه اوند graphic

da hisabdaray saroonkay *n.* د حسابدارارونکی auditor

da ibadat koochnay zay *n.* د عبادتکوچنیای chapel

da ibadat marasim *n.* دعبادت مراسم ritual

da ibadat marasimo pori arwand *a.* دعبادتمراسموپور اوند ritual

da ibtidayee bashareeyat dawr *a.* دابتدايبشريتدور primeval

da ida leek la makhi toranawal *v.t.* دادعاليکلهمختورنول indict

da ilat aw malool tar manz areeka *n* دعلتاومعلولترمنايکه causality

da imaley darmal *n.* داماالدرمل purgative

da inkar toray na *adv.* دانکارتوری نه nay

da insan dawla beezo *adj.* دانسان ولهبيزو anthropoid

da insan pa waseela pa karowal *v.t.* دانسانپهوسيلهپهکاروول man

da insanano da zhwand da nawi dabareeney dawra *a.* د انسانانودژوونددنوبريندوره neolithic

da insanee fikree taraw fan *n.* د انسانيفکریتاوفن telepathy

da intiqad hunar *n* دانتقادهنر critic

da iqrar *a.* داقرار promissory

da ishq naz nakhrey kawal *v.i* د عشقنازنخرهکول flirt

da istiwa karkha n داستواکره
equator

da itihadeeyey gharay n. داتحادیـ غی
unionist

da izafat toray n. داضافت توری
preposition

da iztirab halat n. داضطراب حالت
spasm

da jadee myasht n دجدي میاشت
Capricorn

da jama nakha; musbat n دجمع نه،مثبت
plus

da jamnastic da lobo mahir n. د جمناسک دلوبو ماهر
gymnast

da jamnastic lobi n. دجمناسک لوب
gymnastics

da jamnastic pa arwand; chust a. دجمناسک په اوند،چست
gymnastic

da jamo almaray n. دجامو الماری
wardrobe

da jamo da gul booto patay n. د جامو دل بوو پ
streamer

da jamo darz n. دجامو درز
seam

da jamo gonji keydo wala darz n دجاموونجکدووالادرز
crease

da janayatkarano naray n. د جنایتکارانو ن
underworld

da janazey lmoonz n. دجناز لموـ
requiem

da janazey marasim n. دجناز مراسم
funeral

da jandaro pa yaw zay zeygeydalee mashooman n د جانداروپه یوای زیدلي ماشومان
brood

da jangee tadbeeroono fan n. د جني تدبيرونو فن
strategy

da jangee tadbeeroono mahir n. دجني تدبيرونو ماهر
strategist

da jarahay daktar n. دجراحاکر
surgeon

da jarahay meela n دجراحميله
probe

da jargey gharay n دجرغی
convener

da jashan war a دجشنو festive

da jast unsar n. دجستعنصر zinc

da jazibey da qawey pa waseela harakat kawal v.i. دجاذبدقوپه وسیلهحرکت کول gravitate

da jismoonu da harkat mubhis n. دجسمونودحرکتمبحث
dynamics

da jorabo aw banaynoono jorawona ya ploranzay n. د جورابواوبنینوجوونهیاپلورني hosiery

da jorabo band n. دجورابوبند
garter

da jormaney da mawado sarkaree nazir n. دجرماند مواد وسرکاريناظر bailiff

da juram peykheydo pa mahal bahana kawal n. دجرمپدوپه مهالبهانه کول alibi

da kab hagay n. دکبه spawn

da kab hagay achawal v.i. دکبه اچول spawn

da kaghaz yawa raseed n. دکاغذ یوهرسید coupon

da kaghazee nuskho masheen bandi naqal jorawal v.t. د کاغذينسخوماشینباندنقلجوول xerox da kaghazee nuskho naqal jorawalo masheen *n.* دکاغذي نسخونقل جوولوماشین xerox

da kakhtay arsha *n* دکتعرشه deck

da kakhtay aw mal aw zan zhghoral *v.t.* دکتاومال اوزان ژغورل salvage

da kakhtay bar; mahmoola *n.* د کتبار،محموله shipment

da kakhtay chalowani war *a.* دکته چلوونو navigable

da kakhtay karmandan *n.* دکته کارمندان crew

da kakhtay langar *n.* دکتلنر anchor

da kakhtay langarzay *n* دکتلنرای anchorage

da kakhtay rashpeyl *n.* دکتراشپل oar

da kakhtay rashpeyl *n.* دکتراشپل row

da kakhtay rashpeyl wahal *v.t.* د کتراشپل وهل row

da kakhtay stayring *n.* دکتسرنگ helm

da kakhtay ya da mal ya da zan zhghorana *n.* دکتیادمال یادان ژغورنه salvage

da kalam nachor *n.* دکلام نچو gist

da kaleesa aw da haghi baharanee deywaloono manz ki chapeyra zmaka *n.* دکلیسااودهغبهرني دوالونو منډ کی چاپره ممکه churchyard

da kaleesa da pap maqam *n.* د کلیسادپاپ مقام papacy

da kaleesa da pap pori arwand *a.* دکلیسادپاپ پوراوند papal

da kaleesa markaz *n.* دکلیسامرکز nave

da kaleesa nazim *n.* دکلیساناظم beadle

da kam shee ghla kawal *v.t.* دکم شي غلاکول pilfer

da kaman pa banra arawal *v.t.* د کمان په بها اول arch

da kanfarans talar *n.* دکانفرانس تالار auditorium

da kankreeto jorawal *v. t* د کانکریو جوول concrete

da kankreeto mada *n* دکانکریو ماده concrete

da kanro dabaro yaw ghond *n.* د کانو برو یو غون rubble

da kar eejaza leek *n.* دکاراجازه لیک licence

da kar haq *n* دکارحق patent

da kar kawalo hunar *n.* دکارکولو هنر workmanship

da kar takrar *n.* دکارتکرار reiteration

da kar zmaka *n* دکرمکه farm

da karakhta dak kar kawal *v.i.* د کخته ک کارکول toil

da karani mahir *n.* دکرنماهر agriculturist

da karayi motar *n.* دکرایموټر cab

da karban filiz ya geys *n.* دکاربن فلزیاس carbon

da katan tukham *n.* دکتان تخم linseed

da katoleekee eesayano rehbar *n.* دکاتولیکي عیسائیانورهبر pope

da kawdoree lokhee *n* دکودویلوی ceramics

da kaynato pa arwand *adj.* د
کائناتوپهاوند cosmic

da keena kakhay war *a* دکینهکو
enviable

da keetab dotanay *n.* دکتابدوتنه
tome

da keetab paysoor *n.* دکتابپایو
postscript

da keetab sareeza *n.* دکتابسریزه
preamble

da keetabtoon charwakay *n.* د
کتابتونچارواکی librarian

da khabaro ataro war *a.* دخبرو
اتروو negotiable

da khabaro saray *a* دخبروسی
conversant

da khakhto da darzoono da
neewani lapara zangari
khata *n.* دختودردزونودنیونلپارهزار
خه lute

da khandawoonko nandaro
honar mand *n.* دخندوونکو
نندارموهنرمند comedian

da khandeydo ghag *n.* دخندهدوغ
laughter

da khandoono pa mrasta
bandeyz *n.* دخنونوپهمرستهبندیز
barricade

da khar bandanay barkhi *n.pl.* د
خارباندنیبرخه outskirts

da khar da shawkhwa seema *n.*
دارد شاوخواسیمه suburb

da khar da shawkhwa seemi
astogan *a.* دارد شاوخواسیم
استون suburban

da khar danana chaleydoonkay
breykhnayee wagon *n.* دار
دننهچلدونکیبرنایيواون tram

da khar nazim *n.* دارناظم mayor

da kharabeydo
makhneewoonkay *a.* دخرابدو
مخنیوونکی preservative

da kharakht ranz *n.* دخارترز
scabies

da kharatay masheen *n.* دخراط
مشین lathe

da kharwee daney *n.* دخرويداز
acorn

da khas moqey pa ara jashan *n*
دخاصموقعپهاهجشن festivity

da khash khash ghag *n.* دخشخش
غ rick

da khatar zang *n* دخطرزر alarm

da khateez pa lor *adv* دختیپهلور
east

da khawro aw shago hifazatee
deywal *n.* دخاورواوشوحفاظتي
دوال rampart

da khawro portanay barkha chi
da wakho reykhi aw wrasta
mawad laree *n.* دخاورروپورتنه
برخهچدوورراوورواستهموادلري turf

da khawro teyl *n.* دخاوروتل
kerosene

da khazi pa seyr kawal *v.t.* دپهر
کول womanise

da khazo oogdey jamey *n.* دواود
جام gown

da kheekhey baksa chi daryayee
makhlooq paki nandarey
lapara satalay shee *n.* دیبکسه
چدریائيمخلوقپکنندارلپارهساتلی
شي aquarium

da kheekhey pyala; kheekha *n.* د
یپیاله،یه glass

da khkuli banri khawand *a.* دکلو خاوند
shapely

da khob kalee *n.* دخوب کالي
nightie

da khob wakht *n.* دخوب وخت
bed-time

da khoofeeya khabaro ataro zay aw wakht *n.* دخفیه خبرواتروای اووخت
tryst

da khoog astoganzay *n.* دخو استونای
sty

da khoog astoganzay *n.* دخو استونای
stye

da khoog da ghwakhi landay *n.* دخودغولاندی
bacon

da khoog ghwakha *n.* دخوغوه
pork

da khoog wazda *n.* دخووازده
lard

da khor pa shan *a.* دخورپه شان
sisterly

da khorakee mawado sandooq *n.* دخوراکي موادوصندوق
crate

da khowanzee da keetabono kasora *n.* دوونی دکتابونو کوه
satchel

da khowanzee pori zdakri *n.* د وونی پورزده کي
matriculation

da khowanzee rayees *n.* دوونی رئیس
principal

da khpali pohi bey zaya khodana *n.* دخپلپوهی بی زیامودنه
pedantry

da khra khazeena *n.* دخرمینه
mare

da khra rambari *n* دخرہ رمبا
bray

da khuday da tolo peykho aw zwakoono majmoo ganral *n.* دخدای دولوپواووا کونومجموعه بلل
pantheism

da khuday pa qudrat bawaree *n.* دخدای په قدرت باوري
pantheist

da khuday pa wajood bawar *n.* د خدای په وجودباور
deist

da khuday paman *interj.* دخدای پامان
good-bye

da khuday qudrat *n.* دخدای قدرت
providence

da khwago ploranzay *n* دخواو پلورنی
confectionery

da khwakhay cheygha *n.* دخوچغه
cheer

da khwakhay war *a.* دخوونو
admirable

da khwandee satani da kar lagakht *n* دخوندی ساتند کارلت
upkeep

da khwaralo war *a* دخولوو
edible

da khwaro jazab aw tarkeeb *n* د خووجذب اوترکیب
assimilation

da khwaro naywleek *n.* دخواو نیولیک
menu

da khwaro seezoona *n.* دخوویزونه
eatable

da khwaro takali wanda *n.* دخواو اکلونه
ration

da khwaro war *a* دخووو
eatable

da kifayat tar kachi *adv* د کفایت تر کچ
enough

da kilseeyum filiz *n* دکلسیم فلز
calcium

da kipsool pa shakal *adj* دکپسول په شکل
capsular

da kirdar katana; neemrukh anzor *n.* دکردارکتنه، نیمرخ انور
profile

da kobalt keymyayee onsar *n* د
کوبالکمیایي عنصر cobalt

da koch salatoaw khorakee
mawado sakha jora doday
n. دکوچ سلاتواوخوراکي موادوسخه
جوهو sandwich

da kolp zabancha *n* دکولپ زبانچه
bolt

da kom seez da gatawartob la
makhi da hagha
matloobeeyat *a.* دکومیزد
ورتوب له مخدهغه مطلوبیت
utilitarian

da kom seez landi karkha
rakkhal *v.t.* دکومیزلاندکره
راکل underline

da koneen bootay *n.* دکونین بوی
quinine

da koni da maqad pa arwand
adj. دکوندمقعدپه اوند anal

da koochnee dimagh pa arwand
adj دکوچني دماغ په اوند cerebral

da koochno pa arwand *a.*
دکوچنوپه اوند infantile

da koochno wazhana *n.* دکوچنو
وژنه infanticide

da koochnyo shayano da
andazey ala *n.* دکوچنیوشیانود
اندازآله micrometer

da koochnyo shayano doorbeen
n. دکوچنیوشیانودوربین
microscope

da koochnyo shayano ilam *n.* د
کوچنیوشیانوعلم micrology

da koohee sarkh *v.t.* دکوهي رخ
windlass

da kookoo marghay *n* دکوکومرغ
cuckoo

da koolmey akhiree barkha *n.* د
کولماخري برخه rectum

da koolmo pa arwand *a.* دکولموپه
اوند intestinal

da kor asbab *n.* دکوراسباب
furniture

da kor da istimal spaki saplay *n.*
دکورداستعمال سپکپل slipper

da kor maloona aw lawazim *n.* د
کورمالونه اولوازم movables

da korwadani ronra aw
khwayndi *n.* دکورودانرونه او
خویند in-laws

da kraki war shakhs *n.* دکرکو
شخص wretch

da kulalay khata *n* دکلالخه clay

da lafzoono lobey *n.* دلفظونولوب
pun

da lafzoono lobey kawal *v.i.* د
لفظونولوب کول pun

da lagyo geyday *n* دلریوی faggot

da lambeydo ya jamo weenzalo
taghara *n.* دلمبدویاجاموووینلو
تغاره tub

da lams his pori arwand *a.* دلمس
حس پوراوند tactile

da lams seez; mahsoos *a.* دلمس و
یز؛محسوس tangible

da lams war *a.* دلمس و palpable

da largee dara *n.* دلري ده splinter

da largee hawara takhta *n.* دلري
هواره تخته plank

da largee naray patay *n.* دلري نرپ
lath

da largee teer *n.* دلري تیر perch

da largee ya ospani panra ya tota *n.* دلرييااوسپنهپلهياوه wedge

da largee yaw pata *n* دلريیوپه ply

da larghono shayano nandarzay دلرغونوشيانونندارای*n*.museum

da laril da wani pa panro psolal shaway a. دلارلدونپهپاوپسولل شوی laureate

da las marwand *n.* دلاسموند wrist

da las pa sat goozar *n.* دلاسپهوزار backhand

da las takya *n.* دلاستکیه maulstick

da las warghaway *n.* دلاسورغوی palm

da laso kasano la manz sakha da yawa hagha wazhal *v.t.* دلسو کسانولهمنخهدیوههغهوژل decimate

da lasoono parkar *n* دلاسونوپکار clap

da laswandoono aw panro zabat *n.pl.* دلاسوندونواوپاوضبط archives

da laswandoono da sabt idara *n.* دلاسوندونودثبتاداره registry

da lateef zoq sakhtan *n.* دلطیف ذوقتن dainty

da law masheen; law garay *n.* د لوماشین؛لوری haverster

da leed war *a.* دلیدو visible

da leed war manzara *a.* دلیدو منظره spectacular

da leed wartya *n.* دلیدوتیا visibility

da leedani katani takalay zay *n.* دلیدذکتناکلیای venue

da leekaneezo wasayalo plooroonkay *n.* دلیکنیزووسایلو پلورونکی stationery

da leekani meyz *n* دلیکنمز desk

da leekani yawa barkha *n.* دلیک یوهبرخه paragraph

da leekee cheenjay *n* دلیکیچینجی book-worm

da leekee nakhan *n.* دلیکینان book-mark

da leekwal khpala leekalay lasleek *n.* دلیکوالخپلهلیکلی لاسلیک autograph

da leelam war *a.* دلیلامو salable

da leelam ya dawtalbay pa muzayda ki wanda akheystal *v.t.* دلیلامیاداوطلبپه مزایده کونهاخستل tender

da leemoo sharbat *n.* دلیموشربت lemonade

da leygdawalo waseela *n.* دلدولو وسیله transport

da leygdawani war *a.* دلدونو portable

da leyri keydani war *a.* دلرکدنو removable

da leywanee spee naroghee *n.* د لونیسپیناروغي rabies

da lmar rakhatana *v.i.* دلمراختل dawn

da lmar ranra ki badan khareydal *v.i.* دلمرياکبدنخدل tan

da lobo dagar *n* دلوبور arena

da lobo yaw dawl panra; kha aw aham saray *n.* دلوبویولپله؛به اواهمسی trump

da lokho khoona n. دلوخوونه
pantry

da loogee la kabala sa
bandeydal v.t. دلویله کبله‌ساه
بندل smother

da loomranee aw dwayam por
tar manz neem por n. دلومني
اودويم‌پورترمننیم‌پو mezzanine

da loy maray khawand; ghag
lweydalay a. دلوی‌مرخاوند؛غ
لوډلی throaty

da loy munshee ya loomree
wazeer danda ya maqam n د
لوی‌منشي‌يالومي‌وزير‌دنده‌يامقام
chancery

da loyi darajey ghonda n. دلویدرج
غونه summit

da loyo koolmo landeenay
barkha n دلویوکولمولاندیني‌برخه
colon

da lughato noomleek n. دلغاتو
نوملیک glossary

da lwar himat khawand a. دلو
همت‌خاوند ambitious

da lweydeez pa lor adv. دلوډیه‌لور
west

da lweydeez pa lor adv. دلوډیه‌لور
westerly

da madey aw naray da shtoon
na manana n. دمادواودشتون‌ننه
مننه nihilism

da maghfirat war a. دمغفرت‌و
pardonable

da maghzo iltihab n. دمغزوالتهاب
meningitis

da maide a. دمعدی gastric

da makh aks n. دمخ‌عکس portrait

da makh anzor eystal v.t. دمخ‌انور
استل portray

da makh da barkhi naqashee n.
دمخ‌دبرخنقاشي portraiture

da makh khwa ta adv دمخ‌خواته
forward

da makh las weenzalo khoona n.
دمخ‌لاس‌وينلوخونه lavatory

da makh palwa ta adv. دمخ‌پلوه‌ته
onwards

da makh seengar kawal a دمخ
سینارکول facial

da makh soorwalay n دمخ‌سوروالی
blush

da makha prep. دمخه past

da makha akheystal v.t دمخه
اخستل forestall

da makha barkhleek takal v.t. د
مخه‌برخلیک‌اکل predetermine

da makha da krismas wraz n. د
مخه‌دکرسمس‌ور advent

da makha sanjawal v.t. دمخه
سنجول premeditate

da makha soch n. دمخه‌سوچ
premeditation

da makhi; makhamakh a دمخ،
مخامخ front

da makhneewee waseela a. د
مخنیوي‌وسیله scotch

da makoo safar kawal v.t. دماکو
سفرکول shuttle

da mal da adloon badloon
tijarat kawal v.t. barter1

da mal leygdawalo kakhtay n. د
مال‌دولوکته barge

da maleeyey war a. دمالیو taxable

da malt aw khumree skhak *n.* د
مالتاوخمریاک mead

da maltey leemoo aw naranj da
postakee khwand *n.* دمالیمو
اونارنجدپوستکيخوند zest

da manalo war *a* دمنلوو
acceptable

da mandi musabiqa kawal *v.i* دمند
مسابقهکول race

da manzanay darajey *a* دمنندرج
medium

da manzanyo peyryo tareekh
pori arwand *a.* دمننیوپیوتاریخ
پوراوند medieval

da mar ghonda tawrataw *n.* دمار
غوندهتاوراتاو serpentine

da maree sozawani lapara da
largyo zangari kota *n.* دمې
سوونلپارهدلریوازکوه pyre

da mareekh seeyara *n* دمریخسیاره
Mars

da marghano zala *n.* دمرغانواله
cote

da marghano zala *n.* دمرغانواله
roost

da marghay bachay *n.* دمرغبچی
nestling

da markaz keenr las ta *n.* دمرکز
کیلاسته mid-on

da markaz khee las ta *n.* دمرکزي
لاسته mid-off

da marmar kanray *n.* دمرمرکانئ
marble

da maro arwagani *n.* دمواراماز
manes

da maro da eero lokhay *n* دمود
ایرولوی urn

da maro dua *n.* دمودعا memento

da maro pa mrasta ghayb
wayana *n.* دموپهمرستهغبوینه
necromancer

da maseehano akhtar *n* دمسیحانو
اختر easter

da masharano jargey pori
arwand *a* دمشرانوجرپوراوند
senatorial

da masheeno ilam *n.* دماشینوعلم
mechanics

da mashoom da zeygoon omeed
shandawal *v.i.* دماشومدزونامید
شنول miscarry

da mashoomano tanga *n.* د
ماشومانوتنه perambulator

da masko khar oseydoonkee *n.* د
ماسکوخاراوسدونکی muscovite

da masoor dal *n.* دمسوردال lentil

da matal pa arwand *a.* دمتلپهاوند
proverbial

da matbooato aw chalandoono
sarana kawal *v. t.* دمطبوعاتواو
چلندونوارنهکول censor

da matbooato aw chalandoono
saroonkay *n.* دمطبوعاتواو
چلندونوارونکی censor

da mati shawi kakhtay parchey
n. دماتشوکتپارچ wreck

da mawarayee tabeeyat ilam *n.* د
ماورایيطبیعتعلم metaphysics

da mawseeqay ala wayloon *n.* د
موسیقآلهویلون violin

da mawseeqay da alato mahir *n.*
دموسیقدآلاتوماهر
instrumentalist

da mawseeqay dala *n.* دموسیقله
orchestra

da mawseeqay pa arwand *a.* د موسيقېپهاوند musical

da mawseeqay pyano ta warta ala *n.* دموسيقېپيانوتهورتهآله xylophone

da maya shee da paymayish yawa paymana *n.* دمايعشي پمائشيوهپمانه litre

da mayar dalbandee *n.* دمعيار لبندي standardization

da mayato lapara payp *n* دمايعاتو لپارهپايپ cask

da maydey tap *n.* دمعلسپ ulcer

da maydey tap pori arwand *a.* د معلسپپوراوند ulcerous

da mazd pa badal ki sarawal *v.t.* دمزدپهبدلكرول agist

da mazooro lakray *n* دمعذورولكه crutch

da meel la makhi sanjawana *n.* د ميللهمخسنجوونه mileage

da meylmastoon ya khwaranzay khidmatgar *n.* دملمستونيا خونایخدمتار waiter

da meylmastoon ya khwaranzay khidmatgara *n.* دملمستونيا خونایخدمتاره waitress

da meyrani khawand *a.* دمازخاوند manful

da meywa bagh *n.* دموهباغ orchard

da meywey ghwakhana barkha *n.* دموغونهبرخه pulp

da meywey oba *n* دمواوبه juice

da meywey oba laroonkay *a.* دمو اوبهلرونكی juicy

da meyzaree koochnay tokray *n.* دمزري كوچنوكر canister

da midal khawand *n.* دمال خاوند medallist

da milee shoora gharay *n.* دملي شوراغی parliamentarian

da mityazo kawalo amal *n.* د متيازوكولوعمل urination

da mla teer *n.* دملاتير backbone

da mla teer *n.* دملاتير spine

da mla teer pori arwand *a.* دملا تيرپوراوند spinal

da moashirat da adabo ilam *n* د معاشرتدآدابوعلم etiquette

da moashirat da adabo keetab *n* دمعاشرتدآدابوكتاب facet

da moondani war *a.* دموندنو traceable

da moosalmanano deenee alim *n.* دمسلمانانودينيعالم mullah

da mor pa shan *a.* دمورپهشان motherlike

da mor plar pa arwand *a.* دمور پلارپهاوند parental

da mor plar wazhana *n.* دمورپلار وژنه parricide

da mosam pa wrandi badleydal; zghamal *v.t.* دموسمپهواند بدلدل؛زغمل weather

da mosam sara sam *a.* دموسمسره سم seasonable

da moseeqay nasta *n.* دموسيقناسته concert

da moseeqay yaw dawl badee ala *n.* دموسيقوولبادیآله bagpipe

da moseeqay yaw geetar chi dayrawee geyda laree *n.* د موسيقويیارچدايرويدهلري banjo da motar brayk *n* دموربرک brake

da motar jak *n.* دمورجک jack

da motar klach *n* دمورکلچ clutch

da motar raghawani ya darawani zay *n.* دمورغونیا درونای garage

da mozayeek anzor *n.* دموزائیک انور mosaic

da mreeni aylan *a.* دمیناعلان obituary

da muchyo kor *n.* دمچیوکور hive

da mujaley khparowoonkay *n* د مجلخپروونکی editor

da mujaley sar maqala *n* دمجلس مقاله editorial

da mukhabiratee sapo leygd raleygd *n.* دمخابراتيپولدرالد transmission

da mukhadira mawado yaw qisam *n* دمخدرومواديوقسم cocaine

da munsifa plawee gharay *n.* د منصفهپلاويغی juror

da munsifa plawee gharay *n.* د منصفهپلاويغی juryman

da muqadaso seezoonu ghla *n.* د مقدسویزونوغلا sacrilege

da muqadaso seezoonu ghla kawoonkay *a.* دمقدسویزونوغلا کوونکی sacrilegious

da musafiro kakhtay *n* دمسافروکت ferry

da mustateelee shakal konj *n.* د مستطیلیشکلکونج nook

da na manani war *a.* دنهمننو incredible

da na manfee kalma *adv.* دنهمنفي کلمه not

da naheeyey da mahkamey reeyasat *n.* دناحيدمحکمرياست magistracy

da naleegay da jorawani chara *n.* دناليدجوونچاره padding

da nandarey fankara najlay *n.* د نندارفنکارهنجل mannequin

da nandarey sahna *n.* دنندارصحنه stage

da nandartoon beyzwee salon *n* دنندارتونبضويسالون amphitheatre

da naqashay da rangoono sakha kar akheystana *n.* دنقاشدرنونو خهکاراخستنه palette

da naqshey jorawalo kaghaz *n.* د نقشجوولوکاغذ chart

da naranj murabba *n.* دنارنجمربا marmalade

da naray ustawayee seema *n.* دز استوایسیم tropic

da naree ranz da darmalani zay *n.* دنريرنددرملناي sanatorium

da nareena jinsee ala *n.* دنارینه جنسيآله penis

da nargas gul *n* دنرسل narcissus

da naroghano da wralo dapara yaw dol kat *n.* دنارونغانودولو دپارهيوولک litter

da naroghay nakha aw arz *a.* د نارونغنهاوعرض symptomatic

da nashayee mawado da preykhwalo mlataray *n.* د نشهيمواودپرولوملاتی teetotaller da nashayee mawado da preykhwalo pa arwand *a.* د نشه‌يي موادو د پرېخوا لو په اوند teetotal

da nasti zangaray meyz *n.* دناستة زنگری مېز dais

da naswaro kadoo *n.* د نسوارو کدو gourd

da natoono pranistalo ala *n.* د نوتونو پرانستلو آله wrench

da nawab meyrman *n.* د نواب مېرمن countess

da nawalo obo bahanzoona *n* د ناولو اوبو بهنونه sewer

da nawalo obo da zmaki landi bahanzoona *n.* د ناولو اوبو د زمک لاندی بهنونه sewerage

da nawalo obo dand *n.* د ناولو اوبو ډنډ swamp

da nawara gato da para jorjaray kawal *n* د ناورو ګاټو د پاره جوجری کول collusion

da naykmarghay oj *n.* د نکمرغی اوج heyday

da naytrojan gaz *n.* دنایتروجن ګاز nitrogen

da naz nakhro tag *n* دناز نخرو تګ strut

da neewani haq *n.* دنیوني حق lien

da neewani hokam *n.* دنیوني حکم injunction

da neewani preykra *n.* دنیوني پرکه caption

da neyzey sooka *n.* دنیزي سوکه spearhead

da nikal unsar *n.* د نکل عنصر nickel

da nikasee obo sooray *n.* دنکاسي اوبو سوری manhole

da niptoon seeyara *n.* دنپتون سیاره Neptune

da nisfun nihar karkha; gharma *a.* دنصف النهار کرښه؛ غرمه meridian

da nizamee dalgay tamzay *n.* د نظامي لتمای cantonment

da nizamee masharano yawa dalgay *n.* د نظامي مشرانو یوه ډله squadron

da noro da subak taqleed *n.* د نورو د سبک تقلید parody

da nyoozeelaynd plazmayna; yaw dawl azad khuley mooza *n.* دنیوزیلنډ پلازمینه؛ یو ول آزاد خولو موزه wellington

da obdani masheen *n* داوبدانماشین loom

da obo bahanz *n* داوبو بهنز aqueduct

da obo band *n.* داوبو بند barrage

da obo band *n* داوبو بند dam

da obo koochnay band *n.* داوبو کوچنی بند weir

da obo pa sar lambo wahal *v.i* د اوبو په سر لامبو وهل float

da obo raeystani masheen *n.* د اوبو رااستنی ماشین pump

da obo sar ta rakhoteydal *v.i.* د اوبو سر ته راخوتیدل well

da obo seyl ratlal *v.t* داوبو سل راتلل flood

da obo sheendani zangaray plasteekee nal *n.* داوبو شیندنۍ زنگری پلاستیکي نل hose

da obo zeyramtoon; tank *n.* داوبو زرمتون، بانک tank

da obo zeyrma *n.* داوبوزرمه rservoir

da ogad wali yawa mecha *n.* د اودوالۍيوه‌ميچه furlong

da oogad meel topak *n.* داودميل ټوپک musket

da oogadwalee meychawalo yaw paymana *n.* داودوالۍ‌ميچولويو پمانه yard

da oogadwalee yaw paymayish *n.* داودوالۍ‌يوپمائش mile

da oogo porta harakat *n* داووپورته حرکت shrug

da or sheendee ghra weelee mawad *n.* داورشيندي‌غره‌ويلي مواد lava

da orgadee aw kakhtay khob khana *n* داورايۍ‌اوکتخوب‌خانه berth

da orgadee karkha *n.* داورايۍ‌کره railway

da ospaneezi lari pa mrasta astawal *v.t.* داوسپنيزلارپه‌مرسته استول transmit

da ospani patlay ghazawal *v.t.* د اوسپنياغول rail

da pachayano koranay *n* دپاچايانو کورنۍ dynasty

da paf awaz khuley na watal *v.i.* دپف‌اواز‌خولنه‌وتل puff

da pakh banay; sagay *n.* دپنۍ‌سی bellows

da pakhlanzee da lokho weenzalo zay *n.* دپخلنۍ‌دلوو وينلوای cesspool

da pakhlee lar khod *n.* دپخلي‌لار ود cuisine

da pam na war *a* دپامه‌و aconsiderable

da pam war lamal *n.* دپاموله‌مل limelight

da pam war miqdar *n.* دپامومقدار slump

da pamp pa waseela raeystal *v.t.* دپمپ‌په‌وسيله‌راستل pump

da parayshanay halat *n.* دپرشانۍ حالت turmoil

da parchoon sawdagar *n.* دپرچون سودار retailer

da pareydani waseela *n.* دپارېدنۍ وسيله stimulus

da parmakhtya pa hal ki *adv.* د پرمختيا‌په‌حال‌ک upwards

da partalani war *a.* دپرتلنو analogous

da pato yaw dawl loba *n.* دپتويو ول‌لوبه rummy

da pawzee lakhkar da yaw tabqey tashkeel *n.* دپوي‌لكرد يوطبقةتشکيل legionary

da pawzee lakhkar yawa tabqa *n.* دپوي‌لكريوه‌طبقه legion

da pawzyano dala *n.* دپوريانوله troop

da payey teer *n* دپايتير skid

da peenzo sawo kaghazoonu bandal *n.* د ۵۰۰ کاغذونوبنل ream

da peesho bachay *n.* دپيشوبچی kitten

da peesho ghag *n.* دپيشوغ mew

da peesho ghag kawal *v.i.* دپيشوغ کول mew

da peesho ghur ghur *n.* دپيشو غُرغُر purr

da peesho ghureydal *v.i.* دپيشو غُرېدل purr

da peykhi da tareekh pa zand leekal *v.t.* دپدتاريخ‌پهزندليکل
post-date

da peyso adayana *n.* دپسواداينه
payment

da peyso kasora *n.* دپسوکوه purse

da peyso kasora *n.* دپسوکوه
wallet

da peyso rakra warkra *n.* دپسو راکهورکه transaction

da peyso rakra warkra kawal *v.t.* دپسوراکهورکه کول transact

da peywand zay *n.* دپونداى
commissure

da peywastoon zay *n.* دپوستوناى
junction

da pkhey khapoona; jora shawi lara *n.* دپخاپونه؛جوهشولاره trail

da pkhey palawan *n* دپپهلوان
bully

da pkhey ya boot talay *n.* دپيابو تلى sole

da pkho pa panjo kkheynastal *v.i.* دپوپهپنجوکناستل squat

da plar mreeni wrusta zeygeydalay *a.* دپلارمينوروسته زدلى posthumous

da plar wazhana *n.* دپلاروژنه
patricide

da pohantoon ya khowonzee laylya *n.* دپوهنتون‌ياووني‌ليليه
hostel

da pohanzee rayees *n.* دپوهني رئيس dean

da pokhtani nakha *n* دپوتننه
interrogative

da pokhtani war *a.* دپوتنو
questionable

da poolas sarandoy *n* دپولس ارندوى constable

da poolo eekhodana *n.* دپولوايودنه
demarcation

da poolo takana *n.* دپولوباکنه
confinement

da poplayn tokar *n.* دپوپلين‌وکر
poplin

da poray dastakee *n.* دپورهدستکي
rung

da postakee yawa chanrasee saree naroghee *n.* دپوستکي‌يوه چاسي‌ساري‌ناروغي ringworm

da pozi danana *n* دپوزدننه nasal

da pozi sooray *n.* دپوزسورى
nostril

da pradeetob ehsas *n.* دپرديتوب احساس nostalgia

da pranasti lamani zanana kot *n.* دپرانستلمنزنانه‌کو skirt

da psa ghwakha *n.* دپسهغوه
mutton

da pust idara *n.* دپُستاداره
post-office

da pust rayees *n.* دپُست رئيس
postmaster

da putas filiz *n.* دپاس‌فلز potash

da putasyum unsar *n.* دپسيم‌عنصر
potassium

da pyano da mawseeqay ala *n.* د پيانو دموسيقه‌آله piano

da pyano da mawseeqay ala ghagoonkay *n.* دپيانودموسيقةآله غوونکى pianist

da pyaz tamatar aw masalo roob *n.* دپيازمار‌او‌مسالوروب
ketchup

da qabar dabarleek *n* دقبربرليک
epitaph

da qachaq danda *n.* دقاچاق‌دنده
jobbery

da qadardanay war *a.* دقدردانو
appreciable

da qanoonee mayar khawand *a.*
دقانوني‌معيارخاوند sterling

da qanoonee rabalani cheetay *n.*
دقانوني‌رابلنڅي summons

da qayd pa arwand *a.* دقيدپه‌اوند
adverbial

da qazee hukam *n.* دقاضي‌حکم
verdict

da qazyano plaway *n.* دقاضيانو
پلاوی judicature

da qutar neemayee *n.* دقطرنيمايي
radius

da radyoyee ya talweezyonee parogram khparawana *n.* د
رايويي‌يالويزيوني‌پروګرام‌خپرونه
telecast

da rag dard *n.* دردرد sprain

da ragheydo pa arwand *a* درغدو
په‌اوند curative

da rahat khoona *n.* دراحت‌خونه
lounge

da rahibanu namazdak *n.* د
راهبانونمزدک minster

da ramzee leekani ilam *n.* درمزي
ليکدعلم cryptography

da rando lapara zangaray leek *n*
دندولپارازنګری‌ليک braille

da rangarang shayano gadola *n.*
درنارنشيانوله miscellany

da ranra aw tyarey tar manz wakht *n* درناواوتيارترمنوخت
dusk

da ranz pr zid wakseen warkawal *v.t.* درنپرضدواکسين
ورکول immunize

da ranzoor da wralo lasee waseela *n.* درنوردولودلاسي
وسيله stretcher

da ratlonke gham khwarana *n* د
راتلونکي‌غم‌خوړنه forethought

da rayi panra *n* درايپاله ballot

da reeyazii pa arwand *a.* درياضي
په‌اوند mathematical

da rehem war *a.* درحمو pitiable

da roghtoon sarpayee narogh *n.*
دروغتون‌سرپايي‌ناروغ outpatient

da rokhantya nashtwalay *a.* د
روبانتيانشتوالی lacklustre

da roohaneeyoonu wakmanee *n.*
دروحانيونوواکمني theocracy

da rooseeyi sika *n.* دروسيسکه
rouble

da sa laroonko da noogi qismoona *n.* دساه‌لرونکودنوګي
قسمونه species

da saboon zag *n.* دصابون lather

da sabt daftar *n.* دثبت‌دفتر register

da safar tokha *n.* دسفرتوه
baggage

da sago iltihab *n* دسوالتهاب
pneumonia

da sahib mansabano lakhta *n* د
صاحب‌منصبانولته baton

da sakht aw teyz ghag awaz *n* د
سخت‌اوتزغاواز slam

da sakino jismoono seyraneeza sanga *n.* دساکنوجسمونونيزمانه
statics

da sakoon darmal warkawal *v.t.*
دسکون‌درمل‌ورکول tranquillize

da salami kaleezi jashan *n.* دسلم
کلیزجشن centenary

da salfar gaz *n.* دسلفرګاز sulphur

da salo la makhi *n.* دسلولهمخ
percentage

da saltanat nayib *n.* دسلطنتنایب
viceroy

da samandar narmi sapey *n.* د
سمندرنرمۍ lop

da samandar sapa *n.* دسمندرپه
tide

da samandar teeta sapa *a.* د
سمندریهپه neap

da samoon nakha *n.* دسموننه tick

da samoon nakha lagawal *v.i.* د
سموننهلول tick

da samwalee shoontya *n.* دسموالي
شونتیا verisimilitude

da sandar bolo marghano yawa
dala *n.* دسندربولومارغانویوهله
lark

da sandar gharo dala *n.* دسندرغاو
له troupe

da sandar gharo dalgay *n.* د
سندرغاوۍ chorus

da sanjawani war *a.* دسنجونو
measurable

da sanobar wana *n.* دصنوبرونه
pine

da sansor jargagay *n.* دسانسورجره
censorship

da sar khoogeydana *n.* دسرخوندنه
headache

da sar pakha *n* دسرپخه dandruff

da sar sangi ghosawal *v.t.* دسرﺍﯽ
غوول lop

da sar shmeyrani karpoh *n.* د
سرشمرنکارپوه statistician

da sarak baj *n.* دسکباج toll

da sarak da ghari meylmastoon
n. دسکدغاملمستون motel

da saree weykhtan *n.* دسيوتان
mane

da sari pa toga *adv.* دساريپهتوه
namely

da sarkh para ya meela *n.* درخ
پرهیامیله spoke

da sarmano ash kawana *n.* درمنو
آش کوونه tannery

da sarwayo tababat pori
arwand *a.* دارویوطبابتپوراوند
veterinary

da sat dad ghmbaray ranz *n.* د
غومبرۍرﻧ mumps

da satani war *a.* دساتنو tenable

da sawdagaray war *a.* دسودارو
marketable

da sayins ilam *n.* دساينسعلم
science

da seemabo kan *n* دسيمابوکان
cinnabar

da seemabo pa dagha alyazh
ghakhoona dakawal *v.t.* د
سيمابوپهدغهالياژغاونهکول
amalgamate

da seemabo yaw alyazh chi da
ghakhoonu dakawalo
lapara pakareygee *n* دسيمابو
یوالیاژچدغاونوکولولپارهپهکاري
amalgam

da seenama masheen *n.* دسينما
projector ماشين

da seenama ya talweezyon parda *n.* دسينماياتلويزيون پرده screen

da seend ghara *n* دسيندغاه strand

da seend pa lori *adv.* دسيندپه‌لور overboard

da seengar khoona *n.* دسينارخونه parlour

da seyri rang *n* درنگ complexion

da shabasee narey *n* دشاباسي‌نار acclamation

da shahadat gota *n* دشهادت‌وته forefinger

da shahzada pa shan *a.* دشاهزاده په‌شان princely

da shakal aw banri badlawona *n.* دشكل‌اوبدلوونه metamorphosis

da shakal aw seyrey badloon *n.* دشكل‌اوربدلون transfiguration

da shakari naroghee *n* دشكر ناروغي diabetes

da shakhseeyat tajassum *n.* دشخصيت‌تجسم personification

da shambey wraz *n.* دشنبور sabbath

da shambey wraz *n.* دشنبور Saturday

da sharab jorawani mawsam *n.* دشراب‌جورونوسم vintage

da sharabkhoray jashan *n.* دشرابخورجشن wassail

da sharabo jam *n* دشراب‌جام stalk

da sharam dagh *n.* دشرم‌داغ stigma

da sharamzay hadookay *n* دشرماى‌هوكى share

da shato da machyo rozana *n.* دشاتودمچيوروزنه apiculture

da shato da machyo zay *n.* دشاتود مچيواى apiary

da shato gabeen *n.* دشاتوبين honeycomb

da shato lokhay *n* دشاتولوى alveary

da shatranj pa loba ki kasht aw mat *n* دشطرنج‌په‌لوبه‌ككشت‌او مات checkmate

da shayr da bahar aw wazan ilam *a.* دشعردبحراووزن‌علم metric

da shayr warostay barkha *n* د شعرورستبرخه epilogue

da shaytan bachay *n.* دشطان‌بچى urchin

da shaytan manray *n.* دشطان‌ما pandemonium

da sheydo arwand shayan *n* د شدواوندشيان dairy

da sheydo qand *n.* دشدوقند lactose

da shmeyrani ilam *n.* دشمرنعلم statistics

da shomal pa lor *adv.* دشمال‌په‌لور northerly

da shomalee amreeka yaw dawl kab *a.* دشمالي‌امريكايول‌كب hesitant

da shomalee amreeka yaw margha chi pa sar soor takay laree *n* دشمالي‌امريكايو مارغه‌چه‌سرسوركى‌لري flicker

da shoora gharay *n.* دشوراغى councillor

da shpey *a.* دشپ nocturnal

da shpey *a* دشپ overnight

da shpey *adv.* دشپ nightly

da shpey la makhi *adv.* دشپلهمخ overnight

da shpey pa asman ki tat gard *n.* دشپپهاسمان کتت,رد nebula

da shtamano wakmanee *n.* د شتمنوواکمني oligarchy

da sinayma filam *n* دسينمافيلم film

da skoondalo ya gareydalo nakha *n.* دسکونلویارهدلونه prick

da sokht teyl *n.* دسوختتل fuel

da soli war *a.* دسولو peaceable

da sook goozar *n.* دسوکـوزار punch

da sook wahani loba *n* دسوکوهن لوبه boxing

da soyo da rozalo zay *n.* دسویود روزلوای warren

da sozawalo mawad *n.* دسوزولو مواد stoker

da spee bachay *n.* دسپيبچی whelp

da spee bachay *n.* دسپيبچی puppy

da spee ghapar *n.* دسپيغپهار woof

da spee khoona *n.* دسپيخونه kennel

da spee kuranjeydana *n.* دسپي کونجدنه bark

da speen sosan gul *n.* دسپينسوسن لل lily

da speenawani war *a.* دسپينونو justifiable

da speengeero da jargey gharay *n.* دسپينيرودجرغی senator

da speengeero jarga *n.* دسپينيرو جره senate

da spogmay tandar neewana *n* د سپومهتندرنيونه eclipse

da sro zaro oba warkawal *v.t.* د سروزرواوبهورکول gild

da sro zaro oba warkray shaway *a.* دسروزرواوبهورک شوی gilt

da stargey shabkeeya *n.* دستر شبکیه retina

da stargi gatay *n* دسترای eyeball

da stargi gol *n.* دستریل cataract

da stargo banra *n* دستروبله eyelash

da stargo dakdar *n.* دسترواکر oculist

da stargo weenzalo doormal *n* د سترووينلودرمل eyewash

da stargo zhghorandoya aynaki *n.* دستروژغورندویهعنک goggles

da stayani sandara *n* دستايندسندره laud

da stayani sandara wayal *v.t.* د ستايندسندرهویل laud

da stayani war *a.* دستاينو laudable

da stayani war *a.* دستاينو praiseworthy

da storo majma\ *n.* دستورومجمع constellation

da storo pa arwand *a.* دستوروپه اوند meteoric

da suroonw jorakht *n.* دسرونو جوت chord

da swayl lor ta *adv* دسولولورته south

da tabar mashra *n.* دبرمشره
matriarch

da tabieeyat haq warqawal *v.t.* د
تابعیت حق ورکول enfranchise

da taboot da eekheydo zay *n* د
تابوت دایو دوای bier

da tafree zay *n* دتفریحای resort

da tahammul war *a.* دتحمل و
tolerable

da tal lapara *adv* دتل لپاره forever

da talgaraf fan *n.* دلراف فن
telegraphy

**da tameed da ghusal na
warkawana** *n* دتعمیددغسل نه
ورکونه anabaptism

da tameed ghosal warkawal
دتعمیددغسل ورکول baptize *+v.t.*

da tameereydo war *a.* دتعمیردوو
raparable

da tandar pa shan ghag kawal
v.i. دتندرپه شان غ کول thunder

da taoon naroghee *n.* دطاعون
ناروغي pestilence

da tap tarani patay ~*n.* دپ تنپ
bandage

da tap zay ya dagh *n* دپ ای یا دا غ
scar

da tapoogano lar *n.* دا پوهانو ل atoll

da taqaid tankha *n.* دتقاعدتنخوا
pension

da taqaid tankha akheystal *v.t.* د
تقاعدتنخوا اخستل pension

**da tareekh aw neytey la makhi
da peykho lar leek** *n.* دتاریخ او
نله مخدپو لاليک chronicle

da tarkanray randa *n* دتر کارنده
plane

da taroon mada *n.* دتون ماده
stipulation

da tasarruf wakht *n.* دتصرف وخت
tenure

da tasbeeh dana *n* دتسبیح دانه
bead

da tashannuj ranz *n.* دتشنج رنز
hysteria

**da tashreefatee meylmastya
bandobast kawal** *v.t.* د
تشریفاتي ملمستیا بندو بست کول
banquet

da tashreefato paband *a.* د
تشریفاتو پابند ceremonious

da taskeen darmal warkawal *v.t.*
دتسکین درمل ورکول sedate

da tawajo war *a.* دتوجه و
noteworthy

da tawan peysey *n.* دتاوان پسـ
ransom

da tawazo la makhi *a.* دتواضع له مخ
lowly

**da tawdokhay daraja pa khpal
zay khwandee satoonkay
lokhay** *n.* دتو دو خدرجه په خپل ای
خوندي ساتونکی لوی thermos
flask

da tawdokhay yaw paymayish *a.*
دتو دو خیو پمائش centigrade

**da tawdokhey da maloomawani
daraja** *n.* دتو دو خدمعلو مو ندرجه
calorie

da tayfoyeed taba *n.* دتایفو ئیدتبه
typhoid

**da tayna loba chi pa yaw salon
ki ta sara keygee** *n.* دنس لوبه چ
په یو سالون کتر سره کي badminton

da taynas loba *n.* دنس لوبه tennis

da taynas loba ki da ghondaski wahana *n.* دننس لوبه كدغونسكي وهنه serve

da tee sooka *n.* دتي وكه teat

da tee sooka *n.* دتي وكه nipple

da teefoos ranz *n.* دتيفوس رنز typhus

da tehqeer cheygha *n.* دتحقير چغه hoot

da tehqeer cheygha wahal *v.i* د تحقير چغه وهل hoot

da teylo leygdawoonki laray *n.* د تلو لادونكلار tanker

da teyro panro aw drey konja zaree laroonki yawa wana *n.* دترو پاو او در كونجه زي لرونكيو ونه beech

da tibat aw mangoleeya haywanoono boodayee mula *n.* دتبت او منوليا هاو دونو بوداي ملا lama

da tibat yaw dawl ghwayay *n.* د تبت يو ول غوايي yak

da tila aw speeno zaro bandi jor nakhan *n.* دطلا او سپينو زرو باند جونان hallmark

da tlo raftar *n* دتلو رفتار pace

da toori pokh *n.* دتوري پو scabbard

da toro aw shakloono da manqooshay panra *n.* دتورو او شكلونو دمنقوشپه stencil

da toro aw shakloono da manqooshay panri pa mrasta naqsh jorawal *v.i.* د تورو او شكلونو دمنقوشپه په مرسته نقش جوول stencil

da tra, mama, ya tror zoy ya loor *n.* دتره، ماما، ياترور زوي يا لور cousin

da trak trak awaz *n* دتك تك اواز snap

da traq traq ghag *n* دتق تق غ rattle

da ulampeek da nareewalo syalo lobgharay *n.* دالمپيک دنيوالو سيالو لوبغاي olympiad

da usoolo pa shakal sargandawal *v.t* داصولو په شكل رندول formulate

da uzley aw maheechey dard *n.* دعضلاو ماهيچ درد myalgia

da wada loomranay myasht *n.* د وادا لومرني مياشت honeymoon

da wada pa ara *a* دوادهپه اه conjugal

da wada rasam *n.* دواده رسم nuptials

da wada war *a.* دواده و marriageable

da wada war *a.* دواده و nubile

da wadanay makh *n* دودانمخ facade

da wahshee zanawar bachay *n* د وحشي ناور بچی cub

da wahshee zanawar zala *n.* د وحشي ناور اله lair

da wajood peenzam unsar *n.* د وجود پنم عنصر quintessence

da wakht sanjawani ala *n* دوخت سنجوزآله chronograph

da wakht teyr watal *v.i.* دوخت تروتل lapse

da wali wana *n.* دولونه willow

da wananay da teer rawatali barkha *n.* دوداندتیرراوتلبرخه corbel

da wani koonda *n.* دوزکونده stump

da wanjoon tijarat *n.* دونجون barter2 تجارت

da wano panri *n* دونوپا foliage

da warandi *adv.* دواند before

da warangi masheen *n.* دوانماشین x-ray

da warangi masheen pori arwand *a.* دوانماشین پواوند x-ray

da warangi masheen sara tibee muayna kawal *v.t.* دوانماشین سره طبی معاینه کول x-ray

da wartya khawand *a.* دوتیاخاوند competent

da warzish karay ilam *n.* دورزش کارعلم athletics

da warzpanri gadoonbaya; nuskha leekana *n.* دورپاونبیه؛ نسخه لیکنه subscription

da wasley masha *n.* دوسلماشه trigger

da wat yaw paymayish *n.* دوایر پمائش metre

da watan yaw paymayish *n.* دوان یوپمائش inch

da watani lar; ikhraj *n.* دوتنلاره؛ اخراج exit

da wato lara *n.* دوتولاره passage

da wawri toopan *n* دواورتوپان blizzard

da wawri warookay ghar *n.* د واوریووکیغر iceberg

da wayna fan *n.* دونافن oratory

da wayyo ghwara kawana *n* د وییوغوره کونه diction

da wazan aw kach pa arwand *a.* دوزناوکچ په اوند metrical

da wazan yaw miqyas *n* دوزن یو مقیاس dram

da wazan yaw paymana *n.* دوزن یوپمانه ounce

da wazan yawa paymana *n.* دوزن یوه پمانه ton

da wazeerano da dalgay khoona *n.* دوزیرانو دلخونه cabinet

da weeda keydani wagon *n.* دویده کدناون sleeper

da weeda keydo kalee *n.* دویده کدوکالی bedding

da weeli keydano war *a.* دویاکدنو و soluble

da weeli keydano wartya *n.* دویا کدنوتیا solubility

da weeni pran shawi tota *n.* دوین پرشووه clot

da weenzalo war *a.* دوینلوو washable

da weykhtano patawalo dasmal *n.* دوتانوپولودسمال scarf

da weykhtano taw aw klokhta *n* دوتانوتاواوکلوته crimp

da weykhto weenzalo maya murakkab *n.* دوتووینلومایع مرکب shampoo

da wrazi khob *n.* دورخوب reverie

da wreykhmo cheenjay *n* دورمو چینجی caterpillar

da wrorwalay tolana *n.* دورورول ولنه confraternity

da yadakhtoono kitabgotay *n* د یادتونو کتابوی diary

dard *n.* درد ache

dard *n.* درد agony

dard *n.* درد pain

dardawal *v.t.* دردول pain

dardnak *a.* دردناک painful

dardnak; tapee *a.* دردناک؛پی sore

dareez warta eekhodal *v.t.* درېز ورتهايودل stage

dareez; mimbar *a.* درېز؛منبر pulpit

dareyda *n* درېدا erection

dareydal *v. t.* درېدل halt

dareydal *v.i.* درېدل stand

dareydana *n* درېدنه halt

dareydana *n* درېدنه stop

dareydana; da dareydo zay *n.* درېدنه،ددرېدوای stand

dareydana; qayam *n* درېدنه،قيام stay

darga *n.* درګه junk

dari wari kawal *v.t.* دوکول smash

darj kawal *v. t.* درجکول book

darja bandee *n.* درجهبندي gradation

darja bandee kawal *v.t* درجهبندي کول grade

darjan *n* درجن dozen

darjan *n* درجن twelve

darlodal *v.t.* درلودل have

darmal *n* درمل drug

darmal *n.* درمل medicine

darmal ploroonkay *n* درمل پلورونکی druggist

darmalana *n* درملنه cure

darmalana *n.* درملنه medicament

darmalana kawoonkay *a.* درملنه کوونکی remedial

darmalana yi kawal *v. t.* درملنهيې کول cure

darmaleez mahlool *n.* درملیز محلول syrup

darmaltoon *n.* درملتون pharmacy

darmaltoon *n* درملتون dispensary

darogh *n* دروغ lie

darogh wayal *v.i.* دروغويل lie

darogh; palma *n* دروغ؛پلمه sham

daroghjan *n.* دروغجن liar

daroghjan khabar *n* دروغجنخبر canard

darowoonakay *a.* اروونکی awful

darowoonkay *a* اروونکی formidable

darowoonkay khob *n.* اروونکی خوب nightmare

dars *n.* درس lecture

dars warkawal *v* درسورکول lecture

dars warkowoonkay *n.* درس ورکوونکی instructor

dars; hidayat *n.* درس،هدايت instruction

darsee keetab *n.* درسيکتاب tutorial

darsee nisab *n* درسينصاب curriculum

darsee; taleemee *a.* درسي،تعليمي tutorial

darshal *n.* درشل threshold

darwagh *a* درواغ bogus

darz *n* درز cleft

darz *n* درز crack

darz *n* درز fissure

darz moondal; mateydal *v. i* درز موندل،ماتدل crack

darz; chawd *n.* درز؛چاود scotch

darz; nifaq *n* درز؛نفاق split

darzoona bandawal *v.t.* درزونه بندول seam

daseesa *n.* دسیسه conspiracy

dasi na chi *conj.* داسنه‌چ lest

dasmal *n.* دسمال kerchief

dasmal *n.* دسمال napkin

dasta; bandal *n.* دسته؛بنل sheaf

dastak; magaway *n.* دستک؛موی picket

dastan *n.* داستان narrative

dastanee *a.* داستانی narrative

dastawayz *n* دستاوز document

dastmal *n.* دستمال handkerchief

daw talab keydal *v.t.* داوطلب کدل volunteer

daw talab; khpal pa khwakhi *n.* داوطلب؛خپل‌په‌خوی volunteer

daw talbana; khpal pa khwakha *a.* داوطلبانه؛خپل‌په‌خوه voluntary

dawa kawoonkay *n.* دعواکوونکی plaintiff

dawam *n.* دوام consistence,-cy

dawam *n.* دوام permanence

dawam kawal *v.t.* دوام‌کول withstand

dawam laral *v. i.* دوام‌لرل continue

dawamdar *a.* دوامدار lasting

dawamdar shay *n.* دوامدارشی perennial

dawlatee aylan *n.* دولتی‌اعلان communiqué

dawoodee gul *n* داودیل daisy

dawra; chapeyryal *n.* دوره؛چاپریال circuit

dawra; da nawee mosam payl *n* دوره؛دنوي‌موسم‌پیل epoch

dawra; dawran *n* دوره؛دوران spell

dawran *n* دوران era

dawrayee; musalsal *a.* دورېیي؛مسلسل serial

dayee *n.* دایی midwife

daymee *a.* دایمي permanent

daymee *a.* دایمي perpetual

daymee pam kawal *v. t* دایمي‌پام کول contemplate

dayra *n.* دایره circle

dayra *n.* دایره sphere

dayrawee *a* دایروي circular

dayrawee *a.* دایروي spherical

dayrawee harakat *n* دایروي‌حرکت whirl

daz bandee *n.* زبندي armistice

deen *n.* دین religion

deen pohana *n.* دین‌پوهنه theology

deendar *a.* دیندار saintly

deenee *a.* دیني religious

deenee aqeeda *n* دیني‌عقیده dogma

deenee aw mazhabee dood *n.* دیني‌او‌مذهبي‌دود sacrament

deewa *n.* دیوه lantern

deeyanat *n.* دیانت honesty

dehleez *n.* دهلیز corridor

dendar *a.* دیندار godly

dew *n.* دو demon

dey dawran ki *prep* ددوران‌ک during

deykhwa; dalta *adv.* دخوا؛دلته here

deyo *n* دو fiend

deyr arkheez fanee aw takhneekee pohantoon *n.* ر اخيزفني او تخنيكي پوهنتون polytechnic

deyr arkheez fanoono pori arwand *a.* ر اخيزفنونو پور راوند polytechnic

deyr bad shakla *a.* ر بدشكله hideous

deyr ghat *a.* ر غ titanic

deyr kam *adv.* ر كم seldom

deyr khandowoonkay *a.* ر خندوونكى hilarious

deyr koochnay *a.* ر كوچنى minute

deyr koochnay cheenjay *n.* ر كوچنى چينجى mite

deyr loy *a* ر لوى enormous

deyr loy *a* ر لوى mammoth

deyr muhim *a.* ر مهم salient

deyr oomar laral *v.i.* ر عمرلرل outlive

deyr pakhwanay *a.* ر پخوانى immemorial

deyr porta kawal *v.t.* ر پورته كول sky

deyr sakht *adj.* ر سخت crucial

deyr sor *a.* ر سو frigid

deyr warta *prep.* ر ورته near

deyr zala *adv.* ر له oft

deyr zala *adv.* ر له often

deyr zarooree *a* ر ضروري dire

deyr zhar *adv.* ر ژر anon

deyr zhar *adv.* ر ژر soon

deyr; zyat *a.* ر؛زيات very

deyra kkhata barkha *n.* ر ه كته برخه nadir

deyrakht *n.* رت immensity

deyrakht *n.* رت increment

deyrakht *n.* رت superabundance

deyrkay *n.* ركى majority

deyrsh *n.* درش thirty

deyrsh *a* درش thirty

deyrsham *a.* درشم thirtieth

deyrshama barkha *n* درشمه برخه thirtieth

deyw *n.* دو giant

deywal *n.* دوال wall

deywal *n.* دوال mural

deywal jorawal *v.t.* دوال جورول wall

deywalee *a.* دوالي mural

deywaleeya keydang *n.* دواليه كدنـ bankruptcy

difa *n* دفاع defence

difa kawal *v. t* دفاع كول defend

difa kawal *v.t* دفاع كول fend

difa kawal *v.i.* دفاع كول plead

difa kawoonkay *n* دفاع كوونكى defendant

difa; rakhteenwalee *n.* دفاع؛ رتينولي vindication

difaee khozakht *n.* دفاعي خوت parry

difaee zawab *n.* دفاعي واب rejoinder

dimagh *n* دماغ brain

dobara chap *n.* دوباره چاپ reprint

dobara raghondawal *v.t.* دوباره راغونول recollect

dobara yaw keydal *v.t.* دوباريو كدل rejoin

dobara zandan ta astawal *v.t.* دوباره زندان ته استول remand

dobara zwanawal *v.t.* دوبارهوانول rejuvenate

dobee *n.* دوبي washer

dobee khana *n.* دوبيخانه laundry

doday *n* دوی bread

doday khwaral *v. t.* دودیخوړل dine

dok *n.* دوک spindle

doka *n.* دوکه cheat

doka *n* دوکه deceit

doka *n* دوکه dodge

doka *n.* دوکه fraud

doka *n.* دوکه wile

doka kawal *v. t* دوکهکول deceive

doka kawal *v.t.* دوکهکول hoodwink

doka kawal *v.t.* دوکهکول lure

doka kawal *v.t.* دوکهکول rook

doka; doka warkawal *n.t.* دوکه، دوکهورکول delude

dokamar *n.* دوکهمار trickster

dokamar *a.* دوکهمار wily

dokamar aw bey haya *n.* دوکهمار اوبحیا rascal

dokey baz *a.* دوکباز fraudulent

dol *n* ول drum

dol wahal *v.i.* ولوهل drum

dol; seengar *n* ول؛سينار fashion

dol; zan sambalawana *n.* ول؛ان سمبالونه mode

dolas *n.* دولس twelve

dolasam *a.* دولسم twelfth

dolasama barkha *n.* دولسمهبرخه twelfth

dolay *n.* ولا palanquin

dolcha *n* ولچه bucket

dolcha *n.* ولچه pail

doobeydal *v.t.* وبدل swamp

doobeydana *n* وبدنه sink

dood *n.* دود custom

dood shaway *a.* دودشوی prevalent

dood; riwayat *n.* دود؛روایت tradition

doodeez; riwajee *n.* دودیز؛رواجي vogue

doodeydal *v.i.* دوددل prevail

dookhmanee *n.* ښنمي feud

doongeydal *v.i.* وندل grumble

doonyawee *a* دنیاوي earthly

doonyawee *a.* دنیوي mundane

doonyayee mal *n.* دنیاییمال pelf

doora *n.* دوه powder

doora achawal; sheendal *v.t.* دوه اچول؛شيندل powder

doorbeenee *a.* دوربيني microscopic

doori *n* دو dust

doori pakawal *v.t.* دوپاکول dust

doori pakawoonkay *n* دوپاکوونکی duster

doshamba *n.* دوشنبه Monday

dostana *adj.* دوستانه amicable

dostana *a.* دوستانه fraternal

dostana majlis *n.* دوستانهمجلس symposium

dotanay; doseeya *n* دوتن؛دوسيه file

dozakh *a.* دوزخ hell

dozakhee *a.* دوزخي infernal

drab drab *n.* دربدرب thud

drab drab kawal *v.i.* دربدرب کول thud

drab; khrap *n.* درب؛خرپ thump

drabowal *v.t.* دربول bang

drabowana *n.* دربوونه bang

drama; nandara *n* رامه؛ننداره drama

drana toora *n.* درنهتوره sabre

dranaway *n* درناوی esteem

dranaway *a.* درناوی reverential

dranaway kawal *v.t.* درناویکول respect

dranaway warkawal *v. i.* درناوی ورکول crouch

dranaway warkawal *v. t* درناوی ورکول esteem

dranaway warta kawal *v. t* درناویورتهکول honour

draz; zarb *n.* درز؛ضرب throb

drazawal *v.t.* درزول thump

drazeydal *v.i.* درزدل palpitate

drazeydal *v.i.* درزدل pulse

drazeydal *v.i.* درزدل throb

drey *n.* در three

drey arkheez *a.* دراخیز tripartite

drey arkheeza taroon *n* دراخیزه تون triplicate

drey chanda *a.* درچنده triplicate

drey chanda kawal *v.t.,* درچنده کول triple

drey chanda kawal *v.t.* درچنده کول triplicate

drey chanda kawana *n.* درچنده کوونه triplication

drey goonay *a.* درونی triple

drey goonaytob; taslees *n.* درونی توب،تثلیث trinity

drey gotay *n.* دروی triangle

drey goteez *a.* درویز triangular

drey kaseeza dala *n.* درکسیزهله trio

drey paya *n.* درپایه tripod

drey rangay *n* دررنی tricolour

drey rangee *a.* دررني tricolour

drey zala *adv.* درله thrice

dreyam *a.* دریم third

dreyam da chi *adv.* دریمداچ thirdly

dreyama barkha *n.* دریمهبرخه third

droond *a.* دروند hefty

droond *a.* دروند weighty

droond aw patman *a.* درونداوپتمن superb

droond goozar *n.* دروندوزار pound

droond; sabit *a.* دروند؛ثابت staid

drost *a* درست correct

drostawal *v. t* درستول correct

drust *a.* درست accurate

drustwalay *n.* درستوال accuracy

dukhman *n* دمن enemy

dukhmanee *n* دمني animosity

dukhmanee *n* دمني enmity

dwa *n.* دوه two

dwa arkheez *n* دوهاخیز double

dwa arkheez *a* دوهاخیز equivocal

dwa arkheez agheyz *n.* دوهاخیزاغز interplay

dwa arkheeza *adj* دوهاخیز amphibious

dwa chanda *a.* دوهچنده twofold

dwa chanda kawal *v.t.* دوهچنده کول redouble

dwa kalan war *adj* دوهکلنوار biennial

dwa khazi larana *n* دوهلرنه
bigamy

dwa makhay; reeya *n.* دوهمخي؛ريا
insincerity

dwa makhee *n* دوهمخي duplicity

dwa myashtanay *adj.* دوهمياشتنه
bimonthly

dwa ooneeza *adj* دوهاونيزه
bi-weekly

dwa pa dwa *n.* دوهپهدوه tete-a-tete

dwa pkhey laroonkay jandar *n*
دوهپلرونكیجاندار biped

dwa raga *a.* دوهره mulish

dwa raga haywan *a* دوهرهحوان
mongrel

dwa raga; dwa jinsa *adj.* دوهره؛
دوهجنسه bisexual

dwa raga; mukhalif *a* دوهره؛
مخالف cross

dwa saray kalang *n.* دوهسریكلن
mattock

dwa sawa kalan *adj* دوهسوهكلن
bicentenary

dwa stargeez doorbeen *n.* دوه
ستریزدوربین binocular

dwa zala *adv.* دوهمله twice

dwa zaray *n.* دوهزی shilly-shally

dwa zaweeyi laroonkay *adj.* دوه
زاویلرونكی biangular

dwa zhabeez *a* دوهژبیز bilingual

dwara *a* دواه both

dwara *a.* دواه two

dwara; ham ... ham *pron* دواه؛هم
هم___ both

dwayam *a.* دویم second

dwayam breedman *n.* دویمبریدمن
lieutenant

dwayma nuskha *n* دویمهنسخه
duplicate

dwey oonay *n.* دواونژ fort-night

dyarlas *n.* دیارلس thirteen

dyarlas *a* دیارلس thirteen

dyarlasam *a.* دیارلسم thirteenth

eejara *n.* اجاره lease

eejara *n.* دار اجاره tenant

eejara daree *n.* اجارهداري
monopoly

eejara kawal *v.t.* اجارهكول lease

eejaradaree *n.* اجارهداري tenancy

eejaza *n.* اجازه permission

eejaza *n.* اجازه permit

eejaza leek *n.* اجازهليك conge

eejaza leek akheystoonkay *n.*
اجازهليكاخستونكی licensee

eejaza leek warkawal *v.t.* اجازه
ليكورکول license

eejaza leek; qarardad *n* اجازه
ليك؛قرارداد charter

eejaza warkawal *v.t.* اجازهورکول
let

eejaza warkawal *v.t.* اجازهورکول
permit

eejaza warkawona *n.* اجازهورکونه
indulgence

eekhodal *v.t.* ايودل position

eekhodal *v.t.* ايودل put

eela *adv.* ايله barely

eela; bas ham domra *a.* ايله،بس‌هم دومره mere

eeman *n* ايمان faith

eemandaree *n.* ايمانداري integrity

eemteeyaz *n.* امتياز privilege

eemtiyaz *n* امتياز distinction

eenam *n* انعام bonus

eenam *n* انعام bounty

eenam *n.* انعام prize

eenam *n.* انعام tip

eenam warkawal *v.t.* انعام‌وركول prize

eenam warkawal *v.t.* انعام‌وركول tip

eengleesee abjoo *n* انليسي‌آبجو ale

eerey *n.* اير ash

eerey kawona *n* اير كونه cremation

eerlayndee *a.* ايرليني Irish

eerlayndee wagaray ya zhaba *n.* ايرليني‌وي‌يازبه Irish

eesaeeyat *n.* عيسائيت Christianity

eesarawal; zandawal *v. t* ايسارول، نول detain

eesawee *a.* عيسوي Christian

eesayee *n* عيسائي Christian

eetalwee *a.* ايالوي Italian

eetalwee wagaray ya zhaba *n.* ايالوي‌وي‌يازبه Italian

eetar; sheen asman *n* ايتر،شين آسمان ether

eezat *n* عزت dignity

eezat kamawal *v. t* عزت‌كمول degrade

eezat mab *n.* عزت‌مآب Highness

ehsan; zhmana *n.* احسان،ژمنه obligation

ehsas *n.* احساس sentiment

ehsasatee aw ghinayee *a.* احساساتي‌اوغنايي lyrical

ehsasee; jazbatee *a.* احساسي، جذباتي sentimental

ehteeyaj *n* احتياج requiste

ehteeyat *n.* احتياط precaution

ehteeyat *n.* احتياط prudence

ehteeyatee *a.* احتياطي precautionary

ehtikar *n.* احتكار speculation

ehtimal *n.* احتمال contingency

ehtimal *n.* احتمال probability

ehtimal; sahee gooman *n.* احتمال، صحيح‌‌گومان presumption

ehtimalan *adv.* احتمالاً probably

ehtiram *n.* احترام compliment

ehtiram *n.* احترام courtesy

ehtiram *n.* احترام homage

ehtiram *n.* احترام honour

ehtiram *n.* احترام respect

ehtiram *n.* احترام obeisance

ehtiram *n.* احترام veneration

ehtiram aw dranaway kawal *v. t* احترام‌اودرناوى‌كول compliment

ehtiram kawal *v.t.* احترام‌كول revere

ehtiram satowoonkay *a.* احترام ساتوونكى considerate

ehtiram warkawal *v.t* احترام وركول dignify

ehtiram yi kawal *v.t.* احترام‌يى‌كول venerate

etifaq ta raseydal *v.t.* اتفاق‌ته‌رسیدل accede

etihadeeya shirkat *n* اتحادیه‌شرکت corporation

eyshawal *v.i.* اشول boil

eysheydal *v.i.* اشدل seethe

eystana *n* استنه eviction

eystana *n.* استنه expulsion

F

faal *a.* فعال strenuous

faal *a.* فعال active

faal; gatawar *a* فعال،بور efficient

faal; hasand *a.* فعال،هاند vivid

faalawal *v.t.* فعالول activate

faaleeyat *n.* فعالیت activity

faaleeyat; gatawartob *n* ، فعالیت ورتوب efficiency

fahashtob *n.* فحشتوب obscenity

fahish *a.* فاحش obscene

fahish insan *n.* فاحش‌انسان prostitute

fahisha *n.* فاحشه cuckold

fahisha *n.* فاحشه whore

fahisha *n.* فاحشه strumpet

fahisha khana *n* فاحشه‌خانه brothel

faks masheen *n* فاکس‌ماشین fac-simile

fal *n.* فال auspice

falij *n.* فالج mutilation

faljawal *v.t.* فلجول mutilate

falsafa *n.* فلسفه philosophy

fan *n.* فن art

fan; tareeqa *n.* فن،طریقه technique

fana *n.* فنا vanity

fanee *a.* فانی mortal

fanee bashar *n* فانی‌بشر mortal

fankar *n.* کار فن actor

fankara *n.* کاره فن actress

faransawee *a.* فرانسوي french

faransawee wagaray ya zhaba *n* فراسوي‌وی‌یاژبه French

farayb *n.* فرب swindle

farayb; wehem *n.* فرب،وهم illusion

faree lar *n* فرعي‌لار bypass

faree mahsool *n* فرعي‌محصول by-product

faree mustajar ta da eejarey haq warkawal *v.t.* فرعي مستاجرته‌داجارحق‌ورکول sublet

faree; mrastyal *a.* فرعي،مرستیال tributary

fareyb *n.* فریب delusion

farhangee *a* فرهني cultural

farigh *a* فارغ leisure

farikhta *n* فرته angel

farman *n* فرمان decree

farman *n.* فرمان order

farman sadirawal *v. i* فرمان صادرول decree

farman warkawal *v.t* فرمان‌ورکول order

farman warkawal; masharee kawal *v. t* فرمان‌ورکول،مشري کول command

farman; masharee *n* فرمان،مشري command

farmanbardar *adj.* فرمانبردار compliant

farmanbardar *a* فرمانبردار docile

farmanbardaree *n.* فرمانبرداري compliance

faryadee *a.* فریادي rowdy

farz kawal *v.i.* فرض کول deem

farzee ya daroghee noom *n.* فرضي‌يادروغي‌نوم alias

fasadee *a* فسادي decadent

fasahat aw balaghat *n* فصاحت‌او بلاغت eloquence

fasahat aw balaghat *a.* فصاحت‌او بلاغت rhetorical

fasakh kawoonkay *a.* فسخ کوونکی irritant

fasee *a* فصيح eloquent

fasfuras laroonkay *n.* فاسفرس لرونکی phosphorus

fasid *a.* فاسد corrupt

fasid saray *n.* فاسدسی villain

fasid; paysa khor *a.* فاسد،پسه‌خور venal

fasidawal *v. t.* فاسدول corrupt

fasiq *n* فاسق debauchee

faskh kawal *v.t.* فسخ کول revoke

faskh kawana *n.* فسخ کوونه revocation

fasq *n* فسق debauchery

fastayee *n.* فسطايي sophist

fata kawal *v.t.* فتح کول overpower

fawara *n.* فواره fountain

fawqul ada *a.* فوق‌العاده terrific

fawree *a* فوري immediate

fawree *a.* فوري prompt

fayda *n.* فایده advantage

fayda mand *a.* فایده‌مند advantageous

fayl ta arwand; qayd *n.* فعل‌ته‌اوند، قد adverb

fayl; kroyay *n.* فعل؛کويی verb

faylwazma; karwazma *a.* فعل وزمه،کوزمه verbal

faysala kon *a* فصله‌کن decisive

faysala kun *a* فصله‌کن conclusive

faza *n.* فضا atmosphere

faza ki garzeydal; zay warkawal *v.t.* فضاکردل،ځای‌ورکول space

fazeelat laroonkay; muttaqee *a.* فضیلت‌لرونکی،متقي virtuous

feedeeya *n.* فدیه scapegoat

feel *n* فيل elephant

feelasof *n.* فيلسوف philosopher

feelasofyana *a.* فيلسوفيانه philosophical

feelwan *n.* فيلوان mahout

fehem *n.* فهم intellect

fidakarana *a.* فداکارانه sacrificial

fikar kawal *v.i.* فکر کول muse

fikar kawal *v.t.* فکر کول think

fikar; and *n.* فکر،آند notion

fikar; arwa *n.* فکر،اروا psyche

fikar; ghor *n* فکر،غور muse

fikarmand *a.* فکرمند mindful

fikree *a.* فکري intellectual

fikree *a.* فکري notional

fikree tamayal *n* فکري‌تمایل complex

fikree taraw laroonkay *a.* فکري تاولرونکی telepathic

fikree twan *n.* فکري‌توان mentality

fikree; jazbatee *a.* فکري؛جذباتي spirited

filam chamtoo kawal *v.t* فيلم چمتو کول film

filiz *n.* فلز metal

filiz ta oba warkawal *v.t.* فلزتهاوبه ورکول galvanize

filiz ta oba warkawal *v.t.* فلزتهاوبه ورکول temper

filizee *a.* فلزي metallic

filizee khwalay *n.* فلزي خول helmet

filizee pokh warkawal *v.t.* فلزي پو ورکول plate

finar; bampar *n.* فنر؛بمپر bumper

firasat *n.* فراست intuition

firasat *n.* فراست keenness

firasat *n.* فراست sagacity

fishar *n* فشار depression

fishar *n.* فشار tension

fishar *n.* فشار pressure

fishar *n* فشار zip

fishar achawal *v.t.* فشاراچول pressurize

fishar landi rawastal *v. t* فشارلاند راوستل depress

fishar landi rawastal *v.t.* فشارلاند راوستل strain

fishar; zor *n* فشار؛زور strain

fitna *n.* فتنه incense

fitna achawal *v.t.* فتنهاچول incense

fitrat *n.* فطرت mettle

fitree *a.* فطري inborn

fitree *a.* فطري natural

fitwa warkawal *v.t.* فتواورکول award

fitwa; bakhana *n.* فتوا؛بنه award

fizeek *n.* فزیک physics

foq bashar *a.* فوق بشر superhuman

foq bashar khusooseeyat laroonkay insan *n.* فوق بشر خصوصیات لرونکی انسان superman

foqul ada *a.* فوق العاده supernatural

fosil *n.* فوسیل fossil

frak *n.* فراک frock

frekvency *n.* فریکوینسی frequency

funji *n.* فنجی fungus

fyooz *n* فیوز fuse

G

gabeen *n.* بین beehive

gad jaryan *n* جریان confluence

gad zhwand sara kawal *v. i* ژوند سره کول co-exist

gad zhwandoon *n* ژوندون co-existence

gada; darweyzgar *n* لدا؛درورزر beggar

gada; nasa *n* اینا dance

gadaval *v.t.* ول intermingle

gadawana; yaw zay kawana *n* رنہ کونهای یو amalgamation

gaday *n.* ا wain

gaday *n.* ای vehicle

gaday chalawal *v. t* ای چلول drive

gaday; da pacha takht *n.* لد؛دپاچا تخت throne

gadayee kawal *v. t.* لدايي کول beg

gadayee kawal *v. i* لدايي کول cadge

gadayee kawal *v.t.* لدايي‌کول maunder

gadey hasi *n* ه collaboration

gadeydal *v. t.* لد dance

gadwad *ash* n. آش گو hotchpotch

gadwad kawal *v.t.* وکول jumble

gadwad saman ya asbab *n.* و سامان‌یااسباب welter

gadwadawal *v.t.* وول mate

gadwadawal *v.i* وول mix

gadwadee *n.* وي chaos

gadwadee *n.* وي muddle

gadwadee palana *n.* پالنه وي anarchism

gadwadee; baghawat *n* وي؛بغاوت anarchy

gadwalay *n* والی combination

gaheez *n.* هي morning

gala badawal *v.t.* غله‌بادول winnow

galal; zeygeydal; zeygawal *v.t* لال؛زدل؛زول bear

galay *n.* ل hail

galay wareydal *v.i* لوردل hail

gam pa gam *a.* ‌‌امپه‌ام gradual

gam pa gam seyral *v.t.* ‌امپه‌ام scan

ganda *a.* نده insane

ganda shay la zaya eestal *v.t.* نده شی‌لمایه‌ایستل weed

gandal *v.t.* نل sew

gandana *n.* نه stitch

gandoonkay *n.* نونکی tailor

gangas kawal *v.t.* نس‌کول puzzle

gangas kawal *v. t* نس‌کول bewilder

gangasawal *v. t* نسول confuse

gangastob *n.* نستوب puzzle

gangosawal *v.t* نوسول astound

ganr bootee *n.* بوي thicket

ganr nafoosa *a.* نفوسه populous

ganr shmeyr khazi larana *n.* شمر لرنه polygamy

ganr shmeyr khazi laroonkay *a.* شمرلرونکی polygamous

ganr syoray *n.* سیوری gloom

ganra *n* ه density

ganra gonra *n* ه‌وه crowd

ganra goonra *n.* swarm

ganra goonra *n.* ه‌وه mob

ganra goonra jorawal *v.i.* ه‌وه جوول swarm

ganra goonra jorawal *v.t.* ه‌وه جوول throng

ganra goonra kawal *v.t.* ه‌وه‌کول mob

ganri wani *n.* وز coppice

gapawoo *n.* ‌پاوو windbag

garam aw namjan *a.* رماونمجن sultry

garam aw tod *a.* رماوتود hot

garam mosam *n* رموسم thaw

garana; ibarat *n.* نه؛عبارت phrase

garanday kawal *v.t* ندی‌کول accelerate

garanday kawal *v. t.* ندی‌کول expedite

garanday; teyz *a* ندی؛تز fast

garandeetob *n* ندیتوب acceleration

garandeetob *n* ندیتوب expedition

garang *n.* ز cliff

gararay; abzar *n.* رار،ابزار gear

garay *n.* clock

gard *n.* درد mist

gard chapeyra *prep.* ردچاپره around

gard; golay *a.* رد،ول round

gardawal; raghondawal *v.t.* ردول؛راغونول round

garday *n.* ردى globe

gardjan *a.* ردجن hazy

gareydal; garawal *v.t.* ردل؛رول scratch

gareydana; nasht *n.* ردنه،نشت scratch

garm aw naram; hosa *a.* گرماو نرم؛هوسا cosy

garmaka; dana *n.* رمكه،دانه pimple

garweygna *n.* رونه inquest

garweygna *n.* رونه interrogation

garz bandee *n* ربندي curfew

garzand *n.* رند rover

garzand ploroonkay *n* رند پلورونكى hawker

garzand plorowoonkay *n.* رند پلوروونكى badger

garzand; mutaharik *a.* رند؛ متحرك mobile

garzanda; mutaharik *adj* رنده؛ متحرك ambulant

garzandoyee *n.* رندويي tourism

garzeydal *v.i.* ردل walk

garzeydana *n.* ردنه mobility

gasht *n* شت patrol

gasht kawal *v.i.* شت كول patrol

gasht kawal *v.i.* شت كول roam

gata *n.* ه profit

gata akheystal *v.t.* هاخيستل advantage

gata kawal *v.t.* ه كول profit

gata rasawal *v. t.* هرسول benefit

gata; fayda *n* ه،فايده benefit

gata; hasil *n.* ه،حاصل income

gatandoya *a.* ندويه profitable

gatandoyay *n.* ندويى profiteer

gatavar *a.* ور fruitful

gatavar *a.* ور lucrative

gatawar *a* ور beneficial

gatoonkay *n.* ونكى winner

gawa *n.* واه witness

gawahee warkawal; tasqeekawal *v.t.* واهي وركول؛ تصديقول attest

gawand *n.* اوند neighbourhood

gawandee *n.* اونى neighbour

gawandyan *n.* اونيان kith

gaz *n.* از gas

gazara *n.* ازره carrot

gdan; bajra *n.* دن؛باجره millet

gebon *n.* كيبون gibbon

gedara *n.* يده fox

geedara *n.* يده vixen

geela *n* يله complaint

geela kawal *v. i* يله كول complain

geela; shikayat *n.* له،شكايت grievance

geera *n* يره beard

geera khrayna *n* يره خرينه shave

geometry *n.* جيوميرى geometry

geyda *n* ه belly

geyda yeez *a.* هيز abdominal

ghond ploroonkay *a* غونډپلوروونکی wholesale

ghonda *n* غونډه conference

ghonda *n* غونډه delegation

ghondaska *n.* غونسکه ball

ghondawal *v.t.* غونول accumulate

ghondawal; jala kawal *v.t.* غونول؛ جلاکول pick

ghondawal; tawowal *v.t.* غونول؛ تاوول furl

ghonday *n.* غوﻧﺪ hill

ghonday *n.* غوﻧﺪ mount

ghondeydal *v. t* غوندل convene

ghondeydal *v.i* غوندل flock

ghondeydana *n* غونيدنه accumulation

ghondla jorawal; saza warkawal *v.t.* غونله جوول؛ سزاورکول sentence

ghondla poha; da nahwi ilam *n.* غونله پوهه؛ دنحو علم syntax

ghondla; saza *n.* غونله؛ سزا sentence

ghonzawal; takhta kawal *v.t* غونول؛ تخته کول wring

ghopa *n* غوپه dive

ghopa kawal *v. t* غوپه کول dip

ghopa kawana *n.* غوپه کونه soak

ghopa kawona *n.* غوپه کونه immersion

ghopa wahal *v. i* غوپه وهل dive

ghor ghor *n.* غورغور grunt

ghor ghor kawal *v.i.* غورغورکول grunt

ghor kawal *v.t.* غورکول mull

ghor kawal *v.t.* غورکول ponder

ghora malee kawal *v. t* غوه مالي کول coax

ghorap ghorap skhal *v.i.* غوپ غوپ ل sup

ghoravy *n.* غوروی hag

ghoraway *n.* غوراوی choice

ghoraway *n.* غوراوی option

ghoraway *n.* غوراوی pre-eminence

ghoraway *n.* غوراوی preference

ghorchanr shaway keetab *n.* غورچاشوی کتاب breviary

ghoreydal *v.i.* غورﺪل snort

ghoreydal *v.i.* غورﺪل whimper

ghoreydal *v.i.* غورﺪل roar

ghoreydana *n.* غورﺪنه roar

ghorzang *n* غورﻧﺪ commotion

ghorzang kawal *v.i.* غورﻧﺪکول sally

ghorzawal *v.t.* غورول throw

ghorzawana *n* غورونه overthrow

ghorzawana *n.* غوروونه throw

ghorzeydana *n* انحطاط غورﺪنه، fall

ghosa *n.* غصه fury

ghosa kawona *n.* کوونه غصه aggravation

ghosawal *v.t.* غوول rip

ghosawana *n* غوونه dissection

ghoswalay *n.* غووالی rift

ghota *n.* غوه knot

ghota kawal *v.t.* غوه کول knot

ghota kawal *v.t.* غوه کول plunge

ghota kawal *v.t.* غوه کول tie

ghota; band *n* غوه؛ بند tie

ghota; ghopa *n.* غوه؛ غوپه dip

ghota; ghopa *n* غوه؛ غوپه plunge

ghotay *n* غو bloom

ghotay *n* غو blossom

ghotay kawal *v.i* غوكول bloom

ghotay kawal *v.i* غوكول blossom

ghozh khwaroonkay *a.* غوژ خوونکی supple

ghrambahar *n.* غمبهار rumble

ghrambar *n* غمبار growl

ghrambeydal *v.i.* غمبدل growl

ghrap *n.* غپ sip

ghreew rawastoonkay *a.* غرو راوستونکی pathetic

ghreew; hya hoo *n.* غرو،هياهو hubbub

ghroombeydal *v.i.* غومبدل rumble

ghulam jorawal *v.t.* غلامجوول enslave

ghuncha *n.* غنچه wisp

ghusa *n.* غصه anger

ghusa *n.* غصه rage

ghusa keydal *v.t.* غصهکدل loathe

ghusa; pa qahar *a.* غصه،بهقهر angry

ghusanak *a.* غصهناک loath

ghusanak *a.* غصهناک violent

ghusanak keydal *v.i.* غصهناک کدل rage

ghwa *n.* غوا cow

ghwag *n* غو ear

ghwag pakowoonkay *n.* غو پاکوونکی aurilave

ghwakha *n* غوه flesh

ghwakha *n.* غوه meat

ghwakhan *a.* غون pulpy

ghwakhan keydal *v.t.* غونکدل pulp

ghwalaval *v.t* غولول gull

ghwand; da hukoomat wakmanee *n.* غنډ،دحکومت واکمني regiment

ghwar *a.* غو oily

ghwara *a* غوره better

ghwara *a* غوره select

ghwara aw ala *a* غورهاواعلئ classic

ghwara aw mumtaz *a.* غورهاوممتاز superfine

ghwara kawal *v. t.* غورهکول choose

ghwara kawal *v.t.* غورهکول select

ghwara keydal; ghwara kawal *v. t* غورهکدل؛غورهکول better

ghwara mal *n.* غومال minion

ghwaramalee kawal *v. t.* غومالي کول court

ghwarawal *v.t.* غوول lubricate

ghwarowana *n.* غوونه lubrication

ghwarowoonkay mawad *n.* غووونکیمواد lubricant

ghwayay *n* غوایی bull

ghwayay *n.* غویی ox

ghwayee sara loba kawoonkay *n* غويیسرهلوبهکوونکی. matador

glicrine *n.* لیسرین glycerine

gmanz *n* مڼ comb

godam *n.* ودام storage

godam ki satal *v.t.* ودامکساتل store

gokha *v.t.* وه isolate

gokha kawal *v. t* وهکول depose

gokha keydal *n* وهکیدل abdication

gol *n* ل flower

gol gopee *n.* لوپي cauliflower

golalay; safa *a* لالى،صفا fair

golay *n.* لوj tablet

gomaral shaway *n.* ﻣﺎرلﺷﻮى assignee

gombata; maghara *n.* ﻏﻤﺒﺘﻪ،ﻣﻐﺎره vault

gomra kawal *v.t.* ﻏﻤﺮاهﻛﻮل mislead

gond *n* ﻏﻮند faction

gond *n.* ﻏﻮند party

gonda *n.* ﻏﻮﻧﻪ knee

gonda kedal *v.i.* ﻏﻮﻧﻪﻛﻴﺪل kneel

gongosay *n* ﻏﻮﻧﻮﺳﻰ bruit

gonzi *n.* ﻏﻮﻧﺰ wrinkle

gonzi gonzi *a.* ﻏﻮﻧﺰ ﻏﻮﻧﺰ slovenly

gonzi kawal *v.t.* ﻏﻮﻧﺰﻛﻮل wrinkle

gonzi kawana *n.* ﻏﻮﻧﺰﻛﻮﻧﻪ shrinkage

gonzi keydal *v.i* ﻏﻮﻧﺰﻛﺪل shrink

gonzi warkawal *v.t.* ﻏﻮﻧﻮرﻛﻮل crimple

gooman aw atkal kawal *v.t.* ﻏﻮﻣﺎن اواﻛﻞﻛﻮل imagine

gooman kawal *v. t* ﻏﻮﻣﺎنﻛﻮل conjecture

gooman kawal *v.t.* ﻏﻮﻣﺎنﻛﻮل assume

gooman; hod *n.* ﻏﻮﻣﺎن،ﻫﻮ assumption

goombat *n* ﻏﻮﻣﺒﺖ dome

goona *n.* ﻏﻨﺎه misdemeanour

goona *n.* ﻏﻨﺎه sin

goona gar *n.* ﻏﻨﺎﻣﺎر offender

goona kawal *v.t.* ﻏﻨﺎهﻛﻮل offend

goona kawal *v.i.* ﻏﻨﺎهﻛﻮل sin

goonagar *a.* ﻏﻨﺎﻫﺎر sinful

goonagar *n.* ﻏﻨﻬﺎر sinner

goonagar *a.* ﻧﺎﻫﺎر vile

goong *n.* ﻏﻮﻧﮓ owl

goong bayan *n* ﻏﻮﻧﮕﺒﻴﺎن enigma

goonga stoonza *n* ﻏﻮﻧﮕﺎﺳﺘﻮﻧﺰه dilemma

goongay *a* ﻏﻮﻧﻰ dumb

goongtob *n.* ﻏﻮﻧﺘﻮب vagueness

goozan wahal *v.t.* ﻏﻮزﻧﻮﻫﻞ lame

goozan wahalay *a.* ﻏﻮزﻧﻮﻫﻠﻰ lame

goozanr *n.* ﻏﻮز palsy

goozanr *n.* ﻏﻮز paralysis

goozanr wahal *v.t.* ﻏﻮزوﻫﻞ paralyse

goozanr wahalay *a.* ﻏﻮزوﻫﻠﻰ paralytic

goozar kawal; las pri rakakhal *v.t.* ﻏﻮزارﻛﻮل،لاسﭘﺮراﻛﻞ stroke

gopee *n.* ﻏﻮﭘﻰ cabbage

goreela beezo *n.* ﻏﻮرﻳﻼﺑﻴﺰو gorilla

gorkhar *n.* ﻏﻮرﺧﺮ zebra

gosha nasheen zahid *n.* ﻏﻮﺷﻪﻧﺸﻴﻦ زاﻫﺪ hermit

gostakh *a.* ﻏﺴﺘﺎخ insolent

got nastay keydal *v.i.* ﻏﻮﻧﺎﺳﺘﻰﻛﺪل retire

gota *n* ﻏﻮﺗﻪ finger

gota pa ghakh *adv.,* ﻏﻮﺗﻪﭘﻪﻏﺎ agape

gota warwral *v.t* ﻏﻮﺗﻪورول finger

gotmeyshtaytob *n.* ﻏﻮﻣﺸﺘﻰﺗﻮب agoraphobia

gotmo *n.* ﻏﻮﺗﻤﻮ thimble

gran *a* ﮔﺮان expensive

gran *a.* ﮔﺮان herculean

gran *a.* ﮔﺮان lovely

grana joreydal; bey payle preykhodal *v. t.* رانه‌جودل؛بپایل پرودل baffle

grees *n* ريس grease

grees warkawal *v.t* ريس‌ورکول grease

grees warkray shaway *a.* ريس ورکی‌شوی greasy

groha sargandawana *n.* روهه رنډونه suggestion

gul meykhay *n.* ل‌مخ stud

gúl ploroonkay *n* ل‌پلورونکی florist

gul sang *n.* ل‌سنگ moss

gul sanga *n.* ل‌سانه nosegay

gulab *n.* لاب rose

gulabee *a* لابی pink

gulabee rang *n.* لابی‌رنگ pink

gulabee rang ta mayil *a.* لابی‌رنگ‌ته مایل pinkish

gulalay *n* لالی dandy

gulalay *a.* لالی hale

gulalay *a.* لالی handsome

gulalay *a* لالی pretty

gulalay insan *n* لالی‌انسان smart

guldasta *n* لدسته bouquet

guldozee *n* لدوزي embroidery

gulucose *n.* لوکوز glucose

gulwareen *a.* لورين rosy

gulwareen; gulwazma *a.* لورين؛ل وزمه roseate

gustakh *a.* ستاخ petulant

gustakh saray ya khaza *n.* ستاخ سی‌یاه minx

gustakhee *n* ستاخي flippancy

gustakhee *n.* ستاخي petulance

gut *n* و corner

gwakhal *v.t.* وال threaten

had *a.* حاد keen

had *n.* حد extent

had *n.* حد limit

hadaf *n.* هدف objective

hadee seem *n.* هادي‌سيم lead

hadeera *n.* هديره necropolis

hadeeya *n.* هديه offering

hadeeya warkawal *v. t* هديه‌ورکول donate

hadisa *n.* حادثه incident

hadisatee *a.* حادثاتي incidental

hadokeez kawal *v.t.* هوکيزکول ossify

hadookay *n.* هوکی bone

hafiza *n.* حافظه memory

hafiza *n.* حافظه remembrance

hafizey ta rawastal *v. t* حافظته راوستل evoke

hagay *n* هـ egg

hagay dawla *a.* هوله oval

hagha *pron.* هغه he

hagha dem. *pron.* هغه that

hagha ameyl chi da karay pa seyr zareygee *n* هغه‌امل‌چدکپهر ي festoon

hagha chi nawara tolaneez wuzeeyat walaree *n* هغه‌چناوه ولنيزوضعيت‌ولري underdog hagha kach; kala chi; saranga chi *adv.* هغه کچ؛ کله چ؛ رنه چ as

hagha kas chi khwaley kawee; garmowoonkay jakat *n.* هغه کس چ خوا کوي؛ رموونکي جاک sweater

hagha khaza *pron.* هغه she

hagha khwa deykhwa khozeydal *v.t.* هغه خوا دخوا خوځدل rock

hagha khwa leyri *prep.* هغه خوا لري beyond

hagha khwa ta *adv.* هغه خوا ته younder

hagha loybadana beezo chi pa wano ki zhwand kawee *n.* هغه لوي بدنه بيزو چپه ونو کژوند کوي chimpanzee

haghamasheenchipaharakat kawalotrinabreykhnapayda keygee n هغه ماشين حرکت په چ کي پدا برنا ترينه کولو dynamo

hagha ta *pron.* هغه ته him

hagha yaw rel. *pron.* هغه يو that

hagha zai che weele shavi falz pa qalabo ke achavi *n.* هغه ای چه ويلي شوي فلز په قالبو کي اچوي foundry

haghwee ta *pron.* هغوي ته them

hajoom *n.* هجوم irruption

hakakee kawal *v. t* حکاکي کول engrave

hakeem; darmal jorawoonkay *n.* حکيم؛ درمل جووونکي physicist

hakhwa deykhwa harakat kawal *v.i.* هخوا دخوا حرکت کول shuffle

hakhwa deykhwa zambeydal *v.i.* هخوا دخوا مبدل sway

hakhwa ta *adv.* هخوا ته thither

hakim *n* حاکم dictator

hal kaval *v.t* حل کول fathom

hal kawal *v.t* حل کول dissolve

hal kawal *v.t.* حل کول resolve

hal lara *n.* حل لاره solution

hal lara warta moondal *v.t.* حل لاره ورته موندل solve

hal; soorat; sarangwalay *n* حال، صورت؛ رنوالی circumstance

halak *n* هلک boy

halaktob *n* هلکتوب boyhood

halat *n.* حالت standing

halat *n.* حالت situation

halat; keyfeeyat *n.* حالت، کفيت posture

halat; martaba *n.* حالت، مرتبه status

halat; reeyasat; dawlat *n.* حالت، رياست؛ دولت state

halat; shart *n* حالت، شرط condition

halbee lokhay *n.* حلبي لوی can

haleem *a.* حليم meek

haleydana *n.* حلدنه solvency

halta *adv.* هلته there

halweeyat *n.* حلويات sweetmeat

ham *adv.* هم too

ham agangee *n.* هم آهني consonance

ham andtob *n.* هم اندتوب unanimity

ham andtob *n.* هم اندتوب sympathy

ham ara *adj* هم آره cognate

344

ham ghareetob *n.* همغيزتوب
unison

ham khooya *a* همخويه congenial

ham mahala *a* هممهاله
contemporary

ham mana *a.* هممانا synonymous

ham maneez wayay *n.* هممانيزويى
synonym

ham nooma *n.* همنومه namesake

ham por *n* همپو equal

ham rotba *a.* همرتبه co-ordinate

ham taroonay; zhman *n.* ؛همتونى
ژمن ally

ham waznee *b.* هموزني rhythm

hamaysha bahar gul *n.* همشهبهار
ل marigold

hamaysha; tar dey chi *adv.*
همشه،تردچ still

hamda shan *adv.* همداشان
likewise

hamda shan; da ranga *a.* همدا
شان،دارنه such

hamda shan; hamda dawl *adv.*
همداشان،همداول also

hamdardee kawál *v. i.* همدردي
کول condole

hamghardi *a.* همغاى harmonious

hamjinsa *a.* همجنسه
homogeneous

hamkar *n* همکار colleague

hamkaree *n* همکاري co-operation

hamkaree *n* همکاري co-ordination

hamkaree kawal *v. i* همکاري کول
co-operate

hamla *n.* حمله invasion

hamla *n.* حمله onset

hamla; da zang ghag *n* حمله،دزنغ
stroke

hamsafar *n.* همسفر consort

hangeydal *v. i* هندل bray

haq peyzhandana *n.* حقپژندنه
gratitude

haqarat *n* حقارت contempt

haqdar *a* حقدار eligible

haqdar garzeydal *v. t.* حقداورلدل
deserve

haqeeqat *n* حقيقت fact

haqeeqat *n.* حقيقت reality

haqeeqee *a.* حقيقي real

haqeeqee *a.* حقيقي realistic

haqiki *a.* حقيقى intrinsic

haqooqee dawa *n.* حقوقيدعوا plea

haqooqee salakar *n.* حقوقيسلاکار
solicitor

haqul wakala *n.* حقالوکاله
honorarium

har arkheeza manzara *n.* هراخيزه
منظره panorama

har cheyrta *adv.* هرچرته wherever

har dawl rakakhta keydoonkay
chaparkat ya bistara *n* هرول
راکتهکدونکيچپرکيابستره bunk

har kal yaw zal *adv.* هرکاليول
yearly

har kalay *n* هرکلى welcome

har kas *pron.* هرکس each

har lori ta *adv.* هرلورته round

har shay; pa hees dawl *n.* ؛هرشى
پههيول aught

har sok chi; har cha chi *pron.* هر
وکچ،هرچاچ whoever

har sok; har cha *pron* هروک،هر
چا all

har wakht; har kala; kala *adv.*
conj هروخت؛هر کله؛کله
whenever

har yaw *a* هريو each

har yaw *adv.* هريو either

har yaw *a* هريو every

har yaw *pron* هريو whichever

har zay mawjoodgee *n.* هرای
موجودي omnipresence

har zay ta hazir *a.* هرای ته حاضر
omnipresent

hara myasht *adv* هره میاشت
monthly

hara oonay *n.* هره اوونۍ weekly

hara waraz *adv.* هرورز daily

harakat *n.* حرکت motion

harakat *n.* حرکت movement

harakat kawal *v.i.* حرکت کول
motion

harakat warkawal *v.i.* حرکت
ورکول motor

harakat warkawal *v.i.* حرکت
ورکول stir

harakat; takan *n.* حرکت؛ټکان
move

haram *a* حرام taboo

haram ganral *v.t.* حرام کنړل taboo

haran *n.* هارن siren

hararatee *a.* حرارتي thermal

hareef *n.* حريف adversary

hareef; dukhman *n* حريف؛دښمن
foe

harees *a.* حريص voracious

harfi nida; dakhalat *n.* حرف ندا؛
دخالت interjection

hasa *n.* هه attempt

hasa *n.* هه conation

hasa *n* هه effort

hasa *n* هه try

hasa aw hand *n* هه او هاند diligence

hasa kawal *v.t.* هه کول attempt

hasa kawal *v.i.* هه کول try

hasakaval *v.i.* هسکول heave

hasand *n* هاند quick

hasas *a* حساس critical

hasas; nazak *a.* حساس؛نازک
sensitive

hasas; nazak *a.* حساس؛نازک
touchy

hasaseeyat *n.* حساسیت sensibility

hasaseeyat larana *n.* حساسیت لرنه
allergy

hasawal *v.t.* هول persuade

hasawal; kropawal *v.i.* هول؛
کروپول incline

hasawana; tahreek *n.* هوونه؛
تحریک persuasion

hashara khoray mogak *n.* حشره
خوری موک shrew

hasheeya *n.* حاشیه margin

hasheeya warkawal *v.t* حاشیه
ورکول fringe

hasheeya; charma *n.* حاشیه؛چرمه
fringe

hasheeyawee *a.* حاشیوي marginal

hashra *n.* حشره insect

hashra *n,* حشره moth

hashra wazhoonkay *n.* حشره
وژونکی insecticide

hasil *n.* حاصل output

hasil *n.* حاصل product

hasil *n.* حاصل upshot

hasil warkawoonkay *a.* حاصل ورکوونکی prolific

hasil; jama *n.* حاصل،جمع total

hask *n* هسک over

hask; jag *a.* هسک؛ج tall

hask; watalay *a.* هسک،وتلی outstanding

haskawal *v.i.* هسکول tower

hasta *n.* هسته kernel

hastawee *a.* هستوي nuclear

hastee *n* هستي entity

hawa *n* هوا air

hawa meych *n* هوامچ barometer

hawa peyzhand *n.* هواپژاند meteorologist

hawa peyzhandana *n.* هواپژندنه meteorology

hawa rasand *n.* هوارساند ventilator

hawa rasawana *n.* هوارسوونه ventilation

hawa warkawal *v.t.* هواورکول ventilate

hawa zid wasla *a.* هواضدوسله anti-aircraft

hawabazee *n.pl.* هوابازي aeronautics

hawadar star zay *a.* هوادارسترزای palatial

hawakash *n.* هواکش،سومه vent

hawala; rasmee hukam *n.* حواله، رسمي حکم warrant

hawar *n.* هوار plain

hawara sata *a.* هوارهسطح plane

hawarawal *v. t* هوارول even

hawas *n.* هوس longing

hawas *n.* هوس whim

hawas kawal *v.i.* هوس کول hanker

hawasbaz *a.* هوسباز whimsical

hawayee *a.* هوايي aerial

hawayee *a.* هوايي spatial

hawayee *a.* هوايي airy

hawayee toopan *n.* هوايي توپان tornado

hawayee ya samandaree yoon *n.* هوايي ياسمندري يون voyage

hawayee ya samandaree yoon kawal *v.i.* هوايي ياسمندري يون کول voyage

hawayoon *n.* هوايون aviation

hawayoonee *n.* هوايوني aviator

haweeyat; shakhseeyat *n.* هويت، شخصيت personality

hawsala; sabar *n.* حوصله،صبر toleration

haya *n* حيا modesty

hayanak *a.* حياناک modest

hayatee awakhtoon *n.* حياتي اوتون metabolism

haybatnak *a.* هبتاک horrible

hayjan *n.* هجان sensation

hayjanee *a.* هجاني sensational

hayran *a.* حيران aghast

hayranawal *v.t.* حرانول mystify

hayranawal *v.t.* حرانول perplex

hayranawal *v.t.* حرانول stun

hayranawal *v.t.* حرانول surprise

hayranawal *v.t.* حرانول stupefy

hayranawoonkay *a.* حرانوونکی marvellous

hayranawoonkay *a.* حرانوونکی wonderful

hayranawoonkay *a.* حرانوونکی wondrous

hayranawoonkay warzashee kartab kawal *v.t.* حرانوونکی ورزشي کرتب کول stunt

hayranawoonkay; ajeeb *a.* حرانوونکی،عجیب stupendous

hayraneydal *v.i.* حراندل wonder

hayrantya *n.* حرانتیا surprise

haywad pal *a.* هوادپال patriotic

haywad palana *n.* هوادپالنه partiotism

haywad wal *n.* هوادوال patriot

haywanee shaoor *n.* حوانی شعور instinct

haywanee shaoor laroonkay *a.* حوانی شعور لرونکی instinctive

hayz *n.* حض menses

hazaf; faskh *n* حذف،فسخ cancellation

hazafawal *v. t* حذفول delete

hazafawal *v.t.* حذفول omit

hazafawana *n.* حذفونه omission

hazam; mujalla *n.* هضم،مجله digest

hazima *n* هاضمه digestion

hazir zawabee *n.* حاضروابي repartee

hazirawal *v.t.* حاضرول manifest

haziree akheystana *n.* حاضري اخستنه roll-call

haziree; sar *n.* حاضري،بار attendance

hazireydal; pam kawal *v.t.* حاضردل،پام کول attend

hazmawal *v. t.* هضمول digest

hazrat eesa alayhissalam *n.* حضرت عیسی علیه السلام Christ

hazyanee *a.* هذیانی frantic

heefazat kawal *v.t.* حفاظت کول secure

heefazat; masuntya *n.* حفاظت، مصئونتیا immunity

heela kawal *v. t* هیله کول expect

heela laral *v.i* هیله لرل long

heela man *a* هیله من desirous

heela man; arzoo man *adj.* هیله من،آرزومن appetent

heela; arzoo *n.* هیله،آرزو ambition

heela; ishteeyaq *n.* هیله،اشتیاق appetence

heela; tama *n.* هیله،طمع expectation

heelaman *n.* هیله من aspirant

heelaman *adj.* هیله من avid

heelaman *a.* هیله من hopeful

heelaman *a.* هیله من zealous

heelaman; narama *a.* هیله من،نارامه solicitious

heelay *n.* هیل duck

hees *adv.* هیڅ any

hees cheyrta *adv.* هیڅ چرته nowhere

hees yaw *pron.* هیڅیو none

hees; har *a.* هیڅ،هر any

hees; nafee *n* هیڅ،نفی no

heesab *n.* حساب account

heesab beyrta warkawal *v.t.* حساب برته ورکول refund

heesab speenawal *v.t.* حساب سپینول recompense

heesabawal *v. t.* حسابول enumerate

heeskala *adv.* هيكله nothing

heeskala *adv.* هيكله none

heeskala; hees wakht *adv.* هيكله؛ هيوخت never

heesok *pron.* هيوک nobody

heyl *n.* هل cardamom

heyranawal *v.t.* حرانول astonish

heyranawal *v. t* حرانول daze

heyranawal *v.t.* حرانول amaze

heyranawoonkay *n.* حرانوونکی marvel

heyranawoonkay *a.* حرانوونکی phenomenal

heyraneydal *v.i* حراندل marvel

heyrantya *n.* حرانتيا amazement

heyrantya *n.* حرانتيا astonishment

heyrantya *n* حرانتيا daze

heyrawal *v.t* هرول forget

heyrawana *n.* هروونه oblivion

heywad *n.* هواد country

heywan *n* حيوان beast

heywan dawla *a* حيوانوله beastly

hifazat ki satal *v.t.* حفاظت کساتل ward

hija; sapa *n.* هجا؛ په syllable

hijayee; da yawey sapey astazay *n.* هجايي؛ديوپاستازی syllabic

hijoleekoonkay *n.* هجوليکونکی satirist

hilzonee sadaf *n.* حلزونيصدف conch

himaqat *n.* حماقت infatuation

himaqat kawal *v.t.* حماقتکول infatuate

himat kawal *v. i.* همتکول dare

hindee imlee *n.* هندياملي tamarind

hindee; hindoostanee *a.* هندي؛ هندوستاني Indian

hindsee mumayish *n.* هندسينمايش graph

hindsee zay *n.* هندسيای locus

hindsi *a.* هندسی geometrical

hindwana *n.* هندوانه melon

hindwanra *n.* هندواه water-melon

hiras *n.* حرص avarice

hiras *adv.* حرص avidity

hiras *n.* حرص greed

hirasee *a.* حرصي greedy

his *n.* حس sense

hisabawal; tareekh maloomawal *v. t* حسابول؛تاريخمعلومول date

hisabdaree *n.* حسابداري accountancy

hisar *n.* حصار enclosure

hisar; khoona *n.* خونه حصار؛ ward

ho; aw *adv.* هو،او yes

hod *n.* هو intent

hod laral *v.t.* هولرل purpose

hojam *n* حجم bulk

hokam chalawal *v. t* حکمچلول dictate

hokam; hakimeeyat *n* حکم؛ حاکميت dictation

honar *n* هنر craft

honar *n.* هنر forte

honar mand *n* هنرمند craftsman

honaree *a.* هنري artistic

honaree lasleek *n.* هنريلاسليک monograph

honarmand *n.* هنرمند artist

hookhyar *a.* هويار clever

hookhyar *a.* هويار intelligent

hookhyar *a.* هوښیار sagacious

hookhyar *a.* هوښیار sage

hookoomat kawal *v.t.* حکومت کول rule

hoora *n.* حوره sylph

hujam; miqdar; tolga; jild *n.* حجم،مقدار،بوله،جلد volume

hujra *n.* هجره forum

hukam *n.* حکم ordinance

hukam *n.* حکم ruling

hukam *n.* حکم precept

hukam; sanad *n.* حکم،سند writ

hukamranee *n.* حکمراني governance

hukamranee kawal *v.t.* حکمراني کول govern

hukoomat *n.* حکومت government

hukoomat kawal *v.i.* حکومت کول reign

hukoomatee nizam *n.* حکومتي نظام regime

hunar *n.* هنر skill

ibadat *n* عبادت cult

ibadat *n.* عبادت worship

ibadat kawal *v.t.* عبادت کول worship

ibadat kawoonkay *n.* عبادت کوونکی worshipper

ibadat zay *n.* عبادتای temple

ibadatee *a.* عبادتي liturgical

ibadatzay *n.* عبادتای sanctuary

ibarat *n* عبارت clause

ibarat karawana; kalma bandee عبارت کاروونه،کلمهبندي *n.* phraseology

ibarat; matan *n.* عبارت،متن text

ibham *n.* ابهام obscurity

ibham wayal *v.i.* ابهامویل quibble

ibham; goongtob *n.* ابهام،بونتوب ambiguity

ibtidayee *a.* ابتدايي preliminary

ibtidayee *a.* ابتدايي preparatory

ibtidayee *a.* ابتدايي primary

ibtidayee *a* ابتدائي elementary

ida kawal *v.t.* ادعاکول affirm

idama *n.* ادامه resume

idama darawal *v.t* ادامهدرول discontinue

idama laral *v.i.* ادامهلرل last

idama warkawal *v.t.* ادامهورکول maintain

idama warkawal; khwandee satal *v.t.* ادامهورکول،خوندي ساتل sustain

idara *n.* اداره administration

idara *n.* اداره organization

idara kawal *v.t.* اداره کول administer

idara kawal; pa so ghwandoono weyshal *v.t.* اداره کول،پهسوغنونو وشل regiment

idara kawoonkay *n.* اداره کوونکی operator

idaree *a.* اداري administrative

idaree charwakay *n* اداريچارواکی official

idaree charwakay *n.* اداري چارواکی rum

idaree mamoor *n* ادارى‌مأمور bureaucrat

idaree sanga *n* ادارى‌انه department

idaree taseesat *n.* ادارى‌تأسيسات Bureacuracy

idaree; masoolee *a.* ادارى؛مسؤولى officious

idrak *n* ادراك conception

idrak *n.* ادراك sentience

idrak *n.* ادراك realization

idrakee *a.* ادراكى perceptive

idrakee *a.* ادراكى sentient

iftikhar ta raseydana *n* افتخارته رسدنه accession

iftikharee; rasmee *a.* افتخارى؛ رسمى titular

ihanat *n.* اهانت insolence

ihata kawal *v. t* احاطه‌كول encompass

ihata kawal *v.t.* احاطه‌كول surround

ihda *n* اهداء grant

ijara kaonke *n.* اجاره‌كوونكى lessee

ijaza warkawal *v.t.* اجازه‌وركول allow

ijra kawal *v. t.* اجراكول enforce

ijra kawal *v.t.* اجراكول perform

ijra kawoonkay *n.* اجراكوونكى performer

ijraywee charwakay *n.* اجرايوي چارواكى sergeant

ijtinab *n* اجتناب refrain

ijtinab kawal *v.i.* اجتناب‌كول refrain

ikhlaqee keesa *n* اخلاقى‌كيسه apologue

ikhlas *n* اخلاص devotion

ikhrajawal *v. t.* اخراجول expel

ikhtilaf *n.* اختلاف conflict

ikhtilaf *n* اختلاف discord

ikhtilaf laral *v. i* اختلاف‌لرل disagree

ikhtilaf peyda keydal *v. i* اختلاف پداكدل conflict

ikhtilaf; tawpeer *n.* اختلاف؛توپير variance

ikhtira *n.* اختراع concoction

ikhtira kawal *v. t* اختراع‌كول concoct

ikhtira kawal *v. t* اختراع‌كول devise

ikhtira kawal *v.t.* اختراع‌كول invent

ikhtiraee *a.* اختراعى inventive

ikhtisas *n.* اختصاص specialization

ikhtisasee; malkeeyatee *a.* اختصاصى؛ملكيتى proprietary

ikhtyar *n.* اختيار liberty

ikhtyaree *a.* اختيارى optional

iktibas kawal *v. t* اقتباس‌كول extract

iktishaf *n* اكتشاف exploration

iktishafee safar kawal *v.t* اكتشافى سفركول explore

ilaha *n.* الهه goddess

ilahee; khuday *n* الهى؛خداى divinity

ilaj *n.* علاج remedy

ilaqa *n.* علاقه county

ilham *n.* الهام oracle

ilhamee *a.* الهامي oracular

iltihab; sozeydana *n.* التهاب؛سوذنه inflammation

iltihabee *a.* التهابي inflammatory

iltihabee parsob *n* التهابي؛پسوب blain

iltimas kawal; murajia kawal *v.t.* التماس كول؛مراجعه كول appeal

iltimas; zaree *n.* التماس؛زاري appeal

ilzam lagawal; adaa kawal *v.t.* الزاملول؛ادعاكول allege

ilzam; adaa *n.* الزام؛ادعا allegation

imala; tazreeq *n.* اماله؛تزريق injection

imteeyazee *a.* امتيازي preferential

imtihan akheystal *v. t* امتحان اخستل examine

imtihan akheystoonkay *n* امتحان اخستوونكى examiner

imtihan warkowoonkay *n* امتحان وركوونكى examinee

imtihan; azmoyana *n* امتحان، آزموينه test

imza kawal *v. t.* امضاكول countersign

infijaree *a* انفجاري explosive

infiradee *a.* انفرادي sporadic

inglastan ki tar shahzada landi laqab *n* انلستان كتر شاهزاده لاند لقب duke

inhidam *n.* انهدام subversion

inhiraf *n* انحراف lapse

inhisar laral *v. i.* انحصارلرل depend

inhisar laroonkay *n* انحصارلرونكى dependant

inhisaree eemteeyaz akheystal *v.t.* انحصاري؛امتيازاخستل monopolize

inhisaree haq warkawal *v.t.* انحصاري؛حق؛وركول patent

inhitat; kamzortya *n* انحطاط، كمزورتيا wane

inikas *n.* انعكاس reflection

inikas *n.* انعكاس reflex

inikasee *a.* انعكاسي reflective

injeel *n* انجيل bible

injeel *n.* انجيل gospel

injeel *n.* انجيل testament

inkar *v.t.* انكار gainsay

inkar *n* انكار abnegation

inkar *n.* انكار repudiation

inkar kawal *v. t* انكاركول abnegate

inkar kawal *v. t.* انكاركول deny

inkar kawal *v.t.* انكاركول renounce

inkar kawal *v.t.* انكاركول repudiate

inqilabee *a.* انقلابي revolutionary

inqilabee wagaray *n* revolutionary

insan *n.* انسان man

insan pal *n.* انسان؛پال philanthropist

insan pala *a.* انسان؛پاله philanthropic

insanawal; saray kawal *v.t.* انسانول؛سى كول humanize

insanee *a.* انساني human

insanee *a.* انساني manlike

insanee ghag *n.* انساني غ voice

insanee nizhad *n.* انساني نژاد mankind

intikhab *n.* انتخاب selection

intikhabatee hoza *n* انتخاباتي حوزه constituency

intikhabawal *v. t* انتخابول constitute

intikhabee *a.* انتخابي selective

intikhabee plaway *n* انتخابي پلاوى electorate

intiqad *n* انتقاد criticism

intiqal keydoonkay *a.* انتقال كدونكى transferable

intiqal; badloon *n.* انتقال،بدلون transition

intishar; tableegh *n.* انتشار،تبليغ propagation

intizam kawal *v.t.* انتظام كول manage

intizar *n.* انتظار wait

intizar eestal *v.i.* انتظار ايستل wait

intizar eystal *v.t.* انتظار استل await

inzimam; zameema kawana *n* انضمام،ضميمه كونه annexation

iqama; yawa zangaray wuzeeyat *n.* اقامه،يو هانى و ضعيت pose

iqrar *n* اقرار confession

iqrar kawal *v. t.* اقرار كول confess

iqrarawal *v.t.* اقرارول admit

iqtibas; bayan *n.* اقتباس،بيان quotation

iqtisad *n* اقتصاد economy

iqtisad pohana *n.* اقتصاد پوهنه economics

iqtisadee *a* اقتصادي economic

iqtisadee parsob *n.* اقتصادي پسوب inflation

irada kawal *v.t.* اراده كول intend

irada; nyat *n* اراده،نيت animus

iradee *a* ارادي deliberate

irtiash *v.i.* ارتعاش shiver

irtibat *n.* ارتباط correlation

irtibat laral *v.t.* ارتباط لرل associate

irtibat laral *v.t.* ارتباط لرل relate

irtibat warkawal *v.t.* ارتباط ور كول correlate

irtibat; nisbat *n.* ارتباط،نسبت relation

isam; noom *n.* اسم،نوم noun

ishal *n* اسهال diarrhoea

ishara *n.* اشاره gesture

ishara *n.* اشاره hint

ishara kawal *v.i* اشاره كول hint

ishara kawoonkay *a.* اشاره كوونكى indicative

ishara kawoonkay *n.* اشاره كوونكى indicator

ishara warkawal *v.t.* اشاره ور كول beckon

ishara; khabartya *n.* اشاره،خبرتيا intimation

ishara; peywand *n.* اشاره،پيوند slur

ishqeeya; jinsee *a* عشقيه،جنسي erotic

ishtiba kawal *v.i.* اشتباه كول fumble

isla *n.* اصلاح reformation

isla *n.* اصلاح modification

isla kawal *v.t.* اصلاح كول modify

isla kawal *v.t.* اصلاح كول restore

isla kawal v.t. اصلاح کول revise

isla kawal v.i. اصلاح کول rectify

isla kawoonkay n. اصلاح کوونکی reformatory

isla kawoonkay a اصلاح کوونکی reformatory

isla; naway nazar n. اصلاح؛نوی نظر revision

isla; samowoonkay n. اصلاح؛ سموونکی rectification

israf n اسراف extravagance

israf kawal v.t. اسراف کول lavish

israf kawoonkay a اسراف کوونکی extravagant

israfee a. اسرافي lavish

israr n. اصرار insistence

israr n. اصرار persistence

israr kawal v.i. اصرار کول haggle

israr kawal v.t. اصرار کول insist

israr kawal v.i. اصرار کول persist

israr kawoonkay a. اصرار کوونکی insistent

israr kawoonkay shakhs n. اصرار کوونکی شخص stickler

isteyhsalee adj. استحصالي corrosive

istiara n. استعاره metaphor

istifa n. استعفا resignation

istifada n استفاده gain

istikhbarat n. استخبارات intelligence

istikhdamawal v. t استخدامول engage

istikhdamowoonkay n استخداموونکی employer

istimal n. استعمال use

istimbat n. استنباط inference

istiqamat laral v.i. استقامت لرل persevere

istiqbal kawal v.t استقبال کول welcome

istirahat n. استراحت repose

istirahat kawal v.i. استراحت کول repose

istisna n استثناء exception

itaat n. اطاعت obedience

itaat n. اطاعت subordination

itaat n. اطاعت subjection

itaat n. اطاعت subjugation

itaat kawal v.t. اطاعت کول subordinate

itaat kawoonkay n اطاعت کوونکی subordinate

italat n. عطالت inertia

itehadeeya n. اتحادیه league

itifaqan adv. اتفاقا occasionally

itifaqee a. اتفاقي occasional

itihadeeya n. اتحادیه union

itisal n. اتصال juncture

itmaynan n. اطمینان surety

itminan n اطمینان confidence

izafee a اضافي extra

izafee a اضافي spare

izafee a. اضافي superfluous

izafee a. اضافي supplementary

izafee a. اضافي additional

izafee adj اضافي adscititious

izafee kar n اضافي کار overtime

izafee kar kawal v.i. اضافي کار کول overwork

izafee maleeya n. اضافي ماليه surcharge

izafee maleeya lagawal v.t. اضافي
ماليه لول surcharge

izhar n. اظهار expression

iztirab n اضطراب distress

iztirab n اضطراب unrest

iztirab n. اضطراب panic

J

jaba n جبه bog

jaba n جعبه cist

jaba ki doobeydal v.i جبه کوبدل
bog

jadoo n. جادو witchcraft

jadoo n. جادو witchery

jadoo kawal v.t جادوکول bewitch

jadooyee a. جادويي magical

jadwalee a. جدولي tabular

jag awaza zang n. زنگ آواز جگ gong

jagara n. جگ warfare

jagara kawal v.t. جگ کول wage

jagara pal a. جگ پال warlike

jageerdarana a. جايردارانه
manorial

jagh n. جغ yoke

jagra n جگ combat1

jagra kawoonkay n جگ کوونکی
belligerent

jagra mar n جگمار combatant1

jagra mar a. جگمار militant

jagra maree a. جگماری combatant

jagra maree n جگماری militant

jagramaree n جگماري belligerency

jagran n جگن major

jagrawoo a جاوو bellicose

jagrayeez; jagrawoo a جگييز؛جاوو
belligerent

jagtooran; mashar n. جگتورن؛مشر
captain

jahalat n. جهالت nescience

jahayz n جهز dowry

jahayz n. pl جهز paraphernalia

jai n. ج hemisphere

jajoora n. ججوره craw

jaka n. جکه jerk

jakat n. جاک jacket

jakat dawla kamees n جاکوله
کميس blouse

jal n. جال net

jal n. جال network

jal ghorawal v.t. جال غورول net

jal kari n جعل کاری forgery

jal saz n. جعل ساز counterfeiter

jal ta warta a. جال ته ورته webby

jal; looma n. جال،لومه mesh

jal; tanasta n. جال،تنسته web

jala kawal v. t جلاکول divide

jala kawal v.t. جلاکول insulate

jala kawal v.t. جلاکول seclude

jala kawal v.t. جلاکول separate

jala kawal v.t. جلاکول sequester

jala kawal n. جلاکونه severance

jala kawana n. جلاکونه pick

jala kawoonkay n. جلاکوونکی
insulator

jala keydal v. i. جلاکدل depart

jala keydana n جلاکدنه departure

jala keydoonkay a. جلاکدونکی
separable

jala shaway *a.* جلاشوی secluded

jala shaway *a.* جلاشوی separate

jalad; tameelawoonkay *n.* جلاد، تعميلوونکی executioner

jalatob *n.* جلاتوب seclusion

jalatob *n.* جلاتوب segregation

jalatob *n.* جلاتوب separation

jalawatan kawal *v. t* جلاوطن کول exile

jalawatnee *n.* جلاوطني exile

jalib *a.* جالب interested

jalibeeyat *n.* جالبيت interest

jalwa warkawal *v.t* جلوه ورکول foil

jam *n.* جام goblet

jama *a.* جمع plural

jama kawal *v.t.* جمع کول total

jama kawal *v.t.* جمع کول sum

jamadar *n* جمعدار foreman

jamay *a* جامع overall

jamay *n.* جامع precise

jamhooree *a* جمهوري democratic

jamhooree *n.* جمهوري republic

jami *n.* جام clothes

jami *n* جام dress

jami aghostal *v. t* جاماغوستل clothe

jami aghostal *v. t* جاماغوستل dress

jamid *a.* جامد solid

jamieeyat *n.* جامعيت universality

janab *n* جناب excellency

janat *n.* جنت heaven

janat *n.* جنت paradise

janayat *n* جنايت crime

janayat kar *n* جنايت کار criminal

janayatkar; bey nazma *a.* جنايتکار، بنظمه wanton

janayee *a* جنايي criminal

janeen *n* جنين embryo

jang *n* جن battle

jang *n.* جن war

jangay; tar zangoonano land patloon *n. pl.* جانی، ترزنونانو لۀ پتلون shorts

jangee *a.* جني martial

jangee beyray *n* جني بېړۍ fleet

jangee chal *n.* جني چال strategem

jangee krachay *n* جني کراچۍ chariot

jangeydal *v. i.* جندل battle

jangeydal *v. t.* جندل combat

jangeydal *v.i.* جندل militate

jangeydal *v.i.* جندل war

jangyalay *n.* جنيالی warrior

janjal *n* جنجال affray

janjal *n* جنجال botheration

janjal joreydal; tasadum kawal *v.t.* جنجال جودل، تصادم کول rush

janjal kawal *v.i.* جنجال کول quarrel

janjal; hasa aw hand *n.* جنجال، هه او هاند strife

janjalee *a.* جنجالي quarrelsome

jar wahal *v. t* جاروهل blare

jarahee *n.* جراحي surgery

jaraseem *n.* جراثيم germ

jaraseem *n.* جراثيم leech

jaraseem *n.* جراثيم parasite

jaraseem wazhoonkay *n.* جراثيم وژونکی germicide

jarchee; aylchee *n.* جارچي، الچي herald

jaree *a* جاري continuous

jaree *n.* جاري instant

jaree *a.* جاري affluent

jareeda *n.* جريده journal

jareema *n* جريمه fine

jareema *n.* جريمه penalty

jareema kawal *v.t* جريمه کول fine

jareema kawal *v.t.* جريمه کول penalize

jareema warkawal *v.t* جريمه ورکول forfeit

jarga *n.* جره assembly

jaroo *n* جارو broom

jaryan *n* جريان circulation

jaryan *n.* جريان progress

jaryan laral *v.i.* جريان لرل progress

jashan *n.* جشن ceremony

jashn *n* جشن carnival

jasoor *adj.* جسور hardy

jasoos *n* جاسوس emissary

jawahirat ploranzay *n.* جواهرات پلورنی jewellery

jaydad *n* جايداد estate

jaydad *n.* جايداد property

jazam *n.* جذام leprosy

jazamee *n.* جذامي leper

jazamee *a.* جذامي leprous

jazayee *a.* جزايي penal

jazba *n* جذبه emotion

jazba *n.* جذبه passion

jazba; bey hokhee *n.* جذبه؛بهوي trance

jazbatee *a* جذباتي emotional

jazbatee *a.* جذباتي passionate

jazbawal *v.t* جذبول absorb

jazbawal *v. t* جذبول devour

jazbawal; gharqawal *v.t.* جذبول؛ غرقول immerse

jeel *n.* جيل lake

jeereb *n.* جريب acre

jeerebana *n.* جريبانه acreage

jeyb *n.* جب pocket

jeyb ki eekhodal *v.t.* جب کايودل pocket

jibran *n* جبران compensation

jibranawal *v.t* جبرانول compensate

jibranawal *v.t.* جبرانول recoup

jilogeeree *n.* جلويري repression

jins; qisam *n.* جنس؛قسم sort

jins; shahwat *n.* جنس؛شهوت sex

jinsee kamzortya *n.* جنسي کمزورتيا impotence

jisam warkawal *v. t.* جسم ورکول embody

jisman; yaw zay *adv.* جسم؛يوای bodily

jismee twan *n.* جسمي توان fortitude

jogha *n* جوغه aigrette

jola; obdoonkay *n.* جولا؛اوبدونکی weaver

jongara *a.* جونه shanty

joodar; tor ghanam *n.* جودر؛تور غنم rye

jooma *n.* جمعه Friday

joomat *n.* جومات mosque

joowar *n.* جوار maize

joowaray *n* جواری corn

jor *n* جو make

jor jaray *n.* جوجای accord

jor jaray *n.* جوجای harmony

jor jaray kawal *v.i.* جوجای کول tamper

jor jaray kawoonkay *n.* جوجای کوونکی negotiator

jor jaree *n.* جوجاي assent

jor jaree kawal *v.i.* جوجاي کول assent

jora *n* جوه couple

jora *n* جوه mate

jora *n.* جوه pair

jora *n.* جوه mediation

jora kawal *v. t* جوه کول couple

jora kawal *v.t.* جوه کول mate

jora kawal *v.i.* جوه کول mediate

jora keydal *v.t.* جوه کدل pair

jora; ghbargolay *n.* جوه؛غبرولی twin

jora; naqlee *a* جوه؛نقلي duplicate

jorabey *n.* جوراب sock

jorakht *n* جوت build

jorakht *n* جوت formation

jorakht *n.* جوت structure

jorakht aw tarkeeb *n.* جوتاو ترکیب norm

jorakhtaneez *a.* جوتیز structural

jorat; himat *n.* جرأت؛همت daring

jorawal *v. t.* جوول construct

jorawal *v.t.* جوول make

jorawal; wadanawal *v.t* جوول؛ ودانول set

jorawana; sakht *n* جوونه؛ساخت fabrication

jorjaray; astogna *n.* جوجای؛استونه settlement

jorowoonkay *n.* جووونکی maker

josh *n* جوش boil

josh aw kharosh *n* جوش او خروش enthusiasm

josh aw kharosh *n.* جوش او شوق verve

joshawoonkay *n* جوشوونکی boiler

judagana *n.* جدالانه aside

juft; jora *a* جفت؛جوه even

juram *n.* جرم guilt

juram *n.* جرم offence

juz *n* جز portion

juz; wasayil *n* جز؛وسایل appurtenance

juzee *n.* جزیي nuance

juzyee jagara *n.* جزیي جه skirmish

juzyee rang *n.* جزیي رن tinge

juzyee rang warkawal *v.t.* جزیي رن ورکول tinge

K

ka kor khaza *n.* د کوره matron

ka sa ham *conj.* کهههم albeit

ka sa ham *conj* کهههم however

ka sa ham *conj.* کهههم nevertheless

ka sa ham *conj.* کهههم notwithstanding

ka sa ham *adv.* کهههم though

ka sa ham *conj.* کهههم although

ka sa ham *conj.* کهههم whereas

ka; ay kash *conj.* که؛ای کاش if

kab *n* کب fish

kab neewal *v.i* کب نیول fish

kab neewoonkay *n* کب نیوونکی fisherman

kabar *n.* کبر pride

kabar kawal *v.t.* کبر کول pride

kabarjan *a.* کبرجن arrogant

kabarjan *a.* کبرجن haughty

kabarjan; adee *v* کبرجن؛عادي snobbish

kach; miqdar *n* کچ؛مقدار amount

kach; miqdar *n.* کچ؛مقدار quantum

kach; miqyas *n* کچ؛مقیاس criterion

kachar *n.* کچر mule

kada kawal *v. i* که کول decamp

kada kawal *v.i.* که کول migrate

kadar kawal; daghee kawal *v.t.* کدر کول،داغي کول tarnish

kadoo *n.* کدو pumpkin

kadwal *n.* کوال immigrant

kadwal *n.* کوال migrant

kadwalee *n.* کوالي migration

kadwaltob *n.* کوالتوب immigration

kafan waraghostal *v.t.* کفن وراغوستل shroud

kafan; pokh *n.* کفن؛پو shroud

kafara *n.* کفاره atonement

kafara warkawal *v.i.* کفاره ورکول atone

kafee *a* کافي enough

kafee keydal *v.i.* کافي کدل suffice

kafee; poora *a.* کافي؛پوره sufficient

kafoor *n.* کافور camphor

kaga karkha *n* که کره slant

kagal; lookha *n.* کال،لوخه thatch

kagawana *n* کونه stoop

kageydal *v.i.* کدل stoop

kageydal *v.i.* کدل tilt

kageydal; kagawal *v. t* کدل، کول bend

kagh kagh kawal *v. i.* کاغ کاغ کول caw

kaghaz *n.* کاغذ paper

kaghaz bad *n.* کاغذباد kite

kagleych *n.* کلچ labyrinth

kagleych laroonkay *a.* کلچلرونکی tortuous

kahil *a.* کاهل indolent

kahil *n.* کاهل slothful

kahilee *n.* کاهلي sloth

kahintob; mulatob *n.* کاهنتوب، ملاتوب priesthood

kahkashan *n.* کهکشان galaxy

kajawa *n.* کجاوه sedan

kajeer *n.* کجیر vulture

kajoora *n.* کجوره palm

kakar *a.* کک infectious

kakar *a.* کک nasty

kakarawal *v.t.* ککول infect

kakarawal *v.i* ککول mess

kakarawal *v.t.* ککول muddle

kakari wahal *v. i* ککوهل cackle

kakartya *n.* ککتیا infection

kakhtay *a* کتنی downward

kakhtay *n* کت ark

kakhtay *n.* کت ship

kakhtay chalawal *v.i* کتچلول boat

kakhtay chalawal *v.i.* کتچلول navigate

kakhtay chalawoonkay *n.* کښ چلوونکی sailor

kakhtay ki tlal *v.i.* کښ کتلل sail

kal *n.* کال year

kala *n.* کلا castle

kala *n.* کلا fort

kala chi *conj.* کله چ when

kala chi *conj.* کله چ whereat

kala chi *conj.* کله چ while

kala chi *adv.* کله چي then

kala na kala *adv.* کله ناکله sometime

kalanay *a.* کلنی annual

kalanay *a.* کلنی yearly

kalanay moash *n.* کلنی معاش annuity

kalang; zanra *n* کلن؛زاه crane

kalay *n.* کلی village

kalbad peyzhandana *n.* کالبد پژندنه anatomy

kalbad; jorakht *n.* کالبد؛جوت skeleton

kalee *n* کالی clothing

kalee *n.* کالی garb

kalee *n.* کلی key

kalee aw saman *n.* کالي او سامان belongings

kalee weenzoonki khaza *n.* کالي وینونکه laundress

kalee; marham *n* کالي؛مرهم dressing

kaleesa *n.* کلیسا church

kaleesha aw feelam barabarawal *v.t.* کلیشه او فیلم برابرول stereotype

kaleesha; da kaleeshey jorawani fan *n.* کلیشه؛دکلیشې جوړونفن stereotype

kaleewal *n.* کلیوال peasant

kaleewal *a.* کلیوال rural

kaleewal *n.* کلیوال villager

kaleewal saray *n* کلیوال سی rustic

kaleewal zhwand kawal *v.t.* کلیوال ژوند کول rusticate

kaleewala khooy *n.* کلیواله خوی peasantry

kaleewalee banra warkawana *n.* کلیوالي بهوروکوونه rustication

kaleewalee kor *n.* کلیوالي کور villa

kaleeza *n.* کلیزه almanac

kaleeza; har kal *n.* کلیزه؛هرکال anniversary

kalhindara *n.* کالهنداره calendar

kali pa aghostal *v.t* کالی پهاغوستل garb

kalma bandee kawal *v.t.* کلمه بندي کول phrase

kaltoor *n* کلتور culture

kam *a.* کم lesser

kam arzakhta *a* کم ارزته economical

kam arzakhta seez *n.* کم ارزتهیز trifle

kam asal *a.* کم اصل ignoble

kam asla *a* کم اصله bastard

kam kharsa *a.* کم خره inexpensive

kam khorakee *n.* کم خوراکي malnutrition

kam na kam had *a* کم نه کم حد minimum

kam oomra *n* کم عمره young

kam ratlana *n.* کمراتلنه shortcoming

kam; lag *a.* کم،لگ minor

kam; naseez *a.* کم،ناییز slight

kamakht *n* کمت dearth

kamakht *n* کمت decrease

kamakht *n.* کمت lack

kamakht *n.* کمت shortage

kamakht *n.* کمت rabate

kamakht *n.* کمت mitigation

kamakht; sapma *n.* کمت،سپما retrenchment

kaman *n.* کمان arch

kaman *n* کمان bow

kamanee lara *n* کماني لاره arcade

kamar band *n* کمربند belt

kamarband taral *v.t* کمربندتل girdle

kamawal *v.t.* کمول assuage

kamawal *v. t* کمول decrease

kamawal *v. t* کمول dwindle

kamawal *v. i* کمول ebb

kamawal *v.t.* کمول lack

kamawal *v.t* کمول lessen

kamawal *v.t.* کمول reduce

kamawl *v.t.* کمول deduct

kamay *n.* کمی reduction

kamedonkay *a* کمیدونکی flexible

kameen warta neewal *n.* کمین ورتەنیول ambush

kameenatob *n.* کمینەتوب meanness

kamees *n.* کمیس shirt

kamees landi aghostal keydoonkay khazeena laman *n.* کمیس لانداغوستل کدونکینەلمن petticoat

kameydana *n* کمدنه ebb

kamil *a.* کامل full

kamil *a* کامل utter

kamil; mukamal *a.* کامل،مکمل implicit

kamila khwakhee *n* کاملەخوي bliss

kamila mati *n* کاملەماتۍ rout

kamilan *adv* کاملاً downright

kamilan *adv.* کاملاً utterly

kamilan *adv.* کاملاً wholly

kamilan roond *n.* کاملاوند purblind

kamilan; hamda ranga *adv* کاملاً؛ همدارنه even

kamooneezam *n* کمونیزم communism

kamtar *a.* کمتر inferior

kamtaree *n.* کمتري inferiority

kamyab *a.* کمیاب scarce

kamyab *a.* کامیاب well-to-do

kamyabay lapara sakht intizar kawal *v. t* کامیابلپارەسخت انتظار کول bide

kamyabee *n* کامیابي win

kamyabeydal *v.i.* کامیابدل prosper

kamyabeydal *v.t.* کامیابدل win

kamzoray *a* کمزوری feeble

kamzoray *v.t.* کمزوری کول handicap

kamzoray *a.* کمزوری weak

kamzoray *n.* کمزوری weakling

kamzoray aw teet awaz n.
كمزورى‌اوېآواز undertone
kamzoray insan a. كمزورى‌انسان
sickly
kamzoray keydal v.i كمزورى‌كدل
faint
kamzoray keydal v.i. كمزورى‌كدل
wane
kamzoray; bey zra a كمزورى؛بزه
faint
kamzoree n. كمزورې weakness
kamzortia n. كمزورتيا incapacity
kamzortya n كمزورتيا debility
kamzortya n. كمزورتيا sickness
kamzortya n. كمزورتيا swoon
kan keendoonkay n. كان كيندونكى
miner
kan peyzhandana n. كان‌پژندنه
mineralogy
kan peyzhandoonkay n. كان
پژندونكى mineralogist
kan; madan n كان؛معدن mine
kanastal v.t. كنستل dig
kanaya; hikayat n. كنايه؛حكايت
allegory
kanda n. كنده cavity
kanda n كنده ditch
kanda n. كنده pit
kanda n. كنده moat
kanda keendal v.t. كنده‌كيندل
moat
kandak n كنك battalion
kanee dabar n. كانى‌بر mineral
kanee dabara n. كانى‌بره ore
kanee kheekha n. كانى‌يه mica

kanee; madanee a كانى؛معدنى
mineral
kanfarans n. كانفرانس convention
kangal keydal v.i. كنل‌كدل freeze
kangi n كاز vomit
kangi kawal v.t. كازكول vomit
kanjkaw; daqeeq a كنجكاو؛دقيق
curious
kanjoos n. كنجوس miser
kanray n. كانى rock
kanree dabari raistal v.i. كانى‌بر
راائستل quarry
kanzal kawal v.t. كنل‌كول scold
kar n. كار function
kar n. كار work
kar akheestana n. كاراخيستنه
usage
kar bandeyz kawal; weeshtal v.t.
كاربندزكول؛وېشتل strike
kar kawal v.i كاركول function
kar kawal v.t. كاركول work
kar poh n كارپوه expert
kar ta hasawal v. t كارته‌هول
employ
kar; chara n. كار؛چاره task
kara a كره exact
kara katana n. كره‌كتنه perusal
kara katana n. كره‌كتنه scrutiny
kara katana kawal v.t. كره‌كتنه
كول scrutinize
karakht a. كرخت obtuse
karal v. t كرل cultivate
karal; nyalawal v.t. كرل؛نيالول
plant
karana n كرنه agriculture
karaneez a كرنيز agricultural

karaneeza zmaka *adj* کرنیزهمکه arable

karanpohana *n.* کرنپوهنه agronomy

karaw *n.* کاو torment

karaw; la zehmata dak kar *n.* کاو،لهزحمتهکـکار toil

karaw; mazdooree *n.* کاو،مزدوري labour

karawal *v.t.* کارول utilize

karawal *v.i.* کول pine

karawal *v.t.* کول torment

karawal; amal ki rawastal *v.t.* کارول؛عمل کراوستل implement

karawalay *n.* کرهوالی precision

karawana *n.* کاروونه utilization

karawona *n.* کارونه implement

karay *n.* ک curl

karay *n.* ک link

karay *n.* ک ring

karay; dawra *n.* ک؛دوره round

karaya *n* کرایه fare

karaya *n.* کرایه rent

karaya kawal *v.t* کرایهکول hire

karaya kawal *v.t.* کرایهکول rent

karaya; eejara *n.* کرایه،اجاره hire

karee baheer *n.* کاريبهیر proceeding

karee dawra *n.* کاريدوره process

karee khoona *n.* کاريخونه studio

karee plan *n.* کاريپلان programme

karee plan jorawal *v.t.* کاريپلان جوول programme

kareekatoor *n.* کاریکاور cartoon

kareeza nakha *n.* کیزهنه ringlet

kareydoonkay *a.* کاردونکی practicable

kargadan *n.* کرگدن rhinoceros

kargar *n.* کارګر worker

kargheyran *a.* کرغن obnoxious

kargheyran *a.* کرغن offensive

karhanra; baghbanee *n.* کرهه، باغباني husbandry

karkay *n.* کک window

karkha *n.* کره line

karkhana *n* کارخانه factory

karmand *n* کارمند employee

karmand *n.* کارمند workman

karmandan *n.* کارمندان staff

karmandan *n.* کارمندان personnel

karpoh *n.* کارپوه detective

karpoh *a.* کارپوه skilful

karpoh *n.* کارپوه specialist

karpoh shakhs *n.* کارپوهشخص tactician

karray *n* کری cricket

kart; panra *n.* کارت،پله card

kartoon *n* کارون comic

kartoos; marmay *n.* کارتوس،مرم cartridge

karwanda *n.* کرونده plantation

karwandagar *n* کروندر farmer

karwandagar *n.* کروندر ploughman

karzay *n.* کارای workshop

karzay; daftar *n.* کارای،دفتر office

kasa *n* کاسه bowl

kasab; danda *n.* کسب،دنده profession

kasabee; mahir *a.* كسبي،ماهر professional

kasad; rakood *n.* كساد،ركود stagnation

kasafat *n.* كثافت garbage

kasafat aw chatalay *a.* كثافات او چل paltry

kasar; mateydana *n.* كسر،ماتدنه fraction

kasat akheystal *v.t.* كسات اخستل avenge

kasat akheystal *v.t.* كسات اخستل revenge

kasat; ghach *n.* كسات،غچ revenge

kashar *n.* كشر junior

kashee kawdoray *n.* كاشي كودوى tile

kashee kawdoray lagawal *v.t.* كاشي كودوى لول tile

kashish *n.* كشش gravitation

kashish *n.* كشش traction

kashmalay *n.* كشمالى basil

kashogha *n.* كاشوغه spoon

kasora *n.* كوه bag

kasora *n.* كوه pouch

kasora ki achawal *v. i.* كوه كاچول bag

kasora laroonkay *n.* كوه لرونكى marsupial

kata pri eekhodal *v.t.* كته پرايودل panel

katal *v.i* كتل look

katal aw palatal *v.t.* كتل او پلل peruse

katal; leedal *v.t.* كتل،ليدل see

katana *a* كتنه look

katanee tokar *n.* كتاني وكر linen

katar pri ragarzawal *v.t* كاره پر راوول fence

katar; leeka *n.* كتار،ليكه queue

katara *n* كاره fence

katara *n.* كاره railing

kateeba *n.* كتيبه inscription

katoleek eesayee *a.* كاتوليك عيسائ catholic

katoonkay *n.* كتونكى on-looker

katoray *n* كورى beaker

kawal *v. t* كول do

kawsay *n* كو lock

kawsheyr *n.* كوشر solder

kawsheyrawal *v.t.* كوشرول solder

kawtara *n.* كوتره culvert

kawtara *n* كوتره dove

kawtara *n.* كوتره pigeon

kayfeeyat *n.* كفيت modality

kayfeeyat *n.* كفيت phenomenon

kayk *n.* كك cake

kayla *n.* كله banana

kayla *n.* كله plantain

kaynat *n.* كائنات universe

kedonkay *a* كيدونكى feasible

keemyagaree *n.* كيماري alchemy

keena *n.* كينه spite

keena *n.* كينه rancour

keena *n.* كينه vengeance

keena kakh *a* كينه ك envious

keena satal *v. t* كينه ساتل envy

keendana *n* كيندنه dig

keendana *n.* كيندنه excavation

keendawal *v. t.* كيندول excavate

keendoonkay *n.* كيندونكى pitman

keenr *a.* كي left

keenr lasay *a.* کیلاسی sinister
keesa *n.* کیسه tale
keesa *n.* کیسه story
keesa kawal *v.t.* کیسه کول narrate
keesa leekoonkay *n.* کیسه لیکونکی novelist
keesa; bayan *n.* کیسه،بیان narration
keetab *n.* کتابي bookish
keetab lostay *a.* کتاب لوستی studious
keetabgotay *n* کتابوی booklet
keetabploray *n.* کتاب پلوری stationer
keetabtoon *n.* کتابتون library
keydal *v. i* کدل become
keydal (da shtoon rabita fayl) *v.t.* کدل(دشتون رابطه فعل) be
keyday *n* bundle
keyday shee; shayad *adv.* کدای شي،شايد perhaps
keydoon *n.* کدون possibility
keydoonay *a.* کدونی likely
keydoonay *a.* کدونی possible
keydoonay *a.* کدونی workable
keymya poh *n.* کمیاپوه chemist
keymya pohana *n.* کمیاپوهنه chemistry
keymyayee *a.* کیمیايي chemical
keymyayee mawad *n.* کیمیايي مواد chemical
kha *a.* ه good
kha *adv.* ه well
kha arzakht warkawal *v.t.* ه ارزښت ورکول treasure
kha noom laral *v.t.* ه نوم لرل repute

kha noom; aytibar *n.* ه نوم،اعتبار reputation
kha nyat *n.* ه نیت goodwill
kha raghalay; har kalay *n.* ه راغلی،هر کلی reception
kha shagoon *n.* ه شون mascot
kha wada kawal *v.i.* ه وده کول thrive
kha walay *n.* ه والی goodness
kha; ghwara; nayk *a.* ه،غوره،نک well
khabar panra *n* خبرپاه bulletin
khabar panra *n.* خبرپاه prospectus
khabara oogdawana *n.* خبره اودونه verbosity
khabara ya lost takrarawal *v.t.* خبره يالوست تکرارول repeat
khabardaray *n.* خبرداری caution
khabardaray warkawal *v. t.* خبرداری ورکول caution
khabardaray warkawal *v.t* خبرداری ورکول forewarn
khabardaree *n.* خبرداری premonition
khabardaree *n.* خبرداری warning
khabardaree warkawal *v.t.* خبرداری ورکول warn
khabari *n* خبر talk
khabari atari *n.* خبراتر chat1
khabari atari kawal *v. i.* خبراتر کول chat2
khabari atari kawal *v. t* خبراتر کول communicate
khabari atari kawal *v.t.* خبراتر کول converse
khabartya *n* خبرتیا cognizance
khabartya *a.* خبرتیا notice

khabartya; aylan *n.* خبرتيا؛اعلان announcement

khabaryal *n.* خبريال correspondent

khabaryal *n.* خبريال reporter

khabasat *n.* خباثت malignity

khabees *a.* خبيث malignant

khabees *a.* خبيث wicked

khabrawal *v.t.* خبرول apprise

khabrawal *v.t.* خبرول inform

khabrawal *v.t.* خبرول notice

khabrawana *n.* خبروونه notification

khabrawona *n.* خبرونه news

khabrawoonkay *n.* خبروونکی informer

khabroona *n. pl.* خبرونه tidings

khach pach kawal *v.t.* خچ پچ کول squash

khach pach shaway *n* خچ پچ شوی squash

khachantob *n.* خچنتوب insanity

khadim *a.* خادم ministrant

khadim *n.* خادم steward

khadim; karwandagar *n.* خادم؛ کروندګر yeoman

khafa; nakam *a.* خفه،ناکام unhappy

khageena *n.* خاينه omelette

khaghalay *n.* اغلی Messrs

khaghalay *n.* اغلی mister

khaghalay; hazrat *n.* اغلی؛حضرت sir

khaj *n* خج accent

khaka *n* خاکه contour

khaka *n* خاکه diagram

khakhawal *v. t.* خول bury

khakhowana *n* خوونه burial

khakhta *n.* ختـه adobe

khakhta *n* ختـه brick

khakrayz *n.* خاکرزـ mound

khaksar *a.* خاکسار humble

khaksaree *n.* خاکساري humility

khal *n.* خال mole

khal *n.* خال tattoo

khal khal *n.* خال‌خال mottle

khal wahal *v.t.* خال‌وهل inoculate

khal wahal *v.i.* خال‌وهل tattoo

khal wahana *n.* خال‌وهنه inoculation

khalee; pooda *a.* خالي؛پوده hollow

khaleefa *n.* خليفه prelate

khaleej *n.* خليج gulf

khaliq *n* خالق creator

khalis *a* خالص net

khalq *n.* خلک people

kham *a* خام crude

kham *a.* خام raw

kham aw nawara *a.* خام‌او‌ناوه maladroit

khamar *n* امار dragon

khamdar *adj* خم‌دار anfractuous

khameera *n.* خميره paste

khamosh *a.* خاموش mum

khamosh *a.* خاموش serene

khamosh *a.* خاموش taciturn

khamosh *a.* خاموش mute

khamosh *a.* خاموش reticent

khamosh aw janjal sakha leyri prot insan *n.* خاموش‌او‌جنجال خه‌لرپروت‌انسان stoic

khamoshawal *v. t.* خاموشول calm
khamoshawal *v.i* خاموشول hush
khamoshawal *v.t.* خاموشول lull
khamoshawal *v.t.* خاموشول pacify
khamoshawal *v.t.* خاموشول slake
khamoshee *n.* خاموشي calm
khamoshee *n.* خاموشي stillness
khamoshee *n.* خاموشي reticence
khamosheydal *v.i.* خاموشدل subside
khand darawal; katara tri tawowal *v.t* خندرول؛کاره تر تاوول hurdle2
khand keydal; bandawal *v.t* خندکدل؛بندول block
khand keydana *n.* خندکدنه impediment
khand ya katara ratawowal *v.t* خنياکاره راتاوول hedge
khand; katara *n.* خند؛کاره hedge
khand; katara tawowan *n.* خند؛کاره تاوونه hurdle1
khand; muzahimat *n.* خند؛مزاحمت hindrance
khanda *n.* خندا laugh
khanda *n.* خندا smile
khandal *v.i* خندل laugh
khandan *a.* خندان cheerful
khandan *adj.* خندان convivial
khandawoonkay *a* خندونکی comic
khandawoonkay *a* خندونکی comical
khandawoonki hunaree nandara warandi kawal *v.t.* خندونکي هنري نندارهواندکول parody

khandawoonki nandara *n.* خندونکننداره comedy
khandoonkay *a.* خندونکی jocular
khandoonkay *a.* خندونکی laughable
khandowoonkay *n.* خندونکننداره mime
khandowoonkay *n.* خندونکی funny
khandowoonki nandara *n* خندونکننداره farce
khangar wazma *a.* خانوزمه ticklish
khanjar *n.* خنجر dagger
khanqa *n.* خانقا abbey
khanqa *n.* خانقا cloister
khanqa *n.* خانقا monastery
khap; asar *n.* خاپ؛اثر trace
khapa *a.* خپه sad
khapa kawal *v. t* خپهکول displease
khapa kawal *v.t.* خپهکول sadden
khapa kawoonkay *a.* خپهکوونکی muggy
khapara *n.* خپه paw
khaparak *n* اپرک bat
khapeyray *n* اپر fairy
khapgan *n* خپان displeasure
khapgan *n.* خپان sorrow
khapgan kawal *v.i.* خپانکول regret
khapgan; pkheymanee *n* خپان؛پماني regret
khapori *n* خاپو crawl
khapori kawal *v. t* خاپوکول crawl
khar *n.* خر ass
khar *n* خر donkey

khoosa kawal; soolawal v. t خوسا کول،سولول erode

khooshaya n خوشایه dung

khooshbooya a. خوشبویه fragrant

khooy n خوی conduct

khooy n. خوی temperament

khor n. خور sister

khora deyr adv. خورار full

khora deyr a. خورار immense

khora deyr a. خورار superabundant

khorak n. خوراک meal

khorawal v.t. خورول jog

khorma; neyta n خرما؛نه‌یه date

khorwa n خوروا broth

khorwa n. خوروا soup

khorwa pakhowoonkay n. خوروا پخوونکی stew

khorwalee n. خورولي sisterhood

khosa a. خوسا morbid

khosh khalqa a. خوش‌خلقه affable

khoshal a. خوشال glad

khoshala a. خوشاله gay

khoshala a. خوشاله jubilant

khoshala a خوشاله merry

khoshala a. خوشاله vivacious

khoshala kawal v.t. خوشاله‌کول gladden

khoshalawal v. t. خوشالول delight

khoshalee n خوشالي delight

khoshalee n. خوشالي frolic

khoshalee n. خوشالي hilarity

khoshalee n. خوشالي merriment

khoshalee kawal v.i. خوشاي‌کول frolic

khoshaleydal v.i. خوشالدل rejoice

khoshay kawal v.t. خوشی‌کول relinquish

khoshbakhtee adv. خوشبخت‌سره luckily

khoshbooya n. خوشبو odour

khoshbooya a. خوشبویه odorous

khoshbooya kawal v. t خوشبویه کول embalm

khoshhalee n. خوشحالي prosperity

khota; khuseeya n. خوه؛خصیه testicle

khotawal v.t. خوول agitate

khowal v.t. وول show

khowan n. وون tutor

khowana n. وونه show

khowana aw rozana n. وونه‌اوروزنه lore

khowana aw rozana n. وونه‌اوروزنه pedagogy

khowana kawal v.t. وونه‌کول instruct

khowana; tarbeeya n وونه؛تربیه education

khowanzay n. وونی school

khowanzay tar sara kawal v.t. وونی‌ترسره‌کول matriculate

khowoonkay n. وونکه governess

khowoonkay n. وونکی monitor

khowoonkay n. وونکی pedagogue

khowoonkay n. وونکی teacher

khozakht manoonkay a. خوت منونکی movable

khozakht warkawal v.t. خوت ورکول jostle

khozanda aw khwayanda shaga n. خونده‌اووینده‌شه quicksand

khozanda meela n. خوندهميله piston

khozanda waseela n. خوندهوسيله motor

khozawoonkay n. خووونکی mover

khpal haywad ta beyrta ragarzeydal v.t. خپلهوادتهبرته راورلدل repatriate

khpal haywad ta beyrta staneydana n. خپلهوادتهبرته ستندنه repatriation

khpal haywad ta staneydoonkay n خپلهوادتهبرتهستندونکی repatriate

khpal karay a. خپلکاری automatic

khpal lasay zhwand leek n. خپل لاسیژوندليک autobiography

khpal palana n. خپلپالنه nepotism

khpal saray a. خپلسری headstrong

khpal saray a. خپلسری perverse

khpal saray a. خپلسری stubborn

khpal saree n. خپلسري perversion

khpal saree; fasad n. خپلسري، فساد perversity

khpal zat n خپلذات ego

khpal; zanee a. خپلزاني own

khpala groha khkara kawal v.t. خپلهروهمکارهکول suggest

khpalawal v.t. خپلول adopt

khpalawana n خپلونه adoption

khpalawana n. خپلونه occupancy

khpalwak hukoomat a خپلواک حکومت autonomous

khpalwaka a. خپلواکه independent

khpalwaka hookoomat n خپلواکه حکومت autocracy

khpalwaka preykhodal v.t. خپلواکهپرودل indulge

khpalwaka preykhodalay shaway a. خپلواکهپرودلیشوی indulgent

khpalwakee n. خپلواکي independence

khpalwalee n. خپلولي kinship

khpalwan n. خپلوان kin

khpalwan n. خپلوان relative

khparandoy n. خپرندوی publisher

khparawal v. t خپرول broadcast

khparawana n خپرونه broadcast

khparaway n. خپراوی prevalance

khparaway; wayna n. خپراوی،ونا utterance

khpor shaway; parakh a. خپور شوی؛پراخ rampant

khuday n. خدای deity

khuday n. خدای god

khuday n. خدايي godhead

khuday di mal sha interj. خداید مل شه bye-bye

khuday di mal sha n. خدایدیمل شه adieu

khuday pa amanee interj. خدایپه اماني adieu

khuday warkaray shay n. خدای ورکیشی godsend

khulasa n خلاصه abstract

khulasa shaway a. خلاصهشوی compact

khulasa; iqtibas n خلاصه،اقتباس extract

khuloos n. خلوص sincerity

khush tabee *n.* خوش طبعي humour

khuskay *n.* خوسکی calf

khusoosee *a* خصوصي especial

khwa badoonkay *a.* خوابدوونکی odious

khwa; arkh *n.* خوا؛اخ side

khwabadee *n.* خوابدي resentment

khwaga jorowoonkay *n* خواه جوروونکی confectioner

khwaga patasa *n.* خوه پتاسه lollipop

khwaga sandara *n.* خوه سندره melody

khwagawal *v.t.* خوول sweeten

khwakh *a.* خو happy

khwakh tabee *n.* خو طبعي pleasantry

khwakhawal *v.t.* خوول like

khwakhee *n.* خوی revelry

khwakhee *n.* خوي happiness

khwakhee *n.* خوي jubilation

khwakhoogee *n* خواخوي condolence

khwakhoogee khkara kawal *v.i.* خواخوي کاره کول sympathize

khwalay *n.* خول cap

khwalay *n.* خول hat

khwaley *n.* خول sweat

khwaley keydal *v.i.* خوا کدل sweat

khwana *a.* خوانا legible

khwand *n* خوند smack

khwand akheystal *v. t* خونداخستل enjoy

khwand akheystal *v.t.* خونداخستل relish

khwand aw booy *n* خونداوبوی flavour

khwand warkawal *v.t.* خوندورکول please

khwandawar *a* خوندور delicious

khwandawar *n.* خوندور joyful, joyous

khwandawar *a.* خوندور tasteful

khwandawar *a.* خوندور tasty

khwandawar sharab *n.* خوندور شراب nectar

khwandee kawoonkay *n.* preservative

khwandee satal *v.t.* خوندي ساتل preserve

khwandeeyeena *n.* خونديينه preservation

khwandeyana; satana *n.* خونديينه؛ ساتنه sustenance

khwar *a.* خوار abject

khwar *a* خوار despicable

khwara *n* خواه food

khwara *n* خواه feed

khwara chamtoo kawal *v.* خواه چمتو کول cater

khwara warkawal *v.t* خواه ورکول feed

khwara warkawal *v.t.* خواه ورکول nourish

khwara; ghaza *n.* خواه؛غذا aliment

khwaral *v. t* خول eat

khwaranzay *n.* خونای restaurant

khwaree ke *a.* خواري کی laborious

khwasheenawoonkay *a* خواشينوونکی deplorable

khwasheenee *a* خواشيني cheerless

khwasheenee *a.* خواشيني sorry

khwasheenee kawal *v.t.* خواشينى كول incur

khwayand *a.* ويند slippery

khwayandoy *n.* ويندوى roller

khwayeyda *n.* ويدا jostle

khwayeydal *v.t.* ويدل glide

khwayeydal; khoshay kawal *v.i.* ويدل؛خوشى كول slip

khwayeydal; takar khwaral *v.t.* ويدل؛ٯكرخول trip

khwayeydana *n* ويدنه slide

khyal palana *n.* خيال پالنه idealism

khyal parasta *a.* خيال پرسته quixotic

khyal parastee *n.* خيال پرستي vagary

khyal; fikar *n.* خيال؛فكر idea

khyalee *a.* خيالي imaginary

khyalee *a.* خيالي utopian

khyalee banra warkawal *v.t.* خيالي بهور كول idealize

khyalee insan *n.* خيالي انسان idealist

khyalee insan *n.* خيالي انسان visionary

khyalee keesa *n.* خيالي كيسه myth

khyalee; mafroozee *a.* خيالي؛ مفروضي hypothetical

khyalee; tasawwuree *a.* خيالي؛ تصوري ideal

khyanat *n.* خيانت dishonesty

khyanat *n.* خيانت treachery

khyanat kawal *v.i.* خيانت كول conspire

ki; da ... pa lori *prep.* كه؛د___په لور at

kifayat; kafee miqdar *n.* كفايت؛ كافي مقدار sufficiency

kimkhab *n* كمخاب brocade

kinaya *n.* كنايه quibble

kinayawee; ramzee *a.* كنايوي؛ رمزي allusive

kinayee *a.* كنايي sarcastic

kitab peyzhand *n* كتاب پژاند bibliographer

kitab peyzhandana *+n* كتاب پژندنه bibliography

kitabgotay *n* كتابوى brochure

kkhata *adv* كته down

kkhata *a.* كته low

kkhata aw porta top *n* كته او پورته وپ skip

kkhata kawal *v.t.* كته كول lower

kkhata kawal; raparzawal *v. t* كته كول؛راپرول down

kkhata keydal *v. i.* كته كدل descend

kkhata keydana; nasal *n.* كته كدنه؛نسل descent

kkhata walay *n.* كته والى lowliness

kkheynastal *v.i.* كناستل sit

klak *a.* كلك adamant

klak *a* كلك concrete

klak *a* كلك firm

klak *a.* كلك tight

klak aw rasikh *a.* كلك او راسخ impenetrable

klak hod *n.* كلك هو vow

klakawal *v.t.* كلكول tighten

klakawal *v.t.* كلكول stiffen

klakawal; twanawal *v.t.* كلكول؛ توانول toughen

kochay *n.* کوچی nomad

kochay; kadwal *n.* کوچی؛کوال
vagabond

kochyana *a.* کوچیانه nomadic

kod warkawal *v.t.* کودورکول
manure

kod; ramzee shmeyra *n* کو؛رمزي
شمره code

kodgar *n.* کو ر magician

kodgar *n.* کودر sorcerer

kodgar *n.* کو ر wizard

kodgara *n.* کو ره witch

kodgaree *n.* کوري sorcery

kodi *n.* کوي talisman

kodi kawal *v.i.* کوکول conjure

kodi; dam durha *n.* کو؛دمدرها
amulet

kog *adj.* کو crump

kog rakog *n* کوراکو bight

kog stargay keydal *v.i.* کوستری
کدل squint

kog stargtob *n* کوسترتوب squint

kog walay *n* کووالی curve

kog walay warkawal *v. t* کووالی
ورکول curve

kog; da spee pa seyr yaw
zanawar *n.* کو؛دسپیپهرپوناور
hyaena, hyena

kogwalay *n* کووالی bend

kogwalay *n* کووالی bent

kogwalay *n.* کووالی tilt

kogwog tlal *v.t.* کوتلل wind

kokhakh *n.* کو quest

kokhakh kawal *v.t.* کوکول quest

kokhakh; fishar *n.* کو؛فشار stress

kolp *n.* کولپ lock

kolp bandawal *v. t* کولپبندول
bolt

kolp laroonki almaray *n.* کولپ
لرونکالمار locker

kolpawal *v.t* کولپول lock

kom *pron.* کوم which

kom kas *pron.* کومکس somebody

kom kas; yaw sok *pron.* کومکس؛
یووک someone

kom sa chi; har sa chi *pron.* کومه
چ؛هرهچ whatever

kom yaw chi *a* کومیوچ which

kom zay *adv.* کومهای whither

kom; kom seez *a.* کوم؛کومیز what

komakee *a.* کومکي helpful

komakee *a.* کومکي subsidiary

konatay *n* کونای buttock

konatay *n* کونای hip

kond *n.* کوز widower

konda *n* کونده bloc

konda *n.* کونده log

konda *n.* کونه widow

kondawal *v.t.* کونول widow

konj; gokha *n* کونج؛گوه angle

konr *a* کونز deaf

koocheydal *v.i.* کوچیدل immigrate

koochnay *n.* کوچنی babe

koochnay *n.* کوچنی baby

koochnay *a.* کوچنی small

koochnay *a.* کوچنی tiny

koochnay *n.* کوچنی infant

koochnay *n* کوچنی minor

koochnay *a.* کوچنی least

koochnay as *n.* کوچنیاس pony

koochnay astoganzay *n.* کوچنی
استونای lodge

koochnay baks *n* کوچنۍبکس casket

koochnay botal *n.* کوچنۍبوتل vial

koochnay dabarleek *n.* کوچنۍ برلیک miniature

koochnay dabay *n.* کوچنۍبی packet

koochnay dara *n* کوچندره dale

koochnay darwaza; da krikat da lobi drey chooki *n.* کوچ دروازه؛ دکر کدلوبدرچوک wicket

koochnay drey payey laroonkay gaday *n.* کوچنۍدرپایلرونکیای rickshaw

koochnay ghonday *n.* کوچنغوز hillock

koochnay kakhtay *n* کوچنکته boat

koochnay kalay *n.* کوچنۍکلی hamlet

koochnay kawal *v. t* کوچنۍکول diminish

koochnay khakh; tareeqa *n.* کوچنۍیاخ؛طریقه twig

koochnay khaleej *n* کوچنۍخلیج bay

koochnay khaleej *n.* کوچنۍخلیج creek

koochnay khoona *n.* کوچنخونه cabin

koochnay khoona *n.* کوچنخونه snug

koochnay klaka sheereenee *n.* کوچنکلکهشیرینی toffee

koochnay koranay charg *n.* کوچنۍکورنیچر bantam

koochnay la sheydo beylawal *v. t* کوچنۍلهشدوبلول ablactate

koochnay largeena khoona *n.* کوچنلرینهخونه stall

koochnay meykh *n.* کوچنۍمخ pin

koochnay miqnateesee sapa *n.* کوچنمقناطیسیپه microwave

koochnay panra *n.* کوچنۍپاڼه leaflet

koochnay reybaz; bors *n* کوچنۍ رب؛بورس whisk

koochnay seegar *n.* کوچنۍسیار cigarette

koochnay shama *n* کوچنۍشمع taper

koochnay sooray *n.* کوچنۍسوری pore

koochnay taj *n.* کوچنۍتاج coronet

koochnay wyala *n.* کوچنویاله streamlet

koochnay; warookay *a.* کوچنۍ؛ ووکی minuscule

koochneetob *n.* کوچنیتوب infancy

koodala *n.* کوله hut

koog *n.* خو pig

koohay *n.* کوهی well

kooki *n* کوک howl

kooki kawal; cheyghi wahal *v.t.* کوککول؛چغوهل howl

koolmey *n.* کولمه intestine

koolmey aw ahsha *n.* کولماواحشاء inside

koonda; reekha *n.* کونده؛ریه stub

koonr kawoonkay ghag *a.* کو کوونکیغ strident

koorkaman *n.* کورکمن turmeric

koosa *n.* کوه lane

koosa *n.* کوه street

koosa dabay saray *n.* کوهبیسی loafer

koosa dabay; wrusto pati shaway n. کوهبی؛وروستوپاتا شوی straggler

koosa; lara n. کوه؛لاره alley

koota kawal v.t. کوه کول mow

kooza n. کوزه pitcher

kopra n کوپره coconut

kopray n کوپ scalp

kopray n. کوپ skull

kor n. کور home

kor; sray n کور؛سرای house

koranay n کورن family

koranay khowoonkay n. کورنی وونکی pedant

koranay marghay n. کورنمرغ sparrow

koranay noom n. کورنی نوم nickname

koranay noom n. کورنی نوم surname

koranay noom eekhodal v.t. کورنی نوم ایودل nickname

koranay seez n کورنی یز domestic

koranay; ahlee a. کورنی؛اهلي tame

koranay; aslee a کورنی؛اصلي domestic

koranjeydal v.i. کونجدل whine

koranjeydana n کونجدنه whine

korba n. کوربه host

kornastay a. کورناستی sedentary

kot n کو coat

kotangay n کوته cottage

krachay n. کراچ cart

kragh kragh n. کاغ کاغ caw

kragha; kargha n کاغه؛کارغه crow

kraka n. کرکه hate

kraka n. کرکه malice

kraka n. کرکه abhorrence

kraka kawal v.t. کرکه کول abhor

kraka kawal v. t کرکه کول despise

kraka kawal v. t کرکه کول dislike

kraka kawal v.t. کرکه کول hate

kraka kawal v.t. کرکه کول weary

kraka; na khwakhee n کرکه؛نا خوي dislike

krakjan a کرکجن abominable

krakjan a. کرکجن revengeful

krakjan a. کرکجن malicious

krana n. کنه action

kranjay n کنجی creak

kranjeydal v. i کنجدل creak

kranlara n. کنلاره policy

kranlara warta jorawal v.t. کنلاره ورته جوول systematize

kranlara; mimbar n. کنلاره؛منبر platform

krap n. کپ click

krasan a. کسن brittle

krati prati kawal v. t. کپت کول chatter

kreeka wahal v.i. کریکه وهل shout

kreeka; faryad n. کریکه؛فریاد shout

krega kawal n. کریه کول gobble

krismis (da eesayano akhtar) n کرسمس (دعیسائیانو اختر) Christmas

kubra mar n کبرامار cobra

kuch n کوچ butter

kufar kawal *v.t.* کفرکول profane

kulal *n.* کلال potter

kulalee *n.* کلالي pottery

kura *n.* کره orb

kursay *n.* کرسۍ chair

kwata *n.* کوه pile

kwata kawal *v.t.* کوه کول pile

L

---

la ... leyri *adv.* له___ لر far

la ... porta *adv.* له___ پورته beyond

la ... sakha *prep.* له___ خه from

la ... sakha sha ta *prep.* له___ خه شا ته behind

la ... sakha warandi *prep* له___ خه واند before

la arakha *adv* له اخه by

la aytibar sakha zyat tar lasa shaway *n.* له اعتبارخه زيات ترلاسه شوی overdraft

la bad sakha khwandee zay *n.* له بادخه خونديای lee

la beykha rakkhal *v.t.* له بيخه راکل wrest

la beykha rakkhal *v.t.* له بيخه راکل uproot

la blarbakht sakha makhneeway *n.* له بلاربت خه مخنيوی contraception

la dandi rukhsatawal *v. t.* له دند رخصتول dismiss

la dandi sakha kharijawal *v.t.* له دندخه خارجول sack

la darda ghonjeydal *v.i.* له درده غونجدل writhe

la dey amala *adv.* له دامله accordingly

la dey kabala *adv.* له دکبله thereby

la dey kabala; par dey asas *adv.* له دکبله؛ پر داساس so

la dey khwa hagha khwa ta *prep.* له دخواهغه خواته athwart

la dey lamala *adv.* له دلامله hence

la dey lamala *adv.* له دلامله therefore

la dey parta *adv.* له دپرته otherwise

la dey sara sara *adv.* له دسره سره nonetheless

la dey sara sara *adv.* له دسره سره notwithstanding

la dey sara sara *adv.* له دسره سره yet

la dooda bahar *a* له دوده بهر anomalous

la dwa hindso jor *adj* له دوهندسو جو binary

la dwa sakha yaw *a.,* له دوهخهيو either

la garda dak *a.* له ردهک misty

la garway sakha khlasawal *v.t.* له روخه خلاصول redeem

la garway sakha khlasoon *n.* له رو خه خلاصون redemption

la ghag porta *a.* له غپورته supersonic

la gharmey makhki *n* له غرمه مخکا forenoon

la ghusey khoteydal *v.i.* له غصه خودل simmer

la had sakha zyata stayana *n.* له
ستاینه حدسخهزیاته apotheosis

la hada zyat *adv* لهحدهزیات extra

la hagha lori chi *adv.* چهلوري لهغه
thence

la hagha wakhta chi *adv.* لهغه
چهوختهچ since

la haqooqo mahroomawal *v.t* له
حقوقومحرومول outlaw

la harakata ghorzawal *v.t.* له
حرکتهغورول stall

la ilaj *a.* لاعلاج incurable

la insanano aw basharee tolani
sakha beyzara insan *n.* له
انسانانواوبشريهولنخهبزارانسان
misanthrope

la josha dak *a* لهجوشهک
enthusiastic

la kamakht aw zyadakht parta
adv. لهکمتاوزیادتپرته sharp

la kara ghorzawana *n.* لهکاره
غورونه sterilization

la kara lweydalay *a.* لهکارهلودلی
obsolete

la karawa dak *a.* لهکاوهک
arduous

la karawa daka azmoyana *n.* له
کاوهکهآزموینه ordeal

la khatar sakha khabrawal *v.t* له
خطرخهخبرول alarm

la khatar sara makahmakhawal
v. t. لهخطرسرهمخامخول
endanger

la khatara daka chara *n.* لهخطره
کهچاره venture

la khato aw laho dak zay *n.* لهخو
اولهوکـای slough

la khawro sakha raeestal *v.t.* له
خاوروخهرایستل unearth

la kholi sakha leyri *adj* لهخولیخه
لیری aboral

la khudaya monkar *n* لهخدایهمنکر
atheist

la khwaro da makha ishtiha
rawastoonkay skhak *n* لهخور
دمخهاشتهاراوستونکیاک
appetizer

la koma zaya *adv.* لهکومایه
whence

la kor sakha leyri *adv.* لهکورخهلر
forth

la kora watalay *n* لهکورهوتلی
without

la kraghi da koranay yaw
margha *n.* لهکاغدکورنیومارغه
jay

la landi sakha *adv.* لهلاندیخه
underneath

la lari *prep.* لهلار via

la lasa warkawal *v.t.* لهلاسهورکول
miss

la lasa wrakawal *v.t.* لهلاسهورکول
lose

la lori; pa wasta *prep.* لهلور؛په
واسطه through

la lwagi mreydal *v.i.* لهلومدل
starve

la makhi yi *conj.* لهمخي whereupon

la maleeyey sakha maf *a.* لهمالیخه
معاف scot-free

la manza tlal *v. i* لهمنهتلل collapse

la manza tloonkay *a.* لهمنهتلونکی
perishable

la manza waral *v.t.* لهمنهول
annihilate

la manza wral v.t لهمنهول abolish

la manza wral v. t لهمنهول
eliminate

la manza wral v. t لهمنهول
eradicate

la manza wral v.t. لهمنهول slay

la manza wral v.t. لهمنهول wipe

la manza wrana v لهمنهونه
abolition

la manza wrana n. لهمنهونه
removal

la markaz sakha rakhkoonkay
adj. لهمرکزسخهراکونک
centrifugal

la mashoom sara lobi kawal v.t.
لهماشومسرهلوبکول dandle

la maskharo dak a. لهمسخروک
ridiculous

la meeni dak adj لهمينک amatory

la mehdood a. لامحدود infinite

la mehdood a. لامحدود limitless

la mehdoodeeyat n. لامحدوديت
infinity

la nacharay sakha adv. لهناچارىخه
needs

la nakamay sakha adv. لهناکامخه
perforce

la nal sakha jor shaway a. لهنلخه
جورشوى tubular

la nasyal sara wada kawoonkay
a. لهناسيالسرهوادهکوونکى
morganatic

la nawee sara raghawal v.t. لهنوي
سرهرغول renovate

la nizam sara sam a. لهنظامسرهسم
systematic

la noro sara weyshal v.t. لهنورو
سرهوشل share

la palatani parta qazawat kawal
n. لهپلنپرتهقضاوتکول prejudice

la pkho achawal v.t. لهپواچول
overthrow

la pkho lweydal v.i. لهپولوىدل
succumb

la qanoon sara barabarawal v.t.
لهقانونسرهبرابرول regulate

la qanoon sara sam a. لهقانونسره
سم statutory

la qanoonee lari zay sakha
weystal v. لهقانونىلاراىخه
وستل evict

la qazayee preykri aw hod parta
a. لهقضايىپرکاوهوپرته
subjudice

la reekhtanee tareekh sakha
makhki tareekh wayal n له
ريتنىتاريخخهمخکىتاريخويل
antedate

la sakht kaghaza jora shawi
naray gata n. لهسختکاغذه
جوهشونرته cardboard

la sami lari arawal v.t. لهسملاراول
pervert

la sara adv. لهسره afresh

la sara ada kawal v.t. لهسرهاداکول
repay

la sara adaygee n. لهسرهاداىي
repayment

la sara bya sanjawana n. لهسرهبيا
سنجونه overhaul

la sara shmeyral v.t. لهسرهشمرل
recount

la sara zeyrma kawal v.t. لهسره
زرمهکول replenish

la sara; dobara *adv.* لەسره،دوباره anew

la sarkey aw meywey jor skhak *n.* لەسرکاومیوهجواک shrub

la saza sakha bakhana *n.* لەسزاخه بنه impunity

la shahay sara yaw zay takhteydal *v. i* لەشهسرهیوای تتدل elope

la sharmeydo makh sooreydal *v.i* لەشرمدومخسورهدل blush

la sheydo beyleyda *n* لەشدوبلدا ablactation

la sheydo dak *a.* لەشدوک milky

la shmeyra awreydal *v.t.* لەشمره اودل outnumber

la shora dak *a.* لەشورهک uproarious

la shta pangi sakha deyr akheystal *v.t.* لەشتهپانخمر اخستل overdraw

la storo dak *a.* لەستروک starry

la tareekh sakha da makha dawri loy feel *n.* لەتاریخخهد مخهدورلوىفیل mammoth

la tashreefato sara tar sara kawal *v.t.* لەتشریفاتوسرهترسره کول solemnize

la toko aw maskharo dak anzor *n.* لەتوکواومسخروکانور caricature

la trakahar sara matawal *v.t.* لە تکهارسرهماتول snap

la wada makhkeenay *a.* لەواده مخکینی premarital

la wada warandi *adj.* لەوادهواند antenuptial

la wakhta awookhtal *v. t* لەوخته اوتل elapse

la wara *adv.* لەورا afar

la warandi; da makha *adv.* لە واند،دمخه beforehand

la watana sharal *v.t.* لەوطنهشل banish

la watana sharal *v.t.* لەوطنهشل deport

la watana sharana *n.* لەوطنهشنه banishment

la wrandi chamtoo shaway; muayyan *a* لەوراندچمتوشوى، معین set

la yada lostal *n.* لەیادهلوستل recitation

la yada wayal *v.t.* لەیادهویل recite

la yawa sara; har dawal *adv* لەیوه سره،هرول all

la zan sara ghageydana *n.* لمان سرهغدنه soliloquy

la zan sara khandal *v. i* لمان سره خندل chuckle

la zaya porta kawal *v.t.* لمایهپورته کول remove

la zaya top wahal *v.t.* لمایهپوهل startle

la zeygeydoon warandi *adj.* لە زلدونواند antenatal

la zor asar sara ara laroonkay *n* لەزوعصرسرهاهلرونکی anachronism

la zyan sakha khwandee *a* لەزیان خهخوندي proof

laas *n* لاس hand

laas achawal *v.t.* لاساچول infringe

laas pa las khparowoonki khabartya n. لاس‌په‌لاس خپروونكخبرتيا handbill

laasee kaar n. لاسی‌كار handiwork

laasee sanat n. لاسي‌صنعت handicraft

laasi kitab n. لاسی‌كتاب handbook

lafi n لاف boast

lafi aw bati n. لافاوبا vainglory

lafi wahal v.i لافوهل boast

lafzee a. لفظي literal

lafzee n. لفظي textual

lafzee shkhara n لفظي‌شخه row

lag a. ل little

lag a. ل less

lag lag n. لل stork

lag lag ratlal; saseydal v.i. للراتلل؛ سل trickle

lag miqdar n. لمقدار little

lag sa adv. له little

lag sa khwara n. له‌خواه snack

lag shan n. لشان handful

lag wakht makhki adv. لوخت‌مخك recently

lag zhawar n. لژور shoal

lag; kam a. لږكم scant

lagakht n لت consumption

lagakht n. لت cost

lagakhtoona kamawal v.t. لتونه كمول retrench

lagawal v.t. لول abate

lagawal v.i. لول adhere

lagawal v.t. لول affix

lagawana n. لونه abatement

laghar a. لغ nude

laghara mujasima n لغه‌مجسمه nude`

laghartob n. لغتوب nudity

laghata n لَغته clamp

laghata n. لغته kick

laghata wahal v.t. لغته‌وهل kick

lagkay n. لكی minority

lagtob n. لتوب paucity

lagya kawal v.t. لياكول occupy

lahoo adv. لاهو afloat

lajanzar n. لجنزار marsh

lajanzara a. لجنزاره marshy

lak n لاک lac, lakh

lak; neygh a لك؛نغ erect

laka; ghondi pron. لكه؛غوند as

lakara; amsa n. لكه؛امسا stick

lakara; musafir khana n. لكه؛ مسافرخانه cane

lakay n. لك tail

lakay wal storay n لكوال‌ستوری comet

lakay wal storay n. لكوال‌ستوری meteor

lakhta n. لته wand

lakhtay n لته drain

lakhtay n. لتی gutter

lakhtleek jorawana n. لتليک جورونه tabulation

lakhtleek jorawoonkay n. لتليک جوورونکی tabulator

lalo lalo n. للولو lullaby

lamal garzeydal v.t لامل‌ردل cause

laman warachawal v.t. لمن‌وراچول skirt

lamanleek adj. لمنليک adscript

lamba n لمبا bath

lamba *n* لمبه flame

lamba keydal; zor akheystal *v.i* لمبه‌كدل؛زوراخستل blaze

lamba warta kawal *v.i* لمبه‌ورته كول flame

lambeydal *v. t* لمبدل bathe

lambo wahal *v.i.* لامبووهل swim

lambo wahana *n* لامبووهنه swim

lambo wahoonkay *n.* لامبووهونكى swimmer

lambowahana *n* لامبووهنه buoyancy

lambozan tokay *n* لامبوزن‌توكى buoy

lamda karee ora *n* لمده كي‌اوه dough

lamdawal *v. i.* لمدول dabble

lamdawal *v. t.* لمدول damp

lamdawal *v.t.* لمدول steep

lamdawal *v.t.* لمدول soak

lamdeydal *v.i.* لمددل sob

lamdwalay *n* لمدوالى damp

lamehdood *a.* محدود لا immeasurable

lams *n* لمس touch

lams kawal *v.t.* لمس كول touch

lams; ehsas *n* لمس،احساس feeling

lamsawal *v.t.* لمسول abet

lamsawal *v.t.* لمسول incite

lamsawal *v.t.* لمسول instigate

lamsawal; darak kawal *v.t* لمسول؛درك كول feel

lamsawana *n.* لمسونه provocation

lamsawona *n* لمسونه agitation

lamsawoonkay *a.* لمسوونكى provocative

lamsawoonkay *n.* لمسوونكى tempter

lamsoon *n.* لمسون abetment

lamsoon *n.* لمسون instigation

lamsoon *n.* لمسون temptation

lanat *n* لعنت curse

lanat warkawal *v. t* لعنت‌وركول curse

lanat wayal *v. t.* لعنت‌ويل damn

lanatee *a.* لعنتي accursed

land *a* لنډ curt

land *a.* لنډ short

land *a* لنډ summary

land fikray *a.* لنډفكرى insular

land fikree *n.* لنډفكري insularity

land mahala astogna kawal *v.t.* لنډ مهاله‌استوننه‌كول lodge

land mahalay zand *n.* لنډمهالى adjournment

land mahalay; nasapee *a* لنډمهالى؛ نلاپي snap

land mahalee *a.* لنډمهالي temporary

land mahalee astogna *n* لنډمهالي استوننه sojourn

land mahalee bandobast *a.* لنډ مهالي‌بندوبست provisional

landa aw teyza sa akheystal *v.i.* لنډه‌او‌تزه‌ساه‌اخستل pant

landa azmoyana *n.* لنډه‌آزموينه quiz

landa keesa *n.* لنډه‌كيسه anecdote

landa keesa *n.* لنډه‌كيسه novelette

landa weyna *n* لنډه‌وينا aphorism

landawal *v.t.* لنډول abbreviate

landawal *v.t* لنډول abridge

landawal *v.t.* لنول shorten

landay ya koochnay *a.* لدی‌یاکوچنی puny

landeenay *a.* لاندینی nether

landeenay *a* لاندینی under

landeenay *prep.* لاندینی underneath

landeenay jamey *n.* لاندینجامه underwear

landeenay por *n.* لاندینی‌پو basement

landeez *n* لنیز abbreviation

landeez *n* لنیز abridgement

landi *prep* لاند below

landi *prep.* لاند under

landi kawal *v.t.* لاندکول overtake

landi khwa ta *adv* لاندخواته downwards

landi; teet *prep* لاند،یت beneath

landoon *n* لنون brevity

landoon *n.* لنون summary

landoon; ghorchanr *n.* لنون،غورچا precis

lang mahalee orband *n.* لنمهالي اوربند truce

langar zay *n.* لنرای dock

langaree; hawan *v.t.* لنر،هاون mortar

langarzay *n.* لنرای harbour

lanja kawal *v.i.* لانجه‌کول tussle

lanzaka *n* لانکه doll

lapara *prep* لپاره for

lapara; haq *n.* لپاره،حق sake

lapaya pohana *n.* لاپایه‌پوهنه omniscience

lapreydal *v.i.* لپدل shudder

lapreydana *n* لپدنه shudder

laqab *n.* لقب title

lar khod *n.* ودلار guide

lar khod lar leek *n.* لارودالیک index

lar khowana *n.* لاروونه guidance

lar khowana *n.* لاروونه lead

lar khowana kawal *v.t.* لاروونه کول guide

lar khowoonki khabara *n* لار وونکی‌خبره cue

lar leed *n.* لرلید background

lar leek *n.* الیک catalogue

lar leekanay *n.* لرلیکنی telegram

lar moondal *v.t.* لارموندل orientate

lar wrakay *a* لارورکی erroneous

lara *n.* لاره way

lara yi bandawal *v.t.* لاره‌یبندول thwart

laral *v.t.* لرل own

laram *n.* لم scorpion

laramay *n.* له nettle

larana; neewana *n.* لرنه،نیونه possession

laraway *n.* لاروی passenger

laraway *n.* لاروی wayfarer

laray *n.* لار truck

laray *n.* لار lorry

laray *n.* ل series

laray; tarteeb *n.* لب ترتیب range

laray; tasalsul *n.* تسلسل لب sequence

largay *n.* لری timber

largay *n.* لری wood

largay khoray *a.* خوری لری xylophagous

largeen *a.* لرين wooden

largeen satak *n.* لرين سک maul

largeena lakara *n* لرينه لکه stake

larghon peyzhandoonkay *n* لرغون پژندونکی antiquarian

larghon peyzhandoonkay *n.* لرغون پژندونکی antiquary

larghonay *a.* لرغونی ancient

larghonay a. لرغونی antiquarian

larghonay *a.* لرغونی antique

larghonay; zor *a.* لرغونی؛زو archaic

larghonee *a* لرغوني classical

larghonee asar *n.* لرغوني آثار relic

larghonee oloom *n* لرغوني علوم classic

larghonee tamaddun pori arwand *a.* لرغوني تمدن پور اوند primitive

larghoni zamana *n.* لرغونزمانه antiquity

lari *n.* لا saliva

larkhod *n* لارود forerunner

larkhod *n.* لارود precepter

larkhod *n.* لارود leader

larkhod *n.* لارود usher

larkhod keetabgotay *n* لارود کتابوی directory

larkhowana *n.* لاروونه leadership

larleed *n.* لرليد landscape

larleed *n.* لرليد outlook

larleed; qyafa *n.* لرليد،قيافه prospect

laroonkay; malik *n.* لرونکی؛مالک owner

laryoon *n* لاريون march

larza *n.* لزه quiver

larza *n* لزه shake

larzand *a.* لزاند seismic

larzanda taba *n* لزنده تبه ague

larzeydal *v. i* لرزدل erupt

larzeydal *v.i.* لزدل pulsate

larzeydal *v.i.* لزدل quake

larzeydal *v.i.* لزدل quiver

larzeydal *v.i.* لزدل shake

larzeydal *v.i* لزدل wobble

larzeydal *v.t* لزدل flicker

larzeydal *v.t* لزدل flutter

larzeydana *n* لرزدنه eruption

larzeydana *n* لزدنه flutter

larzeydana *n* لزدنه quake

larzeydoonkay *a.* لزدونکی shaky

las akheystal *v. i.* لاس اخستل cease

las aw greywan keydal *v.i.* لاس او روان کدل grapple

las aw greywan keydana *n.* لاس او روان کدنه grapple

las kakhana *n* لاس کنه manual

las laka *n.* لس لکه million

las magho *n.* لاس ماغو glove

las neeway *n.* لاس نيوی adhesion

las paki wahal *v.t.* لاس پکوهل retouch

las raseydana *n* لاس رسدنه access

las ta rawastal *v.t.* لاس ته راوستل achieve

las ta rawastal *n* لاس ته راوستل acquest

las ta rawastana *n.* لاس ته راوستنه acquisition

las ta rawral *v.t.* لاس ته راول get

las ta rawral *v.t.* لاس ته راول obtain

las ta rawral *v.t.* لاستهراول seize

las tapawal *v.t.* لاسپول grope

las warkawal *v.t.* لاسورکول palm

las warsakha akheystal *v.t.* لاس ورخهاخستل quit

las zara *n.* لسزره myriad

las zareez *a* لسزريز myriad

las; lasama shmeyra *n., a* لس؛ لسمهشمره ten

lasama barkha *n.* لسمهبرخه tithe

lasee *a.* لاسي manual

lasee bam *n.* لاسيبم grenade

laseeza *n* لسيزه decade

lashkhor zanawar ya margha *n.* لاشخورزناوريامارغه scavenger

lasleek *n.* لاسليک signature

lasleekoonkay *n.* لاسليکونکی signatory

lasoona aw nookan seengarawal *n.* لاسوناونوکانسينارول manicure

lasoona parkawal *v. i.* لاسونهپکول clap

lasploray *n.* لاسپلوری vendor

lasposay; goodagay *n.* لاسپوی؛ای puppet

lastay *n.* لاستی handle

lastay; kalawa *n.* لاستی؛کلاوه skein

lastay; mootay *n.* لاستی؛موی winch

lastee loya pyala *n.* لاستيلويهپياله jug

lastonr khula *n* لستوخوله cuff

lastonr khula warchawal *v. t* لستوخولهوراچول cuff

lastonray *n* لستوی sleeve

lat saray *n.* لسی sluggard

latarawal *v.t.* لتاول afflict

lateef *a.* لطيف dainty

lateef *a* لطيف delicate

lawang *n* لونځ clove

lawda *n.* لوده idiot

lawda *a* لوده stupid

lawda; bey aqla *a.* لوده؛بېعقل indiscriminate

lawda; ganr *a* لوده؛ dense

lawdatob *n.* لودهتوب stupidity

lawgaree; da law masheen *n.* لوری؛دلوماشين reaper

lawreena *a* لورينه bountiful

laya *n.* لايه layer

lazat *n* لذت enjoyment

lazat *n.* لذت pleasure

lazat *n.* لذت joy

lazimee fayl *a. verb* لازميفعل intransitive

lazimee kawona *n.* لازميکوونه imposition

lazmee *a* لازمي compulsory

lazoom *n* لزوم must

leed; manzara *n.* ليد؛منظره perspective

leedal *v.t.* ليدل sight

leedal *v.t.* ليدل view

leedal keydoonay; tar pam landi *a.* ليدلکدونی؛ترپاملاند sightly

leedal; katal *v.t.* ليدل؛کتل watch

leedana *n.* ليدنه sight

leedana katana *n.* ليدنهکتنه meeting

leedana; saat *n.* ليدنه؛ساعت watch

leedoonkay *n.* ليدونکی spectator

leedoonkay n. ليدونکی seer

leek n ليک letter

leek lost n. ليکلوست literacy

leek ya saman pa pust leygdawal v.t. ليکياسامان په پُستلدول post

leeka n ليکه column

leeka n. ليکه row

leeka leeka kawal v.t. ليکهليکهکول stripe

leeka pri kakhal v.t. ليکهپرکل line

leekal v.t. ليکل write

leekal; pa band ki achawal v.t. ليکل،په بندکاچول pen

leekali zhmana n. ليکلژمنه treatise

leekanay banra n ليکنبه calligraphy

leekay n ليکی book

leekay satoonkay n ليکیساتونکی book-keeper

leekee plorowoonkay n ليکي پلورونکی book-seller

leekoonkay n. ليکونکی notary

leekwal n. ليکوال author

leekwal n. ليکوال writer

leelam n ليلام auction

leelamawal v.t. ليلامول auction

leemoo n. ليمو lemon

leendakay n. ليندکه parenthesis

leenday wala; khakht karay n ليندوالا،خت کاری archer

leengay n. لينی shin

leesansa sar ta rasawal v.i. ليسانسهسرتهرسول graduate

leeyaqat n. لياقت merit

leeyaqat n. لياقت prowess

leeyaqat laral v.t لياقتلرل merit

leeyaqat; twan n. لياقت،توان potency

lehen; ahang n. لحن،آهنَ tune

lehja; garana n. لهجه،نه idiom

lehjawee a. لهجوي idiomatic

levaltia n ليوالتيا fervour

leycha n لجه forearm

leygd raleygd n. لدرالد transportation

leygdawal v.t. لدول send

leygdawal v.t. لدول transport

leygdawana n. لدونه carriage

leygdawana n. لدونه portage

leygdawoonkay n. لدوونکی carrier

leyri a لر distant

leyri a لر far

leyri a. لر remote

leyri a. لر younder

leyri kawal; ghorzawal v. t لر کول،غورول dispose

leyri kawona n لرکوونه disposal

leyri walay n لروالی far

leyri; pa gokha ki adv. لر،پهوهکه aloof

leyri; yaw lori ta adv. لر،يولورته away

leywa n. لوه wolf

leywal a لوال eager

leywal; munasib a. لوال،مناسب apt

leywanay a لونی crazy

leywanay n. لونی maniac

leywanay a. لونی lunatic

leywanay kas n. لونیکس lunatic

leywanay kawal v.t لونیکول dement

leywantob *n.* لونتوب lunacy

leywantob *n* لونتوب mania

leywantob *n.* لونتوب psychosis

leywantob *v.i.* لونتوب کول rampage

libas *n.* لباس attire

libas *n.* لباس costume

lifafa *n* لفافه envelope

lmanzal *v. t. & i.* لمانل celebrate

lmanzana *n.* لماننه celebration

lmar *n.* لمر sun

lmar khwalay *n* لمرخول belvedere

lmar rakhatana *n* لمرراختنه dawn

lmar ta eekhodal *v.t.* لمرتەایودل sun

lmareen *a.* لمرین solar

lmareen *a.* لمرین sunny

lmareen *a.* لمرین shiny

lmoonz *n.* لمونز prayer

lmoonz kawal *v.i.* لمونزکول pray

loab *n.* لعاب mucilage

loba *n.* لوبه play

loba *n.* لوبه sport

loba kawal *v.i.* لوبه کول sport

loba panra *n* لوبه پله foolscap

loba; musabiqa *n.* لوبه؛مسابقه game

lobeydal *v.i.* لوبېدل toy

lobghalay *n.* لوبغالی gymnasium

lobghalay *n.* لوبغالی stadium

lobgharay *n.* لوبغای player

lobgharay *n.* لوبغای sportsman

lobi kawal *v.i.* لوبکول play

lobsaray *n.* لوباری referee

lobtaka *n.* لوبتکه toy

lobya *n.* لوبیا bean

lochak *n.* لوچك scoundrel

loga *n* لوه hunger

logareetam *n.* لوباریتم logarithim

lokhay *n* لوی dish

lokhay *n.* لوی plate

lokhay *n.* لوی vessel

lokhay *n.* لوی pot

lokhee aw largee *n.* لوی اولرپی utensil

loochak *a.* لوچک profligate

loochak aw koosa dabay zwan *n.* لوچک او کوه بی وان hooligan

loochkay *n.* لوچکي profligacy

loogay *n.* لوی smoke

loogay *n.* لوی soot

loogay keydal *v.i.* لوی کدل smoke

loogay laroonkay *a.* لوی لرونکی vaporous

loogay wahalay *a.* لوی وهلی smoky

looma *n.* لومه noose

looma *n.* لومه snare

loomranay *a.* لومنی premier

loomranay; muhim *a.* لومنی؛مهم prime

loomranee maqam ta stanawal *v.t.* لومني مقامته ستنول reinstate

loomray *a* لومی first

loomray *n* لومی preliminary

loomray gam porta kawal *v.t.* لومی ام پورته کول initiate

loomray wraz *n* لومور first

loond *a.* لوند wet

loondawal *v.t.* لوندول wet

loondwalay *n.* لوندوالی wetness

loor *n* لور daughter

loosawal *v.t.* لوول denude

loot talan *n.* تالان لو ravage

loota *n.* لوه clod

lootal *v.t.* لول depredate

lootal *v.i.* لول maraud

lootal *v.t.* لول plunder

lootal *v.t.* لول rob

lootal; tala kawal *v.t.* لول؛تالاكول ravage

lootmar *n.* لومار marauder

lor *n.* لور sickle

lor *n.* لور scythe

lor ta *prep.* لورته towards

lora *n.* لوه oath

lorand *a.* لوراند merciful

lorand; mehraban *a.* لوراند؛مهربان amiable

loreenee; mehrabanee *n.* لوريني؛مهرباني amiability

los; barband *a.* لو؛بربند bare

lost *n.* لوست lesson

lostal *v.t.* لوستل read

lostay *a.* لوستى literate

lostoonkay *n.* لوستونكى reader

loy *a* لوى big

loy askar *n.* لوىسم cavern

loy asqaf *n.* لوىاسقف archbishop

loy aw azeem *a.* لوىاوعظيم massive

loy badanay *a.* لوىبدن gigantic

loy badanay *a.* لوىبدنى massy

loy chamanzar *n.* لوىچمنزار meadow

loy jageer *n.* لوىجاير manor

loy kar kawal *v. t* لوىكاركول exploit

loy khamar *n.* لوىهامار python

loy khar pori arwand *a.* لوىهارپور اوند metropolitan

loy loy gamoona akheystal *v.i.* لوىلوىهامونهاخستل stride

loy loy leekal *v.t* لوىلوىليكل engross

loy munshee; loomray wazeer *n.* لوىمنشي؛لومىوزير chancellor

loy or *n* لوىاور bonfire

loy samandar *n.* لوىسمندر ocean

loy toray *a.* لوىتورى capital

loy wat *n.* لوىوا avenue

loy; hajeem *a.* لوى؛حجيم voluminous

loya darwaza *n.* لويهدروازه gate

loya gol dabara *n* لويهول بره boulder

loya karnama *n* لويهكارنامه feat

loya keygday *n.* لويهكد pavilion

loya khoona *n.* لويهخونه saloon

loya lar *n.* لويهلار highway

loya lara *n.* لويهلاره thoroughfare

loya musafiree kakhtay *n* لويه مسافري كت cruiser

loya namray *n.* لويهنم gulp

loya sapa *n* لويهپه billow

loya sawdagaree *n* لويهسوداري enterprise

loya teyrwatana *n* لويهتروتنه blunder

loya tota *n.* لويهلوه lump

loyawal; loyeydal *v.i.* لويول؛لويدل zoom

loyee *n.* لويي grandeur

loyee *n.* لويي magnanimity

loyeydana; teyz harakat *n.* لويدنه، تزحرکت zoom

loyidal *v.t.* لويدل lump

lozh *n.* لوژ gallery

lugho kawal *v. t.* لغوکول abrogate

lughwa kawal *v.t.* لغوهکول countermand

lughwa kawal *v.t.* لغوهکول annul

luqma *n.* لقمه mouthful

lwaga; qahtee *n.* لوه،قحطي starvation

lwar awazay *a.* لواوازی loud

lwar ghag *n.* لوغر alp

lwar narkh warandi kawal *v.t.* لو نرخوراندکول outbid

lwar poray *n* لوپوی eminance

lwar poray hakim *n.* لوپویحاکم paramount

lwar poray rahib *n* لوپویراهب prior

lwar pori rahiba *n.* لوپوراهبه prioress

lwar walay *n.* لووالی altitude

lwar walay maloomowoonkay *n* لووالیمعلوموونکی altimeter

lwar zhawar *a.* لوژور rough

lwara alwatana kawal *v.i.* لوه الوتنهکول soar

lwara baya warkawal *v.t.* لوهبیه ورکول overrate

lwara sapa *n.* لومپه surge

lwara sata *n.* لوهسطح plateau

lwara sawkay *n.* لوموک stool

lwarawal *v. t* لوول elevate

lwarawal *v.t.* لوول heighten

lwarawana *n* لووونه elevation

lwaraway *n.* لواوی reverence

lwaraway *n.* لواوی supremacy

lwarwalay *n.* لووالی height

lweydal *v.i.* لودل tumble

lweydeez *n.* لودیز west

lweydeez *n.* لودیز occident

lweydeez bad *n.* لودیزباد zephyr

lweydeez pori arwand *a.* لودیپور اوند westerly

lweydeez wal *a.* لودیوال west

lweydeeza *a.* لودیه western

lweydeeza naray *a.* لودیزهنه occidental

lweyshtakay *n* لوشتکی dwarf

lweyshtakay saray *n.* لوشتکیسی midget

lweyshteenak insan *n.* لوشتینک انسان pygmy

M

ma khpala *pron.* ماخپله myself

ma la *pron.* ماله me

maaf; khwandee *adj* معاف،خوندي exempt

maafawal *v.t* معافول excuse

maafawal; takhfeefawal *v.t.* معافول،تخفیفول remit

maafeeyat *n.* معافیت remission

maafeeyat; bakhana *n* معافیت، بخنه excuse

maamila *n.* معامله issue

mach *n* مچ fly

machak *n.* مچک goad

machay *n.* مچ bee
machnoghza *n.* مچنوغزه sling
macho *n.* مچو kiss
macho kawal *v.t.* مچوکول kiss
mada *n.* ماده matter
mada *n* ماده material
mada parastee *n.* مادهپرستي
materialism
mada; seez *n.* ماده،بيز stuff
mada; zat *n.* ماده،ذات substance
madanee *a* مدني civic
madanee oloom *n* مدنيعلوم civics
madanee; oolasee *a* مدني،اولسي
civil
madawam *adj.* مداوم continual
madee *a.* مادي material
madee banra warkawal *v.t.* مادي
بهورکول substantiate
madha *n.* مدحه panegyric
mafad *n.* مفاد content
mafad aw gata *n.* مفاداوه scope
mafhoom; mana *n.* مفهوم،مانا
purport
mafhoomee kawal *v.t.* مفهومي کول
purport
mafrooza; yaw khyal *n.* مفروضه،
يوخيال hypothesis
mafsal *n.* مفصل joint
mag; wray *n.* مږ،وری ram
magar da chi *prep* مرداچ but
magar da chi *conj.* مرداچ unless
magar da chi *prep* مرداچ save
magar; prata la *prep* مر،پرتهله
except
magaway; sanjaq *n.* موی،سنجاق
peg

maghfirat *n.* مغفرت pardon
maghroor *n* مغرور swagger
maghroorana *a.* مغرورانه lofty
mahal *n.* محل locality
mahal *n.* مهال time
mahaleez *n.* مهاليز periodical
mahaleez *a.* مهاليز temporal
mahalweysh *n.* مهالويش schedule
mahalweysh ki wakht warkawal
v.t. مهالويش کوخت‌ورکول
schedule
maharat *n.* مهارت speciality
maharat *n.* مهارت tact
maharat *n.* مهارت manipulation
maharat *n.* مهارت mastery
maharat *n.* مهارت sleight
maharat *n.* مهارت proficiency
maharatoona aw tadbeeroona *n.*
مهارتونه‌اوتدبيرونه tactics
mahbal; teykay *n.* مهبل،تکی
vagina
mahboob *a* محبوب beloved
mahboob *n* محبوب sweet
mahdood *a* محدود finite
mahdood *a.* محدود limited
mahdoodawal *v. t* محدودول
confine
mahdoodawal *v. t* محدودول curb
mahdoodawal *v.t.* محدودول limit
mahdoodawal *v.t.* محدودول
restrict
mahdoodawoonkay *a.*
محدودوونکی restrictive
mahdoodeeyat *n.* محدوديت
limitation
mahfooz *a.* محفوظ safe

mahir *n.* ماهر adept

mahir *a.* ماهر proficient

mahir *a.* ماهر versed

mahir; chalbaz *a* ماهر،چلباز crafty

mahirana *a* ماهرانه elaborate

mahirana *a.* ماهرانه tactful

mahkama *n.* محکمه tribunal

mahkamey ta hazirawal *v.* محکم ته‌حاضرول arraign

mahrak *n.* محرک locomotive

mahramana *a.* محرمانه confidential

mahroomawal *v. t.* محرومول bereave

mahroomeeyat *n* محرومیت bereavement

mahsool *n.* محصول tariff

mahsool warkawal; ata kawal *v.t.* محصول‌ورکول،اعطاکول yield

mahsoor zay *n.* محصورای closure

mahwa kawal *v. t* محوه‌کول erase

mahwa kawal *v.t.* محوه‌کول obliterate

majazee; kanayawee *a.* مجازی؛ کنایوي allegorical

majazee; waqiee *a* مجازي؛واقعي virtual

majboor *a.* مجبور needful

majboorawal *v. t* مجبورول compel

majboorawal *v.t.* مجبورول induce

majlis *n* مجلس congress

majlis *n.* مجلس session

majmooa jorawal *v.t.* مجموعه جورول aggregate

makab *n* مکعب cube

makab dawla *adj.* مکعب‌وله cubiform

makabee *a* مکعبي cubical

makalima *n.* مکالمه parley

makan; tar wadanay landi zmaka *n.* مکان؛تروداذلاندهمکه site

makar; heela *n.* مکر؛حیله guile

makar; mozee *a.* مکار،موذي sly

makashifa *n.* مکاشفه revelation

makatiba *n.* مکاتبه correspondence

makatiba kawal *v. i* مکاتبه‌کول correspond

makh *n* مخ face

makh aw sha ta harakat kawal *v.i.* مخ‌اوشاته‌حرکت‌کول wag

makh khwa ta *a.* مخ‌خواته onward

makh pa kkhata *adv* مخ‌په‌کته downward

makh pa shomal *adv.* مخ‌په‌شمال north

makh pa zwar *prep* مخ‌پمو down

makh pa zwara *adv.* مخ‌پمو‌ه backward

makha *n.* مخه front

makha dap kawal *v.t.* مخه‌پ‌کول resist

makha dap kawal *v.t.* مخه‌پ‌کول restrain

makha kha *n* مخه farewell

makha neewal *v.t.* مخه‌نیول tackle

makha neewana; karee wasayal *n.* مخه‌نیونه،کاري‌وسایل tackle

makha yi ragarzawal *v.t.* مخه‌یه رارول rein

makham *n* مالم evening

makham *n.* مالم supper

makhamakh keydal *v.t* مخامخ کدل face

makhamanay doday *n* ماامنو ډوډي dinner

makhfee *adj.* مخفي clandestine

makhfee *a.* مخفي underhand

makhfee *a.* مخفي occult

makhfee kawal; patawal *v.t.* مخفي کول،پټول stow

makhkakh *n.* مخکخ pioneer

makhkanay; warandi *n.* مخکنی؛ واند antecedent

makhki *adv.* مخکی ahead

makhki *adv.* مخکه ago

makhki keydal *v.* مخکه کدل precede

makhki keydal *v.t.* مخکه کیدل advance

makhki la dey chi *conj* مخکله دچ before

makhki la dey; qablan *adv.* مخکه له دي،قبلا already

makhki la makhki chamtoo kawal *v.t* مخکله مخکه چمتو کول forearm

makhki la; albata *adv.* مخکله،البته rather

makhlooq *n* مخلوق creature

makhloot shaway shorba *n.* مخلوط شوی شوربا porridge

makhloot taleem *n.* مخلوط تعليم co-education

makhloot; gadola *n* مخلوط،ګوله blend

makhlootawal *v. t* مخلوطول blend

makhneeway *n* مخنیوی control

makhneeway *n.* مخنیوی interception

makhneeway *n.* مخنیوی inhibition

makhneeway *n.* مخنیوی prevention

makhneeway aw waqaya *n.* مخنیوی او وقایه repercussion

makhneeway kawal *v. t* مخنیوی کول control

makhneeway kawal *v.t.* مخنیوی کول inhibit

makhneeway kawal *v.t.* مخنیوی کول prevent

makhneeway kawoonkay *a.* مخنیوی کوونکی obstructive

makhneewoonkay *a.* مخنیوونکی preventive

makhneewoonkay *a.* مخنیوونکی repellent

makhooka *n* موکه beak

makhroot *n.* مخروط cone

makhsoos *a.* مخصوص extraordinary

makhsoos *a.* مخصوص specific

makhtaray *n.* مختای prefix

larghonaya. *a* مکنون latent

makoo *n.* ماکو shuttle

makoos; makoos fayl *a* معکوس؛ معکوس فعل reflexive

makoosawana *n.* معکوسوونه reversal

mal *n* مل fellow

mal *n.* مال lucre

mal keydal *v.t.* مل کیدل accompany

mal; shtamanee *n.* مال،شتمني wealth

malak; khan *n.* خان،ملک squire

malakush shoara *n* ملک‌الشعرا laureate

malamat ganral *v. t* ملامت blame

malamatawal *v. t.* ملامتول condemn

malamatawal *v. t.* ملامتول convict

malamatawal *v.t.* ملامتول impute

malamatawal *v.t.* ملامتول rebuke

malamatawal *v. t.* ملامتول chide

malamatee *n.* ملامتي reproach

malamatya *n* ملامتيا condemnation

malamatya *n.* ملامتيا rebuke

malamatya; ilzam *n* ملامتيا،الزام blame

malande *n.* ملن lampoon

malande kawal *v.t.* ملنکول lampoon

malandi *n* ملن gibe

malandi pri kawal *v.i.* ملنپرکول mock

malandi wahal *v.i.* ملنوهل gibe

malandi; peyghor *adj* ملن؛پغور mock

maldara; shtaman *n.* مالداره،شتمن millionaire

malee *a* مالي fiscal

malee mrasta *n.* مالي‌مرسته subsidy

malee mrasta kawal *v.t.* مالي‌مرسته کول subsidize

maleeya *n.* ماليه revenue

maleeya *n.* ماليه tax

maleeya eekhodana *n.* ماليه‌ايودنه taxation

maleeya lagawal *v.t.* ماليه‌لول tax

maleeyat *n* ماليات finance

maleeyat *n.* ماليات levy

maleeyat lagawal *v.t.* ماليات‌لول levy

maleeyatee *a* مالياتي financial

maleeyatee jareema *n.* مالياتي جريمه surtax

malga *n.* ماله salt

malga pri mokhal *v.t* ماله‌پرمول salt

malga pri mokhal *v.t.* ماله‌پرمول season

malgaray *n* ملرى accomplice

malgaray *n.* ملرى comrade

malgaray *n.* ملرى friend

malgaray *n.* ملرى mate

malgaray; mal; warsara *adv.* ملرى؛مل؛ورسره along

malgartya; ashnayee *n.* ملرتيا، آشنايي amity

malgary *n.* ملرى companion

malgeen *a.* مالين saline

malgeen *a.* مالين salty

malghalara *n.* ملغلره pearl

malham *n.* ملهم balm

malham *n.* ملهم ointment

malik *n.* مالک proprietor

malika *n* ملکه empress

malika *n.* ملکه queen

malkee wagaray *n* ملکي‌وى civilian

malmal *n.* ململ mull

maloom *a.* مالوم conspicuous

maloom *a.* معلوم overt

maloomat *n.* معلومات information

maloomawal *v.t.* معلومول ascertain

maloomawal *v. t* معلومول detect

maloomawal v. t معلومول diagnose

maloomeydal v.i. معلومدل loom

maloona lootal v.t. مالونهلول ransack

malt laroonkay skhak jorawal n. مالت لرونکی ښ ک جوول malt

malta n. ماله lime

maltya n ملتا accompaniment

malyatee wazeeyat; atkal n. مالياتي وضعيت،اكل assessment

mamas n. مماس tangent

mamnooa a. ممنوعه prohibitive

mamnooa a. ممنوعه prohibitory

mamoli a. معمولى mean

mamoolan adv. معمولاً usually

mamoolee a. معمولي ordinary

mamoor n. مأمور commissioner

mamoor; amil n. مأمور،عامل functionary

mamooreeyat n. مأموريت commission

man aw salwa n. منّ او سلوا manna

mana n. مانا meaning

mana akheystal v.t ماناا خستل mean

mana kawal v. t. منع کول debar

mana kawal v. t منع کول dissuade

mana kawal v.t منع کول forbid

mana kawal v.t. منع کول rebuff

mana warkawal v.t. مانا ورکول signify

mana; loyakht n. مانا،لويت signification

mana; radawana n. منع؛ردونه rebuff

manadee n. منادي precursor

manakhta kawal v.t. منته کول avow

manal & منل accept

manana n. مننه thanks

manana warta wayal v.t. مننهورته ويل thank

manandoy a. منندوى grateful

manandoy a. منندوى thankful

manay n. مانع obstacle

manay kawal v.t. مانع کول mar

manay keydal v.t. مانع کدل impede

manay keydal v.t. مانع کدل obstruct

manay; khazan n. مني؛خزان autumn

mand; asar n منه؛اثر wake

mand; da pkhey zay n. منه؛دپای track

manda n. منه run

manda wahal v.i. منهوهل run

mandana; danana kawana n منه؛ دننه کونه thrust

mandaroo n. منداو churn

manfee a. منفي no

manfee a منفي minus

manfee a. منفي negative

manfee adad n. منفي عدد negative

mangol n. منول toe

mangol lagawal v.t. منول لول toe

mangoley n منول claw

mangoli prey khakhawal v.t. منول پرخول paw

manoonkay; darak kawoonkay a. منونکی؛درک کوونکی receptive

manra *n.* مه apple

manray *n* ما bungalow

manray *n* ما edifice

manray *n.* ما palace

manroo *n.* مارو mariner

manroo *n.* مارو navigator

mansoobawal *v.t.* منسوبول ascribe

mansoojat; tokar *n* منسوجات،توکر textile

mansookh *a.* منسوخ outdated

mansookh shaway *a.* منسوخ شوی antiquated

mantaj *a* منتج consequent

mantaq *n.* منطق logic

mantaq poh *n.* منطق پوه logician

mantaqa *n.* منطقه zone

mantaqee *a* منطقي coherent

mantaqee a. منطقي logical

mantaqee banra warkawal *v.t.* منطقي په ورکول rationalize

manz *a.* منز mid

manz *a.* منز middle

manzanay barkha *a.* منزبرخه innermost

manzanay had *n.* منى حد average

manzani takay *n.* منى کى mean

manzar *n.* منظر scenery

manzar; nazar *n.* منظر،نظر view

manzara *n.* منظره scene

manzara; larleed *n.* منظره،لرلید vista

manzara; tamasha *n.* منظره،تماشا spectacle

manzgaray *n.* منى arbitrator

manzgaray *a.* منى intermediate

manzgaray *n.* منى mediator

manzgartob *n.* منتوب arbitration

manzil *n* منزل destination

manzoor *a.* منظور intent

maqad *n.* مقعد anus

maqala *n* مقاله article

maqala *n* مقاله tract

maqala leekal *v. t.* مقاله لیکل essay

maqala leekoonkay *n* مقاله لیکونکی essayist

maqala; namoona *n.* مقاله،نمونه essay

maqam laral *v.t.* مقام لرل rank

maqam; halat *n.* مقام،حالت position

maqam; poray *n.* مقام،پو rank

maqar *adj.* مقعر concave

maqawam; payand *a.* مقاوم،پایند resistant

maqawmat *n.* مقاومت resistance

maqbara *n.* مقبره mausoleum

maqbara *n.* مقبره sepulchre

maqbara *n.* مقبره sepulture

maqool *a.* معقول reasonable

maqooleeyat; hookhyaree *n.* معقولیت،هویاري sobriety

maqsad *n.* مقصد goal

mar *a* مه dead

mar *n.* مار serpent

mar *n.* مار snake

mar keydal *v. i* مکدل decease

mar peych; bandol *n.* مارپیچ،بنول spiral

mar postakay ghorzawal *v.t.* مه پوستکی غورول slough

maraka *n* مرکه dialogue

maraka *n.* مرکه interview

maraka kaval v.t. مركه كول interview

maraka kawal v. t. مركه كول discuss

marawal v.t. مَول glut

maray n. مه morsel

maray n می corpse

maraz; krak n. مز،کرک quail

marboot a. مربوط pertinent

marboot a. مربوط relative

mardana; la jinsee palwa faal a. مردانه،له جنسي پلوه فعال virile

mareez n مريض patient

marg ta sparal v. t. مرته سپارل doom

margee a مري fatal

margee hal a. مري حال moribund

margharay n. مرغى gland

marhala n. مرحله phase

marifat; fikree zhawarwalay n. معرفت،فكري ژوروالى profundity

marifee kawal v.t. معرفي كول introduce

marifee kawana n. معرفي كوونه representation

marjan n مرجان coral

markaz n مركز center

markaz n مركز centre

markaz n مركز middle

markaz; sazman n. مركز،سازمان institution

markazee a. مركزي central

markazee barkha n. مركزي برخه midst

markazee hasta n. مركزي هسته nucleus

markazi a مركزى focal

markheyray n. مرخى mushroom

marmay n مرم bullet

marmay; da nakhi weeshtana n. مرم،دنويشتنه shot

marseeya n مرثيه elegy

marseeya n. مرثيه monody

martaba n. مرتبه grade

masadira n. مصادره requisition

masadira kawal v.t. مصادره كول requisition

masahat n مساحت area

masala n. مساله spice

masala pri doorawal v.t. مساله پري دوول spice

masala; qayda n. مسئله،قاعده theorem

masaleydar; khwandawar a. مسالدار،خوندور spicy

masana n مثانه bladder

masawee a مساوي equivalent

masawee ganral v. t مساوى ل equate

masawee kawal v. t. مساوي كول equalize

masaweetob n. مساويتوب parity

masee alayhis salam n. مسيح عليه السلام messiah

maseehee naray n. مسيحي ن Christendom

mashahoor a. مشهور renowned

mashahoor a. مشهور well-known

mashar a مشر elder

mashar saray n. مشرسى senior

mashar; rahbar n مشر،رهبر premier

mashar; zor *a.* مشر،زو senior

masharee *n.* مشري captaincy

masharee *a* مشرى elderly

masharee kawal *v.i.* مشري کول preside

mashartob *n.* مشرتوب seniority

mashboo kawal *v.t.* مشبوع کول saturate

masheen *n* ماشين engine

masheen poh *n.* ماشين پوه mechanic

masheenee saray *n.* ماشيني سى robot

mashghola *n.* مشغولا hobby

mashghulawal *v.t.* مشغولول amuse

mashghultya; tafreeh *n* مشغولتيا؛ تفريح amusement

mashhoorawal *v.t.* مشهورول popularize

mashkook *a.* مشکوک suspect

mashoom *n.* ماشوم kid

mashoom *n* ماشوم child

mashoom la sheydo warkawalo beylawal *v.t.* ماشوم لهشدو ورکولوبلول wean

mashoom; khidmatgar *n.* ماشوم؛ خدمتار wench

mashoomana *a.* ماشومانه childish

mashoomana *a.* ماشومانه puerile

mashoomtob *n.* ماشومتوب childhood

mashooq *n* معشوق beloved

mashoor *a.* مسحور captive

mashoorawal *v. t.* مسحورول captivate

mashq kawal *v.t.* مشق کول practise

mashq; tajruba *n.* مشق،تجربه practice

mashra; rahbara *n.* مشره،رهبره premiere

mashroob *n.* مشروب liquor

mashwara *n* مشوره consultation

mashwara *n.* مشوره tip

mashwara kawal *v. t* مشوره کول consult

mashwara warkawal *v.t.* مشوره ورکول tip

mask aghostay lobgharay *n.* ماسک اغوستى لوبغاى mummer

maskan *n* مسکن abode

maskhara *n.* مسخره bantling

maskhara *n* مسخره buffoon

maskhara *n* مسخره clown

maskhara *n.* مسخره joker

maskhara kawal *v.t.* مسخره کول satirize

maskhara; malanda *n* مسخره،ملنده sneer

maskharey *n.* مسخرى raillery

maskharey *n.* مسخر ridicule

maskoona aghostee lobgharee *n.* ماسکونه اغوستي لوبغاي pantomime

maslak *n.* مسلک sect

maslakee *a.* مسلکي sectarian

maslihat *n* مصلحت advisability

maslihat *n.* مصلحت opportunism

maslihatee gatawar *a* مصلحتي ور expedient

masnad *n.* مسند predicate

masnad; mutee *a* مسند،مطيع subject

masnooee *a.* مصنوعي artificial

masnooee *a.* مصنوعي counterfeit

larghonaya *a* مصنوعي fictitious

masnooee *a.* مصنوعي synthetic

masnooee khobawana *n.* مصنوعي خوبونه mesmerism

masnooee seez *n* مصنوعي‌يز synthetic

masnooee weykhtan *n.* مصنوعي وتان wig

masool *a.* مسؤل liable

masool *a* مسؤل accountable

masoolana *a* مسؤلانه amenable

masooleeyat *n* مسؤليت post

masooleeyat *n.* مسؤليت liability

masooleeyat warkawal *v.t.* مسؤليت‌ورکول sponsor

masraf *n* مصرف consumption

masraf keydal *v. t* مصرف کدل consume

masraf; lagakht *n.* مصرف،لت expense

masrafawal *v. t* مصرفول expend

masrafawal *v.t.* مصرفول spend

mast *a.* مست jolly

mast; nasha *a.* مست،نشه tipsy

mastawal *v. t* مستول bemuse

mastawal *v. i* مستول booze

mastee *n.* مستي spree

mastey *n* مستة curd

mat *n.* مه arm

mat band *a* مه‌بند armlet

matal *n.* متل adage

matal *n* متل byword

matal; zareena wayna *n.* متل،زرينه ونا proverb

matam *n.* ماتم lamentation

matam *n.* ماتم mourning

matam kawal *v.i.* ماتم کول mourn

matam kawal *v. t* ماتم کول bewail

matam kawoonkay *n.* ماتم کوونکی mourner

matawal *v. t* ماتول contradict

matawal *v.t* ماتول fracture

matawal; beylawal *v.i.* ماتول،بلول split

matey warkawal *v. t* ماتور کول crush

mateydal; matawal *v. t* ماتدل، ماتول break

mateydana *n* ماتدنه breakage

mateydoonkay *n* ماتدونکی cracker

mati *n* ماتٍ defeat

mati warkawal *v. t.* مانور کول defeat

matlab rasawal *v.t.* مطلب‌رسول intimate

matrah kawal *v.t.* مطرح کول propound

matrooka *n.* متروکه scourge

matwalay *n.* ماتوالی fracture

matwalay; zand *n* ماتوالی،ځ break

mawafiqi areeki *n.* موافقايک rapport

mawarayee tabeeyat pori arwand *a.* ماورايي‌طبيعت‌پور‌اوند metaphysical

maweez *n.* مويز raisin

mawhoom parast *a.* موهوم‌پرست superstitious

mawhoom parastee *n.* موهوم‌پرستي superstition

mawjood *a* موجود available

mawjood *a.* موجود present	mayla *n.* ملا fair
mawjood; zeyrma shaway *a.* موجود،زرمه‌شوی stock	mayla *n* مله festival
mawjooda *a* موجوده current	maymar *n.* معمار architect
mawjoodgee *n.* موجودي presence	maymaree *n.* معماري architecture
mawroosee *n.* موروثي hereditary	mayna *n.* ماينه wife
mawseeqee *n.* موسیقی music	mayni aw mantaqey pori arwand *a.* مناومنطقه‌پوراوند zonal
mawseeqee jorawoonkay *n.* موسیقی‌جووونکی musician	mayoosa kawal *v.t.* مأيوسه‌کول frustrate
mawzoo *n.* موضوع؛مقاله theme	mayoosawal *v. t* مايوسول deject
mawzoo; mubhas *n.* موضوع؛مبحث topic	mayoosawal *v. t.* مأيوسول disappoint
mawzoo; wayna *n* موضوع؛ونا discourse	mayoosee *n* مايوسي dejection
mawzooatee *a.* موضوعاتي topical	mayoosee *n.* مأيوسي frustration
mawzooee *a.* موضوعي thematic	maza akheystal *v.t.* مزه‌اخستل savour
mawzooee; failee *a.* موضوعي،فاعلي subjective	mazanak *a.* مزه‌ناک palatable
mawzoon; ham wazan *a.* موزون؛هموزن rhythmic	mazay; spanrseen *n.* مزی؛سپسین yarn
mawzoonawal *v. t* موزونول co-ordinate	mazay; tar *n.* مزی؛تار string
maya *n* مايع liquid	mazd; fees *n* مزد؛فیس fee
maya kawal *v.t.* مايع‌کول liquefy	mazd; zeyra *n.* مزد؛یره allowance
maya kawal *v.t.* مايع‌کول liquidate	mazdeegaray meylmastya *n.* مازدیرملمستیا matinee
mayan *n.* مین lover	mazdoor *n.* مزدور hireling
mayantob *n.* مینتوب affection	mazdoor *n.* مزدور labourer
mayar *n.* معيار standard	mazdooree kawal *v.i.* مزدوري‌کول labour
mayaree *a* معياري standard	mazhabee hukoomat *n.* مذهبي حکومت hierarchy
mayaree kawal *v.t.* معياري‌کول standardize	mazhabee qanoon *n* مذهبي‌قانون canon
mayda keydal *v.i.* مده‌کدل grind	mazhabee tarana *n.* مذهبي‌ترانه hymn
maydawal *v. t* مدول crumble	mazhabee tashreefat *n.* مذهبي تشریفات rite
maydawal *v.t* مدول mash	
maydawal *v.t.* مدول shatter	
mayl laral *v.i.* ميل‌لرل tend	

mazoor *n* معذور handicap

mazroob *n.* مضروب multiplicand

meela; lakara *n.* ميله،لكه rod

meelan *n.* ميلان trend

meena *n* مينه love

meena kawal *v.t.* مينه كول love

meena toree *a.* ميناتوري miniature

meena warkawal *v.t* مينهوركول endear

meena; ishq *n* مينه،عشق amour

meenakaree *n* ميناكاري enamel

meenanak *a.* مينهناك adorable

meenanak *a.* مينهناك affectionate

meenanak *a.* مينهناك loving

meenanak *a.* مينهناك sociable

meenawal; shoqeen *n.* مينهوال، شوقين amateur

meenzal *v.t.* مينل leach

meeras *n.* ميراث heredity

meeras *n.* ميراث heritage

meeras *n.* ميراث legacy

meeras *n.* ميراث inheritance

meeras ki preykhodal *v. t.* ميراث كپرودل bequeath

meerasee *a.* ميراثي inherent

meesaq *n.* ميثاق treaty

mehboob *n* محبوب darling

mehboob *a.* محبوب lovable

mehfooz *a.* محفوظ immune

mehfooz *a.* محفوظ secure

mehraban *adj* مهربان benign

mehraban *adj.* مهربان complaisant

mehraban *a.* مهربان courteous

mehraban *a.* مهربان humane

mehraban *a* مهربان kind

mehrabana *a.* مهربانه gracious

mehrabanee *n.* مهرباني complaisance

mehrabanee; har kalay *a.* مهرباني،هر كلى welcome

mehroomawal *v. t* محرومول deprive

mehsoosawal *v.t.* محسوسول sense

melma; leedoonkay aw katoonkay *n.* ملمه،ليدونكىاو كتونكى visitor

meyda meyda kawal *v.t.* مدهمده كول mince

meydawoonkay *a* مدوونكى molar

meydeydana *n* ميلدنه bruise

meyga *n* مه ewe

meygay *n* مى ant

meykh toombal *v.t.* مخومبل pin

meykha *n.* مه buffalo

meykhanikee *a* ميخانيكي mechanic

meykhanikee *a.* ميخانيكي mechanical

meyl *n.* مل liking

meylma *n.* ملمه guest

meylma pal *a.* ملمهپال hospitable

meylmastoon *n.* ملمستون hotel

meylmastya *n.* ملمستيا hospitality

meylmastya; jashan *n* ملمستيا، جشن feast

meyra *n* مه husband

meyrana *n* مانه bravery

meyrana *n.* مانه valour

meyranay *a.* منى valiant

meyrgee *n* مري epilepsy

meyrman *n.* مرمن dame

meyrman *n.* مرمن lady

meyrman *n.* مرمن mistress

meysht kawal *v.t* مشت کول house

meysht kawal *v.t.* مشت کول populate

meysht zay *n* مشتءای dwelling

meysht zay *n.* مشتءای lodging

meysht zay *n.* مشتءای residence

meywa *n.* موه fruit

meyz *n.* مز table

midal *n.* مال medal

milawawal *v.t.* ملاوول meet

milee kawal *v.t.* ملی کول nationalize

milee keydana *n.* ملی کدنه nationalization

milee sarood *n* ملی سرود anthem

milee shoora *n.* ملی شورا parliament

milee; amoomee *a.* ملی؛عمومي public

mileeyat *n.* ملیت nationality

milkeeyat *n.* ملکیت ownership

mimbar; dareez *n.* ممبر،درې rostrum

miqnatees *n.* مقناطیس magnet

miqnatees *a.* مقناطیسي magnetic

miqnateeseeyat *n.* مقناطیسیت magnetism

miqyas *n.* مقیاس meter

mis *n* مس copper

misgar *n.* مسر smith

miskeen *a.* مسکین poor

misree haram *n.* مصري هرم pyramid

mityazanray *n.* متیاز urinal

mityazi *n.* متیاز urine

mityazi kawal *v.i.* متیاز کول urinate

mizaj *n.* مزاج mood

mizaj *n.* مزاج temper

mizajee *a.* مزاجي temperamental

mla *n.* ملا waist

mla tar kawal *v.t* ملاتر کول uphold

mla wastanay *n.* ملاوستن girdle

mla wastanay; kamar band *n.* ملاوستن،کمربند waistband

mlatar kawal *v.t.* ملاتر کول prop

mlatar kawal *v.t.* ملاتر کول support

mlataray *n.* ملاتی support

moadab *a* مؤدب decent

moadab; satandoy *n* مؤدب، ساتندوی gallant

moallaq *prep.* معلق pending

moama *n.* معما conundrum

moamila *n* معامله deal

moamila *n.* معامله entreaty

moamila kawal *v. i* معامله کول deal

moamila kawoonkay *n* معامله کوونکی dealer

moamilagar *n.* معاملهر coper

moannas *a* مؤنث feminine

moash akheystoonkay *n* معاش اخیستونکی annuitant

moassar *a.* مؤثر impressive

moassisa *n.* مؤسسه institute

moattar kawal *v.t.* معطر کول scent

moayina; imtihan *n.* معاینه،امتحان examination

moayna *n* معاینه check

moayna kawal *v. t.* معاینه کول check

mobariza ghokhtoonkay *n.* مبارزه غوتونکی appellant

mochee *n* موچی cobbler

modaee *n* مدعي claimant

moeen *a* معین definite

mogak *n.* موک mouse

mogak *n.* موک rat

moheet; parkar *n* محیط،پرکار compass

mohrik *n.* محرک incentive

mohtaram *a* محترم dear

mohtaram *n.* محترم gentleman

mohtaram *a.* محترم honourable

mojee harakat *n* موجي حرکت sway

mojiza *n.* معجزه miracle

mojizatee *a.* معجزاتي miraculous

mokha *n.* موخه aim

mokha; hadaf *n.* موخه،هدف purpose

mokha; hadaf *n.* موخه،هدف target

mokhal *v.t.* مول massage

mokhana *n.* مونه friction

mokhana *n.* مونه massage

mokhowoonkay *n.* مووونکی masseur

mom *n.* موم wax

mom warkawal *v.t.* موم ورکول wax

momin *n.* مؤمن monotheist

momyayee shaway maray *n.* مومیایی شوی می mummy

mooda *n* موده duration

mooda *n.* موده term

mooda; dama *n.* موده،دمه interval

mooda; sa wakht *n.* موده،بهوخت while

moolakh *n.* ملخ locust

moolay *n.* مول radish

moondal *v.t* موندل find

moondal *v.t.* موندل procure

moondana *n.* موندنه discovery

moondana *n.* موندنه procurement

moosafar khana *n.* مسافرخانه inn

mootay wahal *v.i.* مویوهل masturbate

mootay; sook *n* موی،سوک fist

moqa *n.* موقع occasion

moqa *n.* موقع opportunity

moqa rapeykheydal *v.t* موقعراپدل occasion

moqa; fursat *n.* موقع،فرصت chance

moqarraba farikhta *n* مقربهفرته archangel

moqeeyat *n.* موقعیت location

mor *n* مور mother

mor *n* مور mum

mor *n* مور mummy

mor plar *n.* مورپلار parent

mor wazhana *n.* موروژنه matricide

mor wazhoonkay *a.* موروژونکی matricidal

moram *v.i.* مرام aim

moranay *a.* مورنه motherly

moranay *a.* مورني maternal

morchal *n.* مورچل trench

morchal jorawal *v.t.* مورچلجوول trench

morwalay *n.* موروالی motherhood

mosam *n.* موسم climate

404

mosam *n.* موسم season

mosam *n* موسم weather

mosam sara zan adatawal *v.t* موسم‌سرمان‌عادتول acclimatise

mosamee *a.* موسمي seasonal

moseeqee wala meylmastoon *n.* موسیقي‌واله‌ملمستون cabaret

mosh khurma *n.* موش‌خرما marten

mosh khurma *n.* موش‌خرما mongoose

mosh khurma *n.* موش‌خرما squirrel

moshahida kawal *v. t* مشاهده‌کول behold

moska kawal *v.i* smile

mostaqeem *adv* مستقیم aright

mostaqeeman *adv.* مستقیما aright

motabar *a* معتبر creditable

motabar *a.* معتبر valid

motadil *a.* معتدل mediocre

motadil *a.* معتدل moderate

motadil kawal *v.t.* معتدل‌کول moderate

motamadin garzawal *v. t* متمدن‌ګرزول civilize

motanawab; tar dwa barkho pori zangaray *n.* متناوب،ترڅوه برخوپورانی alternative

motar *n.* موټر automobile

motar *n.* موټر car

motar chalowoonkay *n.* موټر چلوونکی motorist

motarwan *n.* موټروان chauffeur

motarwan *n* موټروان coachman

motasib kas *n* متعصب‌کس bigot

motor wan *n* موټروان driver

motor wanee *n* موټروانی drive

mozeekala drama *n.* موزیکاله‌رامه opera

mrasta *n* مرسته aid

mrasta *n.* مرسته assistance

mrasta *n* مرسته help

mrasta ghoshtal *v.t.* مرسته‌غوشتل invoke

mrasta kawal *v.t* مرسته‌کول aid

mrasta kawal *v.t.* مرسته‌کول assist

mrasta kawal *v.t* مرسته‌کول hand

mrasta kawal *v.t.* مرسته‌کول help

mrasta warsara kawal *v.t.* مرسته ورسره‌کول staff

mrastandoy *n.* مرستندوی auxiliary

mrastandoya *a.* مرستندویه auxiliary

mrastandoya *a* مرستندویه co-operative

mrastyal *n.* مرستیال assistant

mraway *n.* ماوی low

mraway keydal *v.i* ماوی‌کدل fade

mraway keydal *v.i.* ماوی‌کدل languish

mraway keydal *v.i.* ماوی‌کدل wither

mrayay *n.* مریی slave

mrayay *n.* مریی thrall

mrayay *n.* مریی serf

mrayay dawla *a.* مریی‌وله slavish

mrayeetob *n* مریی‌توب bondage

mrayeetob *n.* مریی‌توب slavery

mrayeetob ta wral *v.i.* مریی‌توب‌ته ول slave

mreena *n* مینه death

mreena *n* مینه decease

mreena *n.* مينه mortality

mreestoon *n.* ميستون cemetery

mreestoon *n.* ميستون morgue

mreydal *v. i* مدل die

mrich *n.* مرچ chilli

mrich *n.* مرچ pepper

muahida *n.* معاهده pact

mualija *n.* معالجه therapy

muallaq *n.* معلق suspense

muallaq kawal; zandawal *v.t.* معلق کول؛نول suspend

muash *n.* معاش livelihood

muayna kawal *v.t.* معاينه کول observe

mubadil *n.* مبادل interchange

mubadila kawal *v. t* مبادله کول exchange

mubadila kawal *v.* مبادله کول interchange

mubadila; safaree *n* مبادله؛صرافي exchange

mubahisa *n* مباحثه contention

mubahisa *n* مباحثه controversy

mubahisa; daleel *n.* مباحثه؛دليل argument

mubaligha *n.* مبالغه exaggeration

mubaligha kawal *v. t.* مبالغه کول exaggerate

mubaligha wayna *n.* مبالغه ونا hyperbole

mubarak *a.* مبارک auspicious

mubarakee *n* مبارکي congratulation

mubarakee wayal *v. t* مبارکي ويل congratulate

mubariza *n.* مبارزه campaign

mubariza *n.* مبارزه challenge

mubarizey ta tlal *v. t.* مبارزتهبلل challenge

mubhim *a.* مبهم obscure

mubhim; goong *a.* مبهم؛وڼ vague

mubhim; shakman *a.* مبهم؛شکمن ambiguous

mudaee *n.* مدعي suitor

mudafay wakeel *n* مدافع وکيل advocate

mudafay wakeel *n.* مدافع وکيل pleader

mudakhila *n.* مداخله intervention

mudakhila kawal *v.i.* مداخله کول intervene

mudakhila kawoonkay *v.i.* مداخله کوونکی meddle

mudarris *n.* مدرس lecturer

mudat; takal shaway wakht *n.* مدت؛باکل شوی وخت span

mudeer *n.* مدير administrator

mudeer *n.* مدير director

mudeer *n.* مدير manager

mudeeree *a* مديري editorial

mudeeree *a.* مديري managerial

mudeereeyat *n.* مديريت management

mudeereeyat *n.* مديريت superintendence

mufakkir *n.* مفکر intellectual

mufassir *n* مفسر commentator

mufeed *a.* مفيد subservient

mufeed *a.* مفيد useful

mufeedeeyat *n.* مفيديت utility

mufrad; yaw *a.* مفرد؛يو singular

muhafiza kar *a* محافظه‌کار conservative

muhafiza karee khokhawoonkay *n* محافظه کاري‌خوونکی conservative

muhakama *n.* محاکمه trial

muhamat; aslaha *n.* مهمات،اسلحه ammunition

muhandis *n* مهندس engineer

muhar lagawal *v.i.* مهرلول stamp

muhar; tapa *n* مهر،پاپه die

muhasib *n.* محاسب accountant

muhasira kawal *v. t* محاصره‌کول besiege

muhasira; kalabandee *n.* محاصره،کلابند siege

muhazzab *a.* مهذب politic

muhazzab *a.* مهذب urbane

muheet *n.* محیط milieu

muhim *n* مهم adventure

muhim *a.* مهم chief

muhim *a* مهم earnest

muhim *a* مهم principal

muhim *a.* مهم significant

muhim shakhseeyat *n.* مهم شخصیت personage

muhimatee *a.* مهماتي adventurous

muhkam *a* محکم consistent

muhkam *a.* محکم tenacious

muhlal *n* محلل solvent

muhlat *n.* مهلت ultimatum

muhrak *n.* محرک motive

muhtaj *a.* محتاج needy

muhtajee *n.* محتاجي necessity

muhtaram *a.* محترم respectful

muhtaram; moazzaz *a.* محترم؛ معزز venerable

muhtat *adj.* محتاط circumspect

muhtat *a.* محتاط painstaking

muhtat *a.* محتاط prudential

muhtat *a.* محتاط prudent

muhtat insan *n.* محتاطانسان prude

muhur; tapa *n.* مهر،پاپه seal

mujala *n.* مجله circular

mujala *n.* مجله gazette

mujarrad *adj* مجرد abstract

mujassam *a.* مجسم incarnate

mujassam kawal *v.t.* مجسم‌کول incarnate

mujassam kawal *v.t.* مجسم‌کول materialize

mujassam kawal *v.t.* مجسم‌کول visualize

mujassam kawana *n.* مجسم‌کوونه portrayal

mujassima *n.* مجسمه statue

mujassima *n.* مجسمه sculpture

mujassima dawla *a.* مجسمه‌وله sculptural

mujassima jorawoonkay *n.* مجسمه‌جوونکی sculptor

mujrim *n* مجرم convict

mujrim *a.* مجرم guilty

mujrimeeyat *n* مجرمیت conviction

mukalima *n* مکالمه conversation

mukamal aw bashbar insan *n* مکمل‌او‌بشپانسان ideal

mukamal kawal; ada kawal *v.t.* مکمل‌کول،اداکول utter

mukarrar *n.* مکرر frequent

mukhabiratee sapey leygdawoonkay aw astawoonkay masheen n. مخابراتي‌پلادوونكی‌او‌استوونكی ماشین transmitter

mukhalif prep. مخالف against

mukhalif a مخالف contrary

mukhalif a. مخالف hostile

mukhalif n. مخالف opponent

mukhalif a. مخالف opposite

mukhalif a. مخالف repugnant

mukhalif mafhoom warkawal v.t. مخالف‌مفهوم‌ورکول contrapose

mukhalif; dukhman n. ،مخالف دمن antagonist

mukhalif; par zid pref. مخالف؛پر ضد anti

mukhalifa raya n. مخالفه‌رایه veto

mukhalifa raya warkawal v.t. مخالفه‌رایه‌ورکول veto

mukhalifana ihsas n. مخالفانه احساس antipathy

mukhalifat n. مخالفت hostility

mukhalifat kawal v.t. مخالفت‌کول antagonize

mukhalifat kawal v.t. مخالفت‌کول oppose

mukhalifat kawal; zawab warkawal v. t مخالفت‌کول، واب‌ورکول counter

mukhalifat khkara kawal v.i مخالفت‌کاره‌کول frown

mukhalifat; dukhmanee n مخالفت؛دمني antagonism

mukhatib n. مخاطب addressee

mukhlis a. مخلص sincere

mukhtalif a مختلف different

mukhtalif a مختلف unlike

mukhtasar a مختصر abstract

mukhtasar a. مختصر brief

mukhtasar a مختصر concise

mukhtasar leekal v.t. مختصرلیکل jot

mulaqat n. ملاقات meet

mulaqat aw khabari atari n. ملاقات‌او‌خبراتر rendezvous

mulawwis kawal v.t. ملوث‌کول taint

mulayam adj. ملایم daft

mulayim a. ملایم temperate

mulazim; nawkar n. ملازم؛نوکر retinue

mulhidtob n ملحدتوب atheism

mumtaz a ممتاز distinct

munakis jisam n. منعکس‌جسم reflector

munakis kawal v.t. منعکس‌کول reflect

munakis shaway a منعکس‌شوی reflex

munakisawal v.t. منعکسول mirror

munakkis keydal v.i. منعکس‌کدل resound

munara n. مناره minaret

munasib a. مناسب adequate

munasib adj مناسب apposite

munasib a. مناسب appropriate

munasib a مناسب due

munasib a مناسب fit

munasib a مناسب optimum

munasib a. مناسب proper

408

munasib; da ijra war *a.* مناسب،د اجراو applicable

munasibat *n.* مناسبت relevance

munasibat; wartya *n.* مناسبت،وتیا appropriation

munasibawal; zangaray kawal *v.t.* مناسبول،بانی کول appropriate

munazira *n.* مناظره moot

munazza; mehfooz *a.* منزه،محفوظ inviolable

munazzam *a.* منظم regular

munazzam *a* منظم rum

munazzam *a.* منظم tidy

munazzam harakat *n.* منظم حرکت march

munazzam kawal *v.t.* منظم کول tidy

munazzamwalay *n.* منظموالی tidiness

munfajira mawad *n* منفجره مواد dynamite

munharif *adv.,* منحرف astray

munharif kawal *v.t.* منحرف کول shunt

munharif keydal *v. i* منحرف کدل deviate

munqabiz kawal *v. t* منقبض کول condense

munqal; nagharay *n.* منقل،نغری hearth

munqata kawal *v. t* منقطع کول disrupt

munsarif kawal *v. t* منصرف کول divert

munshee *n.* منشي secretary

muntaqil kawal *v.t.* منتقل کول transfer

muqabil takee *n.* مقابل کي antipodes

muqabila *n.* مقابله confrontation

muqabila kawal *v. t* مقابله کول contest

muqadas *a.* مقدس holy

muqaddas *a.* مقدس sacred

muqaddas; na badleydoonkay *a.* مقدس،نابدلدونکی sacrosanct

muqadima *n.* مقدمه prelude

muqadima chamtoo kawal *v.t.* مقدمه چمتو کول prelude

muqannana plaway *n.* مقننه پلاوی legislature

muqaribat; moamila *n.* مقاربت، معامله intercourse

muqawee darmal *n.* مقوي درمل tonic

muqawee; ghagan *a.* مقوي،غن tonic

muqawmat *n.* مقاومت opposition

muqtazee *a.* مقتضي advisable

muraba *n.* مربا jam

muraba; zangari inhisaree seema *n.* مربا،بانه انحصاري سیمه preserve

murafia *n.* مرافعه litigation

murafia kawal *v.t.* مرافعه کول litigate

murafia kawoonkay *n.* مرافعه کوونکی litigant

murafia; yawa jor jamey *n.* مرافعه،یوه جوړ جام suit

murajia *n.* مراجعه recourse

murajia kawal; beyrta katana
kawal *v.t.* مراجعه کول،برته کتنه
کول refer

murakab *a* مرکب compound

murakab *n* مرکب multiple

murakab *a* مرکب twin

murakab jisam *n* مرکب جسم
compound

murakab; gadola *n.* مرکب،وله
mixture

muratab kawal *v. t* مرتب کول
concert2

murda khana *n.* مرده خانه
mortuary

murdaree *n.* مرداري squalor

mureed *n* مرید follower

mureed; shagard *n* مرید،شاگرد
disciple

murtahin *n.* مرتهن mortagagee

murtakib keydal *v. t.* مرتکب کدل
commit

musabiqa *n.* مسابقه competition

musabiqa *n.* مسابقه contest

musabiqa *n* مسابقه match

musabiqa kawal *v.i* مسابقه کول
game

musabiqana *a* مسابقانه
competitive

musadira *n* مصادره confiscation

musadira kawal *v. t* مصادره کول
confiscate

musafar *n.* مسافر ،voyager

musafar *n.* مسافر traveller

musakkan darmal *n* مسکن درمل
sedative

musalihat kawoonkay *n.* مصالحت
کوونکی intermediary

musallam *a.* مسلم indisputable

musallam ganral; sahee gooman
kawal *v.t.* مَسَلهل،صحیح و مان
کول presume

musallat *a.* مسلط imposing

musallatawal *v.t.* مسلطول impose

musalsal dard laral *v.t.* مسلسل
درد لرل nag

musarat *n.* مسرت gratification

musawida *n* مسوده draft

musawida chamtoo kawoonkay
a مسوده چمتو کوونکی draftsman

musawwida *n.* مسوده script

musbat *a* مثبت affirmative

musbat *a.* مثبت plus

musbat *a.* مثبت positive

musbat agheyz laroonkay *a.*
مثبت اغز لرونکی salutary

mushabay *a.* مشابه identical

mushal; pakowoonkay *a* مُسهل،
پاکوونکی purgative

mushk *n.* مشک musk

mushkil *a* مشکل difficult

mushtarik amil *n.* مشترک عامل
coefficient

mushtree *n.* مشتري jupiter

musraf *a.* مُسرف prodigal

mustaid *a.* مستعد gifted

mustaid *a.* مستعد prone

mustaqar kawal; tamzay ki
preykhwal *v.t.* مستقر کول،تمای کی
پرول station

mustaqbil *n* مستقبل future

mustaqeem *a* مستقیم through

mustaqeeman *adv.* مستقیما
outright

mustaqeeman *adv.* مستقيماً
straightway

mustaqil *a* مستقل constant

mustasna garzawal *v. t* مستثنی رول
exclude

mustasna kawal *v. t* مستثنی کول
except

mustasna kawal *v. t.* مستثنی کول
exempt

**mustasna kawal; sarf nazar
kawal** *v.t.* مستثنی کول؛صرف نظر
کول waive

mustateel *n.* مستطیل oblong

mustateel *n.* مستطیل rectangle

mustateel shakal laroonkay *a.*
مستطیل شکل لرونکی rectangular

mutaadad *a.* متعدد many

mutaadil; zra rakhkoonkay *a.*
متعادل؛زه رکونکی trim

mutaal; tar tolo lwar *a.* متعال؛تر
تولو لوړ supreme

mutaasib shakhs *n* متعصب شخص
fanatic

mutaasib; mutashadad *a* متعصب،
متشدد fanatic

mutabiat kawal *v.t* متابعت کول
follow

mutabiq; arwand *a.* مطابق،اوند
relevant

mutakhassas keydal *v.i.* متخصص
کدل specialize

mutalia; lost *n.* مطالعه،لوست study

mutanasib *a.* متناسب symmetrical

mutanasib *a.* متناسب proportional

mutanasib *a.* متناسب
proportionate

mutanasib kawal *v.t* متناسب کول
fit

mutanasib kawal *v.t.* متناسب کول
proportion

mutanaway *a.* متنوع
miscellaneous

mutaqabal amal kawal *v.t.* متقابل
عمل کول reciprocate

mutaqabal; mutanawab *a.* متقابل،
متناوب reciprocal

mutaqabil warandeyz *n.* متقابل
واندز paradox

mutaqabil zawab *n.* متقابل واب
retort

mutaqabil zawab warkawal *v.t.*
متقابل واب ورکول retort

mutaqaid *n.* متقاعد pensioner

mutasavi ul azla *a* متساوی الاضلاع
equilateral

mutasil *a.* متصل adjacent

mutasil *adj.* متصل conjunct

mutasil kawal *v.t.* متصل کول
adjoin

mutasirawal *v.t.* متاثرول impress

mutasirawal *v.t.* متاثرول inspire

mutawajo *a.* متوجه attentive

mutawajo *a.* متوجه wary

mutawajo kawal *v.* متوجه کول
advert

mutawajo keydal *v.t.* متوجه کدل
overlook

mutawajo oseydal *v.i.* متوجه اوسدل
beware

mutawasit *a.* متوسط average

mutawatir *adj.* متواتر consecutive

mutawazeeul azla *n.* متوازی
الاضلاع parallelogram

mutazad *a.* متضاد paradoxical

mutee *a* مطیع dutiful

mutee *a.* مطیع submissive

mutee kawal v.t. مطیع کول subdue

mutmain *a.* مطمئن confident

muwafaq; khoshhala *a.* موفق، خوشحاله prosperous

muwafiq *a.* موافق agreeable

muwafiq *a.* موافق suitable

muwafiq keydal *v.t.* موافق کیدل accord

muwafiq keydal; pa mawzoon ahang wayal *v.t.* موافق کدل،په موزون آهنویل tune

muwafiqat *n.* موافقت suitability

muwafiqat kawal *v.i.* موافقت کول agree

muzahimat kawal *v.i.* مزاحمت کول scuffle

muzahimat; shormashor *n.* مزاحمت؛شورماشور scuffle

muzakira *n.* مذاکره nagotiation

muzakira kawal *v.t.* مذاکره کول negotiate

muzakira kawal *v.i* مذاکره کول parley

muztarib *a.* مضطرب anxious

muztarib kawal *v. t* مضطرب کول distress

myashay *n.* میاشی mosquito

myasht *n.* میاشت month

myashtanay *a.* میاشتنی monthly

myashtanay mujala *n* میاشتنی مجله monthly

N

na *adv.* نه no

na amalee *a.* ناعملي impracticable

na amaleetob *n.* ناعملي‌توب impracticability

na andwaltob *n.* ناانولتوب odds

na arama *n* نارامه disquiet

na arwand *a.* نااروند incoherent

na awreydoonkay *a.* نه‌اورېدونکی inaudible

na badleydoonkay; na kageydoonkay *a.* ، نه‌بدلدونکی نه‌کدونکی inflexible

na basya; pati raghalay *a.* نابسیا؛ پاتراغلی insolvent

na beyleydoonkay *a.* نه‌بلدونکی inseparable

na cheez *a.* ناچیز negligible

na darana *n.* نادارنه intrepidity

na gholeydoonkay *a.* نه‌غولدونکی infallible

na hazmeydana *n.* نه‌هضمدنه indigestion

na hazmeydoonkay *a.* نه هضمدونکی indigestible

na heelay keydal *v. i* ناهیلی کدل despair

na heelee *n* نا هیلي despair

na ijra *a* نااجرا pending

na istimaleyda *n.* نه‌استعمالدا redundance

na jor *a.* ناجو inapplicable

na kharabeydoonkay *a.* نه خرابدونکی incorruptible

na khu *conj.* نه‌خو neither

na khu *conj* نه خو nor

na khwakhee khkara kawal *v.t.* ناخوښي كاره كول resent

na leeda *n* نه ليدا blindness

na leedoonkay *a.* نه ليدونكى invincible

na lostal keydal *n.* نه لوستل كدل illegibility.

na lostal keydoonkay *a.* نه لوستل كدونكى illegible

na manal; lughwa kawal *v.t.* نه منل،لغوه كول repeal

na manana *n* نه مننه denial

na manana *n.* نه مننه refusal

na manana *n.* نه مننه refutation

na manana *n* نه مننه repeal

na mard; bey la insana da waseelay *a.* نامرد،بله انسان دوسيله unmanned

na mashroo gad zhwand *n.* نا مشروع ژوند concubinage

na mateydoonkay *n.* نه ماتدونكى adamant

na mehraban *a.* نامهربان inhospitable

na mehsoos *a.* نامحسوس intangible

na munasib *a.* نامناسب improper

na mushakhkhas *a.* نامشخص indistinct

na mustaqeem *a.* نامستقيم indirect

na omeeda *a.* نااميده hopeless

na oomeeda *a* نااميده desperate

na pak *a.* ناپاك unwell

na peywastoon *n.* نه پوستون non-alignment

na poh *a.* ناپوه witless

na qararee *n.* ناقراري malaise

na radeydoonkay *a.* نه ردېدونكى irrefutable

na ragheydoonkay *a.* نه رغدونكى incorrigible

na raz *n* ناراض malcontent

na raza *a.* ناراضه malcontent

na razayat kawal *v. t.* نارضايت كول dissatisfy

na razee keydoonkay *a.* نه راضې كدونكى insatiable

na roghwalay *n* ناروغوالى morbidity

na sam *a* ناسم abnormal

na seez ganral *v.i* نا يزل trifle

na sharha keydoonkay *a.* نه شرحه كدونكى indescribable

na shmeyri khabari kawal *v.t.* نا شمري خبر كول jabber

na shukree *n.* ناشكري ingratitude

na tajroba kar *n.* نا تجربه كار inexperience

na tajruba kar *a.* ناتجربه كار junior

na wada shawi khaza *n.* ناوادهشو مه maid

na wara kar kawona *n.* ناوه كار كوونه malpractice

na wara nyat *a.* ناوه نيت malafide

na wara; kharab *a* ناوه،خراب evil

na wayla keydana *n.* نه ويلكدنه insolvency

na waylay keydoonkay *n.* نه ويلا كدونكى insoluble

na yawazi *conj* نه يواز both

na zghamana *n.* نه زغمنه intolerance

na zghamowoonkay *a.* نه زغمونکی intolerable

na zghamowoonkay *a.* نه زغمونکی intolerant

na zhghoroonkay *a.* نهژغورونکی indefensible

na zhranda shawi wareeji *n.* نه ژرندهشوورﯦج paddy

naarama *n* ناآرامه discontent

naaramee *n* ناآرامي discomfort

naashna *a.* ناآشنا strange

nabaligh *a.* نابالغ premature

nabaryalay balal *v. t.* نابرﯦالیبلل disqualify

nabatee koch *n.* نباتي کوچ margarine

nabatee koochnee sporawan *n.* نباتي کوچنيسپورونه pollen

nabatee sheera *n.* نباتيشیره sap

nabatee zhwand *n.* نباتيژوند vegetation

nabatee; sabzay pori arwand *a.* نباتي;سبزیپوراوند vegetable

nabawara kawal *v. t.* ناباورهکول distrust

nabawaree *n* ناباوري distrust

nabawee *a.* نبوي prophetic

nabaz *n.* نبض pulse

nabee *n.* نبي prophet

naboowat *n.* نبوت prophecy

nachar *a.* ناچار inevitable

nachar kawal *v.t.* ناچارکول oblige

nacheez *a.* ناچیز petty

nadooda *a.* نادوده outmoded

nadrust *a.* نادرست inexact

nafar; shakhs *n.* نفر,شخص person

nafarman *a.* نافرمان insubordinate

nafarman *a.* نافرمان wayward

larghonayn. *n* نافرماني insubordination

nafee *n.* نفي negation

nafoos *n.* نفوس population

nafooz kawal *v.t.* نفوذکول pervade

nafooz; nanawatana *n.* نفوذ;ننوتنه penetration

nafrat *n.* نفرت repugnance

naftee mawad *n.* نفتيمواد petroleum

naghdey *a.* نغدي pecuniary

naghdi peysey *n.* نغدپیسه cash

nagheeree kawal *v.t.* ناغيرکول shirk

nagheeree kawoonkay *n.* ناغي کوونکی shirker

naghota kawoonkay *a.* نغوته کوونکی suggestive

nagokheydal *v.i.* نوډل plod

naha *n.* نهه nine

naham *a.* نهم ninth

nahang *n* نهڼ alligator

nahang *n* نهڼ crocodile

nahawar *a.* ناهوار rugged

nahawarawal *v.t.* ناهوارول ruffle

naheelay kawal *v. t* ناهیلیکول daunt

naheeya *n.* ناحیه region

naheeya *n.* ناحیه sector

naheeya; ilaqa *n.* ناحیه;علاقه parish

najabat *n.* نجابت nobility

najeeb zada *n.* نجیبزاده magnate

najlay *n.* نجلۍ girl

najlay ghokhtal *v.t.* نجلۍغوتل woo

414

najlay ghonde *a.* نجلاغوند girlish

nak *n.* ناک pear

nakafee *a.* ناکافي insufficient

nakafee *a.* ناکافي scanty

nakamee *n* ناکامي failure

nakamee *n* ناکامي fiasco

nakar; lat *a.* ناکار،لت sluggish

nakara shay *n.* ناکارهشی trash

nakarara *a* ناکراره fitful

nakeydoonay *a.* ناکدونی unlikely

nakha eekhodal *v. i* نهايودل
denote

nakha eekhoodoonkay *n.* نه
ايودونکی marker

nakha laroonkay *a.* نهلرونکی
symbolic

nakha weeshtoonkay *n.* نه
ويشتونکی marksman

nakhalis; barjasta *a* ناخالص،
برجسته gross

nakhan *n.* نان mark

nakhan lagawal *v.t* نانلول mark

nakhana; teekat *n.* نانه،ٮک token

nakhcha *n* نخچه map

nakhcha akheestana *n.* نخچه
اخيستنه topography

nakhcha akheestano pori
arwand *a.* نخچهاخيستنوپوراوند
topographical

nakhcha jorawal *v.t.* نخچهجووّل
map

nakhcha kakh *n.* نخچهکښ
topographer

nakhlawal *v.t.* نلول attach

nakhleydal; pa lakari wahal *v.t.*
 نلدل،پهلکوهل stick

nakhleydal *n* نخر,مکز flirt

nakhtar *n* نتر fir

nakhteyzal *v.t* نتل nip

nakhteyzal *v.t.* نتل twist

nakhwakh *a.* خو نا disagreeable

nakhwakhee *n.* ناخوي
disagreement

nakhwakhee *n* ناخوي disapproval

nakhwakhee *n.* ناخوي reluctance

nakreezi *n.* نکرۍ myrtle

nal *n.* نل tube

nal; nawa; fawara *n.* نل،ناوه،فواره
spout

nal; necha *n* نل،نیچه fistula

nal; soornray *n.* نل،سوری pipe

nalay *n.* نا nozzle

nalayiq *a.* نالائق incompetent

nalbakay *n.* نالبکی saucer

naldawan; sarp kar *n.* نلدوان،
سرپکار plumber

naleedalay *a.* نالیدلی invisible

naloono ki oba rasawal *v.i* نلونوکه
اوبهرسول pipe

nam *a* نم damp

nam *n.* نم moisture

nam payda kawal *v.t.* نمپداکول
moisten

namafhooma shor aw zwag *n*
نامفهومهشوراوزو babel

namahirana peywandawal *v. t*
ناماهرانهپوندول botch

namak haram *a* نمکحرام
disloyal

namaqool *a.* نامعقول illogical

namaqoola *a.* نامعقوله irrational

namasaid halat *n.* نامساعدحالت predicament

namjan *a.* نمجن moist

namjan; loond *a.* نمجن،لوند humid

namnak *adj.* نمناک dank

namoona *n* نمونه mould

namoona *n.* نمونه sample

namoona *n.* نمونه parable

namoona khodal; da mayar banra warkawal *v.t.* نمونه و دل؛دمعياربهوركول typify

namoona; beylga *n.* نمونه،بله instance

namoona; mayar *n.* نمونه؛معيار paragon

namtoo *a* نامتو brilliant

namtoo; alee janaba *a* نامتو،عال جنابه eminent

namunasib *a.* نامناسب irrelevant

namzadgee *n.* نامزدي betrothal

nan da shpey *adv.* نندشپ tonight

nan shpa *n.* ننشپه to-night

nan wraz *n.* ورنن today

nana estana *v.t.* ننهايستنه jab

nanawatal; dakhileydal *v. t* ننوتل؛ داخلدل enter

nanawatana *n.* ننوتنه admittance

nanawatana *n* ننوتنه entrance

nanawatana *n* ننوتنه entry

nanaweystal; zayawal *v.t.* ننوستل؛ ايول insert

nanaweystana *n.* ننوستنه insertion

nandara *n.* ننداره exhibit

nandara jorawoonkay *n* ننداره جووونکی dramatist

nandaray wahal; nandaray *v. i.* ناندروهل؛ناندر *n &* brawl

nandarey ta zahirawal *v. t* نندارته ظاهرول display

nandarey; nandarey wahal *n&.* ناندر؛ناندروهل *v.i* clack

nandari ta wrandi kawal *v. t* نندارتهوراندکول exhibit

nandartoon *n.* نندارتون exhibition

naneydal *v.i.* نندل ooze

naneydal; teetawal *v. t.* نندل؛تيتول sprinkle

naneydana; sheendana *n.* نندنه؛ شيندنه spray

napakee *n.* ناپاکي impurity

napawal; wazan kawal *v.t.* ناپول؛ وزنکول scale

napaydar *a* ناپايدار fickle

napaydar *n.* ناپايدار transitory

napoh *a.* پوه نا apish

napoh *n* ناپوه fool

napoh *a.* ناپوه ignorant

napohee *n* ناپوهي folly

napohee *n.* ناپوهي ignorance

napohee; kam taleemee *n.* ناپوهي؛ کمتعليمي illiteracy

napukhta *a.* ناپخته immature

napukhtagee *n.* ناپختي immaturity

naqab *n.* نقاب mask

naqab achowal *v.t.* نقاباچول mask

naqal *n* نقل copy

naqal jorawal *v. t* نقلجورول copy

naqal jorawal *v. t* نقلجورول duplicate

naqal jorawana n. نقل‌جوونه transcription

naqanoona a. ناقانونه wrongful

naqashee; anzorgaree n. نقاشي؛ انوروري painting

naqis a. ناقص imperfect

naqras n. نقرس gout

naqrayee a نقرهيي silver

naqsh kawal v.t. نقش‌كول inscribe

naqsh; banra n نقش،به figure

naqsh; muhar n. نقش،مهر stamp

nar khazay n نرى eunuch

nar pashay n. نرپشى tomcat

nara; shuar n. ناره،شعار slogan

naram a. نرم lenient

naram a. نرم mellow

naram a. نرم mild

naram a. نرم polite

naram aw teeng a. نرماوينذ sedate

naram bad n نرم‌باد waft

naram saqa; tak n. نرم‌ساقه،تاك vine

naram; lateef n. نرم،لطيف soft

naram; lateef a نرم،لطيف tender

naram; sayqalee a. نرم؛صيقلي sleek

narama a. نارامه inconvenient

narama a. نارامه restive

narama kawal v.t. نارامه‌كول hinder

narama kawal v.t. نارامه‌كول obsess

narama kawal v.t. نارامه‌كول perturb

naranj n. نارنج orange

naranjee a نارنجي orange

narasmee jangyalay n. نارسمي جنيالى guerilla

narawa a. ناروا inadmissible

narawa kar kawal v.t. ناروا‌كاركول wrong

narawa; armoonay a. ناروا؛ارمونى illegitimate

narawa; ghalat a. ناروا،غلط wrong

narawal v.t. نول subvert

naray a. نرى thin

naray n. ن world

naray kawal v.i. نرى‌كول taper

naray lakhta n. نرلته withe

naray ranz n. نرى‌رنز tuberculosis

naray warakht n نرى‌ورت drizzle

naray warakht wareydal v. i نرى ورت‌ورېدل drizzle

naraypal n. نپال worldling

nareekhtoonay a نارېتونى sham

nareekhtoonay; armoonay a. نارېتونى؛ارمونى spurious

nareena a. نارينه male

nareena a. نرينه masculine

nareena as n. نارينه‌اس stallion

nareena jinsee zwak; nareentob n. نارينه‌جنسي‌واك،نارينتوب virility

nareena sra gowaza n. نارينه‌سره وزه stag

nareentob n. نارينتوب manhood

nareentob n نارينتوب manliness

nareewal a. نيوال global

nareewal a. نيوال international

nareewal a. نيوال universal

narey soorey a. نارسور outcry

narey soorey *n* نار سور yell

narey soorey kawal *v.i.* نارسور کول yell

nareydal *v.i.* ندل topple

nareydalay *a.* ندلی subversive

narkh; sharah *n.* نرخ؛شرح rate

narma khata *n.* نرمه‌خه ooze

narma oogda sawkay *n.* نرمه‌اوده وکو sofa

narmakht *n.* نرمت lenience, leniency

narmakht *a.* نرمت rickety

narmawal *v.t.* نرمول masticate

narmawal *v.t.* نرمول smooth

narmawal; mulayim keydal *v.t.* نرمول؛ملایم کدل soften

narmee *n.* نرمی laxity

narmee *n.* نرمی politeness

narmeydal *v.i.* نرمدل relent

narogha *a.* ناروغه sick

naroghee *n.* ناروغی ailment

narogheydal *v.t.* ناروغدل ail

nasab *n.* نسب parentage

nasab kawal; toghawal *v.t.* نصب کول؛توغول pitch

nasab shaway zay *n.* نصب‌شوی‌ای pitch

nasabnama *n.* نسب‌نامه pedigree

nasal *n.* نسل generation

nasal *n.* نسل posterity

nasam *a.* ناسم inaccurate

nasam chaland kawal *v.i.* ناسم چلندکول misbehave

nasam darak kawal *v.t.* ناسم‌درک کول misapprehend

nasam karawal *v.t.* ناسم‌کارول misuse

nasam karowana *n.* ناسم‌کارونه misuse

nasam khodal *v.t.* ناسم‌ودل misrepresent

nasam poheydal *v.t.* ناسم‌پوهدل misconceive

nasam poheydal *v.t.* ناسم‌پوهدل misunderstand

nasam shay *n.* ناسم‌شی misfit

nasam shmeyral *v.t.* ناسم‌شمرل miscalculate

nasam tabeerawal *v.t.* ناسم‌تعبیرول misconstrue

nasam; najor *adv.* ناسم؛ناجو ill

nasama larkhowana *n.* ناسمه لاروونه misdirection

nasama shmeyra *n.* ناسمه‌شمره miscalculation

nasamee *n.* ناسمی mal adjustment

nasapa *a* ناپه abrupt

nasapa *adv.* ناپه forthwith

nasapa breed *n* ناپه‌برید pounce

nasapa breed landi neewal *v.i.* ناپه‌برید لاندی‌نیول swoop

nasapa kharabtya *n* breakdown

nasapa lambey lageydal *v.i* لمب ناپه لدل flare

nasapa surat zyatawal *v.i.* ناپه سرعت‌زیاتول spurt

nasapa takan *n.* ناپه‌مکان jolt

nasapa takar *n* ناپه‌مکر crash

nasapaee breed kawal *v.i.* ناپه‌برید کول storm

nasapee *n* ناپی abruption

nasapee *a* ناپی dramatic

nasapee aw chatak faaleeyat *n.* نساپواوچک‌فعاليت sally

nasapee aw gadwad harakat *n.* ناپي‌اووحركت rush

nasapee badloon *n.* ناپي‌بدلون upheaval

nasapee breed *n* ناپي‌بريد swoop

nasapee dalayeez harakat *n.* ناپي لەييزحركت stampede

nasapee dar *n.* ناپي‌ار fright

nasapee darawal *v.t.* ناپي‌ارول frighten

nasapee hasa *n* ناپي‌هه spurt

nasapee park ya baheer *n* ناپي پک‌يابهير flush

nasapee parkeydal ya baheydal *v.i* ناپي‌پکدل‌يابهدل flush

nasapee peykha *n.* ناپي‌په sudden

nasapee toghawona *n.* ناپتوغونه lunge

nasapeetob *n.* ناپي‌توب spontaneity

nasapi *a.* ناپي haphazard

nasar *n.* نثر prose

nasaz *a.* ناساز indisposed

nasbawal *v. t* نصبول erect

nasbawal *v.t* نصبول fix

nasbawoonkay *n* نصبوونکی fitter

naseehat *n* نصيحت advice

naseehat *n.* نصيحت maxim

naseehat kawal *v.t.* نصيحت‌کول advise

nasha kawal *v.t.* نشه‌کول intoxicate

nasha kawona *n.* نشه‌کونه intoxication

nasha saray *n* نشه‌سی drunkard

nashar; khparaway *n.* نشر، خپراوی publication

nashayee mawad *n.* نشه‌يي‌مواد narcosis

nashayee mawad *n.* نشه‌يي‌مواد narcotic

nashayee skhak *n.* نشه‌ياک intoxicant

nashoonay *a.* ناشونی impassable

nashoonay *a.* ناشونی impossible

nashoontya *n.* ناشونتيا impossibility

nashrawal *v.t.* نشرول publish

nasht *n.* نشت nil

nasht; sifar *n.* نشت،صفر nought

nasht; sifar *n.* نشت،صفر zero

nashtoon; da manfee alama *n* نشتون،دمنفي‌علامه minus

nashukra *a.* ناشکره thankless

nasj *n.* نسج tissue

nasoor; changakh *n.* ناسور،چنا cancer

naswar *n.* نسوار snuff

naswaree *a* نصواري brown

naswaree rang *n* نصواري‌رن brown

nasyan; heyrawana *n* نسيان،هرونه amnesia

natajruba karee *n.* ناتجربه‌کاري naivety

natakmeel *a* . ناتکميل incomplete

natanzeemee *n.* ناتنظيمي mal administration

nateeja *n.* نتيجه conclusion

nateeja *n.* نتيجه result

nateeja warkawal *v.i.* نتيجه‌ورکول result

nateekawtob *n.* ناېکاوتوب
instability

natwan *a* ناتوان disabled

natwan *a.* ناتوان incapable

natwan *a.* ناتوان unable

natwan kawal *v.t.* ناتوان کول
impoverish

natwana kawal *v. t* ناتوانه کول
disable

natwana kawal *v. t.* ناتوانه کول
enfeeble

natwana kawal; natwana keydal
v.t&.i ناتوانه کول;ناتوانه کدل
weaken

natwanee *n* ناتواني disability

natwanee *n.* ناتواني inability

nawa; kanal *n.* ناوه، کانال groove

nawab *n.* نواب nabob

nawada kari najlay *n.* ناواده کنجل
spinster

nawakht *n.* نوت invention

nawakht *n.* نوت novelty

nawakhtgar *n.* نوتر inventor

nawalay *a.* ناولی impure

nawalay *n.* ناولی rubbish

nawalay kawal *v.t.* ناولی کول
pollute

nawalay shay *n.* ناولشی mess

nawalay; kheyran *a.* ناول;خرن foul

nawaleetob *n.* ناولیتوب pollution

nawali aw chatali oba *n.* ناولاوچل
اوبه sewage

nawara *a* ناوه abusive

nawara *a.* ناوه bad

nawara *a.* ناوه heinous

nawara aw past saray *n.* ناوهاو
پستسی skate

nawara banra warkawal *v.t.* ناوه
بهورکول uglify

nawara bawar *n.* ناوهباور
misbelief

nawara chaland *n.* ناوهچلند
misbehaviour

nawara chaland *n.* ناوهچلند
miscarriage

nawara chalowana *n.* ناوهچلوونه
mismanagement

nawara gata porta kawal *v. i* ناوه
هپورتهکول encroach

nawara ghageydal *v. i* ناوهغدل
blether

nawara istimal *n.* ناوهاستعمال
misapplication

nawara khabari *n* ناوهخبر yap

nawara leekana *n* scrawl

nawara peykha *n.* ناوهپه
misadventure

nawara saray *a* ناوهسی forlorn

nawara teyrwatana kawal *v.i* ناوه
تروتنهکول blunder

nawara yawwalay *n.* ناوهیووالی
misalliance

nawara; nasam *adv.* ناوه،ناسم
amiss

nawara; wazhoonkay *a* ناوه،وژونکه
deadly

nawarta *a* ناورته dissimilar

nawarta walay *n* ناورتهوالی
disparity

nawartob *n.* ناوتوب impropriety

nawartob *n* ناوتوب
disqualification

nawartya *n* ناوتيا demerit

naway *a.* نوى new

naway *a.* نوى novel

naway askar *n.* نوىعسكر recruit

naway baday shaway *n.* نوىباى شوى upstàrt

naway kadwal *n.* نوىكوال settler

naway kar *n.* نوىكار novice

naway pohantoonee zdakryal *n.* نوىپوهنتونيزدكيال undergraduate

naway tawleed *n.* نوىتوليد regeneration

naway zwan *n.* نوىوان teenager

nawbatee *a.* نوبتي periodical

nawee *n.* نوي ninety

nawi *n* ناو bride

nawi banra warkawal *v.t.* نوبه وركول modernize

nawi banra warkawal *v.* نوبه وركول transform

nawi zwanee *n.* نوواني rejuvenation

nawkar *n.* نوكر lackey

nawkar *n* نوكر menial

nawkar sifatee *n.* نوكرصفتي servility

nawyam *a.* نويم ninetieth

nayab *a* ناياب extinct

nayab *a.* ناياب rare

nayib; zaynastay *n.* نايب،زايناستى vicar

naylon *n.* نايلون nylon

naymat *n* نعمت boon

naz nakhra *n* نازنخره ogle

naz; bati *n* ناز،با brag

nazak *a.* نازك frail

nazak; wreykhmeen *a.* نازك، ورخمين sheer

nazakat *n* نزاكت decency

nazam *n.* نظم verse

nazam leekal *v.t.* نظمليكل versify

nazam leekana *n.* نظمليكنه versification

nazam warkharabawal *v.t.* نظم ورخرابول unsettle

nazar *n.* نذر oblation

nazarat *n.* نظارت surveillance

nazarat *n.* نظارت supervision

nazarat kawal *v.t.* نظارتكول supervise

nazaree *a.* نظري theoretical

nazaree ilam *n.* نظريعلم theory

nazaree seyrani kawal *v.i.* نظري كول theorize

nazaree teyrwatana *n.* نظريتروتنه oversight

nazawal *v. t.* نازول caress

nazawal *v. t.* نازول cherish

nazawal *v.t* نازول fondle

nazawal *v.t.* نازول pat

nazawal *v.t.* نازول pet

nazawalay; gran *n.* نازولى،ران pet

nazawana *n* نازوونه pat

nazeydal *v. i* نازدل brag

nazhad *n* نژاد caste

nazhdey *adv.* نژد anigh

nazhdey *a.* نژد approximate

nazhdey *prep.* نژد nigh

nazhdey *a.* نژد proximate

nazhdey *a.* نژد near

nazhdey ashnatob *n.* نژداشناتوب
intimacy

nazhdey keydal *v.t.* نژدکدل
approach

nazhdey keydal *v.i.* نژدکدل near

nazhdey leedana *n.* نژدلیدنه
myopia

nazhdey leeday *a.* نژدلیدی myopic

nazhdey malgaray *n.* نژدملری
counterpart

nazhdeywalay *n.* نژدوالی
proximity

nazhdeywalay *n.* نژدوالی vicinity

nazhdeywalay; las raseyda *n.*
نژدوالی؛لاس‌رسدا approach

nazir *n.* ناظر controller

nazir *n.* ناظر supervisor

nazir; peyra dar *n* ناظر؛پره‌دار
chamberlain

nazir; qanoonee wakeel *n.* ؛ناظر
قانوني‌وکیل proctor

nazm; qayda *n* نظم؛قاعده
discipline

nazowana *n.* نازوونه endearment

nazuk *a.* نازک fragile

nazuk *a.* نازک slim

**neekana; da plar neeka pa
arwand** *a.*
نیکانه؛دپلارنیکه‌په
اوند ancestral

neekoona aw plaroona *n.* نیکونه‌او
پلرونه predecessor

neel *n* نیل blue

neem *a* نیم half

neem kakha *adv.* نیم‌که ajar

neema shpa *n.* نیمه‌شپه midnight

neemawal *v. t* نیمول bisect

neemayee *n.* نیمایي half

neemayee kawal *v.t.* نیمایي‌کول
halve

neemayee wraz *n.* ور نیمایي
midday

neemgaray *a.* نیمی sketchy

neemgartya *n* نیمتیا deficit

neemgartya *n.* نیمتیا imperfection

neewa *v. t.* نیول catch

neewaka *n.* نیوکه objection

neewaka kawal *v. t.* نیوکه‌کول
castigate

neewaka kawal *v. t* نیوکه‌کول
criticize

neewal *v.t.* نیول arrest

neewal *v.t.* نیول nab

neewal; taskheerawal *v. t.* نیول؛
تسخیرول capture

neewana *n.* نیونه capture

neewana *n.* نیونه catch

neewana *n.* نیوونه seizure

neewana; tawqeef *n.* نیونه؛توقیف
arrest

neewani sakha eystal *v.t.* نیونخه
ایستل decontrol

neewoonkay *n.* نیوونکی occupant

neewoonkay *n.* نیوونکی occupier

neygh *a.* نغ straight

neygh pa neygha *a* نغ‌په‌نغه direct

neygh; sam *a.* نغ؛سم right

neygh; walar *a.* نغ؛ولا upright

neykee *n* نکي good

neykh laroonkay *a.* نلرونکی
stingy

neykhtar *n.* نتر lancet

neykmargha *a.* نکمرغه fortunate

neykmargha *a.* نکمرغه lucky

neyza *n* نزه bayonet

neyza *n.* نزه lance

neyza *n.* نزه spear

neyza wahoonkay *n.* نزه‌وهونکی lancer

nghota kawal *v.i.* نغوته‌کول allude

nghota; ishara *n* نغوته،اشاره allusion

nijat *n.* نجات emancipation

nijat warkawal *v.t.* نجات‌ورکول rescue

nijat; khlasoon *n* نجات،خلاصون rescue

nika *n.* نکاح wedlock

nisab *n.* نصاب quorum

nisbat; sharah *n.* نسبت،شرح ratio

nisbatan loy *a.* نسبتاًلوی sizable

nishasta *n.* نشاسته starch

nizamee dalgay *n.* نظامی‌ډله squad

nizamee zwak *n.* نظامی‌واک militia

nkhalawal *v.t.* نلول ally

nobat; halat *n* نوبت،حالت bout

nobatee bad wa baran *n.* نوبتی‌باد وباران monsoon

nobatee taba *n.* نوبتی‌تبه malaria

nobatee; beylgayeez *a.* نوبتی،بله‌ییز typical

nook *n.* نوک nail

noolas *n.* نولس nineteen

noolasam *a.* نولسم nineteenth

noom *n.* نوم name

noom lar *n.* نوم‌لٱ nomenclature

noom leekana *n.* نوم‌لیکنه registration

noom leekana kawal *v. t* نوم‌لیکنه کول enlist

noom leekana kawal *v. t* نوم‌لیکنه کول enrol

noom pri eekhodal *v.t.* نوم‌پرایودل term

noom warakay *n.* نوم‌ورکی anonymity

noom warkawal *v.t.* نوم‌ورکول name

noomand *n.* نوماند candidate

noomand *n* نوماند nominee

noomand kawal *v.t.* نوماندکول nominate

noomawana *n.* نومونه nomination

noomawaray *n* نوموی celebrity

noomeez *a.* نومیز nominal

noomleek *n.* نوملیک list

noomoona leekal *v.t.* نمونه‌لیکل list

noompohana *n.* نومپوهنه terminology

noompohaneez *a.* نومپوهنیز terminological

noomyalay *a* نومیالی famous

noomyaleetob *n.* نومیالیتوب prominence

noomzaray *n.* نومزری pronoun

nooranee *a.* نورانی radiant

nooranee kawal *v.t.* نورانی‌کول transfigure

nooranee shpol *n.* نورانی‌شپول nimbus

nooraneeyat *n.* نورانیت radiance

noorlas kalan zwan *n. pl.* نورلس کلن‌زون teens کلنوان

nor *a.* نور more

423

noro sakha jala kawal *v.t.* نوروخه جلاکول segregate

notaka; nyal; sooka *n* نوتکه،نیال، وکه sprout

numayanda *n.* نماینده representative

numayinda *n.* نماینده proxy

numayinda *n* نمائنده deputy

numayindagee kawoonkay *a.* نمایندگي کوونکی representative

numayish *n* نمایش display

numayish *n.* نمایش manifestation

numayishee *a.* نمایشي gaudy

nuqs *n* نقص defect

nuqsan *n.* نقصان damage

nuqsan *n.* نقصان decrement

nuqtey eekhodana *n.* نقطه ایودنه punctuation

nuqz *n* نقض breach

nuqzee *adj.* نقضي deficient

nuskha *n.* نسخه prescription

nuskha warkawal *v.t.* نسخه ورکول prescribe

nuskha; formool *n.* نسخه؛فورمول recipe

nuskha; naqal *n.* نسخه،نقل replica

nuskha; riwayat *n.* نسخه،روایت version

nutfa *n.* نطفه sperm

nutfa; tukham *n.* نطفه،تخم semen

nutfawee *a.* نطفوي seminal

nyabatee *a.* نیابتي vicarious

nyal; qalma *n.* نیال،قلمه sapling

nyat baday *a.* نیت بدی jealous

nyat badee *n.* نیت بدي jealousy

nyaw *n.* نیاو justice

nyawgar *a.* نیاوګر just

oba *n.* اوبه water

oba kawal *v. t* اوبه کول drench

oba malham *n.* اوبه ملهم balsam

oba na akheestoonkay *a.* اوبه نه اخیستونکی watertight

oba warkawal *v.t.* اوبه ورکول water

obawal *v.t.* اوبول irrigate

obawana *n.* اوبوونه irrigation

obdal *v.t.* اوبدل knit

obdal shaway *a.* اوبدلشوی textile

obdal shaway khazeena jakat *n.* اوبدلشوی ینه جاک jersey

obdana; tanasta *n.* اوبدنه،تنسته texture

obgarzanay *n.* اوبرنی whirlpool

oblan *a* اوبلن dilute

oblan *a.* اوبلن watery

oblan kawal *v. t* اوبلن کول dilute

oblan khorak *n.* اوبلن خوراک mash

obo ki ghopa keydal *v.i.* اوبو کغوپه کدل duck

obo ki lahoo keydal *v.i* اوبو کلاهو کدل drown

obzad garzawal *v.t.* اوبضدرول waterproof

obzad; na loondeydoonkay *a.* اوبضد،نه لوندیدونکی waterproof

odal *v.t.* اول arrange

odal *v.t.* اول array

odoon *n.* اوون arrangement

ofqee karkha *n.* افقي کره horizon

oj *n.* اوج climax

oj ta raseydal *v.i.* اوجته رسدل culminate

oj; ghwara wakht *n.* اوج;غوره وخت prime

oj; teyra sooka *n.* اوج;ترموکه pinnacle

omeed *n* امید hope

omeed laroonkay *a.* امیدلرونکی optimistic

ooga *n.* اوه garlic

ooga warkawal *v. t* اوهورکول encourage

ooga; walay *n.* اوه;ولی shoulder

oogad *a.* اود verbose

oogad *a.* اود lengthy

oogad aw azad kamees *n.* اوداو ازادکمیس robe

oogad aw azad kamees aghostal *v.t.* اوداوازادکمیس اغوستل robe

oogad aw dangar *a.* اوداونر lank

oogad aw teyra ghakh *n.* اوداوتره غا tusk

oogad dastkash *n.* اوددستکش gauntlet

oogad mahala *a.* اودمهاله chronic

oogad sadar *n.* اودادر toga

oogad zhwand *n.* اودژوند longevity

oogadwalay *n.* اودوالی length

oogadwalay *n.* اودوالی prolongation

oogda *a.* اود long

oogda *a.* اود oblong

oogda aw la qahra daka wayna *n.* اودهاولهقهره کهونا tirade

oogda mukhtalif rangoona laroonki patay *n.* اودهمختلف رنونهلرونکپ stripe

oogda sawkay *n* اودموک bench

oogda zhawara dara *n.* اودهژوره دره ravine

oogdawal *v. t* اودول extend

oogdawal *v.t.* اودول lengthen

oogdawal *v.t.* اودول prolong

oogdey khazeena jorabey *n.* اود ینهجوراب stocking

oogey porta khozawal *v.t.* اوپورته خوول shrug

oogey spakawal *v.t.* اوسپکول parry

ookh *n.* او camel

ookhka *n.* اوکه tear

oomar *n.* عمر age

oomar khwaralay *a.* عمرخولی old

oomar khwaralay insan *a.* عمر خولیانسان senile

oonay *n.* اوون week

ooneez *a.* اوونیز weekly

ooray; sareykh *n.* اور;سر gum

oqab *n* عقاب eagle

or *n* اور fire

or akheystoonkay *a.* اوراخیستونکی inflammable

or balawal *v.t.* اوربلول kindle

or lagawal *v.t* اورلول fire

or wazhal *v.t* اوروژل extinguish

ora *n* اوه flour

ora dawla *a.* اوهوله mealy

orakht *n* اورت rain

orakht wareydal *v.i.* اورت‌وریدل rain

orbal *n* اوربل forelock

orgaday *n.* اورپای rail

orgaday *n.* اورپای train

orlageet *n.* اورلیت match

orlageet balowal *v.i.* اورلیت‌بلوول match

ornay *adj* اونی aestival

orsheenday *a.* اورشیندی volcanic

orsheenday ghar *n.* اورشیندی‌غر volcano

ortak *n.* اورک lighter

os *adv.* اوس now

os mahal *adv.* اوس‌مهال presently

oseydal *v.i* اوسدل abide

oseydoonkay *n* اوسدونکی resident

ospana *n.* اوسپنه iron

oto kawal *v.t.* اوتوکول iron

oto kawal *v.t.* اوتوکول mangle

owa *n.* اووه seven

owallas *n., a* اولس seventeen

owallasam *a.* اوولسم seventeenth

owam *a.* اووم seventh

owama *a* اوومه seven

P

pa ... ki; pa ... manz ki *prep.* په ___ک؛په___مذک among

pa ... manz ki; la ... dali sakha *prep.* په___مذک؛له___لخه amongst

pa adab sara *a.* په‌ادب‌سره mannerly

pa adat sara *adv.* په‌عادت‌سره ordinarily

pa adilana toga *adv.* په‌عادلانه‌توه justly

pa akhira ki *adv.* په‌آخره‌که ultimately

pa ala natoona pranistal; rashkawal *v.t.* په‌آله‌نونه پرانستل؛راشکول wrench

pa amoomee rayo sara sharal *v.t.* په‌عمومی‌رایوسره‌شل ostracize

pa ara reybal *v.t.* په‌اره‌ربل saw

pa aram sara *adv.* په‌آرام‌سره leisurely

pa asal ki *adv.* په‌اصل‌ک mainly

pa asantya sara *adv.* په‌آسانتیاسره readily

pa azabawal *v.t.* په‌عذابول agonize

pa badnyatay sara *a.* په‌بدنیته‌سره niggardly

pa badraga malgartya kawal *v. t* په‌بدره‌ملرتیاکول escort

pa bal nama *adv.* په‌بل‌نامه alias

pa bala akhta kawal *v.t.* په‌بلااخته کول plague

pa bala panra *adv.* په‌بله‌پله overleaf

pa balakht sar eekhodal *v.t.* په بالت‌سرایودل pillow

pa barkho weyshal *v.t.* په‌برخو وشل portion

pa barkho weyshal *v.t.* په‌برخو وشل segment

pa bashpar dawl *adv.* پهبشپول
altogether

pa bashpar dawl *adv.* پهبشپول
fully

pa bashpar dawl *adv.* پهبشپول
stark

pa bata gota soolawal *v.t.* پهبهوته
سولول thumb

pa beera leekal *v.t.* پهبيهليكل
scrawl

pa beera leekal *v.t.* پهبيهليكل
scribble

pa beeri sara takhteydal *v.i* پهبي
سرهتتدل scamper

pa bey khabray sara *adv.* پهبخبر
سره unawares

pa bey rahmay sara jinsee
khwand akheystoonkay *n.* په
برحمسرهجنسيخونداخستونكى
sadist

pa beydya ki *adv.* پهبديا ک afield

pa beykh ki prot *a.* پهبخ کپروت
terminal

pa beylchey sara arawal *v.t.* په
بلچسرهاول spade

pa bistar ki *adv.* پهبستركى abed

pa bukhar alwatal *v. i* پهبخارالوتل
evaporate

pa bukhar arawal *v.t.* پهبخاراول
vaporize

pa campyootar tasneefawal *v. t*
په کمپيورتصنيفول compose

pa chatak harakat leyri kawal
v.t. پهچک حرکتلرکول whisk

pa chatakay *adv* پهچک early

pa chatakay sara *adv* پهچکسره
fast

pa chatakay sara *adv.* پهچکسره
speedily

pa chatakay sara zghaleydal *v.i.*
پهچکسرمغلدل speed

pa chatkay sara *adv.* پهچکسره
apace

pa cheekaro nanawistal *v.t.* په
چيکوننوستل mire

pa cheygho faryad kawal *n.i.* په
چغوفريادكول bawl

pa chrap chrap sara khwaral
v.t. پهچپ چپسرهخول smack

pa dabaro pokhal *v.t.* پهبروپول
pave

pa dabaro weeshtal ya mokhal
v.t. پهبروويشتليامول stone

pa dadman dawl *adv.* پهامنول
surely

pa daftar ki sabtawal *v.t.* پهدفتر ک
ثبتول register

pa daftaro ki da istiqbal oogad
meyz *n.* پهدفترو کداستقبالاودمز
counter

pa daga wayal *v.t.* پهاهويل profess

pa dakhil pori arwand *adv.* په
داخلپوراوند inside

pa dal sara zhghoral *v.t.* پهالسره
ژغورل shield

pa dala ki harakat kawal *v.i* پهله
کحرکتكول troop

pa dala tlal *v. t* پهلهتلل delegate

pa dalayalo walar *a.* پهدلايلوولا
rational

pa dalo weyshal *v.t.* پهلووشل
group

pa danda da ghondaski wahalo
loba kawal *v. i* پهنهدغونسک
وهلولوبهكول bat

pa danda ghondaska wahoonkay lobgharay *n.* پهنه غونسکهوهونکیلوبغای batsman

pa dang peyalee *a.* پهانپیلی straightforward

pa daqeeqa toga *adv.* پهدقیقهتوه minutely

pa dar zarawona *n.* پهدارونه. gallows

pa darawano da peyso wasooltya *n* پهارونودپسو وصولتیا blackmail

pa dard khwarana *n.* پهدردخونه subservience

pa dard rawastal; rag awakhtal *v.t.* پهدردراوستل،راوتل sprain

pa daro daro weyshal *v.t.* پهدودو وشل plank

pa daw talbana dawl *adv.* پهداو طلبانهول voluntarily

pa dawat rabalal *v.t.* پهدعوترابلل convoke

pa dayrawee lori bandi harakat kawal *n.i.* پهدایرويلورباند حرکتکول whirl

pa dey barkha ki *adv* پهدبرخهک over

pa dey dawl *adv.* پهدول thus

pa dey dawran *adv.* پهددوران meanwhile

pa dey shawkhwa ki *adv.* پهد شاوخواک hereabouts

pa dey wakhtoono ki *adv.* پهد وختونوک today

pa difaee toga *adv.* پهدفاعيتوه defensive

pa diqat sara palatal *v.i.* پهدقت سرهپلل pry

pa doodeez deen bawar laroonkay *n.* پهدودیزدینباور لرونکی orthodoxy

pa doodeez deen bawaree *a.* په دودیزدینباوري orthodox

pa eesaeeyat ki asqaf *n* پهعیسائیت کاسقف bishop

pa eesaeeyat ki da tameed ghosal *n.* پهعیسائیت کدتعمید غسل baptism

pa eesaeeyat ki yaw mazhabee mashar *n.* پهعیسائیت کيومذهبي مشر cardinal

pa faaleeyat rawastal *v.t.* پهفعالیت راوستل prompt

pa fikree taraw bawaree *n.* په فکريتاوباوري telepathist

pa fishar sara jorawal *v.t.* پهفشار سرهجوول imprint

pa fuzla shayano da yaw zai laral *v.t.* پهفاضلهشیانو ديوای‌لل litter

pa gada kar kawal *v. i* پهکارکول collaborate

pa gada sara *adv.* پهسره jointly

pa gada sara *adv.* پهسره together

pa gada zhwand kawal *v. t* په ژوندکول cohabit

pa gadwad dawl *adv.* پهوول pell-mell

pa gadwaday sara *adv.* پهوسره chaotic

pa gamoono sara andaza neewana *n* پهامونوسرهاندازه نیونه stride

pa ganro khudayano bawar *n.* په وخدایانوباور polytheism

pa ganro khudayano bawar laroonkay *n.* پەخدايانوباور لرونکی polytheist

pa ganro khudayano pori arwand *a.* پەخدايانوپوراوند polytheistic

pa garandee dawl; nasapa *adv.* پەندیول،ناپه suddenly

pa ghakho shkawal *v.t.* پەغاو شکول nibble

pa ghalata ghag kawal *v.t.* پەغلطه غکول miscall

pa ghaleez dawl *adv.* پەغليظول thick

pa ghaltay sara *adv.* پەغلطسره wrong

pa ghamyo khkulay kawal *v.t.* پە غميوکلیکول jewel

pa ghazab kawal *v.t.* پەغضب کول outrage

pa ghla ghla katal *v.i.* پەغلاغلاکتل peep

pa ghla ghla tlal *v.i.* پەغلاغلاتلل sneak

pa ghla katana *n* پەغلاکتنه peep

pa ghosa kawal *v.t.* پەغصه کول aggravate

pa ghosa kawal *v. t* پەغصه کول enrage

pa ghrap ghrap skhal *v.t.* پەغپ غپل sip

pa ghwara dawl *adv.* پەغوره ول better

pa godam ki satal *v.t* پەمودام کساتل warehouse

pa got nastay *n.* پەموناستی retirement

pa gul meykho seengarawal *v.t.* پەملمخوسینارول stud

pa hagha shawkhwa ki *adv.* پەهغه شاوخواک thereabouts

pa halbi loi kawal; *v. t.* پەحلبيلویکاچول **nakhleydal;** *v. t.* can

pa haqeeqat ki *adv.* پەحقيقت ک substantially

pa har hal *adv.* پەهرحال anyhow

pa har sa poh *a.* پەهرپوه omniscient

pa harakat rawastal *v.t.* پەحرکت راوستل propel

pa hawa arawal *v.t.* پەهوااول aerify

pa hayjan rapaseydal *v.i.* پەهجان راپاڈل rouse

pa heela mana toga *adv* پەهيلهمنه توه avidly

pa hodman dawl *adv.* پەهومنول purposely

pa hor wreetawal *v.t.* پەهوروریتول toast

pa ibtidayee toga *adv.* پەابتدایيتوه primarily

pa ida leek sara makh torawona *n.* پەادعاليکسرهمخ تورنونه indictment

pa ilahee charo pori arwand *a.* پەالهيچاروپوراوند theological

pa infiradee toga *adv.* پەانفرادیتوه solo

pa ishara sara har kar ta chamtoo keydal *n.* پەاشارهسره beck هرکارتهچمتوکدل

pa isharo pohawal *v.t.* پەاشارو
پوهول signal

pa iztirab akhta *n* پەاضطراباخته
agonist

pa jak sara *v.t.* پەجکسرەپورته
کول jack

pa jal ki rageyrawal; akhta
kawal *v.t.* پەجالکراول؛اخته
کول tangle

pa jama pori arwand *n.* پەجمعپور
اوند plurality

pa janjal oreydal *v. t* پەجنجالاوﺪل
bustle

pa jaryan rawastal *v.t.* پەجریان
راوستل mobilize

pa jazar aw mad pori arwand *a.*
پەجذراومﺪپوراوند tidal

pa jibran pori arwand *a.* پەجبران
پوراوند remunerative

pa jinayat kakartya *n.* پەجنایت
ککتیا implication

pa jinayat ki las laral *v.t.* پەجنایت
کلاسلرل implicate

pa jinsee toga kamzoray *a.* پە
جنسيتوهکمزوری impotent

pa kakhtay ki *adv* پەکتۍ aboard

pa kakhtay ki leygdawal *v.t.* پەکتۍ
کلﺪول ship

pa kakhtay ki safar *n.* پەکتۍسفر
sail

pa kakhtay ki tafree ta tlal *v.i.* پە
کتۍکتفریحتەتلل cruise

pa kakhtay ki wral *v. t* پەکتۍکول
embark

pa kalee sara khlasawal *v.t* پەکلۍ
سرەخلاصول key

pa kaleesa ki saroodee dalgay *n*
پەکلیساکسرودیﺉ choir

pa kam miqdar *adv.* پەکممقﺪار
less

pa kamila toga *adv* پەکاملەتوه
entirely

pa kanda ki achawal *v.t.* پەکنﺪهک
اچول pit

pa kar achawal *v.t.* پەکاراچول
install

pa kar achawal *v.t.* پەکاراچول use

pa kar achawona *n.* پەکاراچوونه
installation

pa kar achowana *v.t.* پەکاراچول
operate

pa karaw akhta kawal *v. t.* پەکاو
اختەکول encumber

pa kashak taral *v.t.* پەکشکتل
zip

pa kashoga sara khwaral *v.t.* پە
کاشوغەسرەخول spoon

pa kha andaz *adv.* پەخەانﺪاز pretty

pa khabaro ataro ki land *a.* پە
خبرواتروکﺪ laconic

pa khanjar wahal *v.t.* پەخنجروهل
stab

pa khatar ke achaval *v.t.* پەخطرک
اچول imperil

pa khatar ki achawal *v.t.* پەخطرک
اچول peril

pa khato ki raghreydal *v.i.* پەخوک
رغﺪل wallow

pa khato laral *v.t.* پەخولل silt

pa khawra bandi poza mokhal
v. پەخاورهبانﺪپوزهمول nuzzle

pa khkara dawl *adv.* پەکارهول
openly

pa khob ki garzeydana *n.* پەخوب
کرﺪنه somnambulism

pa khob ki garzeydoonkay *n.* somnambulist

pa khpal gooman *a.* پهخپلومان would-be

pa khpal zay *adv* پهخپلای duly

pa khuday bawar *n.* پهخدایباور theism

pa khuday bawar laroonkay *n.* پهخدایباورلرونکی theist

pa khwakhay cheygha wahal *v. t.* پهخوچغهوهل cheer

pa ki *prep.* پهکی in

pa kodo hazirawal *v.t.* پهکو حاضرول conjure

pa kom kar gumaral *v.t.* پهکومکار ـمارل task

pa konato khwayeydal *v.i.* په کوناتوویدل backslide

pa kor danana *adv.* پهکوردننه indoors

pa lakara wahal *v. t.* پهلکهوهل cane

pa landa toga *adv.* پهلنهتوه short

pa landa toga *adv.* پهلنهتوه shortly

pa landa toga *adv.* پهلنهتوه summarily

pa landa toga bayanawal *v.t.* پهلنه توهبیانول summarize

pa lando *prep.* پهلنو across

pa langar zay ki da kakhtay darawalo lagakht *n.* پهلنرای کـ دکهتردرولولت wharfage

pa lar ki *adv.* پهلرکـ within

pa largee ki zhwand kawoonkay *a.* پهلری کژوندکوونکی xylophilous

pa largee ya lakari pori taral *v.t.* پهلریيالکپورتل stake

pa larghono eetalweeyano pori arwand *a.* پهلرغونوایالویانوپور اوند italic

pa las ki neewal *v.t.* پهلاسکنیول grip

pa las ki neewana *n* پهلاسکنیونه grip

pa las ki takhtawal *v.t.* پهلاسک تتول grab

pa las rawral *v. t* پهلاسراول earn

pa las samawal *v.t* پهلاسـمول handle

pa las sara samawal *v.t.* پهلاسـره ـمول manipulate

pa laso aw pkho porta tlal *v. i* په لاسواوپوپرتهتلل clamber

pa laso aw pkho tlana *n* پهلاسواو پوتلنه scramble

pa leed pori arwand *a.* پهلیدپور اوند optic

pa leeka darawal *v.t.* پهلیکهدرول line

pa leeka ki shamilawal *v.t.* پهلیکه کشاملول deploy

pa leeka tlal *v.i.* پهلیکهتلل file

pa leekalee shakal ki rawastal *v.t.* پهلیکلیشکلکراوستل transcribe

pa lifafa ki achwal *v. t* پهلفافهک اچول envelop

pa lokhee ki achawal *v.t.* پهلویک اچول pot

pa looma ki geyrawal *v. t.* پهلومهک رول entrap

pa looma ki geyrawal *v.t.* پهلومهک رول noose

pa looma ki rageyrawal *v.t.* پهلومه کرارول snare

pa loomi sara neewal *v.t* پهلومسره نیول mesh

pa lor sara reybal *v.t.* پهلورسرهربل scythe

pa lostana palatal *n* پهلوستنهپلل browse

pa loy kach *adv.* پهلوی کچ highly

pa lwar ghag *adv.* پهلوغ aloud

pa lwar ghag aylanawal *v.i.* پهلوغ اعلانول trumpet

pa lwar ghag maloomat warkawal *v.t.* پهلوغمعلومات ورکول page

pa lwar ghag sara ralwaydal *v.t* پهلوغسرهرالودل stump

pa lwar ghag wayal *v.i.* پهلوغویل rattle

pa lwara *adv* پهلوه above

pa magwee razwarandawal *v.t.* پهموي ره اوندول peg

pa maharat bashparawal *v. t* په مهارت بشپول elaborate

pa maharat sara karawal *v.t.* په مهارت سره کارول wield

pa makha di kha *interj.* پهمخهده farewell

pa makhooka wahal *v.i.* پهموکه وهل peck

pa manda warandi keydal *v.t.* په منهواندکدل outrun

pa manz ke *a.* پهمنزکی inmost

pa manz ki *prep.* پهمنزک amid

pa manz ki *prep* پهمنزک between

pa maqtaee dawl khodal *v.t.* په مقطعیول ودل profile

pa maree pasi khayrat *n.* پهمی پسي خرات pittance

pa marpeychee dawl harakat kawal *v.i.* پهمارپچيول حرکت کول snake

pa maskharo sara ghageydal *v.i* پهمسخروسره غدل sneer

pa masnooee dawl da weeda kawalo amal aw ilam *n.* په مصنوعيول دویده کولوعمل او علم hypnotism

pa masnooee dawl weeda kawal *v.t.* پهمصنوعيول ویده کول hypnotize

pa masooleeyat takal *v.t.* په مسؤليت اکل post

pa matrooka wahal *v.t.* پهمتروکه وهل lambaste

pa mawzoon qadam tlal *v.i* په موزون قدمتلل march

pa meena aw shor mashor sara lobeydal *v.i.* پهمینهاو شورماشور سره لوبدل romp

pa meena majzoobawal *v. t* پهمینه مجذوبول enamour

pa meeras rawral *v.t.* پهمیراثراول inherit

pa mehrabanay sara *adv* پهمهرباني سره benignly

pa mehrabanay sara *adv.* پهمهرباني سره kindly

pa mehwar taweydal *v.t.* پهمحور تاودل pivot

pa merda barach wahal *a.* پرمیه بچوهل henpeck

pa meylmastya rabalal *v.i* په ملمستیارابلل feast

pa miqdar ya peymayish ki barabareydal *v.* په‌مقداريا پمائش کبرابرلدل amount

pa miqnateesee khob weedawal *v.t.* په‌مقناطيسي‌خوب‌ويدول mesmerize

pa mityazo pori arwand *a.* په متيازوپوراوند urinary

pa mukhtalifo tabqo bandi jala kawal *v.t.* په‌مختلفو‌طبقو‌باند‌جلا کول laminate

pa munasib dawl *adv* په‌مناسب‌ول appositely

pa munasib dawl *adv.* په‌مناسب‌ول fairly

pa munasib dawl *a.* په‌مناسب‌ول seemly

pa munasiba toga *adv* په‌مناسبه‌ته pat

pa munazzama toga *a.* په‌منظمه‌ته orderly

pa mushkil sara *adv.* په‌مشکل‌سره scarcely

pa mustaqeem dawl *adv.* په‌مستقيم ول straight

pa muzayda ki warandey kawoonkay *n* په‌مزايده‌کوانلز کوونکی bidder

pa muzayda ki warandeyz *n* په مزايده‌کوانلز bid

pa muzayda ki warandeyz warkawal *v.t* په‌مزايده‌کوانلز ورکول bid

pa nakha kawal; daghee kawal *v.t.* په‌نه‌کول؛داغي‌کول spot

pa nakho alamo khkara kawana *n.* په‌نو‌علامو‌کاره‌کونه symbolism

pa nakho nakhano sara pohawal *v.t.* په‌نونانو‌سره‌پوهول sign

pa nakhro katal *v.t.* په‌نخرو‌کتل ogle

pa nama kawal *v. t* په‌نامه‌کول betroth

pa nareentob sara *a.* په‌نارينتوب سره manly

pa nasam zay ki karawal *v.t.* په ناسمه‌ی‌کارول misplace

pa nawara dawl *adv.* په‌ناوه‌ول badly

pa nawara toga *adv* په‌ناوه‌ته‌وه malafide

pa naz nakhro tlal *v.i.* په‌نازنخرو تلل strut

pa naz palal *v.t.* په‌نازپالل pamper

pa nazar ratlal *v.i.* په‌نظرراتلل seem

pa nazaree ilam poh *n.* په‌نظري‌علم پوه theorist

pa neyza ghosawal *v.t.* په‌نزه‌غوول spear

pa neyza ghosawal *v.t.* په‌نزه‌غوول spike

pa neyza wahal *v.t.* په‌نزه‌وهل lance

pa nika pori arwand *a.* په‌نکاح‌پور اوند nuptial

pa nishasta klakawal *v.t.* په‌نشاسته کلکول starch

pa nookano nakhlawal *v.t.* په نوکانونلول nail

pa noom kawal *v. t.* په‌نوم‌کول entitle

pa noom lar ki zayawal *v.t.* په‌نوم‌ا کايول tabulate

pa obo ki ghopa keydal *v.i.* پەاوبو
کغوپەکدل submerge

pa obo weenzal *v.t.* پەاوبووینل
rinse

pa obo ya sheydo ki eysheydalee
da joowaro ora *n.* پەاوبویاشدو
کاشدلیدجوارواوه mush

pa oogadwalee *adv* پەاودوالي long

pa oogey sara zor kawal *v.t.* پەاو
سرەزورکول shoulder

pa or teyl achawal *v.t.* پەاورتل
اچول stoke

pa owa wrazo ki *adv.* پەاووەورو ک
weekly

pa pam ki neewal *v. t* پەپامکنیول
consider

pa pam war kach *prep.* پەپامورکچ
considering

pa pana matawal *v.t.* پەپانەماتول
wedge

pa panra ray warkawal *v.i.* پەپه
رایورکول ballot

pa parakha kacha *adv.* پەپراخه
کچه wholesale

pa parchoon dawl ploral *v.t.* په
پرچونولپلورل retail

pa pardey sara pokhal *v.t.* پەپرد
سرەپول screen

pa paree taral *v.t.* پەپیتل rope

pa pat dawl *adv* پەپول under

pa pata sara *adv.* پەپەسره
stealthily

pa patay sara taral *v.t* پەپسرەتل
tape

pa pay ki *adv.* پەپایک eventually

pa payla ki *adv.* پەپایلەک last

pa payla ki waqay keydal *v.i* په
پایلەکواقعکدل ensue

pa pensal jorawal ya leekal *v.t.*
پەپنسلجوولیالیکل pencil

pa peych nakhlawal *v.t.* پەپچنلول
screw

pa planwalee sara *adv.* پەپلنوالي
سرە wide

pa pokh ki achawal *v. t* پەپوک
اچول encase

pa poza kash kawana *n* پەپوزەکش
کوونه sniff

pa poza pori arwand *a.* پەپوزەپور
اوند nasal

pa pranistani pori arwand *a.* په
پرانستنیپوراوند inaugural

pa preymanay *adv.* پەپرماز galore

pa pyaz pori arwand yaw dawl
sabzee *n.* پەپیازپوراوندیوول
سبزي leek

pa qalee sara pokhal *v.t.* پەقلعی
سرەپول tin

pa qamcheena wahal *v.t.* په
قمچینەوهل whip

pa qanoonee palwa taqeebawal
v.t. پەقانونيپلوەتعقیبول
prosecute

pa qarara *adv.* پەقراره slowly

pa qaraval *v.t.* پەقارول irritate

pa qasdee dawl orbalawona *n* په
قصديولاوربلوونه arson

pa qeero laral; tarkol lagawal
v.t. پەقیرولل؛تارکوللول tar

pa qismoono ki weyshal *v.t* په
قسمونوکوشل sort

pa qulf bandawal *v.t.* پەقلفبندول
interlock

pa radeeyo khparawal *v.t.* پەرايو
خپرول radio

pa rakhteenee dawl *adv.* پەرتيني
ول quite

pa rakhteenee dawl *adv.* پەرتيني
ول really

pa rasmee toga *adv.* پەرسمي‌توه
officially

pa ratloonkee pori arwand *a.* په
راتلونكي‌پوراوند prospective

pa reekhteenee dawl *adv.* پەريتيني
ول indeed

pa reekhtya sara *adv.* پەريتياسره
actually

**pa reeyakaray zan baryalay
kawona** *n.* پەريا‌كاران‌بريالى
كوونه hypocrisy

pa roghtya pori arwand *a.* په
روغتياپوراوند hygienic

pa rohaneeyoono pori arwand *a*
پەروحانيونوپوراوند clerical

pa sa dawl; sanga *adv.* پەهول،نه
how

pa sahil bandi *adv.* پەساحل‌باند
ashore

pa sakani sara prey kawal *v. t.* په
سكنسره‌پر‌كول chisel

pa sakhtay sara *adv.* پەسختسره
hardly

pa sakhtay sara wahal *v.t.* پەسخته
سره‌وهل ram

pa salor gotee pori arwand *a. &
n.* پەلوروي‌پوراوند quadrilateral

pa saloro barkho weyshal *v.t.* په
لوروبرخوويشل quarter

pa sama toga *adv* پەسمه‌توه right

**pa samandaryoonee toghondee
weeshtal** *v.t.* پەسمندريوني
توغوندي‌ويشتل torpedo

pa sandan bandi takawal *v.t* په
سندان‌باندكول forge

pa sangal wahal *v.t.* پەنل‌وهل
nudge

pa sapeyra wahal *v.t.* پەپه‌وهل
whack

pa sar chapa dawl *adv* پەسرچپه‌ول
topsy turvy

pa sar khwali eekhodal *v. t.* پەسر
خوا‌ايو‌دل cap

pa sargand dawl *adv* پەمرندول
clearly

pa sarka ki eekhodal *v.t* پەسر‌كه‌ک
ايو‌دل pickle

pa sarsaree dawl *a* پەسرسري‌ول
cursory

pa sat *n* په abaction

pa sat *a.* په backward

pa sat keydana *v.t.* په‌كدل reverse

pa sat keydana; shakast *n* په‌كدنه،
شكست reverse

pa sat keydoonkay *a.* په‌كدونكى
reversible

pa sat tloonkay *n* پەتلونكى abactor

pa sata swazawal *v.t.* پەسطح‌سوول
scorch

pa satak wahal *v.t* پەسک‌وهل
maul

pa seemee paree taral *v. t.* پەسيمي
پي‌تل cable

**pa seeyasat ki azad khwakhay
shakhs** *n* پەسياست‌كآزادخوى
شخص leftist

pa seher majzoobawal *v. t.* پهسحر مجذوبول charm2

pa seyr; yaw shan *a.* پهر؛یوشان similar

pa sfanj pakawal *v.t.* پهسفنجپاکول sponge

pa sha *adv* پهشا behind

pa sha keydal *v.i.* پهشاکدل recede

pa sha tambawal *v.t.* پهشاتمبول repel

pa sha tambawal *v.t.* پهشاتمبول repress

pa sha tlal; munakkis keydal *v.i.* پهشاتلل؛منعکس کدل recoil

pa sha tlana *n.* پهشاتلنه recession

pa shampoo weykhta weenzal *v.t.* پهشامپووتهوینل shampoo

pa shatag *adv.* پهشاټ recoil

pa shatranj ki mat aw mabhoot *n.* پهشطرنج کماتاومبهوت stalemate

pa shaw khwa ki *adv* پهشاوخواکه around

pa shaw khwa ki *prep.* پهشاوخواکه within

pa shidat wahal *v. i.* پهشدتوهل dash

pa shoghlo *adv.* پهشغلو aflame

pa shoghlo rokhan *adv.* پهشغلو روان aglow

pa shomal ki *a.* پهشمالکه northerly

pa shumalee qotab pori arwand *n* پهشمالیقطبپوراوند Arctic

pa simanto jorawal *v. t.* پهسمنو جوول cement

pa skarwato pakhawal *v.t.* په سکرووپخول bake

pa skarwato pakhowoonkay; nanway *n.* پهسکرووپخوونکی؛ نانوای baker

pa so so zala *adv.* پهوولله retail

pa so zhabo poh *n.* پهوژبوپوه polyglot1

pa so zhabo poheydana *a.* پهوژبو پوهدنه polyglot2

pa sook wahal *v.t.* پهسوکوهل punch

pa sotee wahal *v. t* پهسويوهل belabour

pa speeno zaro pokhal *v.t.* پهسپینو زروپول silver

pa swayl ki prot *a.* پهسولکهپروت southerly

pa sweylee qotab pori arwand *a.* پهسوليقطبپوراوند antarctic

pa syoree ki satal *v.t.* پهسیريکه ساتل shade

pa tabiee dawl *adv.* پهطبيعيول naturally

pa tadbeer sara kar akheystal *v.i.* پهتدبیرسرهکاراخستل manoeuvre

pa tadbeer sara kar akheystana *n.* پهتدبیرسرهکاراخستنه manoeuvre

pa takabbur tlal *v.i.* پهتکبرتلل swagger

pa takalee wakht dama kawal *v.t.* پهاکليوختدمهکول relay

pa takan sara ghosawal *v.t.* پهکان سرهغوول slash

pa talgaraf khabrawal *v.t.* پهلراف خبرول telegraph

pa taloo pori arwand *a.* پهتالوپور اوند palatal

pa talweezyon khparawal *v.t.* په
لويزيون خپرول televise

pa tama kawal *v.t.* په طمع کول
allure

pa tambal sara *a.* په مبل سره
slatternly

pa tangsa ki achawal *v.t.* په تنسه کې
اچول straiten

pa tasmey sara taral *v.t.* په تسم
سره تل strap

pa tawdo obo weenzal *v.t* په تودو
اوبو وينل foment

pa taylafoon ghageydal *v.t.* په
تلفون غدل telephone

pa teengar sara zhmana kawal
v.t. په ينار سره ژمنه کول vow

pa teylo ghwarawal *v.t* په تلو غوول
oil

pa teylu ghwarawal *v.t.* په تلو غوول
anoint

pa teyra shee sooray kawal *v.t.* په
ترهشي سوري کول pierce

pa teyzay sara harakat kawal *v.t*
په تز سره حرکت کول flog

**pa tol takano ki da ray
warkawalo haq** *n.* په ول اکنو کې
درای ور کولو حق suffrage

pa tol wazhna las pori kawal *v.t.*
په ول وژنه لاس پور کول slaughter

pa tolaneez dawl *adv.* په ولنيزول
throughout

pa toleez dawl *adv.* په وليزول
generally

pa tonday palatal *v.t.* په تونډپلل
rifle

pa toora wahal *v.t.* په توره وهل
sabre

pa toto weyshal *v.t.* پهووشل
parcel

pa wajad rawastal *v. t* پهوجد
راوستل enrapture

pa wak ki laral *v.t* پهواک کلرل
hold

pa wak ki laral *v.t.* پهواک کلرل
possess

pa wak ki rawastal *v.t.* پهواک کې
راوستل subject

pa wakseen warkawalo mamoor
n. پهواکسين ور کولومامور
vaccinator

pa warta dawl *prep* پهورتهول like

pa waseela *prep.* پهوسيله per

pa weeno laralay *a* پهوينوللی
bloody

pa wilayat arawana *n.* پهولايت
اوونه provincialism

pa wrandi *prep.* پهواند versus

pa wrandi; porta la *adv.* پهواند،
پورتهله up

pa wro wro tlal *v.i.* پهووروروتلل
slow

pa wrostyo wakhtoono ki *adv.* په
وروستيووختونوکې lately

pa yad rawastal *v.t.* پهيادراوستل
remember

pa yad rawastana *n.* پهيادراوستنه
recall

pa yad rawastana *n.* پهيادراوستنه
recollection

pa yad rawastoonkay *n.* پهياد
راوستونکی reminder

pa yakh khwayeydal *v.t.* پهيخويدل
skate

pa yaw dawl *adv.* په یووړل
somehow

pa yaw khas andaza tlal *v.i.* په یو
خاص اندازه تلل pace

pa yaw khwandee zay kkheynastal *v.i.* په یوخونديای
کنستل perch

pa yaw shee warghorzeydal *v.i.*
په یوشي ورغورېدل pounce

pa yaw zay deyr bachyan zeygoonkay *a.* په یوای ربچیان
زونکی multiparous

pa yaw zay ki darawal *v.t.* په یوای
کدرول park

pa yawa dam *a* په یوه دم outright

pa yawa dam nareydal *v.i.* په یوه
دمندل slump

pa yawa karkha ki darawal *v.t.*
په یوه کره کدرول align

pa yawa khula *a.* په یوه خوله
unanimous

pa yawa lori ki *adv.* په یوه لور ک
aside

pa yawa nazar *adv.* په یوه نظر
prima facie

pa yawa wakht *a.* په یوه وخت
simultaneous

pa yawa zangaree wuzeeyat ki anzor eystal *v.i.* په یومانی
وضعیت کانور استل pose

pa yawazi *adv.* په یوازی only

pa yawazi sara *adv.* په یوازه سره
singularly

pa zamanat khlasawal *v. t.* په
ضمانت خلاصول bail

pa zamanat preykhwal *v.t.* په
ضمانت پرول parole

pa zan pak wachawal *v.t.* پمان
پاک وچول towel

pa zanee toga; bey ikhtyara *a.* په
انی توه،باختیاره spontaneous

pa zarawartob *adv.* په زه ورتوب
heartily

pa zat bandi khabeestob *n.* په ذات
باندخبیثتوب proclivity

pa zawab masool; zawabday *a.*
په واب مسؤول،بوابده answerable

pa zay *conj.* پمای for

pa zay kawal *v.t.* پمای کول place

pa zeegzag dawl *a.* په زیزاول
zigzag

pa zeegzag dawl harakat kawal *v.i.* په زیزاول حرکت کول zigzag

pa zehmat sara par makh tlal *v.i.* په زحمت سره پر مخ تلل
scramble

pa zhaba satal *v.t.* پاپه ژبل lick

pa zhabanee dawl *adv.* په ژبني ول
orally

pa zhabanee toga *adv.* په ژبني توه
verbally

pa zhabi sara *adv.* په ژبسره
viva-voce

pa zmaka da sarkh nakha *n.* په
مکه درخنه rut

pa zmaka kkheynastal *v.i.* پمکه
کناستل land

pa zmaka prot *a.* پمکه پروت
prostrate

pa zmaka wahal *v.t* پمکه وهل
floor

pa zolam wazhal *v. t* په ظلم وژل
butcher

pa zor akheestana *n.* پهزوراخیستنه usurpation

pa zor aw lwar ghag sara bandawal *v.t.* پهزوراولوغسره بندول slam

pa zor sara idara kawal *v.t.* پهزور سرهاداره کول manhandle

pa zor sara mandal *v.t.* پهزورسره منل thrust

pa zor sara par makh beywal *v.t.* پهزورسرهپرمخبیول shove

pa zor zana kawal *v.t.* پهزورزنا کول rape

pa zora dakawal 2 *v.t.* پهزورهکول stuff

pa zora drazawana *n* پهزورهدرزونه pop

pa zora kashawal *v.t.* پهزورهکشول tug

pa zora trapawal *v.i.* پهزورهتپول pop

pa zra pori *a* پهزهپور desirable

pa zra pori *a.* پهزهپور interesting

pa zra pori *a.* پهزهپور pleasant

pa zra pori *a.* پهزهپور remarkable

pa zra pori arwand *adjs* پهزهپور اوند cardiacal

pa zra pory *n* پهزهپوری favourite

pa zyadtar miqdar sara *adv* په زیادترمقدارسره more

pa zyarat ki eekhodal *v. t* پهزیارت کایودل enshrine

pa zyaree akhta kawal *v.t.* پهزیي اختهکول jaundice

pacha *n.* پاچا king

pacha *n* پچه lot

pacha *n.* پاچا sovereign

pacha achowana *n* پچهاچوونه draw

pacha ahowana *n.* پچهاچونه lottery

pacha kawal *v. t* پاچاکول enthrone

pacha kawal *v.t.* پاچاکول throne

pacha wazhoonkay *n.* پاچاوژونکی regicide

pachahee *a.* پاچاهي imperial

pachahee *n.* پاچاهي sovereignty

pachahee *n.* پاچاهي kingdom

pachahee *n.* پاچاهي royalty

pachahee *a.* پاچاهي regal

pachahee dawra *n* پاچاهيدوره reign

padree *n.* پادري priest

paf; da khuley da hawa awaz *n.* پف،دخولهدهوااواز puff

pak *a.* پاک chaste

pak پاک clean

pak *a.* پاک neat

pak; ganjay *a.* پک،بنجي bald

pakawal *v. t* پاکول efface

pakawal *v. t* پاکول clean

pakawal *v.t.* پاکول purify

pakawal; imala kawal *v.t.* پاکول، امالهکول purge

pakawana *n.* پاکوونه wipe

pakbazee *n.* پاکبازي chastity

pakh *n* پ blacksmith

pakhawal *v. t* پخول cook

pakheydal *v.i* پخدل mature

pakheydal *v.i.* پخدل ripen

pakhlanzay *n.* پخلناۍ kitchen

pakhlay *n* پخلی cook

pakhleegar *n* پخلي ر cooker

pakht *n.* پت lineage

pakhwa *adv.* پخوا once

pakhwa; da makha *adv* پخوا،د مخه formerly

pakhwanay *a.* پخوانی previous

pakhwanay useydoonkay *n.pl* پخوانی او سیدونکی aborigines

pakhwanay; makhkanay *a.* پخوانی؛مخکنی antecedent

paki nafooz kawal *v.t.* پکنفوذ کول penetrate

pakowana *n.* پاکونه lotion

pakowana *n.* پاکونه obliteration

pakwalay; chanrawana *n* پاکوالی؛ چاونه clearance

pal *n.* پال omen

pal; gam *n.* پل،ړام step

pal; naray chara *n.* پل،نرڅاه razor

palal *v.t.* پالل nurture

palal; rozal *v.t.* پالل؛روزل mother

palana *n.* پالنه nurture

palana *n.* پالنه patronage

palang *n* پالنګ bed

palatal *v.t.* پلل search

palatal aw saral *v.t.* پلل اوارل audit

palatana *n.* پلنه audit

palatana *n.* پلنه inspection

palatana kawal *v.t.* پلنه کول inspect

palatoonkay *n.* پلونکی inspector

palaway *n.* پلوی partisan

palaweetob *n.* پلویتوب partiality

palee garzeydal; gam akheystal *v.i.* پلی ګرځيدل،ګام اخستل step

paleed *a* پليد malign

paleedgee *n.* پليلي malignancy

pali lara *n.* لاره پل pedestrian

pali safar kawal *v.t.* پلی سفر کول pad

palistar; leyw *n.* پلستر،لو plaster

palistarawal *v.t.* پلسترول plaster

palmagar *a.* پلمګر shrewd

palmagar; daqeeq *n.* پلمګر؛دقيق subtle

pam *n* پام consideration

pam *n.* پام care

pam kawal *v. i.* پام کول care

pam kawal; fikar kawal *v.t.* پام کول،فکر کول mind

pam larana *n.* پاملرنه observation

pam warta kawal; nazar warkawal *v.t.* پام ورته کول؛نظر ورکول remark

pam; yadawana *n.* پام؛يادوونه remark

pana ghokhtoonkay *n.* پناه غوتونکی refugee

pana warkawal *v.t* پناه ورکول harbour

pana warkawal *v.t.* پناه ورکول shelter

pana warwaral *v.i.* پناه ورول resort

pana warwral *v.t.* پناه ورول seek

pana; kadwaltob *n.* پناه؛کوالتوب refuge

panahzay *n* پناهای asylum

panazay *n.* پناهای haven

panazay *n.* پناهای shelter

pand *n.* پند moral

pandee *n* پني coolie

pandee *n.* پني porter

pandghalay *n.* پنغالی camp

pandukay *n.* پنکی parcel

paneer *n.* پنر cheese

panga *n.* پانه asset

panga achowana *n.* پانه‌اچوونه investment

pangawal *n.* پانوال capitalist

pangawal *n* پانوال financier

panjshamba; da zyarat wraz *n.* پنجشنبه؛دزیارت‌ور Thursday

panra *n.* پاڼه leaf

panra *n.* پاڼه page

pansmanawal *v.t.* پانسمانول invest

panzeydalay *a.* پندلی nascent

panzoon pal *n.* پنون‌پال naturalist

panzos *n.* پنوس fifty

panzowoonkay *adj.* پنوونکی creative

par ... bar seyra *adv* پر---برسره besides

par deenee aqeedi arwand *a* پر دینی‌عقیداوند dogmatic

par izafee aydato maleeya *n.* پر اضافی‌عایداتومالیه supertax

par khorak mayan *n.* پرخوراک مین glutton

par khpal wakht *a.* پرخپل‌وخت timely

par makh beywal *v.t.* پرمخ‌بیول promote

par makh tlal *v.i.* پرمخ‌تلل proceed

par makh tlal; rasawal *v.t* پرمخ تلل؛رسول forward

par makh tlalay *a.* پرمخ‌تللی forward

par makh waral *v. t* پرمخ‌ول boost

par makh warana *n* پرمخونه boost

par makh wral *v.t* پرمخول further

par makhtag *n.* پرمخته development

par seena khwayeydal *v. i* پرسینه ویدل creep

par sha tag *n.* پرشاتګ withdrawal

par sha tagay; mukhalif *a.* پرشا تی‌مخالف reactionary

par sha tlal *v.i.* پرشاتلل retreat

par shatag; beyrta garzeydana *n.* پرشاتګ؛برتہرتدنه rebound

par wakht; da wakht paband *a.* پروخت؛دوخت‌پابند punctual

par zay *a.* پرای apposite

par zay *a.* پرای opportune

par zay chaland *n* پرای‌چلند decorum

par zay; pa munasib wakht *a.* پر ای؛بهمناسب‌وخت well-timed

par; bandi *prep.* پر؛باند on

par; da pasa *prep* پر؛دپاسه upon

parakh *a.* پراخ large

parakhawal *v.t.* پراخول amplify

parakhtya *n.* پراختیا expansion

parakhtya *n.* پراختیا magnitude

parakhtya warkawal *v. t* پراختیا ورکول enlarge

parakhtya warkawal *v.t.* پراختیا ورکول expand

parakhtya warkawal *v.t.* پراختیا ورکول span

parakhtya warkawoonkay *n.* پراختیاورکوونکی prompter

parakhtya; intishar *n.* پراختیا؛ انتشار spread

parakhtya; pyawartya *n* پراختيا؛ پياوتيا amplification

parakhwalay *n* پراخوالی breadth

parastish *n.* پرستش adoration

parawal *v.t* پارول acerbate

parawal *v. t.* پارول entice

parawal *v.t.* پارول inflame

parawal *v* پاروول motivate

parawal *v.t.* پارول stimulate

parawana *n.* پاروانه irritation

parawoonkay *n.* پاروونکی stimulant

paray *n.* پی rope

paray *n.* پی tether

parayshan *a.* پرشان pensive

parayshan *a.* پرشان uneasy

parayshana *a.* پرشانه moody

parayshana kawal *v. t* پرشانه کول disturb

parayshana kawal *v.t.* پرشانه کول vex

parayshana kawal *v.t.* پرشانه کول upset

parayshana keydal *v.i.* پرشانه کدل mope

parayshana keydal *v.i.* پرشانه کدل worry

parayshanee *n* پرشاني vexation

parayshanee *n.* پرشاني worry

parayshanee *n.* پرشاني stumble

parayshanee; zyat diqat *n.* پرشاني؛زيات دقت solicitude

parchoon plorana *n.* پرچون پلورنه retail

parchoon ploroonkay *a* پرچون پلورونکی retail

parda *n* پرده curtain

parda *n.* پرده lobe

parda kawal *v.t.* پرده کول veil

parda; burqa *n.* پرده؛برقع veil

pareyshana kawal *v.t.* پرشانه کول nonplus

parganpal *n,a* پرنپال socialist

parganpalee *n* پرنپالي socialism

parhayzgar *a.* پرهزگر pious

parhayzgar *a.* پرهزار righteous

parheyz *n.* پرهز spare

parheyz; taqdees *n.* پرهز؛تقديس taboo

parheyzgar saray *a.* پرهزارسی smug

parheyzgaree *n.* پرهزاري sanctity

park *n.* پک twinkle

park wahal *v.t* پک وهل flash

park; zaleydana *n* پک؛بلدنه shine

parkand *a.* پکند refulgent

parkeydal *v.i.* پکدل twinkle

parkeydal *v.i.* پکدل shine

parkeydana *n.* پکدنه lightening

parkha *n.* پرخه dew

parkha *n.* پرخه frost

parla pasey *adv* پرله پس consecutively

parla pasey wrandeyz *a.* پرله پس واندز alternative

parla pasi ~*a.* پرله پس ceaseless

parla pasi *a.* پرله پس successive

parla pasi dazi kawal *v.t* پرله پسز کول volley

parla pasi goozaroona warkawal *v.t.* پرله پسوزارونه ورکول pound

parla pasitob *n.* پرله‌پستوب
succession

parmakhtyayee *a.* پرمختيايي
progressive

parnara *n.* پرناه chimney

paro *n.* پارو manure

paroon *n.* پرون yesterday

paroonay; obash *n.* پوني؛اوباش
hood

parora; boos *n* پروه؛بوس fodder

parowana *n.* پاروونه motivation

parowoonkay *n.* پاروونکی irritant

parozha *n.* پروژه project

parozha jorawal *v.t.* پروژه‌جوول
project

parqeydal *v.i.* پقدل glitter

parqeydana *n* پقدنه glitter

parsob *n* پسوب swell

parsob; sokalee *n.* پسوب؛سوکالي
weal

parta *adv.* پرته asunder

parta la *prep.* پرته‌له beside

parta la dey chi *adv.* پرته‌له‌دچ
without

partalaeez *a* پرتله‌ييز comparative

parwazgah *n* پروازگاه aerodrome

parzawal *v.t* پرول fell

parzawoonkay *n.* پروونکی
wrestler

pas *a* پ blunt

pas aw ghabee saray *n* پاوغبي‌سی
dunce

pas la dey *adv.* پس‌له henceforth

pas la dey *adv.* پس‌له
henceforward

pas laronki *a.* پاس‌لرونکی reverent

pas pas kawal *v.t.* پس‌پس‌کول
mouth

pas pas kawal *v.t.* پس‌پس‌کول
whisper

pas pasay; pati khabari *n* پس
پسی؛پوخبر whisper

pasarlanay; taza aw tand *a.*
پسرلنی؛تازه‌او‌تاند vernal

pasey *prep.* پس after

pasey *adv.* پس afterwards

pasi keydal *v.t.* پس‌کدل pursue

pasi keydana *n.* پس‌کدنه pursuance

pasi keydana *n.* پس‌کدنه pursuit

pasoon *n.* پاون uprising

pasoon *n.* پاون revolution

pasoon *n.* پاون revolt

pasoon aw balwa *n.* پاون‌او‌بلوا
outburst

pasoon kawal *v.i.* پاون‌کول revolt

pasra kawoonkay *a.* پاسره‌کوونکی
thrifty

pasra shawi shtamanee *n.* پاسره
شوشتمني thrift

past *a.* پست menial

past; lag *n.* پست؛لا slight

pat aw ghalay *a.* پاوغلی
subterranean

pat harakat *n* پحرکت sneak

pat kar *n.* پکار undercurrent

pata eejaza *n.* په‌اجازه connivance

pata keydal *v.i.* پاته‌کدل remain

pata shaway *n.* پاته‌شوی remainder

pata shaway *a.* پاته‌شوی residual

pata shaway barkha *n.* پاته‌شوبرخه
residue

pata shawee; maree *n.* پاته‌شوی، مي remains

pata shoonay; izafee *n.* پاته‌شوني، اضافي surplus

pata; katara *n.* په،کاره bar

patang *n* پتنگ butterfly

patanzay; morchal *n.* پناي،مورچل stronghold

patasa *n.* پتاسه candy

patawal *v. t.* پول conceal

patawal *v.t* پول hide

patawana *n.* پونه hide

patay pri lagawal *v.t.* پپرلول tag

patay trina chapeyra kawal *v.t.* په ترنه‌چاپره‌کول gird

patay; karay *n.* پ،کې band

patay; naray tasma *n.* پ،نرتسمه strip

patay; tar *n.* پ،تار tape

patay; taranga *n.* پ،تانه ribbon

pati keydal; meysht keydal *v.i.* پاتکدل،مشت‌کدل stay

pati ratlal *v.i* پاترا‌تلل fail

patkay *n.* پکې turban

patloon *n.* پتلون pantaloon

patloon n.pl پتلون trousers

patnoos *n.* پتنوس tray

patokay tri arawal *v.t* پوکې‌تراول skin

pawlad *n.* پولاد steel

pawz *a.* پو military

pawzee *n* پوي military

pay *n.* پای end

pay ta rasawal *v. t* پای‌ته‌رسول end

pay ta rasawal *v.t* پای‌ته‌رسول finish

pay ta rasawal *n* پای‌ته‌رسونه completion

pay ta rasawal *a.* پای‌ته‌رسدونی terminable

pay; akhar *n* پای،آخر extreme

pay; intiha *n* پای،انتها finish

pay; khatmeyda *n.* پای،ختمدا termination

paya; ospaneeza geera *n.* پايه، اوسپنیزه‌ګرا staple

paya; satoon *n.* پايه،ستون pedestal

payakht laroonkay *a.* پايت‌لرونکی perennial

paydar *a* پايدار abiding

paydar *a* پايدار binding

paydar *a* پايدار durable

paydar *a.* پايدار interminable

paydawar; bar *n* پداوار،بار yield

paydayshee *a.* پدايشي natal

payey aw stani ta warta *a.* پاياو ستنته‌ورته stellar

payey warkawal *v.i.* پايور‌کول skid

paygham *n* پغام errand

paygham *n.* پغام message

paygham laroonki leekana *n.* پغام لرونکليکنه missive

paygham wroonkay *n.* پغام‌وونکی messenger

payl *n* پيل commencement

payl *n* پيل start

payl kawal *n* پيل‌کول begin

payl kawal *v.t.* پيل‌کول start

payl; sar *n.* پيل،سر beginning

payla *n* پايله consequence

payla *n.* پايله outcome

payleydal *v. t* پيلدل commence

payleydana *n.* پېلدنه outbreak

payli ta raseydal *v. t* پایلته رسدل conclude

paylot; jalawan *n.* پیلو؛جاله وان pilot

paylotee kawal; rehnumayee kawal *v.t.* پیلوي کول؛رهنمايي کول pilot

paymalawal *v.t.* پایمالول trample

paymalawal *v.t.* پایمالول suppress

paymalawana *n.* پایمالوونه suppression

paymayish *n.* پمائش measure

paymayish *n.* پمائش measurement

paymayish kawal *v.t* پمائش کول measure

payshnihad *n* پشنهاد offer

paysoor *n.* پایر appendage

paysoor *n.* پایر appendix

peeka *a* پیکه pale

peeka banafsh rang *n.* پیکه بنفش رن lilac

peeka keydal *v.i.* پیکه کدل pale

peeka rang *n.* پیکه رن tint

peeka rang warkawal *v.t.* پیکه رن ورکول tint

peeka zyar rang *n* پیکه زیرن buff

peelama; sareeza *n.* پیلامه؛سریزه overture

peenza *n* پنه five

peenza gotay *n.* پنځوی pentagon

peenzalas *n* پنلس fifteen

peesho *n.* پیشو cat

peeska *n* پیکه edge

peghor *a.* پغور ironical

peghor *n.* پغور irony

pensal tarashay *n.* پنسل تراشی sharper

pensal; da naqashay burs *n.* پنسل،دنقاشبرس pencil

peych *n.* پچ screw

peych kash *n.* پچ کش spanner

peychal *v.t.* پچل muffle

peychalay *a* پچل complex

peychalay *a.* پچلی intricate

peychalay kawal *v. t* پچلکول complicate

peychalay kawal *v.t.* پچلی کول intrigue

peychaltya *n.* پچلتیا complication

peychaltya *n* پچلتیا intrigue

peychaltya *n.* پچلتیا perplexity

peychowoonkay *n.* پچوونکی winder

peydayakht *n* پدایت creation

peyghambaree kawal *v.t.* پغمبري کول prophesy

peyghla *n.* پغله damsel

peyghla *n.* پغله maiden

peyghla *n.* پغله miss

peyghla; pak lamana *n.* پغله،پاک لمنه virgin

peyghor *n.* پغور sarcasm

peyghor *n.* پغور skit

peyghor *n.* پغور jest

peyghor warkawal *v.i.* پغوورکول jeer

peyghor warkawal *v.i.* پغوورکول jest

peyghor wazma *a.* پغوروزمه sardonic

peykh lar; tareekhcha *n.pl.* پل، تاريخچه annals

peykh leekana *n.* پليكنه chronology

peykh leekana *n.* پليكنه journalism

peykh leekoonkay *n.* پليكونكى journalist

peykha *n* په accident

peykha *n.* په occurrence

peykha; mreena *n.* په،مينه casualty

peykha; waqia *n* په،واقعه event

peykhey kawal *n.* پخكول mockery

peykheydal *v. t* پدل befall

peykheydal *v.t.* پدل happen

peykheydal *v.i.* پدل occur

peykheydana *n.* پدنه happening

peykhi kawal *v.t* پكول mimic

peykhi kawona *n.* پكونه mimesis

peyraway *n* پروى cream

peyrawee *n* پروى buttermilk

peyrawee kawal; naqal kawal *v.t.* پروي كول؛نقل كول imitate

peyrawee; taqleed *n.* پروي،تقليد imitation

peyray *n* پرى elf

peyray; saleeza *n.* پ،سليزه century

peyrodal *v.t.* پرودل purchase

peyrodana *n.* پرودنه purchase

peyrodoonkay *n.* پرودونكى buyer

peyrodoonkay *n..* پرودونكى client

peyrodoonkay *n* پرودونكى customer

peysey *n.* پس money

peysey astawana *n.* پساستوونه remittance

peysey naghdawal *v. t.* پسنغدول cash

peysey tar lasa kawoonkay *n.* پس ترلاسه كوونكى payee

peysh band *n.* پشبند apron

peyso lapara zana kawal *v.t.* پسو لپاره زنا كول prostitute

peytawee ta kkheynastal *v.i.* پتاويته كناستل bask

peytay *n* پ carton

peywand *n.* پوند graft

peywand lagawal *v.t* پوندلول graft

peywand lagawal *v.t.* پوندلول patch

peywandawal *v.t.* پوندول join

peywandawal *v.t.* پوندول transplant

peywandawal; gandal *v.t.* پوندول، ل stitch

peywandee bootay ya fasal *n* پوندي،بوىيافصل hybrid

peywandee; dwa ragay *a.* پوندي، دوهرى hybrid

peywasteydal *v. i.* پوستدل cling

peywasteydal *v.i.* پوستدل copulate

peywastoon *n.* پوستون alliance

peywastoon *n.* پوستون association

peywastoon; yaw keyda *n.* پوستون،يوكدا incorporation

peyzhandana *n.* پژندپه passport

peyzhandana *n.* پژندنه presentation

peyzhandana *n.* پژندنه recognition

peyzhandgalwee *n.* پژنلوي acquaintance

peyzhandgalwee *n.* پژندلوي introduction

peyzhandgalwee; shanakht *n.* پژندلوي؛شناخت indentification

peyzwan *n* پزوان bridle

peyzwan *n.* پزوان harness

peyzwanawal *v.t* پزوانول moor

peyzwanawal *v.t.* پزوانول picket

peyzwanee kawal *v.t.* پزواني کول tether

pkha *n.* په leg

pkhey pri eekhodal *v.t.* پپرايودل tread

pkheymanee *n.* پماني repentance

pkheymaneydal *v.i.* پماندل repent

plan *a* پلن flat

plan jorawal *v.t.* پلان جوول plot

plana panra *n.* پلنه‌پاه sheet

plana takhta *n* تخته پلنه paddle

planawal *v.t.* پلنول widen

planwalay *n.* پلنوالی width

plar *n* پلار father

plar neekoona *n.* پلارنيکونه ancestor

plaranay *a.* پلرنی paternal

plaranay meeras *n.* پلرنی ميراث patrimony

plaranay; koranay *n.* پلرن؛کورن ancestry

plarneeka *n* پلارنيکه forefather

plaway *n* پلاوی committee

plaway *n* پلاوی corps

plazmayna *n.* پلازمنه metropolis

plazmeyna; panga *n.* پلازمنه،پانه capital

ploral *v.i.* پلورل shop

plorana *n.* پلورنه sale

ploranzay *n.* پلورنی shop

ploroonkay *n.* پلورونکی salesman

ploroonkay *n.* پلورونکی seller

podeena *n* پودينه mint

poh; aqil *a.* پوه،عاقل quaint

poha *n* پوهه comprehension

poha *n.* پوهه knowledge

pohand *n.* پوهاند professor

pohaneez sayr *n.* پوهنيز سر excursion

pohaneez; andeykhman *a.* پوهنيز، اندلمن apprehensive

pohaneeza baghwanee *n.* پوهنيزه باغواني horticulture

pohaneeza sanga *n* پوهنيزمانه faculty

pohanghond *n.* پوهنغوند encyclopaedia

pohanleek *n.* پوهنليک thesis

pohantoon *n.* پوهنتون university

pohanzay *n* پوهنی college

pohawal *v.t.* پوهول grasp

pohaway *n* پوهاوی grasp

pohaway; darak *n.* پوهاوی،درک apprehension

poheydal *v. t* پوهدل comprehend

poheydal *v.t.* پوهدل know

poheydal *v.t.* پوهدل understand

poheydal; darakawal *v.t.* پوهدل، دَرَکول apprehend

pokh *a.* پوخ ingrained

pokh *a* پوخ ripe

pokh bawar *n.* پوخ‌باور certainty

pokh shaway *a.* پوخ‌شوی mature

pokh warkawal *v. t* پوورکول cushion

pokh; jild *n.* پو؛جلد cover

pokh; teykay *n.* پو؛تکی pod

pokhakh *n.* پو casing

pokhakh *n* پو coating

pokhal *v. t.* پول cover

pokhal; sadar pri ghwarawal *v.t.* پول؛ادرپرغوول sheet

pokhal; shanal *v. t* پول؛شنل bestrew

pokhowoonkay; lang *n.* پوونکی؛ لد wrapper

pokhtal *v.t.* پوتل ask

pokhtal *v.t.* پوتل inquire

pokhtal *v.t.* پوتل question

pokhtana *n.* پوتنه inquisition

pokhtani garweygni *n.* پوتنروز query

pokhtanleek *n.* پوتنلیک questionnaire

pokhtawargay *n.* پوتوری kidney

pokhtay *n.* پوۀ rib

pokhtoonkay *a.* پوتونکی interrogative

pol *n* پل bridge

polee *a.* پولي monetary

pooch; bey adaba *a.* پوچ؛بادبه vulgar

poochtob *n* پوچتوب absurdity

pookanra *n* پوکاله bubble

poola *n* پوله border

poola *n* پوله boundary

poola laral *v.t* پولهلرل border

poomba *n* په foot

poonba *n.* پنبه cotton

poonda *n.* پونده heel

poora *a* پوره absolute

poora *a* پوره entire

poora kawal; bashparawal *v.t.* پوره کول؛بشپول perfect

poora walay; kamal *n.*؛ پورهوالی؛ کمال perfection

poora; mutlaq *a* پوره؛مطلق thorough

poora; zabardast *a.* پوره؛زبردست perfect

poozay *n.* پوز mat

popanak wahalay *a.* پوپنکوهلی musty

por *n* پور debit

por *n* پور debt

por *n.* پور loan

por akheystal *v. t* پوراخستل borrow

por akhistoonkay *n* پوراخستونکی creditor

por kawal *v. t* پورکول debit

por kawal *v.t.* پورکول loan

por waray *n* پوروی debtor

por waray keydal *v.t* پورویکدل owe

por warkawal *v.t.* پورورکول lend

poray *n.* پو ladder

poray; martaba *n.* پو؛مرتبه stair

pori *adv.* پور across

pori watal *v.i.* پوروتل pass

pori watal; ghosawal *v. t* پوروتل؛غوول cross

pori watana *n* پوروتنه pass

porta *prep.* پورته above

porta *prep.* پورته up

porta *a.* پورته upward

porta kawal *v.t.* پورته‌کول hoist

porta kawal *v.t.* پورته‌کول lever

porta kawal *v.t.* پورته‌کول raise

porta kawal *v.t.* پورته‌کول lift

porta kawona *n.* پورته‌کوونه hold

porta kawona *n.* پورته‌کوونه lift

porta keydal *v.i.* پورته‌کدل arise

porta tlal *v.t.* پورته‌تلل ascend

porta wral *v.t.* پورته‌ول uplift

porta; bar seyra *adv.* پورته؛برسره aloft

portanay *a.* پورتنی upper

portanay zama *n.* پورتنزامه maxilla

portanay; ghwara *a.* پورتنی؛غوره superior

portawalay *n.* پورته‌والی superiority

poshta *n* پشته embankment

postakay *n.* پوستکی husk

postakay *n.* پوستکی peel

postakay achawal *v.i.* پوستکی اچول moult

postakay achawal *v.t.* پوستکی اچول peel

postawal *v. t. & i* پوستول blanch

poz; lakhkar *n.* پو،لکر army

poza *n.* پوزه nose

poza mokhal *v.t* پوزه‌مول nose

pozay; meyzaray *n.* پوزی؛مزری straw

pozband *n.* پوزبند muzzle

pozband *n.* پوزبند gag

pozband taral *v.t.* پوزبندتل gag

pozband warachawal *v.t* پوزبند وراچول muzzle

praday *a.* پردی alien

praday *a.* پردی outlandish

praday *n.* پردی outsider

praday *n.* پردی stranger

prakh *a* پراخ broad

prakh *a.* پراخ capacious

prakh *a.* پراخ vast

prakhtya *n.* پراختیا capacity

praneydal *v. t* پردل clot

prang *n.* پاز leopard

prang *n.* پاز panther

prang *n.* پاز tiger

pranistal *v.t.* پرانستل open

pranistal *v.t.* پرانستل loosen

pranistal *v.t.* پرانستل sever

pranistana *n.* پرانستنه inauguration

pranistana *n* پرانیستنه adjuration

pranistana kawal *v.t.* پرانستنه‌کول auspicate

pranistana; sooray *n.* پرانستنه؛ سوری opening

pranistay *a.* پرانستی open

pranistay *a.* پرانستی widespread

pranj *n* پرنج sneeze

pranjeydal *v.i.* پرنجدل sneeze

prata la dey *adv* پرته‌له‌دی else

prey kawal *v. t* پرکول cut

preykanda *a.* پرکنده categorical

preykanda izhar kawal *v.t.* پرکنده‌اظهارکول assert

preykanda; akheyree *a* پرکنده، آخري final

preykawal *v.t.* پرکول slice

preykhodal *v.t,* پرودل abdicate

preykhodal *v. t* پرودل discard

preykhodal *v.t.* پرودل leave

preykhodal *v.t.* پرودل release

preykhodana *n* پرودنه release

preykhowal *v.t.* پروول abandon

preykhowana; las tri akheystana *n.* پروونه،لاس تر اخستنه renunciation

preykoon *n.* پرکون interruption

preykra *n* پرکه decision

preykra kawal *v. t* پرکه کول decide

preymana; mufsal *a.* پرمانه،مُفصل ample

preymanee *n* پریماني abundance

preyshana kawal *v. t* پرشانه کول commove

pri akhta kawal *v. t* پراخته کول entangle

pri bawar na kawal *v.t.* پرباورنه کول mistrust

pri breed kawal *v.t* پربریدکول overrun

pri draneydal *v.t.* پردرندل out-balance

pri khatal *v.t.* پرختل mount

pri makhki keydal *v.t.* پرمخ کدل transcend

pri makhtaray zyatawal *v.t.* پر مختای زیاتول prefix

pri musallat kawal *v.t.* پرمسلط کول overrule

pri toki kawal *v.t.* پروکوکول banter

pri zyateydal *v.t.* پرزیاتدل surmount

prora *n.* پروه hay

prot; bey parwa *a.* پروت،بپروا slipshod

proteen *n.* پروتین protein

psa *n.* پسه sheep

pukhla kawal *v.t.* پخلاکول conciliate

pukhlayana *n.* پخلاینه reconciliation

pukhlayana; sola *n.* پخلاینه،سوله peace

pur ahang *a.* پرآهن melodious

pur mana *a.* مانا پُر meaningful

pur omeed *n.* پُرامید optimism

purasrar *a.* پُراسرار mysterious

puraysh *a.* پُرعیش mirthful

purfehem *a* پُرفهم comprehensive

purjosh *a* پُرجوش fervent

purtameen *a.* پرتمین glorious

purtameena nandara *n.* پرتمینه ننداره pageantry

pust *n.* پُست mail

pust leygal *v.t.* پُست لل mail

pust rasan *n.* پُست رسان postman

pust; da pust idara *n.* پُست،د پُست اداره post

pustee *a.* پُستي postal

pustee tikat *n.* پُستي ک postage

pyada *adv.* پیاده afoot

pyada pawz *n.* پیاده پو infantry

pyala *n.* پیاله cup

pyala; geelas *n.* پیاله،یلاس tumbler

pyawaray *a.* پیاوی potent

pyawaray azam *n.* پیاوی عظم steadiness

pyawaray kawoonkay;
zwakmanawoonkay *n* پياوى
كوونكى،بواكمنوونكى
amplifier
pyawaray; loy *a.* پياوى؛لوى huge
pyawaray; zorlaroonkay *a.*
پياوى؛زورلرونكى
potential
pyawartya *n.* پياوتيا pontentiality
pyaz *n.* پياز onion

Q

qabar *n.* قبر grave
qabar *n.* قبر tomb
qabeela *n.* قبيله horde
qabeela *n.* قبيله tribe
qabeelawee *a.* قبيلوى tribal
qabil *n.* قابل genius
qabil khalk *n.* قابل خلک
intelligentsia
qabil salakar *n.* قابل سلاكار mentor
qabileeyat *n* قابليت ability
qabili zamanat *a.* قابل ضمانت
bailable
qablawal *n* قبلول acceptance
qablawal *v.t.* قبلول adhibit
qabrasee khwaga sharab *n.*
قبرسي خواه شراب malmsey
qabz *n.* قبض constipation
qabz narmowoonkay *n.* قبض
نرموونكى laxative
qabzeeyat zid *a* قبضيت ضد
laxative
qachaq kawoonkay *n.* قاچاق
كوونكى smuggler

qachaqawal *v.t.* قاچاقول smuggle
qachaqchee *n.* قاچاقچي jobber
qad; badanee banra *n.* قد؛بدني به
stature
qadar *n* قدر estimation
qadar kawal *v.t.* قدركول admire
qadar kawal *v.t.* قدركول adore
qadar; mafhoom; ahmeeyat *n.*
قدر،مفهوم،اهميت significance
qadardanee *n.* قدرداني
appreciation
qadardanee kawal *v.t.* قدرداني كول
appreciate
qadari mutlaq *a.* قادر مطلق
almighty
qafeeya *n.* قافيه rhyme
qafeeya jorawal *v.i.* قافيه جوول
rhyme
qafeeya sazee *n.* قافيه سازي
rhymester
qafila *n.* قافله caravan
qahar *n.* قهر indignation
qahar; tap *n.* قهر؛پ tear
qaharmanee *a.* قهرماني heroic
qahraman *n.* قهرمان knight
qahramanee kawal *v.t.* قهرماني
كول knight
qahrawal *v.t.* قهرول infuriate
qahreydalay *a.* قهردلى indignant
qahwa *n* قهوه coffee
qahwa khana *n.* قهوه خانه cafe
qahwayee; qahwayee rang *n., a.*
قهويي؛قهويي ر tan
qalam *n.* قلم pen
qalamraw *n* قلمرو domain
qalbee *a* قلبي cordial

qalee *n.* قلعي tin

qalib *n.* قالب mould

qalib; chawkat *n* قالب؛چوکا frame

qalibawal *v.t.* قالبول frame

qalibawal *v.t.* قالبول mould

qam *n.* قام nation

qam pal *n.* قامپال nationalist

qam palana *n.* قامپالنه nationalism

qamcheena; shalakha *n.* قمچينه؛ شلاخه whip

qamee *a.* قامه national

qamoos *n* قاموس dictionary

qamoos *n.* قاموس lexicon

qanaat; marakht *n.* قناعت؛مت satiety

qanay kawal *v. t* قانع کول convince

qanay kawal *v.t.* قانع کول satiate

qanay keydoonkay *a.* قانع کدونکی satiable

qanay; rizayee *a.* قانع؛رضايي satisfactory

qand laroonkay *a.* قندلرونکی saccharine

qanoni haq *n.* قانوني حق franchise

qanoon *n.* قانون law

qanoon *n.* قانون statute

qanoon landi rawastal *v.t.* قانون لاندراوستل normalize

qanoon pohana *n.* قانونپوهنه jurisprudence

qanoon waza kawal *v.i.* قانونوضع کول legislate

qanoon waza kawona *n.* قانون وضع کوونه legislation

qanoonee *a.* قانوني legal

qanoonee *a.* قانوني legislative

qanoonee kawal *v.t.* قانوني کول legalize

qanoonee layha; bil *n* قانوني لايحه؛ بل bill

qanoonee taqeeb *n.* قانوني تعقيب prosecution

qanoonee wak *n.* قانوني واک jurisdiction

qanoonee wakeel *n.* قانوني وکيل prosecutor

qanooneetob *n.* قانونيتوب legitimacy

qanooneeyat *n.* قانونيت legality

qanoonpoh *n.* قانونپوه jurist

qanoonpoh *n.* قانونپوه lawyer

qanoonsaz *n.* ساز قانون legislator

qar qar kawal *n.* قرقرکول croak

qarabat *n* قرابت affinity

qarardad kawal *v. t* قرارداد کول contract

qarshavi *a.* قارشوی irate

qarzdar *a.* قرضدار indebted

qasab *n* قصاب butcher

qasad *n.* قصد determination

qasad *n.* قصد intention

qasam khwaral *v.t.* قسم خول swear

qasar *n.* قصر mansion

qasdee *a.* قصدي intentional

qasdee kawal *v. i* قصدي کول deliberate

qaseeda *n.* قصيده ode

qash *n.* قاش slice

qashar tri speenawal *v.t.* قشرتر سپينول shell

qashar; postakay n. قشر،پوستکی shell

qasid n. قاصد courier

qasoor; deywaleeya n. قصور،دوالیه default

qata kawal v.t. قطع کول interrupt

qata kawal v.t. قطع کول intersect

qata kawal; ghosawal v.t. قطع کول،غوول hew

qatal; wazhana n. قتل،وژنه assassination

qatil n. قاتل assassin

qatilana a. قاتلانه murderous

qatlawal v.t. قتلول assassinate

qatlawal v.t. قتلول massacre

qavi a قوی forceful

qawee a قوي energetic

qawee keydal; qawee kawal v.t. قوي کدل،قوي کول strengthen

qayas; partalana n. قیاس،پرتلنه analogy

qayda; farmool n قاعده،فارمول formula

qayda; nizam n. قاعده،نظام system

qayda; tanzeem n. قاعده،تنظیم regularity

qaz (nar) n. قاز(نر) gander

qaza pori arwand a. قضاپوراوند judicious

qazawat n. قضاوت judgement

qazawat n. قضاوت advocacy

qazawat kawal v.t. قضاوت کول adjudge

qazawat kawal; manzgartob v.t. قضاوت کول،منتوب کول arbitrate

qazayee a. قضایِ judicial

qazayee dalgay n. قضایي دلگی jury

qazayee faysala kawal v.i. قضایي فصله کول judge

qazayee hukam n. قضایي حکم judge

qazayee wayna n قضایي وینا dictum

qazayee zwak n. قضایي واک judiciary

qazayee; salisana a. قضائي،ثالثانه arbitrary

qazee n. قاضي magistrate

qazee n. قاضي arbiter

qeechee n. قیچي scissors

qeemat; arzakht n. قیمت،ارزت worth

qeematee a. قیمتي costly

qeematee a. قیمتي precious

qeematee a. قیمتي valuable

qeematee kanray n. قیمتي کانی jewel

qeer; tarkol n. قیر،تارکول tar

qeerat n. قیراط carat

qeeyafa n. قیافه semblance

qilat n. قلت scarcity

qisam n. قسم kind

qisam; dawl n. قسم،ول type

qisam; kheyl n. قسم،خل variety

qismat n. قسمت fortune

qist n. قسط instalment

qita n. قطعه nugget

qomandan n قومندان commandant

qomandan n. قوماندان prefect

qomar baz n. قمارباز gambler

qomar bazee n قماربازي gamble

qomar kawal v.i. قمار کول gamble

qoowat; payakht *n.* قوت،پايت strength

qorban zay *n.* قربانای altar

qos *n.* قوس arc

qudrat *n.* قدرت nature

qufal chi la dwaro khwaw sakha pranistal shee *n.* قفل چله دواو خواوخه پرانستل شي latch

qurbanawal *v.t.* قربانول sacrifice

qurbanee *n.* قرباني sacrifice

qutab; stan *n.* قطب،ستن pole

qutbee storay *n.* قطبي ستورى loadstar

qyamat *n* قيامت doom

R

rabalal *v. t.* رابلل call

rabalowoonkay *n* رابلوونكى caller

rabarseyra kawal *v. t* رابرسره كول expose

rabita *n.* رابطه communication

rabita *n.* رابطه contact

rabita *n.* رابطه liaison

rabita kawal *v. t* رابطه كول contact

rabita shandawal *v.t.* رابطه شنول intercept

rabra *n.* ربه hardship

rabrawal *v.t.* ربول trouble

rabrawana *n.* ربوونه trouble

rabrawoonkay *a.* ربوونكى troublesome

rach; larz *n.* چ؛لز thrill

---

rachapeyrawal *v.t* راچاپېرول engulf

rachawal *v.t.* چول thrill

racheydal *v.t.* چدل jolt

rad rad katana; waranga *n.* رر کتنه،وانه stare

rad; inkar *n.* رد،انكار refuse

radawal *v.t.* ردول confute

radawal *v. t* ردول disapprove

radawal *v.t.* ردول negative

radawal *v.t.* ردول refuse

radawal *v.t.* ردول refute

radawal *v.t.* ردول reject

radawal; pa laghata wahal *v.t.* ردول،په لغته وهل spurn

radawana *n.* ردوونه rejection

radeeyo *n.* رايو radio

radyoyee ya talweezyonee parogram khparawal *v.t.* رايوي يا لويزيوني پروګرام خپرول telecast

raftar *n.* رفتار speed

rag awukhtal *n* راوتل wrick

rag; wareed *n.* رګ،وريد vein

ragarzeydana; badla *n.* راګرزېدنه، بدله return

rageyrawal *v. t.* راګیرول encircle

rageyrawal; jeyb wahal *v.t.* راګیرول،جب وهل purse

raghawal *v.i.* رغول heal

raghawal *v.t.* رغول mend

raghawal; samawal *v.t.* رغول، سمول amend

raghawana *n.* رغوونه repair

ragheydoonkay *a* رغدونكى curable

raghokhtal *v.t.* راغوتل muster	**rakhchina** *n* رخچينه coif
raghond *a.* راغوز thick	**rakhna** *n* رخنه gap
raghondawal *v.t.* راغونول amass	**rakhna** *n.* رخنه leak
raghondawal *v. t* راغونول collect	**rakhna** *n.* رخنه leakage
raghondawana *n* راغونونه collection	**rakhna payda kawal** *v.i.* رخنهپدا كول gape
raghondawana *n.* راغونونه convocation	**rakhteenay** *a.* رتينه actual
raghondawana *n* راغونونه muster	**rakhteenay** *a.* رتينى veritable
raghondawoonkay *n* راغونوونكى collector	**rakhtoonay** *a.* رتونى true
raghorzeydal *v.i.* راغورمدل fall	**rakhtoonay** *a.* رتونى truthful
raghreydal *v.i.* رغدل wriggle	**rakhtya** *n.* رتيا truth
raghreydal *v.i.* رغدل slide	**rakhtya wayana** *n.* رتياوينه veracity
raghreydana *n* رغدنه wriggle	**rakhtyapal** *n.* رتياپال realist
raghreydana *n.* رغدنه tumble	**rakhtyapala** *n.* رتياپاله realism
raghreydana; bey laritob *n.* رغدنه،بلارتوب slip	**rakkhata keydoonkay aw ospaneeza war** *n.* راكته كدونكىاوسپنيزهور shutter
raghyanra *n.* رغيله oasis	**rakra warkra** *n.* راكهوركه bargain
rahat *n.* راحت convenience	**rakra warkra kawal** *v.t.* راكهوركه كول bargain
rahbaree kawal *v.t* رهبريكول head	**rakra warkra; danda** *n* راكهوركه، دنده business
rahib *n.* راهب monk	**ralwaydana** *n* رالودنه downfall
rahib; rahiba *n.* راهب،راهبه votary	**ram kawal** *v.t.* رامكول subjugate
rahiba khaza *n.* راهبمه nun	**rama** *n.* رمه herd
rakab *n.* ركاب stirrup	**rama; gala** *n* رمه،بله flock
rakab *n.* ركاب pedal	**ramatowana; rakagawana** *n* راماتوونه،راكونه fold
rakad keydal; bey harakata keydal *v.i.* راكدكدل،بحركته كدل stagnate	**ramawal** *v.t* رامول harness
rakashawal *v. t* راكشول drag	**rambari wahal** *v. i* رمباوهل bellow
rakashawana *n* راكشونه drag	**ramzee toray** *n.* رمزيتورى cipher, cipher
rakhatal *v.* راختل rise	**ranaqlawal** *v.t.* رانقلول quote
rakhatal; rakhkareydal *v. i* راختل،راكاريدل emerge	**randa** *n.* رنده grate
rakhatana *n.* راختنه rise	**randa kawal** *v.t* رندهكول grate

rang *n* رنگ colour

rang *n.* رنگ paint

rang alwatay; dangar *a.* رنگالوتی؛ دنگر wan

rang warkowana *n* رنگورکونه dye

rang; sayqal *n* رنگ؛صقل polish

ranga anzor *n.* رنگانور pastel

ranga rang *a.* رنگارنگ varied

ranga rang *a.* رنگارنگ various

ranga rang khwara; makoolat *n.* رنگارنگخواړه؛ماکولات *pl* victuals

ranga rang; beyla beyl *a.* رنگارنگ؛بېلا بېل sundry

ranga rangtob *n.* رنگارنگتوب versatility

rangarang *a.* رنگارنگ motley

rangarang *a.* رنگارنگ multifarious

rangarang *a* رنگارنگ diverse

rangawal *v. t* رنگول colour

rangawal *v. t* رنگول dye

rangawal *v.t.* رنگول paint

rangawal *v. t.* نول demolish

rangawal *v.t.* رنگول tincture

rangawoonkay *n.* رنگوونکی painter

rangharal *v.t.* رانغال wrap

ranra *n.* رڼا light

ranrawal *v.t.* رڼول light

ranrookay *n* رڼوکی temple

ranz *n* رنځ disease

ranzara; nanzara *n.* رانه؛ننه turpentine

ranzoor *a.* رنځور ill

ranzoor pal *n.* رنځورپال nurse

rapor *n.* راپور inkling

rapor warkawal *v.t.* راپورورکول report

rapor; khabar *n.* راپور؛خبر report

rapor; mufassil bayan *n.* راپور؛مفصلبیان recital

raqabat *n.* رقابت rivalry

raqabat kawal *v.t.* رقابتکول rival

raqeeb *n.* رقیب rival

raraseydal *v.i.* رارسدل arrive

raraseydana *n.* رارسدنه arrival

rasam gasht *n.* رسمگشت parade

rasam gasht kawal *v.t.* رسمگشت کول parade

rasam palana *n.* رسمپالنه observance

rasaseydal *v.i.* رادل seep

rasawal *v. t* رسول deliver

rasawal *v.t.* رسول supply

rasawana *n* رسونه delivery

rasawoonkay; da tadarikato masool *n.* رسوونکی؛دتدارکاتو مسؤل supplier

rasay *n* رسه cord

raseed *n.* رسید receipt

raseydal *v.t.* رسدل reach

rasha darsha *n.* راشهدرشه visit

rasha darsha kawal *v.t.* راشهدرشه کول visit

rashpeyl wahal *v.i.* راشپلوهل paddle

rashpeyl wahoonkay *n.* راشپل وهونکی oarsman

rasman warandi kawal *v.t.* رسماً واندکول present

rasmawal *v. t.* رسمول depict

rasmee *a* رسمي formal

rasmee bayan warkawal *v.t.* رسميبیانورکول opine

rasmee eejazat laral; tazmeenawal *v.t.* رسمي‌اجازت لرل;تضمينول warrant

rasmee haq *n.* رسمي‌حق prerogative

rasmee maqam neewal *v.i.* رسمي مقام‌نيول officiate

rasmee ya roohanee kalee *n.* رسمي‌يا‌روحاني كالي vestment

ratal *v.t.* رِل reprimand

ratal *v.t.* رِل taunt

ratal; nakhwakhee kawal *v.t* رِل، ناخوي‌كول upbraid

ratal; radawal *v.t.* رِل;ردول snub

ratana *n.* رنه reprimand

ratana *n* رنه taunt

ratana; radawana *n.* رنه;ردوونه snub

ratawowal; ramatawal *v.t* راتاوول;راماتول fold

ratlal *v. i.* راتلل come

ratloonkay *a.* راتلونكى forthcoming

ratloonkay *a.* راتلونكى future

ratloonkay *a.* راتلونكى next

ratloonki peykhey; afsana *n.* راتلونكپ;افسانه sequel

ratolawal *v.t.* راولول gather

ratoobat *n.* رطوبت humidity

rawa *a.* روا admissible

rawa *a.* روا lawful

rawa *a.* روا legitimate

rawan *a* روان fluent

rawral *v.t.* راول adduce

rawral *v. t* راول bring

rawral *v.t* راول fetch

ray warkawal *.v. i* راى‌وركول comment

ray; intiqad *n* راى;انتقاد comment

raya *n.* رايه vote

raya *n.* رايه opinion

raya *n.* رايه poll

raya warkawal *v.t.* رايه‌وركول poll

raya warkawal *v.i.* رايه‌وركول vote

raya warkawoonkay *n.* رايه وركوونكى voter

rayees *n* رئيس boss

rayees *n* رئيس chairman

rayees; aslee *a* رئيس;اصلي arch

rayi ghokhtal *v. t.* رايغوتل canvass

raz *n.* راز mystery

raz *n.* راز secret

raz satal *v.t.* رازساتل secrete

raz satana *n.* رازساتنه secrecy

raz satana *n.* رازساتنه secretion

raz sparal *v. i* رازسپارل confide

raza *n.* رضا willingness

razalat *n.* رذالت roguery

razdar *n* رازدار confidant

razee *adj.* راضي complacent

razee *a.* راضي content

razee *a.* راضي willing

razee kawal *v.t.* راضي‌كول consent3

razee kawal *v. t* راضي‌كول content

razee kawal *v.t.* راضي‌كول satisfy

razee kawal *v.t.* راضي‌كول suit

razee keydal *v. i* راضي‌كدل consent

razee keydana *n.* راضي‌كدنه consent

razeel saray *n.* رذيل‌سى rogue

razmee shair ya shairee *n* رزمي شاعريا شاعري epic

reekha; tana *n.* ره،تنه stem

reekhteenwalee *n* ريتينولي fidelity

reetara; patay *n.* ريتاه،پ tag

reetara; tasma *n.* ريتاه،تسمه strap

reeya kawal *v.t* رياكول feign

reeyakar saray *n.* رياكارسى hypocrite

reeyakar; bey mukhlis *a.* رياكار،بې مخلص insincere

reeyakarana aw dwa makhee *a.* رياكارانه او دو ه مخي hypocritical

reeyasatee *a.* رياستي presidential

reeyazat *n* رضايت contentment

reeyazat kawoonkay *n.* رياضت كوونكى ascetic

reeyazee *n* رياضي mathematics

reeyazee poh *n.* رياضي پوه mathematician

rehbaneeyat *n* رهبانيت monasticism

rehbaree kawal *v.t.* رهبري كول lead

rehbaree kawal *v.t.* رهبري كول pioneer

rehem; taqwa *n.* رحم،تقوا piety

rehen *n.* رهن mortgage

rehen kawal *v.t.* رهن كول mortgage

rehnumayee kawal *v.t.* رهنمايي كول usher

reybal *v.t.* ربل reap

reyband *a.* ربند oblique

reyband kawal; kog aw pa dada tlal *v.t.* ربند كول؛كواوپه دداتلل slant

reybanda zmaka *n.* ربنده مكه slope

reybandtob payda kawal *v.i.* ربند توب پدا كول slope

reybaz *n.* رب sweep

reybaz wahoonkay *n.* ربوهونكى sweeper

reybazawal *v.i.* ربول sweep

reygdeyda *n.* رددا pulsation

reygdeyda *n* رددا pulse

reygdeydal *v.i.* رددل oscillate

reygdeydal *v.i.* رددل tremble

reygdeydal *v.i.* رددل vibrate

reygdeydana *n.* رددنه oscillation

reygdeydana *n.* رددنه vibration

reygdeydana *n.* رددنه tremor

reykha *n.* ريه root

reykha peyzhandana *n.* ره پژندنه etymology

reykhanda kaga toree *n.* رنده كاه توري italics

reykhi ghazawal *v.i.* ريغول root

reykht; tarkeeb *n* رخت،تركيب form

reykhta garee; qalib ki achawana *n* ريختهري،قالب كې اچونه casting

reypat *n.* رب rivet

riayat *n.* رعايت conformity

riayat kawal; ehtiram kawal *v.t.* رعايت كول،احترام كول regard

riayat; ehtiram *n.* رعايت،احترام regard

rifat *n.* رفعت sublimity

rifat; sar lwaree *n* رفعت؛سرلوي uplift

risala *n* رساله brochure

risala *n.* رساله pamphlet

risala leekoonkay *n.* رساله‌لیکونکی pamphleteer

risalat; khidmat ta leywaltya *n.* رسالت؛خدمت‌ته‌لوالتیا vocation

riwajee *a* رواجی customary

riwayatee *a.* روایتی traditional

rizayat *n.* رضایت satisfaction

rodal; tay rodal *v.t.* رودل؛تی‌رودل suck

rodana *n.* رودنه suck

rogdawal *v.t.* رودول accustom

rogdawal *v.t.* رودول addict

rogday *a.* رودی accustomed

rogday *a.* رودی wont

rogday kawal *v. t.* رودی‌کول habituate

rogdeez *a* رودیز routine

rogdeez *a.* رودیز wonted

rogdtya *n.* رودتیا rote

rogdwalay *n.* رودوال addiction

rogh *a.* روغ sound

rogh ramat *a* روغ‌رمه maiden

rogh ramat *a.* روغ‌رمه sane

rogh ramat *a.* روغ‌رمه wholesome

rogha jora *n* روغه‌جوه compromise

rogha jora kawal *v. t* روغه‌جوه‌کول compromise

roghtoon *n.* روغتون hospital

roghtya *n.* روغتیا health

roghtya *n.* روغتیا sanity

roghtya pohana *n.* روغتیاپوهنه hygiene

roghtyayee *a.* روغتیایی sanitary

rohaneeyoon *n* روحانیون clergy

rokhan fikra kawal *v. t.* روان‌فکره کول enlighten

rokhan fikray *n.* روان‌فکري liberalism

rokhana *a.* روانه luminous

rokhana jisam *n.* روانه‌جسم luminary

rokhana kawal *v. t* روانه‌کول elucidate

rokhanawal *v.i.* روانول alight

rokhanawal *v. t* روانول brighten

rokhanawal; pakawal *v. t* روانول؛ پاکول clear

rokhandan *n.* روندان loop-hole

rokhantya *n.* روانتیا illumination

roman; da meeni keesa *n.* رومان؛د مینه‌کیسه romance

rond walay *n.* رووالی lustre

rooh *n.* روح soul

rooh; arwa *n.* روح؛اروا wraith

rooh; asal *n* روح؛اصل essence

roohanee *a* روحاني divine

roohanee *a.* روحاني spiritual

roohanee larkhod *a.* روحاني‌لارخود pastoral

roohanee pal *n.* روحاني‌پال spiritualist

roohaneeyat *n.* روحانیت spirituality

roohee *a.* روحي psychic

roohee tadawee *n.* روحي‌تداوي psychotherapy

roond *a* وند blind

roonr *a.* رو transparent

roonr anday *a.* روآندی liberal

roonrtya *n.* روتیا lucidity

rostaray *n.* روستای suffix

rostaray jorawal *v.t.* روستای‌جوول suffix

rozal *v.t* روزل breed

rozal; tarbeeya warkawal *v.t.* روزل؛تربیه‌ورکول rear

rozana *a* روزانه daily

rozana *n.* روزنه nourishment

rozantoon *n.* روزنتون nursery

rozha *n* روژه fast

rozha neewal *v.i* روژه‌نیول fast

rujoo kawal *v.i.* رجوع‌کول revert

rukhsat *n.* رخصت discharge

rukhsat *n.* رخصت leave

rukhsatawal *v.t.* رخصتول assoil

rukhsatawal *v. t* رخصتول discharge

ruman; ishqeeya keesa *n* رُمان؛ عشقیه‌کیسه novel

ruswa kawal *v.t.* رسواکول scandalize

ruswayee *n* رسوایي scandal

rutba warkawal *v. i* رتبه‌ورکول distinguish

rutba warkawal *v. t.* رتبه‌ورکول ennoble

S

sa *n* ساه breath

sa *interj.* څه what

sa akeystal *v.i.* ساه‌اخستل respire

sa akheystal *v. i.* ساه‌اخیستل breathe

sa akheystana *n.* ساه‌اخستنه aspiration

sa kakhana *n.* ساه‌کنه respiration

sa shay; sa *pron.* څه‌شی؛څه what

sa wakht; kala *adv.* څه‌وخت؛کله when

sa warbandawana *n.* ساه‌وربندوونه suffocation

sa yi warbandawal *v.t* ساه‌یووربندول suffocate

saada *n.* ساده gull

saat; da zang awaz *n.* ساعت؛دزنگ آواز dial

saba *n.* سابه spinach

saba *n.* سبا tomorrow

saba ta *adv.* سباته tomorrow

sabab *n.* سبب cause

sabab *n.* سبب inducement

sabab; daleel *n.* سبب؛دلیل reason

sababee *adj.* سببي causal

sabandaval *v. t* سابندول belch

sabar *n.* صبر patience

sabar kawoonkay *a.* صبرکوونکی patient

sabit qadam *a.* ثابت‌قدم steadfast

sabit qadam satal *v.t.* ثابت‌قدم‌ساتل steady

sabit qaḍam satal *v.t.* ثابت‌قدم‌ساتل poise

sabit tamzay *n.* ثابت‌تمای standpoint

sabitawal *v.t.* ثابتول prove

saboon *n.* صابون soap

saboon pri mokhal *v.t.* صابون‌پر مول soap

saboonee *a.* صابوني soapy

saboot *n* ثبوت evidence

sabt; yadakht *n.* ثبت،يادت record

sabtawal; pa tarteeb sara eekhodal *v.t* ثبتول؛په‌ترتيب‌سره ايودل file

sabtawal; pa yad rawastal *v.t.* ثبتول؛به‌يادراوستل record

sabtawoonkay *n.* ثبتوونكى recorder

sabtawoonkay *n.* ثبتوونكى registrar

sabzee *n.* سبزي vegetable

sabzee khor *n.* خور سبزي vegetarian

sabzee khor *a* سبزي‌خور vegetarian

sabzee ploranzay *n.* سبزي‌پلورنای grocery

sabzee ploroonkay *n.* سبزي پلورونكى grocer

sada *a.* ساده frugal

sada *n.* ساده moron

sada *a.* ساده naive

sada *a.* ساده sheepish

sada kawal *v.t.* ساده‌كول simplify

sada kawang *n.* ساده‌كوز simplification

sada nakhcha jorawal *v.t.* ساده نخچه‌جوول sketch

sada nakhcha; tarha *n.* ساده‌نخچه، طرحه sketch

sada; asan *a.* ساده،آسان simple

sada; asana ساده،آسانه cozy

sada; khandoonay *a.* ساده،خندونی rustic

sada; mutlaq *a* ساده،مطلق slick

sada; pak *a* ساده،پاک blank

sada; wazeh *a.* ساده،واضح explicit

sadar *n.* سادر mantel

sadatob *n.* سادەتوب naivete

sadatob *n.* سادەتوب simplicity

sadiq *a* صادق downright

sadirat *n* صادرات export

sadirawal *v.i.* صادرول issue

sadma; goozar *n* صدمه،بوزار . shock

saf; katar *n.* صف،كتار tier

safa kawal *v.t.* صفاكول mop

safa kawoonkay tokar *n.* صفا كوونكى‌وكر mop

safar *n.* سفر journey

safar *n.* سفر trip

safar *n* سفر travel

safar kawal *v.i.* سفركول journey

safar kawal *v.i.* سفركول tour

safar kawal *v.i.* سفركول travel

safarat *n* سفارت embassy

safarat kar *n* سفارت‌كار diplomat

safarat karee *n* سفارت‌كاري diplomacy

safaratee *a* سفارتي diplomatic

safayee *n* صفائي cleanliness

safeer sara arwand charwakay *n.* سفيرسره‌اوندچارواكى attache

safeer; seeyasee zaray *n.* سفير، سياسی‌ری ambassador

safra *n* صفرا bile

sagak *n* سک buckle

sagay *n* سی lung

sahar sark *n* سهارورک twilight

saharanay *n* سهارنز breakfast

sahee *a.* صحيح authentic

sahil *n* ساحل coast

sahil n. ساحل shore

sahilee adj. ساحلي costal

sahilee oba n. ساحلي اوبه offing

sahoolat n سهولت facility

sahoolat warkawal; tahweelawal v.t. سهولت ورکول؛تحويلول render

sajeeda kawal v.t. سجده کول prostrate

sajeeda; farmanbardaree n. سجده،فرمانبرداري prostration

sakana n سکنه chisel

sakhawat n سخاوت benevolence

sakhawat n. سخاوت generosity

sakhawat n. سخاوت profusion

sakhawat kawal v. t سخاوت کول benevolent

sakhee a سخي benevolent

sakhee a. سخي generous

sakht a. سخت hard

sakht a. سخت rigid

sakht a. سخت rigorous

sakht a. سخت strict

sakht a. سخت onerous

sakht aw shadeed a. سخت او شديد impetuous

sakht baran n. سخت باران shower

sakht goozar khwaral v.t. سخت وزارخول shock

sakht kar n. سخت کار perspiration

sakht kar kawal v.i. سخت کار کول perspire

sakht shay n سخت شی solid

sakht zaray a. سخت زی callous

sakht zaray a. سخت زی relentless

sakht; kanjoos a. سخت؛کنجوس stringent

sakht; khatarnak a. سخت، خطرناک grave

sakht; nawara a سخت،ناوه burdensome

sakht; treekh a. سخت،تريخ austere

sakhta azmoyana n. سخته آزموينه tribulation

sakhta hamla n. سخته حمله onslaught

sakhta neewaka n. سخته نيو که censure

sakhta neewaka kawal v. t. سخته نيو که کول censure

sakhtawal v.t. سختول harden

sakhtee aw shiddat n. سختي او شدت impetuosity

sakhtgeer n. سختير martinet

sakhtgeer a. سختير stern

sakhtgeer insan n. سختير انسان stern

sakhtgeeree n. سختيري stringency

sakin n. ساکن static

sakin a. ساکن stationary

sakoon n. سکون tranquility

sakoon; dareydana n. سکون،درېدنه standstill

sal n. سل hundred

sal kaleeza adj. سل کليزه centennial

salaheeyat; taleem n. صلاحيت، تعليم qualification

salakar n. سلاکار counsellor

salakaree kawal v. t. سلاکاري کول counsel

salakaree; salakar *n.* سلاکاري؛
سلاکار counsel

salam achawal *v.t* سلاماچول hail

salam achawal *v.t.* سلاماچول
salute

salam dua *n.* سلامدعا salutation

salam kawal *v.t.* سلامکول greet

salam; dranaway *n* سلام؛درناوى
salute

salam; rogh ramat *a.* سالم؛روغرمه
whole

salama *n* سلمه cent

salama kaleeza *n* سلمهکلیزه
centenarian

salamat *a.* سلامت healthy

salana; feesadee *adv.* سلنه؛فیصدي
per cent

salanday *n.* ساهلنى asthma

salata *n.* سلاته salad

salb *n.* صلب loin

saleeb *n.* صلیب rood

saleebee jihad *n* صلیبيجهاد
crusade

salees; hawar *a.* سلیس؛هوار
smooth

salfar laroonkay *a.* سلفرلرونکى
sulphuric

salgay *n.* سل hiccup

salgay *n* سل sob

salim *a.* سالم intact

salor *n.* لور four

salor barkheez *a.* لوربرخیز
quadruple

salor ghbarga kawal *v.t.* لورغبرگه
کول quadruple

salor gooteeza banra warkawal;
jor jaray kawal *v.t.* لورویزهبه
ورکول؛جوجاىکول square

salor gotay *n.* لوروى quadrangle

salor gotay *n.* لوروى square

salor goteez *a.* لورویز
quadrangular

salor goteez *a* لورویز square

salor myashtanay *a.* لورمیاشتنى
quarterly

salorama *n.* لورمه quarter

saltanat *n* سلطنت empire

saltanat *a.* سلطنت realm

salweykht *n.* لوت forty

sam aw jadee *a* سماوجدي
bonafide

sam kar na kawal *v.i.* سمکارنهکول
misfire

saman *n.* سامان luggage

samandar *n.* سمندر sea

samandar landi pawzee beyray
n. سمندرلاندپوىب submarine

samandaree *a.* سمندري marine

samandaree *a.* سمندري maritime

samandaree *a.* سمندري nautical

samandaree *a.* سمندري naval

samandaree *a.* سمندري oceanic

samandaree changakh *n.* سمندري
چنا lobster

samandaree feel *n.* سمندريفیل
walrus

samandaree hoora *n.* سمندري
حوره mermaid

samandaree khapeyray *n.*
سمندريهاپر nymph

samandaree khoog *n.* سمندريخو
seal

samandaree nareena makhlooq *n.* سمندري نارينه مخلوق merman

samandaree sragh *n* سمندري براغ beacon

samandaree toopan *n.* سمندري توپان typhoon

samandaree zwak *n.* سمندري ېواک navy

samandaryoon *n.* سمندريون navigation

samandaryoonay toghonday *n.* سمندريوني توغوندی torpedo

samawal *v.t.* سمول adapt

samawal *v.t.* سمول adjust

samawal *v.t.* سمول ameliorate

samawal; samsorawal *v.t.* سمول، سمسورول improve

samawana *n.* سمونه renovation

samawana; jorakht *n.* سمونه، جوت amelioration

samawona *n* سمونه correction

sambalawal *v.i.* سمبالول minister

samdalasa *adv.* سمدلاسه just

sameemana *a.* صميمانه whole-hearted

sameydal *v.t.* سمدل right

samlastal *v.t.* سملاستل lay

samlastal *v.i.* سملاستل rest

samoon; islah *n.* سمون، اصلاح amendment

samoonpal *n.* سمونپال reformer

samoontya *n.* سمونتيا reform

samoontya ramanz ta kawal *v.t.* سمونتيا رامنته کول reform

samsa *n.* مه ladle

samsar *n* سمسار broker

samsara *n.* سمساره lizard

samsortya *n.* سمسورتيا improvement

san *n.* سان muslin

sanad *n.* سند muniment

sanad; daraja *n* سند، درجه degree

sanat *n.* صنعت industry

sanatee *a.* صنعتي industrial

sanatgar *n.* صنعتر artisan

sanatoree *a.* سناتوري senatorial

sanay gharoonkay; taw warkawoonkay *n.* سنغونکي، ور کوونکي تاو spinner

sand *n.* سن jute

sanda *n* ه brim

sanda *n.* ه verge

sandan *n.* سندان anvil

sandara *n* سندره chant

sandara *n.* سندره song

sandara wayal *v.i.* سندره ويل sing

sandarbol *n.* سندربول songster

sandarbol; sandar gharay *n.* سندربول، سندرغای vocalist

sandargharay *n.* سندرغای singer

sandooq *n* صندوق box

saneeya *n* ثانيه second

sanf; tolay *n.* صنف، ټولی guild

sang par sang *adv* نبرنه abreast

sanga *n* لانه bough

sanga *n* لانه branch

sanga *adv.* نه wherein

sangal *n* نل elbow

sangal *n* نل ancon

sangar; morchal *n.* سنر، مورچل fortress

sangaroona jorawal v.t. سنرونه جوول fortify

sangeen; jiddee a. سنین؛جدي solemn

sangfarshee n. سنفرشي pavement

sangi sara mrasta n. سنگسرهمرسته adjunct

sanjawana; churt n سنجوونه؛چرت deliberation

sanjawona n سنجوونه comparison

sanwee; da dwayami darajey a. ثانوي؛ددويمهدرج secondary

saood n صعود mount

saood kawal; miqdar laral; zyateydal v.i صعودکول؛مقدار لرل؛زیاتدل amount

sapa n. په ripple

sapa n. په surf

sapa n. په wave

sapa payda kawal v.t. پهپداکول ripple

sapand keydal; takan khwaral v.t. پاندکدل؛څکانڅول wave

sapandwalay n. پاندوالی undulation

sapara n پره booth

sapara n پره bower

sapayeez kawal v.i. پهییزکول undulate

sapayeez; da mawjoono pa arwand a. پهییز؛دموجونوپهاوند sinuous

sapeedar n. سپدار poplar

sapey jorawal; sapand keydal v.i. پجوول؛پاندکدل surge

sapey wahal v.i پوهل billow

sapeyra n. په slap

sapeyra porta kawal v.t. پهپورته کول slap

sapray n. پر canopy

sar n. سر cape

sar n. سر head

sar badala a. سربداله giddy

sar beyra adv. سربره on

sar beyra par dey prep. سربرهپرد over

sar chapa a. سرچپه topsy turvy

sar chapa kawal v. i. سرچپهکول capsize

sar chapa kawal v. t سرچپهکول convert

sar chapa kawana n سرچپهکونه conversion

sar chapa par hookoomat bandi n. سرچپهپرحکومتباند coup

sar cheena n. سرچینه rudiment

sar cheena n. سرچینه source

sar cheena n. چینه سر originator

sar cheena akheysta; top wahal v.i. سرچینهاخستل؛ټوپوهل spring

sar cheena keydal v.t. سرچینهکدل originate

sar danga n. سردنه protagonist

sar ghandaway; sar laray n. سرغندوی؛سرلاری van

sar gharand a. سرغاند unruly

sar gharawana n سرغونه deviation

sar gharaway n. سرغاوی obstinacy

sar gharaway n. سرغاوی transgression

sar gharaway n. سرغاوی rebel

sar gharaway kawal *v.i.* سرغاوی کول rebel

sar gharaway; teyray *n.* سرغاوی، تری violation

sar ghosawal *v. t.* سرغوول behead

sar jama *n.* سرجمع overall

sar kakh *a.* سرکخ mettlesome

sar kashee *n* سرکشي defiance

sar khoogay *n.* سرخوی migraine

sar khozawal *v.i.* سرخوول nod

sar khozawana *n.* سرخوونه node

sar khreyana *n.* سرخرینه tonsure

sar koozay *n.* سرکوزی swine

sar lakhkar *n* سرلکر commander

sar lakhkar *n* سرلکر marshal

sar lobsaray *n.* سرلوباری umpire

sar lobsaree kawal *v.t.,* سرلوباري کول umpire

sar parast *n.* سرپرست overseer

sar parast *n.* سرپرست warden

sar parastee *n.* سرپرستي wardship

sar patoonay *n.* سرپونی wimple

sar pokh *n.* سرپو lid

sar sharee; tawleedee wartya *n.* سرشاري،تولیديوتیا productivity

sar shmeyrana *n.* سرشمرنه census

sar shmeyrana *a.* سرشمرنه statistical

sar ta rasawana; ijra *n.* سرته رسونه،اجرا performance

sar tamba *a.* سرمبه sturdy

sar tamba *a.* سرتمبه obstinate

sar tar sara *prep.* سرترسره throughout

sar tar sara; la payla tar paya *adv.* سرترسره،لهپیلهترپایه through

sar teyray *n.* سرتری trooper

sar zay *n.* اړای observatory

sar zay *n.* ای pasture

sara *n* ساه cold

sara *n* سره fertilizer

sara areeki khatmawal *v. t.* سره ایکختمول boycott

sara gadawal *v. t* سره ول combine

sara gandal *v.t.* سرهنل rivet

sara na joreydal *v.t.* سرهنه جولدل mismatch

sara nakhlawal *v.t.* سرهنلول table

sara peywandawal *v.t.* سرهپوندول weld

sara pukhla kawal *v.t.* سرهپخلا کول reconcile

sara sanjawal *v. t* سرهسنجول compare

sara tawawal *v.i.* سرهتاوول rove

sara; warsara *prep.* سره،ورسره with

sarab *n.* سراب mirage

sarak *n.* سک road

saral *v. t.* ارل chase1

saral *v.t.* ارل oversee

saral *v.t.* ارل invigilate

saral; pa naz nakhro tlal *v.i.* ارل، پهنازنخروتلل stalk

saran *n.* ارن invigilator

sarana *n.* ارنه invigilation

sarana kawoonkay *a.* ارنهکوونکی monitory

sarana; taqeeb *n.* تعقیب،نه ارن chase2

saranay; wahshee *a.* وحشي،ني سارا wild

sarandoy sarteyray *n.* سروندی ار ترى sentinel

saranga chi *conj.* چ رنه as

sarani lapara weekh pati keydana *n.* ارنلپاره ویپاتکدنه vigil

sarawal *v.i.* رول graze

sarawal *v.t.* رول pasture

sarawal *v. i.* سول cool

sarawana *n* روونه graze

saray *n* سارى example

saray *n* سى male

sarayee orbasha *n.* سارايياوربشه oat

sardar *n.* سردار chieftain

sareeza *n* سریزه foreword

sareeza *n.* سریزه prologue

sareeza *n.* سریزه preface

sareeza leekal *v.t.* سریزهلیکل preface

sareeza; ibtidayee *a.* ابتدایي،سریزه introductory

sareykh سر glue

sareykh *n.* سري adhesive

sarf kawal *v.t. & i.* صرفکول conjugate

sargand *a.* رند apparent

sargand *a.* رند manifest

sargand topeer *n* رندتوپیر contrast

sargand topeer larl *v. t* رندتوپیر لرل contrast

sarganda *a.* رنده evident

sargandawal *v.t.* رندول unshcathe

sargandawal; dalalat kawal *v.t.* رندول؛دلالتکول indicate

sargandeydal *v.i.* رندل appear

sargar *n.* ارر spy

sargaray *n* ارى scout

sargardan garzeydal *v.i.* سردان رل wander

sargardan kawal *v.t.* سردانکول ramble

sargardan; koosa dabay *a* سردان؛ کوهبى stray

sargardanee *n.* سردانی quandary

sargardanee *n* سرداني ramble

sargardanee *n* سرداني stray

sargaree kawal *v.i* اروي کول scout

sargaree kawal *v.i.* اروي کول spy

sargharawana kawal *v. t* سرغونه کول disobey

sarhadee sawkay *n.* سرحديوک outpost

sarka *n.* سرکه vinegar

sarka keydal *v.* سرکهکدل acetify

sarkas *n.* سرکس circus

sarkh *n.* رخ axle

sarkh *n.* رخ pulley

sarkh; da akasay da feelam sarkh *n.* رخ؛دعکاسدفیلمهرخ reel

sarkh; paya *a.* رخ؛پایه wheel

sarkhanay *n.* رخنی whirligig

sarkhandoy *n.* رخندوی revolver

sarkhawal *v.t.* رخول wheel

sarkhawal; tawawal *v.i.* ؛رخول تاوول spin

sarkhay *n.* رخى clew

sarkheydal *v.i.* رخدل lurch

sarkheydal *v.i.* رخدل reel

sarkheydoonkay masheen *n.* رخدونکیماشین turbine

sarkondai *n.* سرکوز somersault

sarleek *n.* سرلیک heading

sarmakhkay *n.* رمکه reptile

sarman *n.* رمن leather

sarman *n.* رمن skin

sarmaya *n.* سرمایه fund

sarnawakht *n.* سرنوت predestination

sarokha *n.* سوخه chill

sarood; choonrar *n* سرود؛چوهار warble

sarood; naghma *n* سرود؛نغمه carol

sarowoonkay *n* سوونکی cooler

sarparast *n.* سرپرست superintendent

sarparastee kawal *v.t.* سرپرستي کول superintend

sarpee *a.* سرپي leaden

sarsaree jangeydal *v.t.* سرسري جندل skirmish

sarsaree; kam zhawar *a.* سرسري؛کمژور shallow

sarshar *a.* سرشار profuse

sartambagee *n.* سرتمبي obduracy

sartanee ghota *n.* سرطانيغوه tumour

sarwa *n.* سرو cedar

sarway; salor pkhey laroonkay *n.* ساروی؛بلورپلرونکی quadruped

sas *n.* ساس sauce

sasawal; wro wro wahal *v.t.* ول؛ ورورووهل tap

saseydal *v. i* لدل drip

saseydal *v.i.* لدل leak

saseydal; la lasa ghorzeydal *v. i* لدل؛لهلاسهغورلدل drop

saseydana *n* لدنه drip

saskay *n* لکی drop

sast *a.* سست loose

sastawal *v.t.* سستول loose

sastee *a.* سستي slack

sastee *n.* سستي slowness

sata *n.* سطح level

satak *n.* کے hammer

satal *v.t.* ساتل keep

satal ta warta lokhay *n.* سطلته ورتهلوی peck

satal; palal *v.t.* ساتل؛پالل patronize

satana *n.* ساتنه maintenance

satana *n* نه lick

satana *n.* ساتنه retention

satana ki akheystal *v* ساتنهکاخستل custody

satandoy *n.* ساتندوی bodyguard

satandoy *n.* ساتندوی patron

satandoy *n.* ساتندوی safeguard

satandoy *n.* ساتندوی warder

satanzay *n* ساتنای cache

sathee maloomat *n.* سطحيمالومات smack

satoonkay *n* ساتونکی custodian

satoonkay *n.* ساتونکی keeper

satoonkay *a.* ساتونکی retentive

sawal; pokhtana *n.* سوال؛پوتنه question

sawda *n.* سودا obsession

sawda *n.* سودا mart

sawdagar *n.* سودار trader

sawdagar *n.* سوداگر tradesman

sawdagar *n.* سوداگر merchant

sawdagaree kawal *v.t* سوداري کول market

sawdagaree saman *n.* سوداري سامان merchandise

sawdagareeza moassisa *n.* سوداريزه‌مؤسسه firm

sawdagareeza rakra warkra *n.* سوداريزه‌راکه‌ورکه dealing

sawka kawal *v.t.* سوکه‌کول retard

sawka kawal; sastawal *v.t.* سوکه کول؛سستول slacken

sawka; pasawana *n.* سوکه؛پوونه retardation

sawkeedar *n.* وکيدار sentry

sayhat man; qawee *a.* صحت‌من؛ قوي robust

sayins poh *n.* ساينس‌پوه scientist

sayinsee *a.* ساينسي scientific

sayl; jaryan *n* سل؛جريان current

saylab *n.* سلاب torrent

saylabee *a.* سلابي torrential

sayqalee kawal *v.t.* صقلي‌کول polish

saza *n.* سزا punishment

saza warkawal *v.t.* سزاورکول inflict

saza warkawal *v.t.* سزاورکول punish

sazayee *a.* سزايي punitive

seekhak; teyra rawataltya *n.* سيخک؛ته‌ره‌راوتلتيا spur

seelanee *n.* سيلاني tourist

seelay *n.* سيله gust

seem *n.* سيم wire

seem aw mazee ghazawal *v.t.* سيم اومزي‌غول wire

seem ghazawana *n.* سيم‌غوونه wiring

seem ya mazay warachawal; kash kawal *v.t.* سيم‌يامزى وراچول؛کش‌کول string

seema *n.* سيمه locale

seema *n.* سيمه territory

seemab *n.* سيماب quicksilver

seemab *n.* سيماب mercury

seemabee *a.* سيمابي mercurial

seemayeez *a.* سيمه‌ييز local

seemayeez *a.* سيمه‌ييز regional

seemayeez *a.* سيمه‌ييز territorial

seemayeez kawal *v.t.* سيمه‌ييزکول localize

seemayeez padree *n.* سيمه‌ييزپادري parson

seemayeez; mahalee *a.* سيمه‌ييز؛ محلي vernacular

seemayeeza lahja aw wayang *n.* سيمه‌ييزه‌لهجه‌اوويند vernacular

seemee paray *n.* سيمي‌پى cable

seena *n* سينه bosom

seena band *n* سينه‌بند bodice

seenama *n.* سينما cinema

seend *n.* سيند river

seend kakhana *n.* سيندکنه lexicography

seengar *n.* سينار cosmetic

seengar *n* سينار decoration

seengar pori arwand *a.* سينارپور اوند ornamental

seengar; samawana *n* سينار؛ سموونه trim

seengarawal v.t. سينارول adorn

seengarawal v.t. سينارول attire

seengarawal v. t سينارول decorate

seengarawal v.t. سينارول ornament

seengarawal v.t. سينارول prune

seengarowoonkay a. سينروونکی cosmetic

seengarpal a سينارپال fashionable

seerat n. سيرت character

seeri kawal v.t. يرکول rupture

seeri weeri kawal v.t يروير کول tatter

seeri weeri shay n. يروير شی tatter

seeriwalay n. يروالی rupture

seeyahee n. سياهي ink

seeyara n. سياره planet

seeyarawee a. سياروي planetary

seeyasat pohana n. سياست پوهنه politics

seeyasatdaree n. سياست داري polity

seeyasatwal n. سياست وال politician

seeyasatwal n. سياستوال statesman

seeyasee a. سياسي political

seher; khkula n. سحر،ښکلا charm1

selai n. سيل gale

seyl n. سل spate

seyra n. ره aspect

seyra peyzhandana n. ره پژندنه physiognomy

seyra; qeeyafa n. ره،قيافه countenance

seyra; shakal n ره،شکل feature

seyra; zahiree banra n. ره،ظاهري به visage

seyral aw sparal v.i. لاوسپل rummage

seyrana aw sparana n نه اوسپنه rummage

seyray wuna n. ونه oak

sfanj n. سفنج sponge

sha; mla n. شا،ملا back

shaar n. شعار motto

shaar n. شعار watchword

shaayar n شعائر doctrine

shabahat laral a. شباهت لرل akin

shabaka n. شبکه lattice

shabasay warkawal v.t شاباسی ورکول felicitate

shabasay; neykmarghee n شاباسی،نکمرغي felicity

shabash; d khoshalay yaw awaz interj. شاباش،دخوشاليو آواز hurrah

shadab a. شاداب lush

shadab a. شاداب youthful

shadal saray n شلسی boor

shadeed a. شديد intense

shadeed a. شديد intensive

shadeed a. شديد severe

shadeed a. شديد tense

shadeed a. شديد harsh

shadeed gham aw weer n. شديد غم اووير woe

shadeed; tond a. شديد،توند vehement

shado n شادو ape

shafa warbakhal v.t شفاوربل remedy

shafaf a. شفاف lucent

shafahee azmoyana *n* شفاهي آزموينه viva-voce

shafqat *n.* شفقت pathos

shaftaloo *n.* شفتالو peach

shaga *n.* شه pebble

shaga *n.* شه sand

shagardee *n.* شاردي apprentice

shaghal *n.* شغال jackal

shaglana *a.* شلنه sandy

shahadat *n.* شهادت martyrdom

shahadat nama *n.* شهادت‌نامه certificate

shahadat nama *n.* شهادت‌نامه testimonial

shahana *a.* شاهانه majestic

shahay *n.* شه paramour

shahee *a.* شاهي royal

shahee taj *n.* شاهي‌تاج tiara

shaheed *n.* شهيد martyr

shaheen *n* شاهين hawk

shahid keydal; shahidee warkawal *v.i.* شاهدكدل، شاهدي‌وركول witness

shahidee leekoonkay *n.* شاهدي ليكونكى deponent

shahkar *n.* شاهكار masterpiece

shahkar kartab *n* شهكاركرتب stunt

shahwanee *a.* شهواني lascivious

shahwanee *a.* شهواني lustful

shahwanee *a.* شهواني sensual

shahwanee *a.* شهواني sensuous

shahwanee *a.* شهواني sexual

shahwanee *a.* شهواني voluptuous

shahwaneeyat *n.* شهوانيت sexuality

shahwat *n* شهوت cupidity

shahwat *n.* شهوت lust

shahwat parast *a.* شهوت‌پرست lewd

shahwat parast *n.* شهوت‌پرست sensualist

shahwat parastee *n.* شهوت‌پرستي sensuality

shahwat paray *n.* شهوت‌پارى sexy

shahwat parowoonkay *a.* شهوت پاروونكى lusty

shahwatee *a.* شهوتي licentious

shahwatran *n.* شهوت‌ران voluptuary

shahzada *n.* شاهزاده prince

shahzadgay *n.* شاهزاد princess

shair *n.* شاعر bard

shair *n.* شاعر poet

shair gotay *n.* شاعروى poetaster

shaira khaza *n.* ه شاعره poetess

shairana *a.* شاعرانه poetic

shairana khkula *n.* شاعرانه‌كلا poetics

shairay ki hagha kaleema chi qafeeya yi da bali haghi qafeeyi sara jora wee *n.* شاعر كى هغه كليمه‌چقافيه‌يدبلاهغله‌قافيه‌سره جوه‌وي crambo

shairee *n.* شاعري poetry

shairee; deewan *n.* شاعري،ديوان poesy

shak *n* شك doubt

shak *n.* شك suspicion

shak laral *v. i* شك‌لرل doubt

shakal *n.* شكل shape

shakal bandee *n.* شكل‌بندي outline

shakal warkawal v.t شکل ورکول shape

shakh; neygh n. شخ؛نغ stiff

shakhsee a. شخصي personal

shakhseeyat na warkawal v.t. شخصیت نه ورکول impersonate

shakhwalay n. شخوالی rigour

shakman a. شکمن sceptical

shakman n شکمن suspect

shakman a. شکمن suspicious

shakman a. شکمن uncertain

shakmanee n. شکمني scepticism

shal n. شال shawl

shal a. شل lax

shal n شل twenty

shal shoot n شل شو cripple

shalag a شل coarse

shalag shalag a. شل شل threadbare

shalam a. شلم twentieth

shalam a. شلم twenty

shalama barkha n برخه شلمه twentieth

shama n. شمع candle

shamil a. شامل inclusive

shamilawal v.t. شاملول include

shamilawal v.t. شاملول merge

shamilawoonkay n. شاملوونکی merger

shamileydal v. i شاملدل consist

shamooltya n. شمولتیا inclusion

shamshatay n. شمشته turtle

shan; shawkat n. شان؛شوکت pomposity

shanakht n. شناخت identity

shanakht kawal v.t. شناخت کول identify

shanal aw sparal v.i. شنل او سپرل research

shanana aw sparana n ننه او سپنه research

shanawoonkay; tajzeeyatee a شننوونکی؛تجزیاتي analytical

shand; bey hasila a. شن؛بحاصله sterile

shandar a. شاندار pompous

shandar a شاندار fine

shandar a. شاندار tremendous

shandar; waswasee a شاندار؛ وسواسي fantastic

shandtob n. شنتوب sterility

shanshob n. شنشوب sediment

shaoor n شعور conscience

shaoor n. شعور wit

shaqol n. شاقول perpendicular

shar n شا barren

sharab n شراب alcohol

sharabkhana n. شرابخانه tavern

sharal shaway n. شل شوی outcast

sharal shaway kas n. شل شوی کس outlaw

sharal; eystal v.t. شل؛استل hurl

sharam n. شرم shame

sharamnak a. شرمناک shameful

shararat n. شرارت prank

sharay n شری measles

sharay n ش blanket

sharay n ش wrap

sharbal; kuch jorawal v. t. & i. شاربل؛کوچ جوړول churn

shareef a. شریف noble

shareef saray n. شریف سی noble

shareef saray *n.* شريف سى nobleman

shareek *a.* شريک mutual

shareek; mrastandoy *a.* شريک؛ مرستندوى associate

shareekeydal *v.i.* شريکدل partake

shareer *a.* شرير mischievous

shareer *a.* شرير naughty

shareer; khabees *a.* شرير؛خبيث vicious

sharha kawal *v.t.* شرحه کول illustrate

sharha kawal; azada leekal *v.t.* شرحه کول،آزادليکل paraphrase

sharha; tawzee *n.* شرحه؛توضيح illustration

sharmandookay *a.* شرمندوکى bashful

sharmawal *v.t.* شرمول abash

sharmawal *v. t* شرمول embarrass

sharmawal *v.t.* شرمول shame

sharmawal; ruswa kawal *v.t.* شرمول؛رسوا کول reproach

sharmeendookay *a.* شرميندوکى timorous

sharmeydal *v.i.* شرمدل shy

sharmeydalay *a.* شرمدلى ashamed

sharminda *adv* شرمنده ablush

sharmindookay *n.* شرمندوکى shy

sharoonkay *n* شرونکى repellent

shart *n* شرط bet

shart *n.* شرط proviso

shart taral *v.i* شرط طتل bet

shart taral *v.i.* شرط طتل wager

shart tarana *n.* شرط طتنه wager

shart; artya *n.* شرط،اتيا requirement

sharteeya *a* شرطيه conditional

shat; sheera *n* شات،شيره molasses

shata pati keydal *v.i.* شاته پاته کدل lag

shata pati shakhs *n.* شاته پاته شخص laggard

shatag *n.* شا ت retread

shateer *n.* شاه تير girder

shatranj *n.* شطرنج chess

shaw khwa *prep* شاو خوا about

shawq *n* شوق craze

shawq *n.* شوق zeal

shawqeen *a* شوقين fond

shawqeen *n.* شوقين zealot

shawqeen; leywal *a.* شوقين،لوال ardent

shay *n.* شى item

shay *n.* شى object

shay; seez *n.* شى،يز thing

shayan teet aw park eekhowal *v. t* شيان تيت او پرک ايوول clutter

shayr *n.* شعر poem

shayree band *n.* شعري بند stanza

shaytan *n.* شطان satan

shazalmay *n.* شلمى bridegroom

shazalmay *n.* شلمى groom

sheen rang *n* شين رنگ green

sheen yaqoot *n.* شين ياقوت sapphire

sheendal *v.t.* شيندل sift

sheendal; da hasharato zaharjan darmal pashal *v.t.* شيندل؛دحشراتوزهرجن درمل پاشل spray sheenkay *n.* شينکى greenery

sheera tri eystal *v.t.* شيره‌تراستل sap

sheerdan; sooray; nalka *n.* شيردان،سورى،نلکه tap

sheereen *a.* شيرين luscious

sheereenee raneewal *v. t.* شيرينى رانيول candy

shehed *n.* شهد honey

sheyba *n.* شيه moment

sheyba *n.* شيبه minute

sheydatob *n.* شداتوب frenzy

sheydey *n.* شد milk

sheydey warkawal *v.t.* شدورکول foster

sheydey warkawal *v.i.* شدورکول lactate

sheydey warkawal *v.t.* شدورکول milk

sheydey warkawal *v.t.* شدورکول suckle

sheydey warkowoonkay *a.* شد ورکوونکى milch

sheyr khat *n* شرخط toss

sheyr khat *v.t.* شرخط‌کول toss

sheytan *n* شطان devil

shidat *n.* شدت severity

shiddat zyatawal *v.t.* شدت‌زياتول intensify

shiddat; da fayl zamana *n.* شدت، دفعل‌زمانه tense

shiddat; pyawartya *n.* شدت، پياوتيا vehemence

shikayat *n.* شکايت protest

shikayat kawal *v.i.* شکايت‌کول protest

shikayat; sarganda nakhwakhee *n.* شکايت،پرندهناخوي protestation

shirakat *n.* شراکت partnership

shirkat *n.* شرکت company

shirkat *n.* شرکت participation

shirkat kawoonkay *n.* شرکت کوونکى participant

shirkat laral *v.i.* شرکت‌لرل participate

shkanja *n.* شکنجه persecution

shkanja kawal *v.t.* شکنجه‌کول persecute

shkanja kawal *v.t.* شکنجه‌کول rack

shkanja kawal *v.t.* شکنجه‌کول torture

shkanja; rabrawana *n.* شکنجه، ربوونه torture

shkeydal *v.t.* شکدل lacerate

shkhara *n* شخه dispute

shkhara *n.* شخه encounter

shkhara *n* شخه fight

shkhara *n.* شخه quarrel

shkhara *n.* شخه wrangle

shkhara kawal *v. t* شخه‌کول bicker

shkhara kawal *v. i* شخه‌کول dispute

shkhara kawal *v. t* شخه‌کول encounter

shkhara kawal *v.t* شخه‌کول fight

shkhara kawal *v.i.* شخه‌کول wrangle

shkhara; lanja *n.* شخه،لانجه tussle

shkhara; mobahisa *n.* شخه،مباحثه altercation

shkhwand wahal *v.i.* شخوندوهل
ruminate

shkhwand wahana *n.* شخوندوهنه
rumination

shkhwand wahoonkay *n.* شخوند
وهونکی rodent

shkhwand wahoonkay *a.* شخوند
وهونکی ruminant

shkhwand wahoonkay sarway *n.*
شخوندوهونکیساروی ruminant

shlakha *a.* شلاخه lash

shlawal; shkawal *v.t.* شلول؛شکول
tear

shmeyr *n.* شمر calculation

shmeyr *n.* شمر number

shmeyr pohana *n.* شمرپوهنه
arithmetic

shmeyr pohaneez *a.* شمرپوهنیز
arithmetical

shmeyra *n.* شمره count

shmeyra kawal *v. t.* شمرهکول
count

shmeyra; karkha *n.* شمره؛کره
score

shmeyral *v. t.* شمرل calculate

shmeyral *v.t.* شمرل number

shmeyral *v.t.* شمرل score

shmeyral; andaza lagawal *v.t.*
شمرل؛اندازهلول reckon

shmeyroonkay *n.* شمرونکی
numerator

shmeyroonkay *n.* شمرونکی scorer

shmeyroonkay masheen *n*
شمرونکیماشین calculator

shobal *n* شوبل hurt

shobda baz *n.* شعبدهباز juggler

shobda bazee kawal *v.t.* شعبده
بازیکول juggle

shoghal; danda *n* شغل؛دنده
employment

shoghla *n* شوغله blaze

shohrat *n.* شهرت renown

shoja *a.* شجاع gallant

shomal *n.* شمال north

shomalee *a* شمالی north

shomalee *a.* شمالی northern

shooka *n.* شوکه robbery

shookawana; takhtawana *n.*
شوکونه؛تتوونه snatch

shookmar *n.* شوکمار robber

shool pool *a* شولپول flabby

shoonay *a.* شونی obtainable

shoonay *a.* شونی probable

shoonda *n.* شونه lip

shoondak; poz *n.* شونک؛پوز snout

shoontya *n.* شونتیا likelihood

shoora *n.* شورا council

shoorayee *a.* شورایی parliamentary

shor mashor *n.* شورماشور fuss

shor mashor jorawal *v.i* شورماشور
جوول fuss

shormashor *n.* شورماشور ado

shoro kawal *v.t* شروعکول initial

shpa *n.* شپه night

shpa teyrawal; zay warkawal
v.i. شپهترول؛ځایورکول roost

shpag; shpagam *n., a.* شپږ؛شپږم six

shpagam *a.* شپږم sixth

shparas; shparasam *n., a.* شپاس؛
شپاسم sixteen

shparasam *a.* شپاسم sixteenth

shpeylak *n* شپلک whistle

shpeylak wahal *v.i.* شپلک‌وهل whistle

shpeylay *n* شپلا bugle

shpeylay *n* شپلا flute

shpeylay wahal *v.i* شپلوهل flute

shpeyta *n., a.* شپته sixty

shpeytam *a.* شپتم sixtieth

shpoon *n.* شپون herdsman

shpoon *n.* شپون shepherd

shranga *n.* شرنا clink

shrangeydal *v.i.* شرندل jingle

shranghar *n.* شرنهار jingle

shtaman *a.* شتمن opulent

shtaman kawal *v. t* شتمن‌کول enrich

shtamanee *n.* شتمني mammon

shtamanee *n.* شتمني riches

shtamanee *a.* شتمني richness

shtoon; wajood *n* شتون؛وجود being

shuhrat *n.* شهرت popularity

shuja *a.* شجاع stout

shukawal; tolawal *v.t.* شکول؛ټولول pluck

shumalee ya sweylee qutab *n.* شمالي‌يا‌سولي‌قطب polar

shuro *n.* شروع outset

shutar murgh *n.* شترمرغ ostrich

sifat *n.* صفت adjective

sigrat *n.* سر cigar

sika *n* سکه coin

sika jorawal *n* سکه‌جوول coinage

sika jorawal *v.t.* سکه‌جوول mint

silool; koochnay zandan; hajra *n.* سلول؛کوچني‌زندان؛حجره cell

siloolee *adj* سلولي cellular

silsila; so barkheeza feelam ya keesa *n.* سلسله؛وبرخيزه‌فيلم‌يا‌کيسه serial

simant *n.* سمنت cement

sinama *n.* سينما movies

siraf *conj.* صرف only

sirinj *n.* سرنج syringe

sirinj wahal *v.t.* سرنج‌وهل syringe

skala; payshnihad *n.* سکاله؛پیشنهاد proposition

skarwata *n.* سکروه spark

skatlandee wagaray *n.* اسکلندي‌وی Scot

skhak *n* ښاک drink

skhak *n* ښاک beverage

skhak jorawal *v. t.* brew

skhak jorawana *n* ښاک‌جوونه brewery

skhal *v. t* ښل drink

skoondal *v.t* سکونل goad

skoondal; chokhawal *v.t.* سکونل؛چوخول prick

smas *n.* سم cave

so arkheez *a.* واخيز multilateral

so arkheez *a.* واخيز versatile

so chanda *a.* وچنده manifold

so chi *prep.* وچ until

so goonay *a.* وونی multiple

so shaklay *n.* وشکلی multiform

so zaya mat aw munkasir khat *n.* وايه‌مات‌او‌منکسر‌خط zigzag

so; so goonay *a* وؤونه several

soba; kamyabee *n.* سوبه؛کاميابي victory

sodagareez mal *n.* سوداريزمال commodity

sofiana au zahidana jwand *n* صوفيانه اوزاهدانه ژوند benefice

sohan *n* سوهان file

sohanawal *v.t* سوهانول file

sok; kom yaw *pron.* وک؛ کوميو some

sok; kom yaw *pron.* وک؛ کوميو who

sok; yaw kas *pron.* وک؛ يو کس one

solayeez *a.* سوله ييز peaceful

somia *n* صومعه convent

somrawalay *n.* ومروالى quantity

somrayeez *a.* ومره ييز quantitative

sond *n.* سوند ginger

sonreydal *v.i* سوندل hiss

sonreydana *n* سوندنه hiss

soocha *a* سوچه pure

soocha *n* سوچه virgin

soocha gata las ta rawral *v.t.* سوچه ګته لاس ته راول net

soochawalay *n.* سوچوالى purity

soochawalay ghokhtoonkay *n.* سوچوالى غوتونکى purist

sood khor *n.* سودخور usurer

sood khwarana *n.* سودخونه usury

soofee *n* صوفي mystic

soofyana *a.* صوفيانه mystic

sooka *n.* سوکه tip

sooka; da zaweeyi ras *n.* سوکه؛ د زاويرأس apex

sooka; makhooka *n.* سوکه؛ موکه peak

sooka; oj *n.* سوکه؛ اوج top

soolawal *v.t.* سولول rub

soolawana *n* سولونه rub

sooleydana *n* سولدنه erosion

soon *n* سون burn

soor *a.* سور red

soor banjan *n.* سوربانجان tomato

soor garanday *n* سورندى cockroach

soor kawal *v.t.* سورکول redden

soor rag *n.* سوررګ artery

soor rang *n.* سوررن red

soor ranga hashrat *n.* سوررنه حشرات vermillion

sooray *n.* سورى aperture

sooray *n* سورى hole

sooray *n.* سورى hollow

sooray kawal *v. t* سورى کول bore

sooray kawal *v.t* سورى کول hole

sooray kawal *v.t.* سورى کول perforate

sooray kawal *v.t.* سورى کول slit

sooray keydal; shleydal *v.t.* سورى کدل؛ شلدل puncture

sooray; shleydalay *n.* سورى؛ شلدلى puncture

soorbakhan *a.* سوربخن reddish

soorbakhan khurmayee rang *a* سوربخن خرمايي رن maroon

soorbakhan qahwayee rang *n.* سوربخن قهوه يي رن mahogany

sooreydana *n* سوردنه crimson

sor *a* سو cold

sor *a* سو cool

sorb saray *n* وربسى fat

sotak khwaroonkay *a.* سوک خوونکى malleable

sotay *n* سوى cudgel

soya *n.* سويه hare

soya *n.* سويه rabbit

sozanda; khoonee *a* سوزنده؛خوني fiery

sozawal *v.t.* سوزول singe

sozawal aw eerey kawal *v. t* سووله اوايركه ل cremate

sozawoonkay *a.* سوزوونكی caustic

sozeydal aw loogay kawal *v.i.* سوزدلاولوی کول smoulder

sozeydana *n* سوزدنه singe

spaga *n.* سپه louse

spak aw bey tarbeeyey saray *n* سپکاوبتربيسی cad

spak ganral *v.t.* سپکـل scorn

spak khob *n.* سپکخوب slumber

spak khob kawal *v. i* سپکخوب کول doze

spak khob kawal *v.i.* سپکخوب کول slumber

spak nazar kawal *v.t.* سپکنظر کول slight

spak shakhs *n* سپکشخص churl

spak tia *n* سپکتيا disrepute

spak; nakas *a.* سپک،ناکس base

spaka lasee nayza *n.* سپکهلاسینزه javelin

spakawal *n* سپکول affront

spakawal *v. t.* سپکول debase

spakaway *v.t.* سپکاوی affront

spakaway *n.* سپکاوی insult

spaki saplay *n.* سپکپل sandal

spakwalay *n* سپکوالی abasement

spakwalay *n.* سپکوالی levity

spara askar *n.* سپارهعسکر cavalry

sparakhtana warta kawal *v.t.* سپارتنهورته کول recommend

sparakhtana; tawseeya *n.* سپارتنه، توصیه recommendation

sparal *v.t.* سپارل assign

sparal *v.t.* سپارل vest

sparana *n* سپارنه surrender

sparana; tohmat *n.* سپارنه؛تهمت charge

spareydal *v.t.* سپردل ride

sparghay badawal *v.i.* سپرغبادول scintillate

sparlay *n* سپرل ride

spay *n* سپ bitch

spay *n* سپی dog

spayee *n.* سپآيي soldier

spayee joreydal *v.i.* سپايجودل soldier

speen *a.* سپين white

speen geeray *n* سپينيری elder

speen goya *a.* سپينويه frank

speen goyee *n.* سپينويي candour

speen rang *n* سپينرن white

speen rang warkawal *v.t.* سپينرن ورکول whiten

speen sandal *n.* سپينصندل sandalwood

speen wazma *a.* سپينوزمه whitish

speen zar *n.* سپينزر silver

speena wayna kawoonkay *a.* سپينهوناکوونکی outspoken

speenawal *v.t.* سپينول justify

speenawal; weenzal *v. t* سپينول؛ وينل bleach

speenawana *n.* سپينونه justification

speyda dagh *n* سپيدهداغ aurora

spogmakay *n.* سپومک sputnik

spogmakay; pleewanay *n.* سپومکي؛
پليوني satellite

spogmay *n.* سپوږمه moon

spogmeez *a.* سپوږميز lunar

sra kari ghwakha *n* سره کغوه fry

sra sharab *n.* سره شراب wine

sra zar *n.* سره زر gold

sragh *n.* راغ lamp

sragh *n.* راغ torch

srak kawal *v.i.* رک کول spark

srakeydal *v.i.* رکدل sparkle

srakeydana *n.* رکدنه sparkle

srangeez *a.* رنيز qualitative

srangwalay; mayar *n.* رنوالی؛معيار
quality

sreeka *n.* یکه pang

sreykhawal *v.t.* سرول paste

sreykheydoonkay kaghaz *n.*
سردونکي کاغذ sticker

sreykhnak *a.* سريناک adhesive

sreykhnak *n.* سرناک sticky

sreykhnak *a.* سرناک slimy

sreykhnaka *adj* سرناکه cohesive

stan *n.* ستن needle

stana wahal *v.t.* ستنه وهل inject

stana; mlataray *n.* ستنه؛ملاتی prop

stana; paya *n.* ستنه؛پايه pillar

staneydal *v.i.* ستندل recur

staneydal *v.i.* ستندل return

staneydana *n.* ستندنه recurrence

staneydoonkay *a.* ستندونکي
recurrent

star *a.* ستر grand

star kar *n* ستر کار exploit

star ploranzay *n.* سترپلورنی store

staray kawal *v.t* ستی کول fatigue

staray keydal; staray kawal *v.t.*
ستی کدل،ستی کول tire

staray; beyzara *a.* ستی؛بزاره
weary

starga *n* ستره eye

starga patawal *v.i.* سترهپول nap

starga patawana *n.* سترهپوونه nap

stargak *n* سترک wink

stargak wahal *v. t. & i* سترک وهل
blink

stargak wahal *v.i.* سترک وهل
wink

stargey pri patawal *v.t.* سترپرپول
ignore

stargi breykheydal *v. t.* ستربرځل
dazzle

stargi patawana *n* سترپوونه
elusion

stargi pri patawal *v. t* سترپرپول
evade

stargi taral *v. t* ستر تل blindfold

stari byatee *n. pl.* ستربياتي shears

stariwalay *n* ستوالی fatigue

stayal *v. t* ستايل commend

stayalay *a.* ستايلی commendable

stayana *n* ستاينه commendation

stomana *a.* ستومانه lethargic

stomana *n.* ستوماني tedium

stomana kawal *v. t.* ستومانه کول
exhaust

stomana kawal; beyzara keydal
v.t. & i ستومانه کول،بزاره کدل
weary

stomana kawoonkay *a.* ستومانه
کوونکی irksome

stomana kawoonkay *a.* ستومانه کوونکی mawkish

stomana kawoonkay *a.* ستومانه کوونکی tedious

stomana kawoonkay *a.* ستومانه کوونکی tiresome

stomana kawoonkay safar kawal *n.* ستومانه کوونکی سفر کول trek

stomana keydal *v.i.* ستومانه کدل moil

stomana safar *v.i.* ستومانهسفر trek

stomanee *n.* ستوماني laziness

stomanee *n.* ستوماني lethargy

stoonay *n.* مر ستوني؛ throat

stoonay wartakhta kawal *v.t.* ستونیورتخته کول throttle

stoonay; ghara *n.* ستوني؛غاه throttle

stoonez *a.* ستونیز guttural

stoonza *n* ستونزه difficulty

stoonza *n.* ستونزه problem

stoonzman *a.* ستونزمن inexplicable

stoonzman *a.* ستونزمن problematic

stoonzmanawal *v.i.* ستونزمنول snarl

stor peyzhand *n.* ستورپژاند astronomer

stor pohana *n.* ستورپوهنه astrology

stor pohand *n.* ستورپوهاند astrologer

stor ween poh *n.* ستوروینپوه astronomy

stor yoonay *n.* ستوریونی astronaut

storay *n.* ستوری star

storgay (da nakha *) *n.* ستوری(دا) نه(*) asterisk

storsaray larween *n.* ستورساریلروین telescope

storsaray larweenee *a.* ستورساری لروینی telescopic

suroor *n.* سرور glee

swa; korma *n.* سوه،کومه hoof

swarlas *n.* وارلس fourteen

swayl *n.* سول south

swaylee *n.* سولي south

swaylee *a.* سولي southern

swazawal *v. t* سوزول burn

sweesee *a* سویسي swiss

sweesee wagaray ya zhaba *n.* سویسيوىیاژبه swiss

swich; tanray *n.* سوچ،ت switch

syal shay *a.* سيالشی liquid

syal; jora *n.* سيال،جوه peer

syal; maya *a* سيال،مايع fluid

syalee *n* سيالي competence

syalee kawal *v* سيالکول envy

syalee kawal *v. i* سيالي کول compete

syalee kawal *v. i* سيالي کول contend

syalee; da mandi musabiqa *n.* سيالي،دمندمسابقه race

syalee; raqabat *v.i.* سيالي،رقابت vie

syoray *n.* سيوری shade

syoray *n.* سيوری shadow

syoray laroonkay *a.* سيوریلرونکی shadowy

syoray laroonkay *a.* سيوریلرونکی sombre

syoray pri achawal *v.t* سيوریپر اچول shadow

T

ta pakhula kedonkay *a.* ته‌پخلا کیدونکی irreconcilable

taahud kawal *v.t.* تعهدکول pledge

taahud; zhmana *n.* تعهد،ژمنه pledge

taajjub *n* تعجب wonder

taayyun *n.* تعیین specification

taayyun kawal *v.t.* تعیین کول specify

taba *n* تبه fever

taba kawal *v.t.* تباه کول mortify

taba kawal *v.t.* تباه کول wreck

taba kun *a* تباه کن disastrous

taba; wagaray; mada; jisam *n.* تبعه،وی،ماده،جسم subject

tabah kar *a.* تباه کار maleficent

tabahee *n.* تباهي wreckage

tabar *n.* تبر axe

tabay *a* تابع dependent

tabay *a.* تابع obedient

tabay *a.* تابع subordinate

tabayeeyat; inhisar *n* تابعیت، انحصار dependence

tabdeel *n.* تبدیل substitution

tabeeb *n.* طبیب medico

tabeed; daktar *n* طبیب،اکر doctor

tabiee kawal *v.t.* طبیعي کول naturalize

tabieeyat *n.* تابعیت allegiance

tabieeyat; madanee haqoona aw dandi *n* تابعیت،مدني حقونه او دند citizenship

tableeghat *n.* تبلیغات propaganda

tableeghat *n.* تبلیغات publicity

tableeghatee plaway *n.* تبلیغاتي پلاوی missionary

tableeghawal *v.t.* تبلیغول propagate

taboot *n* تابوت coffin

tabqa; por *n.* طبقه،پو storey

tabqa; qashar *n.* طبقه،قشر stratum

tabyat *n.* طبیعت temperance

tadarikat; jins *n* تدارکات،جنس supply

tadawee kawal *v.t.* تداوي کول redress

tadawee; talafee *n* تداوي،تلافي redress

tadbeer *n.* تدبیر plan

tadbeer jorawal *v.i.* تدبیرجوړول scheme

tadbeer kawal *v.t.* تدبیر کول plan

tadbeer; tarha *n.* تدبیر،طرحه scheme

tadbeeree *a.* تدبیري strategic

tadeel *n.* تعدیل adjustment

tadeelawal *v.t.* تعدیلول modulate

tadreejee talqeen kawal *v.t.* تدریجي تلقین کول instil

tadweenawal *v. t* تدوینول compile

tafakur *n* تفکر contemplation

tafakurree *a.* تفکري meditative

tafree *n.* تفریح recreation

tafreehee chakar *n* تفریحي چکر canter

tafreehee chakar *n.* تفریحي چکر outing

tafreehee kakhtay *n.* تفریحي کښتي yacht

tafreehee kakhtay ki samandaryoon kawal *v.i* تفریحي کټ کسمندریون کول yacht

tafreeq *n.* تفریق subtraction

tafreeqawal *v.t.* تفریقول subtract

tafseel *n* تفصیل detail

tafseel warkawal *v. t* تفصیل ورکول detail

tafseer *n* تفسیر commentary

tafteesh kawal *v.t.* تفتیش کول interrogate

tafteesh; palatana *n.* تفتیش،،پلنه search

tafteeshee *a* تفتیشي detective

tafzeelee *n.* تفضیلي superlative

tag kawal *v.t* ډګ کول ambulate

tag loray; madar *n.* تلوری؛مدار orbit

tag ratag *n* تراټ haunt

tag ratag kawal *v.t* تراټ کول ferry

tag ratag kawal *v.t.* تراټ کول haunt

tag ratag kawal *v.i.* تراټ کول traffic

tagay *adj.* تږی athirst

tagay *a.* تږی thirsty

tagay keydal *v.i.* تږی کېدل thirst

taghara *n.* تغاره kit

taghara *n.* طغرا monogram

taghayyur *n.* تغییر variation

tagloray *n.* تلوری route

tagloray; lar *n.* تلوری؛لار path

tahdeed *n* تهدید menace

tahdeedawal *v. t.* تهدیدول bully

tahleel wayana *n.* تهلیل وینه antiphony

tahreef; gholawana *n.* تحریف؛ غولوونه sophistication

tahreekawal *v.t.* تحریکول provoke

tahreekawal *v.t.* تحریکول tempt

tahseel *n.* تحصیل acquirement

tahseelawal *v.t.* تحصیلول acquire

tahseelee *a* تحصیلي academic

tahweelkhana *n* تحویلخانه bunker

tahweelkhana *n* تحویلخانه depot

taj *n* تاج crown

taj eekhodana *n* تاج اودنه coronation

taj poshee kawal *v. t* تاج پوشي کول crown

taj; jogha *n* تاج؛جوغه crest

tajaddud; tazatob *n.* تجدد،تازه توب modernity

tajamul *n.* تجمل luxury

tajamulee *a.* تجمل luxurious

tajaray *n.* تجر safe

tajassum *n.* تجسم substantiation

tajasum *n* تجسم embodiment

tajir *n* تاجر businessman

tajleel *n.* تجلیل glorification

tajleelawal *v.t.* تجلیلول glorify

tajroba *n* تجربه experience

tajroba kar *a* تجربه کار expert

tajroba kawal *v. t.* تجربه کول experience

tajruba kar *a.* تجربه کار veteran

tajrubawee *a.* تجربوي tentative

tajweez *n.* تجویز proposal

tajweez warkawal *v.t.* تجویز ورکول propose

tajweez; tasweeb *n.* تجویز؛تصویب approval

tajzeeya *n.* تجزیه decomposition

tajzeeya kawal *v.t.* تجزیه کول
analyse

tajzeeya kawal *v. t.* تجزیه کول
decompose

tajzeeya kawal *v. t* تجزیه کول
disperse

tajzeeya nigar; zeyrowoonkay *n*
تجزیه نار؛ زروونکی analyst

tajzeeya; shanana *n.* تجزیه؛شننه
analysis

tak *n.* ژ gait

tak sheen *a.* تک شین verdant

tak soor *a.* تک سور vermillion

takal *v. t* اکل elect

takal *v.i.* اکل opt

takal; gomaral *v.t.* اکل؛گمارل
appoint

takan; jatka *n.* کان؛جکه hitch

takana; da mulaqat zhmana *n.*
اکنه،دملاقات ژمنه appointment

takar *n* کر collision

takar *n.* کر clash

takar kawal *v. i.* کر کول collide

takar kawal *v.t.* کر کول hit

takar wahal *v. t.* کر وهل clash

takar; mayda shawi tota *n* کر؛
مده شوو ه smash

takar; tasadof *n* کر،تصادف hit

takawal *v.t.* کول knock

takawal; kotra kawal *v.t.* کول؛
کوتره کول thresh

takay *n* ک ace

takay *n* کی dot

takay lagawal *v. t* لول کي dot

takay lagawal; ishara kawal *v.t.*
کی لول؛اشاره کول point

takay pa takay *a.* کی پهکی
verbatim

takay; sooka *n.* کی؛بو که point

takay; zay *n.* کی،بای spot

takee aw nuqtey eekhodal *v.t.*
کي او نقطای ودل punctuate

takeeya kawal *v.i.* تکیه کول lean

takeeya kawona *n.* تکیه کو ونه lean

takeydalay *a.* کدلی jerky

takhallus *n.* تخلص pseudonym

takhcha *n.* تاخچه niche

takhcha *n.* تاخچه shelf

takhcha jorawal *v.t.* تاخچه جوول
shelve

takheer *n.* تاخیر postponement

takhfeef *n* تخفیف discount

takhfeefawal *v.t.* تخفیفول mitigate

takhmeenawal; arzawal *v.t.*
تخمینول؛ارزول appraise

takhneek pori arwand *a.* تخنیک
پوراوند technological

takhneekee *n.* تخنیکی technical

takhneekee garana *n.* تخنیکي نه
technicality

takhneekee karpoh *n.* تخنیکي
کارپوه technician

takhneekee karpoh *n.* تخنیکي
کارپوه technologist

takhneekee peyzhandana *n.*
تخنیک پژندنه technology

takhnrawal *v.t.* تخول tickle

takhreeb *n.* تخریب sabotage

takhreebawal *v.t.* تخریبول
sabotage

**takhsees warkawal; pa arwand
ganral** *v.t.* تخصیص ورکول؛په اروند
اوندنل attribute

483

takht; istirahat zay *n.* تخت، استراحتای couch

takhta kawal *v. t.* تخته کول compress

takhtawal *v.t.* تول abduct

takhtawal *v.t.* تول kidnap

takhtawana *n* تونه abduction

takhteydal *v.i* تدل abscond

takhteydal *v.i* تدل escape

takhteydal *v.i* تدل flee

takhteydoonkay *n.* تتدونکی fugitive

taklees kawal *v. t* تکلیس کول coke

takmeel *n.* تکمیل fullness

takmeel kawal *v.t.* تکمیل کول supplement

takmeel; zameema *n.* تکمیل، ضمیمه supplement

takra *a.* تکه agile

takra *a.* تکه adept

takrar *n.* تکرار repetition

takrar; tamreen *n.* تکرار، تمرین rehearsal

takratob *n.* تکه توب agility

takya kawal *v* تکیه کول abut

takzeeb *n* تکذیب contradiction

tal *n.* تل abeyance

tal *n.* تل procrastination

tal pati *a.* تل پاتی everlasting

tal sheen *n* تل شین evergreen

tal zhwanday *a.* تل ژوندی immortal

tal; beykh *n* تل، بخ bottom

tal; hameysha *adv* تل، همشه always

tal; heeskala *adv* تل، هیکله ever

tala; heesab *n.* تله، حساب balance

tala; paymana *n.* تله، پمانه scale

tala; qaharmana *n.* تله، قهرمانه heroine

talafee *n.* تلافی recovery

talafee; jibran *n.pl.* تلافی، جبران amends

talaffuz *n.* تلفظ pronunciation

talaffuz kawal *v.t.* تلفظ کول pronounce

talaq *n* طلاق divorce

talaqawal *v. t* طلاقول divorce

talasum; zra rakkhana *n.* طلسم، زړه راکنه glamour

taleem; khowana *n.* تعلیم، ښوونه tuition

taleemee *a* تعلیمی didactic

taleemee sanad *n* تعلیمی سند diploma

taleeq; darawana *n.* تعلیق، درونه suspension

taleydal *v.i.* الدل procrastinate

talf kawal *v.i.* تلف کول perish

talf kawal *v.t.* تلف کول squander

talf kawal *v.t.* تلف کول waste

talf kawana *n.* تلف کونه wastage

talgaraf *n.* لراف telegraph

talgaraf karpoh *n.* لراف کارپوه telegraphist

talgarafee *a.* لرافی telegraphic

talim yafta khalak au da tarbiye sakhtanan *n.* تعلیم یافته خلک او د تربیتنان gentry

taloo *n.* تالو palate

talpati *a.* تلپاتی imperishable

talpati kawal *v.t.* تلپاتۍکول immortalize

talpatitob *n.* تلپاتوب immortality

talqeen kawal *v.t.* تلقین کول inculcate

talweezyon *n.* لویزیون television

tamancha *n.* تمانچه pistol

tamas *n.* تماس engagement

tambakoo *n.* تنباکو tobacco

tambal *n.* مبل lazy

tambal saray *n.* مبل سۍ slattern

tambalee kawal *v.i.* مبلي کول laze

tambawana *n.* تمبوونه repulse

tambawana *n.* تمبوونه repulsion

tambawoonkay *a.* تمبوونکی repulsive

tambeeya *n.* تنبه admonition

tambeydal *v.i* تمبدل falter

tameel *n* تعمیل execution

tameelawal *v. t* تعمیلول execute

tameerawal *v. t* تعمیرول build

tameerawal *v.t.* تعمیرول repair

tamreen kawal *v.t.* تمرین کول rehearse

tamzay; markaz *n.* تمای؛مرکز station

tan pa tan jagara *n* تن په تن جه duel

tan pa tan jagara *n.* تن په تن جه melee

tan pa tan jangeydal *v. i* تن په تن جندل duel

tana payda kawal *v.i.* تنه پدا کول stem

tana; da wani kanda *n.* تنه؛دوني کنده trunk

tanab aw paray gharal *n.* طناب او پیغل marl

tanasub *n.* تناسب proportion

tanda *n.* تنده thirst

tandar *n.* تندر thunder

tandar ta warta *a.* تندرته ورته thunderous

tanday *n* تندی forehead

tandi wari *n.* تندیوری lambkin

tang *a.* تنگ narrow

tangawal *v.t.* تنول constrict

tangawal *v.t.* تنول narrow

tangsa *n.* تنسه poverty

tanha *a.* تنها lone

tanha *a* تنها sole

tanha *a.* تنها solitary

tanhayee *n.* تنهایي celibacy

tanhayee *n.* تنهایي loneliness

tanhdeedawal *v.t* تهدیدول menace

tankha *n.* تنخوا stipend

tankha; ajoora *n.* تنخوا؛اجوره salary

tanoor *n.* تنور furnace

tanoor *n.* تنور oven

tanraka *n* تاکه blister

tanray *n* ت button

tanray bandawal *v. t.* تبندول button

tanz *n.* طنز scoff

tanz kawal *v.i.* طنز کول scoff

tanzeem *n.* تنظیم orderly

tanzeem *n.* تنظیم regulation

tanzeem kawal *v.t.* تنظیم کول model

tanzeemawal *v.t* تنظیمول marshal

tanzeemawal *v.t.* تنظیمول straighten

tanzeeya *a.* طنزیه satirical

taoon zad amil *n.* طاعون‌ضدعامل pesticide

tap *n.* پ wound

tap jorawal; ghosawal *v.t.* پ جوول؛غوول hack

tap zay pa patay taral *v.t* پای‌په‌پ تل bandage

tapa *n* ٿاپه cachet

tapa *n.* ٿاپه label

tapa lagawal *v.t.* ٿاپه‌لول label

tapana *n.* تپنه daub

tapay *n.* ٿاپی speck

tapee kawal *v.t.* پی‌کول injure

tapee kawal *v.t.* پی‌کول wound

tapoo *n.* ٿاپو island

tapoo wazma *n.* ٿاپوروزمه isle

taq *a.* طاق odd

taqat *n.* طاقت power

taqato *n.* تقاطع intersection

taqatwar *a.* طاقتور powerful

taqaza *n* تقاضا request

taqaza kawal *v.t.* تقاضاکول petition

taqaza kawal *v.t.* تقاضاکول request

taqaza kawal; zaray kawal *v.t.* تقاضاکول؛زارکول solicit

taqcha *n.* طاقچه rack

taqdeer *n* تقدیر destiny

taqdees *n.* تقدیس sanctification

taqdeesawal *v.t.* تقدیسول consecrate

taqdeesawal *v.t.* تقدیسول hallow

taqdeesawal *v.t.* تقدیسول sanctify

taqeebawal *v. t* تعقیبول dog

taqeebawal *v.t.* تعقیبول trace

taqeebawal *v.t.* تعقیبول track

taqeebawal *v.t.* تعقیبول sue

taqleed kawal *v.t.* تقلیدکول ape

taqleed kawal *v. t* تقلیدکول emulate

taqleed kawoonkay *n.* تقلید کوونکی imitator

taqleed shaway *a.* تقلیدشوی stereotyped

taqleedee *a.* تقلیدي mimic

taqreeban *adv* تقریباً about

taqreeban *adv.* تقریبا almost

taqreeban *adv.* تقریبا near

taqreeban *adv.* تقریبا nearly

taqreeban *adv.* تقریبا nigh

taqteer *n* تقطیر distillery

tar *n* تار fibre

tar *n.* تار thread

tar ... landi *adv* تر___لاند below

tar akhira awreydal *v.t.* ترآخره اوریدل overhear

tar aw taza *a.* تراوتازه sprightly

tar azmayakht landi karmand ya zandanee *n.* ترآزمایت‌لاند کارمندیازندانی probationer

tar cha da makha keydal *v.t.* تر چادمخه‌کدل outwit

tar chat landi zay *n.* ترچت‌لاندای loft

tar dey chi *conj* تردچ until

tar dey chi *n. conj.* تردچ till

tar dey wrosta *adv.* تردوروسته hereafter

tar fishar landi rawastal *v.t* تر فشارلاندراوستل stress

tar goona warteyridana *n.* ترناه ورتردنه condonation

tar hagha mahala *prep.* ترهغهمهاله till

tar har sa da makha *adv* ترهرهد مخه first

tar jagh landi rawastal *v.t.* ترجغ لاندراوستل yoke

tar jamo landi achowoonkay kamees *n* ترجامولانداچوونکی کمیس chemise

tar khpal agheyz landi seemo ta da pacha garzand astazay *n..* ترخپلاغزلاندسیموتهدپاچارند استازی missis, missus

tar lag miqdar *prep.* ترلهمقدار less

tar lasa kawal *v.t.* ترلاسهکول gain

tar lasa kawal *v.t.* ترلاسهکول receive

tar lasa kawoonkay *n.* ترلاسه کوونکی receiver

tar mreeni wrusta *a.* ترمینوروسته post-mortem

tar mreeni wrusta moayna *n.* تر معاینه وروسته مین post-mortem

tar osa *adv.* تراوسه hitherto

tar osa *conj.* تراوسه yet

tar paki achawal *v.t* تارپکاچول thread

tar pokhtani landi neewal *v.t* تر پوتهلاندنیول query

tar samandar landi *a* ترسمندرلاند submarine

tar sara kawal *v.t.* ترسرهکول fulfil

tar sara kawona *n.* ترسرهکوونه fulfilment

tar sha *adv.* ترشا back

tar sifar kam *prep.* ترصفرکم minus

tar syooree landi *a.* ترسیوريلاند overcast

tar takalee wakht zyat *adv.* تر اکلیوختزیات overtime

tar tolo akheyr *adv.* ترولوآخر lastly

tar tolo bad wuzeeyat ta beywal *v.t.* ترولوبدوضعیتتهبیول worst

tar tolo deyr *a* ترولور further

tar tolo deyr *a.* ترولور utmost

tar tolo ghwara *a* ترولوغوره foremost

tar tolo ghwara *a.* ترولوغوره pre-eminent

tar tolo hask maqam *n.* ترولو هسکمقام zenith

tar tolo kam kach ta rasawal *v.t.* ترولوکمکچتهرسول minimize

tar tolo kam miqdar *n.* ترولوکم مقدار minimum

tar tolo kha *a.* ههولو تر superlative

tar tolo khwakh *a* ترولوخو favourite

tar tolo koochnay *n.* ترولوکوچنی minim

tar tolo lag *a.* ترولو minimal

tar tolo loy miqdar *n* ترولولوی مقدار most

tar tolo lwar ghag *n* ترولولوغ alto

tar tolo lwar zay moondal *v.t.* ولولوای موندل top

tar tolo nawara *a* ترولوناوه worst

tar yawa hada *adv.* تریوه‌حده
somewhat

tar yawey andazey *adv.* تریوانداز
something

tar zand wrosta *adv.* ترزوروسته
late

tar zangana pori land patloon *n.*
ترزنانه‌پورلدپتلون breeches

tar zeyrmo dak *a.* ترزرموک
replete

tar zmakay landi soora *n* ترمک
لاندسوه burrow

tarafdar *a.* طرفدار partisan

tarafdaree *n.* طرفداری adherence

tarafdaree kawal *v.t.* طرفداری‌کول
advocate

tarah kawal *v. t.* طرح‌کول design

tarah; khaka *n.* طرح؛خاكه design

taral *v.t* تل bind

taral *v. t* تل close

taral *v.t* تل fasten

taral; bandawal *v.t.* تل؛بندول seal

taral; mamnoo garzawal *v.t* تل،
ممنوع‌رول bar

taralay zay *n.* تلی‌ای close

taranga *a.* تانه littoral

taranga *n* تانه brace

taraqee *n.* ترقي advancement

taraqee kawal *v.t.* ترق‌کول
meliorate

taraqee warkawal *v. t.* ترقي‌ورکول
develop

taraqee yafta *n.* ترقي‌يافته advance

taraw *n.* تاو attachment

taraw *n* تاو connection

taraw laral; zyatawal *v.t.* تاولرل،
زياتول append

tarbeeya warkawal *v. t* تربيه
ورکول educate

tarbeeya warkawal *v.t.* تربيه
ورکول train

tareef *n* تعریف definition

tareefawal *v. t* تعريفول define

tareekawal *v. t* تاریکول blear

tareekh leekoonkay *n.* تاریخ
ليكونكی annalist

tareekh leekoonkay *n.* تاریخ
ليكونكی historian

tareekh sakha makhkeenay *a.*
تاریخ‌خه‌مخكينی prehistoric

tareekh; peykh lar *n.* تاریخ؛پل
history

tareekhee *a* تاریخي historic

tareekhee *a.* تاریخي historical

tareekhee yadgar *n.* تاریخي‌يادار
monument

tareeqa *n.* طریقه manner

tareeqa *n.* طریقه procedure

tareeqa *n.* طریقه method

tareeqa kar *n.* طریقه‌کار
mechanism

tareeqa laroonkay *a.* طریقه‌لرونكی
methodical

tarha *n.* ترهه scare

tarha *n.* ترهه horror

tarha *n.* ترهه intimidation

tarha jorawana *n.* طرحه‌جوونه
projection

tarha kawal *v.t.* طرح‌كول outline

tarha kawal *v. t* طرحه‌كول draft

tarha; namoona *n.* طرحه؛نمونه
pattern

tarhagar *n.* ترهر terrorist

tarhagaree *n.* ترهري terrorism

tarhawal *v.t.* ترهول horrify

tarhawal *v.t.* ترهول intimidate

tarhawal *v.t.* ترهول scare

tarhawal *v.t.* ترهول terrify

tarhawal *v.t.* ترهول terrorize

tarhowoonkay *n* ترهوونکی breakneck

tarhowoonkay *a* ترهوونکی dread

tarjee *n.* ترجیح priority

tarjee warkawal *v.t.* ترجیح‌ورکول prefer

tark kawal *v.t.* ترک‌کول forsake

tarkanr *n.* ترکا carpenter

tarkanr *n.* ترکا joiner

tarkanree *n.* ترکاپی carpentry

tarkeeb *n* ترکیب composition

tarkeeb *n* ترکیب compost

tarkeeb *n* ترکیب mould

tarkeeb; yaw zayakht *n.* ترکیب،یو‌زایت synthesis

tarkeebawal *v. i* ترکیبول compound

tarkeebawal *v.t.* ترکیبول mingle

tarkeebawal *v.t.* ترکیبول symbolize

tarkeebawal; seyra warkawal *v.t.* ترکیبول،سېره‌ورکول form

tarkeebawal; weeli kawal *v.t.* ترکیبول،ویلی‌کول fuse

tarkeebee joz *n.* ترکیبی‌جز ingredient

tarman *a.* تمن lukewarm

taroon *n.* تون affiliation

taroon *n.* تون agreement

taroon kawoonkay *n* تون‌کوونکی contractor

taroon lasleekawal *v.t.* تون لاسلیکول stipulate

taroon; beyt *n.* تون،بیعت plight

taroona sara gandal *v.t.* تارونه‌سره ‌ندل weave

tarteeb *n.* ترتیب array

tarteebawal *v.t.* ترتیبول organize

tarteebawal *v.t.* ترتیبول range

tarteebawoonkay; satandoy *n.* ترتیبوونکی،ساتندوی ranger

tarz *n.* طرز style

tarz; dood *n.* طرز،دود mode

tasadofee *a.* تصادفی casual

tasadufee *a* تصادفي accidental

tasalsul *n* تسلسل continuity

tasano *n* تصنع affectation

tasarruf kawal *v.t.* تصرف‌کول preoccupy

tasarruf; da loomreetob haq *n.* تصرف،دلومړیتوب‌حق preoccupation

tasawee *n* تساوي equation

tasawor kawal *v. t* تصورکول conceive

tasawwuf *n.* تصوف mysticism

tasawwur kawal *v.t.* تصورکول suppose

tasawwur; farz; khyal *n.* تصور، فرض،خیال supposition

tasawwur; gholawoonkay zahir *n.* تصور،غولوونکی‌ظاهر phantom

tasawwur; gooman *n.* تصور،ګومان imagination

tasawwur; khyal n. خيال،تصور imagery

tasawwuree a. تصوري imaginative

tasawwuree; khyalee a. تصوري، خيالي visionary

tasbee n. تسبيح rosary

tasbeet shaway a. تثبيت شوى stable

tasdeeq v. تصديق acknowledge

tasdeeq n. تصديق confirmation

tasdeeq n. تصديق verification

tasdeeq n. تصديق testimony

tasdeeq kawal v.t. تصديق كول recognize

tasdeeqawal v. t. تصديقول certify

tasdeeqawal v.i. تصديقول testify

tasdeeqawal v.t. تصديقول verify

tasees n. تأسيس establishment

taseesawal v. t. تأسيسول establish

tasfeeya kawal v.t. تصفيه كول sublimate

tasfeeya kawoonkay a. تصفيه كوونكى sublime

tash a تش empty

tash lasay n. تش لاسى pauper

tash lasay a. تش لاسى penniless

tash zay n. تش ای vacancy

tash zay; naleekali panra n تش ای،ناليكلپه blank

tash; khalee a خالي،تش devoid

tash; khalee a. تش،خالي vacant

tashannuj wahalay shakhs a. تشنج وهلى شخص hysterical

tashannujee a. تشنجي spasmodic

tashawal v تشول empty

tashawal v. t تشول evacuate

tashawal v.i. تشول teem

tashawal; bey kara kawal v.t. تشول،بكاره كول vacate

tashawal; khalee kawal v.t تشول، خالي كول hollow

tashawana n تشونه evacuation

tashbee n. تشبيه simile

tashkhees n تشخيص diagnosis

tashkheesawal v.t. تشخيصول assess

tashreefat n تشريفات complement

tashreefatee a. تشريفاتي ceremonial

tashreefatee meylmastaya n. تشريفاتي ملمستيا banquet

tasht n. تشت basin

tashweesh n تشويش concern

tashweesh laral v. t تشويش لرل concern

tashyal; khala n. تشيال،خلا vacuum

taskeen n. تسكين solace

taskeenawal v.t. تسكينول solace

taskeenawal; khamoshawal v.t. تسكينول،خاموشول appease

tasleem keydal v.t. تسليم كدل submit

tasleemawal v.t. تسليمول concede

tasleemeydal v. t تسليمدل capitulate

tasleemeydal v.t. تسليمدل surrender

tasma; chingak n تسمه؛چنك clasp

tasmeemawal v. t تصميمول determine

tasneefawoonkay *n* تصنیفوونکی compositor

tasob *n* تعصب bias

tasob *n* تعصب bigotry

tasob kawal *v. t* تعصب کول bias

taspod payda keydal *v.i.* تسپودپیدا کدل swell

tasweeb *n.* تصویب approbation

tasweebawal *v.t* تصویبول approbate

tasweebawal *v. t.* تصویبول endorse

tasweebawal *v.t.* تصویبول subscribe

tasweebawal *v.t.* تصویبول ratify

tasweebawal; muwafiqat kawal *v.t.* تصویبول،موافقت کول approve

tasweer *n* تصویر photo

tasweer; shakal *n.* تصویر؛شکل image

tat *a* تت dim

tat *n.* ا canvas

tat *a.* تت opaque

tat; nasargand *a* تت؛نارند dark

tatabuq *n.* تطابق symmetry

tatar *n* ر chest

tatar *n.* ار tinker

tatawal *v. t* تول dim

tatawal *v.t.* تول obscure

tatay *n.* toilet

tatbeeqawal *v.t.* تطبیقول tally

tateydana *n* تتدنه blur

tatmee; bramta *n* تطمیع؛برامتا allurement

tatwalay *n.* تتوالی opacity

taw khwaral *v.i.* تاوخول swing

taw khwaralay *a.* تاوخولی wry

taw khwarana *n.* تاوخونه spin

taw rataw *a* تاوراتاو crisp

taw rataw *a.* تاوراتاو spiral

taw rataw zeena *n.* تاوراتاوزینه maze

taw shaway seez *n.* تاوشوییز roll

taw; da faaleeyat dawra *n* تاو؛د فعالیت دوره swing

tawafuq *n.* توافق adaptation

tawafuq *n.* توافق concord

tawafuq sara peykheydal *v. i* توافق سره پدل coincide

tawajo *n.* توجه attention

tawajo *n.* توجه concentration

tawajo *n* توجه focus

tawajo *n.* توجه tendency

tawajo *n* توجه heed

tawajo kawal *v.t* توجه کول focus

tawajo kawal *v.t.* توجه کول heed

tawajo satal *v. t* توجه ساتل concentrate

tawan *n.* تاوان harm

tawan akheystal *v.t.* تاوان اخستل ransom

tawan arowoonkay *a.* تاوان اوونکی noxious

tawan rasawal *v.t* تاوان رسول harm

tawan warkawal *v. t.* تاوان ورکول damage

tawan warkawal *v.t.* تاوان ورکول remunerate

tawan warkawal *v.i.* تاوان ورکول retaliate

tawan warkawana *n.* تاوان ورکونه remuneration

tawan warkawana *n.* تاوان ورکونه retaliation

tawan; awaz *n.* تاوان؛عوض recompense

tawan; jareema *n* تاوان؛جريمه forfeit

tawan; jibran *n.* تاوان؛جبران indemnity

tawan; zarar *n* تاوان؛ضرر disadvantage

tawaquf *n* توقف stoppage

tawas *n.* طاوس peacock

tawazo *n* تواضع deference

tawda; deyr garam *a.* توده؛برم torrid

tawdawal *v.t* تودول heat

tawdokha *n.* تودوخه heat

tawdokha *n.* تودوخه warmth

tawdokhee *n.* تودوخي temperature

tawdokhmeych *n.* تودوخمچ thermometer

taweydal; sarkheydal *v.i.* تاودل؛ رخدل turn

tawheed *n.* توحيد monotheism

tawheen *n* توهين disdain

tawheen *n.* توهين humiliation

tawheen kawal *v. t.* توهين کول disdain

tawheenawal *v.t.* توهينول humiliate

tawkal *n.* توکل reliance

tawleed shaway mawad *n.* توليد شوی مواد production

tawleed; hasil *n.* توليد؛حاصل produce

tawleedawal *v. t* توليدول create

tawleedawal *v.t.* توليدول generate

tawleedawal *v.t.* توليدول manufacture

tawleedawal *v. t* توليدول beget

tawleedawal *v.t.* توليدول produce

tawleedawana *n* توليدوونه manufacture

tawleedawoonkay *n.* توليدوونکی generator

tawleedawoonkay *n* توليدوونکی manufacturer

tawleedee *a.* توليدي productive

tawowal *v.t.* تاوول convolve

tawpeer *n* توپير difference

tawpeer laral *v. i* توپيرلرل differ

tawpeer laral *v.t.* توپيرلرل vary

tawpeer moondana *n* توپيرموندنه discrimination

tawpeerawal *v. t.* توپيرول discriminate

tawqeef *n* توقيف curb

tawqeef kawal *v.t.* توقيف کول intern

tawzee *n.* توضيح demonstration

tawzee *n.* توضيح gloss

tawzee kawal *v. t.* توضيح کول explain

tawzee warkawal *v. t* توضيح ورکول demonstrate

tawzee; daleel *n* توضح؛دليل explanation

tay *n.* تی mamma

tay laroonkay *n.* تيلرونکی mammal

tayarawal *v.t.* تيارول prepare

tayaray *n.* تياری preparation

tayaree; muqarrarat takal *n.* تياری؛مقرراتاکل provision

tayeed; afwa *n.* تاييد،عفوه grace

tayeedawal *v. t* تائيدول confirm

tayeedawal *v. t.* تائيدول consign

taylafoon *n.* تلفون phone

taylafoon *n.* تلفون telephone

taylafoonee aw da rabitey areeki *n.* تلفوني او د رابطه ايك telecommunications

tayzab *n* تيزاب acid

tayzabee *a* تيزابي acid

tayzabeeyat *n.* تيزابيت acidity

taza *a.* تازه fresh

taza *a.* تازه up-to-date

taza intikhabawal *v.t.* تازه انتخابول recruit

taza kawal *v.t.* تازه کول refresh

taza kawal *v.t.* تازه کول renew

taza kawana *n.* تازه کوونه refreshment

taza kawana *n.* تازه کوونه renewal

taza; naway *a.* تازه،نوی recent

taza; naway *a.* تازه،نوی modern

tazad *n.* تضاد antithesis

tazad khwakhay *n* تضادخوی antitheist

tazahar kawal *v.t.* تظاهر کول prtend

tazahar; bahana *n.* تظاهر،بهانه pretension

tazahur kawal *v.i.* تظاهر کول sham

tazatob; mastee *n.* تازه توب،مستي vivacity

tazee spay *n.* تازي سپی greyhound

tazkeer aw tanees *n.* تذکير او تأنيث gender

tazkeeya *n.* تزکيه refinement

tazkeeya kawal *v.t.* تزکيه کول refine

tazkira kawal *v. t* تذکره کول cite

tazkiree *a.* تذکري reminiscent

tee *n* تي breast

teekala *n.* ټيکله loaf

teekalay; disc *n.* ټيکلی،ټسک disc

teekat *n.* ټکټ ticket

teekaw *n.* ټيکاو perseverance

teekaw *n.* ټيکاو stability

teekaw warbakhal *v.t.* ټيکاوور بخل stabilize

teeng azama; sar pa las *a.* ټينګ عزمه،سر په لاس resolute

teengakht *n.* ټينګت tenacity

teengakht *n.* ټينګت stabilization

teengar *n* ټينګار emphasis

teengar *n* ټينګار urge

teengar kawal *v. t* ټينګار کول emphasize

teengar sara ghokhtal *v.t* ټينګار سره غوتل urge

teengar warkawal *v.t.* ټينګاور کول stable

teengawal *v. t.* ټينګول consolidate

teengeydoonkay *a.* ټينګدونکی persistent

teengwalay *n* ټينګوالی consolidation

teer *n* تير beam

teet park *a.* تيت پرک sparse

teet; kog *n* کوږ،تيت bow

teetakay *n.* ټيټکی pigmy

teetawal *v.t.* ټيټول abase

teetawal; shanal *v.t.* تيتول،شنل strew

teeteydal *v. t* ټيټيدل bow

tehqeeq *n.* تحقیق inquiry

tehqeeq *n.* تحقیق investigation

tehqeeq kawal *v.t.* تحقیق کول investigate

tehqeeqee; tafteeshee *a.* تحقیقی، تفتیشی inquisitive

tehqeer *n.* تخقیر scorn

tehreefawal *v.t.* تحریفول invert

tehreekawal *v. t* تحریکول excite

tehseen *n.* تحسین admiration

tehseen *n.* تحسین praise

tehseen; stayana *n.* تحسین،ستاینه applause

teredal *v.t* تیریدل forgo

teygh *n.* تغ blade

teykhta *n* تخته escape

teyl *n.* تل oil

teyla kawal *v.t.* لهکول push

teyla; kokhakh *n.* لمه،کو push

teynas *n.* نس racket

teypar *n.* پر turnip

teyr *a.* تر past

teyr eystal *v. t* تراستل bluff

teyr eystal *v. t* تراستل dodge

teyr eystal *v.t.* تراستل sophisticate

teyr eystana *n* تراستنه bluff

teyr eystana *n.* تراستنه sophism

teyr mahal *n.* ترمهال past

teyr mahal ta nazar achawana *n.* ترمهالتهنظراچوونه retrospection

teyr mahal ta staneyda *n.* ترمهال ستندا ته retrospect

teyr watal *v.t.* تروتل mistake

teyr watal *v.i.* تروتل stumble

teyr watana *n* وتنه تر misapprehension

teyr watana *n.* تروتنه mistake

teyra *a.* تره sharp

teyra kawal *v.t.* ترهکول sharpen

teyra kawal; parawal *v.t.* ترهکول، پارول whet

teyra kawoonkay *n.* ترهکوونکی sharpener

teyra sooka *n.* ترموکه nib

teyra wraz *adv.* ترهور yesterday

teyrawalay *n.* ترهوال acumen

teyray *n* تری aggression

teyray *n.* تری intrusion

teyray kawal *v.t.* تریکول intrude

teyray kawal *n.* تریکول trespass

teyray kawal; tawheen kawal *v.t.* تریکول،توهینکول violate

teyray kawoonkay *a.* تیریکوونکی aggressive

teyreydana *n.* تریدنه transit

teyreydana; da watalo lar; mukhalifat *n.* تردنه،دوتلولار، مخالفت crossing

teyro peykho pori arwand *a.* ترو پوپوراوند retrospective

teysha; kawdar *n.* تشه،کور hatchet

teyz *a.* تیز acute

teyz *a.* تز rapid

teyz asmanee rang *n.* تزآسمانیرن indigo

teyz khwazeydal *v.t.* تزخودل wallop

teyz; faryadee *a.* تز،فریادي shrill

teyza aw stargi wroonki ranra *n* تزهاوسترونکیرا flare

teyza sa akheystal *v.i* تزه ساه اخستل
gasp

teyza sa akheystana *n.* تزه ساه
اخستنه gasp

teyzee; shiddat *n.* تزي،شدت
intensity

teyzwalay *n.* تزوالى velocity

tib; fizeek *n.* طب،فزیک physic

tibbee *a.* طبی innate

tibee *a.* طبي medical

tibee botay *n.* طبي بوی herb

tibee ghwagay *n.* طبي غو
stethoscope

tibee katanzay *n.* طبي کتنای clinic

tijarat *n* تجارت commerce

tijarat *n.* تجارت trade

tijarat kawal *v.i* تجارت کول trade

tijaratee *a* تجارتي commercial

tijaratee *a.* تجارتي mercantile

tijaratee nakha *n* تجارتي نه brand

tiksee *n.* کسي taxi

tiksee ki tlal *v.i.* کسي کتلل taxi

tilayee *a.* طلایي golden

timsal *n* تمثال effigy

tlal *v.i.* تلل go

toba kawal *v.t.* توبه کول forswear

tobagar *a.* توبه گار repentant

tod; garam *a.* تود،ګرم warm1

todawal; garmawal *v.t.* تودول،
ګرمول warm

togal; trashal *v. t.* تول،تراشل carve

toghanday *n.* توغندی rocket

toghanday *n.* توغوندی missile

toghawal *v.t.* توغول launch

toghawal keydoonkay jisam *n.*
توغول کدونکی جسم projectile

toghawal shaway *a* توغول شوی
projectile

toghawal; weeshtal *v.t.* توغول،
ویشتل shoot

toghawana *n.* توغوونه launch

tok *n* وک episode

toka *n.* وکه hoax

toka *n.* وکه joke

toka *n.* وکه witticism

toka kawal *v.t* وکه کول hoax

tokal *v.t.* وکل contuse

tokampalana *n.* توکمپالنه
racialism

tokar *n* وکر cloth

tokar ploroonkay *n* وکر پلورونکی
draper

tokar; kalbad *n* وکر،کالبد fabric

tokham; rozana *n* تخم،روزنه breed

tokhay *n.* وخی cough

tokheydal *v. i.* وخدل cough

tokhmar kawal *v.t* تخمر کول
ferment

tokhmar; hayjan *n* تخمر،هجان
fermentation

toki *n.* وک fun

toki *a.* وک humorous

toki kawal *v.i.* وک کول joke

toki kawal *v.i* وک کول mime

tokmar *n.* وکمار banter

tokmar *n.* وکمار humorist

tokmar *n* وکمار mimic

tokmar *n* وکمار wag

tokmar *a.* وکمار witty

tokmaree *n* وکماري mimicry

tokmeez; nazhadee *a.* توکمیز،
نژادي racial

tokray *n.* وکر basket

tol *n* ول all

tol *a.* ول total

tol *n* ول whole

tol takana *n* ولاکنه election

tol umree *a.* ولعمري lifelong

tol wazhana *n* ولوژنه carnage

tol wazhana *n.* ولوژنه massacre

tol wazhna *n.* ولوژنه slaughter

tol; bashpar *a.* ول،بشپر all

tolana *n.* ولنه community

tolana *n.* ولنه society

tolaneez *a* ولنیز collective

tolaneez *n.* ولنیز social

tolaneez parmakhtag *n.* ولنیز
پرمخته civilization

tolaneeza khayr kheygara *n.*
ولنیزه خیره commonwealth

tolanpohana *n.* ولنپوهنه sociology

tolawana *n* ولونه pluck

tolay *n.* ولی mass

toley peysey; majmooa *n.* ولپس،
مجموعه sum

tolga *n* وله set

tolo barkho ki badloonoona
rawastal *v.t.* ولوبرخوکیبدلونونه
راوستل overhaul

tolpokhtana *n.* ولپوتنه referendum

tolwak *n* ولواک emperor

tolwak *n.* ولواک monarch

tolwakee *n.* ولواکي monarchy

tolwakpal *n.* ولواکپال royalist

tomatee *a.* تومتي slanderous

tomna *n* تومنه ferment

tomna *n.* تومنه yeast

tond *a.* تند poignant

tond aw teyz awaz *n.* تونداوتزباد
hurricane

tond khooya *a.* تند خویه sullen

tond khooyee; mukhalifat *n.* توند
خویي،مخالفت frown

tond; teyz; chalak *a.* توند،تز،
چالاک smart

tondee *n.* توندي poignancy

tondee *n* توندي hurry

tondee kawal *v.t.* توندي کول hurry

tookanri *n* توکا spittle

tookanri *n.* توکا spittoon

tookanri tookal *v.i.* توکاتوکل spit

tookanri; lari *n* توکا،لا spit

tookeydal; notaki kawal *v.i.*
وکدل،نوتککول sprout

toolul balad *n.* طول البلد longitude

toomaree harakat *n.* طوماري
حرکت scroll

toonal keendal *v.i.* تونل کیندل
tunnel

toonal; da eystani bahanz *n.*
تونل،داستبهن tunnel

toopan *n.* توپان tempest

toopan; sooran *n.* توپان،سوران
storm

toopanee *a.* توپاني tempestuous

toopanee *a.* توپاني windy

toopanee; hayjanee *a.* توپاني،
هجاني stormy

toopoona wahal *v.i.* توپونه وهل skip

toora *n.* توره sword

tooryalay *a* توریالی brave

toot *n.* توت mulberry

top i. وپ bound

top *n.* وپ jump

top *v.i.* وپ leap

top *n.* وپ vault

top wahal *v.i* وپوهل jump

top wahal *n* وپوهل leap

top wahal *v.i.* وپوهل vault

top wahoonkay *n.* وپوهونکی skipper

topak *n.* وپک gun

topak *n* وپک rifle

topak wal *n.* وپکوال musketeer

topkhana *n.* توپخانه artillery

topkhana *n.* توپخانه ordnance

topoona wahal *v. i* وپونهوهل hop

tor *a* تور black

tor kargha *n.* تورکارغه raven

tor kargha *n.* تورکارغه rook

tor lagawal *v.t.* تورلول accuse

tor lagawal *v. t.* تورلول calumniate

tor lagawana *n* تورلونه accusation

tor postakay *n.* تورپوستکی nigger

tor postay ghulam *n.* تورپوستیغلام maroon

tor postay saray *n.* تورپوستیسی negro

tor posti khaza *n.* تورپوسته negress

tor rangay *a.* توررنی swarthy

tor ya badgoomanee leyri kawal *v.t.* توریابدسومانیلرکول vindicate

tora kahruba *n.* توره کهربا jet

tora khawra *n.* توره خاوره muck

toran *n.* تورن accused

toran; ghal *n* تورن؛غل culprit

toranawal *v. t* تورنول denounce

toranawal *v.t.* تورنول impeach

toranawal *v.t.* تورنول incriminate

toranawal *v.t.* تورنول vilify

torawal *v. t.* تورول blacken

torawona; taqeeb *n.* تورورونه؛تعقیب impeachment

toray; tahal *n.* توری؛طحال spleen

torsh *adj* ترش acerb

toshaka *n.* توشکه mattress

toshakcha *n.* توشکچه pad

tota *n.* وه piece

tota kawal *v. t* وهکول chop

tota tota kawal *v. t* وهوهکول dissect

tota tota kawal *v.t.* وهوهکول splinter

tota tota keydal *v. i* وهوهکدل crash

tota; barkha *n.* وه؛برخه fragment

tota; peena *n* وه؛پینه patch

totee *n.* طوطي parrot

totla keydal *v.i.* توتلهکدل stammer

totlatob *n* توب توتله stammer

toy shaway seez *n* تویشویيز spill

toyawal; narawal *v.i.* تویول؛نول spill

tra; kaka *n.* تره؛کاکا uncle

trakeydal *v.t.* ټکدل crackle

trashal *v.t.* تراشل whittle

trashal; hajamat jorawal *v.t.* تراشل؛حجامتجوول shave

trashal; tarteebawal *v.t.* تراشل؛ترتیبول trim

trawa tanda *n.* نه تروه scowl

trawa tanda neewal *v.i.* ترومنهنیول scowl

trawey oba *n* ترواوبه brine

treekh *a* تریخ bitter

treekh *a.* تریخ pungent
treekh aw khwandawar *a.* تریخ‌او خوندور piquant
treekhawal *v. t* تریخول embitter
treekhawal *v.t.* تریخول pepper
treekhwalay *n* تریخوالی acrimony
treekhwalay *n.* تریخوالی pungency
treew *adj* تریو acescent
treew *a.* تریو sour
treewwalay *n.* تریووالی salinity
tri ... landi *adv* تر ــ لاند beneath
tri gata akheystal *v.t.* تری‌ه‌اخستل avail
tri teyray kawal *v.t.* ترتری‌کول transgress
tri warandi keydal *v.t.* تروراندکدل antecede
tri wrandi keydal *v.i* تروراندکدل excel
trom; shpeylay *n.* تروم؛شپل trumpet
tror *n.* ترور aunt
troshawal; naraza kawal *v.t.* تروشول؛ناراضه‌کول sour
tuhmat *n* تهمت defamation
tuhmat *n.* تهمت libel
tuhmat lagawal *v. t.* تهمت‌لول defame
tuhmat lagawal *v.t.* تهمت‌لول libel
tukham shanal *v.t.* تخم‌شنل sow
tukhamdan *n.* تخمدان core
tukhamdan *n* تخمدان matrix
tukhamdan *n.* تخمدان ovary
tukhamdan *n.* تخمدان uterus
tukhmi badyan *n* تخم‌بادیان aniseed

twan *n.* توان energy
twan *n* توان main
twan *n.* توان might
twan; zhwand zwak *n.* توان،ژوند زواک stamina
twan; zor *n* توان،زور force
twaneydal *v.* تواندل can
twaneydal *v* تواندل may
twanmand *a.* توانمند tough
tyara *n* تیاره dark
tyara *a.* تیاره gloomy
tyara kawal *v.t.* تیاره‌کول overshadow
tyara ki pateydal *v.i.* تیاره‌کپدل darkle
tyatar *n.* تیاتر theatre
tyatar pori arwand *a.* تیاترپوراوند theatrical
tyoob *n* تیوب cylinder

umeed bakhoonkay *a.* امیدبونکی promising
umeedwara *a.* امیدواره pregnant
unsar *n* عنصر element
usmanee turkeeya *n.* عثمانی‌ترکیه ottoman
usool *n.* اصول principle
usooleeyat; aqlaneeyat *n.* اصولیت؛عقلانیت rationality
ustad *n.* استاد master
ustadana *a.* استادانه masterly
ustadana *a.* استادانه scholastic

ustadee *n.* أستادي artifice

ustadee kawal *v.t.* استادي کول master

ustawayee *a.* استوايي tropical

uzlatee *a.* عضلاتي muscular

uzwee *a.* عضوي organic

W

waaz *n.* وعظ sermon

waaz kawal *v.i.* وعظ کول preach

waaz kawal *v.i.* وعظ کول sermonize

waaza (qalach) *n* واژه(قلاچ) fathom

waba *n.* وبا pest

waba; taoon *a.* وبا؛طاعون plague

wabayee n وبايي epidemic

wach *adj.* وچ arid

wach *a* وچ dry

wach klak; tanha *n.* وچ کلک؛تنها stark

wach; dad awaz *a.* وچ؛آواز husky

wacha pakha lara n وچه پخه لاره causeway

wachawal *v. t* وچول drain

wachawana *n* وچونه drainage

wacheydal *v. i.* وچدل dry

wachi ta watana *n.* وچته وتنه landing

wachkakhpak *n.* وچکپاک rubber

wachkalee *n* وچکالي famine

wachtya *n* وچتيا draught

wachtya *n* وچتيا drought

wada *n.* واده marriage

wada *n.* واده matrimony

wada *n.* وده promotion

wada *n.* واده spousal

wada *n.* وده germination

wada *n* وعده promise

wada *n.* واده wedding

wada kawal *v.t.* واده کول marry

wada kawal *v.i* وده کول flourish

wada kawal *v.i.* وده کول germinate

wada kawal *v.t.* وده کول grow

wada kawal *v.t* وعده کول promise

wada kawal *v.t.* واده کول wed

wada kawoonkay; amalee *a.* وده عملي کوونکي؛ viable

wada na makhki da halak aw najlay tar manz meena naki khabari *n.* واده نه مخکدهلک او نجلاتر منمينه ناکخبر courtship

wada warkawoonkay; paloonkay *n.* ودوركوونكي؛ پالونکی grower

wada; karhanra *n.* وده؛کرهه growth

wadanawal *v.t.* ودانول piece

wadanay *n* وداز building

wadanee jorawal *n* وداني جوول construction

wafadar *n.* دار وفا loyalist

wafadar; sabit qadam *a.* وفادار؛ ثابت قدم staunch

wafadaree *n.* وفاداري loyalty

wagay *n* وی bunch

wagay *a.* وی hungry

wagi *n.* وا rein

wagma *n* ومه breeze

wagma *n.* ومه whiff

wagon; bar leygdawoonki waseela *n.* واون؛بارلدوونکوسیله wagon

wahal *v. t.* وهل beat

wahal dabawal; kar bandeyz *n* وهل‌بول؛کاربدنز strike

wahoonkay *n.* وهونکی striker

wahshat *n.* وحشت savagery

wahshatnak *a.* وحشتناک terrible

wahshee *a.* وحشي savage

wahshee khoog *n* وحشي‌خو boar

wahshee marghano khkari *n.* وحشی‌مارغانوکاری fowler

wahshee zanawar *n* وحشي‌ناور brute

wahshee zanawar ya insan *n* وحشي‌ناوریاانسان savage

wahsheetob; bayaban *n.* وحشيتوب؛بیابان wilderness

waiz *n.* واعظ preacher

wajad *n.* وجد rapture

wajeeba; danda *n* وجیبه؛دنده duty

wajib *a.* واجب obligatory

wajood *n* وجود؛شتون existence

wajood laral *v.i* وجودلرل exist

wajood warkowana *n.* وجود ورکونه incarnation

wak warkawal *v.t.* واک‌ورکول authorize

wak warkawal *v. t* واک‌ورکول empower

wak; hookoomat *n.* واک؛حکومت rule

wak; preykhla *n.* واک؛پرله authority

wakalat kawoonkay; mahir *n.* وکالت کوونکی؛ماهر practitioner

wakeel *n.* وکیل attorney

wakeel *n.* وکیل barrister

wakha *n* واه cockle

wakha *n* واه grass

wakhay *n* وی bracelet

wakht barabarawal *v.t.* وخت برابرول؛وخت‌اکل time

wakht peyzhandana *n.* وخت‌پژندنه punctuality

wakht teyrawal *v.t.* وخت‌ترول while

wakht yi poora keydal *v.i.* وخت یِ پوره کدل expire

wakht zandawal *v.i.* وخت‌نول linger

wakht zaya kawal *v.i.* وخت‌ضائع کول loaf

wakht; dawran *n.* وخت؛دوران period

wakman *a.* واکمن authoritative

wakman *n.* واکمن ruler

wakman; hakim *n* واکمن؛حاکم despot

wakmanee *n* واکمني dominion

wakseen *n.* واکسین vaccine

wakseen warkawal *v.t.* واکسین ورکول vaccinate

wakseen warkawana *n.* واکسین ورکونه vaccination

wal *n.* وَل loop

walar *a.* ولا perpendicular

walee *n.* والي governor

walee *n.* ولي guardian

walee; buzurg *n.* ولي؛بزرگ saint

wali; da sa lapara *adv.* ولي؛دهلپاره why

walja *n* ولجه booty

walja; ghaneemat *n* ولجه؛غنيمت plunder

walwala; leywaltya *n.* ولوله؛لوالتيا ardour

wana *n.* ونه tree

wand; skakht *n.* وند؛سکت share

wanda *n* ونه contribution

wanda *n.* ونه lot

wanda akheystal *v.i* ونهاخستل mass

wanda wal *n* ونهوال co-partner

wanda wal; shareek *n.* ونهوال؛ شريک associate

wanda wanda kawal *v. t* ونهونه کول distribute

wanda warkawal *v. t* ونهورکول contribute

wanda warkawal *v.t.* ونهورکول involve

wanda warkawal; gata pa barkha kawal *v.t.* ونهورکول؛به په برخه کول impart

wanda; tol lagakhtoona *n.* ونه؛ول لتونه input

wandawal *n.* ونهوال partner

waqaf *n* وقف dedication

waqaf kawal *v. t* وقف کول devote

waqaf kawal *v. t* وقف کول endow

waqaf kawoonkay *n* وقف کوونکی devotee

waqar; tashreefat *n.* وقار؛تشريفات solemnity

waqfa *n.* وقفه pause

waqfa *n.* وقفه recess

waqfa kawal *v.i.* وقفه کول pause

waqiee *a.* واقعي objective

waqiee; muwassaq *a.* واقعي؛موثق substantial

war *n* ور door

war *a* و able

war *a.* و capable

war garzawal *v. t* ورول و enable

war garzeydal; rutba moondal *v.i.* ورول؛رتبهموندل qualify

war khatayee *n* خطايي وار confusion

war; kaman laroonkay war *n.* ور؛کمانلرونکیور portal

wara man *a* من واره favourable

wara tota *n* وه وه nibble

waraktoon *n.* وکتون kindergarten ;

waral; bar waral *v. t.* ول؛بارول carry

warandeenay *prep.* واندينی afore

warandeyz kawal *v.t.* واندز کول offer

warandwayana *n* واندوينه forecast

warandwayana *n.* واندوينه anticipation

warandwayana *n* واندوينه foresight

warandwayana kawal *v.t.* واندوينه کول anticipate

warandwayana kawal *v.t* واندوينه کول forecast

warandwayana kawal *v.t* واندوينه کول foresee

warandwayana kawal *v.t* واندوينه کول foretell

warang achawal; teer achawal واناچول،تیراچول beam v. i

waranga n. وانه ray

waranga achawal v.i. وانهاچول irradiate

warastawal; muntaqilee n. وراستول،منتقلي transfer

waray n و fleece

waray n. و wool

waray shookawal v.t وشوکول fleece

waraz n ور day

warazpanra n. ورپهره daily

warbakhal v.t. وربل grant

warbakhal v.t. وربل spare

warbandi beyrta tlal v.t وربانډ برتهتلل retrace

warbashi n. وربش barley

wareen a. وین woollen

wareen astar n وین استر nap

wareen tokar n. وین وکر serge

wareen tokar n وین وکر woollen

wareena gharal shawi sanay n. وینهغلشوسنه worsted

wareez n. وري cloud

wareezan a ورین cloudy

wareezhi n. وريژ rice

wareydal v.i. ورېدل pour

wareydana n. ورېدنه affluence

warghaway katana n. ورغوی کتنه palmistry

warghaway katoonkay n. ورغوی کتونکی palmist

waridat n. واردات import

waridawal v.t. واردول import

waris n. وارث heir

warkawal v.t. ورکول give

warkh n. ورخ valve

warkh; patam n. ورخ؛پم sluice

warkhatal v.i ورختل climb

warkhatana n. ورختنه climb1

warookay kheekhayee botal n. ووکیيېبوتل phial

warookay shay ya insan n ووکی شیيانسان small

warooktya adv. ووکتیا smallness

warpasey conj. ورپس after

warpasey a. ورپس subsequent

warpayadawal v.t. ورپهیادول remind

warpori khandal v.t. ورپورخندل ridicule

warrasawal v. t. وررسول convey

warsakha draneydal v.t. ورخه درندل outweigh

warsakha gokha keydal v.i. ورخه وهکدل secede

warsakha khabrawal v.t. ورخه خبرول portend

warsakha makhki keydal v.t. ورخهمخککدل surpass

warsara barabaray kawal v.t. ورسرهبرابريکول offset

warsara makhamakheydal v. i ورسرهمخامخدل cope

warsara malgartya kawal v. t. ورسرهملرتیاکول befriend

warta a. ورته like

warta aw mushabay kawal v.t ورتهاومشابهکول fabricate

warta barabarawal v.i. ورته برابرول provide

warta darmal warkawal *v.t.* ورته درمل ورکول physic

warta ghag laroonkee toree sara da parla pasey kalmo peyleydana *n.* ورته غلرونکي توري سره دپرله پس کلمو پيلدنه alliteration

warta heela laral *v.t.* ورته هيله لرل hope

warta kawal *v.t.* ورته کول liken

warta makh kawal *v.t* ورته مخ کول front

warta shakhseeyat warkawal *v.t.* ورته شخصيت ورکول personify

warta walay *n.* ورته والى conformity

warta walay *n.* ورته والى like

wartatob *n.* ورته توب likeness

wartawalay *n.* ورته والى similarity

wartlana *n.* ورتلنه reference

wartya *n.* وتيا capability

wartya *n.* وتيا talent

warya *adv.* ويا gratis

warzash ta zan chamtoo kawal *v.t.* ورزش تمان چمتو کول limber

warzashee *a.* ورزشي sportive

warzda kawal *v.t.* ورزده کول teach

warzish *n.* ورزش exercise

warzish kar *n.* ورزش کار athlete

warzish kawal *v. t* ورزش کول exercise

warzishee syalee *n.* ورزشي سيالي tournament

wasayil *n* وسايل equipment

wasayil *n* وسايل means

wasayil pa las warkawal *v.t* وسايل په لاس ورکول outfit

waseela *n.* وسيله resource

waseeyat kawal *v.t.* وصيت کول will

washarmeyga ! *interj* اوشرمه! fie

waskat *n.* واسک vest

wasl kawal *v. t.* وصل کول connect

wasla *n.* وسله armament

wasla *n.* وسله weapon

wasla toon *n.* وسله تون armoury

wasla wal kawal *v.t.* وسله وال کول arm

waslatoon *n.* وسله تون arsenal

wasleen *n.* واسلين vaseline

wasley *n.* وسلي munitions

wast *a.* وسط middling

wastee *a.* وسطي median

waswas *n.* وسواس caprice

waswas *n.* وسواس melancholia

waswas *n.* وسواس melancholy

waswasee *a.* وسواسي capricious

waswasee *a.* وسواسي melancholic

waswasee *adj* وسواسي melancholy

watalay aw barjasta *a.* وتلي او برجسته prominent

watalay; ramzee *a.* وتلي؛رمزي signal

watan *n* وطن distance

watanee *n* وطني native

wawra *n.* واوره ice

wawra *n.* واوره snow

wawra wareydal *v.i.* واوره وريدل snow

wawreen *a.* واورين icy

wawreen *a.* واورين snowy

wayal *v.t.* ويل say

wayal *v.t.* ويل tell

wayand *n.* وياند spokesman

wayand; shmeyroonkay *n.* ،وياند
شمرونكى teller

wayay pa wayay *adv.* ويى‌په‌ويى
verbatim

wayay; lughat *n.* ويى،لغت word

wayee panga; qamoos *n.* ،ويى‌پانه
قاموس vocabulary

waylon *n* وايلون fiddle

waylon ghagawal; apalti wayal
v.i وايلون‌غول،اپلتويل fiddle

wayloon ghagoonkay *n.* ويلون
غوونكى violinist

wayna *n.* ونا locution

wayna *n.* ونا oration

wayna kawana *n.* وناكونه speech

wayna; bayan *n.* ونا؛بيان parlance

wayna; khabara *n.* ونا؛خبره say

waynawal *n.* وناوال orator

wayroos; da fasad tomna *n.*
ويروس؛دفسادتومنه virus

waza kawal; rol lobawal *v. t* وضع
كول؛رول‌لوبول enact

wazahat *n* وضاحت clarification

wazahat kawal *v. t* وضاحت‌كول
clarify

wazan *n.* وزن gravity

wazan *n.* وزن weight

wazan kawal *v.t.* وزن‌كول weigh

wazan larana *n.* لرنه وزن
weightage

wazan laroonkay *a* وزن‌لرونكى
bulky

wazar *n.* وزر wing

wazar; banraka *n* وزر،بكه feather

wazarat *n.* وزارت ministry

wazay *a.* واضح obvious

wazda weeli kawana aw
ghwarawana *n.* وازده‌ويلكوونه
اوغووونه tallow

wazeefa; rol *n.* وظيفه،رول role

wazeer *n.* وزير minister

wazeh *a.* واضح intelligible

wazeh *a.* واضح patent

wazgar wakht teyrawal *v.i.* وزار
وختترول loiter

wazhal *v.t.* وژل kill

wazhal *v.t.* وژل murder

wazhana *n.* وژنه homicide

wazhana *n.* وژنه kill

wazhana *n.* وژنه murder

wazhghona *n* وژغونه bristle

wazhoonkay *a.* وژونكى lethal

wazhoonkay *n.* وژونكى murderer

weeda *adv.* ويده asleep

weeda keydal *v.i.* ويده‌كدل sleep

weejarawal *v. t* ويجاول destroy

weejarawal *v.t.* ويجاول raze

weejarawal *v.t.* ويجاول scourge

weejarawal *v.t.* ويجاول ruin

weejarawana *n* ويجاونه
annihilation

weejaree *n* ويجاي destruction

weejaree *n.* ويجاي ruin

weekh *a.* ويښ alert

weekh *a* ويښ awake

weekhawal *v.t.* ويول arouse

weekhawal; weekheydal *v.t.*
ويول؛ويدل wake

weekheydal; weekhawal *v.t.*
ويدل؛ويول awake

weekhtob; sarani ta weekh pati keydana *n.* ویتوب،بار نته وپات کیدنه vigilance

weekhwalay *n.* ویوالی alertness

weekhwalay *n* ویوالی wake

weeli keydal *v.i.* ویلکدل melt

weeli keydal *v.i* ویلکدل thaw

weeli keydana *n.* ویلکدنه fusion

weeli keydoonkay; halawoonkay *a.* ویلکدونکی،حلوونکی solvent

weeli shaway *a.* ویلیشوی molten

weena *n* وینه blood

weena lagay *n* وینهلي anaemia

weena toyawana *n* وینهتویونه bloodshed

weenayeez *a.* وینهییز sanguine

weeney ta nanawatalay chark *n.* وینهتهننوتلیچرک sepsis

weeni keydal *v. i* وینکدل bleed

weenzal *v. t* وینل cleanse

weenzal *v.t.* وینل launder

weenzal *v.t.* وینل wash

weenzana *n.* ویننه purification

weenzana *n* ویننه wash

weer *n* ویر lament

weer *n* ویر wail

weer kawal *v.i.* ویرکول lament

weer kawal *v.i.* ویرکول wail

weer laralay *a.* ویرللی wistful

weer laralay *a.* ویرللی tragic

weer larali peykha *n.* په ویرلا tragedy

weerawal; ghwarawal *v.i.* ویول، غوول spread

weerjan *a.* ویرجن woebegone

weeshtana; da booto rawataltya *n* ویشتنه،دبووراوتلتیا shoot

weetameen *n.* ویامین vitamin

weeyareydal *v. i* ویامدل exult

wehem; khyal *n* وهم،خیال fancy

wehem; khyal *n* وهم،خیال figment

wehshee *a.* وحشی barbarous

wehshee insan *n.* وحشیانسان barbarian

wehsheetob *n.* وحشیتوب barbarism

wehsheeyana *a.* وحشیانه barbarian

wehsheeyana amal *n* وحشیانهعمل barbarity

werawonki *a.* ویروونکی ghastly

weykhta *n* وته hair

weyra *n* وره dread

weyra *n* وره fear

weyrawal *v.t* ورول dread

weyreydal *v.i* ورمدل fear

weyreydal *a.* ویریدل afraid

weyrowoonkay *a.* وروونکی fearful

weysh *n* وش distribution

weysh *n* وش division

weysh *n.* وش partition

weysh; takhsees *n.* وش،تخصیص allotment

weyshal *v.t.* وشل apportion

weyshal *v.t.* وشل partition

weyshnal; zay pa zay kawal *v.t.* وشنل،بایپمایکول scatter

weystana *n* وستنه elimination

wilayat *n.* ولایت province

wilayatee *a.* ولایتی provincial

woolas *n.* ولس public

woolas mashr *n.* ولسمشر president

woolaspal *n* ولسپال republican

woolaspala *a.* ولسپاله republican

woolaswakee *n* ولسواکي democracy

woolaswalee *n* ولسوالي district

wraga *n.* وره flea

wrakeydal *v. i* ورکدل disappear

wrakeydal *v.i.* ورکدل vanish

wraktob *n* ورکتوب disappearance

wrana rawrana; tag ratag *n.* ونه راونه؛تراﺗ traffic

wranawoonkay *n.* ورانوونکی wrecker

wranay; kharabay *n.* ورانی؛خرابی wrack

wrandeenay *a.* واندینی prior

wrandi *n.* واند precedent

wrandi sakha gooman *n.* واندخه ومان presupposition

wrandi sakha gooman kawal *v.t.* واندخومان کول presuppose

wranditob *n.* واندتوب precedence

wrankaray *a.* ورانکاری untoward

wrara *n.* وراره nephew

wray *n.* وری lamb

wrazanay *adv* ورﻧ adays

wrazanay *a.* ورﻧی workaday

wrazanay chari *n.* ورﻧﭽﺎر routine

wreen *a.* ورین nice

wreentob *n.* ورینتوب nicety

wreet shaway *a* وریتشوی roast

wreeta shawi ghwakha *n* وریﺗﻪشو غوه roast

wreetawal *v.t.* وریتول fry

wreetawal *v.t.* وریتول parch

wreetawal *v.t.* وریتول roast

wreez *n* وریز brow

wreykham *n.* ورم silk

wreykhmeen *a.* ورمین silken

wreykhmeen *a.* ورمین silky

wreyra *n.* وررﻩ niece

wro wro chakar wahal *v.i.* ورو ورو چکروهل stroll

wro wro eyshawal *v.t.* ورو ورو اشول stew

wro wro kamzoray kawal *v.t.* وروورو کمزوری کول undermine

wro; sast *a* ورو؛ﺳﺖ slow

wroon; panday *n.* ورون؛پﻪ thigh

wror *n* ورور brother

wror wazhana *n.* وژنه ورور fratricide

wrorwalee *n* وروروﻟﻲ brotherhood

wrost *adj* وروﺳﺖ addle

wrosta *adv* وروﺳﺘﻪ after

wrosta la *adv.* وروﺳﺘﻪﻟﻪ next

wrostanay *n* وروﺳﺘﻨﻲ last

wrostanay barkha *n.* وروﺳﺘﯿﺑﺮﺧﻪ rear

wrostay *a.* وروﺳﺘﻲ last1

wrusta la *prep.* وروﺳﺘﻪﻟﻪ since

wrusta la *adv.* وروﺳﺘﻪﻟﻪ thereafter

wrusta; badan *adv.* وروﺳﺘﻪ؛ﺑﻌﺪﻟ post

wrustanay tamzay *n.* وروﺳﺘﻨﻲﺗﻤﺎی terminus

wrustawal; kharabawal *v.t.* ورﺳﺘﻮل؛ﺧﺮاﺑﻮل spoil

wurmeyg *n.* ورم nape

wuzeeyat; waqar *n* وضعيت؛وقار poise

wuzgartob; rukhsatee *n.* وزارتوب؛رخصتي vacation

wyala *n.* ویاله brook

wyala *n.* ویاله canal

wyala *n.* ویاله stream

wyala *n.* ویاله rivulet

wyareydal *v. t* ویالدل cocker

wza *n.* وزه goat

yadakht *n.* یادت notation

yadakht *n.* یادت memoir

yadakht *n* یادت memorandum

yadakhtawal *v.t.* یادتول note

yadawaree *n* یادآوري anamnesis

yadgar *n.* یادار keepsake

yadgar *n.* یادار souvenir

yadgar *n.* یادار memorial

yadgaree *a.* یاداري monumental

yadgaree *a.* یاداري memorable

yadgaree dabar leek *a* یاداري؛بر لیک memorial

yadgaree dabara *n.* یاداري؛بره megalith

yadowana *n.* یادوونه mention

yag *n* یږ bear

yahoodee *n.* یهودي Jew

yak shamba; yoonay *n.* یک شنبه؛ یون Sunday

yakh *a* یخ chilly

yakh aw taza satana *n.* تازه او یخ ساتنه refrigeration

yakh satal *v.t.* ساتل یخ refrigerate

yakhchal *n.* یخچال fridge

yakhchal *n.* یخچال glacier

yakhchal *n.* یخچال refrigerator

yam (loomray kas; laka: za yam) یم(لومى کس؛لکه:زه یم) am

yana *n.* ینه liver

yaq dol salor araba beza bagai *n.* یوولدلورارابه بیزه بـ barouche

yaqeenan *adv.* یقیناً certainly

yaqeenee *a* یقینی certain

yaqoot *n.* یاقوت ruby

yar; shareek *n.* یار؛شریک pal

yarghal *n.* یرغل raid

yarghal gar *n.* یرغلر aggressor

yarghal kawal *v.t.* یرغل کول raid

yarghal rawral *v.t.* یرغلراول attack

yarghalgar *n* یرغلر offensive

yarghmal *n.* یرغمل hostage

yateem *n.* یتیم orphan

yateem kawal; yateem keydal *v.t* یتیم کول؛یتیم کدل orphan

yateemano da astogni zay *n.* یتیمانو داستوناي orphanage

yaw *a.* یو a

yaw *a.* یو one

yaw (laka yaw kas; yaw keetab) یو(لکه یو کس؛یو کتاب) an

yaw arkheez *a* یواخیز ex-parte

yaw aroopayee koochnay gharsa roe *n.* یواروپایي کوچنغره

yaw awaz larana *n* یوآوازلرنه monotony

yaw awazay *a.* يوآوازى
monotonous

yaw bal *a* يوبل another

**yaw botal chi pa labratwar ki
kareygee** *n* يوبوتل چپه لابراتوار کې
کاري flask

yaw cheyri; pa kom zay ki *adv.*
يوچر؛به کومای ک somewhere

**yaw dandi sakha arzee bali
dandi ta arawal** *v.t.* يودندخه
عارضى بلدندته اول second

yaw dawal; warta *a.* يوول؛ورته
alike

**yaw dawl amreekayee
gharsanay** *v.i* يوول امريکايي غرۀ
mouse

yaw dawl bootay *n.* يوول بوى sage

yaw dawl bootay *n.* يوول بوى
mistletoe

**yaw dawl bootay; parta la
juftgeeray zeygeydalay** *n* يو
ول بوى؛برته له جفت يرزدلا agamist

yaw dawl chanrey *n.* يوول چ pea

yaw dawl chogha *n.* يوول چوغه
cloak

yaw dawl da dabaro skara *n.* يو
ول دبرو سکاره lignite

yaw dawl da kheekhey botal *n.*
يوول ديبوتل jar

yaw dawl darmal *n.* يوول درمل
tincture

yaw dawl dastkash *n.* يوول دستکش
mitten

**yaw dawl gaya chi zyar gulan
laree** *n.* يوول ياچزيلان لري
dandelion

**yaw dawl gharanay aw wehshee
bakam laroonkay ghwayay**
n يوول غرنى اوو حشي بکام لرونکى
غوايى bison

yaw dawl ghat mosh khurma *n.*
يوول غموش خرما mink

yaw dawl ghwakheen sas *n.* يوول
غوين ساس pudding

yaw dawl gopee *n.* يوول وپي
broccoli

yaw dawl heelay *n.* يوول هيل
marionette

yaw dawl jakat *n.* يوول جاک
pullover

**yaw dawl kab chi da kakhtay
beykh pori nakhalee** *n* يوول
کب چد کتيخ پورنلي barnacles

yaw dawl keymyayee mada *n* يو
ول کميايي ماده chlorine

**yaw dawl khkulay koochnay
khkaree spay** *n.* يوول کلى
کوچني کاري سپى terrier

yaw dawl khwaga *n.* يوول خواه
comfit

yaw dawl khwaga khwara *n.* يو
ول خواه خواه jelly

yaw dawl khwali *n* يوول خول
bonnet

yaw dawl khwaranzay *n.* يوول
خوناى canteen

yaw dawl koochnay goongata *n.*
يوول کوچنونه weevil

yawdawlkoochnaykhorakeekab
v.t. يوول کوچني خوراکي کب
smelt

**yaw dawl koranay toora aw
speena kawtara** *n.* يوول کورذ
توره او سپينه کوتره magpie

yaw dawl manra *n.* يوول‌مه
nonpareil

yaw dawl margha *n.* يوول‌مارغه
leghorn

yaw dawl naray spaka toora *n.*
يوول‌نرسپكه‌توره rapier

yaw dawl pasta doday *n.* يوول
پسته‌و toast

yaw dawl patloon *n.* يوول‌پتلون
jean

yaw dawl qaseeda *n.* يوول‌قصيده
ballad

yaw dawl sandar bola marghay
n. يوول‌سندربوله‌مرغ warbler

yaw dawl saranay bootay *n.* يوول
ساراني‌بوى weed

yaw dawl sharab *n* يوول‌شراب
brandy

yaw dawl sharab *n.* يوول‌شراب
whisky

yaw dawl spay *n* يوول‌سپى bulldog

yaw dawl stara ghombasa *n.* يو
ول‌ستره‌غومبسه hornet

yaw dawl teyl *n.* يوول‌تل castor oil

yaw dawl treekh bootay *n.* يوول
تريخ‌بوى wormwood

yaw dawl wana *n.* يوول‌ونه birch

yaw dawl wana *n* يوول‌ونه rush

yaw dawl wana *n.* يوول‌ونه teak

yaw dawl wareen kalee *n.* يوول
وين‌كالي masquerade

yawdawlzalawarkawoonkimada
n. يوول‌ولاوركوونكماده varnish

yaw deyr star badanay kab *n.* و يو
كب بدني ستر whale

yaw dol botay che tal sheen we *n*
يوول‌بوى‌چه‌تل‌شين‌وى ivy

yaw dol kab *n.* يوول‌كب herring

yaw hija *n.* يوهجا monosyllable

yaw hijayee kalma *a.* يوهجايي‌كلمه
monosyllabic

yaw kam miqdar *n* ايو‌كم‌مقدار less

yaw kar takrarawal *v.t.* يو‌كار
تكرارول reiterate

yaw kaseez wayna *n.* يو‌كسيزونا
monologue

yaw kaseeza sandara *n* يو‌كسيزه
سندره solo

yaw kawal *v.t.* يو‌كول incorporate

yaw kawal *v.t* يو‌كول link

yaw kawal *v.t.* يو‌كول unite

yaw kawana *n* يو‌كوونه weld

yaw kawang *n.* يو‌كوز unification

yaw keydana *n* كدنه‌يو coalition

yaw khas kaleeza *n.* يو‌خاص‌كليزه
jubilee

yaw khas tarz ki sandara wayal
v.i. يو‌خاص‌طرزكسندره‌وىل
warble

yaw khyalee haywad *n.* يو‌خيالي
هواد utopia

**yaw lar nabatee aw heywanee
meykroboona** *n.* يو‌لنباتي‌او
حواني‌مكروبونه bacteria

yaw loy samandaree kab *n.* يولوى
سمندري‌كب shark

yaw margha *n.* مارغه‌يو swan

yaw misree eenzar *n.* يو‌مصري‌اينر
sycamore

yaw nawakht; dadman *a.*
يونواخت؛امن steady

**yaw oogdey pkhey laroonkay
margha** *n.* يواودپلرونكى‌مارغه
stilt

yaw pa baḷ bandi takia *n.* يوپهبل باندتکيه interdependence

yaw pa baḷ bandi takia *a.* يوپهبل باندتکيه interdependent

yaw pa bal pasey ratlal *v.t.* يوپهبل پسراتلل alternate

yaw pa manz ki; motanawab *a.* يوپهمنزکې،متناوب alternate

yaw qeematee kanray *n.* يوقيمتي کانئ jade

yaw radyoekteef aw tashashee unsar *n.* يورايواکتيفاوتشعشعي عنصر radium

yaw rangarang khkulee rangoona laroonki mada chi ghamee tri joreygee *n.* يو رنارنکليرنونهلرونکمادهچغميتر جوي opal

yaw sa mooda *adv.* يوهموده awhile

yaw saat *n.* يوساعت hour

yaw samandaree sadaf *n.* يو سمندريصدف oyster

yaw seez; yaw shay *pron.* يويز،يو شی something

yaw shan *a* يوشان equitable

yaw shan *adv* يوشان alike

yaw shan *a.* شان يو same

yaw shan kawal; jazab kawal *v.* يوشان کول،جذب کول assimilate

yaw shaway *adj.* يوشوی corporate

yaw shaway *a.* يوشوی incorporate

yaw so *a* يو و few

yaw sok *n.* يووک somebody

yaw star topak *n.* يوسټروپک cannon

yaw stargeez *a.* سټريز يو monocular

yaw stargeeza aynak *n.* يوسټريزه عينک monocle

yaw unsar *n.* يوعنصر manganese

yaw unsar *n.* يوعنصر neon

yaw wahshee as *n.* يووحشيآس mustang

yaw walay *n.* يووالی unity

yaw warta ghag laroonkee toree sara da parla pasi kalmo peyleydal *v.* يوورتهغلرونکي توريسرهدپرلهپسکلموپيلدل alliterate

yaw zaharjana mada *n.* يوزهرجنه ماده nicotine

yaw zghastee syalee *n.* يوغاستي سيالي marathon

yaw zyat miqdar *n.* يوزياتمقدار multitude

yaw; tanha *n.* يو،تنها single

yawa dabareena panra *n.* يوهبرينه پله slate

yawa karkha ya lika ki darawana *n.* يوه کرهياليکه ک درونه alignment

yawa khaza laroonkay *a.* يومه لرونکی monogynous

yawa lor ta meelan laral *v.i.* يوه لورتهميلانلرل trespass

yawa mom dawla mada *n.* يوهموم ولهماده paraffin

yawa paysa; da amreeka sika *n.* يوهپسه،دامريکاسکه penny

yawa qandee mada *n.* يوهقنديماده saccharin

yawa salor konja tota *n.* يوملور کونجهوه pane

yawa sandarghari wara marghay *n.* يوه‌سندرغاوه‌مرغ wren

yawa sreykhnaka khoshbooya mada *n.* يوه‌سرناکه‌خوشبويه‌ماده myrrh

yawa tal shna wana *n.* يوه‌تل‌شنه‌ونه laurel

yawa tota *n.* يوموه monolith

yawa tota; laga barkha *n* يوموه،له برخه bit

yawazeenay; infiradee *a.* يوازينی؛ انفرادي solo

yawazey *a.* يواز alone

yawazeytob *n.* يوازتوب singularity

yawazi *a.* يواز lonely

yawazi *a.* يواز only

yawazi insan *n.* انسان يواز recluse

yawazi preykhodal *v.i.* يوازپرودل strand

yawazi tlal; yaw keydal *v.t.* يواز تلل؛يو کدل single

yawazi; tanha *a* يوازی؛تنها exclusive

yawazi; yaw kaseez *a.* يواز؛يوکسيز single

yawazitob *n.* يوازتوب celibacy

yawazitob *n.* يوازتوب individualism

yawazitob *n.* يوازتوب isolation

yawey khwa ta tlal *v.i.* يوخواته‌تلل side

yawolas *n* يوولس eleven

yawoon *n.* يوون unit

yawrangwalay *n.* يورنوالی resemblance

yawrangwalay laral *v.t.* يورنوالی لرل resemble

yawshantob *n.* يوشانتوب parallelism

yawshanwalay *n.* يوشانوالی par

yawtob *n.* يوتوب oneness

yeywi *n.* ييو plough

yeywi shawi zmaka *n* ييوشومکه fallow

yeywi shawi zmaka *n.* ييوشومکه furrow

yoon; safar *n.* يون،سفر tour

yoonanee *a* يوناني Greek

Z

za *pron.* زه I

zaboor *n.* زبور psalm

zabtawana *n* ضبطونه forfeiture

zaeef *a.* ضعيف infirm

zaeef kawal *v.t.* ضعيف کول depauperate

zafran *n.* زعفران saffron

zag kawal *v.t* کول foam

zag; kaf *n* کف ، foam

zagh zagh *n.* غ غ sizzle

zahar *n.* زهر poison

zahar *n.* زهر venom

zahar warkawal *v.t.* زهرورکول poison

zahar zad *n.* زهرضد mithridate

zaharjan a. زهرجن poisonous

zaharjan *a.* زهرجن venomous

zaharjan *a.* زهرجن virulent

zaharjantob; wayrooseetob n.
زهرجنتوب؛ويروسيتوب
virulence

zahid a. زاهد ascetic

zahid a. زاهد piteous

zahir; shakal n. ظاهر،شكل guise

zahiree banra n ظاهري به format

zahireydal v.t ظاهرېدل evolve

zahoor; banra n ظهور،به
appearance

zaka conj. كه because

zaka conj. كه so

zakha n. زخه wart

zakham n. زخم injury

zakham n زخم sore

zakheem kawal v.i. ضخيم كول
thicken

zakheera n. ذخيره stock

zakheera kawal v.t. ذخيره كول
stock

zala n. اله nest

zala n. لا glare

zala n. لا radiation

zala jorawal v.t. اله جوړول nest

zala jorawal v.i. جوړ اله nestle

zala warkawal v.t. لاوركول
varnish

zala; sapara n. اله،پره cot

zaland adv. لاند ablaze

zaland a لاند bright

zaland a. لاند candid

zaland a. لاند glossy

zaland a. لاند lustrous

zaland a. لاند resplendent

zalanda a لانده clear

zalanda kawal v.t. لانده كول
illuminate

zalandtob n لاندتوب clarity

zalaval v.t. لول glaze

zaleydal v.i لدل glare

zaleydal v.t. لدل radiate

zaleydal; shuhrat payda kawal
v.t. لدل،شهرت پيداكول star

zaleydana n لدنه flash

zalim a ظالم cruel

zalim n. ظالم oppressor

zalim jabir n. ظالم جابر tyrant

zalimana a. ظالمانه oppressive

zalmotay n. زلموی youngster

zalzala n زلزله earthquake

zama pron. زما mine

zama a. زما my

zaman mafhoom v.t. ضمن مفهوم
imply

zamanat n. ضمانت bail

zamanat n. ضمانت guarantee

zamanat n. ضمانت parole

zamanat n. ضمانت warrantee

zamanat n. ضمانت warranty

zamanat leek n. ضمانت ليک
voucher

zamanat warkawal v.t ضمانت
وركول guarantee

zamanat warkawal v.i. ضمانت
وركول vouch

zambeydal v.i. مبدل lounge

zambeydal; rang rang tlal v.i.
ننتلل مبدل، stagger

zambeydana n. مبدنه stagger

zambeydana; ngokheydana n.
مبدنه،نوډدنه shuffle

zameema *n.* ضميمه appendix

zameema kawal; nakhlawal *v.t.*
ضميمه كول؛نلول annex

zameena *n.* زمينه basis

zameena *n.* زمينه conspectus

zameena *n* زمينه context

zameena; da zmaki yawa tota *n.*
زمينه؛دمكيوموه plot

zamin *n.* ضامن warrantor

zamoong *pron.* زمو our

zamrod *n* زمرد emerald

zan dabalshakhseeyatpaseyra
ganral *n.* زاندبل شخصيت پهرمل
impersonation

zan ghokhtana *n* غوتنه زان egotism

zan khodana *n.* زانودنه pretence

zan khodani pori arwand *a.* زان
ودنپوراوند pretentious

zan larzawal *v.i.* زانلزول wince

zan leedana *n.* زانليدنه arrogance

zan pak *n.* زانپاک towel

zan pasi kagal *v.t.* زانپسكال trail

zan raghondawal *v. i.* زانراغونول
cringe

zan sara khwandee satal; zeyrga
kawal *v.t.* زانسرهخونديساتل؛
زرمه كول reserve

zan sara khwandee satana *n.* زان
سرهخونديساتنه reservation

zansarasatal *v.t.* زانسرهساتل retain

zan sara satal *v.t.* زانسرهساتل
withhold

zan seyral *v.i.* زانل introspect

zan seyrana *n.* زانه introspection

zanshatakawal *v.t.* زانشاته كول
resign

zanshatakawal *v.t.* زانشاته كول
retread

zan stayana *n.* زان ستاينه narcissism

zan ta rakkhal; mutasira kawal
زانتهراكل؛متاثره كول *v.t* fancy

zan tri satal *v.t.* زانترساتل shun

zan wazhna *n.* وژنه زان suicide

zan wazhnee *a.* زانوژني suicidal

zan zanee; fardee *n.* زانناني؛فردي
individuality

zan; nafas *n.* زان؛نفس self

zana *n.* زنه chin

zana *n.* زنا adulteration

zana karee *n.* زناكاري adultery

zana kawal *v.t.* زناكول adulterate

zanawar *n.* ناور animal

zanawar ya kaban neewalo
lapara pa dam ki da
khwaro mawad *n* ناورياكبان
نيولولپارهپهدام كدخوومواد bait

zandan *n.* زندان cage

zandanee kawal *v.t.* زنداني كول
imprison

zandaneetob *n.* زندانيتوب captivity

zandawal *v.t.* نول postpone

zandawal *v.t.* نول prorogue

zandawal; zandeydal *v.t. & i.*
نول؛ندل delay

zandaykawal *v. t.* زندكول choke

zanday kawal; khamoshawal *v.t.*
زندكول؛خاموشول stifle

zanday kawana *n.* زندكونه
strangulation

zanday shaway *a.* زندشوى stuffy

zandeydalay *adj.* ندلى belated

zandeydalay *a.* ندلى late

zandeydalee poroona *n.pl.* ندلي پورونه arrears

zandeydaly *a.* ندلۍ overdue

zanee; yawazi zan *a.* زاني؛يوازان individual

zang *n* زنگ bell

zang *n.* زنگ rust

zang na akheystoonkay *a.* زنگ نه اخستونکی stainless

zang wahal *v.t.* زنگ وهل ring

zang wahal *v.i* زنگ وهل rust

zang wahalay *a.* زنگ وهلی rusty

zang wahana *n.* زنگ وهنه rusticity

zangal *n* ځنگل forest

zangal *n.* ځنگل jungle

zangal *n.* ځنگل woods

zangal jorawal *v.t.* ځنگل جوړول afforest

zangal meyshtay *a.* ځنگل مشتی sylvan

zangal poha *n* ځنگل پوهه forestry

zangal wan *n* ځنگل وان forester

zangalee seema *n.* ځنگلي سيمه woodland

zangarana; takana *n.* ځانگه،باکنه allocation

zangaray kawal *v.t.* ځانگی کول allocate

zangaray kawal *v.t.* ځانگی کول allot

zangaray sifat *n.* ځانگی صفت attribute

zangari honaree zhaba *n.* ځانګري هنري ژبه jargon

zangari jamey *n.* ځانجامه livery

zangari zhaba *n.* ځانژبه lingo

zanghwaray *a.* ځانغوای selfish

zango *n* زانګو cradle

zankhkaray; batoo *a.* ځانکاری؛باتو vainglorious

zankhoday *a.* ځانودی proud

zanta kawal *v. t* ځانته کول detach

zanza *n.* زنځه millipede

zanza *n.* زنځه centipede

zanzeer *n* زنځير chain

zaqoom *n.* زاقوم cactus

zar *n.* زر thousand

zar bawara *adj.* زرباوره credulity

zar kala *n.* زرکاله millennium

zar; beeranay *a* زر؛بيرنی early

zara *n* ذره mite

zara *n.* ذره molecule

zara *a.* ذره particle

zara *n.* ذره modicum

zarab *n.* ضرب multiplication

zarab kawal *v.t.* ضرب کول multiply

zarabkhana *n.* ضرابخانه mint

zarafa *n.* زرافه giraffe

zarafat *n* ظرافت elegance

zarafat; da kanjkaway his *n* ظرافت،د کنجکاوحس curiosity

zarakht *n* زت fray

zarakht *n.* زت senility

zarar *n* ضرر mischief

zararnak *a.* ضررناک baleful

zaratee *a.* زراعتي agrarian

zarawal; la moda lweydal *v.t.* زول،لەموەلوېدل stale

zarawee *a.* ذروي molecular

zaray *n.* زی seed

zaray kawal *v.t.* زارکول implore

zarb; wahana *n* ضرب،وهنه beat

zarba; goozar *n.* ضربه،بوزار stroke

zard aloo *n.* زردآلو apricot

zaree dozee *n.* زري‌دوزي fret

zaree dozee kawal *v.t.* زري‌دوزي fret
كول

zaree kawal *v.t.* زاري‌كول entreat

zaree sheendal *v.t.* زي‌شيندل seed

zareeya *n* ذريعه medium

zarfeeyat *n* ظرفيت content

zargar *n.* زرگر goldsmith

zargar *n.* زرگر jeweller

zarghon; taza *a.* زرغون،تازه green

zarobay *n.* وبی cascade

zarobay *n.* وبی waterfall

zarooree *a* ضروري essential

zarooree *a.* ضروري indispensable

zarooree *a.* ضروري integral

zarooree *a.* ضروري major

zarooree *a* ضروري necessary

zarooree shay *n.* ضروري‌شی necessary

zartoray kawoonkay *a.* زتوری كوونكی weary

zatee leywaltya *n.* ذاتي‌لوالتيا appetite

zawab *n* واب answer

zawab *n.* واب response

zawab warkawal *v.t* واب‌وركول answer

zawab warkawal *v.i.* وركول‌واب reply

zawab warkawal *v.i.* واب‌وركول respond

zawab warkawoonkay *n.* واب وركونكی respondent

zawab; difa *n* واب،دفاع reply

zawabee tuhmat *n.* وابي‌تهمت coun025charge

zawal زوال decay

zawal *n* زوال decline

zawal moondal *v.t.* زوال‌موندل decline

zaweeya *n.* زاويه angle

zaweeya laroonkay *a.* زاويه‌لرونكی angular

zaweeyadar kawal *v.t.* زاويه‌دار كول crankle

zawqee kar *n* ذوقي‌كار fad

zay badlawal *v.t.* ای‌بدلول move

zay badlawal *v.t.* ای‌بدلول shift

zay laroonkay *a.* ای‌لرونكی spacious

zay laroonkay; hawadar *a.* ای لرونكی؛هوادار roomy

zay nastay kawal *v.i.* ای‌ناستی‌كول sojourn

zay neewal *v.t.* ای‌نيول contain

zay neewal *v.t.* ای‌نيول replace

zay neewana; taweez *n.* ای‌نيوونه، تعويض replacement

zay takal *v.t.* ای‌كل locate

zay; iwaz *n.* ای،عوض lieu

zaya kawana *n.* ضايع‌كونه waste

zaya; shar *a.* ضايع،شا waste

zayawal *v.t* ايول accommodate

zaybayish *n.* زبائش ornamentation

zaynastay *n.* ايناستی substitute

zaynastay *n.* ايناستی successor

zayqa *n.* ذايقه savour

zayqa *n.* ذايقه taste

zayqa laral *v.t.* ذايقه‌لرل taste

zaytoon *n.* زیتون olive

zaywar *n.* زور ornament

zda kawal *v.i.* زده کول learn

zda kawoonkay *n.* زده کوونکی learner

zda kawoonkay *n.* زده کوونکی pupil

zda kawoonkay *n.* زده کوونکی trainee

zdakra *n.* زده که learning

zdakra kawal; lostal *v.i.* زد که کول،لوستل study

zdakra; tarbeeyat *n.* زده که،تربیت training

zdakro lapara malee mrasta; tehseel *n.* زده کول پاره مالی مرسته، تحصیل scholarship

zdakrotay; leesansa *n* زدکوتی، لیسانسه graduate

zdakryal *n.* زدکیال student

zeen *n.* زین saddle

zeen ya kata eekhodal *v.t.* زین یا کته ایودل saddle

zeeni wakhtoona *adv.* ینی وختونه sometimes

zeeni; yaw shmeyr *a.* ینی،یوشمیر some

zeep; kashak *n.* زیپ،کشک zip

zeeyanman *a.* زیانمن inimical

zeeyar *n* زیار endeavour

zeeyar basal *v.i* زیارباسل endeavour

zeeyar kakh *a* زیارکخ diligent

zeeyar kakh *a.* زیارک industrious

zeg *a.* زیه hoarse

zehen; khyal *n.* ذهن،خیال mind

zeher zid *n.* زهرضد antidote

zehmatawal *v.t* زحمتول bother

zehnee *a.* ذهنی mental

zehnee tawajo *n.* ذهنی توجه aptitude

zer kedal *v.t.* یرکیدل gaze

zer zer katana *n* یریرکتنه gaze

zeygantoon *n.* زنتون maternity

zeyganzay *n.* زنای womb

zeygeydal *v.* زیيدل born

zeygeydalay *adj.* زدلی borne

zeygeydana *n.* زیدنه birth

zeygeydana *n.* زیدنه nativity

zeygowoonkay *a.* زوونکی reproductive

zeyr *a* زر careful

zeyr *a.* زیه yellow

zeyr khana *n* زرخانه cellar

zeyr rang *n* رنزیه yellow

zeyr yaqoot *n.* زیاقوت topaz

zeyr zeyr katal *v.i.* یریرکتل stare

zeyramtoon *n.* زرمتون repository

zeyrawal *v.t.* زیول yellow

zeyray warkawal *v.t* زری ورکول herald

zeyrbakhan *a.* زیبخن yellowish

zeyrmatoon *n.* زرمتون godown

zgeyrway; faryád *n.* زیروی،فریاد moan

zgeyrwee kawal *v.i.* زروی کول groan

zgeyrwee kawal *v.* زیروی کول moan

zghageydal *v.i.* غدل sizzle

zghaland nazar *n.* غلندنظر glance

zghaland nazar *n.* غلندنظر glimpse

zghaland nazar kawal v.i. غلندنظر كول glance

zghalawana n. غلوونه shove

zgham n. زغم tolerance

zghamal v.t. زغمل afford

zghamal v.t. زغمل tolerate

zghamal v.t. زغمل stomach

zghamal v.t. زغمل undergo

zghamoonkay a. زغموونكى tolerant

zghara n. زغره armour

zghara n. زغره mail

zghara; wasla n. زغره،وسله armature

zghastoonkay n. غاستونكى runner

zhaba n. ژبه language

zhaba n. ژبه tongue

zhaba kawal; zhmana kawal v.t. ژبه كول،ژمنه كول undertake

zhabanay a. ژبنى lingual

zhabanay a. ژبنى oral

zhabanay a. ژبنى viva-voce

zhabanay a. ژبنى wordy

zhabawar a. ژبور articulate

zhabdood n. ژبدود grammar

zhabgharand a. ژبغاند talkative

zhabkhod n. ژبود grammarian

zhabpoh n. ژبپوه linguist

zhabpohan n. ژبپوهنه linguistics

zhabpohana n. ژبپوهنه philology

zhabpohand n. ژبپوهاند philologist

zhabpohaneez a. ژبپوهنيز linguistic

zhabpohani pori arwand a. ژبپوهني اوند پور ژبپوهن philological

zhama n. ژامه jaw

zhamanay a. ژمنى wintry

zhamay n. ژمى winter

zhamay teyrawal v.i ژمى ترول winter

zhanrkay n. ژكى youth

zhar stareydoonkay a ژر ستريدونكى rank

zhar tar zhara adv. ژره تر ژر instantly

zhar teyreydoonkay a. ژرتريدونكى fugitive

zhar teyreydoonkay a. ژرتريدونكى momentary

zhar teyreydoonkay; mutadee fayl n. ژرتريدونكى،متعديفعل transitive

zharal v.i. ژل weep

zharghonay a. ژغونى tearful

zhawar a. ژور deep

zhawar a. ژور steep

zhawar dand n ژور دند abyss

zhawar fikra; roonr anda a. ژور فكره،روآنده profound

zhawara n. ژوره snail

zhawarghalay; kasa n. ژورغالى، كاسه socket

zhawartya n ژورتيا depth

zhawlan a ژاولن elastic

zhay n. ژ brink

zhay n. ژ rim

zhbara n. ژباه translation

zhbaral v.t. ژبال translate

zhbaran n. ژبان interpreter

zhbarana kawal v.t. ژبانه كول interpret

zheyrwee n زروى groan

zghamal *v.t.* زغمل endure

zghoral *v.i.* ژغورل guard

zghoral *v.t.* ژغورل protect

zghoral *v.t.* ژغورل save

zghorana *n.* ژغورنه protection

zghorandoy *n.* ژغورندوی saviour

zghorandoy *a.* ژغورندوی protective

zghoroonkay *n.* ژغورونکی protector

zghoroonkay; satoonkay *n* ژغورونکی،ساتونکی guard

zhman plar ya mor *n.* ژمن‌پلاريا مور sponsor

zhmana *n.* ژمنه onus

zhmana matawal *v.i.* ژمنه‌ماتول perjure

zhmana matawana *n.* ژمنه‌ماتوونه perjury

zhmana matawana *n.* ژمنه‌ماتوونه treason

zhmana; moahida *n.* ژمنه؛معاهده compact

zhmna; taroon *n.* ژمنه؛تون covenant

zhobanr *n.* ژوب zoo

zhoblawal *v.t.* ژوبلول hurt

zhopoh *n.* ژوپه zoologist

zhopohana *n.* ژوپوهنه zoology

zhopohani pori arwand *a.* ژوپوهنی پوراوند zoological

zhowal *v. t* ژوول chew

zhowali khabari *v.i.* ژوولخبر mutter

zhowali khabari kawal *v.i.* ژوولخبر کول mumble

zhranda *n.* ژرنده mill

zhranda kawal *v.t.* ژرنده‌کول mill

zhrandagaray *n.* ژرندی miller

zhwand *n* ژوند life

zhwand *n.* ژوند subsistence

zhwand kawal *v. i* ژوندکول dwell

zhwand kawal *v.i.* ژوندکول live

zhwand kawal *v.i.* ژوندکول subsist

zhwand leek *n* ژوندليک biography

zhwand leek leekoonkay *n* ژوند لیک‌لیکونکی biographer

zhwand pohana *n* ژوندپوهنه biology

zhwand pohand *n* ژوندپوهاند biologist

zhwand warbakhal *v. t.* ژوندوربل enliven

zhwand warkawal; zhwand warbakhal *v.t.* ژوندورکول؛ ژوندوربخل animate

zhwanday *a.* ژوندی animate

zhwanday *a.* ژوندی live

zhwanday *a.* ژوندی living

zhwanday kawal *v.t.* ژوندی‌کول vitalize

zhwanday mawjood *n.* ژوندی موجود wight

zhwanday pati keydal *v.i.* ژوندی پاتوکدل survive

zhwanday satal *v. t* ژوندی‌ساتل conserve

zhwanday wajood *n.* ژوندی‌وجود organism

zhwanday; sarshar *a* ژوندی؛ سرشار alive

zhwandoon *n* ژوندون living

zid aw naqeez n. ضداونقيض antonym

zid; makoos a. ضد؛معكوس reverse

ziddi hamoozat adj. ضدحموضت antacid

zikar n. ذكر mediation

zikar kawal v.t. ذكركول meditate

zikar kawal v.t. ذكركول mention

zima war a. ذمهوار responsible

zima waree n. ذمه واري responsibility

zimnee qanoon; seemayeez qanoon n. ضمني قانون؛سيمهييز قانون bylaw, bye-law

zimnee; arkheez a. ضمني؛اخيز tacit

zmaka n. مكه earth

zmaka n. مكه land

zmaka da kakht lapara tayarawal v.t. مكهدكتلپاره تيارول till

zmaka yeywi kawal v.i مكهييوكول plough

zmakmeyshtay hashra khor n. مكمشتيحشرهخور toad

zmakmeyshtay shamshatay n. مكمشتهشمشت tortoise

zmakpeyzhand n. مكپژاند geologist

zmakpeyzhandana n. مكپژندنه geology

zmakpoh n. مكپوه geographer

zmakpohana n. مكپوهنه geography

zmaray n. زمر lioness

zmaray n. زمری lion

zof n. ضعف infirmity

zolana n. زولنه fetter

zolanay n. زولانی anklet

zolanay warachawal v.t زولانۍ وراچول fetter

zoq; khwand n. ذوق؛خوند relish

zor n. زور compulsion

zor a. زو aged

zor achawal v.t زوراچول accentuate

zor azmoyal v.i. زورآزمویل wrestle

zor halat ta staneydal v.i. زوحالت تهستندل relapse

zor karawal v.t زوركارول force

zortokarpeywandawal v.t. زووكر پوندول rag

zor warkawal; takhta kawal v.t. زوررور كول؛تخته كول press

zor zyatay n. زورزياتی tyranny

zor zyatay n. زورزياتی stricture

zor zyatay n. زورزياتی violence

zor; istaydad n. زور؛استعداد potential

zor; khwa badowana n. زور؛ خوابدوونه nuisance

zor; matbooat n. زور؛مطبوعات press

zor; pata shaway a. زو؛پاتهشوی stale

zorandawal v. t زندول dangle

zorawal v.t. زورول annoy

zorawal v. t زورول bedevil

zorawana n. زورونه annoyance

zorawar adj. زورور mighty

zorawar a. زورور strong

zordar a. زوردار emphatic

zoreydal; zghamal *v.t.* ورمل، suffer زغمل

zoreydalay shakhs *n.* وردلی‌شخص nag

zorowoonkay *a.* وروونکی injurious

zorwaka *a* زورواکه autocratic

zoy *n.* زوی son

zra *n.* زه heart

zra keydal *v.t.* زه‌کدل aspire

zra keydal *v.i.* زه‌کدل yearn

zra khoogee *n.* زه‌خوی pity

zra matawal *v. t* زه‌ماتول dishearten

zra na zra keydal *v.i.* زه‌نازه‌کدل hesitate

zra na zratob *n.* زه‌نازه‌توب hesitation

zra nazra keydal *v.i.* زه‌نازه‌کدل waver

zra nazra keydal *v.i.* زه‌نازه‌کدل vacillate

zra nazratob kawal *v.i.* زه‌نازه‌توب shilly-shally کول

zra rahaskeydana *n.* زه‌راهسکدنه nausea

zra rakhkoonay *a.* زه‌راکونی winsome

zra rakkhal *v.t.* زه‌راکل attract

zra rakkhana *n.* زه‌راکنه attraction

zra rakkhowoonkay; jalabowoonkay *a.* زه راکوونکی؛جلبوونکی attractive

zra saway kawal *v. t* زه‌سوی‌کول commiserate

zra saway; rehem *n.* زه‌سوی؛رحم mercy

zra seyzal *v.t.* زه‌سزل pity

zra swanday *n* زه‌سواندي compassion

zra swanday *a.* زه‌سواندی pitiful

zra ta nazhdey *a* زه‌ته‌نژد darling

zra torowoonkay *a.* زه‌توروونکی loathsome

zra tri wral *v. t* زه‌ترول enchant

zra war *a.* ور زه bold

zra war *a.* ور زه courageous

zra wartob *n.* زه‌ورتوب courage

zra wartya *n* زه‌ورتیا boldness

zra wartya warkawal *v. t.* زه ورتیا ورکول embolden

zra wral *v.t* زه‌ول fascinate

zra wrana *n.* زه‌ونه fascination

zraswand *a.* زسواند sympathetic

zratoray *a.* زتوری reluctant

zrawar *a.* زه‌ور chivalrous

zrawar sarteyray *n* زه‌ورسرتری chevalier

zrawar; garam *n* زور،برم stalwart

zrawartob *n.* زه‌ورتوب chivalry

zubanee yadawal *v. t* زباني‌یادول cram

zukam *n.* زکام influenza

zulam *n.* ظلم oppression

zulam kawal *v.t.* ظلم‌کول molest

zulam kawal *v.t.* ظلم‌کول oppress

zulam zyatay *n.* ظلم‌زیاتی molestation

zulm *n* ظلم cruelty

zwag *n* و clamour

zwag *n.* و noise

zwag jorawal *v. i.* وجوول clamour

zwag kawal *v.t.* و کول murmur

zwak warbakhal *v.t.* واک‌وربل reinforce

zwak warbakhana *n.* واک‌وربنه reinforcement

zwakman *a* واک‌من sovereign

zwan *a.* وان young

zwan halak *n.* وان‌هلک lad

zwana najlay *n.* نجلوانه lass

zwanaka *n* وانکه acne

zwanaka *n.* وانکه chit

zwar ghwagay babar spay *n.* و غوی‌ببرسپی spaniel

zwaranda kangal shawi wawra *n.* ونده‌کنل‌شوی‌واوره icicle

zwarandawal *v.t.* وندول hang

zyadakht *n.* زیادت augmentation

zyadakht *n* زیادت increase

zyadakht *n.* زیادت superfluity

zyan *n.* زیان loss

zyan arowoonkay *a.* زیان‌اوونکی pernicious

zyanawal *v.i* زیانول abort

zyar *n* زیار struggle

zyar *n.* زیر pale

zyar kakh *a.* زیارک trying

zyar kakhal *v.i.* زیارکل strive

zyar kakhal *v.i.* زیارکل struggle

zyarat; haj *n.* زیارت؛حج pilgrim

zyarat; haj *n.* زیارت؛حج pilgrimage

zyaratzay *n.* زیارتی shrine

zyat *a* زیات abundant

zyat *n* زیات accessory

zyat *a* زیات excess

zyat *n.* مقدار زیات heap

zyat *a* زیات much

zyat bar *n* زیات‌بار overload

zyat barawal *v.t.* زیات‌بارول overburden

zyat barawal *v.t.* زیات‌بارول overload

zyat darmal khwaral *n.* زیات‌درمل خ‌ور overdose

zyat darmal khwaral *v.t.* زیات درمل‌خور overdose

zyat diqat *n.* زیات‌دقت subtlety

zyat ghageydal *v.i.* غدل زیات prattle

zyat kach *n.* زیات‌کچ plenty

zyat kar *n.* زیات‌کار overwork

zyat kar kawal *v.t.* زیات‌کارکول outdo

zyat kar kawal *v.t.* زیات‌کارکول overact

zyat kar kawal *v.t.* زیات‌کارکول overdo

zyat khalk *n.* زیات‌خلک throng

zyat khorak khwarana *n.* زیات خوراک‌خونه gluttony

zyat khorak; marakht *n* زیات خوراک؛مت glut

zyat khoshala *a* زیات‌خوشاله overjoyed

zyat lagakht *n* زیات‌لت overcharge

zyat lagakht kawoonkay *n.* زیات لت‌کوونکی spendthrift

zyat lagakht rawastal *v.t.* زیات‌لت راوستل overcharge

zyat miqdar warkawal *v.t* زیات مقداورکول heap

zyat na zyat *n* زیات‌نه‌زیات maximum

zyat peychal *v.t.* زیات‌پچل overlap

zyat sara nakhleydalay *n* زيات سرهندلى overlap

zyat shmeyr *n.* زياتشمر multiplicity

zyat tar *a.* زياتتر most

zyat warakht *n* زياتورت downpour

zyat zaleydal *v.t.* زياتللدل outshine

zyata gata kawal *v.i.* زياته کول profiteer

zyata parakhtya moondal *v.t.* زياته پراختيا موندل outgrow

zyata stayana kawal *v. t.* زياته ستاينه کول extol

zyatawal *v.t.* زياتول add

zyatawal *v.t.* زياتول augment

zyatawal *v.t.* زياتول increase

zyatee kawal *v.t* زياتی کول exceed

zyateyda *n.* زياتدا proliferation

zyateydal *v.i.* زياتدل abound

zyateydal *v.i.* زياتدل preponderate

zyateydal *v.i.* زياتدل proliferate

zyattara *adv.* زياتره most

zyattara *adv* زياتره much

zyatwalay *n.* زياتوالی preponderance

zyatwalay *n.* زياتونه addition